RODALE'S

LOW-MAINTENANCE GARDENING TECHNIQUES

RODALE'S

LOW-MAINTENANCE GARDENING TECHNIQUES

Barbara W. Ellis, Joan Benjamin, and Deborah L. Martin

Rodale Press, Inc.
Emmaus, Pennsylvania

OUR MISSION

We publish books that empower people's lives.

RODALE  BOOKS

Copyright © 1995 by Rodale Press, Inc.
Illustrations copyright © 1995 by Frank Fretz, Leslie Flis, and Len Epstein

All rights reserved. No part of this publication may be reproduced or transmitted in any form or by any means, electronic or mechanical, including photocopy, recording, or any other information storage and retrieval system, without the written permission of the publisher.

The information in this book has been carefully researched, and all efforts have been made to ensure accuracy. Rodale Press, Inc., assumes no responsibility for any injuries suffered or damages or losses incurred during the use of or as a result of following this information. It is important to study all directions carefully before taking any action based on the information and advice presented in this book. When using any commercial product, *always* read and follow label directions. Where trade names are used, no discrimination is intended and no endorsement by Rodale Press, Inc., is implied.

Printed in the United States of America on acid-free ♾, recycled ♻ paper, containing 20 percent post-consumer waste

Library of Congress Cataloging-in-Publication Data

Ellis, Barbara W.
Rodale's low-maintenance gardening techniques : shortcuts and time-saving hints for your greatest garden ever / Barbara W. Ellis, Joan Benjamin, and Deborah L. Martin
p. cm.
Includes bibliographical references and index.
ISBN 0–87596–641–1 (hardcover)
1. Gardening. 2. Low maintenance gardening. 3. Organic gardening. I. Benjamin, Joan. II. Martin, Deborah L. III. Title. IV. Title: Low-maintenance gardening techniques.
SB453.E458 1995
635—dc20 95–1026

RODALE'S LOW-MAINTENANCE GARDENING TECHNIQUES EDITORIAL AND DESIGN STAFF

Editor: Barbara W. Ellis
Associate Editors: Joan Benjamin, Deborah L. Martin
Contributing Editors: Fern Marshall Bradley, Jean M. A. Nick
Senior Research Associate: Heidi A. Stonehill
Interior and Cover Designer: John Lotte
Interior Layout: Karen Coughlin
Interior Illustrators: Frank Fretz, Leslie Flis, Len Epstein
Front Cover Photographers: Rodale Stock Images (upper left), Rob Cardillo/Organic Gardening (upper right), T. L. Gettings/Rodale Stock Images (lower left), John P. Hamel (lower right)
Back Cover Photographers: T. L. Gettings/Rodale Stock Images (upper left and lower right), Ed Landrock/Rodale Stock Images (upper right), Patricia Lyn Seip/Rodale Stock Images (lower left)
Copy Editor: Sarah Dunn
Editorial Assistance: Stephanie Snyder
Manufacturing Coordinator: Patrick Smith
Indexer: Ed Yeager

RODALE BOOKS

Executive Editor, Home and Garden: Margaret Lydic Balitas
Copy Manager, Home and Garden: Dolores Plikaitis
Art Director, Home and Garden: Michael Mandarano
Office Manager, Home and Garden: Karen Earl-Braymer
Editor-in-Chief: William Gottlieb

If you have any questions or comments concerning this book, please write to:
Rodale Press, Inc.
Book Readers' Service
33 East Minor Street
Emmaus, PA 18098

Distributed in the book trade by St. Martin's Press

2 4 6 8 10 9 7 5 3 1 hardcover

Contents

PART 3
Saving Time in the Lawn and Landscape

PART 4
Saving Time with Smart Plant Choices

Introduction

There's no doubt about it—gardening takes work. But for most of us, it's work we love to do. Whether we're puttering among our perennials, snipping herbs for a savory stew, or planting seeds for that first early crop of lettuce, there's no place we'd rather be than out in our gardens. But let's face it, there are chores we anticipate with nothing short of dread—like struggling to mow a steep slope or hacking back the shrubs that annually threaten to engulf the house.

Even chores that are fairly easy to accomplish, like weeding and trimming, aren't always so fun. Although you can keep on top of them with regular attention, if you take a vacation or turn your back on them during an especially busy week, you're doomed to play catch-up until they're under control again.

But don't despair—bringing in a road crew and paving your yard isn't the only way to have a low-maintenance garden. *Rodale's Low-Maintenance Gardening Techniques* will show you how to grow beautiful gardens and produce healthy fruits and vegetables with as little work as possible. Throughout, you'll find least-work techniques, time-saving systems, and handy tools that will let you get your gardening done quickly and effectively, with as little physical labor as possible. Browse through the book and you'll discover low-work composting and soil-building systems, tools, and techniques that simplify watering chores, easy ways to dry herbs or trellis vegetables, perennials that never need dividing, roses that are both beautiful and tough as nails, and much more.

Throughout this book, magazine-style articles and headlines make it easy to look for ideas that make sense in your garden. Lists of tips, step-by-step instructions, and plenty of illustrations ensure that you'll spend your time solving problems, not searching for answers.

Pick Your Maintenance

When you start thinking about reducing maintenance in your yard and garden, keep in mind that a task isn't work unless it's work to you. You may love watering but hate weeding; enjoy pruning but loathe mowing. Start planning your low-maintenance landscape by identifying the chores you hate most, or at least the ones you'd like to spend less time and energy on. Look them up in the appropriate chapters to find a host of ideas for making them more manageable. Here's a rundown on what topics you'll find in each part of the book. And if you're looking for something specific, don't forget to use the index.

Part 1: Saving Time with Basic Techniques. Look here for chapters on all the major gardening techniques like planning, soil improvement, composting, and pest control.

Part 2: Saving Time with Fruits and Vegetables. Here, you'll find chapters on vegetables, berries and small fruits, tree fruits, and herbs, as well as on trellising, training, and harvesting.

Part 3: Saving Time in the Lawn and Landscape. In addition to a chapter on lawns and groundcovers, Part 3 features a chapter with easy-to-build projects that will make your yard easier to care for. It also features Problem Sites: Quick Solutions to your Yard's Trouble Spots (Chapter 21)—look here for ideas on dealing with problems like shady, dry, windy, or high-traffic sites.

Part 4: Saving Time with Smart Plant Choices. This is where you'll find great ideas for growing all your favorite ornamentals, including annuals, bulbs, perennials, wildflowers, roses, trees, and shrubs.

Once you've reduced the time you spend on chores you don't enjoy, the gardening activities that are left are recreation and good exercise. And gardening *is* good exercise: One hour spent weeding, trimming, or raking can burn off 300 calories; walking behind a hand mower can burn up over 450 calories an hour.

Starting Out

If you don't quite know where to start to turn your high-maintenance yard into a low-maintenance one, here are some tips to help you.

Pick the right plants. The plants you choose can make a world of difference in the amount of maintenance your landscape requires. They can mean the difference between a high-maintenance landscape and an easy-care one. Before you plant, learn about your site. Find out about the type and quality of the soil, the amount of sun, and the exposure. Then pick plants that will thrive in those conditions. It also pays to know the mature height and spread of each plant you choose before you buy. Otherwise, you're just planting pruning problems.

Use mulch. Keeping your soil covered with a layer of organic mulch is the best thing you can do to reduce landscape maintenance. A 3- to 4-inch layer of bark chips, chopped leaves, straw, grass clippings, or other organic materials controls weeds, holds moisture in the soil so you don't have to water as often, protects the soil from wind and water erosion, and adds organic matter, which in turn improves the soil.

Reduce lawn maintenance. Probably nothing tops lawns as maintenance guzzlers, what with all the mowing, watering, fertilizing, and weeding they need. One of the best ways to reduce lawn maintenance is to reduce the size of your lawn by replacing it with groundcovers, mulch, or even decks and patios, all of which need less maintenance. You'll find more tips for reducing lawn maintenance in Chapter 19, Lawns and Groundcovers.

Reform your pruning practices. Plants that are sheared into unnatural shapes like squares and gumballs take much more work to maintain than ones that are allowed to take a more natural-looking, informal shape. For tips on low-maintenance pruning techniques, see Chapter 9, Pruning. Selecting plants that mature at the size you want is the least-work alternative. They won't require any pruning beyond shaping to remove overlapping or rubbing branches or dead wood. If you do have a plant that's larger than you'd like, you can replace the plant or control the size by removing entire branches. Either cut one or two of the largest stems on a shrub back to the ground each year or selectively remove back to the base of the branch. Some shrubs will withstand being cut back to within 1 foot of the ground, although they may not bloom for a year or two after this drastic treatment. Try this with barberries, deutzia, forsythia, rose-of-Sharon, privets, honeysuckles, mock oranges, and lilacs.

Plan your free time. So what will you do with all that time you've saved once you've cut your yard-care chores to the bone? You can sit back and enjoy your great-looking landscape. Or you can spend time on the gardening activities you do enjoy, like planning that perennial garden you've always wanted. After all, now you'll have time for it.

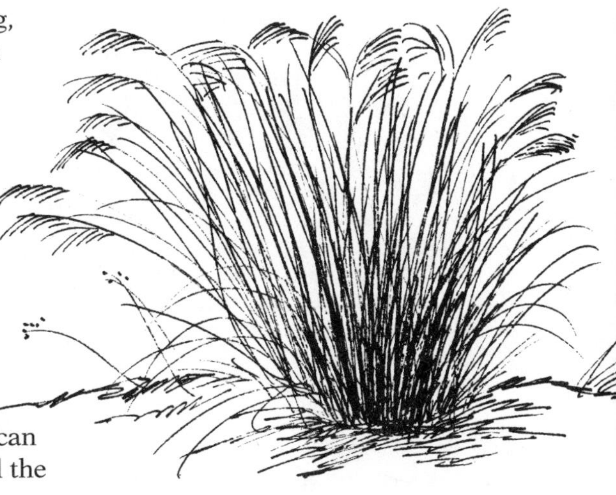

PART 1

Saving Time

with Basic Techniques

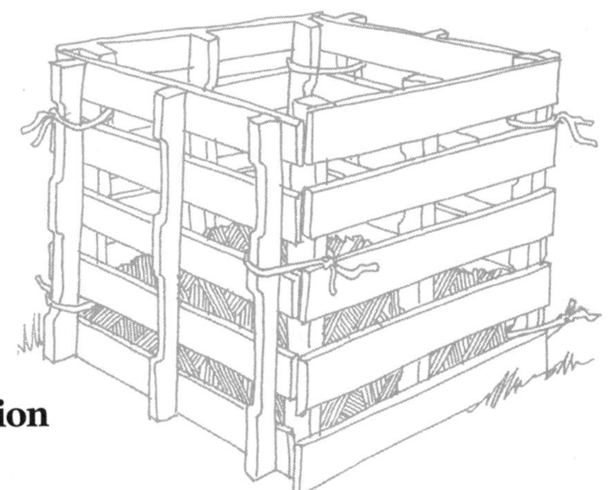

Planning

Planning the Low-Maintenance Way

PLANNING may seem like a mysterious and tiresome garden chore, but there's nothing more straightforward: If you decide what you want before you plant or make changes in your landscape, you'll save time—lots of it. It's just like having a recipe in your hands. One look and you know immediately which steps need to be done first, what materials you should have on hand, and what the final results will look like.

Planning is your opportunity to build convenience and success into your entire landscape. It gives you a chance to evaluate your site and plantings on paper—when it's still simple and inexpensive to make changes. A plan makes it easier to visualize and reach your goals. Drawing one isn't hard, but getting around to doing it may be. That's why this chapter contains tips for getting started, making easy maps, written and picture records, and simple time schedules that make the process fun enough that you'll want to do it!

3 Tips for Jump-Starting the Planning Process

What's the easiest way to start landscape planning? Find out what kind of site, plants, and landscape features you've got to work with first. Then decide what you want from your yard *before* you start digging and planting. You probably have a dream landscape in mind already. These easy tips will help you get it down on paper and turn it into a doable plan.

1. **Sketch a bird's-eye view of your property.** If you have a builder's plan or survey map of your yard and house, make a copy of it. If not, draw a rough sketch on a piece of ¼-inch graph paper. Use circles to represent existing plants, and squares or rectangles for buildings—you're not trying to win an art contest, just get an idea of what you've got to work with. Pace off the distance between plants and buildings so you can place them on the drawing accurately. (Measure if you're a stickler for details.) Label slopes, low spots, and other challenging sites.

2. **Circle your plan with planting sites.** Think of everything you'd like to see in your landscape: gardens, lawn areas, tree plantings, and special features like trellises. Draw a circle to represent each one and label it. Use a pencil and eraser so you can keep moving items around until you find the arrangement you like best. See "Design Your Yard and Garden for Maximum Convenience" on page 8 to make sure you end up with the best locations.

3. **Narrow your sights.** Landscaping your entire yard at once is daunting, so set priorities and take it step by step. What do you want most from your landscape? Quick shade? Fresh vegetables? A flower-filled foundation planting? Pick two or three items you want most of all and make them your goals. It's a great way to discover what's most important to you and reduce your workload. Draw plans of your priority areas first. You can move on to others next year—or whenever you have the time and money.

Plan to Choose Your Chores

A great place to start any garden plan is to sit down with a cup of coffee or tea and make a list of garden chores you don't enjoy. Mowing and trimming the lawn? Hauling hoses? Pruning? Then turn to the chapters that discuss your least favorite chores, and you'll find techniques for cutting them out of your gardening schedule. If problem sites are your biggest headache, turn to Chapter 21 for solutions.

Take a Garden Time Test

When you set a garden goal like planting new shade trees or making enough compost to fertilize your yard, do you know if you'll have time to accomplish it? Take the test below and evaluate your past performance. It will help you determine if your new goals are reasonable, or if they're impossible dreams. Choose the answers that most closely match your gardening practices.

1. I plant all of the garden plants and seeds I buy:

☐ A. As soon as conditions are right.

☐ B. Before the growing season ends.

☐ C. Only in my dreams. I throw out plants or squirrel away lots of unused seed each year that I never got around to planting.

If you chose A, you're in good shape. Your planting goals are in line with the amount of time you have. If you chose B or C, chances are you're biting off more than you can chew. Try cutting back the number of plants or seeds you buy next year by one-half.

Once you get a handle on what you really have time for, order only that much and no more—no matter how tempting the store displays and catalog pictures look.

2. I mulch, fertilize, water, and weed my garden:

☐ A. As soon as it needs it.

☐ B. After my plants all collapse and I know they really need me.

☐ C. ...Well, I was planning on doing it next year.

If you put off garden chores because you don't have time to get to them, reexamine the size of your garden. Cutting it back by one-third will dramatically cut the time you spend on maintenance.

Rescheduling chores may also solve the problem. If you plan to fertilize plants in spring but get overwhelmed by other chores, pick a season when you do have extra time. Add compost to your garden in summer, fall, or winter and your plants will benefit without putting you in a time crunch.

3. I harvest:

☐ A. Most of the fruit and vegetables I grow.

☐ B. Very little of what I grow; most of it rots.

How well does your harvest schedule work? Do you have enough time to put up tomatoes and store apples, or do they rot in the garden and yard? If you aren't using your fruit or vegetable harvest, cut back on the number of plants you set out until you are growing only what you have time for. Or try spreading out your harvest using the tips in Chapters 13 and 18.

TAKE-IT-EASY TIP!

Break Up Garden Tasks

One way to conquer garden chores is to divide them into easy-to-achieve pieces that fit your daily schedule. If you've only got a half-hour to weed your garden each evening, start by snipping off the tops of any weeds that are flowering. That will prevent them from going to seed and buy you some time.

Divide your weeding into doable pieces. See how far you can weed the first evening, then set goals for the rest of the week: one row, one-eighth of your garden, or whatever you can do in a half-hour. If you've got more time, take on a bigger area or take on two chores—watering one section of your garden while you weed another, for example.

Your Garden's Past Can Save You Time in the Future

Garden records are great memory boosters that keep you from repeating mistakes. Just write down what you plant each season, whether the crop was a success or a failure, why, and what you did about it. When it's time to order seeds or deal with a problem, you can look back and see what worked and what didn't. Make record-keeping fun by using a system that appeals to you. Here are some of the options.

An easy way to keep track of the plants you're growing is to cut photos and descriptions from catalogs and tape them on a sheet of notebook paper—one plant per sheet. Jot notes about each plant on its sheet—recommended care, where you planted it—and keep the sheets in alphabetical order in a three-ring binder.

Garden calendars. Choose a basic calendar that just tells you the date or choose one of the more informative calendars. Check your local bookstore and garden magazine ads for calendars that include garden advice and lore, graphs for drawing garden plants, pages for notes, and even inspiring photos and drawings.

Computer records. If you already use a computer to keep household records, add garden notes to your system. You'll be able to keep track of plant orders and plant performance with ease.

Spiral notebooks with pockets. If you like to collect gardening articles, pick a record book with pockets. Stuff all those interesting news notes inside so you'll know where they are. Pockets are handy for storing plant orders, too.

Three-ring binders. These hold lots of pages for notes, and it's easy to add more if you're a prolific note taker. Draw each year's garden design in your notebook for easy comparisons. When you want to rotate your vegetable crops or remember if you ever tried starting blackberry lilies from seed, you'll have the information in your hands.

Garden record books. Specially designed books include features like design tips and sections to keep track of your garden budget. You may appreciate one of these hardcover notebooks as the years go by.

Photo journal. Writing in journals isn't for everyone. If taking notes just isn't your style, take photos instead. Paste them in a notebook and scrawl a few notes so you remember if the picture is of your favorite tomato or a watering system that worked particularly well. You can even include seed packets, information cut from catalogs, and order forms to fill in the gaps.

Take a Low-Maintenance Stand When You Make Garden Plans

Gardens don't need to take up all your spare time and energy to look good. Make these simple changes in your planting plan—or your existing landscape—to get the gorgeous look of a high-maintenance planting without all the work.

▶ **Let clipped shrubs grow out.** Reduce pruning chores by letting closely clipped formal shrubs and hedges grow out and resume their natural appearance. See "Restyle Your Shrubs to Reduce Maintenance" on page 87 for instructions. Replace hedges with dwarf shrubs if you'd rather cut out pruning altogether.

▶ **Insist on plant sizes that fit your landscape.** Unruly plants like Japanese honeysuckle need lots of pruning to keep them in bounds. Substitute well-behaved vines like clematis, or dwarf shrubs that won't overtake your fence or grow higher than your picture window.

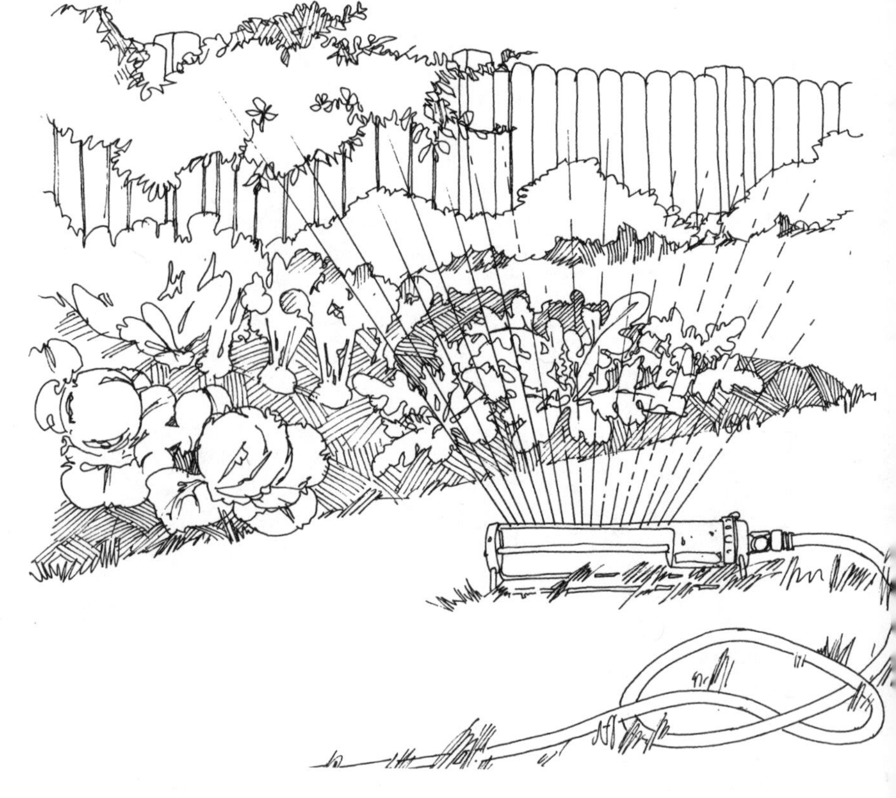

▲ **Prohibit wasteful water systems.** Overhead sprinklers lose water to evaporation, so you have to water a lot. They also keep plant leaves wet, which encourages diseases. Switch to water- and time-saving ooze or soaker hoses that dribble water into the ground and keep leaves dry.

◀ **Demand disease and insect resistance.** Avoid endless struggles with fungus-prone flowers and insect-infested vegetables and trees by choosing highly resistant cultivars. Try 'Centennial' crabapple, for instance, to avoid problems with fire blight. Better yet, skip finicky plants altogether. Replace problem-prone flowers like hybrid tea roses, and plant tough, healthier plants like shrub roses or flowering perennials instead.

▼ **Give finicky plants generous spacing.** Good air circulation keeps diseases away from fungus-prone plants like hybrid tea roses. Give them plenty of room for cleaner leaves and blooms.

▶ **Reshape your edges.** Beds and borders with sharp corners make mowing difficult. Whenever possible, round corners and use gentle curves that you can follow easily with a lawn mower.

▲ **Let staked plants sprawl.** Support flopping plants with shorter, sturdier plants instead of stakes and string. You'll get a beautiful casual cottage garden look as the leaves and flowers mingle.

Design Your Yard and Garden for Maximum Convenience

Plantings that are easy to get to are easy to care for, too. Make sure you consider all the design options when it comes to garden locations and layouts, so you can choose the ones that will save you the most time and effort. The suggestions here should help get you started.

▶ **Put the gardens you work on most closest to your house.** If you spend most of your time in the vegetable patch, put it by the kitchen door and move the flower beds farther away. You'll save more than steps—a garden that's close at hand is easy to monitor, so you'll discover pest and disease problems early, before they become a major headache.

▲ **Leave yourself work space.** Plants that are easy to reach are easy to care for, so leave work space between your garden and the house, a compost bin, or a fence. A 2-foot space is big enough if only you and your trowel or hand pruners need access. If you want to bring your garden cart or wheelbarrow into the garden for mulching or cleanup, leave at least a 3-foot gap.

◀ **Locate gardens within one hose's length of water.** Save yourself from lugging heavy hoses around by keeping gardens near a water source. If that's impossible, use drip irrigation and soaker hose systems. Once installed, the hoses can stay in place all year long.

◀ **Install pathways for easy access.** Place stepping-stones through damp areas or wide beds so plants are easy to get to and maintain. Install a path or steps if you need to travel up a steep slope or reach a distant flower bed. See Chapter 20 for details on installing paths, stairs, and stepping-stones.

◀ **Bring the garden to you with raised beds and containers.** Raise plantings off the ground and you'll bend less and save your back, shoulders, and neck from strain. See "Raising Beds Lowers Labor" on page 200 for instructions for building raised beds. Try flower boxes, pots, tubs, and hanging baskets for individual plants. See Chapter 28 for ideas on putting containers to work for you.

▲ **Size your garden to fit your reach.** Make most beds 4 feet wide or less so you won't have to stretch to reach interior plants. If you have a large property, you'll need bigger beds—up to 10 or 12 feet wide—or they'll look unbalanced. Add one or two paths across the length of the beds to provide easy but hidden access to your plants.

Quick and Easy Garden Design Techniques

Before you plant, picture what your garden will look like and you'll avoid unpleasant surprises. A simple sketch is all it takes to find out if your arrangement will work, or if you've picked out too many flowers or put them too close to the door. But there are lots of other techniques if drawing doesn't appeal to you. Try one described below to get a glimpse of your future garden.

◀ **Photograph your garden site.** Photos can give you a quick, realistic view of the area you've got to work with. Take the photos to a copy center and make enlarged copies.

Experiment with different garden designs by drawing the outline of your bed on the copies. Draw circles to represent plants. When you settle on a look that you like, draw in the basic shape of the plants you'd like to try. Use mail-order catalogs or book and magazine photos to get an idea of what the plants will look like when they are mature.

▶ **Use patterns to make garden layout simple.** Look for designs in everyday objects around your home: quilts, blankets, even a favorite shirt can provide inspiration for plant placement. Stick with simple patterns like zigzags or diamonds. Elaborate designs like those you might find in a Persian rug are too complicated for most gardens. Transfer the pattern to a drawing of your garden's outline and choose plants to fill in the shapes.

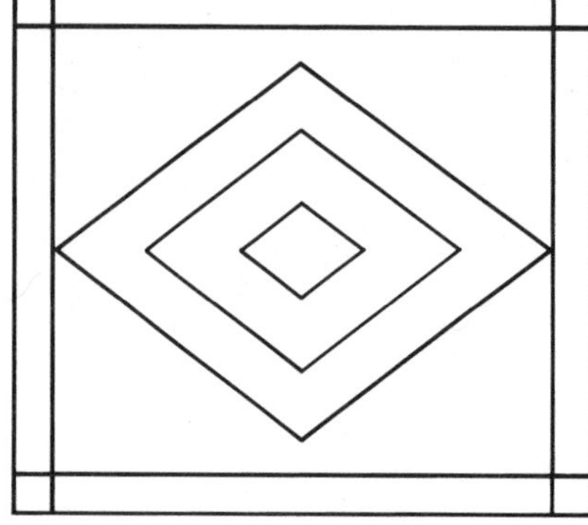

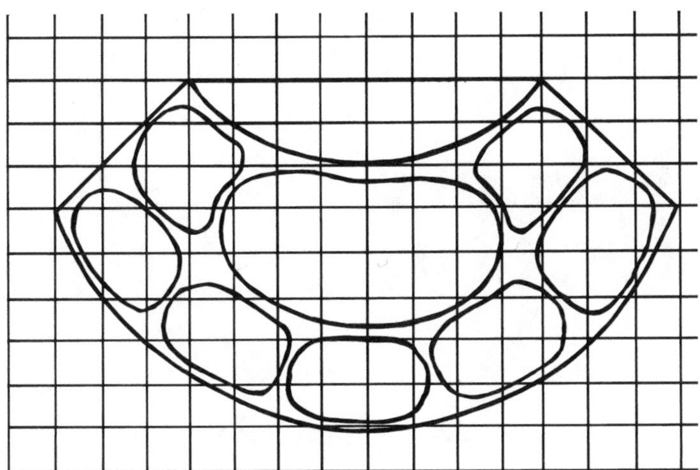

▲ **Draw bubbles.** A piece of graph paper, a pencil, and a rough outline of your proposed garden bed are all you need to draw a simple bubble diagram. Just doodle with shapes, each representing a drift (grouping) of one type of plant, until you get an arrangement you like. Then choose plants to fill in the shapes.

▶ **Test your design with stand-ins.** For a 3-D representation of your design, outline the shape of your future bed with a hose, a piece of rope, or a sprinkling of flour. Use any lightweight or easy-to-move objects to represent trees, shrubs, and flowers. Garbage bags filled with leaves make good shrub stand-ins, or try lawn chairs or your wheelbarrow. Plastic pots can represent flowers of various sizes.

Cut and Paste a Full-Color Garden Design

If you have trouble vizualizing your flower bed using black and white, cut photos of plants or just scraps of color from garden catalogs to colorize your garden plan. Use each shape to represent a flower color. If you enjoy making cut-and-paste plans, go the extra mile and make one for each season; that way you'll be able to imagine what your garden will look like throughout the season. If you don't want to cut up your catalogs, turn pages next to each other so you can see what your choices look like side by side.

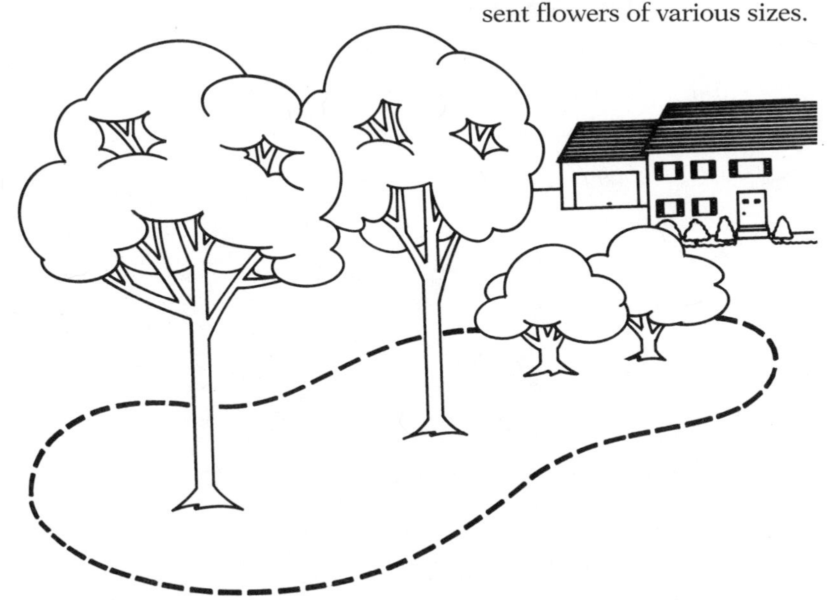

◀ **Design away your problem sites.** You can use existing plantings to help you put a polish on your yard and eliminate problem sites at the same time. For example, if you have a newly planted yard with scattered trees and shrubs, look for ways you can join them together with flowers or groundcovers to cut the size of your lawn and make mowing easier. Shade-loving perennials and wildflowers are excellent options under mature trees.

Chapter 2

Soil Care and Preparation

Soil Care and Preparation the Low-Maintenance Way

Healthy soil is the foundation of a low-maintenance garden. Plants that grow in healthy soil are more vigorous and have fewer pest and disease problems than ones in poor soil. And that means less time spent doctoring sick plants.

Good soil doesn't happen overnight, but you don't have to sweat and slave for it. The basics of good soil care are simple: Use plenty of organic mulch, don't dig the soil when it's too wet or too dry, and don't walk on prepared soil.

In this chapter, you'll find techniques for letting mulch and plants do your soil improvement work for you. And if you decide to dig, you'll find advice on saving your back in the process. For information on pH, see "Be Practical about pH" on page 64.

Make a Garden the Nearly No-Dig Way

Preparing a new garden site—or improving an old one—doesn't mean you have to do any digging. With this simple system, you can build a garden full of great soil with only a shovel for digging up hard-to-kill woody weeds like tree seedlings or poison ivy. It isn't the quickest system for building a garden, so you'll need a bit of patience. And it doesn't totally eliminate work.

The process is basically the same whether you are starting a new garden or renovating an old one. Before you start, mark off the area you intend to improve with stakes and string or a sprinkling of flour.

1. Scalp the weeds in spring. Remove as much of the top growth on existing grass, weeds, and other plants as you can. Mow it off with your mower blade as low as it will go. Dig out all woody plants.

2. Keep 'em in the dark. Cover this scalped area with a thick, light-excluding mulch. Several layers of newspaper (at least 12 sheets) or a layer of corrugated cardboard will work well. Be sure to overlap all the edges so weeds won't come up between them. Don't use inorganic mulches such as black plastic or landscape fabric—they'll smother the plants beneath them, but they'll break down incompletely and are almost impossible to remove.

3. Add organic mulch. Cover the newspaper or cardboard mulch with 8 to 10 inches of an organic mulch such as compost, wood chips, shredded bark, straw, spoiled hay, or leaves.

4. Let it cook through summer. Once you've assembled this soil-building layer cake, all you do is wait. If you wish to brighten the area while it's "cooking," tuck pots of annuals into the mulch and remove them in the fall.

5. Replenish the mulch. In fall, add more compost, wood chips, shredded bark, leaves, spoiled hay, or straw.

6. Plant next spring. By the following year, you can plant right through the mulch into the newly enriched soil below.

For a Fast Soil Test, Weeds Make Easy Reading

Before you pop 'em, pull 'em, or chop 'em, let weeds tell you what your soil needs. Then change the soil conditions, and many of the weeds will leave on their own. Weeds are plant opportunists that often grow in a particular location *because they can and other plants can't.* A dense population of one or two kinds of weeds is a good indication that your soil suits them better than it suits the plants you'd really rather be growing. Use this list of soil conditions and common weeds that thrive there to diagnose soil problems.

A Simple Soil Saver

Walking over newly turned soil is a surefire way to undo your soil improvement efforts because it compacts the soil you just loosened up. Whenever you can, build garden beds that you can reach into from the sides—without walking on them. If you don't build beds, be sure to leave pathways in your garden for walking and working. Or use a portable path, such as a plank or sturdy piece of cardboard, to distribute your weight more evenly when you have to walk on your soil.

Heavy clay or compacted soil. Plantains, dandelions, annual sow thistle, and Canada thistle thrive in heavy or compacted soils.

Poor, acidic soil. Taprooted weeds such as dandelions and Queen-Anne's-lace appear in poor, acidic soil, where their roots grow deep in search of nutrients. Acidic soils are also favored by sorrels, docks, and prostrate knotweed.

Alkaline soil. Mustards and thistles are more prevalent in high pH (alkaline) soils.

Fertile, cultivated sites. Shallow-rooted weeds such as lamb's-quarters, chicory, and chickweed take the forefront in fertile soil—their arrival is an indication that your soil-improving efforts are working.

Waterlogged or poorly drained soil. Coltsfoot, docks, and mosses grow where soil is soggy, acidic, and low in fertility.

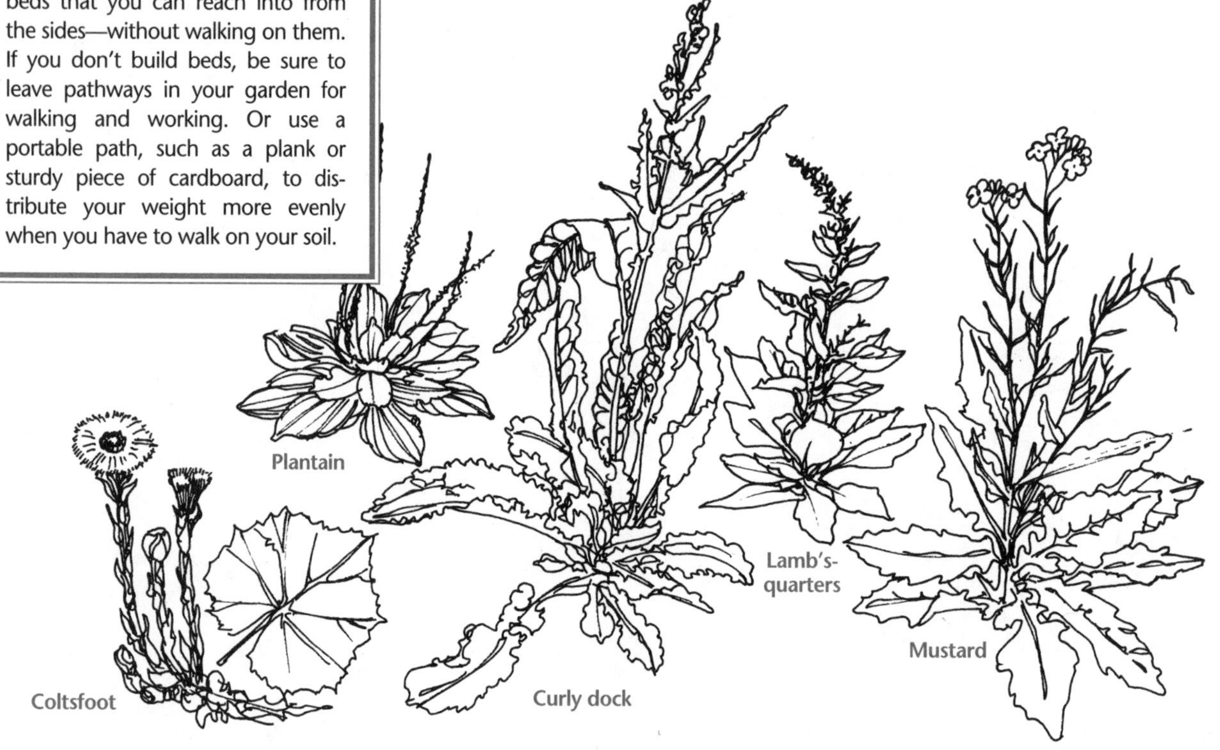

Find Out What Your Soil Needs Most

Before you spend a single dime buying soil amendments—or a single minute gripping a shovel handle—take some time to find out more about your soil. Knowing what problems you're dealing with will save time, effort, and aggravation in the long run.

Check for Sand or Clay

Test for the amount of sand, silt, and clay in your soil (its texture) when the earth is moist but not wet. Two or three days after a rainy spell is a good time. Take a loose ball of soil about the size of a table tennis ball in the palm of your hand. Gently squeeze it between the ball of your thumb and the lower outside edge of your index finger. Sand feels gritty, silt feels slightly greasy or like moist talcum powder, and clay feels slippery.

Squeeze the ball in your hand and release. If it crumbles, it has a reasonably balanced texture. If the soil ball holds its shape, it has a substantial percentage of clay. If you can roll it into a sausage shape, it has even more clay.

Soils that have a lot of sand tend to dry out quickly and don't hold nutrients well. Soils with a lot of clay stay cold in the spring, turn to a cement-like consistency if worked when wet or walked on, and drain slowly or puddle up when it rains. Soils with reasonably balanced texture, which are called loamy soils, shouldn't present problems given good basic care.

Test Soil Drainage

You'll find a simple way to check your soil's drainage below. Or, to see if it drains too rapidly, water a small area of your lawn or garden very thoroughly. Two days later, dig a small hole 6 inches deep where you watered. If the soil is already dry to the bottom of the hole, your soil probably doesn't retain enough water for good plant growth.

Simple Solutions for Problem Soils

Whatever your soil problem—too much sand or clay, too quick or slow to drain, the best thing you can do is add organic matter. If you mulch with compost or other organic matter, earthworms and other soil residents will work it down into the soil for you.

While you can use sand to improve drainage in clay soils, be prepared to add a lot. You'll need to work in at least a 1- to 2-inch-thick layer over the entire area you're amending. In smaller proportions, sand plus clay equals cement. Adding sand to your soil does little beyond improving drainage; you'll still need to add organic matter.

Building raised beds is another option for eliminating problems with poor soil. For more ideas on dealing with difficult soils, see Chapter 21.

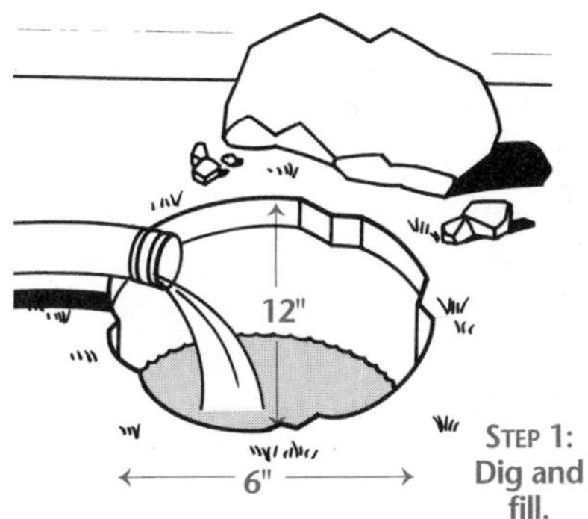

STEP 1: Dig and fill.

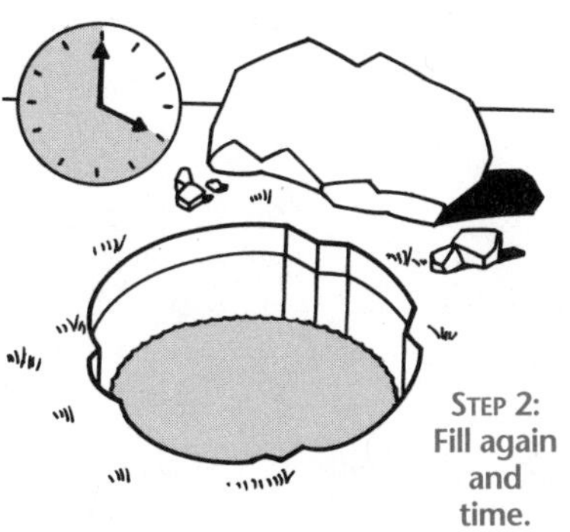

STEP 2: Fill again and time.

To test your soil's drainage, dig a hole 6 inches across and 12 inches deep. Fill it with water and let it drain. As soon as the water has drained completely, fill it again. Keep track of how long it takes the hole to drain the second time. If it's more than 8 hours, you have a drainage problem.

Sow-Easy Soil Improvement While You Wait

Improving poor soil for a new garden bed or rejuvenating the soil in an existing site need not mean hours of backbreaking digging—or tons of soil amendments. If you're willing to give up a few months of growing time, you can get plants to do nearly all the work for you. Cover crops, also called green manures, are plants that will literally lay down their lives for the good of the soil they grow in.

A cover crop will hold water in the soil, prevent erosion, and act as a weed-blocking mulch both while it's growing and after it's dead. As it decays on the soil surface or after it's tilled into the soil, it adds organic matter and nutrients.

You can choose a cover crop that suits your growing season, your soil's needs, and even your ability to mow or till the resulting residue. Yellow-blossom sweet clover, for example, has deep taproots that can help to break up hard clay soils; cowpeas grow quickly in hot weather. Both are pea-family members (legumes) that add nitrogen to the soil.

In most parts of the United States, winter annuals make excellent cover crops. For directions on growing them , see "Cover Crops Step-by-Step" on the opposite page.

If you'd rather give your soil a boost during the growing season, sow a summer annual such as cowpeas, buckwheat, oats, or berseem clover in spring. Let it grow until it blooms or until you're ready to plant your garden.

With any cover crop, you'll get maximum soil benefits from letting the crop grow as close to maturity as possible without allowing it to reseed. Legumes, like clover, vetch, and cowpeas, add the most nitrogen to the soil when they're allowed to bloom. And the amount of organic matter you add to your soil increases as long as you let the crop grow. But if you're itching to start planting, terminate the cover crop by mowing it down or digging it under. You'll still improve the soil and get your crops in on schedule, too.

Not Enough Compost? Here's Where to Turn

Nothing beats compost for satisfying the hungry citizens of your soil or adding organic matter to improve it. But when compost is in short supply, what other soil amendments do you turn to? Here are some to consider.

Manure. Manure nourishes your soil with lots of organic matter. To avoid injuring plants with too much nitrogen, use aged or composted manure. Be careful—it may bring weed seeds with it to your garden. After you add it, watch for seedlings and chop them down with a hoe while they're still young.

Locally available materials. Close at hand and usually free or inexpensive, locally available materials include sawdust, spoiled hay, grass clippings, and chopped or shredded leaves. Whether you add them to your compost pile or work them directly into the soil, they'll add organic matter to feed your soil.

An instant tax refund. Your local government may already be producing compost from yard wastes collected from you and your neighbors. Why not take advantage of already composted material—that your taxes pay for!

Cover Crops Step-by-Step

Winter annuals such as vetch, clover, and rye make good cover crops because they do most of their growing at the ends of the season—in late fall and early spring. They're planted in late summer, left to winter-kill, and allowed to resprout and flower in early summer the following year. By late May, in most places, the soil is improved and the garden is ready for planting. Here's a simple system for using them to improve your soil.

1. Sow in late summer. In mid- to late August, sow seed of winter annuals such as hairy vetch by sprinkling them over a prepared seedbed. Crimson clover, annual ryegrass, and cereal rye also work well with this schedule.

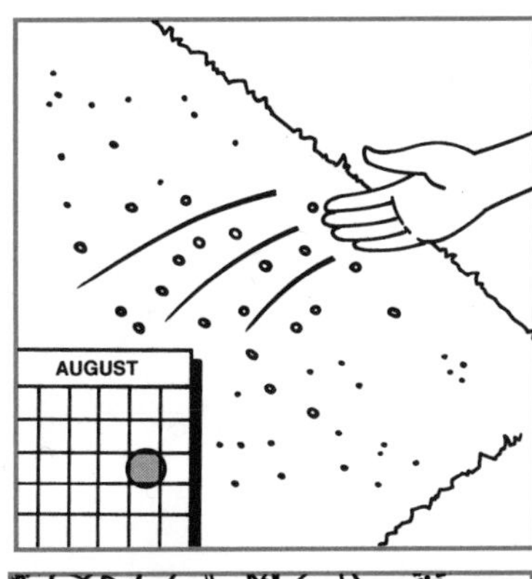

2. Let it grow till frost. The crop will grow until it's winter-killed, leaving a protective mulch of plant residue over your garden through winter.

3. Cut it down to improve the soil. In spring, the vetch will resprout from the roots, reaching flowering size sometime in May. Before the plants set seed, cut the topgrowth down with a scythe or string trimmer (it'll likely be too tough for your lawn mower).

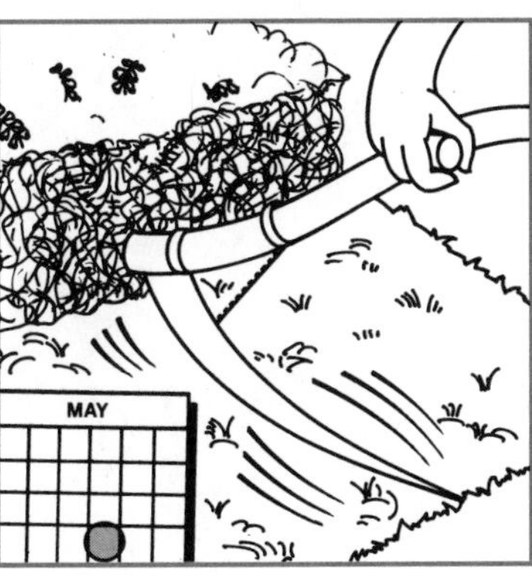

4. Plant into the mulch. Transplant directly into the resulting mulch. Or till or spade the cover crop residue into your soil. If you till in your crop, wait four or more weeks before planting.

Don't Hesitate to Inoculate

Legumes such as vetch, clover, and cowpeas form symbiotic relationships with bacteria in the soil. These relationships allow them to "fix" nitrogen—they take nitrogen from air in the soil and convert it to a form plants can use. Each type of legume needs a specific strain of bacteria to help them fix nitrogen.

The best way to ensure that the right bacteria is there for your cover crop is to coat your seeds with an inoculant at planting time. When you buy seeds of a leguminous cover crop, ask the supplier for the right inoculant to go with them. If you use the same crop in the same place next year, you won't need to inoculate—the bacteria will be available for 3 to 5 years.

For Speedy Soil Improvement, You'll Have to Dig In

Quick soil improvement takes time and muscle power. But if you're in a hurry to plant, it just may be worth it to you. To enrich poor or depleted soil, you'll need to add organic matter and turn it under to at least a shovel's depth. Or you can work it in with a rotary tiller. It's hard physical labor, even with a tiller, but the resulting garden bed will be enriched, improved, and ready to plant when you're done digging.

If you're starting with poor soil, you'll never have a low-maintenance garden unless you dig in and take the time to improve your soil up front. For example, a site with compacted clay soil that's quickly tilled will probably lead to nothing more than a failed garden. And having to plant all over isn't low-maintenance. For very poor soil or compacted sites, double digging may be the answer.

Double digging is labor intensive, but it ensures healthy, fuss-free plants. The initial time investment has a huge payoff: You'll save years of slow soil-building effort and have fewer maintenance chores forevermore. Roots penetrate double-dug soil deeply and easily, so plants suffer less from drought. Organic matter and other soil amendments added during the process provide plenty of food and help the soil hold water better. Before you start, get a soil test to see what your site needs, then follow the directions shown here.

After you've double-dug a bed, all you need to do to keep your plants and soil healthy is to add a top-dressing of manure or compost every other year. When you divide or lift plants, work up and amend the soil in the hole before you replant.

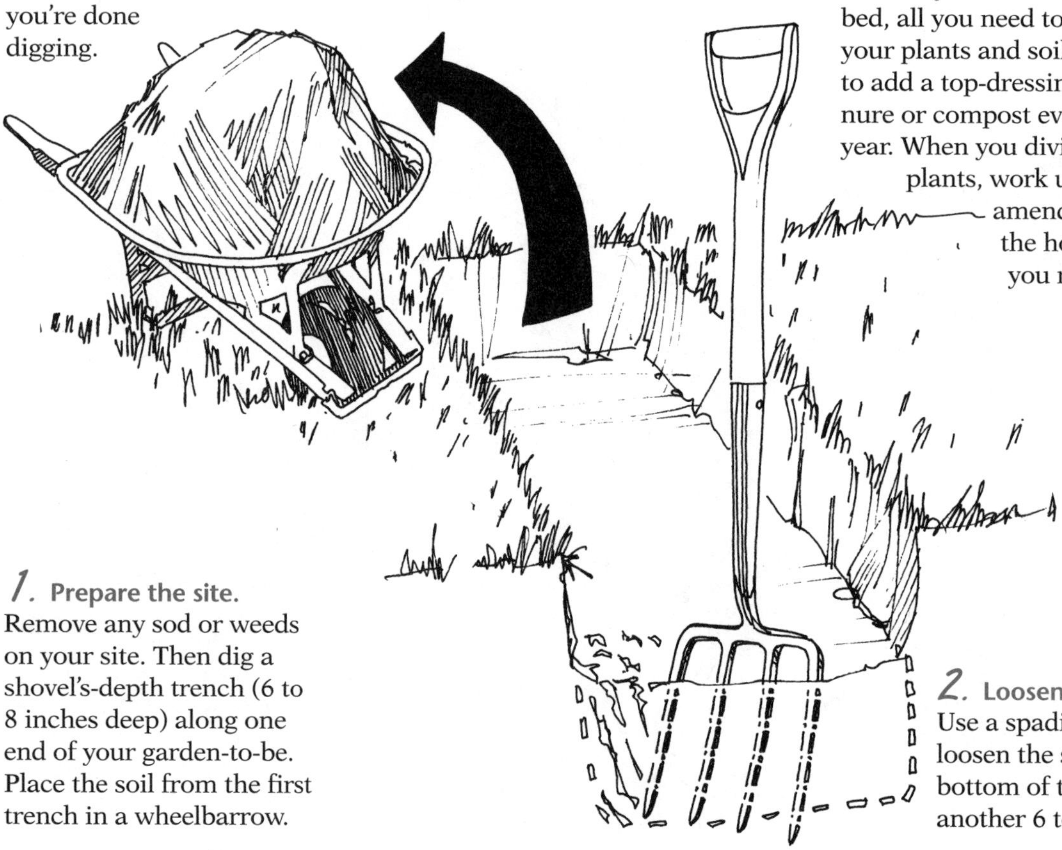

1. Prepare the site. Remove any sod or weeds on your site. Then dig a shovel's-depth trench (6 to 8 inches deep) along one end of your garden-to-be. Place the soil from the first trench in a wheelbarrow.

2. Loosen the soil. Use a spading fork to loosen the soil at the bottom of the trench another 6 to 8 inches.

3. **Dig a second trench.** Dig a new trench beside the first one and use the topsoil to fill in the first trench. Loosen the soil in the second trench just as you did for the first one. Repeat the process, digging and filling trenches until you cover the entire garden area. Fill the final trench with the topsoil in the wheelbarrow.

Finish the project by covering the site with 2 or more inches of organic matter, like compost or manure, and any soil amendments recommended by your soil test. Work the material into the top few inches of soil.

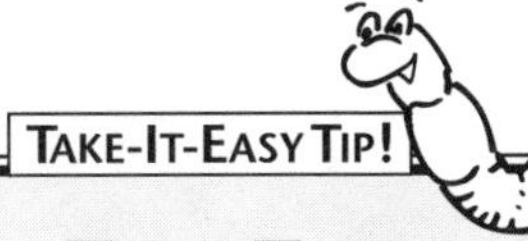

TAKE-IT-EASY TIP!

Try a Tarp

When you're double digging or preparing a planting hole, add a tarp to your list of tools. Spare yourself the effort of lifting soil up into a wheelbarrow or cart—just shovel it onto the tarp. If you need to move the soil, drag the tarp to another spot. When you dig planting holes, pile the soil on a tarp so it won't end up mixed into your lawn grass.

Go Easy on Your Earthworms

Earthworms can do great things for your garden if you'll let them. Worms tunnel through the soil, eating organic matter and excreting nutrient-rich, pH-balanced castings. As they tunnel, they aerate and loosen the soil, easing the way for plant roots.

Fortunately, it doesn't take much effort to keep your earthworms happy and healthy. To keep your earthworm crew busily improving your garden, just give them cool, moist soil covered with a layer of organic mulch.

Too much tilling, on the other hand, makes life tough for worms. Rotary tiller tines chop worms with every pass and leave others exposed to drying sun and wind.

High salt levels are another earthworm enemy. Keep salty chemical fertilizers and sidewalk de-icers far from your garden areas, lest your earthworms pack their bags for more pleasant surroundings.

Turn the Soil, Not Your Spine

Digging and turning the soil is hard work, and it pays to prepare for the effort. Here are some tips to keep you healthy and happy when you dig.

Dress for success. Dress for digging in comfortable, nonrestrictive clothing. Wear sturdy shoes or boots to protect your arches from bruising during repeated foot-powered shovel assaults on rocky or sod-covered soil. Let gravity work in your favor by keeping your shovel's blade—not its handle—vertical as you push it into the soil.

Step in the right direction. When you're digging a planting hole or performing some other task that requires you to move the soil, *lift* your shovelful of soil, keeping it close to your body, then *step* in the direction of your piled soil and *toss* toward it. Turning and tossing without moving your feet puts a strain on your back.

Lift with your legs. Dig with your knees slightly bent to put the weight of your effort on your stronger leg muscles, not your back. Holding your abdominal muscles tight gives your back added support while you dig. Don't overfill your shovel; lifting heavier loads will tire you more quickly and make you more susceptible to injuries.

For a Quick-Start Garden, Add Organic Matter and Grow

If you have a plot that you need to plant within the next few weeks, the quickest way to get it ready is to add finished compost. If you don't have it, use purchased compost or composted cow manure. Work it into the top few inches of the soil before you plant.

Buying compost or manure can be expensive, but don't try to cut corners and add raw organic matter such as leaves, weeds, or clippings directly to the soil shortly before planting—if you add lots of dry, brown (high-carbon) materials such as dried leaves or sawdust directly to your soil, the busy decomposers that feast on such organic matter will use up all the available nitrogen, leaving little for your plants.

If you'd like to improve your soil but don't want to haul compost from the nursery (or your compost pile), see "Say 'Bye' to Your Bin with Sheet Composting" on page 32.

Handy Helpers: Tools to Help with the Big Dig

Admittedly, the most important tool a gardener needs when faced with a digging job is a strong back. A pair of sturdy, comfortable gloves are nice to have, too. And there are a few digging accessories that can ease the effort of the next "big dig."

▲ **U-bar digger.** This odd-looking tool lets you use your body weight to help you break up compacted soil. Push it into the soil with your foot and pull the handles toward you to loosen the soil. Stand straight so you don't strain your knees or back.

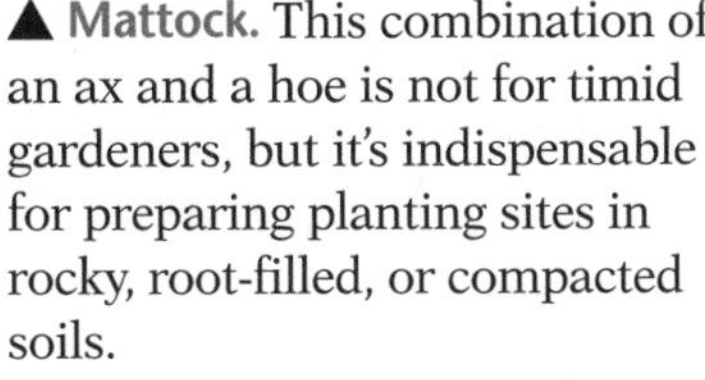

▲ **Mattock.** This combination of an ax and a hoe is not for timid gardeners, but it's indispensable for preparing planting sites in rocky, root-filled, or compacted soils.

◀ **Rotary tiller.** Available in many sizes, with tines in front or in back, rotary tillers can make quick work of seasonal cultivating jobs like working compost or cover crops into the soil. Overusing them can damage the soil and discourage earthworms.

Work Your Soil When the Time Is Right

When you want to get a garden started, it's tempting to dash out and dig the first chance you get. But time isn't the only thing you need when it comes to working the soil. Before you tackle a digging project, make sure the soil isn't too wet or dry.

Digging and turning wet soil compresses it, eliminating the passageways that bring air to your plants' roots. This damage leaves your garden soil with a concrete-like consistency that's hard hoeing for you and hard growing for your plants.

Tampering with too-dry soil is similarly damaging. The churning tines of a tiller can quickly pulverize a dry garden into a dustbowl; the powdery soil that results easily blows away in the wind or washes away in the next rain.

So when do you dig? To find out, grab a small handful of your garden's soil and try to squeeze it into a ball. If it stays in a firm ball when you open your hand—or if water runs out—it's too wet. Wait a few days and test it again. If it crumbles to pieces—or blows away—it's too dry. Moisten it with a hose and test again. A loose ball that crumbles when you prod it means grab the shovel and get to work.

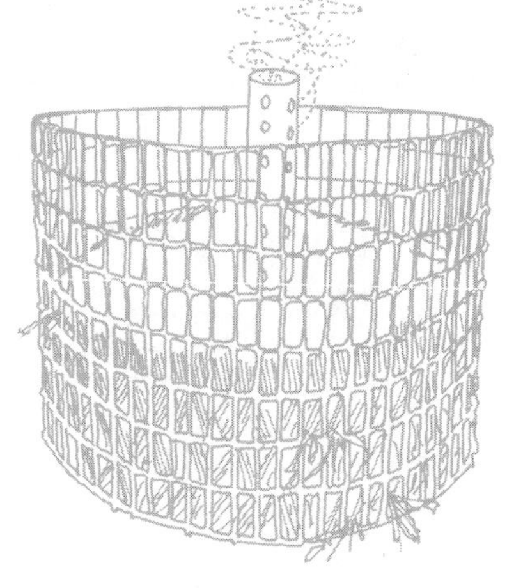

CHAPTER 3

Composting

Composting the Low-Maintenance Way

DO YOU THINK making compost takes too much time and effort? Well, it doesn't have to! Making and using compost is the easiest way to improve your soil or fertilize your lawn. Instead of paying to have your yard waste, grass clippings, and kitchen scraps hauled away (and hauling them to the curb yourself), you can turn them into compost—the gardener's black gold. Making your own compost will save you money and effort normally spent on commercial soil amendments and fertilizers.

There are lots of simple composting techniques that save time, money, and labor. Do you need compost fast? How about a way to make an easy but attractive compost bin to keep you and your neighbors happy? Find out how with the tips that follow.

Make Composting Convenient

Hauling compost around is a real time waster. To save time and energy, make your compost near where you use it and develop easy, efficient ways to get materials to your pile. For example, collect kitchen scraps in a tightly sealed container and carry them out weekly, rather than daily. In the winter, use an interim system. See "Easy Composting for Winter" on page 29 for a system to try.

It's also easier to make compost from ingredients that you have on hand than to collect and haul them to your yard. Use the list below to make a mental inventory of ingredients in your own home, yard, and garden.

Kitchen. Nonmeat, nondairy food scraps like vegetable or fruit trimmings, coffee grounds, tea bags, and eggshells.

Household. Pet or human hair, floor sweepings, sawdust, houseplant trimmings.

Fireplace. Use alkaline wood ashes in moderation.

Newspaper. Shredded or chopped-up newspaper helps balance soggy ingredients like grass clippings or kitchen scraps.

Lawn, garden, and landscape. Grass clippings, leaves, spent plant parts and trimmings.

Trees and shrubs. Twigs and prunings help keep compost loose, but they break down slowly. If finished compost is too chunky, sift out the sticks and add them to the next batch.

Pets and livestock. Composting manure from plant eaters (rabbits, horses, sheep, cows, goats) conserves nitrogen content and reduces the risk of burning plants with fresh manure. Add used bedding from poultry, gerbils, hamsters, or guinea pigs. Don't add droppings from dogs, cats, or other carnivores—they can carry diseases.

Weeds. Add weeds before they go to seed or they'll sprout in your compost or garden.

Make Compost the Easy Way

Don't bother layering. Compost happens; it's as simple as that. If you do nothing but throw your leaves, grass clippings, and kitchen scraps together in a pile, eventually all of the parts will decompose and turn into dark, crumbly compost. Forget about making neat layers of materials, mixing, and stirring. Just make a pile of ingredients you have on hand. Keep adding materials as you get them until your pile reaches about 3 feet tall. Then, start a new pile.

Add handy ingredients and water. Any organic matter will break down into compost. Some commonly available ingredients are kitchen scraps (except meat and dairy products), leaves, grass clippings, straw or hay, spent garden plants, and weeds.

The organisms that break down compost ingredients need evenly moist conditions. Keep your compost pile as wet as a wrung-out sponge: not too wet and not too dry. When you water your yard or garden, give your compost pile a drink, too.

Wait for finished compost. You'll have finished compost at the bottom of the pile in about a year. Keep adding materials to the top of the pile and scoop out compost from the bottom as needed.

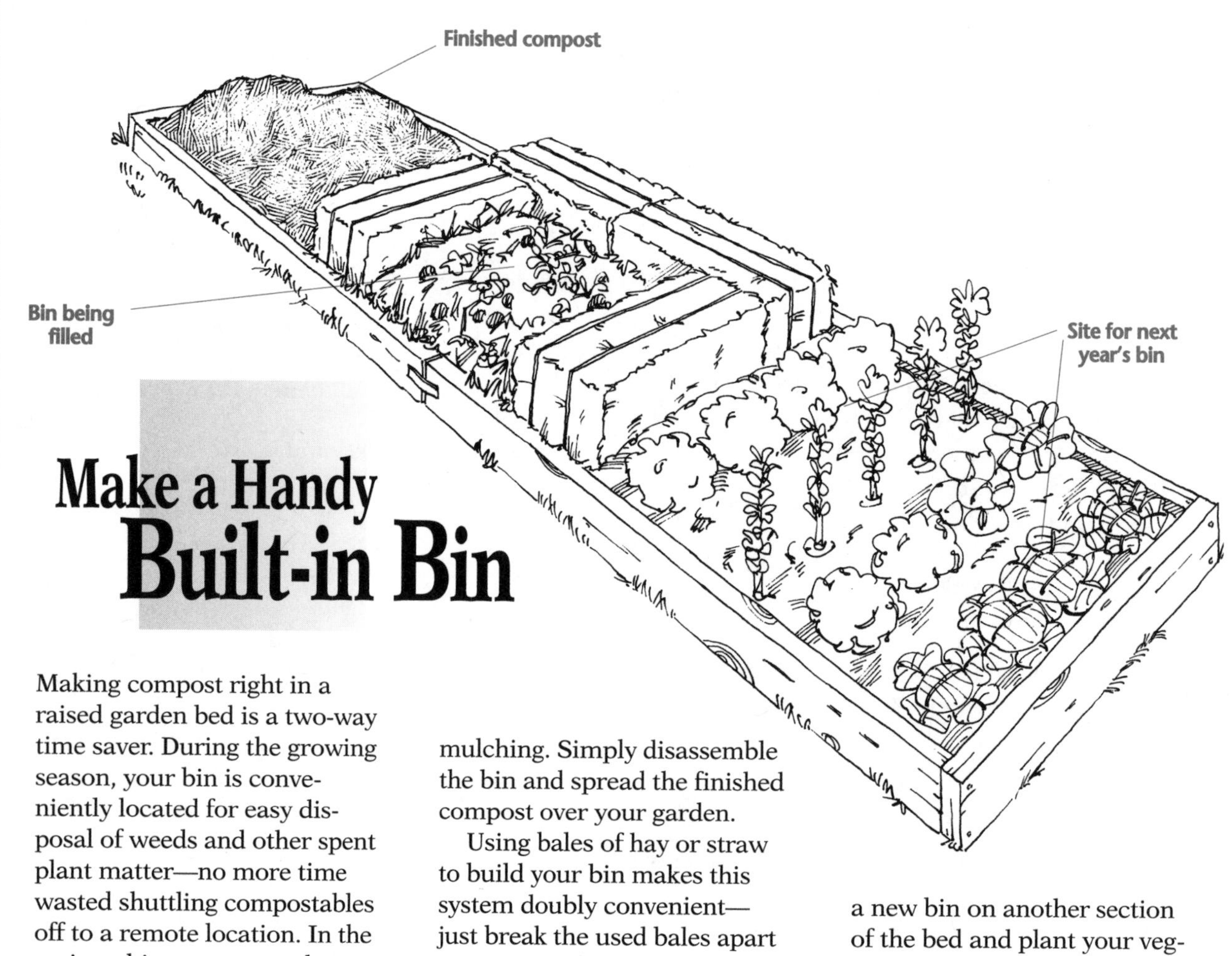

Make a Handy Built-in Bin

Making compost right in a raised garden bed is a two-way time saver. During the growing season, your bin is conveniently located for easy disposal of weeds and other spent plant matter—no more time wasted shuttling compostables off to a remote location. In the spring, this system speeds preplanting soil improvement and mulching. Simply disassemble the bin and spread the finished compost over your garden.

Using bales of hay or straw to build your bin makes this system doubly convenient—just break the used bales apart in spring and use them as mulch. Use fresh bales to form a new bin on another section of the bed and plant your vegetables in the enriched soil where the old bin stood.

Let the Ingredients Do the Work

To speed up the composting process without doing extra work, use the right mix of ingredients. The organisms that make compost will thrive if you serve equal amounts of "brown" and "green" ingredients.

Browns. These high-carbon materials are dry and brown or yellow. They include hay, leaves, paper, pine needles, sawdust, straw, and vegetable stalks.

Greens. High in nitrogen and moist or even sloppy, they include fruit and vegetable wastes, grass clippings, weeds, coffee grounds, cover crops, and seaweed. Because it's very high in nitrogen, manure is also "green."

A pile with all brown ingredients won't decompose; one with all green ingredients will turn slimy and smelly. But mixing a wide variety of greens and browns will make your decomposers happy, and they will produce compost with all the nutrients your plants need.

Take-it-Easy Techniques for Handling Your "Heapables"

Now that you've examined the wealth of compost materials in and around your home, you'll want to use or store them as close as possible to the source. Here are a few hints for the best ways to deal with common compost ingredients before—or instead of—adding them to the compost pile.

Stockpile your scraps. Unless you're aiming for extra exercise, don't dash to your compost pile to toss in kitchen scraps as they happen. Plan on stockpiling stuff like eggshells, banana peels, and coffee grounds in the kitchen for up to a week. A plastic or metal container with a tight-fitting lid is your best bet. To control odors, toss in an occasional handful of wood shavings of the sort sold for pet bedding.

Select a prime site. When you choose a location for your compost pile or bin, think about where your compost ingredients will come from and where the finished compost will go. To reduce the time you spend taking materials to the pile and taking finished compost to your garden, make your compost as close as possible to both these areas. (If your property is hilly, try to keep them both at the same elevation. That way you can push materials or compost across the slope, rather than up and down it.) A spot right next to your vegetable garden can be ideal, allowing you to toss in garden wastes and shovel out finished compost—right where you need it.

Let the clippings fall. Grass clippings make fine mulch and are a valuable addition to your compost pile, especially if you need to balance a lot of dry, brown ingredients like leaves or wood chips. But if you have a lot of lawn, you probably don't need all your clippings. There's no reason to bag up your clippings or rake them up at all if you don't want to. So skip all the trips to the bin by just letting the clippings fall back into the grass. The nutrients they contain will nourish your lawn, reducing the amount of time you'll need to spend fertilizing it, too.

Grow Melons While You Wait

To get double duty from a compost pile you don't turn regularly, grow a crop of melons or pumpkins on top of it. Not only does the foliage cover up the pile and make it more attractive, you get a harvest. Plus, you don't have to move the vines anywhere to compost them!

Build a Basic Bin

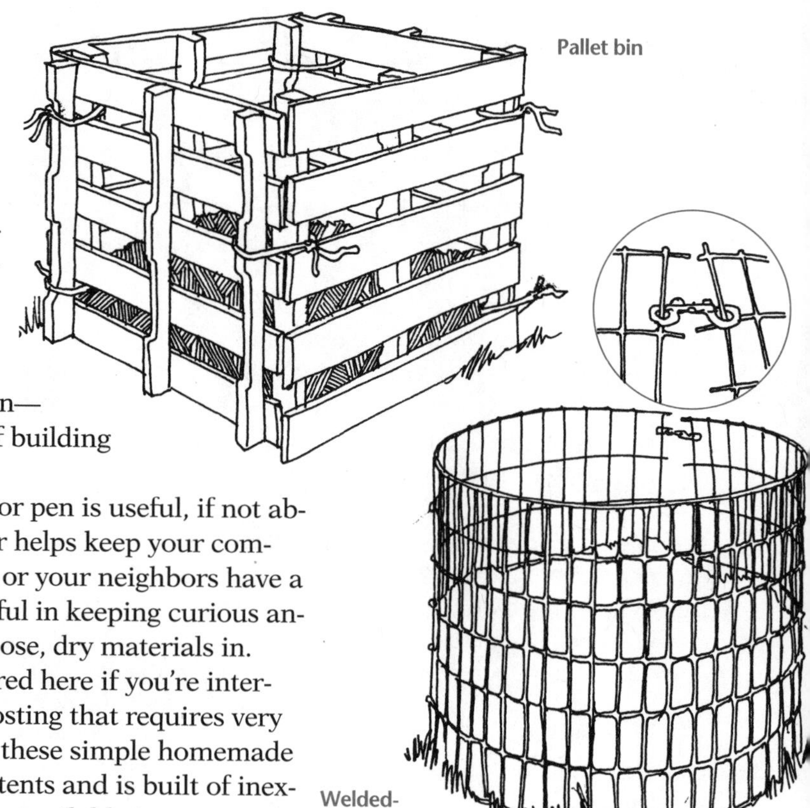

Good compost comes from good ingredients and has little to do with the container it's made in. An uncontained heap of compostable materials produces compost just as well as those same materials in a carefully crafted bin—without the time, effort, and expense of building the composter.

But there are situations where a bin or pen is useful, if not absolutely necessary. A compost container helps keep your composting area tidy—a nice feature if you or your neighbors have a view of that site. A structure is also useful in keeping curious animals out of your pile and in keeping loose, dry materials in.

Assemble one of the basic bins pictured here if you're interested in easygoing, let-it-happen composting that requires very little time and effort from you. Each of these simple homemade containers allows easy access to its contents and is built of inexpensive or free materials that are readily available in most areas.

Best Bets for Bins

Often, the best materials for making a bin are right in and around your home and garden. Old or leftover fencing, cinder blocks, or bricks make fine composters, as do old garbage cans and big, bottomless cardboard boxes. A child's no-longer-needed playpen would serve equally well. Simply make the most of whatever you have available.

Pallet bin. Used wooden pallets are often free for the taking at companies that receive shipments of supplies. Tie or wire four pallets together to form a square bin. Simply untie a corner and swing one side open to add materials, turn the pile, or remove finished compost.

Plastic-coated wire works well for holding together the pallets in this bin. It's durable, flexible, and easy to untie and retie when you need to reach your compost. Use two pieces of wire on the corners for stability; one on the gate corner.

Welded-wire pen. Use a 10-foot length of 48-inch-wide welded-wire fencing to create a circular pen for your compost pile. Hold the ends together with wire, metal fasteners, or twine. Gaining access to your compost is as simple as unfastening the pen and pulling the fencing aside. Or remove the fencing completely, turn your pile onto the space next to it, and set up the fencing around the pile in its new location.

A couple of metal fasteners with spring closures at each end make opening and closing a wire pen a snap. Pull the fencing around your compost so the ends are only a few inches apart, then clip on one fastener near the top and one near the bottom. When you open the pen, leave the fasteners clipped to the fencing so

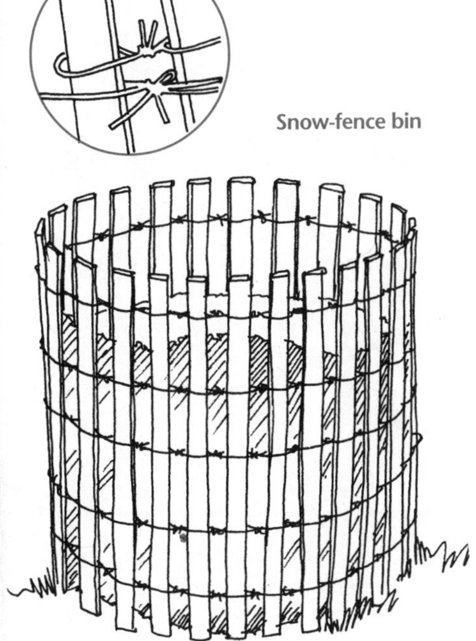
Snow-fence bin

you can find them again when you're ready to close it.

Snow-fence bin. Used or inexpensive snow fencing makes an easy-to-assemble enclosure for your compost. You'll need at least 10 feet of fence to make an adequate-size bin. Arrange the fencing in a circle and fasten the ends together. Or, drive corner posts into the ground and bend the fence around them to form a square or rectangular compost bin.

Snow fencing, which is made of laths woven together with three to five continuous strands of wire, supplies its own built-in fasteners. Loosen the wire around the laths at each end of your piece of fencing and remove a few of them. Straighten out as many of the wires as you'll need to hold the bin closed, then clip off the extras. Close the bin by wrapping or tying together the wires at each end.

Problems?
Here's Help for Your Heap

Busy gardeners barely have time to troubleshoot problems in their gardens and landscapes, let alone ones in the compost pile. Fortunately, composting is a simple process, and most problems are easily prevented. But if odors or obstinately inert ingredients complicate your composting, use the following guide to problems and solutions to set things straight in a hurry.

Problem	Solution
Wet, foul-smelling heap	Aerate the pile by turning or stirring it; add dry, absorbent materials. Protect pile from rain.
Dry heap; little or no decomposition	Aerate the pile by turning or stirring it; add water as you work. Cover pile with plastic to retain moisture.
Warm, damp middle; dry outer materials	Increase volume of pile and moisten.
Damp, sweet-smelling heap with little decomposition	Add nitrogen sources such as fresh grass clippings, blood meal, or manure; aerate the pile by turning or stirring it.
Matted, undecomposed layers of leaves or grass	Break up layers and mix all ingredients well. Shred materials before composting; avoid thick layers of a single ingredient.
Large, undecomposed items in finished compost	Screen out undecomposed materials and add to a new pile.

Cover Crop Your Pile

Here's an easy way to give your compost pile an added boost of nitrogen: Sow an annual cover crop like crimson clover or berseem clover on top of it in the fall or early spring. Dig the crop into the compost when it flowers in early summer.

Sizing Up Buys on Bins

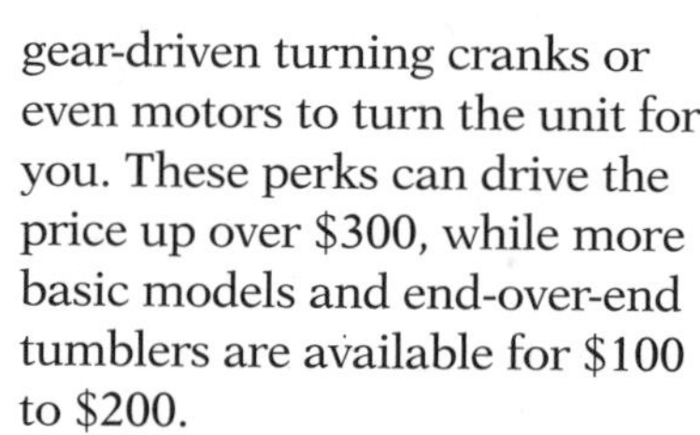

Commercially available composters are generally more expensive than their homemade counterparts, but they do offer some features worthy of consideration. Most conceal their contents well, making them useful where aesthetics are a concern. And once filled, many of them require very little attention from you. Ease of use is another area where manufactured bins excel, although this varies considerably among the different types.

If you choose to buy a bin for any of these reasons—or simply because you haven't the time to make your own—keep the following shortcomings of store-bought composters in mind as well. Few composters on the market have the capacity (about 27 cubic feet) necessary for hot composting. This means that weed seeds and disease organisms may survive composting and return to the garden in your finished compost. Smaller capacity also means commercial models may fall short when yard waste volumes swell—you may have to stockpile grass clippings or leaves until the materials in a full composter finish decomposing.

Drums, Tumblers, and Balls

The many different composters in this category are designed to make turning easy, which allows you to produce finished compost fairly quickly. And since it's easy, the estimates manufacturers provide for the number of days from ingredients to finished compost assume you'll turn your compost regularly.

Barrel types use stands that hold the barrel either on its side for a rolling turning method or upright for end-over-end turning. Look for features such as ease of loading and unloading, interior baffles to help mix contents, and ease of turning when the unit is full. Barrels with a horizontal orientation come with features such as gear-driven turning cranks or even motors to turn the unit for you. These perks can drive the price up over $300, while more basic models and end-over-end tumblers are available for $100 to $200.

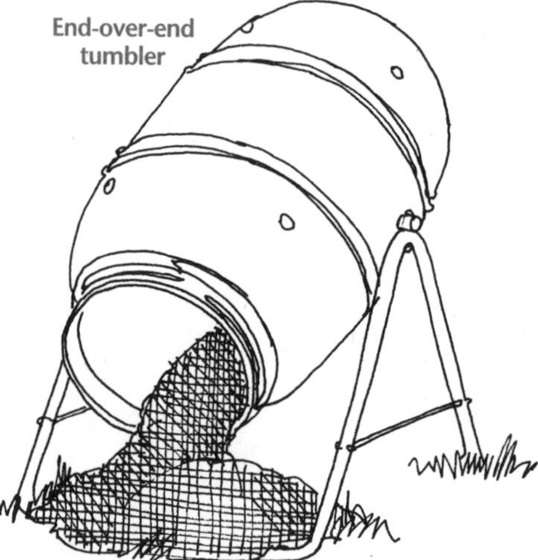

The same turning principles apply to tumblers and balls that you roll on the ground. Turn these rather odd-looking units by pushing or rolling them around your yard to mix their contents. Just roll one to the spot where you want finished compost, open the door, and roll it over to dump the contents. As with barrel tumblers, consider how easily these bins will turn when filled with ingredients; take your yard's slope into account, too, lest turning become an uphill battle. Prices range from $120 to $200, depending on the tumbler's volume.

Conventional Bins

Stationary, enclosed composters come in a range of brands and styles. With these bins, you add materials to the top and remove finished compost at the bottom. Most are made of recycled plastic, which makes them long-lasting and durable.

Like homemade wooden bins, these composters perform best when you occasionally turn their contents. Look for models that allow easy access for aerating and turning options other than moving the entire contents with a pitchfork. Other features to consider include vents for air circulation and a cover that admits some, but not too much, rain. You'll also find a wide price range for such composters, from as low as $70 to over $120, so shop for your best deal and the features you want.

A Simple Cardboard Bin

Cheap, easy, and compostable, too! Manufactured from the recycled liners of corrugated cardboard containers, these bins are colored an eye-pleasing dark green. A cardboard bin will hold your compost for about a year before it's ready to become one with its contents. Then you can just toss it into another cardboard bin and let microorganisms do their thing. Cardboard bins are available by mail from Mellinger's Inc., 2310 West South Range Road, North Lima, OH 44452. The cost is comparable to a homemade welded-wire pen, but with a smaller capacity.

Easy Composting for Winter

Most composting systems slow down when the weather turns cold. The lower temperatures inhibit decomposition, and winter weather also reduces the amount of yard waste destined for the compost pile. But if your compost pile is also your kitchen waste disposal system, you need a wintertime system that really works. Here's a method using a modified plastic garbage can that will help you through the winter months. You may like it well enough to use year-round.

Composting proceeds very slowly in this system—to help things along, insulate the can with bales of hay or straw or bags of dried leaves. A stockpile of chopped, dried leaves or shredded newspaper is useful for tossing in with wet kitchen scraps. When spring arrives, you can add the can's contents to your regular compost pile or simply let them finish composting in the garbage can.

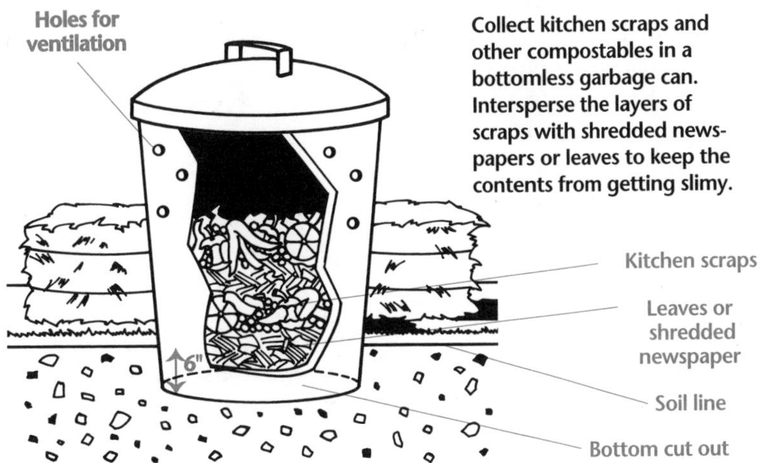

Collect kitchen scraps and other compostables in a bottomless garbage can. Intersperse the layers of scraps with shredded newspapers or leaves to keep the contents from getting slimy.

1. Cut the bottom out of a large plastic garbage can, and cut or drill several 1-inch holes in the sides for ventilation.

2. Select a site near your house to make winter compost treks easier. Then use the cutout from the bottom of the can to measure off a can-size space on the ground where you'll position your winter composter.

3. Following your markings, dig a hole about 6 inches deep and set the bottomless can into the hole.

4. Add compostable materials as you collect them.

Speed Up Your Compost with One Good Turn

Build a pile or fill a bin with a good mix of compostable materials, and you'll eventually have compost. It's that simple. But it could take a year or more to get finished compost—unless you add air and water to the mix. That's because the hungry horde of organisms in your compost pile needs air and water to reduce your scraps and yard waste to black gold. Providing water is easy: Keep your pile about as wet as a wrung-out sponge. Watering a pile in dry climates and covering it in wet regions are the best ways to maintain a good moisture level.

Adding air isn't as easy. Time-honored turning, as often as every 2 to 3 days, is a real back bender, and it takes time to do it right. But when your garden soil cries out for compost and your wallet cries out from too many purchases of bagged organic matter, take your fork in hand and give your pile at least one good turn.

If turning hasn't been a part of your composting plan before, you'll be surprised at how much more quickly a turned pile turns into finished compost. Stirring and turning your compost just once or twice during the growing season can cut composting time down from a year to just a few months. More frequent aeration can further speed the process.

If turning seems like the best tactic for producing the compost you need, try a few of the following tips to ease the trials of turning.

Plan for easy access. One of the biggest hindrances to turning compost is accessibility. Confining bins or cramped spaces quickly frustrate turning efforts by keeping you from getting in there with your fork and getting the job done. An unconfined pile that has space next to it for turning is easiest to deal with; make sure bins allow full-front access.

Form a duet or trio. Removing compost from a bin and turning it back into the same bin makes you move the compost twice. Use two bins, one for composting and one to turn the compost into. A third bin gives you a place to store materials until you're ready to start a new pile.

Lift with your knees, not your back. Ignoring this simple technique can make you vow to never turn again. When you do turn your compost, give your back a break and let your stronger leg muscles do the heavy lifting.

Don't twist when you turn. When moving compost from one pile to another, carry each shovelful or forkful to its new home. Lifting, twisting, and tossing can strain your shoulders and back.

Schedule turning time. Promise not to turn your pile every time you're near it. Set a schedule you can live with—once a month, bi-weekly, whatever works best and produces the compost you need—and tend your pile at those times. Try tending your compost pile at dusk when cooler temperatures make turning more pleasant and fading light limits other garden activities.

Tips for No-Turn Composters

If you're like most gardeners, turning compost ranks high on your list of chores you'd rather avoid, especially when so many other garden tasks await your attention. Or perhaps you'd gladly turn your pile, but can't because it's just too strenuous. Here are some other compost-aerating methods that will let you turn your attention to gardening activities you enjoy more.

Give it a tumble. Barrel composters and compost tumblers give you a mechanical edge when it comes to turning compost. Regularly giving your barrel a spin produces finished compost quickly with little effort. One solar-powered tumbler is even mechanized to turn the barrel for you.

Poke and prod. Compost aerating tools let you aerate your pile by poking holes in it instead of turning it. Poking your pile with a sturdy stick or pipe has a similar effect and is still easier than turning with a pitchfork.

Install ventilation. Build your pile around a "chimney" of PVC pipe or sturdy cardboard tubing with holes drilled into it. Or layer perforated pipes, tubes with holes drilled in them, or sunflower stalks into your pile as you add materials. A pile built atop a pile of loose brush, a pallet, or a raised wire frame also gets more air movement, as the heat of decomposition pulls air up from the ventilated base.

To add air to your compost pile with an aerating tool, push the tool into the compost. When you pull it out, two "wings" at the tip of the aerator open, enlarge the hole and let air into the pile's interior.

Ventilating your pile with PVC pipes or cardboard tubes with holes drilled in them will speed up the composting process. Either build your pile around a single chimney or layer the pipes across it as you build.

Skip the Pile and Go Straight to the Soil

Skip the bins and the piles and try this quick and easy composting method: Just dig a hole 12 to 18 inches deep in your garden and bury your kitchen scraps and fruit and vegetable trimmings. You'll be eliminating the whole process of gathering materials and building and tending a compost pile. Keep in mind, though, that while this method may be convenient, it improves the soil more slowly than spreading finished compost.

You can use a post-hole digger to create these in-ground garbage disposals as you need them. Or from early spring until the ground freezes, leave a row in your garden empty and bury scraps there as they accumulate. Mulch your "compost row" heavily to keep it from becoming weedy. When you need to add new kitchen scraps or other compostables, just pull back the mulch and bury them. To spread out your soil improvement efforts, plant the row with vegetables in the next growing season and start a new row for compostables.

Say "Bye" to Your Bin with Sheet Composting

Here's an easy way to skip the bin, pass up the pile, and go directly to your garden. Sheet composting—a low-labor combination of mulching and composting—can enrich your soil without all the moving, mixing, and managing of traditional composting methods.

To sheet compost, simply top your garden's soil with plant residues—leaves, grass clippings, seed-free weeds—in the fall and leave them there until spring. Then work them into the soil with your shovel or rotary tiller. During the growing season, you can sheet compost between rows or in unplanted parts of your garden.

Sheet composting works best if you chop or shred plant materials before you spread them on your garden. To keep lightweight compostables such as chopped leaves from blowing away, mix them with other ingredients like fresh grass clippings or weeds. Other alternatives are to turn them into the soil or anchor them with heavier materials such as mulch or compost.

If you have a side discharge mower, just blow the clippings onto your garden as you mow around it. Or rake clippings from the surrounding grass onto your garden bed after you mow.

You can make short work of leaves if you have a bagging mower. Instead of raking them up, mow them right off your

1. Mow up your leaves. Collect and chop leaves for sheet composting or mulch in one easy step by mowing them off your lawn with a bagging lawn mower.

2. Cover your beds. Spread a 3-inch layer of chopped leaves right onto your garden bed from the mower bag. Leave in place all winter to decompose.

lawn. Another option is to pile them up on your garden and run the mower over them to chop them up.

By making compost right on top of the soil, you bypass the need to gather ingredients, mix them up, turn them, and transport finished compost back to your garden. However, you also bypass some of the waste-disposal benefits of compost piles and bins. Sheet composting is not a good way to dispose of kitchen scraps. And few gardeners find it useful for beds of ornamentals—it's best on the open expanse of a vegetable garden.

This method is also more appealing if you own or have access to a rotary tiller to help you incorporate your compost into the soil. Some gardeners use this method successfully without turning the soil; they simply pull back the covering materials and plant in the soil below.

3. **Dig or till in the compost.** In early spring the following year, several weeks before you're ready to plant, incorporate last year's compost materials into the soil.

Compost Away Tough Sites

With kitchen scraps, yard clippings, and a little patience, you can turn an unsightly depression—or any other tough site—into a great garden. All you need to do is compost right on the site and spread the compost once it's mature. Here's how.

Start building a compost pile on your problem site by piling up lawn clippings, chopped leaves, weeds that haven't set seed, and kitchen scraps. If you are trying to fill a depression in your lawn or improve a site with poor soil, you can simply build right on the site. If you're working with a slope, build a temporary wall at the base of the slope with heavier materials like clumps of dug-up sod turned upside down to keep your pile in place.

Continue adding materials until the pile is 4 feet high or so. Start another pile next to the first if you are going to need more compost to improve the site. You can plant gourds or pumpkins in the piles to camouflage them, if you like.

Once the pile has broken down into finished compost, spread it over the site, add some topsoil, plant, and mulch. Keep the plants well watered until they are established.

CHAPTER 4

Seed Starting

For Simple Starts, Presprout and Presoak

Give Seeds What They Need to Succeed

Make a Place for Perennials

Wise Buys Are the Start of Success with Seeds

Cover Seeds Lightly

Minimize Work with a Smart-Start Setup

Get the Maximum from Your Medium

Steps to Success When You're Sowing Direct

Sow-Easy Seeding Techniques

Protect Your Posture with the Pea Shooter

Simple Seedlings: Continued Care

Seed Starting the Low-Maintenance Way

STARTING PLANTS FROM SEED may not seem low-maintenance. After all, it takes time, planning, effort, and materials. Why not just buy plants at the garden center and be done with it?

For one thing, starting from seed saves money. And since seed catalogs offer a seemingly limitless selection, it also means you'll be able to choose disease-resistant hybrids or favorite heirloom cultivars, whichever you prefer. Starting from seed also allows you to grow seedlings when you need them. You can grow small batches of plants to provide a continuous harvest, time your seed starting to account for local weather conditions, or grow sets for a late fall crop.

Fortunately, seed starting doesn't need to take huge amounts of time or effort. Use this chapter to help you grow great seedlings without tying up all your time.

For Smooth, Simple Starts, Presprout and Presoak

Here's a technique that will let you start seeds without much space, soil, or light, yet give them the moisture and warmth they need to germinate. Instead of sowing your seeds into prepared containers of planting medium, presprout them using a couple of layers of moistened paper towel and a plastic bag.

This method works well for precious or rare seeds because it lets you lovingly plant each one that sprouts. It saves time if your seeds are old—you don't have to sow lots of seeds to figure out which ones are still viable and will grow.

You can also presprout or presoak seeds and sow them directly into your garden. This method is especially useful for seeds that are particular about germination or for times when the soil is cold or dry. It works well for peas, for example, which germinate best in warm soil but grow best when the air is cool. Also try it to give melons, squash, and their relatives, which need ample warmth to germinate, a head start in the garden. Presprout and plant the sprouted seeds directly into your garden two weeks after your last spring frost.

Presoaking seeds is even simpler than presprouting. Large seeds, such as beans, peas, and okra, will germinate faster if soaked overnight in lukewarm water before planting. And a 20-minute preplanting soak in compost tea (see page 63) will encourage beans, corn, parsley, peas, spinach, and squash, as well as offering some protection against soilborne diseases. Drain seeds after presoaking them and dry them briefly on paper towels for easier handling when you plant.

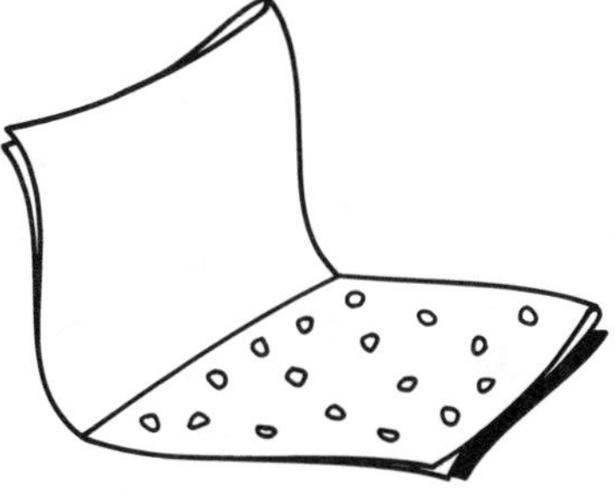

1. **Germinate in paper.** Put your seeds in the middle third of two moistened paper towels. Position the seeds carefully, leaving a little space between the seeds. Fold the two outer thirds of the toweling in over the seeds.

2. **Store in a plastic bag.** Put the folded towel in a plastic bag, along with a label identifying the seeds and the date you started them. You can put several seed/towel packages in one bag, as long as you attach a label to each package or fold it into the towel. Seal the bag loosely—your seeds need air, too. To provide the necessary warmth, put the bag atop your refrigerator or water heater.

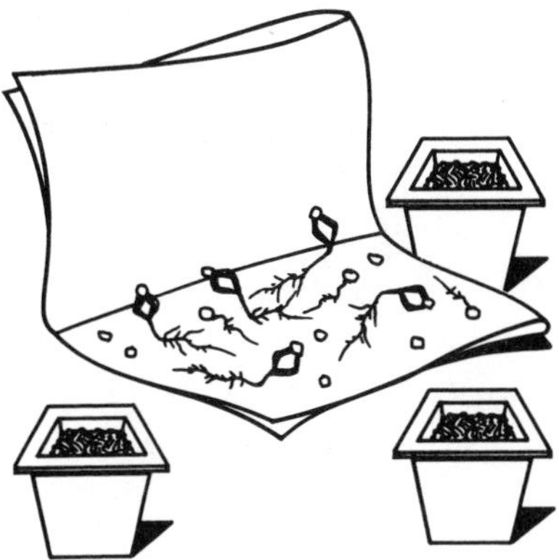

3. **Check for sprouting.** Check your seeds in 2 or 3 days and every day after that. Remove them from the towels as soon as they sprout and plant them, sprout (root) down, in containers filled with soilless medium. Handle each seed by its seed coat, and poke a hole into the moistened medium. Lower the root into the hole and position the seed just below the surface of the medium. Gently press the medium around the seed.

heat & capillary mats -

Easy Ways to Give Seeds What They Need to Succeed

To germinate, most seeds' needs are relatively simple: They need warmth and moisture. While some seeds also require either light or darkness to sprout, most do just fine as long as they're warm and moist. You can take advantage of this by saving growing sites under lights and next to windows for your seedlings and for the few seeds that need light to germinate. Sprout all your other seeds anywhere you can easily keep them warm and moist. Here are some other hints to help you satisfy your seeds' needs with ease.

Make a Place for Perennials

The seeds of many perennial plants require exposure to winter conditions (moist cold) in order to germinate. While you can give seeds such a treatment in your refrigerator, in cold winter areas it's equally simple to sow them into pots and set them outdoors for the winter. A frame made out of stacked bricks, cinder blocks, or timbers and covered with a piece of window screen will protect your seeds from critters and falling leaves until spring.

Pick the right container. Moisture matters when it comes to starting seeds, but so does air. Make sure every container you sow seeds into has a drainage hole in the bottom; if your seeds sit in water, they'll rot. If you're managing a large number of seedlings, uniformly sized containers make it easy to apply water evenly; square containers make best use of limited space under lights or next to windows.

Put an appliance to work. Gentle, constant warmth stimulates seed sprouting. You can buy a heat mat to provide seed-stimulating temperatures, or you can make use of existing sources such as your refrigerator or water heater. You can start seeds atop your TV, too, if it's on a lot.

Take the work out of watering. Try a capillary mat to help keep seed-starting medium moist without extra effort. While not a substitute for regularly checking moisture levels yourself, a wick-watering system protects seedlings from the wide variations that can occur if you forget to water.

Add water with care. In addition to refilling the reservoir for a capillary mat system, you'll probably need to moisten the surface of the medium once in a while. Use a spray bottle that produces a fine shower of water—or a watering can rose with very small holes—to avoid washing young seedlings around in their containers. If you're not wicking water to your seedling containers, bottom-water by setting them in a flat of water for a few minutes. Then lift them out and let excess water drain away.

Maintain moisture. Keeping a cover over containers of newly sown seeds holds in the moisture and substantially reduces the need to water. Purchase rigid plastic covers to fit standard-size flats or simply cover containers with plastic wrap, supported an inch or so above the medium. To prevent disease, remove the cover when your seedlings pop up.

Let there be light. Seedlings need bright light to grow strong and healthy. A greenhouse or sunporch makes an ideal seed-starting spot; a bright window is adequate as well. Seedlings growing next to windows need to be turned regularly since they tend to bend toward the light source.

Artificial lights are an excellent option, too. To keep seedlings from growing leggy as they stretch toward lights above them, start with lights just 2 to 3 inches over your containers. Move the lights up as your seeds start to grow, but keep them no farther than 4 to 6 inches above the plant tops.

Seedlings need 12 to 16 hours of light each day. Use a simple appliance timer to turn the lights on and off for you and to make sure that they get a consistent amount of light each day.

Wise Buys Are the Start of Success with Seeds

Whether you plan to set up a seed-starting system or simply toss a few seeds into the soil, it's worth your time to choose seeds and seed sources with care. Follow the tips below to spend your seed-shopping time and money wisely to get the seeds you want.

Stick to a list. Temptation lingers on every page of seed catalogs. Give in too many times and you'll find yourself with more seeds than you have time, energy, or space to start.

Shop early in the season. Even large seed companies may run out of the most popular cultivars of your favorite garden plants. Visit retailers' seed racks early, and place catalog orders promptly.

Buy only what you need. While extras of most seeds will keep for a year or two, it's a nuisance to store partial seed packets and to find them them when planting time rolls around again. And few seeds, if any, benefit from this aging process. Look for sources that sell seeds in small quantities, or share an order with friends.

Find a reputable source. Buy from seed sellers who guarantee their products and who will answer your questions about planting and growing the seeds they sell.

Bypass "bargain" seeds. Reduced prices often reflect reduced quality; seeds are likely to be older and stored under less-than-desirable conditions. The result: fewer, weaker seedlings that need more care just to survive.

Cover Seeds Lightly

Covering seeds too deeply can reduce germination or cause seeds to sprout unevenly. Most need a covering only three times their diameter (or thickness). To avoid burying small seeds under too much medium, sow them on top of moistened, prepared seed-starting medium, then cover them with a light layer of dry medium. Use a fine-mist spray bottle to dampen the covering.

Minimize Work with a Smart-Start Setup

Germinating seeds and growing them to transplanting size requires careful attention to temperature, moisture, and light. With a little planning, your seed-starting setup can tend to some of these details for you. Features such as light timers and wick-watering systems can save you from becoming a slave to your seeds and seedlings.

Even so, you'll want to check on your seeds and seedlings regularly. Put your seed-starting operation someplace where you're likely to visit it at least every couple of days. A location near a window is handy but unnecessary as long as you plan to provide light; more helpful is a nearby source of water and a spot that you don't mind getting a little messy.

If you're starting just a few seeds, a couple of pots on a windowsill may be just right. For managing multiple flats of seedlings, a little planning up front will help you save time and effort in the long run.

Adjustable-height fluorescent lights

Capillary mat watering system

Pots, Peat, Even Paper—There's a Container to Suit Your Seeds and Needs

The ideal seed-starting and seedling-growing container holds 1½ to 2 inches of soil-like medium and has holes in the bottom for drainage. That's it. All other features of the containers you start your seeds in are up to you. Options include flats, cell packs, peat pots, peat pellets, plastic pots, clay pots, cardboard tubes, newspaper pots, milk jugs or cartons with the sides cut down, egg cartons, virtually any food container, and soil blocks formed of planting medium without any surrounding container.

Convenient container storage
Adjustable-height fluorescent lights
Timer to control lights
Compost collection
Potting medium
grow MIX

Get the Maximum from Your Medium

A good growing medium for seedlings is loose and crumbly, allowing it to hold both moisture and air for healthy root growth. For seed starting, try any of the following materials alone or in combination: vermiculite, milled sphagnum moss, perlite, or screened compost. You can also buy bagged mixes that already contain a combination of materials.

A seed-starting medium does not need to be a source of nutrients; your seedlings will do fine with the food they bring with them until about the time their first true leaves appear. At that point, you can transplant them into a potting mix that contains compost, soil, and/or fertilizers. Or you can begin to foliar-feed them with sprays of fish emulsion or liquid seaweed.

Seed-starting mixes can be hard to wet, particularly when they're completely dry. To overcome this and avoid the need to water seed-starting containers after you've sown your seeds, moisten the medium thoroughly before you put it into containers. Put dry mix into a tub or other large, watertight container, then add warm water and mix until it's well saturated. To spare yourself a lot of stirring, add water and let it sit overnight so it has time to absorb most of the moisture on its own. Then fill your containers and, if necessary, let excess moisture drain away before you plant. Once your seeds are sown, keep a close watch on moisture levels to make sure the medium doesn't dry out again.

A Simple Way to Start

Indoor seed starting need not be an elaborate space- and time-consuming effort. Fill a container with moistened soilless medium, sow your seeds, add a label, then put the container into a loosely closed plastic bag. Remove the bag after the seeds sprout.

Steps to Success When You're Sowing Direct

The simplest way to start seeds is the way nature does it—put them directly on or in the ground. If you live where winters are mild, you can sow seeds outside year-round. In cold-winter areas, the seed-sowing season begins in spring when the ground thaws and continues into early fall.

Start with a weed-free seedbed. Loose, crumbly, well-enriched soil lets seedlings spread their roots and get growing. If you prepared your soil in fall and mulched it over winter, you can pull back the mulch and begin planting in spring. Otherwise, wait until the soil is soft enough to dig and dry enough to crumble in your hand. Don't work your soil while it's wet or your seeds will wake up in concrete.

Sprinkle small seeds lightly over the area you want to plant, or plant in straight rows using a string stretched between two stakes as a guide. Follow seed packet directions for spacing. If the weather's dry when you plant, gently moisten the seedbed, then tack a piece of floating row cover over it to hold in moisture until your seeds germinate.

Sow-Easy Seeding Techniques

The actual delivery of seed to soil is a critical moment in determining how much maintenance lies ahead. Those few seconds when you lovingly tuck a seed into a peat pot or casually toss it into an open furrow can determine whether you'll soon be thinning crowded plants or lounging in a hammock. Try these tips to sow seeds accurately, efficiently, and (almost) effortlessly.

If you sow too thickly, be ready to thin. Whether you're sowing into a flat or directly in your garden, pay attention to spacing. It's tempting (and all too easy) to sow thickly to ensure a full crop, but that means diminished yields unless you spend time thinning out extra plants after seeds germinate. Nobody wants to nip out healthy seedlings, even if they're a bit crowded. It takes a little more time to sow seeds at their proper spacing, but the resulting healthy plants will need less of your attention later on.

It's nice for your nails, too. A common metal nail file makes a great tool for planting tiny seeds into seed-starting containers. Moisten the pointed tip and use it to pick up tiny seeds—they'll stick to it—and to lay them atop the medium. When seedlings are ready for transplanting, use the file for digging under seedling roots and lifting them out and into a new home.

Recycle a shaker. Improve distribution of small to medium seeds by shaking them out of clean, recycled salt or spice shakers. Add dry white sand to very fine seeds to help you see where you're sowing. You can also combine seeds of crops that mature quickly with those of crops that grow more slowly. For example, sow radish and carrot seeds together; you'll thin your carrot crop as you harvest your radishes.

Plant in a different pattern. If you want to sow extra seeds to ensure a full crop, try planting small groups of seeds at the proper spacing. If multiple seeds sprout, you'll still have to thin out all but one, but without worrying about the spacing within the row.

Try a tape. Although commercial seed tapes offer only a very limited selection of plants and cultivars, few other planting methods are as easy. Prepare your planting area as described in "Steps to Success When You're Sowing Direct" on the opposite page and lay the seed tape into a furrow of the proper depth, cover it lightly, and water.

Get mechanically inclined. For large gardens with straight rows, a mechanical seeder can cut your seed-sowing time in half. As you push one of these two-wheeled devices through the garden, it makes a furrow, drops seeds at the proper spacing, covers the seeds, and firms the soil over them.

Protect Your Posture with the Perfect Pea Shooter

Stooping to sow large-seeded crops such as peas, corn, or beans places an unnecessary strain on your spine. Avoid getting the bends over beans by using a length of lightweight tubing, such as PVC pipe, to drop seeds into the soil while you remain standing. Choose a piece of pipe that's long enough to let you stand, with a diameter that lets seeds pass through with ease. Use a permanent marker to draw 1-inch intervals on one end, and use your planter to check planting depth, too.

Simple Seedlings: A Quick-Reference Guide to Continued Care for Your Sprouted Seeds

Once your seeds are up and growing, their needs change somewhat. Here are some hints to help keep your sprouts happy and healthy as you get them ready to move to your garden.

Take off the covers. Remove plastic or glass covers to lower the humidity and give seedlings as much light as possible.

Cut down on watering. Let the top ¼ inch of soil dry between waterings, and resist the urge to feed emerging plants. Overwatering and fertilizing result in soft, tangled growth and rot.

Water carefully. If you water from above, water next to seedlings rather than on top of them. Water as gently as possible. Or water seedlings from below by pouring water into the tray or saucer in which the flats or pots are sitting and letting it soak up into the soil. And water in the morning, not in the evening.

Transplant when true leaves appear. Transplant before seedlings' roots get tangled. The best time is when seedlings have developed their first set of true leaves. When seedlings sprout, they first send up seed leaves, shaped like the seed coat. The leaves that follow are true leaves.

Handle with care. Don't handle seedling stems—they're very fragile and easy to crush. Instead, dig up the seedling with a houseplant trowel or Popsicle stick, then hold it gently by the leaves to move it.

Give each a home of its own. Plant each seedling in a clean cell pack, cup with drainage holes, or plastic pot of its own. Replant at the same depth it grew in the flat, and firm the soil to make sure there's good root-to-soil contact.

Don't delay. Handle seedlings as little as possible; don't leave them lying out. Have your pots set up and the medium moist and ready before you start, and transplant one seedling at a time. The roots can dry out in a matter of minutes.

Keep them comfortable. Protect newly transplanted seedlings until they've reestablished themselves. Keep them in bright but indirect light.

Hold off on feeding. Don't fertilize seedlings until they're established or you'll shock them. Once they start growing again, give them a boost with one-third- to one-half-strength liquid seaweed.

Keep them cool. Don't let your seedlings overheat. They prefer cool temperatures—around 60°F is fine for most species.

Prepare them for life outdoors. Start hardening off your seedlings when frost danger is over and the soil has warmed. Set them outside during the day and bring them in again at night. Select a protected location, such as a spot against a north-facing wall. If possible, mist them in the heat of the day, and put them in the shade or cover them with moist newspaper or a spunbonded row cover like Reemay. Continue this treatment for about a week before planting them out in your gardens.

TAKE-IT-EASY TIP!

Squash Seedlings Need Room for Roots

The seedlings of squash, melons, and their relatives don't grow well when their roots are disturbed. Instead of starting these seeds in seedling flats and transplanting them into larger containers, give them room to grow from the start. Sow squash and their cousins into individual containers filled with potting mix. When it's time to move them to the garden, remove their containers gently to minimize root injury.

CHAPTER 5

Planting

Planting the Low-Maintenance Way

A WELL-DONE planting job is rarely a low-maintenance enterprise. Even in the best soils, planting means at least a little bit of digging, a little removal of existing vegetation, and a little soil preparation. And the bigger the plant, the more of those things you'll have to do. In rocky, compacted, or weedy sites, planting can mean hard work, even for relatively small plants.

But planting properly pays long-term dividends. Why? Because time invested in careful planting means you'll save time later when you're not nursing sickly plants or removing dead ones. Proper planting also helps plants stay healthy and grow vigorously. Not only will your plants look great, but you also reduce your chances of having to deal with pest and disease problems down the road. Finally, if you treat your investments with care at planting time, the money you spend on plants won't go to waste. There's nothing like having to replace a newly planted tree or shrub that didn't survive a slipshod planting job to remind you that it's worthwhile to do it right the first time.

Cut Post-Planting Care with Seasonal Savvy

Wouldn't it be great to just stick a plant into its chosen site and be done with it? Now *that's* low maintenance! Well, you can get away with this no-care approach—and still end up with healthy plants—if you choose the right planting time. To get off to a good start, plants need moist, warm soil for good root growth, as well as ample water to support topgrowth. All you need to do is make the most of the weather in your region.

In most parts of the United States, spring and/or fall are ideal for establishing plants with a minimum of fuss. (In the South, late or early winter are best.) The cloudy days and cool, moist air help reduce transplant shock by keeping moisture losses to a minimum. Here are some guidelines to help you decide which season is best for planting.

Spring planting. In spring, plants are naturally preparing for a flush of new growth, which is just what they'll need to get established in a new location. Spring rains naturally help keep new transplants well watered, too. In areas where cold weather arrives in early autumn and temperatures often fall below –10°F, early spring planting gives plants time to grow and establish themselves before harsh winter temperatures arrive.

Fall planting. Fall planting provides plants with weeks of good root-growing weather—moist soil and warm soil temperatures. Since aboveground growth slows or becomes dormant in the cooler air, the roots have a chance to catch up with topgrowth. Fall transplants also can begin growing in early spring, when the soil is still too wet for planting.

For the best root growth and winter survival, try fall planting only in areas where the soil temperature remains above 50°F for several weeks after the trees become dormant. And plant early in the fall to take advantage of good root-growing weather.

In areas with hot, dry summers and mild winters, fall planting gives new plants time to establish healthy roots before the following spring. By then, the plants' roots are also better prepared to survive the hot summer weather.

Summer planting. You can plant successfully in summer, but summer installations generally demand more watering and care than plantings timed to take advantage of the cooler weather and natural rainfall in spring and fall.

At Planting Time, Put the Weather to Work

Sunny, breezy spring days are guaranteed to set gardeners planting, but such days aren't ideal from a plant's perspective. In warm sun and drying wind, new transplants suffer because their roots can't take up enough water to replace the amount they lose through their leaves. Instead, put in your plants under gray and drizzly skies.

If you *do* plant on a sunny day, make sure plants are well watered before you start, and don't leave them with their roots exposed to sun and wind.

After planting, water well to help plants get growing as quickly as possible. Watering also settles the backfilled soil around the roots and forces out any air pockets that formed during planting. Save fertilizer applications until you see signs of new growth.

Don't Dig Down, Dig Out

Simply digging a hole and plopping a plant into it may seem like the easy way to plant, but it causes long-term problems that may come back to haunt you. Plant roots are likely to circle around in a planting hole without ever extending into the surrounding soil. Eventually, they can choke, or girdle, the plant. A planting hole can also become a "bathtub" of loose soil that traps water around roots and drowns them.

To give your plants the best possible chance for a healthy, problem-free life, give them a prepared planting site. To prepare a planting site, spade or till up a planting area that's about five times the diameter of the plant's root ball. This loosens the soil so the roots can spread freely. Amending the soil over the entire area with organic matter to a shovel's depth is ideal, but it isn't absolutely necessary if you've picked plants suited to your soil conditions. When you plant, dig saucer-shaped holes, as shown in the illustration above.

Preparing planting areas for groups of trees and shrubs is a great idea. Plants growing together in a large, mulched planting area will be healthier and more vigorous than ones planted individually in the lawn.

Instead of digging the deepest hole you can manage, encourage roots to spread out when you plant by loosening the soil to a shovel's depth over a wide area. Dig a saucer-shaped hole two to three times the width of the root ball for each plant. Make the holes just deep enough to set the plant at the same depth it grew at the nursery.

To Plant Right, Pick Right from the Start

To save yourself hours of maintenance, pick plants that like your site from the start. By choosing plants that will thrive in your site's conditions, you'll prevent years of maintenance headaches.

It's a losing battle to plant something in a site that doesn't suit it. You can amend the soil in the sunny border between your house and driveway to get rhododendrons to grow there, but you'll tire of the extra care they'll need every year just to eke out a so-so existence. Eventually, you'll want to replace them with plants that flourish without extra effort. For ideas on plants to grow in challenging situations, see Chapter 21.

Take-It-Easy Planting Tips

On smaller plants, a screwdriver or even a plant tag makes a handy tool for teasing out roots that are circling the container.

Although you shouldn't cut corners when it comes to proper planting, here are some tips to make planting easy.

Wheel, don't carry. Use a garden cart or wheelbarrow to carry everything you need to your site at once—plants, shovel, trowel, mulch, and any other tools you might need.

Slide, don't lift. Rather than carrying large plants, use a large tarp to slide them over rough ground. On smooth surfaces, setting plants on a dolly may do the trick.

Use professional planters. Consider having large trees and shrubs planted by the nursery where you bought them. Large plants can easily weigh over 100 pounds, so professional planting can save your back. Also, many nurseries provide replacement guarantees on plants they install.

Measure before you plant. Make sure your hole is large enough before you set your plant into it. Measuring the height and width of both the hole and the root ball will save you from having to haul the plant out of the hole repeatedly while you make it larger.

Space before you plant. If you're planting a large area of groundcovers or annuals, space out the plants you have over the area you want to plant before you dig.

Spread the roots for no-fail planting. Before you settle container-grown plants into the ground, take a minute to encourage the roots to spread out into the soil. Using a knife or trowel to quarter the root ball seems like a drastic technique, but it's a very effective way to encourage the roots to branch and spread. When you quarter a root ball, cut upward about halfway from the base. Or, for smaller plants, use the technique shown in the illustration above.

When you plant, spread the roots out in the planting hole and backfill around them. If your planting site is newly prepared, set plants slightly higher than they grew in their pots—they'll settle in as the soil settles. Otherwise, plant them at their container-grown depth.

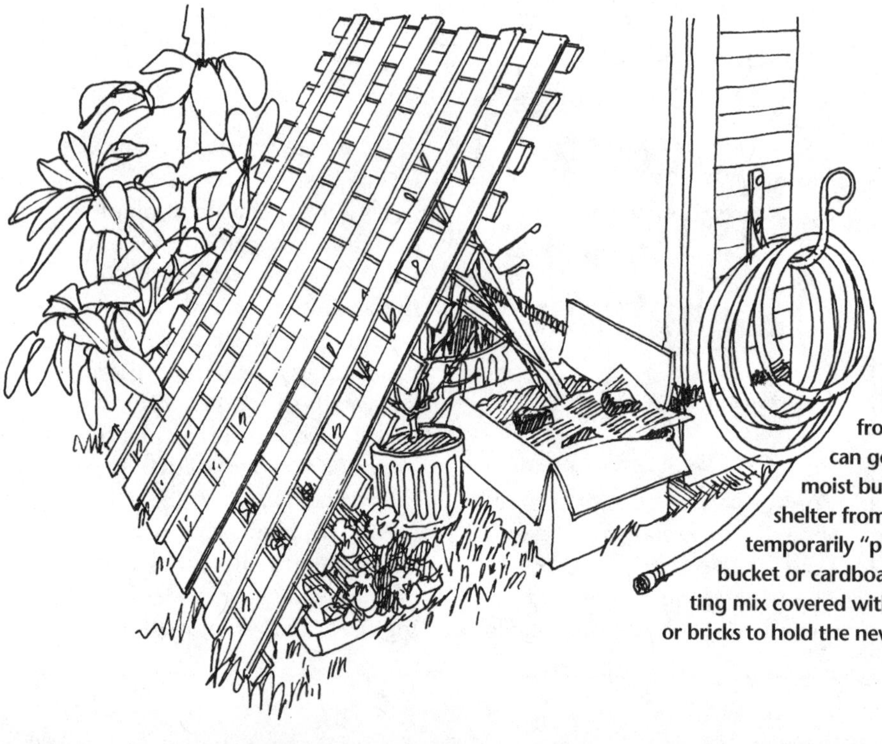

If you don't have time to plant new purchases right away, protect them from stress and harsh conditions until you can get them into the ground. Keep the roots moist but not constantly wet, and provide shelter from strong sunlight and winds. You can temporarily "plant" bareroot purchases in a large bucket or cardboard box of moistened compost or potting mix covered with a layer of damp newspaper. Use rocks or bricks to hold the newspaper in place.

Bareroot Plants
Make for Easy Planting

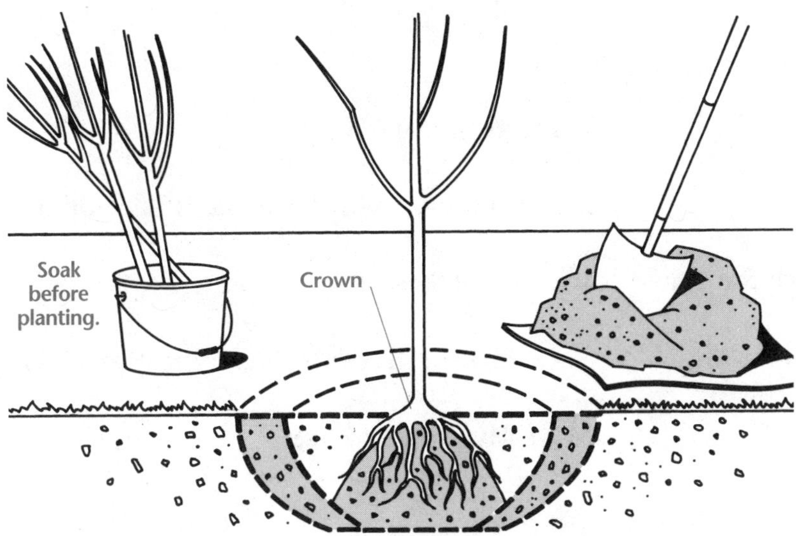

To plant bareroot plants, dig a hole that's wider than it is deep. Then spread the roots over a mound of soil in the bottom of the planting hole. Look for a soil line on the stem and use it as a planting depth guide; if no soil line is evident, backfill soil up to the crown, but not over it. Pat the soil down firmly around the roots and water thoroughly.

Although bareroot plants may seem strange or intimidating, they make lots of sense for low-maintenance gardeners. Since they're sold without all the soil that accompanies container-grown and balled-and-burlapped plants, they're easier to lift and move around your yard. If you're mail-ordering, they're also less expensive to ship. Roses, fruit trees and bushes, strawberries, and grapevines are typically sold bareroot, as are daylilies, irises, and many other perennials. Many trees and shrubs are also sold bareroot.

Fortunately, bareroot plants are easier to handle than they might seem. They're typically shipped dormant, timed to arrive at your door ready for planting. Whenever possible, plant them as soon as you can. If you can't plant right away, moisten their roots thoroughly and pack them in moist potting mix or compost. Try to hold them this way for no longer than three days.

Before you plant, soak the roots in a bucket of water for at least an hour or two. Cut off any dead or damaged roots with sharp scissors or pruning shears. Then plant them as shown above.

Check under the Burlap for Best Buys on B&B

If you buy a field-grown tree or shrub from your local nursery, chances are you'll get it balled-and-burlapped, or B&B. Before you buy, it pays to check what's under the burlap to make sure you spend all your planting efforts on a healthy plant instead of one that has been mistreated.

B&B plants are usually dug while they are dormant, and their root balls are wrapped with burlap. The biggest hazard of buying a B&B tree is that it may not have a large enough root ball.

To check the root ball size of potential purchases, use this rule of thumb: The root ball should be 1 foot in diameter for every inch of the diameter of the trunk at the base. There is no similar rule for shrubs, but bear in mind that the bigger the root ball, the faster the plant will establish itself.

Undersize root balls are a bigger hazard for trees, whose roots extend far beyond their drip lines (the point to which the tree's branches extend). The average B&B tree retains only 5 percent of its original root mass. An illustration showing how to plant a B&B tree appears on page 347.

CHAPTER 6

Mulching

Mulching the Low-Maintenance Way

MULCH is something of a miracle—it's a one-step way to get rid of some of the most tiresome garden chores and make time for the fun stuff. But it doesn't stop there; mulch can provide you with other benefits as well.

Organic mulches, for example, add humus to your soil as they decompose and encourage beneficial organisms and worms to grow and work in your garden. Some mulches can actually repel pests, while other unconventional mulches can save your plants from winter winds and heaving.

The materials you can round up around your home or buy locally will save you the most labor and expense. You won't have far to haul them and they're usually free (or really cheap). Take a look at everything mulch can do for you, then pick and use the materials that make your life easiest.

Haste Makes Waste with Tree and Shrub Mulching

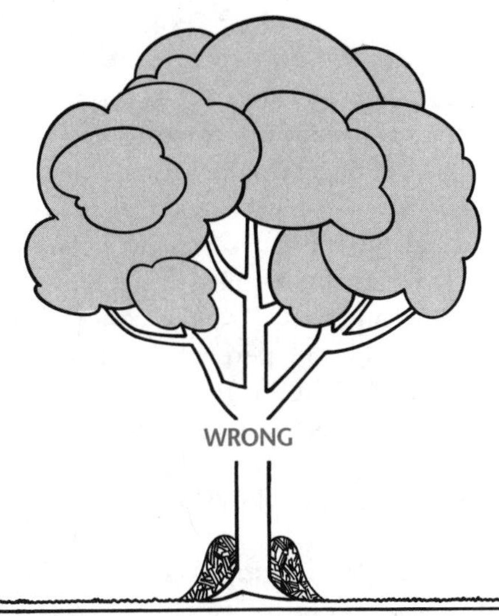

Mulching trees and shrubs is a simple, once-a-year (or less) chore—if you take time to do it right the first time. If you get in a hurry and dump mulch around your plants any old way, you'll soon be back rearranging it to fix pest and weed problems. Here's a simple list of dos and don'ts to keep in mind.

DON'T heap it too high. Deep mulch layers don't let air or water reach the soil easily so roots suffer. Four inches of mulch is plenty for good weed control, so don't strain your back or budget applying deeper amounts.

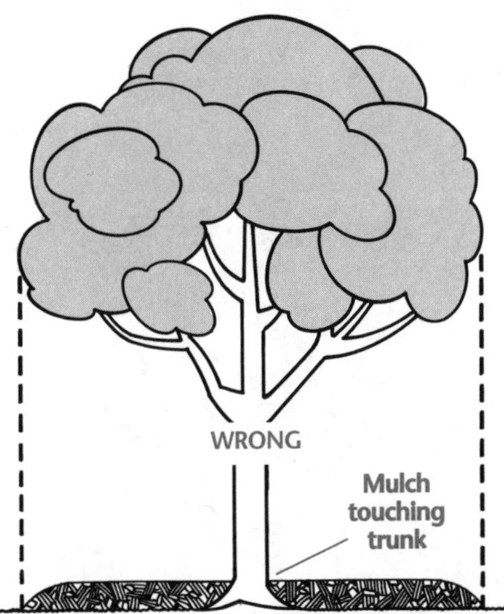

DON'T touch plant parts. Keep mulch 4 inches away from tree bark and plant stems or you'll create a moist hiding place for insects and bark-eating mice and voles.

TAKE-IT-EASY TIP!

Durable Mulches Reduce Your Workload

If you don't enjoy mulching, use long-lasting materials like bark chips or cocoa hulls. They decompose slowly and don't need to be replaced often. Most other organic mulches decompose quickly and need to be topped or replaced yearly. You'll spend a little extra time spreading shorter-lived mulches, but you'll build up your soil's organic matter fast.

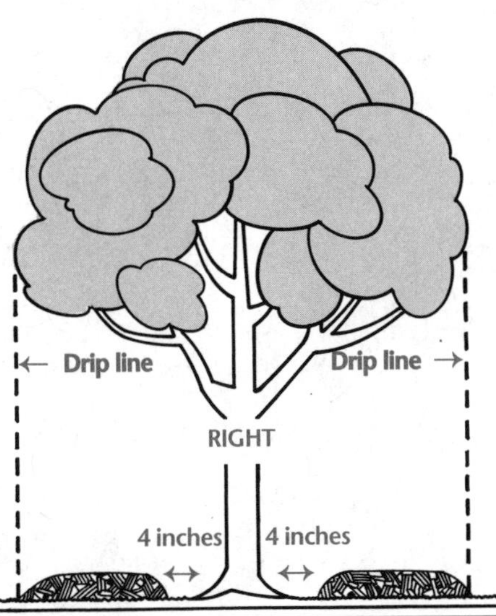

DO stretch mulch to the drip line. You'll protect your trees and shrubs best with wide mulch rings that keep lawn grass, mowers, and weeds far away from trunks and stems.

What Can Mulch Do for You?

Mulch may look pretty passive lying there in your garden, but it's constantly working to save you time and effort. Mulch offers innumerable benefits and can save you hours of time spent doing unpleasant garden chores.

Once you're sold on the idea of mulching, turn to "Which Mulch Means the Least Work for You?" on page 52 to pick the mulching materials that are easiest for you to use. Organic mulches are the most useful. They're made from once-living materials like bark, leaves, or grass clippings that eventually decompose and improve the soil. Inorganic or man-made mulches are long-lasting but don't add humus or nutrients to your garden.

Whichever material you choose, mulching will give you more benefits than any other single gardening chore. Here's what you can expect.

Quicker garden cleanup. When company's coming, an inch or two of a dark, decorative mulch—like wood or bark chips—is all it takes to make your garden look tidy.

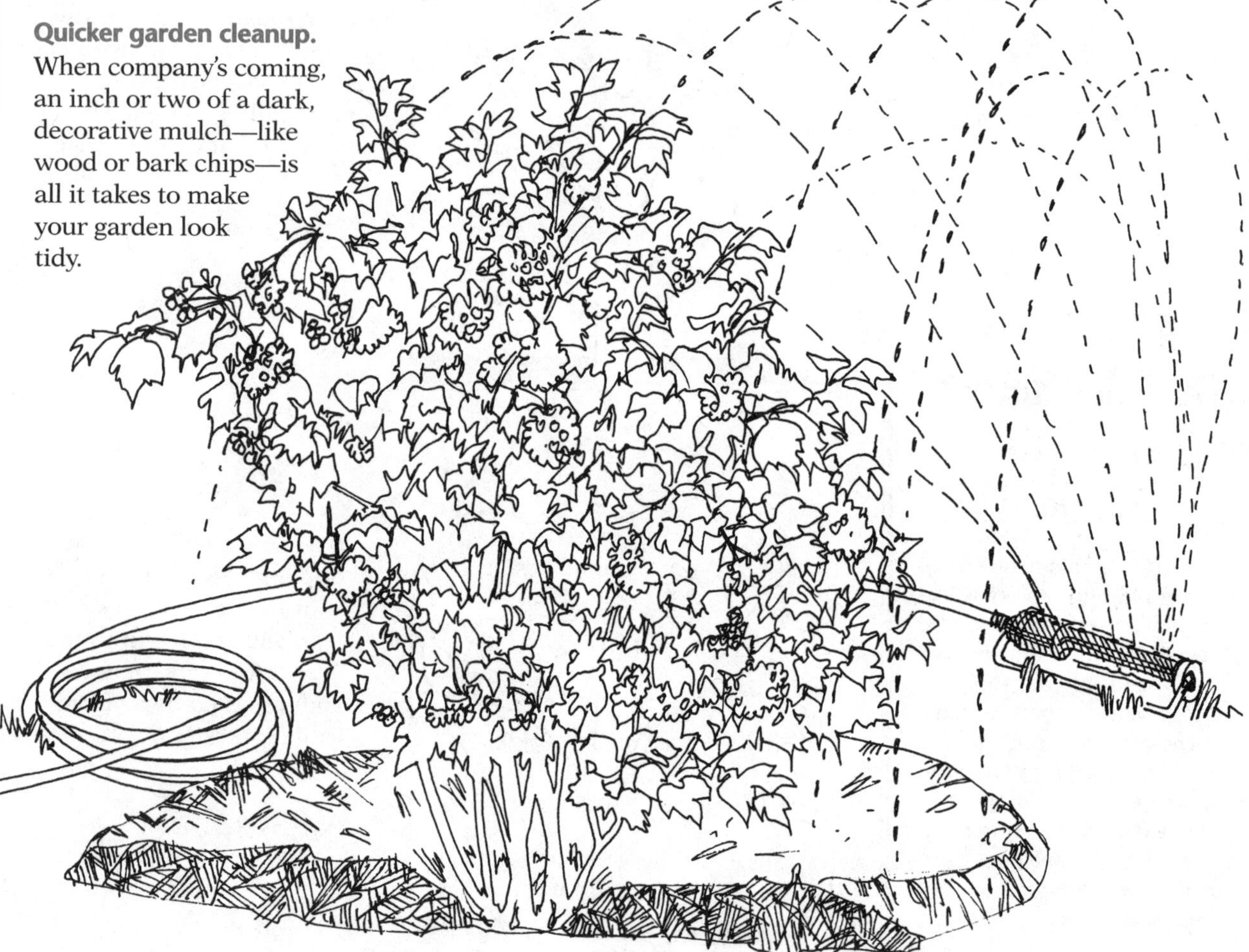

Low-work weed control. To control a minor weed problem, pull or hoe out existing weeds and bring on the mulch—at least a 4-inch-deep layer of organic matter. You won't have to weed again unless seeds blow in and root. If you're coping with tough perennial weeds, see "Fight the Toughest Weeds with Ease with 'Super Mulch'" on page 54. You'll find more on weed control in Chapter 10.

Fewer watering chores. A 3- to 4-inch layer of organic mulch throughout your garden can reduce the amount of water lost to evaporation by at least one-half. That means more water for your plants and less watering for you. Mulch also keeps roots cool so plants need less water.

Simple disease prevention. Rain and water droplets from sprinklers splash soil and the spores that cause fungal diseases onto plant leaves. A cushion of mulch will keep the fungal spores and the soil off your plants.

One-step soil protection. A layer of organic mulch protects the soil from beating raindrops, which prevents crusting and soil compaction. It will also stop heavy rains from washing away valuable topsoil and plants. Mulch can also protect soil from foot traffic.

No-dig soil improvement. When organic mulches break down, they add nutrients to the soil. This gives plants a boost and saves you from fertilizing chores.

Cleaner produce. Surround vegetables and berries with mulch to keep them—and you—free of mud. You'll be able to harvest crops without lots of cleaning fuss, even in wet weather.

Protection from mower blight. A ring of mulch around the base of trees or shrubs keeps you from getting too close with your lawn mower—no more tedious trimming or bark wounds. (See "Keep Grass in Check with Edging and Mulch" on page 187 if you want even more protection.)

Safety from winter's wrath. Plants can heave out of the ground and die when temperatures alternate between freezing and thawing. Mulching after the ground freezes with loose straw or chopped leaves moderates soil temperatures and stops harmful expanding and contracting.

The soil microbes and earthworms that aerate and fertilize the soil for you thrive under mulch. It protects them from temperature fluctuations and provides a moist, inviting home.

Which Mulch Means the Least Work for You?

With the wide variety of mulches available, you may be baffled about which ones to use. Any mulch can control weeds and conserve moisture, so choose one that can do more for you. Organic mulches offer the most benefits. When they break down, they add nutrients and organic matter to the soil and reduce fertilizing chores. Many also improve the appearance of your garden and are available free or at low cost. Inorganic mulches can't improve your soil or your garden's looks, but they may be handy if you need to mulch a large landscape. They have some major drawbacks: They're expensive, don't add any nutrients to the soil, need to be anchored in place, and are ugly. Whenever possible, use an organic mulch instead.

Mulch	Benefits	Relative Cost	How to Use
Organic Mulches			
Burlap	Controls erosion; protects new seedbeds.	Inexpensive.	Spread one layer; hold in place with stakes or metal pins. Will hold soil and plants in place on slopes and protect newly seeded grass or wildflowers.
Cocoa hulls	Attractive; add nutrients and humus; suppress weeds; conserve moisture. Chocolate scent.	Expensive.	Apply a 1-inch layer around flowers or herbs. High in potassium; too much may injure some ornamental plants.
Compost	Attractive if completely rotted; adds nutrients and humus; suppresses weeds; conserves moisture.	Free if you make your own; inexpensive to purchase.	Apply a 1- to 3-inch layer around, but not touching, plants. See Chapter 3 for information on making compost.
Grass clippings	Add nitrogen and humus; fair weed control and moisture conservation.	Free.	Apply a 1- to 2-inch layer around, but not touching, plants. Can become slimy if used in layers more than 2 inches thick. Unattractive unless dried or composted before use; use under more attractive mulches.
Hay	Adds humus; suppresses weeds well; conserves moisture; provides good winter protection.	Free or inexpensive.	Lay 8- to 10-inch layers around, but not touching, plants. Spoiled hay is cheap and won't sprout weed or hay seeds.
Leaves	Add humus; suppress weeds well; conserve moisture.	Free.	Shred leaves with a mower and/or compost them before use. Apply in 3-inch layers. Large, whole leaves blow away or mat down and can keep plants too wet.

Mulch	Benefits	Relative Cost	How to Use
Paper	Suppresses weeds well; conserves moisture.	Free or inexpensive.	Spread whole sections of newspaper up to 1 inch thick to smother weeds. Anchor with soil or stones or use under more attractive mulches. Or shred paper and apply 4- to 6-inch layers.
Seaweed	Adds trace minerals; suppresses weeds well; conserves moisture; may repel pests; offers good winter protection.	Free if you can collect it nearby.	Spread a 4- to 6-inch layer around plants. Spread over tender perennial plants in winter. Use under more attractive mulches.
Stones	Attractive; give fair weed control and moisture conservation when crushed; permanent.	Expensive.	Apply a 2- to 4-inch layer around plants. Use only in landscape situations; difficult to remove. To improve weed control, spread landscape fabric, newspaper, or wool mulch (see page 57) first and cover with stones.
Straw	Adds humus; suppresses weeds well; conserves moisture; provides good winter protection.	Inexpensive to medium priced.	Lay 8- to 10-inch layers around, but not touching, plants. Cover plants with a 4-inch layer for winter protection. May attract slugs.
Wood chips, shredded bark	Attractive; suppress weeds well; conserve moisture; long lasting.	Expensive unless you can get it free.	Spread 1 to 2 inches in flower beds and 4 inches around, but not touching, trees and shrubs. Will wash away during heavy rains.
Inorganic Mulches			
Landscape fabrics	Suppress weeds well; conserve moisture; control erosion; long lasting.	Expensive.	Apply 1 layer with holes cut for plants. Cover with an organic mulch; degrades if exposed to light. Use to cover large landscape areas and on slopes. Roots may become entwined in the fabrics, making it difficult to remove or replace plants.
Plastic	Black and transparent plastics warm the soil for early planting in spring; black prevents weed growth; white reflects extra light for better growth; plastic coated with aluminum paint repels aphids and thrips.	Expensive.	Use in vegetable gardens. Apply a single layer with holes cut for plants and remove in fall. Cover with an organic mulch or anchor with soil. Not useful in ornamental landscapes—it rips, doesn't allow water and air into or out of the soil, and is not biodegradable. Plastics billed as biodegradable are not; they break apart but do not break down. Some recyclable plastics are available.
Plastic, colored	Colored mulches affect plant growth and may boost early crop yields but not enough to be worth the price.	Expensive.	Use in vegetable gardens to warm the soil if you must have an early crop.

Fight the Toughest Weeds with Ease with "Super Mulch"

When tough perennial weeds like thistles and burdock take over your garden, fight back with "super mulch." First, mow or break off tall weeds, then cover the area with a layer of cardboard (boxes that are broken down and cut open work well) or a 1-inch layer of newspaper. Place 8 to 10 inches of spoiled hay or straw over the top. Apply the mulch in summer or fall and you'll smother the weeds in time for planting the following year. The mulch will break down into humus after a couple of seasons and make a fine planting bed.

If you're battling a particularly crafty weed like poison ivy or an invasive plant like spreading bamboo, leave the area covered for one or two years. (See the illustration on page 320 for a technique for controlling invasive garden plants.) Keep 8 to 10 inches of mulch over the area at all times, adding new mulch as the older material breaks down. Don't let the weeds get any light, and they'll give up when their food stores run out.

Mulch and Grow Better Soil

Mulch and compost can turn your poor soil into fertile ground while you grow flowers and vegetables. Follow the simple steps below in late spring, and you'll be able to plant immediately, even on clay or sandy soil.

1. Cut down any weeds or grass in your garden area with a mower and leave the clippings where they fall.

2. Cover the site with a layer of newspaper, 4 or 5 sheets deep.

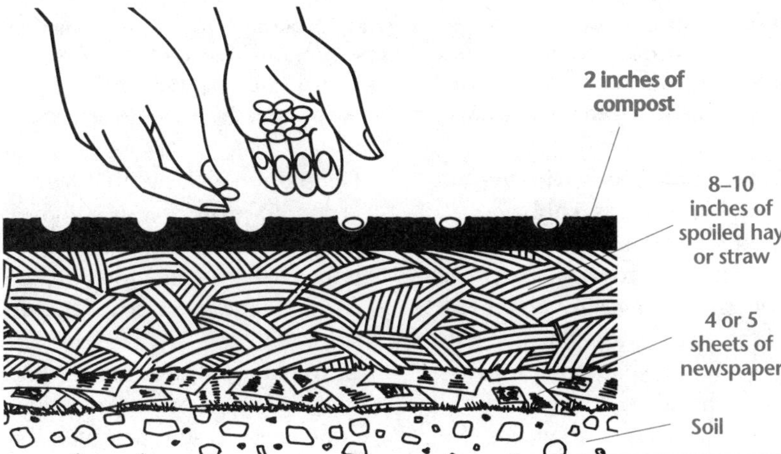

3. Place 8 to 10 inches of spoiled hay or straw over the paper.

4. Top the hay with 2 inches of compost.

5. Dig some earthworms from a good garden spot and place 5 or 10 of them in 3 or 4 spots under the mulch.

6. Plant seeds of strongly rooted annual flowers or vegetables in the compost and you'll be picking flowers or harvesting crops by summer. Meanwhile, the roots and worms will break up and improve the soil texture, and the mulch and compost will break down and improve your soil's health. Try cleome, cosmos, sunflowers, amaranth, beans, and grains for the best results the first year.

Annual Flowers Make the Mulch

Does your newly planted perennial garden have more bare spots than plants? Fill in the blanks with quick-spreading annual flowers. They'll keep your planting weed-free until slower-growing perennials fill in. For an established tree or shrub planting, see "Plant Once, Mulch Forever with Permanent Perennials" on page 56.

Trailing annuals like sweet alyssum and Madagascar periwinkle (*Catharanthus roseus*) shade out weed seedlings before they can get a foothold. Even annuals that grow upright can lend a helping hand if you space them close enough so that they touch each other when they're mature.

Buy inexpensive flats of impatiens to cover bare spots in shade gardens; use French marigolds, melampodium (*Melampodium paludosum*), or narrowleaf zinnias (*Zinnia angustifolia*) as fillers in sunny areas.

Grow Your Own Mulch

Don't let late crops stop you from planting a mulch of cover crops. In late summer, sow oat or purple vetch seeds up to and under the leaves of broccoli, cabbage, lettuce, and other crops that are still producing. Winter's chill will kill off the cover crop before spring and your soil will get a humus boost as the plants decompose.

Are you short on mulch materials or tired of replacing mulches every year? Instead of hauling more organic matter out to your garden, grow a living mulch. Live plants can be as effective as compost or hay at conserving moisture and reducing weeds. Living mulches are particularly good at preventing soil erosion too: They don't just protect the ground from heavy rains, they hold it in place with their roots. For tips on using plants as mulch in the flower garden, see "Annual Flowers Make the Mulch" on page 55 and "Plant Once, Mulch Forever with Permanent Perennials" on this page. For vegetable gardens, read on.

Crowd out weeds with vegetables. Plant beans, cabbage-family crops, salad greens, and peas in wide rows spaced close enough so leaves touch when plants are grown. The dense growth will shade the soil so moisture doesn't evaporate. Cover bare areas so weeds can't get a toehold.

Fill in open areas with cover crops. To protect your soil over winter with very little effort, plug the bare spots in your garden with cover crops in late summer.

To plant cover crops on this schedule, as soon as you're done harvesting vegetables, cut off and compost the tops of plants. Broadcast oat, purple vetch, or hairy vetch seeds over the entire garden area for a quick protective blanket. They'll sprout, grow through the fall, and get killed back in winter.

In spring, plant right through the cover crops; they make a good mulch even when they're dead. In warm areas where cover crops survive winter temperatures, till them into the soil before planting. See "Undersow to Grow Your Own Fertilizer" on page 130 and "Sow-Easy Soil Improvement While You Wait" on page 16 for more cover crops to try.

Plant Once, Mulch Forever with Permanent Perennials

If you've got bare or weedy patches around trees or shrubs, plant groundcovers or other spreading perennials. They're the easiest mulch of all since they don't need refurbishing each year. They'll shade the soil, keep out weeds, and need almost no maintenance once established.

Plant daylilies, ajuga, lilyturf, and English ivy in sun or shade. For shady spots, try hostas, epimediums, lilies-of-the-valley, pachysandra, or sweet woodruff.

Weird Mulches That Work

Lots of great but unusual mulch materials are hidden away waiting for you in your house, yard, and community. See if you're overlooking any of these handy resources.

Carpet. If you just tore out some cotton or wool carpeting, take it to the vegetable garden instead of the dump. Lay strips down between the rows for a long-lasting, weedproof mulch. Only use all-cotton or all-wool carpet since synthetic ones may contain harmful chemicals.

Christmas trees. Evergreen boughs make great plant covers in winter, and you can find a plentiful supply around the holidays. Let neighbors know you'd like their discards, or just collect them from the curb before sanitation workers do. Lop off the limbs and pile them around any perennial plants or shrubs that need protection from winter winds and freezing and thawing temperatures.

Herbs. Lots of gardeners think of herbs like mint and perilla as invasive pest plants. If you've got a large patch of rampant herbs, why fight it? Cut the plants back with hedge shears whenever you need some mulch and place the stems and leaves around your plants. You'll have fragrant weed control that helps repel insects. Other vigorous herbs for mulch include artemesia (*Artemisia* spp.), velvet sage (*Salvia leucantha*), and yarrow.

Snow. If you live in the North, don't overlook the benefits of snow mulch for winter protection. A heavy blanket of the white stuff keeps plants safe from drying winter winds and frigid temperatures. Nature often does all the work for you, but in years with little snow, you can help out by piling it up to cover perennial plants and shrubs.

Weeds. It's hard to believe, but weeds make good mulch if you're selective about what you use. For a low-maintenance living mulch, leave noninvasive weeds like chickweed in your garden if they spring up between vegetables or around trees and shrubs.

Dead weeds. You can use dead weeds as mulch, too, as long as they haven't gone to seed. Use them to anchor newspaper mulch instead of laying them on bare ground: Pulled weeds have been known to reroot in especially rainy seasons. Common weeds that make good mulches include lamb's-quarters, jewelweed, plantain, pigweed, and pokeweed. Avoid Bermuda grass, bindweed, crabgrass, nutsedge, purslane, or any other weed that can reproduce from root sections.

Wool. Nonwoven, feltlike mats made of wool and other natural fibers make a long-lasting (2 years or more) but biodegradable mulch. They're convenient (but expensive) to use since they come in squares or rolls that can be cut with scissors or a knife.

Water the soil first, then cut mats to fit, and place a single layer around but not touching plants. Or apply a layer with holes cut for plants. Anchor with soil, another mulch, wire pins, or rocks.

Look to Your Trees for Mulching Materials

Leaves make great mulch—especially if they're chopped and don't blow around like whole leaves. They're easy to come by: Just mow your yard in fall and collect the chopped leaves in a mower bag. If you don't have enough, collect bags of leaves from neighbors and put them in windrows at home to mow, too. Some municipalites offer free leaves, and you can also check with lawn-care companies and your local parks department.

Move Mulch with Ease

If you're adding 4 inches of mulch to a large vegetable garden, you're in for some work. You can choose lightweight mulches, but even they can be cumbersome if you have to move large quantities around. Try these tips for getting mulch to your garden and placing it around your plants with the least effort.

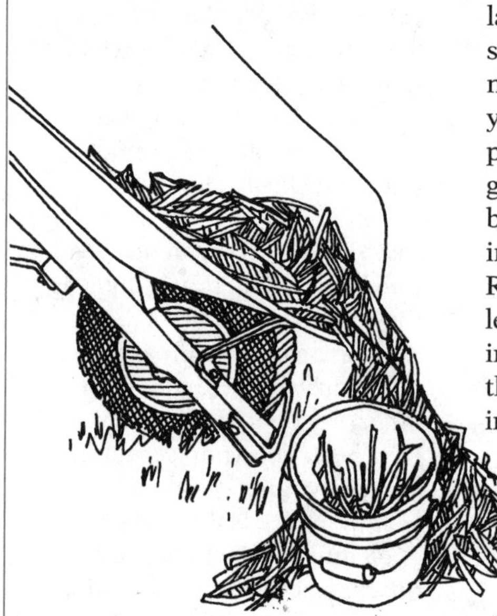

Place barrels or bottomless buckets over plants to protect them when you dump a load of mulch from a wheelbarrow or truck. Cover small plants with plastic flowerpots. Once plants are safe, you can unload and shovel quickly without burying or crushing plants.

Bag it or blow it. Collect grass clippings and leaves with a lawn mower bag and you'll save time raking. Dump the mulch materials directly in your garden or in a compost pile that's in or beside your garden. If you don't have a bagging mower, dump leaves in windrows near your garden. Run your mower over the leaves to chop them, then mow in a single direction to blow the leaves into your garden or into a single row.

Get some wheels. A pickup truck or lawn tractor with a trailer makes it easy to move bulky materials like bales of straw and hay. If they aren't available, carts, wheelbarrows, and even little red wagons can save your back and make mulching easier. You can load mulch directly into these vehicles, push or pull them to your garden, then dump the materials exactly where you need them. To load up extra mulch and keep it from blowing around, fill large plastic garbage barrels, plastic bags, or washtubs, load them into a wheeled vehicle, and drop them off where they're needed.

Rob the laundry. If you don't have wheels, put plastic bags of mulch into a laundry basket. You can slide the basket over your lawn without risking a plastic bag break.

Try a tarp or stuff a sheet. It's easy to drag grass clippings or leaves to your garden if you throw them on a plastic tarp or old bedsheet.

Get double duty from mix-and-match mulches. When you're short on mulch or money, try a mixture of materials to cover your planting beds. For example, use a beautiful, decorative mulch like cocoa beans on top of an uglier, but inexpensive, mulch like grass clippings. Or sprinkle attractive shredded bark over newspaper or straw, or mix several kinds of mulch together, and top with a thin layer of decorative mulch. No one will know the difference but you and your pocketbook.

Bedsheets Make Good Garden Tools

If you use grass clippings for mulch in your vegetable garden, don't struggle with bushel baskets or balancing cut grass on your rake. An old bedsheet is the easiest way to haul clippings to the garden. A sheet lets you haul more grass at one time, and it also takes the weight off your back.

CHAPTER 7

Fertilizing

Fertilizing the Low-Maintenance Way

FERTILIZING is certainly not on the top-ten list of favorite gardening activities. The good news: If you've been managing your soil organically by adding compost and other organic amendments regularly, your plants probably won't need very much fertilizer. Soil that's rich in organic matter generally contains plenty of nutrients that are readily available to plants. Rich soil also is biologically active, so trillions of soil organisms are hard at work breaking down even more nutrients for plants all during the growing season.

In this chapter, you'll learn ways to make the most of fertilizers and also cut the time and effort you spend applying them. You'll also find an explanation of what soil pH means to your plants and how to manage it efficiently.

Just the Facts: What You Need to Know about Feeding Your Plants

Nitrogen, phosphorus, and potassium (N, P, and K) are the primary nutrients plants need to grow. In addition to these three macronutrients, plants also need smaller amounts of calcium, magnesium, and sulfur—the secondary nutrients. Plants also use trace elements, also called micronutrients, in minute amounts. Trace elements include boron, chlorine, copper, iron, manganese, molybdenum, and zinc.

The good news is healthy soil that's rich in organic matter generally contains enough of all of these nutrients to keep plants healthy and growing. Fertilizing becomes necessary either when there aren't enough nutrients in the soil or when nutrients are present but are in forms plants can't take up through their roots. (A pH imbalance, for instance, will cause nutrients to be unavailable.) Of course, gardeners also fertilize to boost plant performance—to produce a bigger crop of tomatoes, for example.

Know How Food Will Make Them Grow

Whatever plants you want to feed, it's helpful to know how nutrients will affect them. In general, nitrogen promotes growth of leaves and stems, phosphorus encourages production of flowers and fruits, and potassium boosts root growth. Although plants need all three of these nutrients to grow, the amount of each varies according to their stage of development.

Fertilizers with different amounts of nutrients allow you to fine-tune your feeding program. For example, plants putting out new growth benefit from fertilizers with higher ratios of nitrogen relative to the other nutrients. Plants that are flowering and setting fruits do better with an increase in phosphorus. You can make sure your plants have everything they need by applying complete fertilizers—those containing all three major nutrients—with varying ratios of nitrogen, phosphorus, and potassium. You can mix your own fertilizers by combining single-nutrient fertilizers, but if your goal is reducing the time you spend fertilizing, buying complete commercial mixes is most efficient.

Keep Feeding Simple

You could easily devote all your time to formulating the right combination of macronutrients, secondary nutrients, and trace elements to satisfy the needs of each and every plant you grow. Fortunately, this is as unnecessary as it is undesirable. Use the following information about the needs of certain plant groups to help you choose the best fertilizers to use.

Leafy crops, foliage plants, trees and shrubs, grasses. A steady supply of nitrogen gives these plants what they need to build lush, green, healthy stems and foliage. Look for products that supply from two to four times as much nitrogen as they do phosphorus or potassium.

Fruits, flowers. Phosphorus enhances the floral display in ornamental plantings and improves blossom and fruit set in fruit-producing plants, including vegetable fruits such as tomatoes, beans, and squash. A complete fertilizer for these plants has twice as much phosphorus as it does nitrogen, with an equal or lesser amount of potassium.

Root crops. As mentioned above, potassium plays a critical role in healthy root growth, so it stands to reason that root crops such as carrots, beets, and potatoes would benefit from a fertilizer ratio that's twice as high in potassium as it is in nitrogen.

Vegetables. Since a vegetable garden contains a mix of crops—root, leafy, and fruit-bearing—it's easier to supply a balanced fertilizer to all crops than to cater to a variety of different nutrient needs. To feed your whole garden select a fertilizer in which the macronutrients are in equal ratio to each other; use single-nutrient sources to satisfy specific crop needs.

Get What You and Your Plants Need—Read the Bag

When shopping for fertilizers, it's important to take time to read the bag. The label on all commercial fertilizers features a three-number NPK ratio, and also the guaranteed analysis. Some, but not all, products provide ingredient information.

The amount of macronutrients a package of fertilizer contains is expressed as a three-number ratio. The first number is the percentage of nitrogen; the second, the percentage of phosphate (the form of phosphorus plants use); and the third, the percentage of potash (the form of potassium plants use).

Commercial fertilizers—both synthetic and organic—supply one, two, or all three of the macronutrients. Some contain secondary nutrients; a few, such as seaweed and compost, also supply all of the micronutrients.

Look for fertilizers that are labeled "Certified Organic," or carefully check the ingredients to make sure all the ingredients are safe and natural. Be wary of any products labeled organic that have an NPK ratio that adds up to more than 15; these products probably have ingredients that aren't organically acceptable.

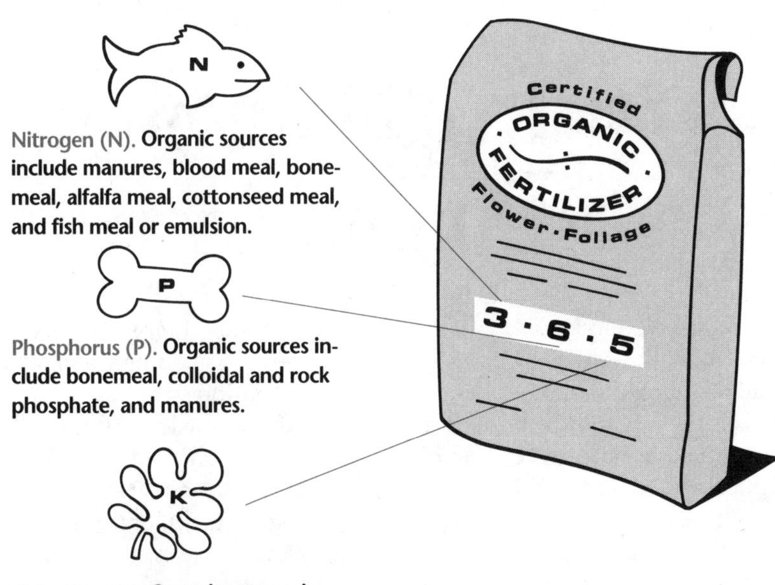

Nitrogen (N). **Organic sources include manures, blood meal, bonemeal, alfalfa meal, cottonseed meal, and fish meal or emulsion.**

Phosphorus (P). **Organic sources include bonemeal, colloidal and rock phosphate, and manures.**

Potassium (K). **Organic sources include wood ashes, greensand, langbeinite, and seaweed or kelp.**

Don't Have a Feeding Frenzy

One of the best ways to save time fertilizing is *not* to fertilize. If you're feeding your soil regularly with compost and keeping it covered with organic mulch, most of your plants won't need any supplemental feedings. So before you haul out the fertilizer, take time to think about which plants truly *need* to be fertilized. Perennials, trees, shrubs, and vines that are growing well will probably continue to do fine without feeding. If they just need a boost, an annual mulching with compost will help control weeds, hold moisture in the soil, *and* feed.

Even in a well-managed organic garden, there are plants that do better when fertilized. Fast-growing vegetables tend to be more productive when they receive added nutrients. Beds of annual flowers may bloom more as well. Perennials that have been in place for a few years also benefit from fertilization to replenish the nutrients they've removed from the soil. And container plants that rely on the soil in their pots will thank you for an occasional boost. By comparison, you may choose not to fertilize your lawn. Not fertilizing has an added benefit: The grass grows more slowly and you have to mow less.

Exercise Your Application Options

Different forms of fertilizer lend themselves to different application methods. Dry fertilizers may be powdered, granular, or pelletized—such products are easily applied over the soil surface. Liquid fertilizers give you the option of spraying nutrients directly on your plants as a foliar feed or watering them into the soil around plants.

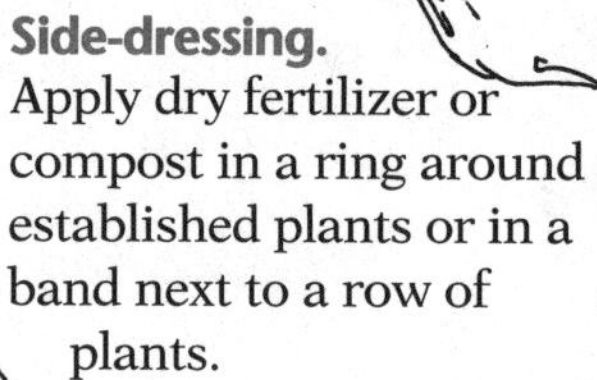

Side-dressing. Apply dry fertilizer or compost in a ring around established plants or in a band next to a row of plants.

Foliar application. Spray liquid fertilizer or compost tea onto plant leaves to give them a boost any time during the growing season.

Top-dressing. A drop-type spreader lets you apply dry fertilizer or screened compost over the top of your lawn.

Broadcasting. To prepare soil for planting, you can broadcast dry fertilizer with a spreader or by hand, then rake it in.

TAKE-IT-EASY TIP!

Strain to Avoid Maintenance

When you fill your sprayer with fertilizer for foliar applications, add this step to help keep your sprayer in good working order and clog-free. Poke a bag made of a double layer of pantyhose or cheesecloth into the opening of your sprayer and secure it around the opening with a rubber band. Pour your solution through this strainer to remove large particles that can clog sprayer parts. Remove the strainer before spraying.

Let Your Irrigation System Do Double Duty

If you have an irrigation system, let it fertilize for you—add a siphon attachment between the tap and the hose. Put the uptake tube into a bucket of concentrated liquid fertilizer and let the system do the rest.

With a drip system, you'll need a proportioner or fertilizer injector that will work with its lower water flow rate. To prevent clogging, filter fertilizer solutions before adding them to your irrigation system, and avoid fish emulsion. After fertilizing, flush your system with clear water for a few minutes.

Siphon attachments, proportioners, and injectors are available at well-stocked garden centers and by mail. See "Sources" on page 355 for suppliers.

Cut Fertilizer Needs with Compost

If you keep only one fertilizer on hand, make it compost. The nutrient content of compost is low when compared to synthetic fertilizers (compost's NPK ratio can range from 0.5–0.5–0.5 to 4–4–4), but it does much more than just add nutrients to the soil. It promotes microorganism populations that increase the availability of nutrients to your plants. As a source of organic matter, it also helps improve soil quality, drainage, and water-holding capacity.

Once you start using compost, you'll understand why good gardeners know you can never have too much of it. See below for some of the best ways to save time and still feed your plants with compost. If you feel like you could never make enough compost to perform all these different functions, check with the agency in your local government that oversees waste collection. Chances are your municipal government, township, or local parks department has a yard waste composting facility where residents can get compost at little or no cost.

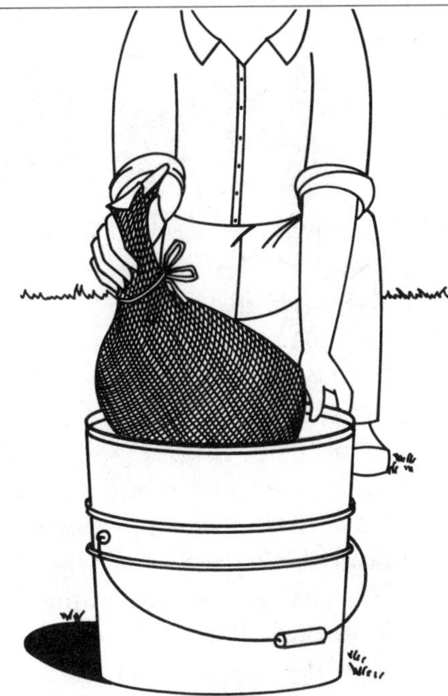

You can feed when you water if you take time to brew a bucketful of compost tea for your plants. Compost tea provides nutrients whether you sprinkle it over leaves or water it around the base of your plants.

Deficient or Diseased?

If your plants are stunted, spindly, and otherwise unhealthy looking, you might assume that they're diseased. But a nutrient deficiency can cause symptoms that mimic those caused by diseases: stunting, dieback, discolored foliage, and misshapen growth. Take a closer look before you draw your conclusion. Unless you see mold, rot, or another definite disease symptom, your plants may be asking for dinner, not doctoring. A foliar application of seaweed spray or compost tea will perk up plants that are wanting for nutrients. And such sprays can also help them fight off disease problems, too—just in case!

Compost mulch. Mulching perennial beds and mixed plantings with compost is enough to adequately feed most established plants. It also reduces the need to water and weed.

Top your vegetable garden in fall. Spreading a 1- to 2-inch layer of compost over your vegetable garden in late fall will protect the soil from the elements through winter and leave it ready for planting when spring arrives.

Side-dress with compost. During the growing season, you can side-dress vegetable crops with compost or use it as a mulch for the garden.

Feed your lawn. If you open your drop-type spreader to its widest setting, you can nourish your lawn with a top-dressing of compost.

Make compost tea. To make a batch of compost tea, put one or two shovelfuls of compost into a coarsely woven or burlap sack. Tie the sack shut, and steep your "tea bag" in a 5-gallon bucket of water for 1 to 7 days. Dilute the resulting liquid to a weak-tea color and use it to water your plants; strain it through cheesecloth to apply as a foliar spray or via drip irrigation. Any plants in need of a boost will respond well to a foliar application of compost tea.

Be Practical about pH

A soil's pH—the measure of its acidity or alkalinity—is important because it affects whether plants can take up the nutrients in the soil through their roots.

Soil pH varies by region and fluctuates with the previous uses of soil, such as cultivation or development. It is expressed as a number from 1.0 to 14.0: 1 is acid, 7 is neutral, and 14 is alkaline.

While some of your plants may have specific pH preferences, most tolerate a fairly wide range of soil pH. And plants that are finicky are simply expressing their need for the nutrients that are unavailable to them when the pH is "wrong."

The easiest thing to do about soil pH is nothing—as long as it's not seriously inhibiting your gardening success, leave it alone. Follow the steps below to do as little as possible about soil pH, while understanding how it affects your plants.

Know your soil's pH. Have a soil test done by a professional, or buy a home pH test kit and find out what your soil's pH is.

Know a little about pH and nutrient availability. Most nutrients plants need are available when the soil pH is between 6.0 and 7.5. When the pH is below 6.0, some nutrients, including nitrogen, phosphorus, and potassium, are less available to the plants. When the pH exceeds 7.5, iron, manganese, and phosphorus availability drop.

Enjoy Your Present pH

250-square-foot garden with pH of 7.2

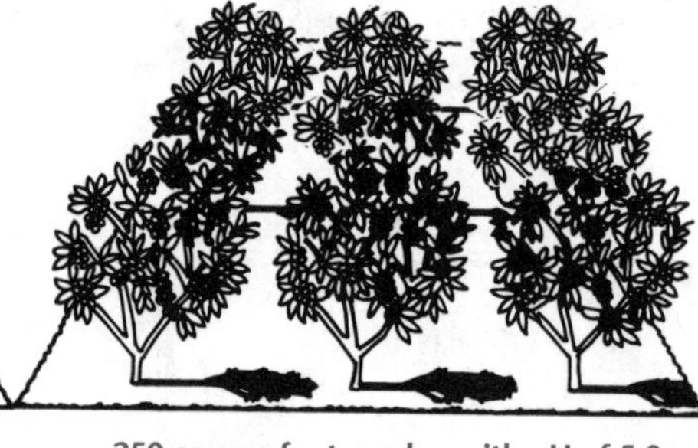

250-square-foot garden with pH of 5.0

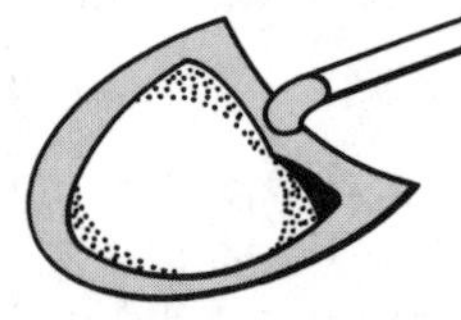

Add 16.5 lbs. of sulfur → pH 5.0

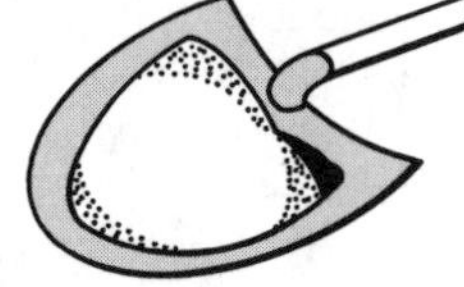

Add 30 lbs. of lime → pH 7.2

The best way to cope with soil pH is to make good use of the pH you already have. The 250-square-foot gardens shown here will produce healthy crops of vegetables (pH 7.2) and luscious blueberries (pH 5.0) with very little extra work. However, to grow blueberries in a soil where you can easily grow vegetables, and vegetables where you can grow blueberries, is another matter altogether. It takes an enormous amount of work, time, and amendments to alter soil pH. In this example, it would take 16.5 pounds of sulfur to lower the pH of the 7.2 garden to 5.0, and 30 pounds of lime to raise the 5.0 garden to 7.2. Plus, substantial pH changes must be made slowly—by amending the soil over two years or more—to avoid severely upsetting the balance of life in the soil. Few soils are in need of such dramatic amendment—be happy with what you have.

Know a little about plants and pH. Most cultivated plants grow best in soils with a pH in the range of 6.0 to 7.0. Common exceptions to this rule include blueberries, potatoes, and rhododendrons, all of which prefer more acidic conditions.

Choose plants accordingly. When you choose landscape plants, take pH into account. You can adjust soil pH by applying soil amendments. However, you'll be more successful if you select plants that are adapted to your soil's pH. Keep in mind that it's easier to amend cultivated soils, such as in vegetable gardens, than sodded or planted areas of the landscape.

Allow time for change. If you find your soil's pH is seriously out of kilter, or if you want to amend a limited area to make way for vegetable crops that won't tolerate existing conditions, start the amendment process early. Many factors, including soil type, organic matter content, and the type of amendment you use, will contribute to how quickly or slowly you can alter soil pH. Follow the specific recommendations you'll get with a complete soil test, and allow time for them to take effect before you plant.

Discover compost. Among its many attributes, compost also includes help for gardeners struggling with unfavorable soil pH. Because compost enhances soil microorganism activity (and because soil microorganisms help make nutrients available to plants), compost serves as sort of a soil pH buffer, reducing plants' dependence on a particular pH range.

More Food Isn't Better!

Many gardeners, especially those who take a casual approach to measuring things, subscribe to the theory that if a little is good, a lot must be better. When it comes to fertilizers, they couldn't be farther from the truth. With few exceptions, plants rarely take up more fertilizer than they need; the nutrients they don't use remain in the soil. Some cause imbalances in soil biology, while other more soluble products end up washing into the groundwater. So don't waste your money or your time: When you apply fertilizer, follow the label's recommendations for how much to use. If you estimate how much you need, err on the low side.

For Easy Applications, Make a Master Measure

Fertilizing your garden is easier if you you don't have to spend time weighing and measuring fertilizers each time you feed. Making a master measure for the fertilizers and soil amendments you use most often will allow you to just scoop and spread—without overfeeding. To make one, first weigh the materials to determine the volume of a pound. Then pour each into a clean, dry plastic container—recycle whatever's handy; an old deli container or a modified milk jug works fine. Then mark the volume with a permanent marking pen on the outside of the container. One good general mix is 3 pounds of alfalfa meal, 2 pounds of bonemeal, and 1 pound of kelp meal for every 100 square feet of growing area.

Use a recycled container to make a handy measure for the fertilizers you use most.

CHAPTER 8

Watering

Watering the Low-Maintenance Way

TIRED OF DRAGGING HOSES and paying ever-increasing water bills? There are ways to stop spinning your wheels and your water meter. End your watering woes by using mulch or exchanging thirsty plants for drought-tolerant ones. There are tools, techniques, and watering systems that can do the work for you—and reduce your water bills—no matter what you grow.

Chances are your yard needs a water-wise makeover. In this chapter, you'll find ways to make your landscape less thirsty. Once you've added mulch and improved your soil, you'll find most established ornamental plantings need extra water only during droughts. Water is more crucial for new plantings, fruits, and vegetables, but in the pages that follow, you'll find a variety of efficient tools and techniques you can use to safely cut back on the time you spend watering them, too.

Spend Your Watering Time Wisely

Mulch can reduce your plants' water needs drastically, but there may come a time when they need a drink. When they do, you'll save time and avoid rotting roots, fungus diseases, erosion, and high water bills by applying the right amount of water when and where it's needed. Here's how.

Any flower bed with closely spaced plants is a good candidate for a soaker hose. Just lay the hose between rows and let water ooze its way down to the roots. Cover the hose with mulch to keep moisture in the soil and hide the hardware.

Water only when plants are thirsty. When plants need a drink, they start to wilt, top leaves first. They droop in the heat of the day, then recover in the evening as the temperature cools down. As days pass and their thirst gets worse, leaf edges curl and leaves may take on a dull look. Eventually they don't perk up when temperatures cool, leaf edges turn brown and crispy, and, finally, they collapse.

To keep plants healthy, give them a drink when they start wilting slightly. If you wait until they are stressed, they'll be more likely to have problems.

Put water where it's needed. You'll waste less water if you use soaker hoses and drip systems to apply it to the ground directly around plants. These systems keep water off pathways, where it encourages weeds to grow, and off sidewalks and driveways, where it's wasted. You'll also have fewer disease problems with these systems since they don't wet plant leaves (which encourages fungal diseases).

Know how much is enough. The best rule is to soak the soil 1 foot deep when your plants get thirsty. Deep watering encourages deep rooting, which helps plants survive drought.

How do you know when you've soaked 1 foot deep? It depends on your soil type. Sandy soils let water pass through quickly, so ½ inch of water is all it takes to reach 1 foot down. If you have a loamy soil, ¾ inch of water will give you the desired results. Clay soils soak up water slowly, so you'll need to apply 1¼ inches of water for clay soil, spread out over several hours to keep water from pooling on the soil surface.

To measure water output for soaker hose and drip irrigation systems, follow the instructions that came with your system—their flow depends on water pressure. Use rain gauges to measure rainfall and water applied from overhead sprinklers.

Water when the time is right. If you're using an overhead sprinkler, the best time to water plants is early morning when the wind is calm and the sun is low. Water evaporates quickly during the heat of day, so much of it never reaches your plants. Plants watered in evening with overhead sprinklers or by hand tend to stay wet all night, which encourages disease. Soaker hoses and drip irrigation systems make it easy and effective to water any time, since evaporation isn't a problem and these systems don't wet the foliage.

Save Time with a Water-Saving Landscape

▲ **Select drought-tolerant shrubs and plant ground-covers.** Drought-tolerant shrubs like hypericum and Northern bayberry are just as attractive in foundation plantings and flower beds as thirstier shrubs like azaleas. And groundcovers need much less water than lawn to look their best. Replacing lawn with groundcovers around trees and shrubs will cut down on the water they need—and your mowing chores as well.

Do you race around your yard in the summer pouring water on every plant in sight? If so, you'll save loads of time and aggravation if you start using plants and techniques, like the ones shown here, that conserve water throughout your yard, landscape, and gardens.

It's best to start new plantings off on the right foot by selecting drought-tolerant plants. For existing gardens, though, it's often easier to change your watering methods than your plants. (You'll find lists of drought-tolerant plants on pages 233 and 234.) One good place to start cutting down on watering chores is to pick out which plants in your yard really need water and which do just fine with what they get from Mother Nature.

To decide what plants to water, determine which ones are essential to you. Do you depend on food from the vegetable garden? Do you have heirloom shrubs or flowers that you just can't live without? Do you have newly planted trees and shrubs that need regular watering until they become established? Will your neighbors harass you if your lawn goes dormant? Try to limit yourself to three areas that absolutely must have additional water and let the others fend for themselves.

▶ **Use drip irrigation.** Install a soaker hose or drip irrigation system in your vegetable garden. Keep a thick layer of straw or other organic mulch on your garden on top of your soaker hoses so you won't lose water to evaporation or runoff.

▼ **Collect free water.** Place a rain barrel under your down-spout for a free water supply.

▶ **Mulch, mulch, mulch.** Keep soil under flowers, trees, and shrubs mulched with wood chips, pine needles, or other organic mulches to hold moisture in the soil. Mulch discourages water-hogging weeds, too.

◀ **Grow drought-tolerant flowers.** In flower gardens, plant drought-tolerant perennials such as coneflowers and other deep-rooted perennials like daylilies. Many ornamental grasses are drought-tolerant, too.

Don't Waste Time on Water Wasters

Overthirsty plants, soil that drains too fast or too slowly, poor watering techniques, and inefficient garden plans not only waste tremendous quantities of water, they also waste your time and money. Look at your yard and garden and see which of the water wasters below are drinking you dry. Then try one or more water-saving solutions for quick relief.

Water Wasters	Water-Saving Solutions
Bare, uncovered soil. Water evaporates quickly from uncovered ground. Since wind and rain can beat at it at will, bare soil is often hard-packed or has an impenetrable crust, so water runs off it without soaking in.	Cover the ground with 2 to 4 inches of organic mulch. Use attractive mulches like bark chips for flower beds, trees, and shrubs, or plant bare areas with groundcovers to help hold moisture in place. Use any handy mulch materials—compost, grass clippings, shredded leaves, straw—for vegetable gardens. For more on mulching, see Chapter 6.
Poor soil. Hard-packed soil, or soil that's either high in clay or high in sand, creates watering problems. Hard-packed or clayey soils may drain so slowly that water puddles and drowns plants or runs off without soaking in. Sandy soils may drain so quickly you spend all your time trying to keep plants from wilting.	Adding organic matter in the form of compost, shredded leaves, or aged manure will improve any type of soil—it improves drainage on hard-packed and clayey soils and helps sandy soils hold water longer. Keeping your soil covered with organic mulches helps add organic matter, but for dramatic improvement, add an inch of organic matter each year, working it into the top few inches of soil. After two to four years, you'll have a yard and garden that needs less water and less care of any kind.
Planting plans that mix moisture-loving and drought-tolerant plants. This arrangement not only wastes water but creates plant health problems, too. If you give moisture lovers enough water, you'll injure or drown their dry-soil companions.	Group plants with similar water needs together. Plant them in different beds if possible. If you can't, cluster them together within beds. You'll be able to water each group according to its needs without wasting water on neighbors that don't want it.
Thirsty flowers, shrubs, trees, and vegetables. Plants that droop and beg for water every time you walk by only mean more work for you.	Keep a 2- to 4-inch layer of organic mulch around plants to conserve moisture. For even more water savings, replace extra-thirsty plants with drought-tolerant ones. Native trees, shrubs, and vines are generally good choices, as are deep-rooted perennials like peonies, yarrows, daylilies, coreopsis, globe thistles, pinks, and sedums. Plant wide rows of closely spaced vegetables to protect soil moisture from evaporating. You'll find more water-saving plant choices in Chapter 21.
Overhead sprinkling. Sprinklers are inefficient at delivering water to plant roots. Much of the water that's shot into the air evaporates as it falls to the ground; winds also send it in unwanted directions. If water pressure fluctuates, sprinklers won't run efficiently or cover the areas you aim at.	Switch to soaker hoses or drip irrigation so water stays on the ground. Or to reduce evaporation, choose sprinklers that create large water droplets that fall more quickly. Watering in early morning instead of during the heat of the day also reduces evaporation. Purchase a pressure regulator to ensure that sprinklers have enough water to operate effectively.

Water Wasters	Water-Saving Solutions
Misdirected sprinklers. Inground or overhead sprinklers that water buildings, pavement, or weeds mean big water bills; the only weeds benefit.	Adjust sprinkler heads to cover only planted areas or purchase ones with spray patterns that fit your plantings. Drip irrigation or soaker hoses spread through planting beds will deliver water exactly where you want it.
Sprinkling plants until the ground looks wet. Watering a thirsty plant just until the soil surface looks damp creates more problems than it solves. Plants watered this way need more frequent watering and develop very shallow roots.	Water less often, but water deeply each time you do it so you soak the entire root zone. This encourages plant roots to grow deep into the soil, making them more drought-resistant. After a watering session, jab your finger into the ground to see how deeply you've really watered. (Or use rain gauges to see how much water you've delivered.) You'll be amazed at how dry soil can be under a surface that "looks" soaking wet.
Lawns. Large expanses of lawn grasses are the greediest water hogs of all. They demand weekly watering to look their best in the heat of summer.	Replace the thirstiest stretches of lawn with drought-tolerant groundcovers that can fend for themselves. If you can't part with even a small bit of your lawn, replace water-demanding grasses like Kentucky bluegrass gradually by overseeding with cultivars that require less moisture. Check with your extension agent or garden center manager for good choices for your area. You can lower your water bill even more if you use drought-tolerant, low-growing grasses like turf-type tall fescue, fine fescue, or buffalograss. (See Chapter 19 for lists of drought-tolerant groundcovers and lawn grasses.)

Make a Custom Watering System for Vegetables

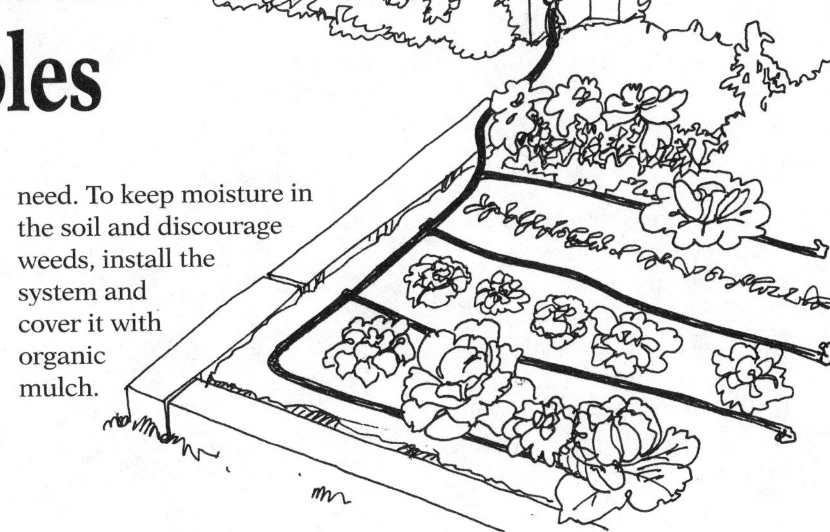

Cut-to-fit irrigation systems are an easy way to make a custom system for watering vegetable gardens with parallel rows. Stretch the main supply line across the top or bottom of your garden, as shown here, and attach sections of rubber ooze hose wherever you have a row of plants. You can cut the ooze hose to any length you need. To keep moisture in the soil and discourage weeds, install the system and cover it with organic mulch.

Make Your Hoses Behave with Handy Hose Tamers

Have you ever given your hose a tug and then looked on in horror as it leveled a row of cherished plants? The hose is not your enemy—it just needs a little guidance. Use the tools amd techniques shown here to make it behave.

Take weight off your back. Wheeled carts and reels can make dragging hoses easier. A cart lets you move several hoses around your yard at once with ease; add a reel and winding and unwinding hoses becomes a simple, nonsnarling task.

Flip tangled hoses free. A flick of the wrist is all it takes to turn a snarled hose into a model of good behavior. Detach your tangled hose from the faucet, grasp a free end, and keep flipping and rolling the hose until all the tangles are worked out.

Hang hoses high. Hoses last longer if you keep them off the ground. Inexpensive metal hangers, which you can attach to a shed, garage, or house, keep hoses organized and ready to use. Freestanding hose hangers are an option if you want to keep your hose near a garden. They're usually made of wrought iron and have prongs that let you anchor them into the ground. They're attractive but pricey.

Connect hoses with quick-release couplers. Stop struggling with hose ends that are difficult to screw onto faucets or other hoses. Brass quick-release couplers make connecting and disconnecting hoses easy: Just screw them onto hose ends, faucets, and all your attachments, and you'll be able to snap all your watering devices together or apart as needed. They're made to swivel so hoses won't kink. Plastic couplers are cheaper than brass ones, but some won't let water out of a faucet unless a hose is attached. Buyer beware!

Direct hoses with homemade guides. To make a simple, inexpensive hose guide, stick a piece of rebar in the soil deep enough so it's sturdy; leave several inches above ground to keep your hose in place. Cover the rebar with a piece of bamboo (if looks are important) or PVC pipe. Place the guides in front of vulnerable plants or anywhere you don't want your hose to go.

Or sink wooden stakes into the ground, leaving 6 to 8 inches exposed, and cover them with plastic soda bottles.

Handy Helpers: Tools to Make Hand Watering a Breeze

You could spend the summer with your thumb hooked over the end of your hose, but it's not only uncomfortable, it's also one of the least efficient ways to complete your watering chores. For the times when hand watering makes sense, the tools shown here will help make hand watering a breeze. They'll cut down on the time you spend hand watering and reduce the amount of water you use. All the items listed are available through garden-supply catalogs and at garden centers.

▼ **Bubblers and water breakers.** These attachments can turn a hard stream of water into a gentle flow or spray, so they're great for watering fragile seedlings and areas that erode easily. Lay them beside a plant and they'll water while you do other work. Move them frequently to prevent flooding.

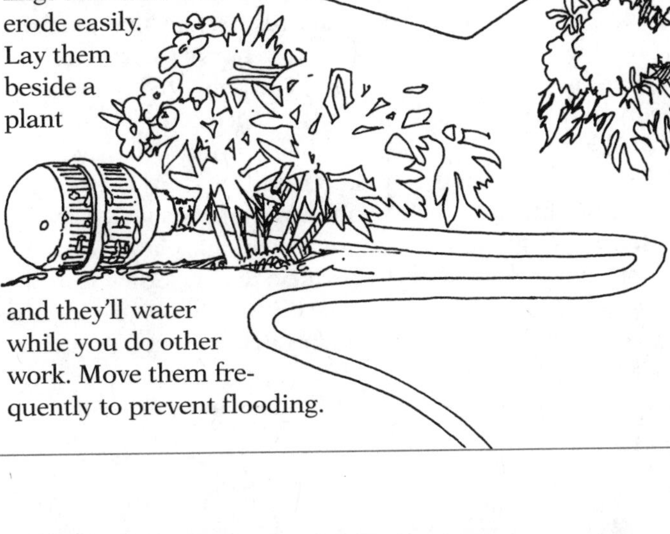

▼ **Water wands.** If you have to water plants in the middle or back of a flower bed, extend your reach and gain control of your hose end with an inflexible, lightweight aluminum or plastic wand. You'll be able to direct water at the base of a plant or along the undersides of leaves to rinse pest insects away.

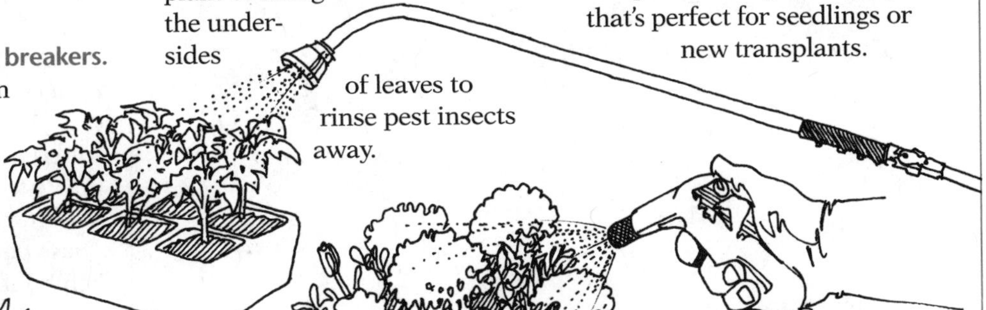

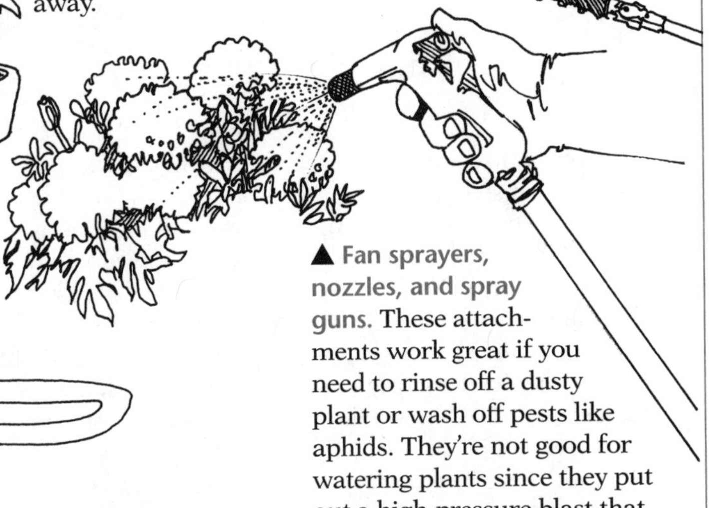

◀ **Watering cans.** For indoor or outdoor container plants, or for a drought emergency in the garden, watering cans are time-saving choices. They let you haul small amounts of water around quickly without lugging out hoses. Consider the filled weight of a can before you buy. Water weighs slightly more than 8 pounds per gallon, so a 2½-gallon can will weigh over 20 pounds filled. Select a smaller can or plan on filling halfway. Attachments can make your life easier, too. The oval "rose" on the spout of this can produces a gentle spray that's perfect for seedlings or new transplants.

▲ **Fan sprayers, nozzles, and spray guns.** These attachments work great if you need to rinse off a dusty plant or wash off pests like aphids. They're not good for watering plants since they put out a high-pressure blast that sends mulch and soil flying.

Collecting Rain Makes Watering Easy

Rain barrels make it easy to collect and distribute rainwater. If you already have gutters and a downspout, all you need is the barrel. You can buy plastic ones with spouts, such as the one shown here, through mail-order garden catalogs. Or make your own barrel out of a plastic trash can if you'd prefer a do-it-yourself model.

Set the barrel under a downspout as close to your garden as possible. Keep it covered to keep mosquitoes out. Then run your downspout into the barrel, attach a garden hose to the spout, and you're in the water business. Run the hose to your garden or a landscape spot downhill for automatic watering. Otherwise, use your rain barrel for filling watering cans or dip water out as needed.

Let Timers Watch Your Watering

If you don't want to spend time monitoring your soaker hoses or sprinklers—or have to ever again worry about remembering to turn them off—let a timer do it for you. Inexpensive ($10–$30) mechanical timers let you turn a dial to set the length of time you want to water; a few let you set the amount of water to apply. Set the dial and go about your business, and the timer will turn the water off automatically.

If you can't always be there when your garden needs you, look into the benefits of battery-operated electronic timers. They're more expensive than the mechanical models ($30–$70), but once you set the watering schedule, they'll turn the water on and off for you at the times and days you specify. These devices are particularly helpful if you're working with water restrictions that limit the days and hours you can irrigate. The only time you're likely to encounter a problem is when it rains. Unless you're home and can turn the system off, it will merrily water or overwater your plants, even during a deluge. Some timers have optional moisture-sensing probes that will turn the water off when the soil is moist and back on again when it's dry.

Easy-Does-It Watering: Fast Fill-Up for a Slow Drip

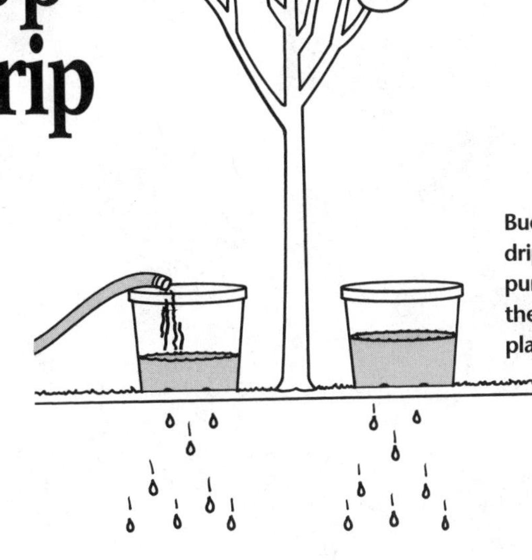

Buckets or milk jugs make ideal drip-waterers in a pinch. Just punch a couple of small holes in the bottom, set them around a plant, and fill them with water.

Watering new plants properly takes time and patience, but it's all-important if they're going to get a healthy start in life. You have to drizzle the water on slowly so it soaks deep into the soil. And you don't just have to water once at planting time—you're looking at a summer of weekly watering sessions. While you could set up an elaborate watering system or spend hours standing over your new plants with a hose, there's an easier and cheaper alternative: Make your own low-tech drip system from containers. Drip containers will let you leave gallons of water around a plant in a flash, and then drip it out slowly into the soil without wasting a drop. Use them for new plants or to provide extra water for particularly water-sensitive ones.

Plastic milk jugs, soda bottles, and plastic buckets make fine containers for drip-watering plants. All you need to do is punch one or two very small nail holes in the bottom of the container. Since you want the water to drip out a drop at a time, put some water in the container and start with the smallest hole you can make. Gradually enlarge it until the water drips out at the rate you want.

To water, place one or more empty drip containers beside a thirsty plant. (The number of containers you use depends on how much water the plant will need; use several containers to give large trees and shrubs several gallons of water; one or two for smaller perennials.) Then fill the container with water from a bucket or garden hose and let the water slowly drip into the soil.

Store-bought drip containers work in a similar way. One, called the Treegator, looks like a heavy-duty plastic sack that opens up so you can place it around a tree. Zip it up and fill its pouch with up to 20 gallons of water; small holes near the bottom let the water drip out at a controlled rate. Treegators are available from Spectrum Products, P.O. Box 18187, Raleigh, NC 27619-8187; (800) 800-7391.

Easy Container Watering

Potted plants can be tricky to water, especially when you're in a hurry. They flood their saucers, and water bounces off leaves and soaks your table or the floor.

You can avoid these problems by using one of the systems described above for watering large tubs and containers. Plastic soda bottles are especially handy for indoor use—their narrow shape fits even medium-size containers. Or try making your own wick-watering system and water from the bottom up. See the illustration on page 315 for directions. You'll avoid the fuss and muss of watering from above, and your plants can get a drink whenever they need it, even if you're away for a few days.

Let Drip Systems Water Your Ornamental Plantings

Mixed plantings of trees, shrubs, and flowers aren't made for watering with sprinklers—some plants get too much water; others, too little. You can avoid the aggravation of watering individual plants with your hose by installing a drip irrigation system. A well-planned system, like the one shown here, is versatile enough to handle a variety of plant sizes and shapes.

Run the main hose line next to the plants you want watered. Emitters set in the line let water drip out at a steady pace and are perfect for wetting closely spaced plants. For shrubs or other plants off the main line, use spaghetti tubes to send water exactly where it's needed. Use one tube for small plants, two or more for large plants. Cover the entire system with mulch to stop evaporation.

Watering Systems That Work for You

Instead of spending your time watering, let a drip, soaker, or sprinkler system do it for you. To pick the system that best fits your space, budget, and schedule, review the highlights below. Nearly all of these systems are available at garden centers or through mail-order catalogs. For inground systems, check around to find a reputable dealer in your area.

Water System	Best Uses	Comments
Inexpensive		
Soaker hose. Water seeps out along entire length of hose; made of canvas, plastic, or rubber.	Level areas where plants are closely spaced; short runs (100 to 200 feet); around flowers, vegetables, shrubs, and trees. Move as needed. Plastic and rubber hoses can be buried permanently and/or mulched.	Plastic or rubber hoses are long lasting and easy to move; difficult to bend into tight curves. Canvas hoses are lightweight; easy to move when empty but sloppy to move when in use. Drain and dry after each use to prevent mildew.
Sprinkler hose. Shoots sprays of water from holes punched along length of hose.	Narrow lawn or garden strips.	Turn the hose so water sprays into the ground instead of the air. Keep the water volume low or you'll blast holes in the soil. Plastic hoses tear easily; rubber ones are long lasting.
Sprinkler. Shoots water through the air. Some spray in set patterns; others oscillate or rotate.	Lawns; choose a sprinkler with a spray pattern that most closely matches the shape of your yard.	Select sprinklers that spray large droplets to reduce evaporation. Traveling sprinklers that "walk" along your outstretched hose are best but are expensive.
Medium-priced		
Drip irrigation. Water drips from emitters placed in hose at set intervals or through spaghetti tubes with emitters at ends.	Use hoses with emitters preinstalled for evenly spaced plants like vegetables. Use spaghetti tubes to reach ornamental plants.	Operates at low water pressure. Clean filters and flush system every few weeks to prevent clogging. Look for a system that flushes automatically. Use a backflow preventer; pressure regulators are optional but keep the system running more efficiently.
Expensive		
In-ground irrigation. Low-maintenance once installed; pop-up heads stay out of sight unless in use and can be mowed over.	Lawns.	Automatic timers make these systems convenient. Effective for covering large lawns. Remove grass when it grows too close to sprinkler heads. Leaks may develop in areas where the soil freezes and thaws during winter, but they can be fixed easily.

CHAPTER 9

Pruning

Pruning the Low-Maintenance Way

THE ABSOLUTE BEST WAY to cut down on the time and labor you spend on pruning is to avoid it altogether. And the secret to that is choosing plants that grow only as tall and wide as your space. Looking for dwarf trees and shrubs is a good start. Also keep your eye out for well-behaved fruit trees and berry bushes—there are new ones being introduced every day. Although buying on impulse is fun and easy, choosing the right plants from the start is worth the extra time it takes: It will save you pruning time and effort for the life of your plants.

But uprooting all the plants in your yard and replacing them isn't often an option. And extreme age, high winds, lightning, or diseases can also ravage plantings. What to do? Haul out the pruning saw and shears. But never fear, with the information that follows you can complete your pruning chores quickly and with confidence.

Pick Your Cuts to Prune Plants Right the First Time

Random hacking takes a lot more effort than proper pruning, and it costs a lot. These cuts come back to haunt you as rotted or diseased areas and lush, uncontrolled growth. As a first step toward reforming your pruning practices, *always* make proper pruning cuts that will shape your plant the way you want it to grow.

When you prune, cut just above a bud, as shown. But don't just select any bud—cut to one that's pointed in the direction you want a branch or stem to grow. Unless your plant has a bare spot in the middle, choose a bud growing away from the center to avoid crowded, crossing branches. If you're removing damaged stems or branches during the growing season, cut just above a healthy leaf to help hide the wound.

To make any pruning cut, make a slanted cut ¼ inch above a bud. The high side should be above the bud to shed water and prevent rotting.

Cut Out Labor

There are two ways to prune trees and shrubs. You can thin them and save time and effort, or head them back and create more work. It's not hard to decide which technique is best for you—or your plants.

Thinning cuts. Prune selectively by cutting branches back to the next larger limb or by removing entire limbs or stems. You'll shape the plant by reducing its height and improve air circulation by opening it up. The result is a healthy, attractive plant that won't need follow-up pruning.

Heading cuts. When you cut the ends off branches, they send up a dense growth of side shoots. This type of pruning makes formal hedges look tidy and full but creates problems. It reduces air circulation and light inside the plants so inner branches are susceptible to insects or diseases; they may even get shaded out completely.

See "Restyle Your Shrubs to Reduce Maintenance" on page 87 for a better solution. If you can't give up your formal hedge, prune it so the top is slightly narrower than the bottom so the entire plant gets light.

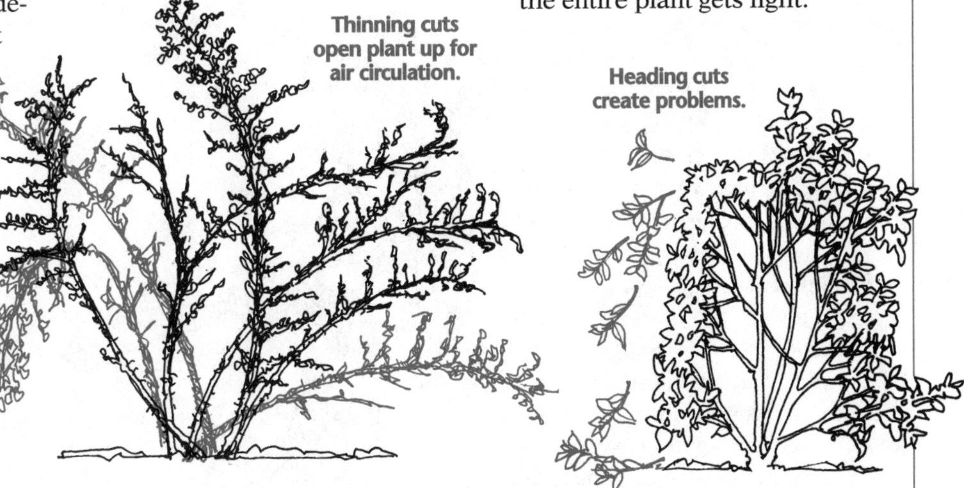

Use Handy Helpers to Make Pruning a Breeze

All you really need for painless pruning are a few good tools. High-quality stainless steel or forged steel blades won't snap under stress, so you'll avoid lots of wasted time and frustration. But even they have limits; treat your tools right and only tackle jobs they're designed for. If it takes lots of effort to cut, you're pruning a branch that's too big for your tool.

A set of hand pruners and a handheld pruning saw should see you through most pruning situations you're likely to encounter. If you have hedges or large plantings of flowers or brambles, a pair of hedge clippers and a pair of loppers will come in handy, too. Pick out tools that feel comfortable in your hand and are lightweight enough so pruning won't exhaust you. Clean the blades after each use, using steel wool if necessary; then wipe them with an oily cloth and they'll last a lifetime. Here's what to look for.

▶ **Hand pruners.** Bypass hand pruners are kinder to fragile stems than anvil types, which tend to crush tender stems as the blade comes to rest on a flat plate. Pointed blades let you reach into tight spots and give a clean cut on stems and twigs under $1/2$ inch thick. Ergonomic models have handles that are set at an angle to the blades so you won't have to bend your wrist as much.

Anvil pruners will cut wood with less effort than bypass pruners, though, and are a good choice if you have limited hand strength.

▼ **Pruning saws.** A curved pruning saw can cut through wood with ease, especially if you select one that cuts on the push *and* pull strokes. Many models only cut on the pull stroke, so there's less pressure on the narrow blade. They're just as useful but not quite as fast. Try out models you see in local hardware stores or garden centers to find one that feels and cuts comfortably. You may find the best selection in mail-order catalogs; see "Sources" on page 355 for a list of tool suppliers.

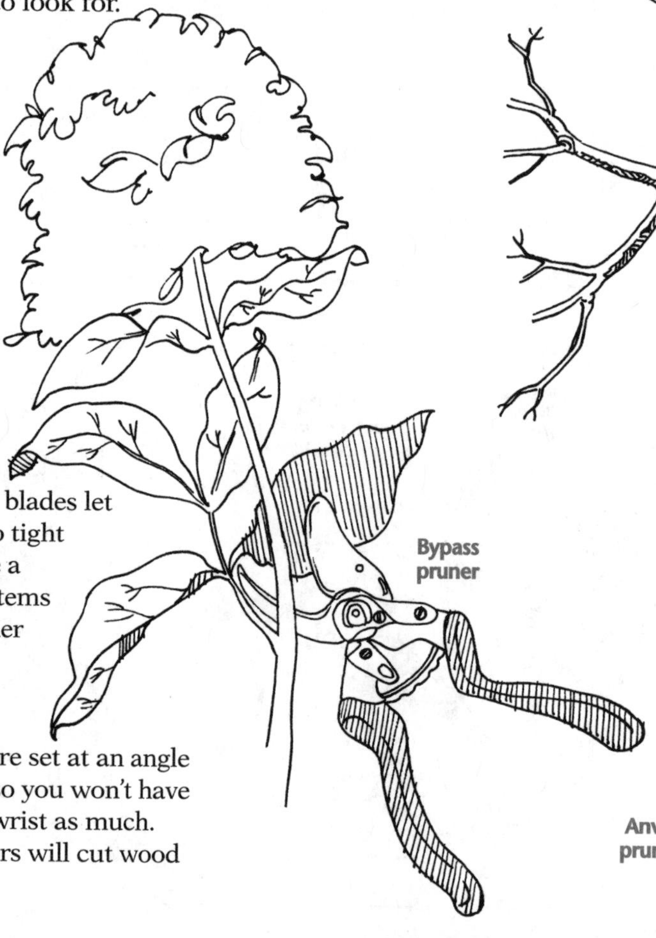

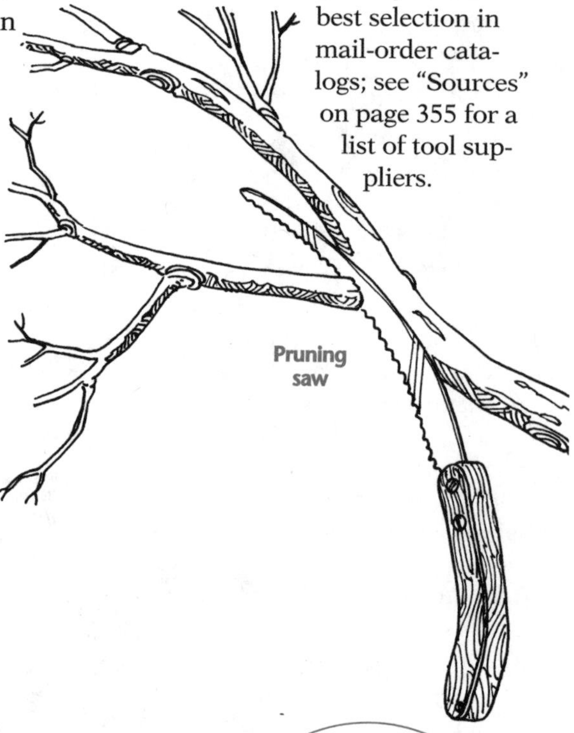

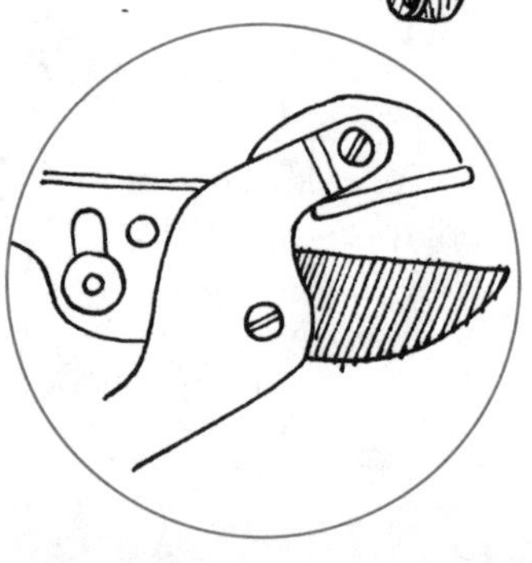

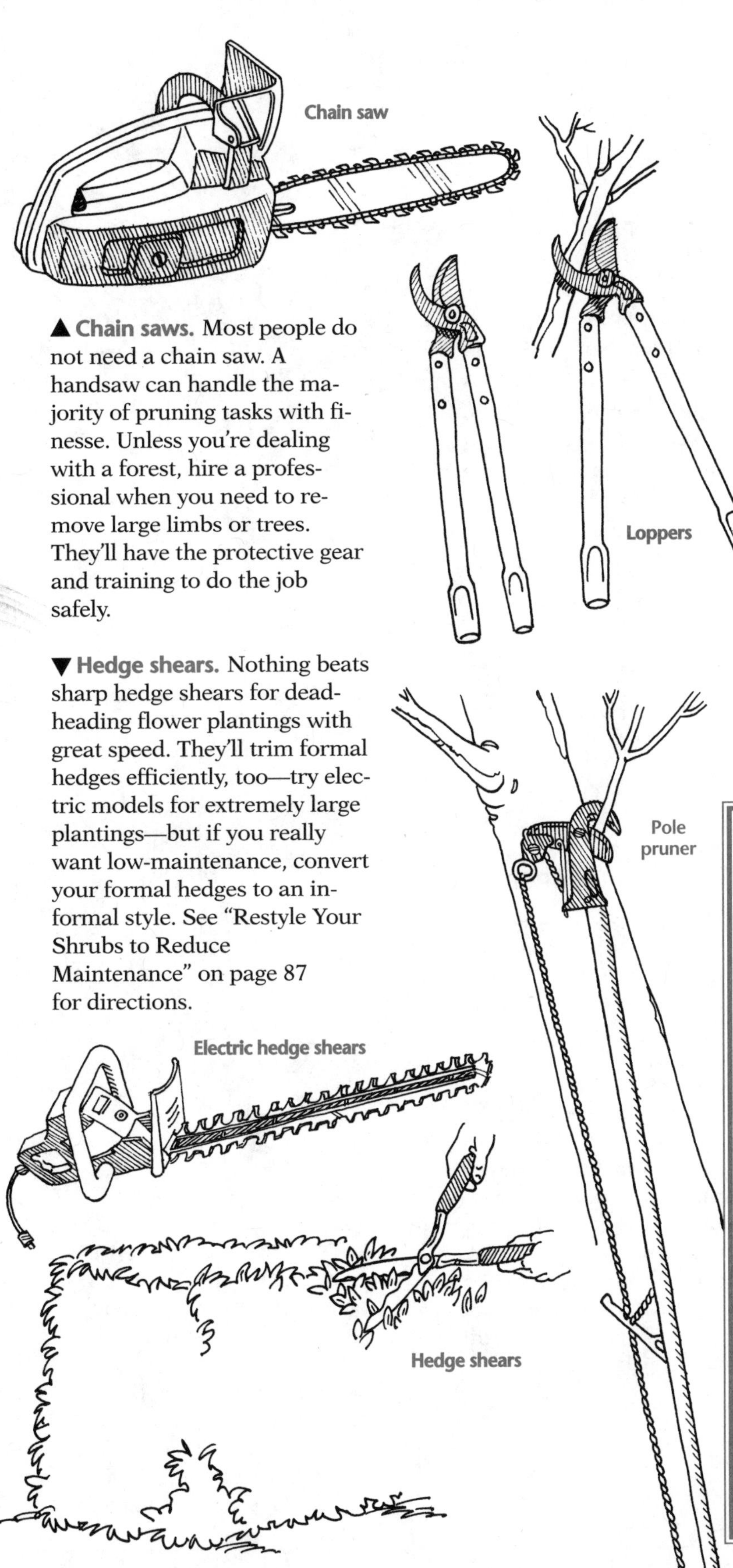

▲ **Chain saws.** Most people do not need a chain saw. A handsaw can handle the majority of pruning tasks with finesse. Unless you're dealing with a forest, hire a professional when you need to remove large limbs or trees. They'll have the protective gear and training to do the job safely.

▼ **Hedge shears.** Nothing beats sharp hedge shears for deadheading flower plantings with great speed. They'll trim formal hedges efficiently, too—try electric models for extremely large plantings—but if you really want low-maintenance, convert your formal hedges to an informal style. See "Restyle Your Shrubs to Reduce Maintenance" on page 87 for directions.

◀ **Loppers.** A good pair of loppers will make short work of pruning chores for branches that are $\frac{1}{2}$ to $1\frac{1}{2}$ inches in diameter. The long handles give you plenty of leverage for cutting tough limbs. Ratchet-style loppers hold the blades in place while you get a better grip. Several small pulls on the handles is all it takes to slice through a stem, so you won't need Herculean strength.

▼ **Pole pruners.** You'll rarely have to use a pole pruner unless you're growing fruit trees. They'll extend your reach but are awkward; it takes practice to balance and cut without injuring nearby limbs. Rent one unless you have lots of trees.

Do You Really Need a Chain Saw?

Sure, chain saws are fast—and great for cutting wood—but they're not so great for pruning. Before you buy, rent, or use one, consider the following:

- Unless you have lots of practice, it's hard to make a proper pruning cut without slicing into healthy tree trunks or branches.
- The only place it's really safe to use a chain saw is when both feet are planted firmly on the ground. Don't be tempted to violate this rule by climbing ladders; it's too easy to injure yourself and the tree.
- A chain saw is incredibly powerful and quick; don't give it a chance to get away from you by raising it above your head.
- Protective gear is a must when using chain saws. You'll need safety goggles, gloves, a helmet, steel-toe boots, earplugs, and heavy-duty trousers. Make it easy on yourself and hire a professional arborist with the proper gear.

Pruning Dos and Don'ts

The way you prune plants makes a huge difference in your workload. Cut limbs correctly, and they'll recover quickly and you won't have any follow-up work to do. Cut them incorrectly, using a misguided technique like topping, and you'll create an ongoing nightmare of yearly corrective pruning. Use the dos and don'ts shown here to make your pruning jobs this year—and every year thereafter—a breeze.

▶ **DO line up your pruning cuts and use three-step branch removal.** Cuts should mirror the angle of the branch bark ridge—that furrow of bark where branch and trunk meet. Your cut should closely parallel the branch collar, but not cut into it. This type of cut gives your tree the best chance to cover over the wound and keep out insects and diseases.

Remove medium and large branches in three easy steps. First, cut part of the branch off to reduce the weight. Holding up a heavy branch while you prune it off the trunk will break your back, your pruning saw, and tear the bark. Then, undercut the remaining stub so the trunk bark won't rip when the stub falls free. Last, make the final cut from the top, beside (but not cutting into) the branch collar.

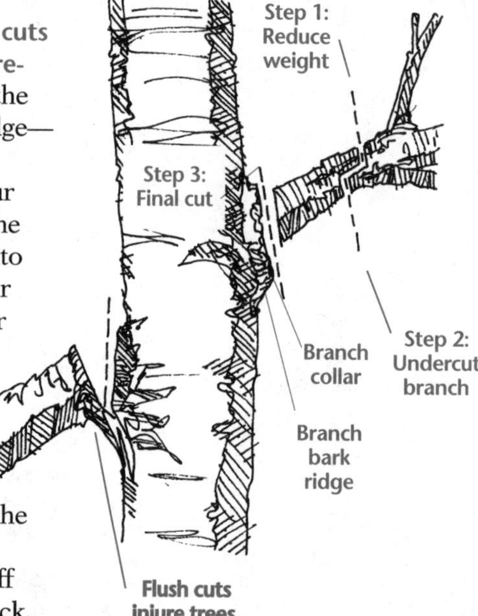

▲ **DON'T make pruning cuts that are too deep or leave branch stubs.** Flush cuts injure trees so badly they can't grow over the wound; enter rot and insects. Stubs rot and give insects and diseases an opening to destroy healthy tissue.

▲ **DO prune branches selectively.** Open up or lower the size of a mature tree by removing overcrowded or long branches at the point where they meet the trunk or a larger branch.

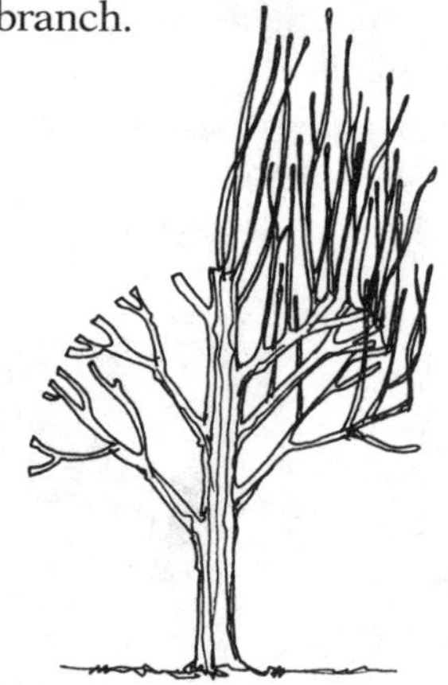

▲ **DON'T top trees, ever!** This so-called method destroys a plant's natural shape and results in unhealthy, malformed trees. A host of new, weak sprouts will rise from the cuts, and they'll need constant pruning to keep them under control. Insects and diseases will find the cut wood inviting.

Pruning Tips for Poorly Placed Plants

Plants always let you know if they're in the wrong spot by growing out of control. Get them back in shape with pruning, then take the steps necessary for a permanent cure; otherwise, you'll be doing fix-it pruning forevermore. Look for these symptoms to identify poorly placed plants.

Weak, spindly growth. Poor soil and insufficient light can cause weak, spindly growth. If you suspect poor soil, prune to reshape the plant, then use compost and organic fertilizer to restore soil fertility. See "Find Out What Your Soil Needs Most" on page 15 for ways to evaluate your soil.

Evaluate light conditions, too; the plant may be getting too much shade. If so, prune back by one-third and transplant to a sunnier spot. Choose a shade-tolerant plant for a replacement.

Awkward shape or branching. Incorrect pruning, storm damage, and winds are just some of the reasons a plant may have an ugly or awkward shape. To correct it, lightly shape the plant by pruning out individual branches. Do not give it a "haircut" with hedge shears; you will only cause lots of additional scraggly growth and make the problem worse.

Determine why the plant grew strangely. Was it injured? Is it in an area with high winds? Storm damage probably won't recur, so pruning is a good cure. Constant, severe winds are another story; provide a windbreak or move the plant to a sheltered area.

If a lawn mower caused the damage by bashing away at the base of stems, prune away the injured area and surround the plant with a wide mulch ring.

Wildly vigorous growth. Plants that smother your house or neighboring plants are definitely in the wrong place. Prune them back by one-third (more if you're dealing with an out-of-control vine) so they are manageable. Then move them to a more appropriate spot or the compost bin.

Choosing the Best Arborist

Any time you have to climb a tree or use a chain saw to prune a branch, think twice. An arborist can save you a lot of time, aggravation, and possible injury. Good ones have the training, equipment, and protective gear to do the job quickly and safely. Remember, one small slip in a tree can mean permanent injury.

Check credentials. Look for a certified arborist; they've had to pass a rigorous exam on tree care and selection. Call or write the International Society of Arboriculture, P.O. Box GG, Savoy, IL 61874; (217) 355-9411.

Consult local experts. Contact nearby botanical gardens to see if they can recommend good arborists. Extension agents, horticulture or forestry professors, or the staff at your local department of conservation may also have ideas.

Beware of incredible deals. Bargain-rate tree-pruning deals are usually a sign of inferior or incompetent work.

Check references. Ask for the names of recent clients. Call them up to see if they were pleased with the work.

Renew Overgrown Shrubs and Trees in 3 Easy Steps

Spread out your pruning chores, and you and your plants won't suffer undue stress. This three-step system works wonders on healthy plants and even offers hope for less vigorous ones. The process is similar whether you're dealing with an ornamental shrub or a fruit tree. Prune plants in late winter or early spring.

Renewing Ornamental Shrubs

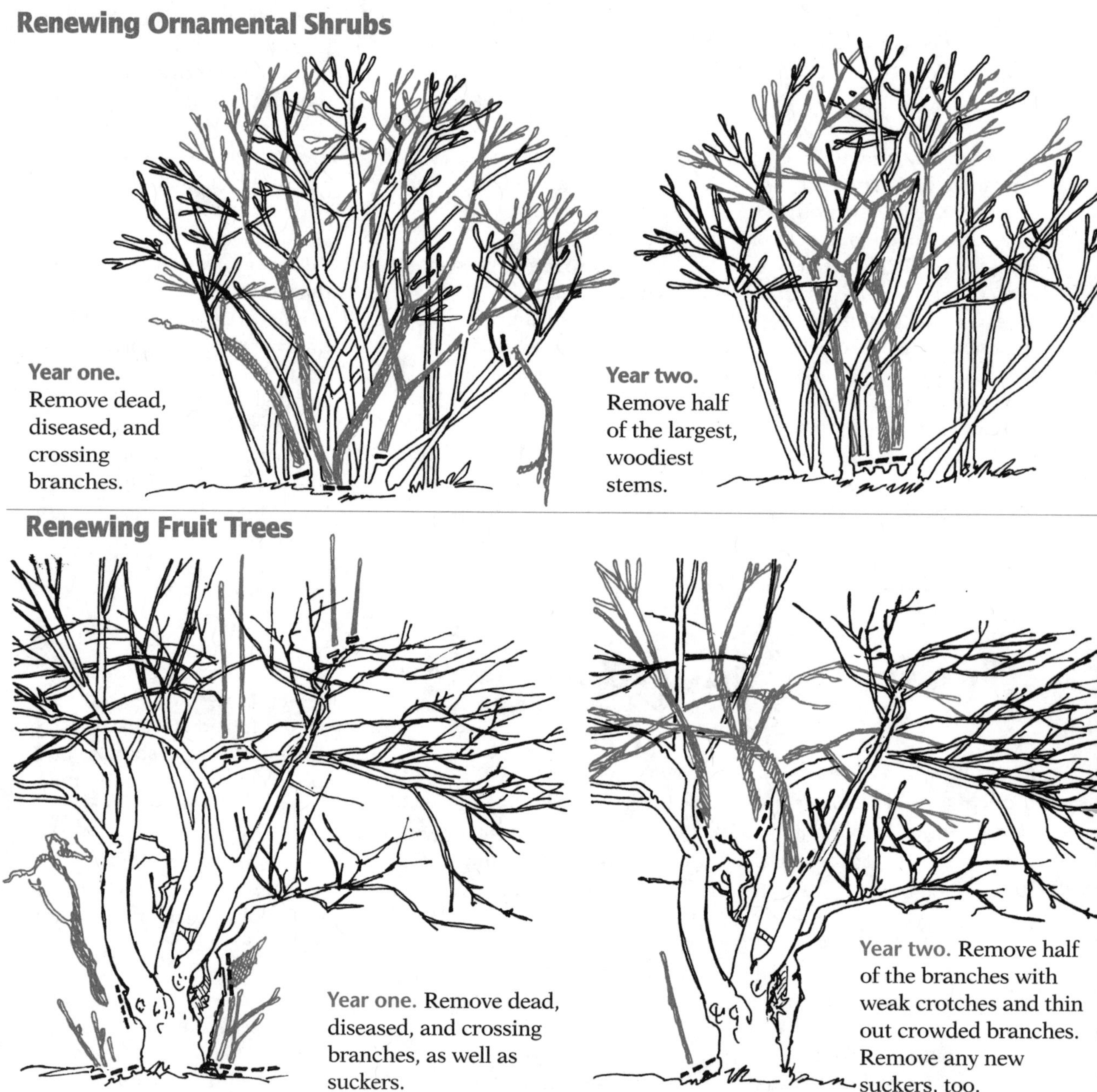

Year one. Remove dead, diseased, and crossing branches.

Year two. Remove half of the largest, woodiest stems.

Renewing Fruit Trees

Year one. Remove dead, diseased, and crossing branches, as well as suckers.

Year two. Remove half of the branches with weak crotches and thin out crowded branches. Remove any new suckers, too.

TAKE-IT-EASY TIP!

Don't Haul Those Twigs Away!

A pile of branches isn't a liability you have to spend hours chipping or dragging to the dump. If your property has a secluded corner, stash your branches there and create an instant wildlife shelter. Birds, squirrels, rabbits, and other creatures will all take advantage of your generosity, and you'll gain the pleasure of their company.

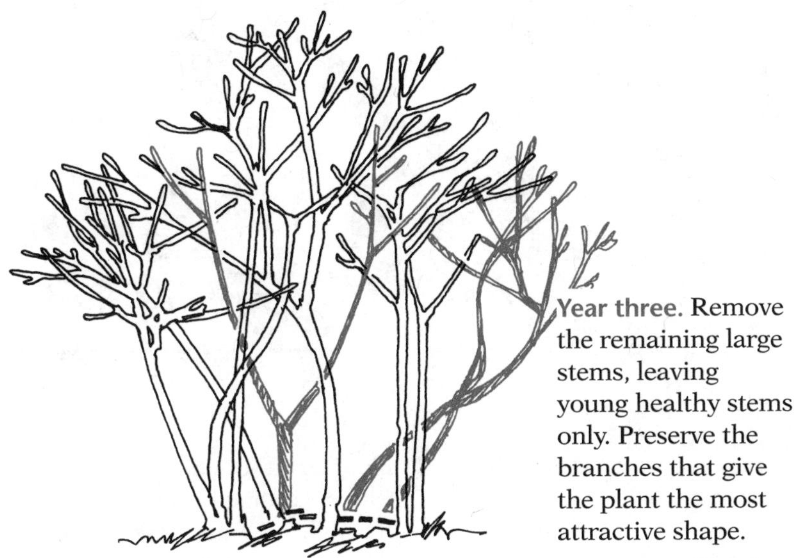

Year three. Remove the remaining large stems, leaving young healthy stems only. Preserve the branches that give the plant the most attractive shape.

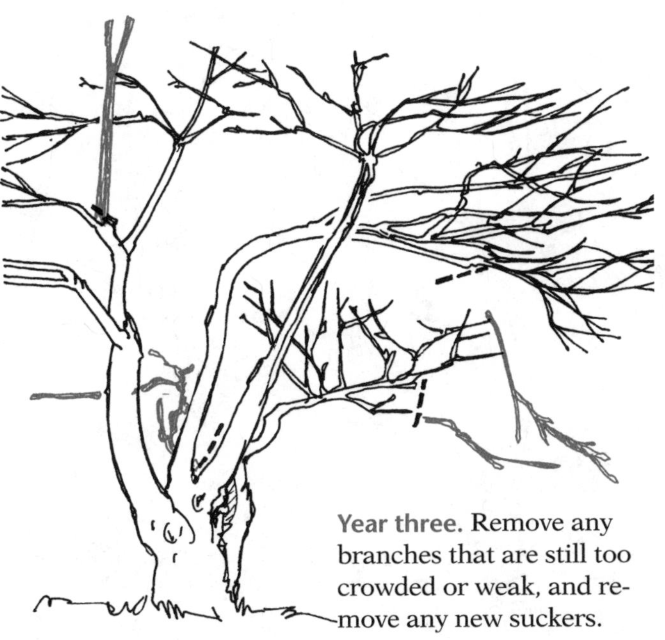

Year three. Remove any branches that are still too crowded or weak, and remove any new suckers.

Pick the Right Size and Shape to Escape Pruning Chores

Have you brought home gorgeous plants, then discovered after they engulfed your house that they were too big when full- or even half-grown? To avoid this problem, measure your planting space before you buy. That way you'll know if a 6-foot-tall, 5-foot-wide shrub will fit under your picture window. You'll save hours and hours of futile labor trying to prune oversize plants to fit. If you have existing plants that are out of bounds, see "Pruning Tips for Poorly Placed Plants" on page 83 for pruning suggestions. Here's how to tell what size plants will eventually reach.

Read the label. Plant labels are a great help since most list mature size and some growing hints. Double-check the label information with garden center personnel before you buy; occasionally, labels get switched with other plants.

Check several sources. For reliable plant sizes and growth habits, head for your local library and ask for good tree and shrub books. You'll find several of the best listed in "Recommended Reading" on page 358.

The Best Time to Prune Flowering Shrubs Is When You Have the Time

Flowering shrubs aren't as choosy about pruning as you might think. Timing schemes for spring- and summer-flowering shrubs guarantee that you won't miss a season of bloom. But there's no crisis if you don't follow them; you'll still get plenty of blooms the following season. What's most important is that pruning gets done, so schedule when it's most convenient for you. If you're faced with badly overgrown plants, see "Renew Overgrown Shrubs and Trees in 3 Easy Steps" on page 84 for the easiest approach.

If you can't stand to miss even one bloom season, all you have to do is follow one simple rule: Prune flowering shrubs after they flower.

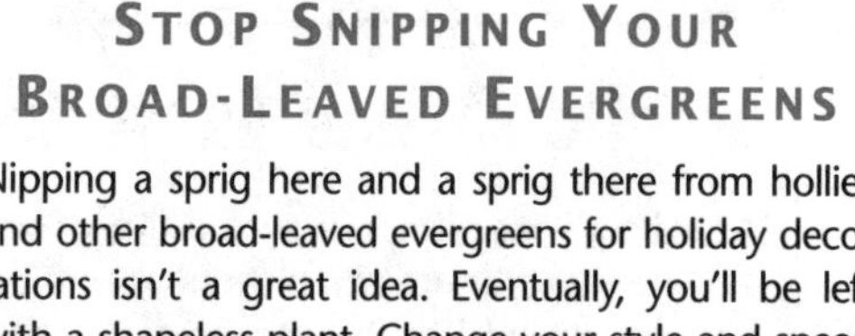

Stop Snipping Your Broad-Leaved Evergreens

Nipping a sprig here and a sprig there from hollies and other broad-leaved evergreens for holiday decorations isn't a great idea. Eventually, you'll be left with a shapeless plant. Change your style and speed up your harvest by removing entire branches or taking them back to a bigger branch. Choose crowded limbs or ones that detract from the plant's form.

Spring-blooming shrubs. Trim forsythias, lilacs, sweet mock orange, and other early bloomers right after flowering. They set next year's flower buds during summer, so if you prune in fall, winter, or the following spring, you'll slice off the next season of bloom. If the plants are severely overgrown, renewal-prune by removing one-third of the stems to ground level each year.

Summer-blooming shrubs. Any time after flowering is fine for pruning hydrangeas, buddleias, rose-of-Sharon, and other summer bloomers. There's no rush as with spring bloomers, though, so take advantage of their foliage through fall and prune in late winter or early spring. Summer bloomers set flower buds on the new season's growth, so hard pruning (cutting stems back to 2 or 3 inches from the ground) will guarantee you the most flowers.

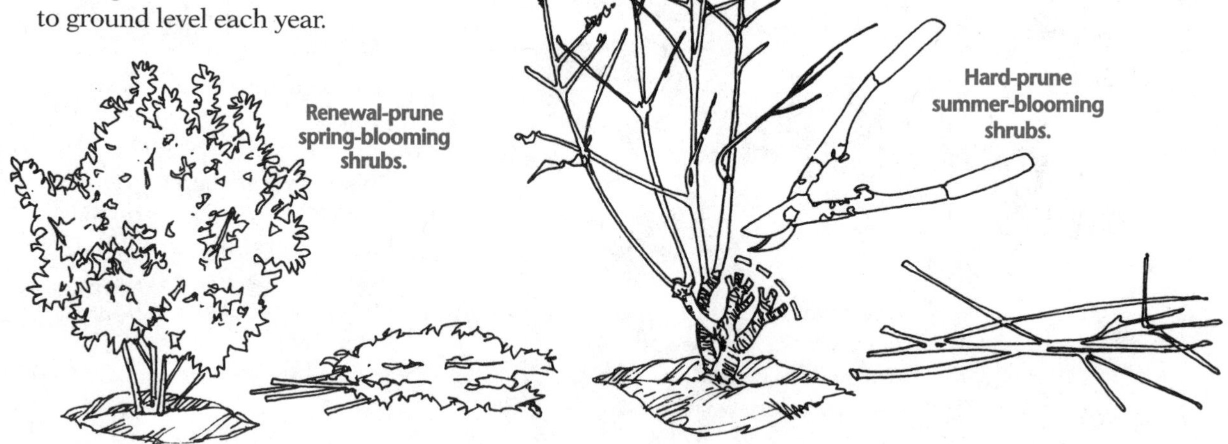

Restyle Your Shrubs to Reduce Maintenance

When it comes to low maintenance, formal, squared-off hedges and closely clipped shrubs don't make the grade. You don't have to be a slave to these maintenance monsters, which need clipping several times a year to look their best. Instead, put your hedge shears away, grab your hand pruners, and help nature rework your plants into beautiful, easy-care informal shapes.

Restyling deciduous shrubs and hedges. Use thinning cuts, not heading cuts, to open up holes in plants to let light in. (This is a good way to rejuvenate an informal hedge, too.) Make the cuts close to the ground or just above low branches; you'll encourage side buds to grow.

Remove one-third of the growth on each plant each year, taking out the most gnarled and woody branches first. Continue the process for three years until all the old growth is gone. Let new growth and suckers form the framework for your informal hedge.

Shrubs that respond well to this treatment include deutzia, forsythia, sweet mock orange, spirea, and old-fashioned weigela.

Restyling evergreen shrubs and hedges. Clean out any dead wood inside the shrubs. Poke holes in the top by reaching inside as far as you can with hand pruners and cutting branches back to larger limbs. You'll end up with an uneven but attractive look if you make sure each cut branch still has some green on it.

Broad-leaved evergreens like hollies and yews will respond to the additional light with new growth, and eventually return to their natural form. Junipers and American arborvitae may not respond at all. In that case, replacing them is the best solution.

Thin for Health

Shrubs, trees, and perennial flowers with overcrowded stems or branches are just the kind of sheltered, humid home insects and diseases like mildew prefer. Remove one-quarter to one-third of shrub or perennial stems from the center of your plants so sunlight and air can reach the inside leaves—diseases and insects hate this! Cut a few limbs out of the center of trees if they're too choked with branches for healthy growth. Take them back to a large branch or the trunk. Repeat each year until the plant has a healthy, open growth habit.

Unusually Effective Pruning Tools

Push mowers and string trimmers make good pruners for large groundcover or perennial plantings. For a fast spring cleanup, set the mower at its highest setting and run it over the plants in early spring before new growth starts. This works on level ground but not on hilly areas or plantings that have heaved out of the ground; they'll get scalped and die.

String trimmers zip through perennials, ornamental grasses, or groundcover foliage on any kind of ground. They'll leave a ragged finish, but new foliage will cover it quickly. You can't beat it when you're short on time.

CHAPTER 10

Weeding

Weeding the Low-Maintenance Way

AFTER SPENDING a few hot, sweaty, dirty, itchy hours ridding your gardens of weeds, it's hard to have anything good to say about them. Yet few plants are as versatile, tough, and tenacious. In poor soils, where few other plants will grow, weeds help prevent erosion by covering the soil and anchoring it with their roots. They also improve the soil they grow in by breaking it up with their extensive root systems. A "weedy" site can attract birds and beneficial insects that will help control pests in your gardens. In fact, perhaps the most low-maintenance thing you can do about weeds is learn to live with them.

However, weeds are not for everyone or for every place. In the landscape and garden, they're not only unattractive, they also compete with desired plants for light, water, and nutrients. They also are hosts and overwintering sites for pests and diseases.

In this chapter, you'll find practical tools and easy techniques for waging war on the weeds in your own backyard.

Make It Easy to Keep Weeds Out of Your Yard and Garden

It's all too easy to encourage or create weed problems when you are planting a garden or installing a new feature in your landscape. Use the following techniques to keep weeds from becoming a perpetual problem.

Don't bare your soil. Bare soil is an open invitation to both weed seeds and aggressive spreaders looking for new territory to colonize. Once you've prepared an area for planting, get your plants in the ground, then add a 2- to 4-inch layer of mulch over any exposed soil to discourage weeds.

Make it easy to mow. Use edgings or mowing strips to eliminate the need to trim and keep weeds and lawn grasses from spreading into garden beds. (Set plastic mowing strips or bricks flush with the soil around beds and mow with one wheel just inside the bed to eliminate hand trimming.) Use a thick layer of mulch around places where it's difficult to control weeds to keep them from becoming established.

Block weeds out. Lay woven or spunbonded landscape fabric, layers of newspaper, or cardboard under paving and decking to control weeds in walkways and patios. Cover it with shredded bark if appearance is an issue.

Give weeds some competition. Don't let weeds fill in the bare spots between slower-growing perennials, trees, shrubs, or vines in a new planting. Instead, give them some competiton by planting fast-growing annuals or groundcovers that can outcompete weeds for the space. If you also keep all your plantings vigorous and healthy, the desirable plants will compete with and help shade out any weeds that venture in.

Use easy lawn weed control. One super-easy way to help control weeds in the lawn is to set your mower blade a little higher. Grass that's allowed to grow taller is more vigorous and will make it tough for broad-leaved weeds to get a foothold.

Keep them in the dark. Soil contains hundreds of thousands of weed seeds, and every time you disturb the soil you expose some of those seeds to the light they need to germinate. So once you've prepared and planted a site, discourage weeds by keeping cultivation to a minimum. Mulch unplanted areas to further exclude light. You can also try doing your cultivating at night when there's no sunlight to trigger germination. Studies have shown that waiting until 3 hours after sunset significantly reduces the number of weeds that wake up after the soil is disturbed.

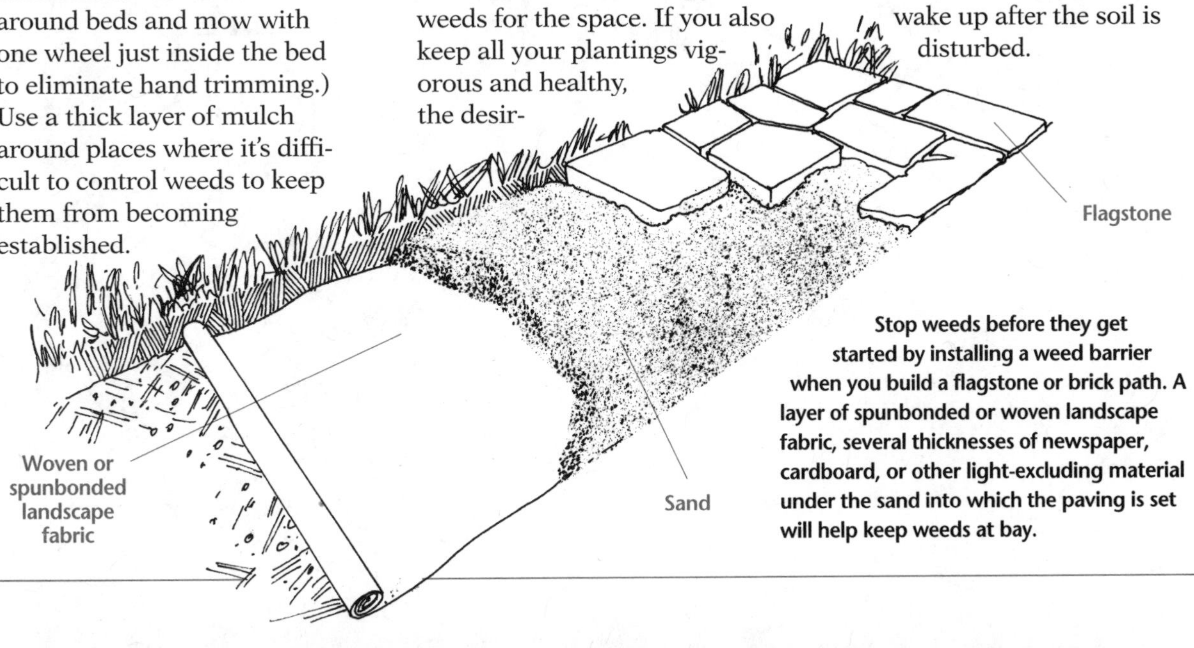

Flagstone

Woven or spunbonded landscape fabric

Sand

Stop weeds before they get started by installing a weed barrier when you build a flagstone or brick path. A layer of spunbonded or woven landscape fabric, several thicknesses of newspaper, cardboard, or other light-excluding material under the sand into which the paving is set will help keep weeds at bay.

When It Comes to Weeding, It Pays to Know Your Foe

Start your war on weeds with a tactical advantage by learning a little bit about the enemy. It may seem like extra work, but it can save you hours of weeding time in the end. That's because with weeds, what and when you weed are as important as how.

While all weeds are easiest to control when they're very young—a quick swipe of the hoe will wipe out a crop of baby weeds in an instant—as they grow older, it pays to know whether you're dealing with annual, perennial, or biennial weeds. So if you don't already have a good weed guide, add one to your garden bookshelf and get to know your foe.

Annual weeds. Chickweed, lamb's-quarters, shepherd's-purse, purslane, pigweed, and other annuals all live and die within one season and reproduce only by seed. Keep them from setting seed, and you've eliminated next year's weed crop. They're easiest to control when very young, but if you don't get to them in time, you absolutely must stop them before they set seeds—some annual weeds form hundreds of thousands of seeds at a time. So even if you don't pull up the plants, be sure to pick the flowers to keep them from setting seed. For information on controlling winter annuals, which germinate in early fall and set seed the following spring, see "Save Time in

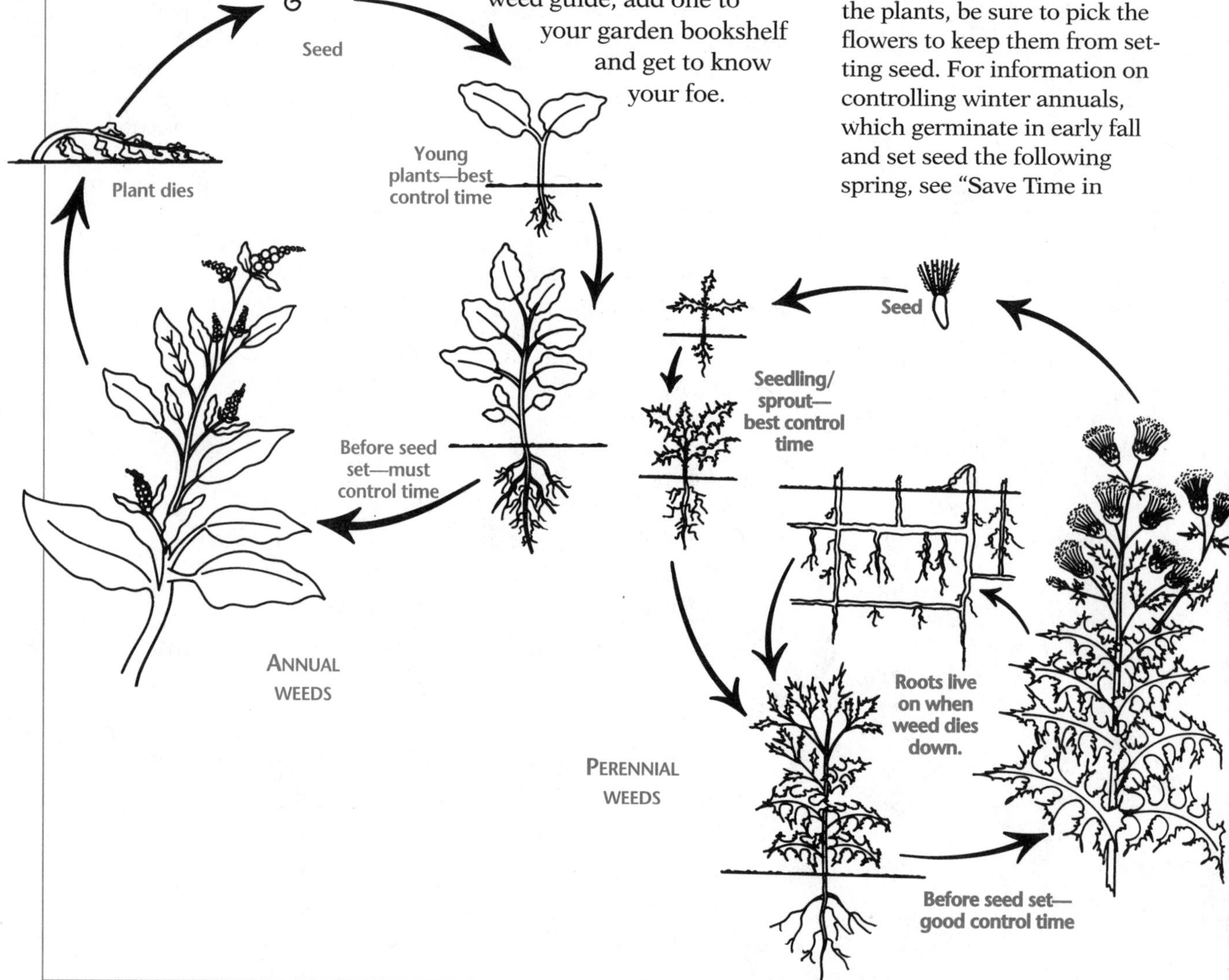

Summer by Weeding in a Winter Wonderland" on this page.

Perennial weeds. Bindweed, dandelions, thistles, dock, and woody perennial weeds like poison ivy are tough customers that can be a challenge to control. They reproduce both by seed and vegetatively, usually via spreading underground stems or roots. Like annual weeds, they're most easily controlled when very young, and it's important to prevent them from producing seeds, but you also have to worry about those wandering roots. Once they're older, they can resprout from roots or root pieces left in the soil, so complete control means removing weeds completely—roots and all.

Biennial weeds. Queen-Anne's-lace, common mullen, and other biennials produce foliage the first year, flowers and seeds the next. For best results, treat them as perennial weeds the first year. The second year, when they set seed and die, treat them as annual weeds.

Save Time in Summer by Weeding in a Winter Wonderland

If winter or cool-season annuals are among the weeds in your gardens, take advantage of what is traditionally a slow gardening time to stop them in their tracks. Winter annuals, such as common chickweed and henbit, germinate in fall and grow slowly until spring, when they flower and set seed. This schedule gives them time to get a firm foothold in your garden, well before you're able to start planting.

Instead of letting these weeds get a jump on your gardens, put an end to their cycle. Wait for an unseasonably warm, mid- to late winter day, when it's too soon to do any real gardening and too nice to stay inside. Then grab a kneeling pad and get out there and remove those potential problems while they're still small, shallow-rooted, and easy to pull. Without insect pests, hot sun, or other waiting garden tasks to trouble you, you can enjoy some early, easy gardening, knowing that you're saving yourself a lot of trouble in the months to come.

Weed When Wet

If a stretch of rain leaves your garden soil too wet to be workable, grab your galoshes and do some weeding. You can pull even tough, taprooted weeds like dandelions and rampant spreaders like bindweed with relative ease from soggy soil. And young, shallow-rooted weeds will come up so easily that it won't seem like work.

While on your wet weed hunt, work from the edges of your garden to avoid compacting the soil. And remove the pulled weeds from your beds—many weeds can reroot easily into wet soil.

Work-Then-Wait
Ways to Wipe Out Weeds

If you find yourself fighting a losing battle with weeds, try one of the following techniques to help you reclaim those spaces. Although each of these methods requires up-front effort from you, the materials you put in place do the rest.

Stop Weeds by Smothering

Plants—weeds included—need light. And without it, eventually even the toughest weeds will call it quits. To clear an area where weeds and brush have taken over, start by doing as much damage to the weeds as you can—mow them off close to the ground or chop them up with your tiller. Dig out the roots of woody perennial weeds such as poison ivy, or use a Weed Wrench to pull them out. (See the opposite page for more on Weed Wrenches.) Then cover the area with a thick, light-excluding mulch. Try a layer of cardboard or several thicknesses of newspaper (12 or more sheets is best), topped with 6 inches of organic mulch.

Once in place, this method asks little of you; just watch out for any weeds that manage to pop through, and pull them out. After several months to a year, you can plant directly into what's left of the mulch. Don't till or turn the mulch under; if you disturb the soil, you'll expose new weed seeds to the light. If you use this method to clear an area infested with poison ivy or field bindweed, you may need to replenish the mulch and leave the site undisturbed for up to two years.

Sizzle Weeds Away with Sunlight

If you can spare space in your garden for 6 weeks in the middle of summer, get the sun on your side and solarize the weeds away. For maximum success with this technique, you need a level, unshaded garden bed that is cleared as if for planting. If your site is sloping or shaded, weed seeds or rhizomes in some parts of the bed may survive the process. Start by watering the soil thoroughly—the moisture helps transmit heat from the sun into the soil. Then stretch a sheet of clear 1- to 4-mil plastic over the moistened bed, tucking the edges of the plastic into a trench around the outside of the bed and sealing them with a covering of soil. Press the plastic down to make sure it has good contact with the soil surface.

Remove the plastic after 4 to 6 weeks. If you don't plan to plant your newly cleared bed right away, cover it with a weed-free mulch such as shredded bark to keep new weed seeds from taking advantage of the vacant site. Disturb the soil as little as possible when you do plant; weed seeds deeper than the top 6 inches of the soil may survive solarization and be ready to germinate if you expose them to light.

Starve
Perennial Weeds with Attention

If you turn your attention to young perennial weeds every two weeks, you can starve them out of your garden over the course of a growing season.

In the first week of a perennial weed's life, food stored in its roots supports its growth. During the second week of growth, it's just breaking even. Beyond 14 days, it starts storing food back to its roots—once this happens, it become much more difficult to control.

The moral to this story is simple: Hoe off or pull up perennial weeds every two weeks, catching them each time at the end of their second week of growth. Each hoeing leaves them less able to resprout from their roots until, finally, they don't come back.

Tools to Take the Work Out of Weeding

Ask some gardeners about their favorite weeding tool. Don't worry; they'll have at least one, maybe several. Look in any garden-supply catalog; you're likely to find a large selection of tools designed specifically for weeding, as well as several others that look as if they'd be handy for that purpose. Here are some guidelines to help you pick the best tools for you.

Try tools on for size. The trick to finding the best tool for tackling the plants that plague you is to suit yourself and your site. Try a gardening friend's favorite tools on for size before you buy. Test the feel of tools as you shop. Look for tools that give you the advantage of leverage, like several of the tools pictured below. Consider the position you'll need to be in when using each tool, and make sure it's right for your height and physical strength. And if your back resents your weeding work, look for tools that minimize the strain by allowing you to remain upright or to exert less force while you weed.

Consider your foes. Annual weeds in a garden are readily leveled with a sharp hoe blade, while deeply rooted perennial weeds demand a digging and cutting tool such as an asparagus (a.k.a. dandelion) fork. And woody or brushy pest plants cry out for tougher tools like mattocks or the back-sparing Weed Wrench.

Pick tools for your site. You can save time and effort by matching your weeding tools to the site you have to weed. Larger tools work well between the rows of a vegetable garden but are unwieldy in tightly spaced perennial beds, where a narrow-bladed weeder is needed. In a large vegetable garden, for example, a wheel hoe can make short work of weeds growing between the rows. In a perennial garden, a small hand weeder works best. Of course, when weeds crop up in a planting of newly sprouted seedlings, your nimble fingers are the best tools to use.

Think about the soil you'll be working in as well—if it's heavy, your weeding tools need to be tougher and heavier to break through with less effort from you.

This handy ball weeder uses leverage to get weeds out. Insert the prongs into the ground and rock back on the ball to pull out the weed.

An asparagus fork is handy for digging deep-rooted dandelions and other perennial weeds.

This heavy-duty Weed Wrench uses leverage to help you pull out large woody weeds. It is available in four sizes, based on the stem diameter of the plants you want to remove. It is available from New Tribe, 5517 Riverbanks Road, Grants Pass, OR 97527.

For no-stoop weeding, try a Weed Popper that uses leverage to pop weeds out of the ground. There are several different styles, but all use foot-activated levers to pull weeds.

Wild and Wacky Ways to Wipe Out Weeds

If battling weeds with conventional weapons takes too much time and energy, consider enlisting a high-tech helper. These specialized tools that fight weeds with fire and water are unlikely to make you abandon your hoe altogether, but they do offer weed-control options that require less physical strength to accomplish the job.

Propane torch weeders. These tools attach an extended nozzle to a standard propane cylinder to let you scorch weeds from a standing position. Weed flamers are excellent for controlling weeds in cracks in sidewalks and driveways, and along roadsides and curbs. With care, you can also use them on weeds growing amid your garden plants. In dry weather, propane flamers can be a fire hazard; under such conditions you'll need to have a hose ready to douse small fires.

Water Needle weeder. This device attaches to your garden hose and concentrates the flow of water into a powerful stream that you can use to loosen the soil surrounding a weed's deep taproot. Once you wash away the soil, even large dandelions pull up easily without snapping the roots. Since water does the work, the Water Needle represents no hazard to garden plants—you can even use it to water established trees and shrubs. And its high-pressure spray makes it useful for washing weeds out of cracks in pavement.

Hot-water weeder. Equipment that lets you scald weeds with superheated water—most notably the Waipuna System from New Zealand—is still sized for large-scale maintenance. Along roadsides and in playground areas, hot-water weeders offer an excellent nonchemical way to control weeds. Around your home landscape, a pan of hot water from the kitchen makes a fine but very nonspecific weed control. Simply pour it over weeds and watch them wilt. Obvious care is needed to avoid scalding desirable plants or yourself.

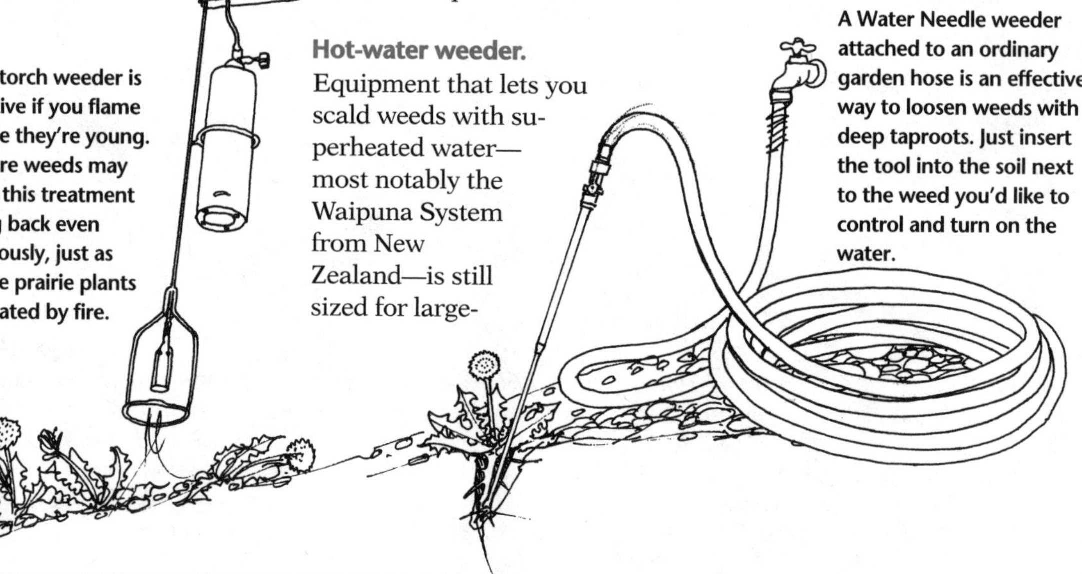

A propane torch weeder is most effective if you flame weeds while they're young. More mature weeds may respond to this treatment by growing back even more vigorously, just as many native prairie plants are rejuvenated by fire.

A Water Needle weeder attached to an ordinary garden hose is an effective way to loosen weeds with deep taproots. Just insert the tool into the soil next to the weed you'd like to control and turn on the water.

Tilling Can Mean Trouble Times Two

The weedy, wide walkways between the rows of your vegetable garden may seem ripe for a quick pass with the rotary tiller. And they may be just that, if the weeds growing between your crops are seed-free annuals. But tilling may double your troubles if perennial weed problems are hiding amid the tomatoes. Most of these tough customers will grow back from the roots after you've tilled off their tops; some of the worst ones—quackgrass, ground ivy, and Canada thistle—will spring to new life from every chopped-up piece your tiller leaves in the garden.

Too Tired to Weed? No Time? Try a Little Light Weeding

Solving the weed problems in your vegetable garden, lawn, and landscape plantings need not mean spending all your limited gardening time pulling weeds. If you spend a small amount of time every week or two, you can get control of weeds in most sites and eliminate some weed problems entirely.

Use the tips that follow to make the most of whatever amount of weeding time you can work into your week.

Get 'em while they're young. Compare hoeing off a 2-inch-tall pigweed seedling to pulling out a 2-foot-tall, mature pigweed plant. Multiply that difference by the hundreds of seeds a mature plant can produce. When do you want to control this plant and others like it? It's worth your while to spend your time with hoe in hand, eliminating tiny weed seedlings. If you don't, rest assured they'll grow into much bigger problems in a relatively short amount of time.

Focus on flowers. Where weeds have grown bigger and more numerous than you can control all at once, it's important to do whatever you can to halt their spread. Use your time to tackle any and all weeds that have started to flower—weeds are remarkably quick at producing seeds once they begin blooming. While you'll still need to go after the roots of perennial weeds, stopping seed production goes a long way toward limiting future problems.

Fine-tune your technique. A brief, weekly weeding session can be much more relaxing than a one-time, all-day, full-out physical effort to wipe out every weed on your property. Choose a hoe that's comfortable for you to use, and keep the cutting edge of the blade sharp to minimize the pushing and pulling needed to cut through weeds. Maintain good posture as you weed: Hoe from an upright position, and let your leg muscles do as much of the work as possible when pushing, pulling, or bending to get closer to the ground. When kneeling, stay close to your work. If you find yourself on all fours, stretching to get to the weeds, move closer to keep your knees at an angle of 90° or less to your body.

Come back for more. Cutting weeds off with a hoe is a less effective control than pulling out entire plants, roots and all. But regular hoeing sessions require less of you physically and, over time, will keep weed populations in check. And, not least of all, quietly hoeing in your gardens gives you time to truly tend each plant, thereby contributing to the overall health of your landscape in a way few other weed-control methods can.

Kill Weeds with Household Helpers

When weeds crop up in the cracks of your pavement, halt their advance with a home remedy. Add ¼ cup of salt to 1 quart of boiling water, and pour the hot liquid over the weeds. Or drench them with vinegar. Both these homespun weedkillers kill *all* plants—they alter soil conditions so little else will grow in the site for some time—so don't use them to kill weeds in gardens. You can also wash away your weeds with commercial "soap" sprays—fatty acid–based products formulated for weed control. Apply soaps with care, too, as they're toxic to most plants they touch.

CHAPTER 11

Pest Prevention and Control

Pest Prevention and Control the Low-Maintenance Way

WHY SPEND YOUR LIFE battling insect explosions and animal attacks? It doesn't take much more than compost and good planning to create a problem-free garden filled with plants that can fight pests on their own. Healthy plants are your first line of defense against insects. Keeping an eye on your plants will also reduce pest-fighting chores because you'll spot problems early.

In this chapter, you'll find tips on attracting beneficial insects and animals to help you in the pest control war, as well as simple ways to prevent pests from reaching your crops at all. You'll also find tips for dealing with problems that do arise.

7 Simple Steps to Prevent Insect Pests

There isn't any magic that will rid your garden of pests once they move in, but there is a low-maintenance solution to pest problems—prevention. Try these seven simple steps to eliminate pest problems before they start.

1. **Build up your soil.** There's no easier or more effective way to grow pest-free plants than by improving your soil. Add an inch or two of compost to poor soil each spring until drainage and fertility are restored. A yearly side-dressing or sprinkle of compost in spring will keep soil in good shape thereafter.

2. **Put up pest barriers.** Keep pests from reaching plants by putting obstacles in their way: Fabric covers, dusts, and cardboard, plastic, or metal collars can all do the trick. See "Let Barriers Control Your Insect Problems for You" on page 98.

3. **Attract beneficials.** Plant flowers that appeal to pest predators. Provide water and shelters as described in "Persuade Beneficials to Become Resident Pest-Control Experts" on page 106.

4. **Rotate crops.** Whenever you pull out a crop, put a different one in. You'll discourage pests that were attracted to the original crop and stop insect populations from building up.

5. **Grow a wide variety of plants.** Large plantings of a single plant draw insects like magnets. Confuse pests by mixing many types of flowers and vegetables. Pests will have trouble finding their favorite plant snacks and may move on to easier pickings.

6. **Plant pest-resistant plants.** Some plant types are naturally pest-free and make good garden choices. Don't give up on susceptible favorites, though; pest-resistant cultivars may be available through catalogs or garden centers.

7. **Clean up waste.** Pests find hiding and breeding places beneath old leaves, stalks, and stems, so remove and compost faded plant parts promptly.

Monitor Plants for Quick Pest Prevention

Spider mite

Most insect problems can be solved in seconds if you spot them in time. Check your plants for pests at least once a week—in early morning if you can—while the air is cool and moist. Insects are cold-blooded and can't move very fast until the sun heats them up.

To monitor pests, flip over a few leaves and search for signs like eggs, insect droppings, or spider mite webbing. At this stage, a blast of water or a pinch of your fingers may be all it takes to stop pests dead in their tracks.

Look before you squish, though. Don't destroy insects that aren't causing problems. Keep a reference book handy until you can distinguish between the bad bugs and the good ones—who may be feasting on the very pests you're trying to control.

Let Barriers Control Your Insect Problems for You

You can fend off all of the vegetable pests pictured here with easy-to-install insect barriers like floating row covers. Barriers keep pests from reaching your plants, so you won't have to beat them off or deal with the damage they cause.

Control jumping, crawling, and flying pests with floating row covers. Light, air, and water easily penetrate floating row covers or lighter-weight insect barrier fabrics, but the pests on these pages can't. Cover seeds or transplants immediately after planting to avoid trapping insects inside. Anchor the fabric to the ground with metal pins or stones and soil spread over the edges. Leave enough slack so plants have room to grow. Remove fabric barriers when insect-pollinated plants like beans, cucumbers, eggplants, melons, peppers, and squash bloom or you won't get any fruit. You can leave crops like carrots and onions covered all season.

Look for floating row covers or insect barrier fabrics in

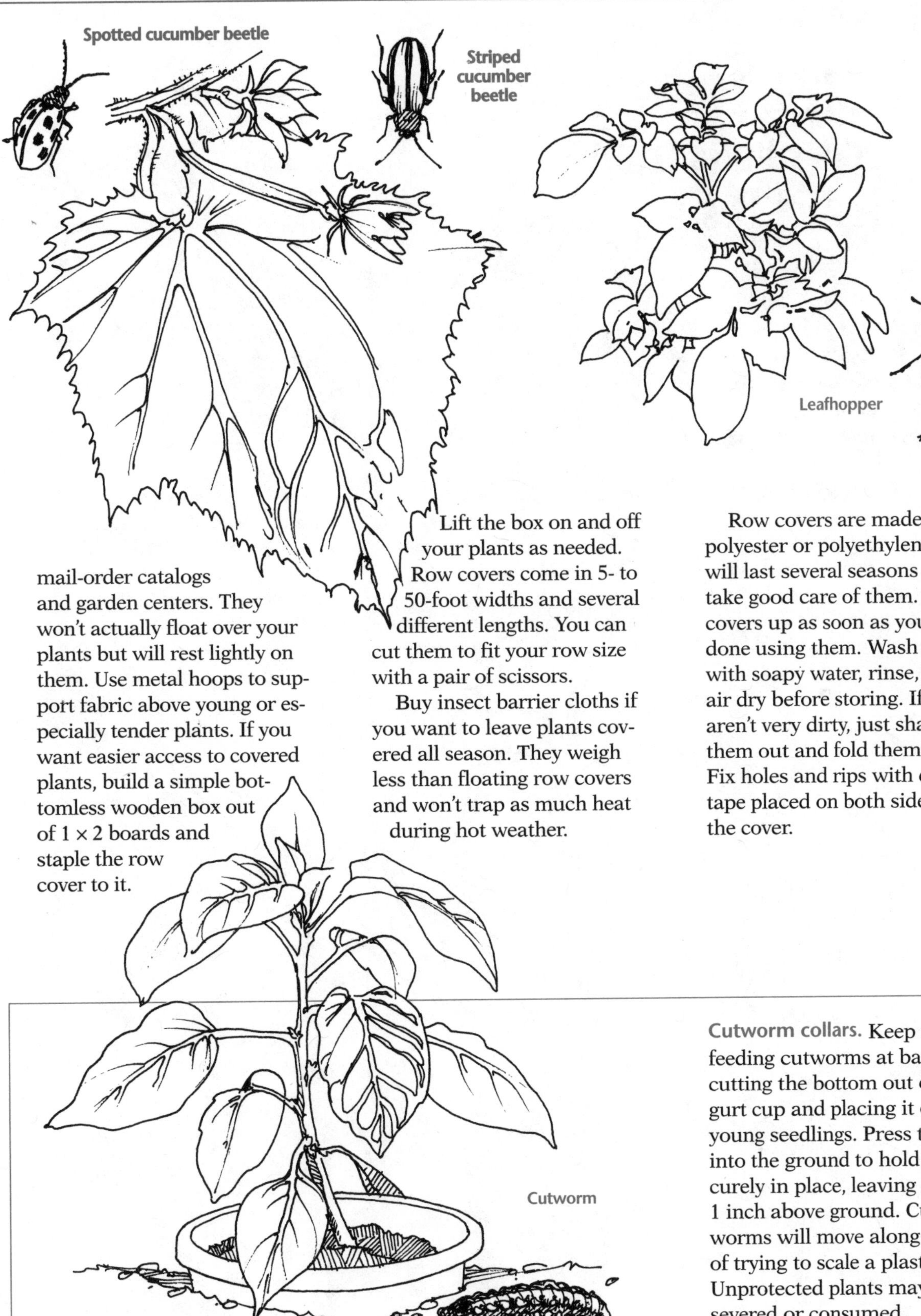

mail-order catalogs and garden centers. They won't actually float over your plants but will rest lightly on them. Use metal hoops to support fabric above young or especially tender plants. If you want easier access to covered plants, build a simple bottomless wooden box out of 1 × 2 boards and staple the row cover to it.

Lift the box on and off your plants as needed. Row covers come in 5- to 50-foot widths and several different lengths. You can cut them to fit your row size with a pair of scissors.

Buy insect barrier cloths if you want to leave plants covered all season. They weigh less than floating row covers and won't trap as much heat during hot weather.

Row covers are made from polyester or polyethylene and will last several seasons if you take good care of them. Pick covers up as soon as you're done using them. Wash them with soapy water, rinse, and air dry before storing. If they aren't very dirty, just shake them out and fold them up. Fix holes and rips with duct tape placed on both sides of the cover.

Cutworm collars. Keep night-feeding cutworms at bay by cutting the bottom out of a yogurt cup and placing it over young seedlings. Press the cup into the ground to hold it securely in place, leaving at least 1 inch above ground. Cutworms will move along instead of trying to scale a plastic wall. Unprotected plants may be severed or consumed.

Quick Picking Protects Plants from Insect Pests

Colorado potato beetles

Unless you're dealing with a major infestation, hand-picking is one of the quickest ways to foil pests. If you're squeamish, wear gloves and drop pests into a bucket of soapy water. Otherwise, just pick and squeeze.

Pull caterpillars off plants. When foliage disappears in a hurry and your plants are coated with droppings, caterpillars are probably the culprits. Look closely to find them since they're often colored to blend in with their surroundings.

Get the drop on beetles. Many pest insects drop off leaves when your hand comes close. Use their actions to your advantage by placing your hand or a bucket under large beetles so you'll catch them when they fall.

Smash pest eggs before they hatch. Look under leaves for pest eggs. Destroy them by rubbing gently, being careful not to tear foliage in the process. If leaves do tear, don't panic. Plants are better off with a rip than an insect infestation.

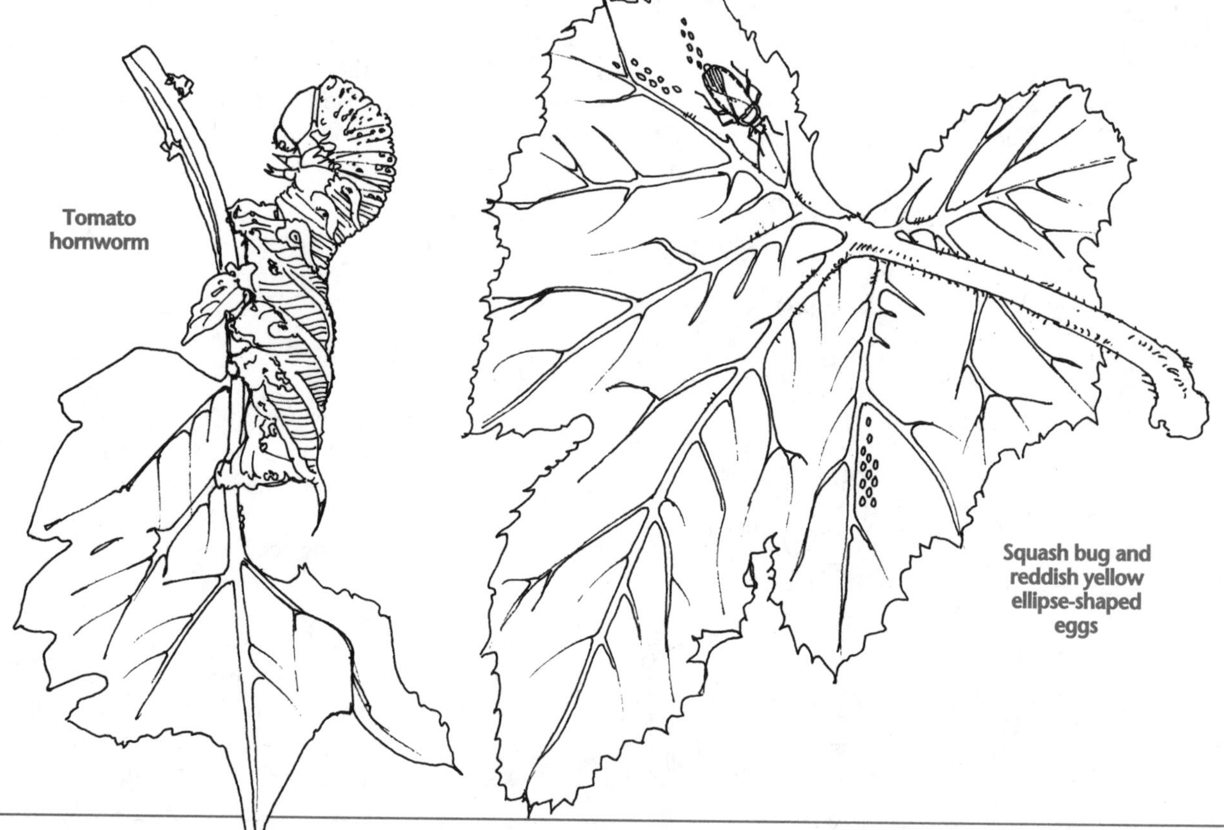

Spray Insect Pests Away

When pests get out of hand, there are easy ways to step up controls. A strong spray of water will control many pests, but if that doesn't do the trick, choose one of the organic sprays listed below.

If you're spraying anything besides water, wear goggles, plastic gloves, a hat, a long-sleeved shirt, and pants to protect yourself from spray drift. Always wait until the weather is calm.

Wash Pests Away with Water

You can stop most insects in their tracks by spraying them frequently (once or twice a week) with a hard jet of water. If you don't kill them, you'll certainly discourage them. Knocking pests off plants disrupts their feeding schedule and lifestyle. As with any spray, it's essential to get thorough coverage. Reach under and through plants to hit the backsides of leaves where pests often hide. Open up curled leaves to rinse pests out of hiding places.

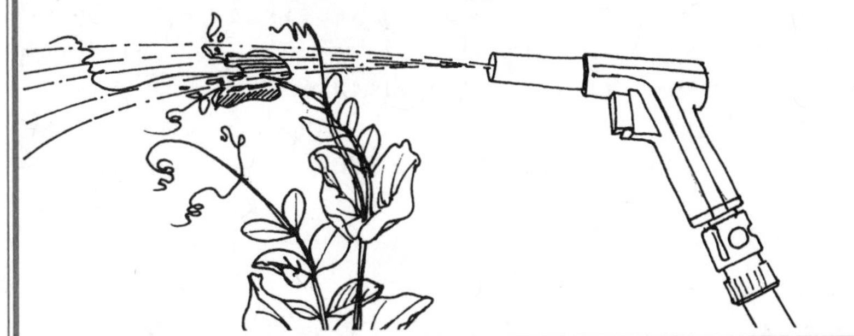

Dehydrate pests with soap. Soft-bodied insects succumb to insecticidal soap spray when they come in contact with it. Make sure you coat foliage until it drips from the tops and bottoms of leaves. Soap sprays work on contact, so rinse them off after ten minutes to avoid burning plant foliage. Repeat applications according to package instructions—the timing is different depending on the pest.

Suffocate bugs with oil. Horticultural oil sprays effectively control pests such as aphids, mealybugs, mites, and scales. Use them in late winter (before trees leaf out) to smother most soft-bodied tree and shrub pests. You can use oil sprays labeled "superior" or summer oils in other seasons. Apply when humidity is low and temperatures won't exceed 85°F, and when plants aren't stressed by drought. You can also try a homemade summer oil. Mix 1 cup cooking oil and 1 tablespoon liquid soap, then add 2½ teaspoons of the mix per cup of water to spray.

Spray with botanical insecticides. Use pyrethrin, rotenone, and sabadilla only as a last resort. They are moderately toxic to people and pets and can be very toxic to beneficials. As a result, *Organic Gardening* magazine no longer recommends them.

Sometimes Sharing Beats Squashing

Parsley worms will devour parsley and dill plants, but show them some mercy. They'll turn into beautiful black swallowtail butterflies if given the chance. Instead of controlling them, why not plant enough parsley for you *and* the parsley worms—and enjoy watching them grow.

Speed through Spraying Chores with the Right Tool

When you decide spraying is the answer to your pest problems, choose the sprayer that makes the job most efficient. Thorough coverage is essential for good results, so make sure your sprayer can reach both upper and lower leaf surfaces. Most nozzles are adjustable, so you can apply a spray that ranges from a fine mist to a hard stream.

▶ **Spray gun.** Hook one up to your water hose and you're ready to blast insects off plants near and far.

▼ **Hand pump sprayer.** Pump the handle on the tank to create pressure, then squeeze the handle on the sprayer to coat plants with spray. Good for small spraying jobs.

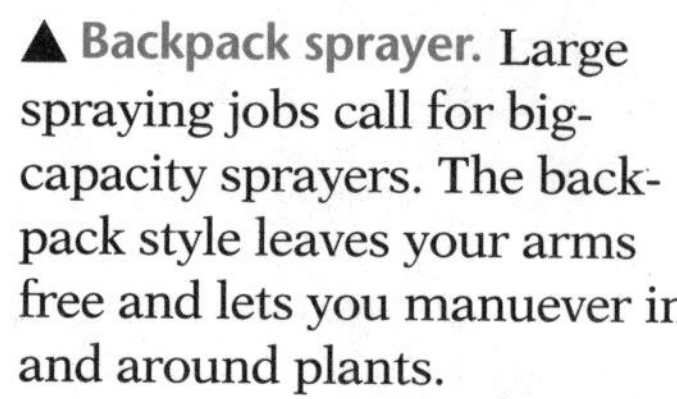

▲ **Backpack sprayer.** Large spraying jobs call for big-capacity sprayers. The back-pack style leaves your arms free and lets you manuever in and around plants.

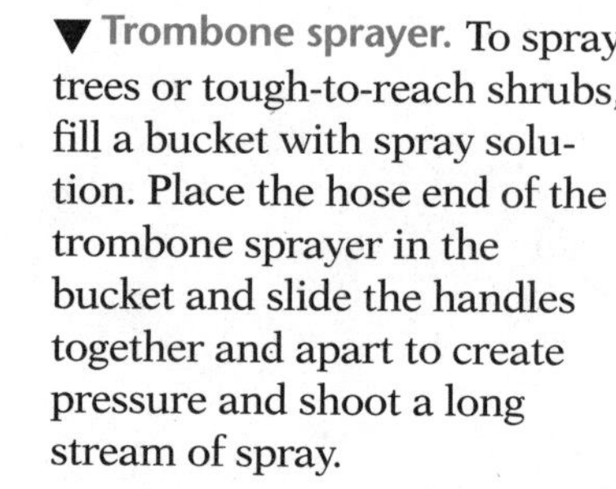

▼ **Trombone sprayer.** To spray trees or tough-to-reach shrubs, fill a bucket with spray solution. Place the hose end of the trombone sprayer in the bucket and slide the handles together and apart to create pressure and shoot a long stream of spray.

Tips for Smart Spraying

Less is best. Only mix as much spray as you can use at one time, or you'll end up storing the excess or wasting it. If you aren't sure how much you'll need, underestimate. It's easier to mix up more spray than to safely store too much.

Keep 'em clean. Rinse spray tools immediately after you use them. They'll last longer, and they're easier to clean before spray residues dry.

To know them isn't to love them, but it is the easiest way to find out how to control slugs. Choose from a variety of materials that irritate these soft-bodied pests by dehydrating or sizzling them.

▼ **Slugs shy away from copper.** Surround plantings with strips of copper; slugs won't cross the barrier even during rainy weather. Handpick any slugs that are inside the barrier when you install it. Wear heavy gloves and watch your feet when working with copper—the edges are sharp!

▲ **Slugs love moist, shady places.** Set a trap for slugs by giving them a hideaway during the heat of the day. Old cabbage or lettuce leaves will give them a place to gather, so you won't have to seek to destroy them. See the illustration on page 105 for another easy slug trap.

Copper barrier

▲ **Slugs don't like dust.** A 2-inch-wide band of diatomaceous earth (DE), lime, or wood ashes makes an irritating barrier when it comes in contact with slimy slug skin. Use a dust mask and plastic gloves when you apply these to keep your lungs dust-free and your hands from drying. Reapply DE and lime after rain.

For Efficient Control, Get to Know Ornamental Plant Pests

Aphid

Find out all you can about the habits of pests, and you can use that information against them. As an example, the pests shown here are easy to identify and control if you know how they act and feed. If you don't already have a garden insect guide, get one. You'll find some listed in "Sources" on page 355.

◀ **Leafminers.** You won't normally see leafminers, but their tunnels are the tip-off that larvae are in your plants' leaves. Pick off leaves with tunnel trails and drop them into soapy water.

Leafminers

▲ **Aphids.** Since these soft-bodied insects tend to cluster around plant tips to suck out juices, pruning shears make a quick control measure. Snip off infested stems and drop them in a bucket of soapy water.

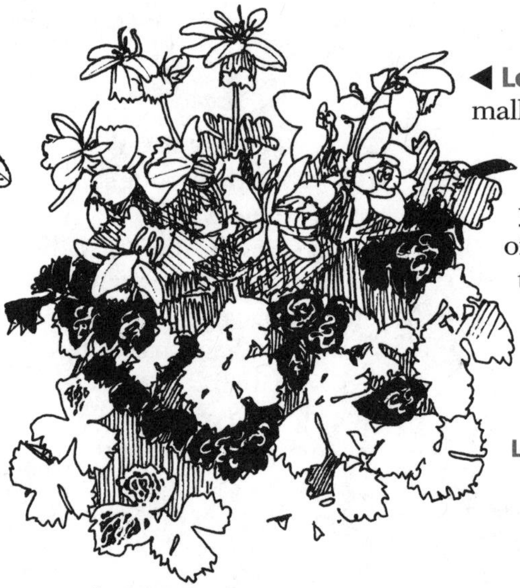

◀ **Lace bugs.** These insects tend to hang out in groups, so you can easily squash them by hand. Look for them on the undersides of leaves with yellow blotches or speckled white or gray patches. They suck plant juice and leave small dark spots of excrement under leaves. Soak lace bugs with insecticidal soap or summer oil spray if there are too many of them to mash.

Lace bug

▶ **Japanese beetles.** If you see skeletonized leaves, you'll also see enough of these metallic-bronze pests around to make a positive I.D. They feed during the day, but drop or fly out of reach when you try to touch them. Grab them in early morning when it's too cool for them to fly. Keep a bucket of soapy water poised beneath beetles and they'll drop right in as you approach.

▼ **Slugs.** Large holes rasped in leaves could be the work of several pests, but slime trails let you know you're dealing with slugs. These slimy creatures can't tolerate hot, dry conditions. Create moist, shady hideaways to lure them away from plants. Turn clay flowerpots upside down and chip small holes out of the edge of the pot so slugs can crawl inside. Check pots when it's hot outside and destroy the slugs you find there. For more ideas for getting a grip on slug problems, see "Simple Ways to Slug It Out with Slugs" on page 103.

▼ **Whiteflies.** Lighty touch your plants to check for these insects. If they're present, they'll rise up in a cloud of white. Whiteflies hang out on the undersides of leaves, so zap them with a spray of insecticidal soap—make sure to coat leaf undersides thoroughly.

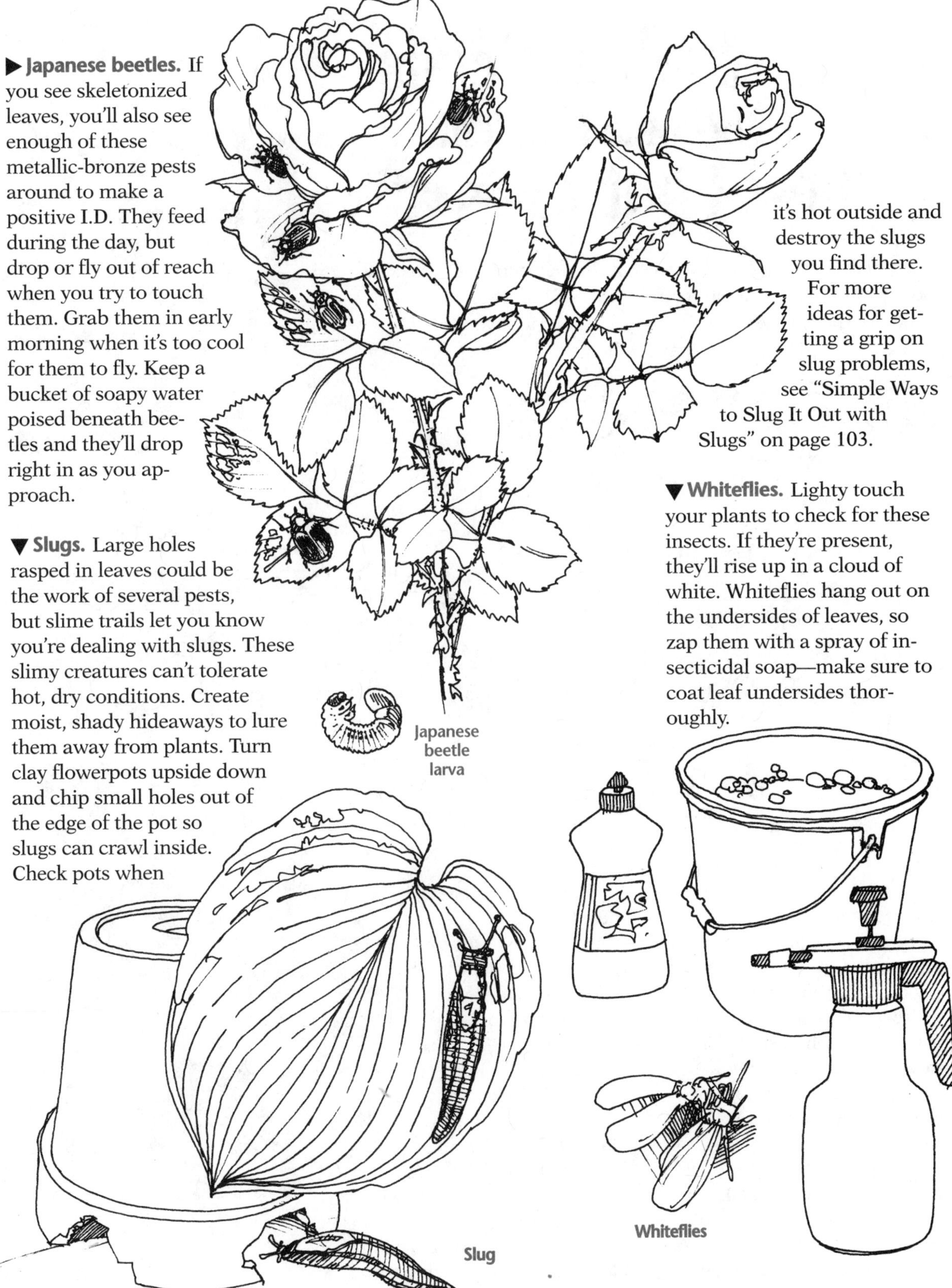

Persuade Beneficials to Become Resident Pest-Control Experts

Toads, ladybugs, lacewings, bees, and other beneficial insects and animals can save you from hand-to-hand combat with pests. Try the tips below to make your yard a haven for these hardworking garden helpers.

Invite birds into your garden. Birds consume an incredible volume of insects as part or all of their diet, depending on species. Don't just put out birdseed: Plant a diversity of plants in your landscape to provide fruits, seeds, and nesting sites for birds. Hang nesting boxes and supply water, too.

Stay away from sprays. Even organically acceptable pesticides, such as oil and soap sprays, can harm beneficial insects like lady beetles. Instead of spraying for pests, provide beneficials with favorite flowers, water, and shelter from high winds. They'll get your pest problem under control and keep it that way.

Don't be squeamish about spiders. They are among the most effective insect predators. Take pains not to disturb webs and certainly don't kill them. Mulch pathways and bare areas after planting to give spiders extra protection.

Attract toads with cool, shady homes. These insect-eaters don't like to go dry, so give them a flowerpot house where they can hide from the heat and stay moist. Chip a doorway in an old clay pot, turn the pot upside down, and place it in your garden; it's as good as a welcome mat.

Foster wild areas. Attract beneficial birds and insects by letting their favorite wild and weedy plants grow. Undisturbed areas provide homes for both insects and birds, so you'll have plenty of natural predators for pest insects.

Plant flowers for food. You can appeal to a wide range of parasitic, predatory, and beneficial insects by planting borders of flowers rich in nectar and pollen. Mix plantings in throughout the garden, too. Small, shallow flowers, like sweet alyssum, provide insects with easy access to food.

Other good choices include members of the parsley family such as angelica, anise, caraway, carrots, cilantro, cumin, dill, and fennel, and, of course, parsley. Also try daisy-family plants like asters, calendulas, cosmos, daisies, feverfew, goldenrod, marigolds, ornamental thistles, sunflowers, yarrow, and zinnias. It's the blooms that lure beneficials, so remember to let herb and vegetable plants flower, too.

Basic Controls for Mammals

Cut branches, smashed or missing fruit, and dug-up areas all indicate that large mammals such as cats, deer, dogs, rabbits, raccoons, possums, or woodchucks have been visiting your garden. Try these controls to make sure *you* get to your crops first.

Fence 'em out. The best way to keep large mammals away is to fence them out before they get used to visiting your garden. Animals will be more determined if they know what they're missing behind a newly installed fence. To keep mammals at bay, build a wire fence 8 feet high for deer, 6 feet high for dogs, or 2 feet high for rabbits—bury the bottom edge 2 to 3 inches below ground to discourage them from digging under.

Cover your crops. Surprisingly, installing row covers or lightweight insect barrier fabric is an easy and effective way to keep animals such as cats, dogs, and woodchucks out of garden beds.

Repel 'em. Try repellants to keep small mammals such as chipmunks, mice, moles, voles, rats, and pocket gophers away from bulbs and plant roots. To make, mix 1 tablespoon castor oil, 2 tablespoons dishwashing soap, and 6 tablespoons water. Stir 2 tablespoons of the mix into a watering can full of water and sprinkle over the ground after a rain.

Keeping Birds at Bay

Birds can chew or poke holes in fruits or vegetables, and they can also steal your crops entirely. Row covers, stiff plastic netting, or insect barrier fabric over plants or beds will keep them away from your crops. Or try stretching strands of monofilament fishing line just above row crops: Space the strands 6 inches apart and raise them as plants grow.

Scarecrows are another effective option, as are inflatable, solid, or silhouetted likenesses of cats, snakes, and owls. Just move them around occasionally so birds don't get used to them.

CHAPTER 12

Disease Prevention and Control

Common Sense Is All You Need

Keep Your Crops on the Move

A Snip in Time Saves Disease Headaches

Control Disease with a Breeze!

Solarize Your Way to Disease-Free Soil

Don't Be Fooled by Diseaselike Symptoms

Disease Prevention and Control the Low-Maintenance Way

THERE'S NOTHING low-maintenance about fighting disease. Surprisingly, keeping diseases out of your garden can be easier than fighting them once they've gained a foothold. The best techniques for keeping diseases at bay are good gardening practices.

Ordinary activities like mulching, taking care of the soil, watering, and careful harvesting help fight disease because they keep your plants healthy and vigorous. And healthy plants are much less susceptible to attack by diseases than unhealthy ones. Filling your yard with a wide variety of plants helps fight disease, too. That's because diversity is a barrier to diseases, many of which infect only certain plants or plant families.

In this chapter, you'll learn about simple steps you can take to prevent disease organisms from infecting plants in your garden and landscape. You'll also find a few hints on how to handle the occasional disease problem that does occur.

Common Sense Is All You Need to Keep Diseases at Bay

Simple, commonsense gardening practices are your best allies when it comes to fighting plant diseases. In the list that follows, you'll find gardening techniques that are already part of your regular routine that also help you fight diseases. You'll also find some ways to fight diseases that you may not yet be using.

Pick plants that will love your site. The absolute easiest thing you can do to avoid disease problems is to grow plants that are suited to your site. Plants that thrive in the soil, light, and other conditions found in and around your landscape will need little care of any kind. And their natural good health will do more to block diseases than any treatment you can give them.

Don't be afraid to move plants that are suffering too many disease problems in a particular site. They may thrive in a new location, and if they don't, you might as well replace them with more durable selections.

Choose disease-resistant plants. Resistance is another way to let your plants take care of themselves. They have built-in defenses against common plant diseases. For example, look for tomatoes identified by the legend VFN, indicating resistance to Verticillium and Fusarium wilts and nematodes. Or select an ornamental crabapple that's known to resist the apple scab that decimates your neighbor's tree each year. Look for details about disease resistance in the plant descriptions of mail-order catalogs; knowledgeable personnel at local nurseries and garden centers will be able to help you select disease-resistant plants.

Keep your plants healthy. Mulching, feeding the soil with organic matter, and other good gardening practices keep your plants healthy, and healthy plants will reward you for your effort by remaining largely trouble-free. If your plant buddies seem a little peaked or show signs of a disease problem, give them a boost with a foliar spray of liquid seaweed (also called liquid kelp). Although seaweed sprays have no known fungicidal or bactericidal activity, they are widely recognized as superb plant-perker-uppers, probably because of the array of micronutrients they supply.

(continued)

Keep insects at bay. In addition to the damage they do by eating your plants, many insects like aphids and leafhoppers also carry diseases from plant to plant, infecting them with every bug-size bite. Cucumber beetles actually do much more damage to vine crops by transmitting bacterial wilt than they do through feeding. Protecting your crops with barriers like floating row covers not only protects them from pests but also helps control the diseases they deliver.

Fight diseases with air flow. Air circulation around your plants helps dry up moisture on leaves and stems, limiting the spread of the many disease organisms that make their way to your plants in a film of water. Position highly susceptible plants such as lilacs, phlox, roses, and zinnias where there's little else to block air movement; thin plantings to increase air flow if disease problems arise.

Don't garden when it's wet. Delicate dew droplets and lingering rainwater seem much less romantic when you realize how many disease organisms each drop can hold. And gardening amid the moisture is a sure way to sprinkle water from one plant to the next, spreading problems as you go. Admire your glistening garden all you want, but try to let it dry before you start to garden. It's also helpful to water your garden in the morning to give plants time to dry off again before nightfall; whenever you can, deliver water to the soil instead of onto your plants.

Keep equipment clean. Soilborne diseases can become toolborne ones if you routinely leave soil clinging to shovels and other tools. Pruners and other tools can also collect disease organisms while you work and then spread them to healthy plants they touch. Keeping your tools clean will help them last longer and also will keep them from transporting diseases about your garden. Brush soil from tool blades before you put them away or after you've been working around a diseased plant. Wipe pruners and other cutting tools clean with isopropyl (rubbing) alcohol as a disinfecting solution after you work around a diseased plant.

Don't create openings for diseases. Many plants do a fine job of keeping diseases from infecting them by blocking the pathogens' entrance with waxy cuticles, hairy or sticky foliage, thick bark, or other impediments. But injuries from lawn mowers, string trimmers, carelessly swung shovels, or wayward boots all make openings in a plant's armor, which puts the welcome mat out for diseases to enter. Avoid tugging or tearing at your crops when you harvest, and work carefully around the bases of trees and shrubs—a ring of mulch or groundcovers around them will keep mowers and trimmers at bay. Treat all your plants with gentle care and you'll avoid making a way for diseases to get past their natural defenses.

Remove diseased plants. In spite of your best preventive efforts, sometimes some of your plants will get sick. The most effective way to deal with this is to remove diseased plants from your garden before their problems spread. If the infected area is limited relative to the size of the plant, simply trimming away affected leaves or pruning out a diseased branch may be sufficient for control.

Keep your garden clean, too. Remove dead or dying plant material and clean up fallen leaves at the end of the growing season to eliminate places where diseases can overwinter.

Keep Your Crops on the Move to Control Soilborne Diseases

Rearranging your vegetable garden from year to year may be all you need to avoid problems with soilborne diseases. Many diseases are host-specific: They attack only a certain plant or plant family.

Avoid growing plants in the same family in the same location. To get the greatest benefit, rotate crops so you don't return them to the same spot for four years. If you have space constraints, plan a two- or three-year rotation instead.

Here's a list of crops, grouped by family, to help you rotate your garden favorites.

- Broccoli, brussels sprouts, cabbage, cauliflower, kale, radishes, turnips
- Cucumbers, melons, squash, pumpkins
- Corn, oats, rye, wheat
- Beans, peas, clovers, vetches
- Onions, garlic
- Tomatoes, peppers, potatoes, eggplant
- Carrots, parsley, dill, fennel, cilantro

A Snip in Time Saves Disease Headaches

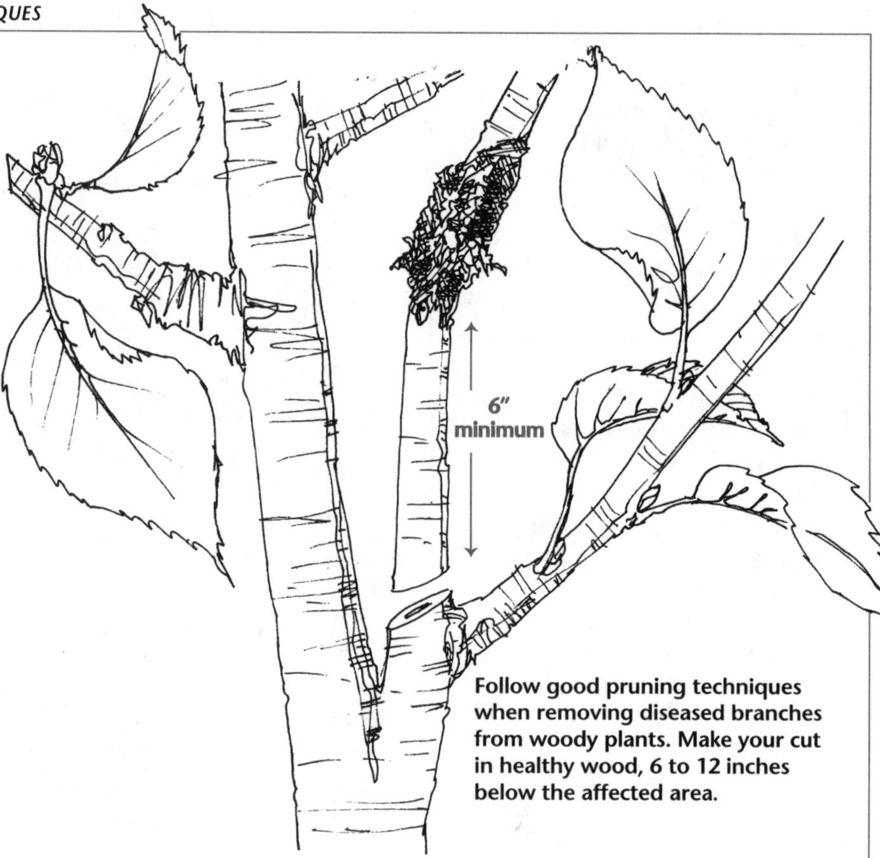

Follow good pruning techniques when removing diseased branches from woody plants. Make your cut in healthy wood, 6 to 12 inches below the affected area.

If a disease problem does rear its head in your garden, it's important to act quickly to prevent its spread. In the vegetable garden or flower bed, snipping off infected leaves or flowers is often all you need to do to control diseases entirely. In severe cases, you may need to remove entire plants.

Pruning is also an effective control for many diseases that affect fruit trees, berry bushes, brambles, and ornamental trees, shrubs, and vines. The techniques you use are basically the same as for any other pruning you do, but when you prune away a diseased plant part, be sure you remove enough of an infected branch or stem to stop the advance of disease. While some disease organisms stay localized near the canker or other diseased area, others can advance past the canker without producing symptoms.

Make your pruning cut in healthy tissue, 6 to 12 inches below the diseased area, to ensure that you remove all the diseased wood. Don't abandon good pruning techniques when removing diseased branches; see Chapter 9.

When pruning to remove diseased tissue, disinfect your pruning tools after each cut. Carry along a container of isopropyl (rubbing) alcohol. After each cut, dip the tool in the alcohol for 15 seconds. When you finish your pruning work, sterilize each tool a final time, then wipe it dry.

Hire Help to Treat Trunk Troubles

If a diseased area appears in a large limb or the trunk of a tree, it's best not to try and correct the problem yourself. Removing the area may jeopardize the tree's stability, making it more susceptible to wind damage, and the resulting wound creates an opening for insect pests and other disease organisms. Call a professional arborist to evaluate the problem and to tell you whether your tree is worth saving.

Dealing with Disease

If, in spite of your conscientious adherence to preventive gardening techniques, your favorite plant in the whole world falls prey to some scurrilous microorganism, you need not give it up for lost. Continue to give the plant care to help maintain its health; protect it from other stress. Using a good plant disease ID guide or through consultation with your local extension agent, identify the problem as specifically as possible. Then select and apply the appropriate organic controls. It may be necessary to apply sprays on a regular basis, until either disease symptoms disappear or the weather conditions that promote infection are past.

Control Disease with a Breeze!

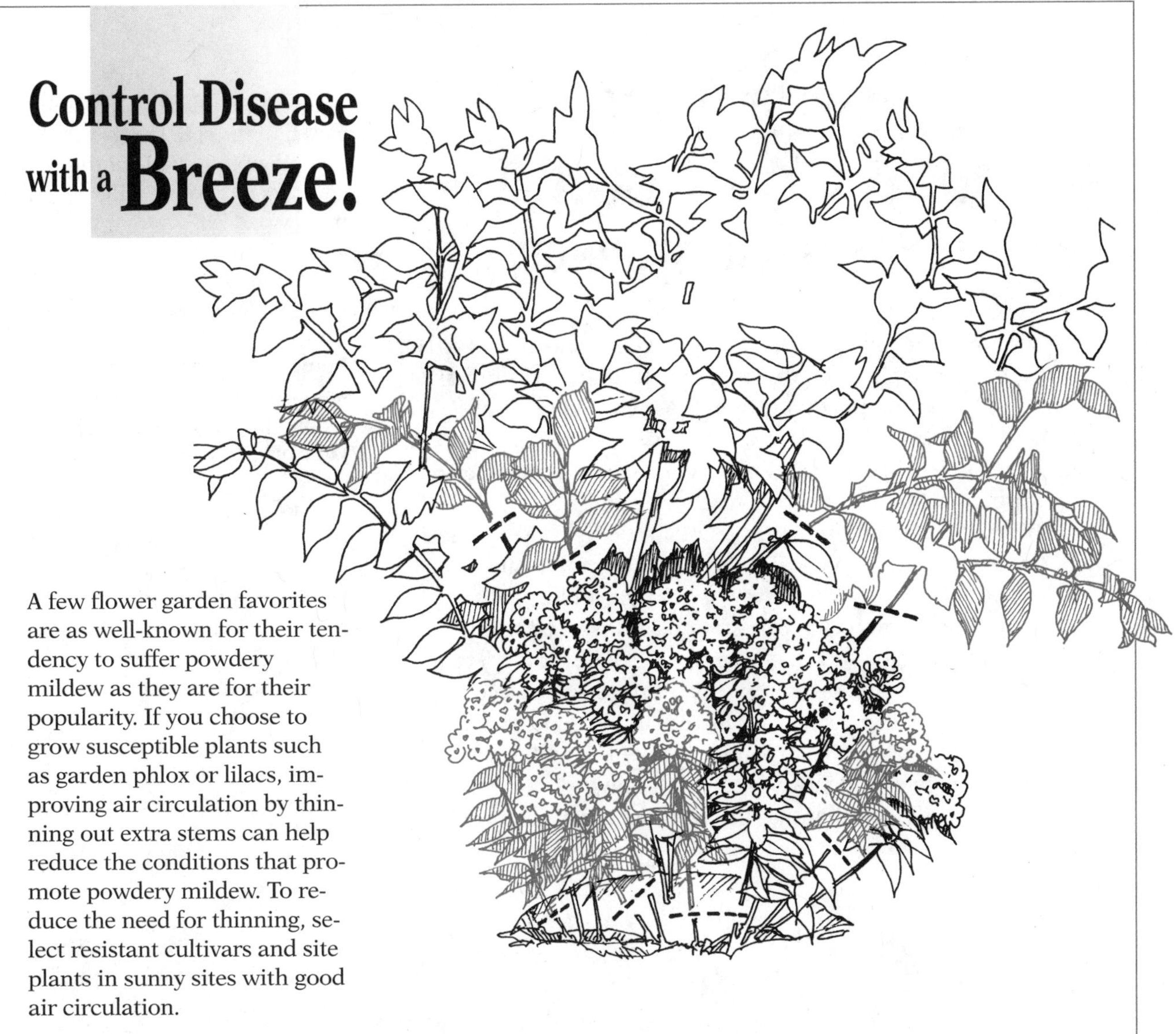

A few flower garden favorites are as well-known for their tendency to suffer powdery mildew as they are for their popularity. If you choose to grow susceptible plants such as garden phlox or lilacs, improving air circulation by thinning out extra stems can help reduce the conditions that promote powdery mildew. To reduce the need for thinning, select resistant cultivars and site plants in sunny sites with good air circulation.

Solarize Your Way to Disease-Free Soil

If soilborne problems like wilts and nematodes plague your plantings, try soil solarization. This easy technique uses the heat of the sun to "cook" the disease organisms in your soil. To solarize a bed, water thoroughly, cover the bed with clear plastic, tuck the edges of the plastic into a trench around the outside of the bed, and cover them with soil. Remove the plastic after 4 to 6 weeks. Mulch if you don't plan to plant right away.

Solarization takes several months to be effective. If you live in the North, prepare your bed a season before you plant. For more on soil solarization, see "Sizzle Weeds Away with Sunlight" on page 92.

Disease or Disorder? Don't Be Fooled by Diseaselike Symptoms

Diseases aren't the only things that can cause plants to look sickly. A plant that's struggling to grow in an unsuitable environment often displays symptoms that mimic those caused by diseases or insects, including early leaf drop, brown or undersize leaves, and general poor growth. Environmentally stressed plants are also more susceptible to attacks from disease organisms and pests.

So before you spend time on a losing battle fighting a nonexistent disease, take time to consider what exactly *is* causing the problem. Look for obvious disease indicators: mold, rot, branch cankers, or other physical manifestations of disease organisms. Without specific signs such as these, your plant's problem may be caused by its environment as much as by any microscopic enemy.

Use the questions and suggestions that follow to help decide if the environment may be your plants' problem. Do what you can to remedy problems you identify—redirect a downspout, for example. If you find your plant is suffering site conditions you can't correct, move it to a better location.

Is the site right? Is the plant suited to the soil, exposure, and other conditions of the site? A plant growing in too much shade will look spindly and unhealthy; one growing in too much sun may have bleached, yellowed leaves. Around the foundation of your home, acid-loving plants may languish in soil that's more alkaline than any place else on your property.

What's the weather been like? Check to see if the soil is either too wet or too dry. Plants growing under the eaves of your home or with dense trees overhead may not have received enough water from recent rains. Or foundation plants may literally be drowning beneath a leaky gutter or badly placed downspout.

Improper pruning. The lower branches on plants that are broader at the top than the bottom may die out; keep plants narrower at the top than on the bottom.

Sites under eaves and downspouts. Check soil moisture; too-wet or too-dry soil can cause yellowed leaves and wilting.

Foundation plantings. Sites along foundations often have alkaline soil; check soil pH and avoid acid-loving plants.

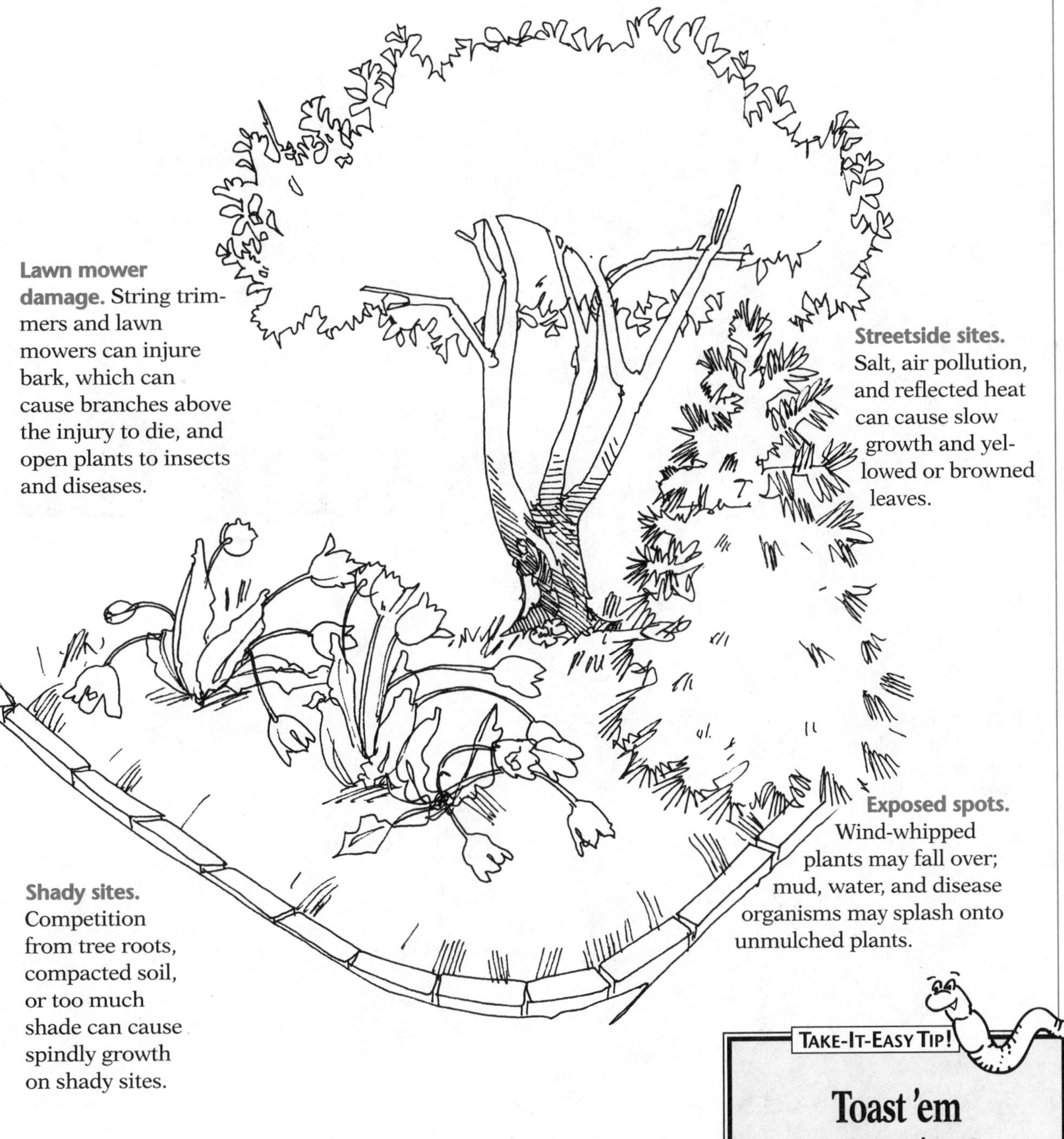

Is traffic a problem? Plants located near roadways can be damaged by cars or suffer the effects of road salt, but other types of traffic can cause problems, as well. Is someone cutting through a bed and compacting the soil around a treasured planting? Are children playing too close to a tree or shrub and damaging it in the process? Both problems can cause plants to grow slowly or look sickly. Look for ways to redirect traffic or move your plants.

TAKE-IT-EASY TIP!

Toast 'em or Toss 'em?

Unless your compost pile is newly made and on its way to a hot 160°F, leave diseased trimmings out of the heap. Instead, dispose of them by burning them, bagging them for waste collection, or burying them in an out-of-the-way corner of your property.

PART 2

Saving Time

with Fruits and Vegetables

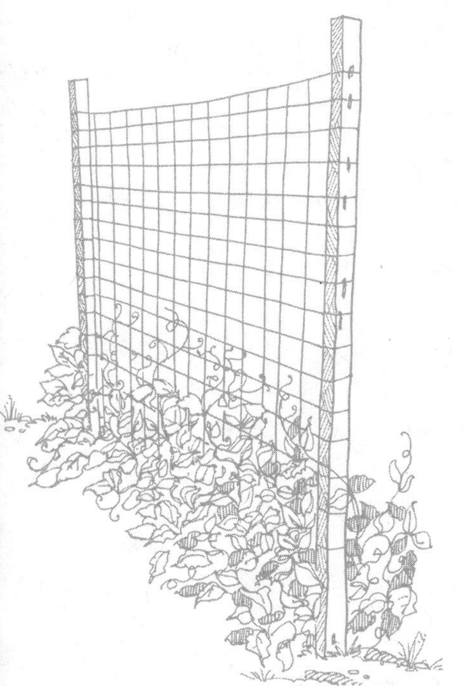

CHAPTER 13

Vegetables

Set Your "Sites" for Success

Plant Just the Right Amount

Design Convenience into Your Garden

Save Work by Making Smart Plant Choices

Tuck In Your Crops

Make a Planting Plan That Saves Time

Should You Grow Row by Row?

Soil Preparation without Tears

Tips for Gardening on Tough Sites

Work Your Soil with Roots

Keep Healthy Soil and Happy Vegetables

Keep Green Manures on Hand

Soil Improvement with Green Manures

Undersow to Grow Your Own Fertilizer

It Pays to Watch the Weather

Mix Seeds and Transplants for Speed

Sow Seeds Evenly to Save Time Thinning

Don't Make Room for Weeds

Tactics for Timely Transplanting

Make the Most of Mulch

Low-Maintenance Tips for Your Crops

Don't Dig Potatoes, Grow Them in Mulch!

It Pays to Inoculate

Which Tomato Type is Best for You?

Vegetables the Low-Maintenance Way

IF YOU DO JUST a little planning before you plant and take the right steps to improve your soil, you'll find that vegetable gardening can take a lot less time and labor than you ever dreamed. This chapter shows you how to design food gardens for easiest care and maximum harvests.

Set Your "Sites" for Success

Before you prepare a new vegetable garden, use your head. Vegetable gardens are easiest to maintain when they have no strikes against them, like deep shade or rocky soil. Here's a checklist of what you need for success. If your site doesn't match up, choose one of the options listed for making it right.

☑ **At least six hours of full sunlight.** What if you don't have enough sun? Consider growing vegetables in containers on the driveway or deck where the increased warmth will boost growth. Otherwise, share a sunny site in a friend's yard. Vegetables simply won't be successful in the shade.

☑ **Good drainage.** If your only sunny site is soggy, building raised beds will pay off big in the long run. They require some work to loosen the soil and heap it up, but once done, you'll have perfect drainage forevermore. Another choice is to build a framed raised bed using lumber or concrete blocks and fill it with good soil. For low-work ways to make garden beds, see "Soil Preparation without Tears" on page 125.

☑ **Convenient access to the hose, house, and compost pile.** Think how many steps you'll save if your vegetable garden is close to your house, and your water source and compost supply are near your vegetables. It's nice to have a dry place to store tools near the garden, as well. If there is no outdoor building handy to the garden, a plastic trash can with a lid makes a quick storage bin for the essentials.

☑ **Limited competition from large trees.** Trees compete with your vegetables for essential water and nutrients, so locate your garden as far as possible from hungry, thirsty tree roots. If you have only a few sunny spots and tree roots are nearby, try planting in containers or framed raised beds to keep your vegetables above the competition.

☑ **Protection from marauding pets and children.** You can use fences, hedges, and even plantings of large perennials like ornamental grasses to channel children and pets away from vegetables. Or keep plants out of harm's way with raised beds.

Plant Just the Right Amount

Growing too much of any vegetable is a waste unless you have hungry neighbors with a real fondness for zucchini. Save labor (and your neighbors) by pacing your plantings to match your appetite. Look over the typical harvests you can expect per plant from these common crops, then plant only as many plants as you need. It's easy to see that you won't need a row of plants like cucumbers unless you plan on lots of pickling.

Design Convenience into Your Garden

You can plant your garden without planning, but you'll pay for it with added effort when it's time to improve the soil, pick produce, water, or fight weeds. You don't need an elaborate plan to save labor. This garden features a variety of ideas that will make your vegetable gardening easier and more enjoyable.

▼ **Have some fun.** This scarecrow, created from an old Batman costume, is an imaginative way to bring a smile to your face and keep pesky birds at bay.

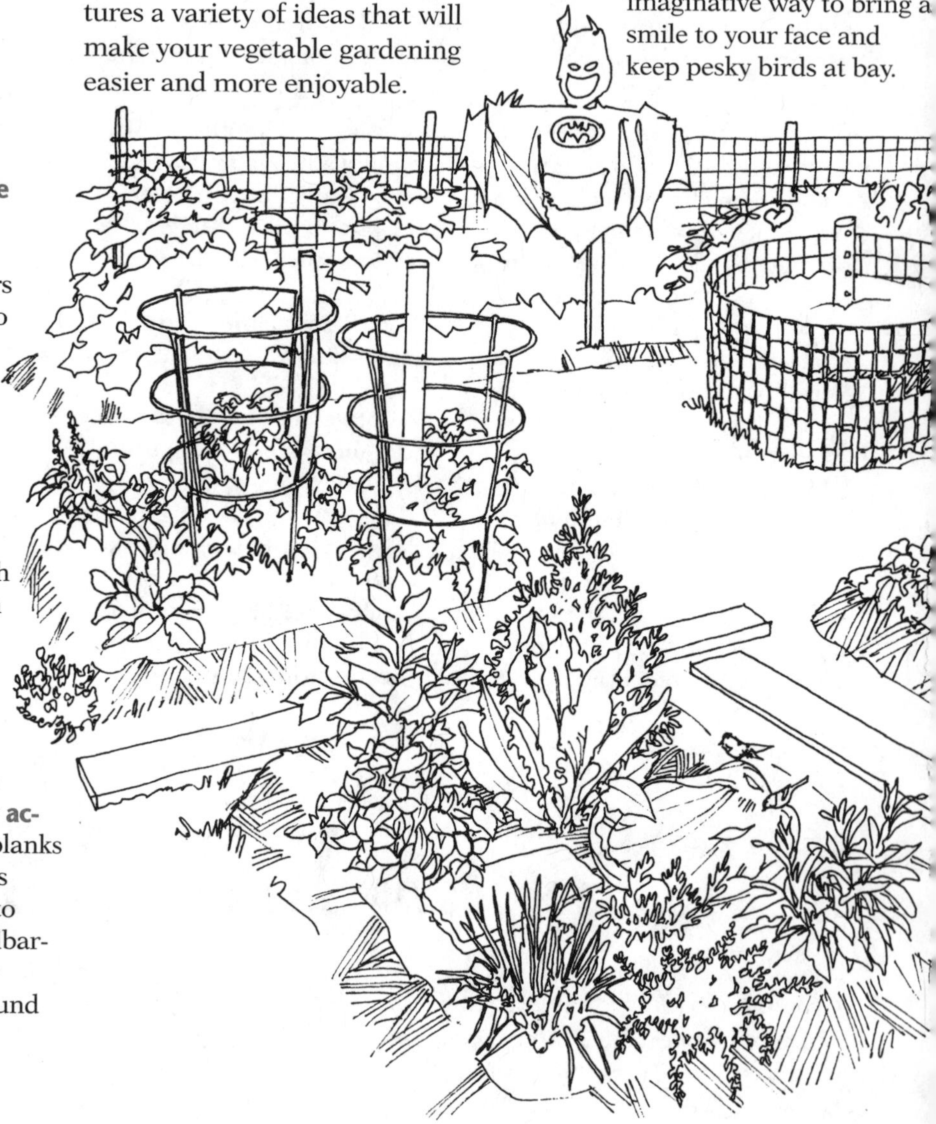

▶ **Train vines to save space.** One way to keep vines like squash or cucumbers from wandering is to train them up a fence. Fruits hang straight down for easy picking.

▶ **Stake tomato cages.** Insert a stake inside each tomato cage to hold it in place and keep it from toppling over under heavy fruit load.

▶ **Use wooden planks for easy access.** Wooden planks in the pathways make it easier to manuver wheelbarrows and other equipment around raised beds.

▲ **Make compost in your garden.** If you make compost right in your beds, you won't have to haul it across the yard when you need to feed your soil or plants.

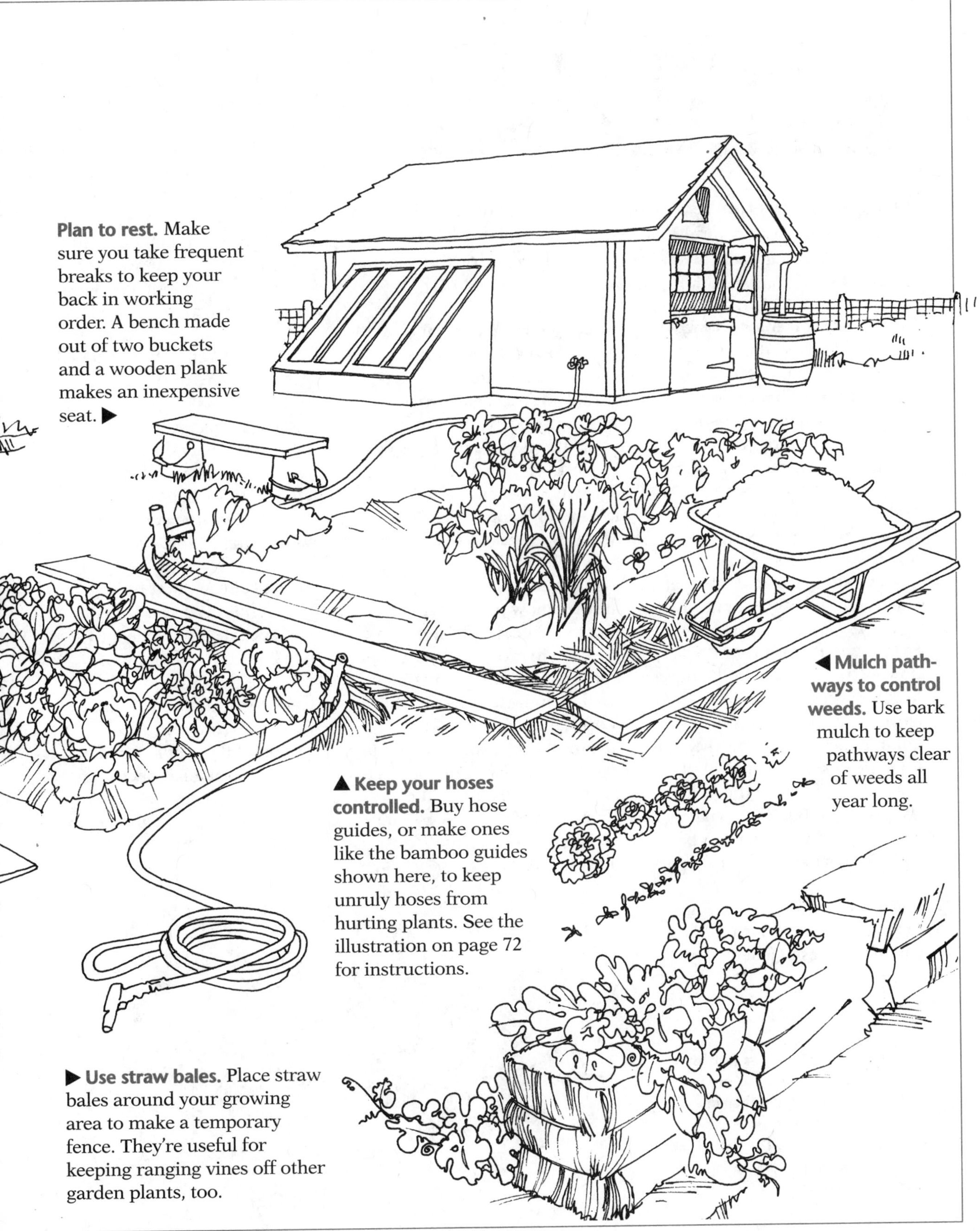

Plan to rest. Make sure you take frequent breaks to keep your back in working order. A bench made out of two buckets and a wooden plank makes an inexpensive seat. ▶

◀ **Mulch pathways to control weeds.** Use bark mulch to keep pathways clear of weeds all year long.

▲ **Keep your hoses controlled.** Buy hose guides, or make ones like the bamboo guides shown here, to keep unruly hoses from hurting plants. See the illustration on page 72 for instructions.

▶ **Use straw bales.** Place straw bales around your growing area to make a temporary fence. They're useful for keeping ranging vines off other garden plants, too.

Save Work by Making Smart Plant Choices

It takes most of us firm resolve (or an avalanche of zucchini) to limit the number and variety of vegetables we plant. But remember, planting decisions frame your workload for the season ahead. Bite the bullet and take these suggestions to heart.

Grow what you enjoy eating. If no one likes broccoli, why bother with it? In other words, grow the crops that are satisfying for you and your family. You may decide to grow arugula or snap peas that you couldn't otherwise afford, for example. Maybe all you really want is fresh sweet corn or tomatoes. If that's the case, don't waste space on crops that end up in the compost pile.

Forget about crops that don't do well in your garden. If you live in the cool Pacific Northwest, heat-loving cantaloupes are a struggle, whereas salad greens and beets will flourish. Likewise, if the frost flattens your 'Big Boy' tomatoes every year in Vermont, maybe it's time to switch to small tomatoes that ripen faster. You'll get big flavor with a cultivar like 'Oregon Spring', which matures in just 60 days.

Select gourmet vegetables that aren't locally available. Why grow the same tomatoes, lettuce, and snap beans you can buy at the nearest produce stand when you can grow more flavorful choices like 'Royal Burgundy' beans, 'Lolla Rosso' lettuce, or 'Tappy's Best' tomato? Many of the tastiest types aren't grown for market because they lose quality rapidly (like baby lettuce, snow peas, or squash blossoms) or simply aren't cost-effective to grow because people don't know about them. (Ever tried mizuna, fava beans, mâche (corn salad), or 'Gilfeather' turnips?) Order some seed catalogs that specialize in gourmet vegetables and choose the plants that pique your palette. See "Sources" on page 355 for suggestions.

Select cultivars adapted to your growing region. There are vegetable cultivars ideal for every growing region. Instead of buying seed from big seed houses that aim for the average growing climate, patronize regional seed companies. Many focus on continuing old cultivars proven in your area and they also search out and develop new strains.

Grow only as much as you will eat. Do you really need ten tomato plants? Using tomatoes as an example, two plants per person is plenty if fresh salads are the main use. All you need are five to six plants if you want to preserve enough for year-round eating.

Select cultivars that bear throughout the season. You can avoid having to deal with one big harvest—and more produce than your family can eat—if you choose vegetables that bear fruit over a long season. If the crops you like tend to ripen all at once, plant a mixture of early, mid-season, and late-maturing cultivars to spread out the harvest.

Sprouting broccoli cultivars such as 'Romanesco' and 'Calabrese' produce many small heads, rather than one large one. The leaves make excellent cooked greens as well. They will often overwinter to supply early spring greens and sprouts.

For example, try planting a mid-season corn cultivar like 'Honey 'N Pearl' (78 days) at the same time as a later-maturing cultivar like 'Silver Queen' (92 days) to avoid a corn glut. The same technique works great for tomatoes too. And since the growth habit of tomatoes also affects your harvest, see "Which Tomato Type Is Best for You?" on page 137 for details on selecting the right plants. Or you can plant reseeding greens like arugula.

Grow what you will be home to enjoy. If you vacation the last two weeks of August, plan your crops around your trip. Plant your corn crop so it will peak before or after your trip, for example. Likewise, if you're going to be away or super-busy when peas need to be picked, skip the peas this season.

Be realistic about putting up the harvest. These days, many time-pressed gardeners are opting to "eat what's in season" instead of spending the time it takes to manage and can or freeze large harvests. You can save time and effort if you grow only as much fresh produce as your family can eat—and not enough to fill the freezer. Consider using the extra garden space for spinach, broccoli, collards, and other hardy crops that you can eat fresh well into winter. Fresh vegetables are always tastier and more nutritious than frozen or canned.

Tuck In Your Crops

Before you dig a new garden, look for ready-made planting areas. You just might find a few places where you can tuck in some lettuce or a packet of snap beans with no more effort than clearing a few weeds and adding some compost.

You also may find spring vacancies in flower beds. Finding a place for a few "spot" gardens may allow you to grow all the salad greens, radishes, and snap beans your family can use without turning up new ground.

MULTIPLE PLANTINGS MEAN MANAGEABLE HARVESTS

By planting crops over several weeks (a technique known as succession planting) rather than all at once, you'll get a steady supply of produce instead of a one-time onslaught. How much you pick at any one time depends, of course, on how much you plant each time. The idea is to get as much as you need for a week or two, plus a little extra if you plan to store any vegetables long-term. That way, you'll never be overwhelmed. Succession planting works best with crops that ripen all at once like lettuce and other salad greens, bush beans, and corn.

To plan on a continuous but not overwhelming harvest, spread out planting times throughout the season. For example, three beds of lettuce, each planted two weeks apart, will be ready for harvest about two weeks apart as well.

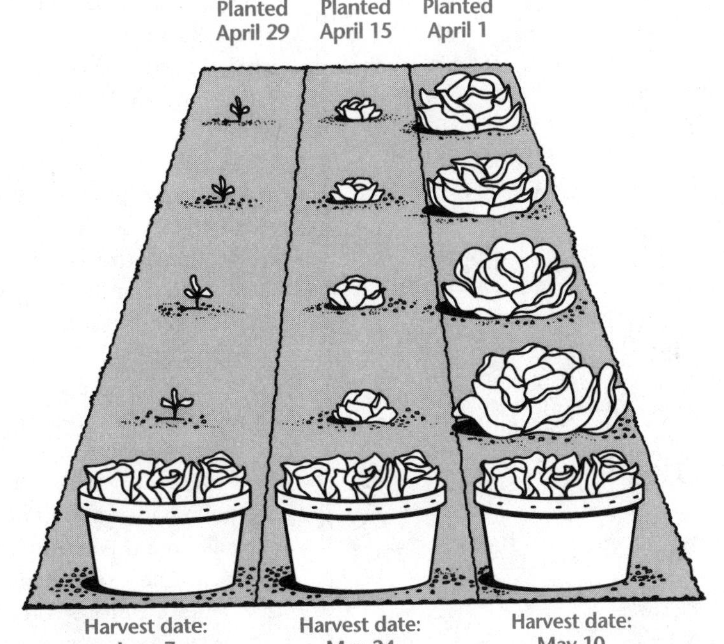

Make a Planting Plan That Saves Time

Before you turn a shovelful of soil in a new garden bed, take time to consider what features will make that bed easy to manage. You'll be living with your design for at least one season, so you'll certainly save enough time, energy, and aggravation to make the planning well worthwhile. Besides, you can do your planning in early spring or late fall when there aren't as many garden priorities.

Consider garden size. Keeping your garden small is the simplest way to keep it low maintenance. If you're a new gardener and don't know how much is too much, begin with an area no larger than 100 square feet. If you've been gardening a while, take a hard look at how much time you want to spend in your garden and which crops will give you the most return.

Picture your space before you dig. Rectangles and squares are the easiest bed shapes for most of us to work with. Preview your garden layout by using a garden hose to represent the perimeter of the garden. Then lay out some newspaper weighted with rocks to mark where the actual beds will be dug. What's left will be the pathways. Then stand back and look at the design and see if it looks workable. Imagine what you're going to plant where. Get out the wheelbarrow and any other garden equipment you use and see if you can reach each bed easily. Consider any hidden hazards, like the septic tank, electrical lines, or the kids' soccer field. Before you put the newspaper away, use stakes to mark the beds. It doesn't hurt to commit your plan to paper, too, before you lose any bright ideas about what you're going to plant where.

Take a look at garden length. Once you've prepared the soil in your beds, you'll have to walk around them to get from one side of the garden to the other. (Walking on the soil will compact it, destroying all your hard-earned soil improvement.) Beds 5 to 15 feet long work well in small gardens. You can increase the length up to 30 feet in larger gardens. If you're planning framed raised beds, plank "bridges" from one edge to the other make it easy to cross from side to side in a long garden.

Keep plants within reach. You should be able to reach the middle of planting areas without trampling the beds—4 feet is a comfortable stretch for most gardeners. If you've never planted in beds before, make some sample patches before you plant; experiment with 3 feet, 3½ feet, and 4 feet and see what feels best to you.

Leave room for you! Pathways between beds need to be at least 1½ feet wide to allow for foot traffic. They should be at least 3 feet wide if you intend to take a wheelbarrow into the garden with you. In a large garden, plan for a central crossroads at least 4 feet wide to accommodate the garden cart and to allow some leeway for hauling mulch, compost, and other supplies.

Grow a Dinner Bucket

Five-gallon buckets by the kitchen door make great planters for quick picks. Since the plants are outside your main vegetable garden and close by for easy inspection, you'll rarely have insect problems. Drill plenty of holes in the bucket to ensure good drainage. Try growing hot peppers, green onions, cherry tomatoes, greens, or zucchini.

Should You Grow Row by Row?

Once you've selected the best site for your vegetable garden and the crops you want to grow, you'll need to decide whether to plant in rows or beds.

Gardening in Rows

Gardens planted in narrow, parallel rows or strips with paths in between are easy to plan. The soil is usually turned over each spring to clear space for new crops; it's a simple matter if you have a tiller. Row gardens are well suited to large crops like corn, pole beans, tomatoes, and potatoes.

On the down side, row gardens require lots of space, and you have to spend time maintaining lots of walkways where you don't grow food. Row gardens generally have less drought resistance, and the large expanses of unplanted soil are an open invitation to weeds. Frequent cultivation also depletes soil organic matter, which increases the need for compost and fertilizer. Mechanical tillers also cause petroleum pollution.

Gardening in Beds

Crops grown in beds are set out in wide areas or blocks not separated by rows. Paths between beds allow easy access to vegetables but minimize wasted space. That means you can grow more vegetables in a smaller area than with row gardens. Beds can be tilled each season—but once you're satisfied with the location and layout, it's easier and more economical to maintain them without tilling. Because plants are spaced close together and you're not maintaining wide walkways, bed gardens need less weeding and less watering. Beds are most suitable for smaller vegetables like greens, root crops, and cole crops.

On the down side, it takes more work to prepare beds the first season. They also may be harder to design at first if you're used to planting in rows, and they aren't well suited to mechanical cultivation.

Pick Your Style

In large gardens, a combination approach works well. Plant the big crops in rows and the smaller stuff, like salad greens, cole crops, and root crops, in beds. For small gardens, beds are the obvious choice since they maximize space. Not only will you harvest more food than if you planted in rows, but grouping vegetables in blocks conserves water and reduces weeding since the leaves shade the soil between plants.

Soil Preparation without Tears

Believe it or not, sweating and straining are optional activities when it comes to making new garden beds. Try the techniques that follow for easy ways to make gardens that produce trouble-free harvests year after year.

You'll find a range of options—from beds you never dig to ones that take some effort initially but are quite easy to maintain ever after. Choose the method that fits your site and lifestyle best.

No-Dig Garden Beds

Yes, you can grow great vegetables without ever turning over the soil! Here's how.

1. Mow the area with the mower blade set as low as it will go.

2. Spread a six-page-thick layer of newspaper over the spot and water it well.

3. Cover the newspaper with at least 2 inches of compost or good soil mix. Add some balanced organic fertilizer at the rate listed on the package.

(continued)

4. Rake the bed smooth and sprinkle it with water until it is evenly moist. Wait a day or two and then plant, cutting through the newspaper if setting out transplants.

Believe it or not, this method works fine the first season for everything but long-rooted crops like carrots. Plus, there's no need to dig these beds every year. Just add 2 inches of compost on top and plant.

After three years you should be able to grow anything, and you can cut back the compost you add each spring to a maintenance amount of 1/8 to 1/4 inch. If you'd rather, add the compost as a side-dressing around plants in the summer.

Just-a-Bit-of-Digging Garden Beds

This method requires a large supply of compost-making materials and a half-hour of shoveling per bed. The advantage is that you'll have terrific soil by the end of one season.

1. **Pile up organic matter.** Start by piling up organic matter as if you were making a compost pile. You're aiming for a pile about 4 feet wide and 2 feet high and as long as you want to make it. The combination of ingredients isn't critical, but an even mix of leafy green stuff and tougher materials like leaves and stalks is ideal. Shredded leaves are a real bonus.

   Sprinkle in a little soil on the pile to start the decomposition process, and moisten the ingredients with water. They should be as wet as a wrung-out sponge.

2. **Dig a path.** Once your pile is in place, dig a path about 2 inches deep and 2 feet wide all around it, pitching the soil over the pile. You want to end up with 2 to 4 inches of soil covering the pile.

3. **Add fertilizer.** Sprinkle on a thin layer (1/8 to 1/4 inch is plenty) of finished compost. Or apply a balanced commercial organic fertilizer at the rate listed on the package.

4. **Rake it smooth.** Rake the bed smooth and then sprinkle it with water until it is evenly moist.

5. **Wait.** Sit tight for a week to allow the pile to settle a bit.

6. **Plant.** That's all there is to it!

This method has two special benefits. First, it provides bottom heat early in the season from all the decomposing organic matter, a real boost in cool climates. Second, all that organic matter decomposes into an excellent foundation for your garden bed.

Finding enough organic matter to make a 4 × 2-foot base isn't as overwhelming as it sounds. Just drive around the neighborhood during leaf-raking and lawn-cutting seasons and you can rescue tons of bagged leaves and grass clippings destined for the landfill. You may want to stock up on bed-making materials in the spring and fall, too, when supplies are abundant.

Lots-of-Digging Garden Beds—But Just This Once

You've probably heard about the benefits of double digging, a method used to create great soil that has excellent drainage, warms early in the season, and provides perfect conditions for intensive planting. But double digging is a lot of work, isn't it?

Well, yes, but once the soil has been prepared this way, you hardly have to lift a finger again. You'll rarely need to water since double-dug beds are rich in moisture-holding organic matter. Your soil will be fertile without fertilizing, so you'll get bumper crops of vegetables—even if you plant close to make the most of your hard-earned space. Of course, close spacing means fewer weeds, so that's another task you can avoid. Plus, you'll have soil that's ready to plant whenever you're ready—even in soggy seasons.

For vegetable gardeners pressed for space or those with serious drainage problems, double-dug raised beds are ideal. For instructions on double digging a new garden bed, see "For Speedy Soil Improvement, You'll Have to Dig In" on page 18.

Tips for Gardening on Tough Sites

When difficult conditions make gardening seem like a lost cause, look for ways to grow around, above, or below the problem. Here are some ideas to get you started.

Grow veggies in the lawn. Is your garden site presently a lawn? If so, consider leaving the grass in place in the pathways and just digging up the growing space you'll need. This minimizes weeds and erosion, and the grass pathways are easy to keep up by mowing. Be sure to make the pathways at least as wide as your lawn mower.

Create instant raised beds. Is poor soil giving you a headache and backache? Cover the growing area with straw bales laid flat and placed end to end. Spread a 2-inch layer of compost on top and then plant. The bales will decompose within a year, creating a wonderful growing base. Good crops to try in "bale beds" include bush beans, peas, greens, okra, and eggplants. Large vining vegetables like squash, melons, and tomatoes also perform well, especially if you make a hole in the bales, pour in a bucket of composted manure and then set in transplants.

Create soil on barren sites. Are you a gardener without any soil? If you live on bedrock, or if the bulldozer that leveled your lot stole your soil, here's a solution. Make an enclosure out of lumber, stone, cinder blocks, or even straw bales. (Or buy a kid's sandbox!) The sides should be at least 8 inches high—1 foot is ideal. Put an inch of gravel or sand in the bottom to ensure good drainage. Then fill the enclosure with a mixture of good soil and compost and plant. If you want to economize on soil, fill the bottom half of the enclosure with a mix of organic matter—shredded leaves, sawdust, rotted manure, and weeds.

Save water with sunken beds. Are you gardening in the desert? Take a hint from ancient Indian tribes and plant your crops in sunken beds that capture and conserve water. To make a sunken bed, dig out a bed 1½ feet deep. Reserve the best soil in a wheelbarrow or on a tarp, and place the rest in the paths. Mix the good soil with some compost, fill the trench with 6 inches of this mix, and you're ready to plant.

Work Your Soil with Roots

Let the roots of robust seedlings cultivate the soil for you before you plant. Here's how.

1. Sow quick-growing seeds like mustard and radish by broadcasting them thickly in early spring. Several weeks later, chop the young plants out with a sharp hoe.

2. Ventilate the soil by rocking the tines of a garden fork back and forth in the soil. Or use a broadfork, which is especially designed for aerating the soil.

Easy Steps for Keeping Your Soil Healthy—and Your Vegetables Happy

Vegetables need fertile soil with lots of organic matter to grow their best and stay problem free. You can keep your soil in tip-top form by mulching and adding compost to the soil every year, but collecting, hauling, and spreading soil amendments takes work. Isn't there an easier way? Absolutely! The tips below will help you maintain your soil but let you relax the endless hunt for tons of compost and mulch-making materials.

Concentrate your efforts in beds. Instead of turning and amending your entire garden area each spring, limit your soil improvements just to your planting beds. It's a lot more economical and less time-consuming to enrich the areas where you'll actually plant crops and leave the pathways alone.

Don't till every season. As long as your soil isn't compacted, there's no need to till or dig every season. Keep your feet out of your beds, and you'll have won the battle against soil compaction.

Let plants do the tilling. Letting plants do your work is better for you *and* the soil. And all you need to do to accomplish this is keep something growing at all times. It's as simple as sowing seeds: As soon as one crop is finished, replace it with another. The constant action of roots and a myriad of other living processes will keep the soil loose and friable.

Grow organic matter for your soil. Instead of making tons of compost to keep your soil provided with plenty of organic matter, carry a single seed packet to your garden and grow green manures. You can plant green manure crops throughout the growing season, whenever it's convenient for you, and they'll produce the organic matter your soil needs right where *you* need it. For more on growing and using green manures, see "Super-Simple Soil Improvement with Green Manures" on the opposite page.

Keep Green Manures on Hand

If you'd prefer to follow through on your intentions to plant green manures (instead of having those plans turn into good intentions), make sure you have seeds on hand year-round. Otherwise, the day that you pick to plant your crop may be the day you realize you forgot (again!) to order the seeds. Instead, order seeds like clover, hairy vetch, or soybeans when you place your next seed order. Whenever you have the time—whether it's spring, summer, or fall—you'll be ready to plant a soil-protecting cover over any garden bare spots. For more ideas for selecting and using green manures, see "Sow-Easy Soil Improvement While You Wait" on page 16.

Super-Simple Soil Improvement with Green Manures

Spring planting can be a snap if you grow green manure crops in summer or fall. With the simple system outlined below, all you'll need to do is rake away the winter-killed green manure and sow your seeds. Plus, you'll have a healthy, productive garden—all without digging, hauling compost, or buying fertilizer. Here's a walk through the seasonal tasks for the easiest garden you can imagine.

First Spring

A few weeks before you're ready to plant your vegetable crops, sow a mixture of seeds like radishes, mustard, or rape—any quick-growing crops that like cool weather—for an early-season green manure crop. Sow the seed thickly. A few days before you're ready to plant your vegetables, chop out these "sacrificial crops," leaving the residues to decompose. If you're preparing a new bed, use one of the methods described in "Soil Preparation without Tears" on page 125, and start using this system in summer.

Summer

Keep something growing in your garden beds at all times. If you have some empty space and you're not ready to plant a food crop, sow warm-weather green manures like buckwheat, cowpeas, or soybeans to fill the vacancies. Chop these crops down when you need the space, working the debris into the soil or using it as mulch as soon as it dries.

Don't let green manure crops get out of hand—they're easier to manage if kept small. Even if you're not ready to plant a food crop, cut them down before they get more than 8 inches tall or start to go to seed. Just plant another round of green manure to keep the process moving until you need the space.

Wait two or three days to plant vegetables after chopping down a green manure crop. (Decomposing plant material draws nitrogen from the soil, which temporarily robs it from any growing plants.) The chopped material will disappear in a day or two in warm weather; it will take a few days longer in cool weather. If you can't wait, simply rake the green manure onto the pathways. Once it dries, rake it back onto the bed as mulch.

Scrape up any mulch that has decomposed in the pathways and use it to cover vegetable crop seeds when you plant. This humus-rich blanket will keep the top of the soil from drying out and give the young seedlings a wonderful nutrient boost.

Early Fall

Remove the remaining summer crops and compost them. Clip the plants off at the soil level, leaving the roots in the ground to rot. In climates with cold winters, sow oats or mustard in the beds by mid-September. (Austrian winter peas are a good choice for the South.) These plants will grow until freezing temperatures hit, and then they die back, forming a mulch blanket.

If you miss planting a fall green manure crop, be sure to cover the bed with shredded leaves. Whatever you do, don't leave the soil uncovered and open to erosion.

Second Spring

About a month before your first spring plantings, push the remains of last year's green manure or any mulch you've used to cover your beds to the side, and plant the spring seed mix again. When it's time to plant early spring crops, chop out the seedlings—use hedge clippers or a string trimmer if a hoe proves difficult. You don't need to remove the roots of green manures—they should be left to rot in the ground. To aerate the bed, use a garden fork to gently lift the soil—no need to turn it over. That's all it takes! You're ready to plant.

Undersow to Grow Your Own Fertilizer

Growing a green manure crop under your main crop is a simple way to grow next year's fertilizer right where you'll need it. You'll avoid all the hassle and expense of buying soil amendments, andwhen used this way, green manure crops act as a living mulch, which conserves moisture and suppresses weeds.

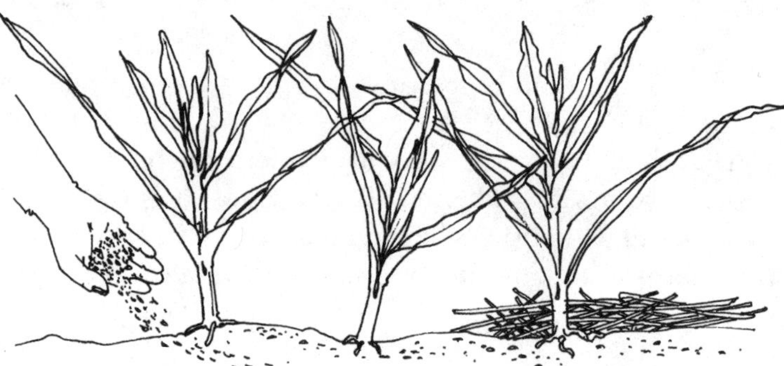

You can undersow corn with hairy vetch, as shown here, but there are many other combinations to try, including tomatoes with oats, corn with soybeans, cabbage with cowpeas, and squash with sweet clover. See "Sow-Easy Soil Improvement While You Wait" on page 16 for other green manure crops to try.

1. Plant your main crop and let it become established before broadcasting seed for your green manure crop. Corn, for example, should be about 10 inches tall before you sow.

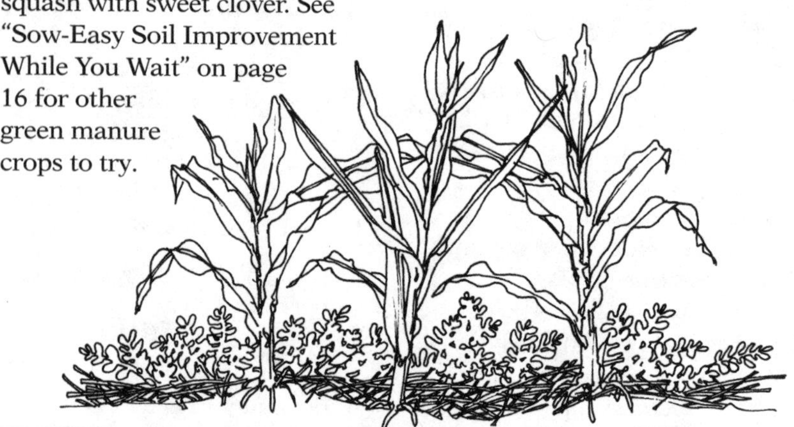

2. To cover the green manure seed, sprinkle the area with compost or mulch it lightly with straw.

3. Let the green manure crop grow through the season and till or dig it under the following spring. It will protect the soil over the winter.

When You're Planting, It Pays to Watch the Weather

The easiest way to plant seeds and transplants in the garden is to wait until the weather is right. There's nothing wrong with trying for an early start, but you'll probably have to replant seeds that were lost to rot or replace transplants blasted by an Arctic wind. In other words, gambling on an early spring is very rarely a low-maintenance venture!

But when is the weather right? Try taking a cue from the trees and plants growing around you. Lilacs and honeysuckle grow almost everywhere, so they make good examples. When their leaves show their first green, it's safe to plant early crops like lettuce, cabbage, and peas. For warm-weather crops like corn and beans, wait until the honeysuckle or lilac blossoms are fully open.

Mix Seeds and Transplants for Speedy Planting

If spring zooms by before you finish planting, speed up the process by using both transplants and seeds. These tips will help you plant and sow your vegetables efficiently.

Tips for transplants. Use transplants for crops that take a long time to grow, like cabbage, broccoli, and tomatoes. Buy the healthiest starts you can find—this is not the place to pinch pennies on root-bound, overcrowded seedlings. Healthy transplants will get off to a faster start, bear a better crop, and crowd out weeds more effectively than sickly ones. If you don't have time to tend to young seedlings daily, use transplants for the majority of your needs. They're successful for all but long-rooted crops like carrots, radishes, turnips and beets.

Suggestions for seeds. Buy seeds for plants that you use in quantity and that grow quickly, such as snap beans, spinach, arugula, and lettuce. Also buy seeds of plants that are so easy to handle that there's no need to spend the extra money on transplants. Examples include crops with big seeds like peas, beans, corn, and squash.

Sow Seeds Evenly to Save Time Thinning

There's no doubt about it, sowing seeds carefully is easier on the nerves than weeding extra seedlings out later. After all, what gardener likes to pull up healthy little plants? But sowing evenly is tough—especially with small seeds like carrots. Here are some simple techniques and tools that will make sowing and thinning easier for you.

Try creasing your seed packet down the middle and tapping the seeds out gently along the crease line. If seedlings still pop up in clumps, thin them out with a metal rake when they are about ½ inch high. Drag the rake across the width of the row so that the teeth dig in only about ¼ to ½ inch. The bed will look terrible for a few days, but the remaining seedlings will soon fill in the gaps. This technique works well for beets, carrots, chard, collards, kale, radishes, spinach, turnips, lettuce, and other salad greens.

If you have a large garden, consider investing in a few specialized seeding tools that make the process more efficient. A mechanical seeder makes planting lots of corn a snap and is very simple to use. These seeders have adjustable seed plates for other sizes of seeds and can be used in wide beds as well as in rows.

Crank seeders save a lot of time for crops that are broadcast—green manures, for example. This device looks a bit like a ricer only it spews out seeds instead of applesauce as you crank the handle. Most garden centers and hardware stores carry these tools.

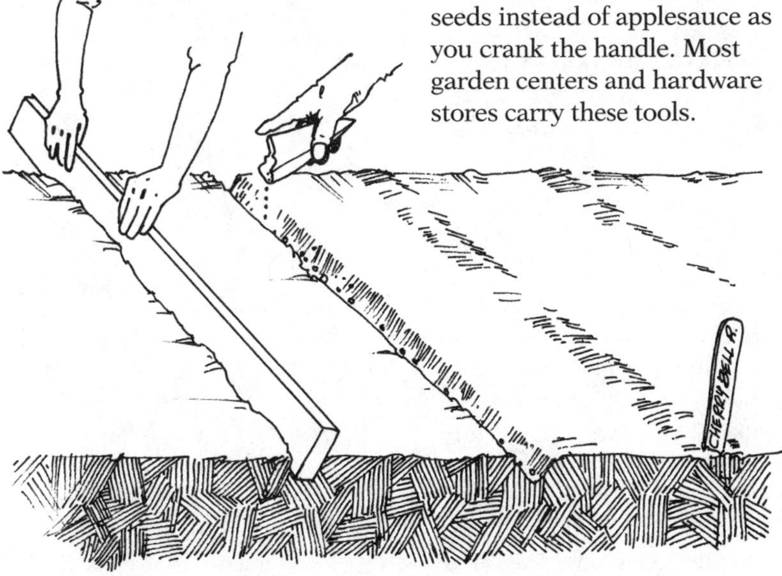

Use a board to make a furrow quickly, then crease seed packets and tap seeds out one by one instead of sowing en masse. Save the leftover seeds for subsequent plantings.

Don't Make Room for Weeds

Where do weeds come from, anyway? The truth is, gardeners plant most of them. Some weed seeds blow in, but the vast majority arrive in compost and mulch. Letting weeds go to seed is another prime source of future weeding headaches. All those weed seeds lie in the soil, waiting for a chance to come to the surface where there is enough light to germinate.

Every time you turn the soil over, you bring up another crop of weed seeds. Knowing all this, what's the low-maintenance way to keep weeds out of your way? Try these tips.

Keep your beds full of growing plants. If all the space is occupied by green manure crops or vegetable crops, weeds won't have room to sprout. (See "Super-Simple Soil Improvement with Green Manures" on page 129 for a method for keeping your soil covered.) In addition, growing your own organic matter with green manures reduces the likelihood you'll bring weed seeds to your garden with compost.

Keep your soil mulched. If you get caught with nothing growing in your beds, keep them mulched with at least 4 inches of materials like shredded leaves, dried grass clippings, or straw. Keep a supply of these materials handy for emergencies.

Rake out uninvited sprouts. If you till up a new area or dig a new bed and don't have time to plant a green manure crop, wait a few days for the weeds to sprout. (If you can, hang in there until the first rain.) Then use a metal rake to scratch the top ½ inch of the soil, which will disrupt any

Tactics for Timely Transplanting

Want to set out your transplants without watering them every day for a week? Let Mother Nature do the job. Sit tight until the weather is right and set in your plants when winds are calm and rain is expected. To give your plants an extra boost, soak them in seaweed solution before taking them out of their pots and give them another good drink once they are in the ground. Make a ring of soil around the base of the plant to help capture and retain water around the roots.

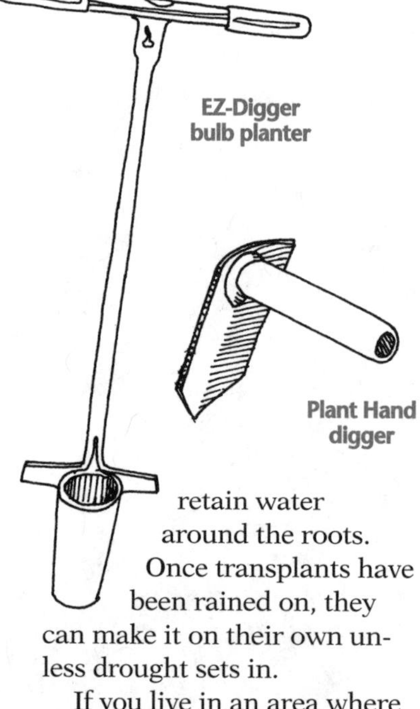

Once transplants have been rained on, they can make it on their own unless drought sets in.

If you live in an area where rain is scarce and you have no irrigation, prick a small nail hole in the bottoms of several plastic gallon jugs, fill them with water, and space them around your plants. The water will drip out slowly, saving you from watering for at least a week.

Transplanting Tools Ease Planting Pains

Why limit yourself to a trowel or shovel when other new or familiar tools can make planting much easier? Hand-diggers shaped like mini-plows let you open up planting holes in one quick swoop. A long-handled bulb planter works as well for transplants as for bulbs (unless the soil is compacted) since you can dig holes without stooping.

germinating weeds without bringing up lots more. This tip is especially useful if you want to grow crops like carrots or lettuce, which are tedious to weed.

Cut unwanted seedlings to the quick. If a few weeds pop up early in the season, snip them off at ground level with sharp scissors while they are still small. For weeds like dandelions that have long roots, push the scissors into the soil and cut off the root as far down as you can reach. This will keep you from uprooting young crop seedlings.

Crowd out weeds with leaves. To keep weeds out of beds planted with crops, space your vegetables as closely as possible. Imagine how big your vegetables will be when they mature, and space or thin the plants accordingly. The leaves of growing plants will form a "living mulch," shading out most weed problems.

Skim the soil. To keep ahead of weeds in more open planting areas, like blocks of corn or hills of squash, chop them out while they are still small. Use a sharp hoe or a spade to skim off the weeds at soil level, and you'll avoid the hassle of digging and pulling. The only secret here is to keep the blades of your tools razor sharp. Once crops have reached full size, you can relax your weeding routine, but never let weeds go to seed!

Make the Most of Mulch

Everybody knows that organic mulches have lots of benefits. They keep weeds down and moisture in, and they return lots of organic matter to the soil as they decompose. But if mulching is not your bag, here are some tips to make the process less painful.

Mulch the pathways. If mulching your whole garden looks overwhelming, just cover the paths. A one-time mulching effort will give you easy access to planting beds all year long. Start with a layer of newspaper at least four pages thick. Pile on a layer of weeds, grass clippings, sawdust, seaweed, straw—whatever organic matter is most available to you. The following season, scrape up the decomposed material in the pathways and use it to cover seeds when you're planting.

Plant green manures throughout the season. A pound of mulch won't go very far, but planting a pound of buckwheat seeds will keep weeds out and feed the soil, too. See "Undersow to Grow Your Own Fertilizer" on page 130 for more on using green manures.

Look for lightweight mulches. Shredded paper is one good example and is often available from local businesses that shred documents. Or make your own shredded paper by feeding newspaper into a leaf shredder sheet by sheet. Cover paper mulch with a thin layer of straw or composted leaves to hold it in place.

Mulch when the time is right. If you're mulching cool-weather crops like lettuce or peas, apply mulch before it gets hot. This keeps the soil cool, which prolongs the harvest. For heat-loving crops like tomatoes and squash, mulch after the plants set fruit to ward off drought and keep the fruit clean and dry. It's best to apply mulch right after it rains so there will be some moisture for the mulch to hold in.

Have mulch delivered. If scavenging for mulch is not your style, buy straw from a local farmer or farm-supply store. In addition, landscaping companies might be glad to dump off leaves and grass clippings. (Just make sure the materials are organic before you ask for a load.)

Use mulches that last. Ever heard of a rug garden? Lay down an old all-cotton carpet, cut out the planting areas, plant, and voilà! Your garden is planted and mulched and will last for several seasons. Wood chips, although they are too coarse and acidic for use directly around vegetable plants, are great for pathways. Put some newspaper or cardboard down first and pathways will be passable with minimum renewal for many years.

Low-Maintenance Tips for Your Favorite Crops

Do you have a favorite vegetable? Check the tips and techniques below for ways to make growing it easier, faster, and more efficient.

Crop	Tips for Sure-Fire Success	Methods to Maximize Efficiency
Beans, snap	Choose cultivars with dark seeds or purple pods for early plantings; they're less likely to rot. Plant small amounts (3 plants per person) every 12 days for a continuous crop and manageable harvests.	Plant snap beans in spaces vacated by lettuce and spinach to return nitrogen to the soil. Train pole beans up a teepee made of saplings to conserve space (1 teepee serves a family of 4).
Beets	Soak seeds overnight to speed germination. Beets need thinning because each "seed" actually contains several seeds. Clip extras with sharp scissors and add to the salad bowl.	For a double crop, harvest beet leaves throughout the season. Leave two-thirds of the leaves so root harvest won't be disturbed.
Cabbage family crops (broccoli, brussels sprouts, cabbage, cauliflower, collards, kale)	Use row-covers to prevent damage from cabbage worms. Row covers also minimize the temperature fluctuations that cause poor heading in broccoli and cauliflower.	Plant kale, collards, and brussels sprouts for nutritious, long-season crops, sowing seeds in the spaces left from early peas or beans. These hardy greens will overwinter in many areas with minimum protection.
Carrots	For better germination, cover seeds with ½ inch of compost. Keep the compost moist until seeds are up and growing.	Sow radish seeds with carrots; radishes keep the soil loose and are ready to harvest before carrots need the space. Planting with onions reduces carrot fly infestations.
Corn	Plant when nighttime air temperatures stay above 40°F. (The soil temperature should be about 50°F.) To deter crows, cover seedbeds with row covers.	Plant a mid-season and a late-season cultivar at the same time so you won't have to remember to plant a later crop. Early cultivars aren't tasty enough to warrant the work.
Cucumbers	Use row covers to thwart cucumber beetles. Remove covers when vines blossom to allow pollination. Plant a second crop as insurance against pests when the first crop blooms.	Trellising pays off in increased cucumber yields.
Eggplant	To combat flea beetles, place white plastic buckets around eggplants. Coat the plastic with sticky Tanglefoot to capture the beetles.	Eggplants love heat—cover them with plastic jugs (remove lids and cut out bottoms) until summer nights are warm.
Lettuce	Plant many types, starting with cold-tolerant strains early in the season. Switch to heat-resistant cultivars as summer draws near.	Sow a 2½- to 3-foot block every 10 days to 2 weeks until the weather gets hot. For longer harvests, keep roots cool with mulch to retard bolting. Row covers allow harvest of many greens well into winter.

Crop	Tips for Sure-Fire Success	Methods to Maximize Efficiency
Onions	Buy sets or transplants instead of seeds for a quick, reliable harvest. Choose small (½-inch-diameter), firm sets since they're less likely to bolt.	Onions are good companions for most crops except peas and beans. Keep a bag of onion sets in the refrigerator and use them to fill in blank spaces all season.
Peas	Soak seeds overnight to speed germination. To avoid trellising, select short cultivars and plant seeds thickly so the vines will support each other.	Interplant with radishes and early greens if space is short; avoid planting near garlic or onions. Pick daily to encourage vines to keep producing.
Peppers	To increase yields, snip off early blossoms on young plants to give them a chance to bulk out before fruiting. Boost with 1 teaspoon Epsom salts to 1 quart of water when plants set fruit.	For easy harvest, uproot hot peppers at the end of the season and hang them to dry in a warm closet. Uprooted sweet peppers will hold for a month in a bucket of water if kept in a cool location.
Spinach	Soak seeds in compost tea for 15 minutes or all night before planting. Plant heat- and bolt-resistant cultivars.	Pick outside leaves only, once they reach 3 to 4 inches long—plants stay productive longer if you harvest the entire plant.
Squash	To prevent squash borer attack, use row-covers until female blossoms appear. Start another plant or two in early summer for added protection.	Pumpkins and winter squash take up a lot of space. Let them ramble over compost piles and steep slopes where other crops can't grow.
Potatoes	A month before planting, put seed potatoes in a bright, dry location, like a basement windowsill. The sprouts will grow slowly in the light. Cut them into sections with two or three sprouted eyes and plant. Crops will be ready almost a month earlier.	Why grow plain white potatoes? Specialty spuds are available in a riot of colors and shapes and are just as easy to grow. Try potatoes with yellow, pink, or blue flesh for flavors that store-bought spuds can't match.
Tomatoes	Buy the best transplants you can find. Seedlings should be bushy with sturdy stems. Choose disease-resistant cultivars. Try an assortment of single plants instead of buying a six-pack of one cultivar. Tomatoes almost always produce, but different cultivars produce better in different weather conditions.	Staking isn't necessary, but staked tomatoes have larger fruit, are easier to pick, and are less prone to rot. If you use tomato cages, buy the tallest, sturdiest ones available. To prevent cages from toppling, drive a stake inside each cage to hold it in place.

Don't Dig Potatoes, Grow Them in Mulch!

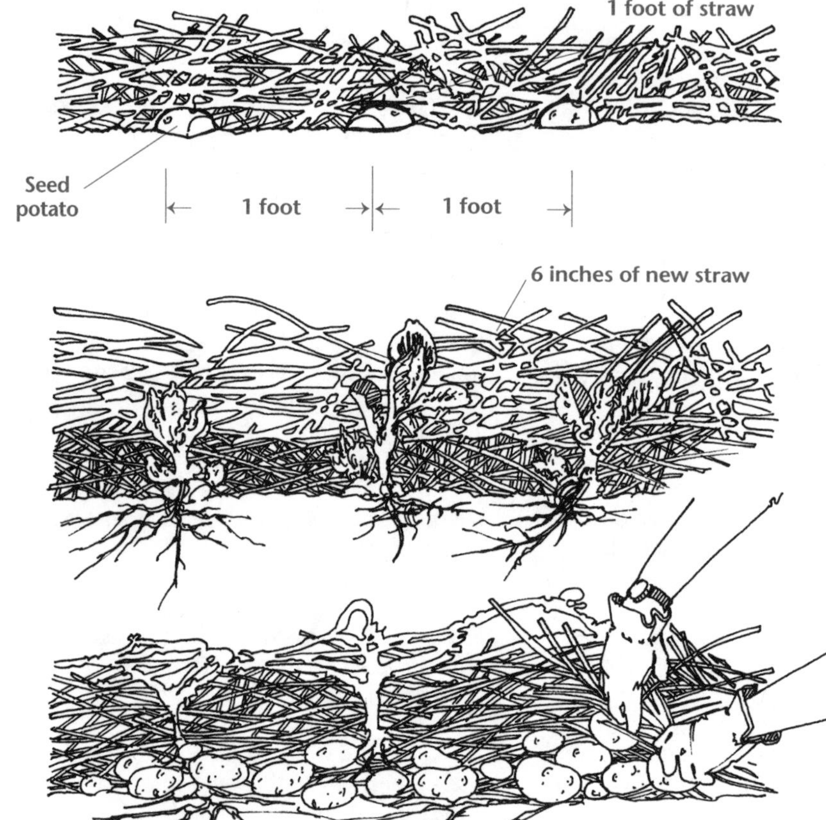

Growing potatoes under mulch couldn't be easier. There's no digging, no tools—just a few bales of straw.

1. Place seed potatoes 1 foot apart on top of the soil and cover them with 1 foot of straw, hay, or shredded leaves. (Be sure each piece of potato has 2 or 3 eyes.)

2. Believe it or not, potato shoots and leaves will eventually poke through the mulch. When they do, add 6 more inches of clean straw mulch around the plants. (Don't cover the leaves.) Peek underneath the mulch periodically to watch the tubers develop and check to make sure they aren't turning green, which is a signal to add more mulch.

3. Begin harvesting new potatoes when the vines flower. Simply lift up the mulch and pick a few baby spuds. Harvest the main crop when the vines begin to die down.

With Beans, Peas, and Other Legumes, It Pays to Inoculate

The first time you plant legumes like peas and beans in your garden, inoculate them with the bacteria they need to fix nitrogen in their roots. Tests show that yields on inoculated crops increased up to 77 percent. To inoculate seeds before planting, moisten them in a flat pan and sprinkle on the black dustlike innoculant powder. Shake the pan to ensure good coverage.

Different legumes need different types of bacteria. The inoculant powder most commonly sold contains a mix suitable for peas, snap beans, and lima beans. If you grow other legumes, like cowpeas or scarlet runner beans, buy the proper inoculant. Once you've planted inoculated crops, you don't need to do it again. The bacteria will remain in the soil.

Which Tomato Type Is Best for You?

The type of tomatoes you plant can mean the difference between a crop that's over in a few short weeks and one that lasts throughout the summer months. That's because tomatoes are either determinate or indeterminate.

Determinate tomatoes set all their flowers and fruit at the same time, then stop growing. Choose them if you have a short growing season—since their fruits ripen all at once, you can squeeze in a complete harvest before frost. Determinate plants stay shorter, so they're easy to grow in cages and a good choice if you hate staking. Canning tomatoes, like 'Heinz' and 'Roma,' are popular determinate cultivars.

Indeterminate tomatoes continue growing and setting flowers throughout the growing season. They usually require staking, although they can be grown fairly well in extra-tall cages. See "Don't Train and Tie Tomatoes, Cage Them" on page 171 for details. On the plus side, though, they'll spread out the harvest so you aren't overwhelmed with too many tomatoes all at once. Most slicing tomatoes, like 'Beefsteak' and 'Better Boy,' are indeterminate cultivars.

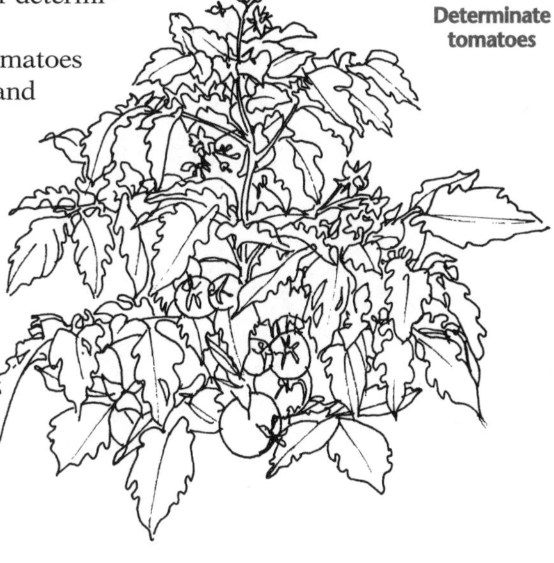

Determinate tomatoes

CHAPTER 14

Fruit Trees

Fruit Trees the Low-Maintenance Way

IS THERE ROOM in the low-care garden for fruit trees? The answer is yes. This is not to say you can plant a tree and expect to pick perfect fruits off it without giving it any care. But you *can* expect to pick lots of super-tasting fruit with only a small time investment.

The trick to getting lots of fruit for a few hours of work is to lavish care on your trees their first few growing seasons. In this chapter, you'll learn easy training and pruning techniques to help baby trees develop into strong, healthy adults. You'll also find tips to help you choose which fruits will grow best in your yard. We'll even tell you about some fruits you really *can* plant and ignore until harvest time.

Choose One of These Fruit Trees—They Thrive on Neglect

Hardy wild trees don't count on gardeners to make life easy for them. To save yourself a lot of work, plant fruits that haven't had all the wildness domesticated out of them. Some of these may be new to you, but they all offer good crops for little or no work.

Cornelian cherry (*Cornus mas*). These trees bear yellow flowers on their bare branches in spring. The small, plumlike fruits are good cooked. Zones 4–8.

Jujube (*Ziziphus jujuba*). Harvest these bite-size morsels when they're ripe and apple-crisp or let them hang longer on the tree for datelike treats. Zones 5–10.

Pawpaw (*Asimina triloba*). This native tree bears oddly shaped fruits with a banana-pineapple-custard flavor. Mulch under them to keep the soil cool, don't prune them, and they will pretty much take care of themselves. Zones 5–8.

Pear (*Pyrus* spp.). Of all the large cultivated fruits, pears are the best low-maintenance choice. They have few pest and disease problems and need very little pruning after the first few years. Choose fire-blight-resistant cultivars. Zones 4–9.

Persimmon (*Diospyros* spp.). American and Asian persimmons need little or no pruning, like almost any soil, and are prone to few pests. The rich orange fruits range from 1 to 4 inches across. American persimmons Zones 5–10; Asians, 7–10.

Quince (*Cydonia oblonga*). While the large, furry, yellow fruits won't win many beauty contests, the aroma and taste of cooked quince is manna from the gods. The trees are small and have few pest problems. Zones 5–9.

Tart cherry (*Prunus cerasus*). These modest-size trees bear heavy crops of tangy red fruits even if you don't prune them at all. Be prepared to fight the birds for your crop. Zones 4–9.

For Years of Problem-Free Fruits, Set Your Sites on Success

Safe Sites

Full sun. Most fruits demand at least a half-day of full sun to do well. All day is best.

Well-drained soil. Fruit trees won't put up with wet feet.

Space. Air should circulate freely through and around the tree. Leave enough space so your fully grown tree won't push up against a wall, hedge, or other tree.

Trouble Spots

Just-vacated sites. Never plant the same kind of fruit tree—or even a closely related one—in a spot where you just removed one. Healthy or sick, that tree you removed left things in the soil that will inhibit or sicken a new one.

Wild cousins. Wild trees can share diseases and pests with your more civilized children. Look for—and consider removing—wild or abandoned fruit trees near a proposed site.

Touchy territory. Not every neighbor wants half a fruit tree sticking out over his picture-perfect lawn—even if you offer him half of the fruit. You're probably better off leaving space between a tree and the edge of your property.

Plant a Pretty Mini-Orchard

Even if they didn't produce a single piece of edible fruit, fruit trees would still be worth growing for the beauty of their spring blossoms. The fragrant flower clusters of cherry, peach, plum, and pear set off the early spring greenery. A couple of weeks later, apple trees catch up, showing off their trusses of sweet-smelling flowers.

Why relegate such decorative trees to an orchard? Set fruit trees in small groups and plant spring flowers under them. Their pink and white blossoms are right at home with other flowers, and their sturdy form adds vertical line and structure. Daffodils, tulips, and small bulbs like sky-blue glory-of-the-snow (*Chionodoxa luciliae*) are good companions, as are early-blooming perennials.

Here are some pointers for making your fruit and flower bed easy to care for.

Think small. Dwarf and semi-dwarf trees are just the right scale for combining with shrubs and perennials.

Mulch thickly. Spread a thick layer of mulch throughout the bed to reduce weed problems all season long.

Give trees elbow room. Leave at least a 4-foot circle unplanted around each tree trunk to reduce competition and help your trees grow vigorously.

Skirt New Trees to Make Easy Weed-Free Zones

While grown-up trees are taller than most weeds, young trees can suffer when weeds press around them too closely. Cut tedious weeding time to almost nothing with this quick fix.

Fold a 3-foot-square of landscape fabric in quarters and snip off the center point to leave about a 4-inch hole. Slip this fabric skirt over the newly planted tree (you may have to hold the branches together with one hand). Smooth the skirt over the ground and pin down the corners with soil staples or rocks. You can cover the fabric with a few inches of mulch if you want a neater look.

This dwarf plum tree makes a nice focal point for a perennial border. In spring its thickly clustered, wonderfully fragrant flowers line every inch of the branches.

Do These Little Jobs; You'll Prevent Big Problems Later

Preventing disease and controlling insect infestations can turn into a big job if you let the problems get out of hand. Help keep things under control by performing these routine chores.

◀ **Snip off problems before they spread.** At the first sign of disease or infestation, remove affected branches. Look for cankers (lumpy masses) on branches or twigs and watch for any deformed leaf growth, including sudden wilting or browning leafy branch tips. Cut off insect tents. Prune off stems afflicted with fire blight (blackened, curled-down branch tips and scorched leaves). Be sure to cut 10 to 12 inches below infected areas.

◀ **Clean up trees after the leaves fall.** Rub trunks with a wire brush or a ball of scrunched-up chicken wire to remove loose flakes of bark where insects hide. Pick off and destroy any dried fruits.

▼ **Pick up and clean up.** Pick up dropped green fruit at least weekly. Put the gatherings in the freezer overnight to kill any residents and compost them. Rake up and remove dropped debris after you've cleaned up the trees in the fall.

For Low-Work Fruit, Plant Trees That Won't Grow Much Taller Than You

Trees that stay short without drastic yearly pruning are the low-maintenance way to go. Short trees mean an easy reach to pick and prune—no ladder or long-handled tools necessary. Here's what to look for in a modest-stature tree.

Dwarf and semi-dwarf trees take up less space than full-size ones, and they bear full-size fruit that's easy to pick.

Naturally small trees. Some trees just won't grow as large as other trees. Tart cherry trees are smaller than sweet cherries, for example, and quinces rarely become large trees.

Genetically small trees. Fruit breeders occasionally come across a tree that grows very slowly. At less than 10 feet tall these so-called "genetic dwarfs" are great low-maintenance trees. 'Garden Bing' sweet cherry, 'Apple Babe' apple, and 'Honey Babe' peach are examples of genetic dwarf cultivars.

Trees with dwarfing roots. Cultivars that would normally grow into large trees will grow much smaller if grafted onto a size-controlling set of roots. Apples, pears, peaches, and sweet cherries are all available on dwarfing roots.

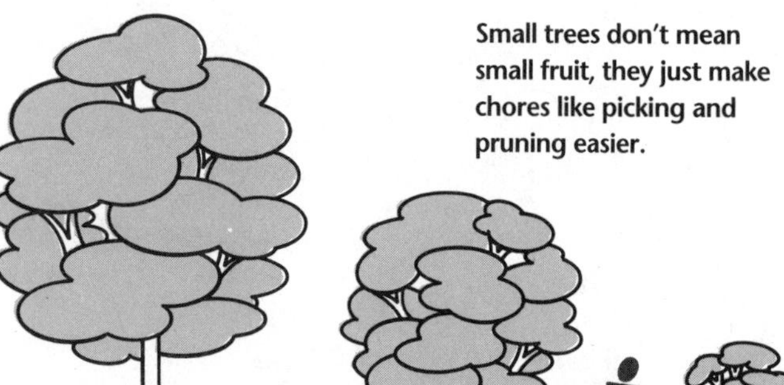

Small trees don't mean small fruit, they just make chores like picking and pruning easier.

Pick Some Little Apples in Spring to Make Big Ones Later

You may not get many supermarket-perfect apples from a low-maintenance tree, but you'll get plenty of edible fruit, as well as bushels for apple butter, jelly, and cider. If you want to make your fruits bigger, try thinning them early in the season. Thinning has the added benefit of eliminating some of the less-than-perfect apples early on.

Thin apples when they're about the size of big jelly beans and after the natural "June drop" or self-thinning period is past. Use sturdy scissors and carefully snip off all but the largest or least-blemished fruit in each cluster. If any clusters are very close together, snip off all the fruits in some clusters to leave just one apple every 6 inches.

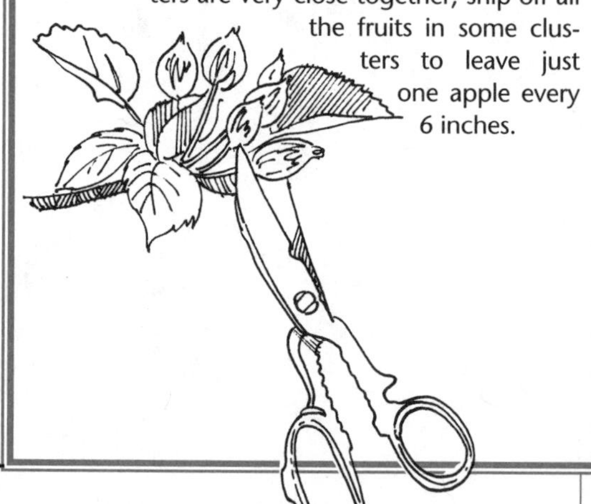

Don't Buy Problems— Stick with Trouble-Free Trees

Don't waste your time growing trees that will need extra care just to survive—they'll yield poorly, if at all. Ask local gardeners and extension agents which fruits to avoid and which are trouble free. Here are some common weather extremes and suggestions for choosing trees in such areas.

Warm winters. Fruits like apples and pears need a certain number of cold days each winter to bear well. Pick "low-chill" cultivars for success.

Cold winters. Match tree hardiness with your winter low temperatures. "High-chill" trees are a good choice if you tend to have midwinter thaws.

Hot and/or humid summers. Some plants can't take extreme heat. Others are simply more prone to disease problems when the weather is humid. Select heat- and disease-resistant cultivars.

Short, cool summers. What good is a healthy fruit tree if the fruit never ripens because your season is too short? Look for early-ripening cultivars.

Stick It to Pesky Pests with These All-Natural Controls

Plant large, tasty fruits like apples and peaches and you'll soon have insect pests lining up for a share of the feast. Here are two simple traps you can use to make sure you get most of that feast for yourself. (You'll find lots more useful traps described in the natural pest control catalogs listed in "Sources" on page 355.)

▼ **Stop trunk drivers in their tracks.** Some pests travel up the trunk highway to get to your tree. Stop them simply like this: Wrap a 12- to 18-inch-wide strip of heavy paper, roofing paper, or cardboard around the trunk, making sure the ends overlap a few inches. Tie a string around the middle of the paper band, then fold the top half down over the bottom half. Check the trap every few days and destroy any pests.

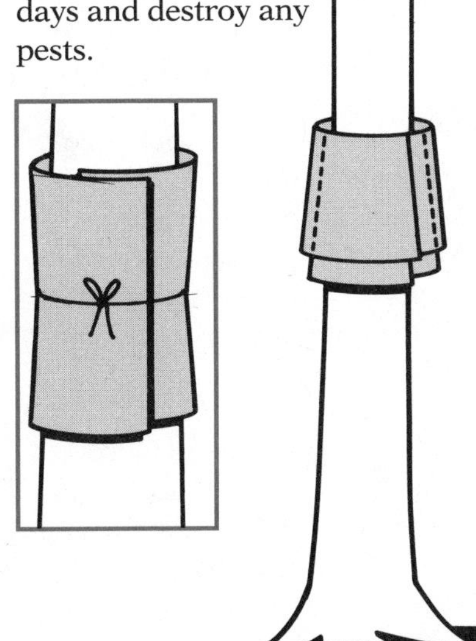

▲ **Fake out flying fruit eaters.** If you live in the eastern or central states and grow apples, you will probably meet some little white apple maggots happily munching their way through your fruit. Control next year's maggot crop by hanging sticky red balls in your trees about a month after your trees bloom. When the females try to lay eggs on the big red "apples" you've hung, they'll find themselves stuck tight. End of problem.

You'll need 1 to 6 traps per tree, depending on its size. And don't fuss with cleaning traps: Buy disposable traps, or slip each reusable trap into a plastic sandwich bag and tie it with a twist tie before coating it with sticky stuff like Tangle-Trap.

Bring Back Birds and Banish Bugs

Sure, some adult birds aren't above eating a cherry or two, but baby birds eat bugs—*lots* of bugs. Foraging parent birds will scour your garden for as many fat, juicy insects as they can find to satisfy their clamoring broods. Invite birds to nest in and around your garden and they will more than pay you back for any fruit they snitch later in the season. Try these tips to make your yard into a bird magnet.

Offer drinking water. A birdbath or other source of water will encourage birds to set up housekeeping in your garden.

Hang out some "For Rent" signs. Mount birdhouses and nesting shelves around your yard. To attract wrens, hang a house with a 1-inch-diameter hole from a branch in a fruit tree 5 to 10 feet above the ground. Bluebirds prefer a house with a 1⅜-inch hole firmly mounted on a post 4 to 6 feet above the ground. Robins and swallows prefer a nesting shelf (a house with no front or sides) mounted 6 to 10 feet above the ground.

Plant or leave a hedgerow. A hedgerow, especially a naturalistic one, will attract nesting species that don't use bird boxes.

TAKE-IT-EASY TIP!

Cut Your Spraying Time with Disease-Resistant Cultivars

No gardener enjoys spraying—even with organic fungicides. Fortunately, you can save time and money by planting disease-resistant cultivars of fruit trees. If you don't know which diseases are a problem in your area, talk with local backyard fruit growers. Or call your extension agent and ask which fruits and cultivars they recommend for organic growing.

Save Pruning Time Later—Train Trees When They're Young

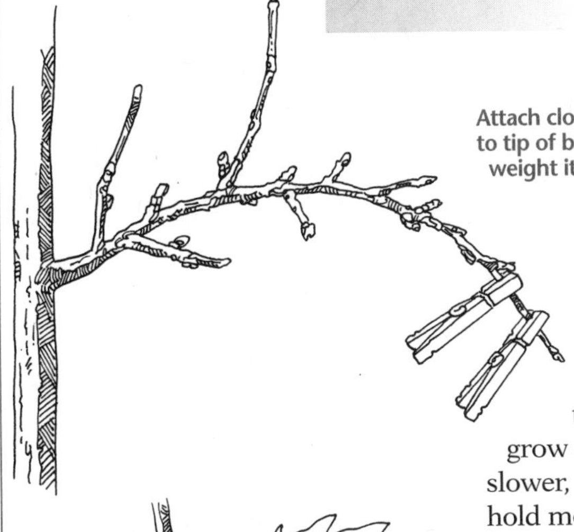

Attach clothespins to tip of branch to weight it down.

Use a clothespin to angle a new branch out.

Training trees when they're young has several low-maintenance advantages. Branches that have been trained to grow out rather than up grow slower, bear fruit sooner, and hold more fruit or winter ice without snapping.

Redirecting branches so they spread out is easy when they're small and actively growing: All you need is a pocket full of clip clothespins. Do this every few weeks for the first two summers, and you'll have a fine tree. Here's how.

Spread new branches down to a 45 to 60 degree angle. Hold the branch down gently with one hand. Clip the clothespin onto the branch and rest the other end against the trunk. Release the branch and adjust the clothespin up or down to get the right amount of spread—halfway between or a little lower than straight up and straight out is ideal. You'll be able to take the clothespin off in a month, after the branch "sets."

Weight branch tips to keep them from growing straight up. Keep branches growing at the proper angle by weighting them with clothespins. You can use this technique on older trees to make a water sprout into a new fruiting branch.

Don't Skip This One-Time, 5-Minute Pruning Job

A few minutes of pruning at the end of a new tree's first growing season will save hours of pruning later. If you train the branches during the first summer as they're growing (see above) and prune once in late summer, you'll have a strong, productive tree.

Pick four sturdy branches. At the end of the first summer, select four vigorous branches. Each branch should be about 4 inches above or below any other and spaced around the trunk pointing to the four corners of the world. Cut all other branches off flush with the main stem. Cut a few inches off the tip of each branch to make them the same length and encourage branching.

Cut the top off the main stem. For peaches, nectarines, and tart cherries, cut the main stem back to 1/4 inch above the top branch. For apples, pears, apricots, and plums, cut the main stem back to 2 feet above the top branch. (If it's less than 2 feet long, leave it alone.) Don't cut sweet cherry stems.

Easy-Does-It Pruning for Young Fruit Trees

All it takes is a few minutes a year to keep your fruit trees in shape. Here's how.

Trees trained in the open-center style have 3 or 4 horizontal scaffold branches.

Apples, Pears, Apricots, Plums, and Sweet Cherries

These trees tend to grow one main trunk and layers of horizontal branches. Commercial orchardists encourage this tendency and call it central-leader training. You did the first step in "Don't Skip This One-Time, 5-Minute Pruning Job" on page 145. Here's how to complete the training process.

Year two. This is basically a repeat of the first summer. Pick another layer of branches a foot or so above the first year's layer (for a total of eight branches). Treat the branch tips and the main stem the same way that you did the first summer.

Year three. Again, repeat the first summer procedure and choose a third layer of branches a foot or so above the second layer (for a total of twelve branches). Shorten the branch tips again, but this year weight the tip of the main stem with a couple of clothespins. As it bends over, it will slow down and start producing fruit buds.

Trees trained in the central-leader style ideally have layers of horizontal scaffold branches. The branches radiate out from the trunk like the spokes of a wheel.

Thereafter. You shouldn't need to do much after the third year. In late summer, snip a few inches off the tip of any overly long shoot and clip a clothespin or two onto any very vertical shoot to make it bend over.

Peaches, Nectarines, and Tart Cherries

These trees grow a cluster of equal-size branches that come out of the trunk at about the same level. Commercial orchardists call this open-center training. You did the main step in "Don't Skip This One-Step, 5-Minute Pruning Job" on page 145. Here's how to continue the training process.

Year two. A few times during the season, clip a clothespin or two onto the tip of any shoot pointing straight up.

Year three. In spring just after the tree blooms, thin out branches a bit. Your tree should be funnel-shaped with a thin, cone-shaped layer of branches all around and nothing in the center. Cut any branches invading the center space back to a main branch. Shorten each branch tip by cutting off about half of last year's growth.

Thereafter. Repeat year three. Cut a few of the oldest medium-size branches back to the main branch each spring. This will keep your tree compact and make new, fruit-producing branches.

Simple Pruning for Big, Overgrown Trees

A huge tree may look like a huge pruning project, and it can take a while, but it doesn't need to be complicated. Follow these straightforward steps.

Remove all dead wood. You can do this any time of year. Start with a pruning saw for the big stuff and finish up with a pole pruner or loppers for smaller branches.

Remove rubbing branches. Cut one of the branches off where it joins either the trunk or a larger branch.

De-sucker the base of tree. During the summer, you can snap off young suckers with your hand. Cut older suckers off flush with the trunk or the roots with hand pruners any time.

Snip off water sprouts. Water sprouts are long, straight shoots that reach for the sky. Snip them off while they're green and growing and they won't grow back as fast. If there's a big gap in a tree that you'd like to fill with a branch, weigh down the end of a water sprout with a bunch of clothespins so it points toward the hole. It will bend over and become a nice new fruit-bearing branch.

Remove a few of the medium and large branches. If the tree is very tall, cut about one-third of the highest branches back to the trunk or a main branch. You may even want to cut the trunk itself back to a side branch. July or August is probably the best time to take out large branches because you'll stimulate less regrowth, but you can do it anytime. Just wait a year before removing any more branches.

Thin things out. If the tree isn't tall, just really dense, thin out some medium and small branches throughout the tree. Always cut back to a larger branch or the trunk so you don't stimulate a lot of new little branches to grow.

Don't Assume You Have to Prune

Many gardeners assume they have to prune fruit trees or they won't get any fruit. This simply isn't true. Here are some reasons why commercial orchardists prune and thoughts about why you may or may not want to.

Commercial Reason	Low-Maintenance Approach
To get more large fruit.	If small and medium fruit suit you, you'll actually get more pounds of fruit if you don't prune.
To make strong branches that won't break when loaded with fruit.	If you're willing to risk an occasional broken branch, you can skip this. Besides, a little early training achieves this goal better.
To keep the tree small so you can reach the fruit.	Don't waste your time trying to keep a large tree pruned down to size. Buy a small tree.
To remove diseased and dead wood.	You should definitely cut out diseased branches as soon as you see them.
To open the tree up so that air and sunshine can reach all parts of the tree.	Sunshine and fresh air need to get to all parts of your tree to prevent disease problems. If a tree is dense, thinning its branches is a healthy idea.

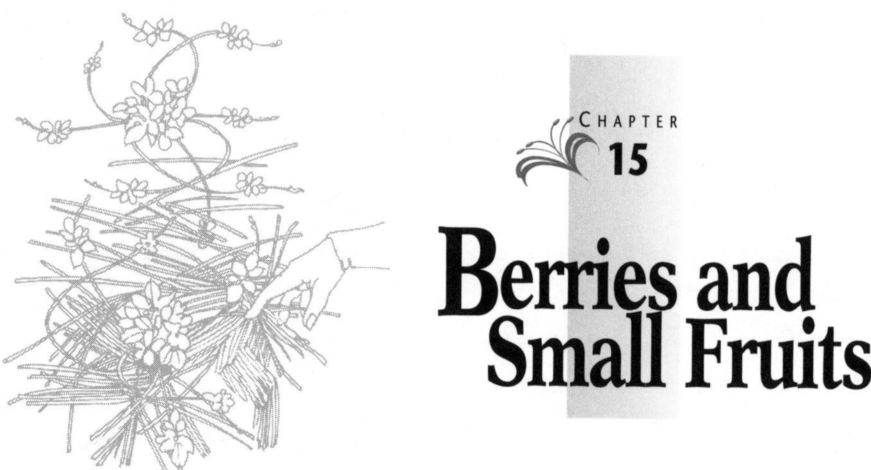

CHAPTER 15

Berries and Small Fruits

Berries and Small Fruits the Low-Maintenance Way

A MORNING OF MAINTENANCE once or twice a year—and a watchful eye—are all the care blackberries and raspberries need. Other small fruits are even more obliging. Small fruits bear quickly and for many years, and they are perfect in the low-maintenance garden.

This chapter will help you choose berries and small fruits that will give you lots of delicious fruit for little or no care in return. You'll also learn tricks for keeping overzealous spreaders in check and quick ways to boost your harvests.

Grow Berries and Small Fruits the Easy Way

Berries and small fruits are tough characters. In the wild, they grow and bear quite happily with no help from anyone. Let them grow wild in your yard if you have room—you'll get plenty of handfuls of berries for your morning cereal. Here are four simple things you can do to civilize your berry patch and increase your harvests.

Mow. Your trusty lawn mower or string trimmer is a fast and easy way to keep the weeds from overwhelming your plants. Mowing also keeps adventuring berry suckers from turning your yard into an impenetrable briar patch. Leave a few inches unmowed around the main stems so you don't damage the plants themselves.

Mulch. Cover the no-mow zone right under your plants with mulch. Straw, old carpet (preferably natural fiber) spread upside down, or even the weeds you just uprooted from the front bed will do fine. If new weeds break through, just stomp them over and dump on more mulch.

Prune. You'll get plenty of fruit from most types of berries and small fruits even if you never snip a twig. But an occasional cut or two will keep plants vigorous, thin out dead wood, and keep the fruits within reach. Only you can decide whether saving time by not pruning is worth a smaller harvest or a struggle with a tangle of thorny canes. If you decide to prune, you'll find low-maintenance pruning tips for various fruits later in this chapter.

Feed and water. Mulching your plants with organic mulch like grass clippings, chopped leaves, or pulled weeds feeds them gradually, helps control weeds, and conserves soil moisture. If you care to do more, add compost under the plants each year as an extra feeding. Watering is optional, too. In dry seasons, if you don't water, the berries will be smaller or may even shrivel up before they ripen. If you aren't content with what nature can provide, keep the plants watered from the time they flower through harvest.

Just Starting Out? Put Your Berry Best Foot Forward

Get your berry plants off to a healthy start before you plant. You'll save yourself unnecessary maintenance later on.

1. **Pick a berry good site.** Put your berries and small fruits where they will be happy. Like vegetables, they want as many hours of full sun as possible, well drained soil, and space so air can move around them. See "Set Your 'Sites' for Success" on page 119 for specifics.

2. **Banish pesky weeds.** It's lots easier to dig up or smother nasty perennial weeds before you plant; otherwise, you'll have to pick through a tangle of berry plants to get them out. See Chapter 10 for the easiest ways to rid your site of weeds.

3. **Buy smart.** Don't be penny-wise and dollar-dumb. Healthy, pest-resistant plants that are suited to your climate are a must for low-maintenance growing. To find out which types of small fruits and berries grow best in your area, call your local extension agent and ask what they have the fewest problems with. Select cultivars that are resistant to extremes (drought, cold, heat, humidity) and as many diseases as possible.

   Buy plants (especially strawberries, raspberries, and blackberries) from a reputable nursery. Cheap plants are rarely a bargain in the long run and, like free plants from a neighbor, they can harbor diseases and pests.

Neglect These Care-Free Berries

It's really as easy as plant-'em-and-pick-'em with certain small fruits and unusual, delicious berries. You'll get loads of tasty fruits without pruning, staking, or other care. Here are some no-sweat possibilities.

Plant small fruits like elderberries and most brambles that spread by suckers where they have room to ramble. Also keep them well away from property lines so they don't become unwelcome visitors in your neighbor's yard.

Alpine strawberry (*Fragaria vesca* 'Alpine'). Compact plants without runners yield small, flavor-packed berries from spring through frost.

Bush cherries and native plums (*Prunus* spp.). Clouds of white flowers, then tart cherry-like fruit, cover these 3- to 10-foot bushes. Fall-bearing types thwart birds.

Currant and gooseberry (*Ribes* spp.). Tangy and translucent, red and white currants hang in clusters from 3- to 5-foot plants. Musky black currants dangle from bushes up to 7 feet tall. Try 'Crandall' for fragrant yellow spring flowers. Gooseberry fruits are larger, but the 3- to 5-foot bushes are quite thorny. Try 'Colossal' or 'Poorman' for fewer thorns.

Elderberry (*Sambucus* spp.). Clusters of creamy flowers as big as dinner plates on 5- to 10-foot stems mature into heavy crops of tart, flavorful berries.

Highbush cranberry (*Viburnum trilobum*). As much an ornamental as a fruit, these 6- to 10-foot beauties sport white spring flowers, reddish fall foliage, and tart red fruits for months.

Juneberry (*Amelanchier* spp.). Dainty white, early-spring flowers grace these shrubs and trees. The blueberrylike pink to purple-blue fruits are also attractive.

Mulberry (*Morus* spp.). While technically a tree, the fruits are definitely berries. Shake the lower branches over a sheet to quickly gather the ripe berries. Keep trees away from walkways—dropping fruits stain.

TAKE-IT-EASY TIP!

Weedproof Your New Bushes

Here's a super-easy way to control weeds around berry bushes—and fruit trees, too. After you've planted, fold a 3-foot-square of landscape fabric in quarters and snip off the center point to leave about a 4-inch hole. Slip this fabric skirt over the plant and smooth it over the ground. Pin down the corners with soil staples or rocks. Berry plants can't sucker through this "no-weed" zone either, so use this tip for nonsuckering plants like highbush blueberries, gooseberries, currants, and bush cherries.

Put Your Berries Where Your Mouth Is

To save time *and* enjoy more berries, plant your berries and small fruits right next to your house or driveway. That way, you won't have to hike out to the back 40 to see if they're ripe or to pick a handful.

Sound unattractive? No way! Many berries and small fruits are very good-looking plants. Some have pretty, fragrant flowers and vibrant fall color. All you need to do is think of edibles instead of ornamentals when you plan your landscape. Here are some suggestions to get you started.

Groundcovers. Strawberries fill in fast as a groundcover on sunny slopes. Mix in some pink-flowered ones for interest.

Flower beds. Alpine strawberries are as pretty an edging plant as anyone could want, and they bear all summer. Try alternating yellow and red cultivars. Red currants drip clusters of eye-catching red jewels in season.

Vines for shade. Grape- or kiwi-covered arbors make for cool outdoor sitting.

Foundation shrubs. Blueberries and highbush cranberries look wonderful behind smaller plants. They offer spring flowers, tasty eats, and fall color—things many foundation shrubs don't rise to.

Blueberries and other acid-loving berries are perfect bedmates for azaleas and rhododendrons. Here, midhigh and lowbush blueberries and ground-hugging lingonberries, with their delicate pinkish spring flowers and intense red fall foliage, are a nice foil for the showier ornamentals. Add a generous sprinkling of spring bulbs to poke through the lingonberries, and you have a bed pretty enough for any front yard.

Plant Some Shady Characters

If you want a few berries and don't have any full sun, don't despair. Try planting some black raspberries or wineberries where they'll receive filtered sun all day. (They even thrive under black walnut trees!) The plants will sprawl but the berries will be large and extra juicy.

Don't Sweat It–Plant a New Strawberry Patch Every Few Years

Strawberry plants are cheap; your time isn't. If you have space for two strawberry beds in you garden, try this simple approach.

Plant a new patch. Every third spring, buy new plants and plant a brand-new strawberry patch. Put it as far away from the old patch as possible to reduce the chance of pests and diseases packing up and moving on over. Harvest the berries as they ripen.

Recycle the old patch. Bid the old patch goodbye as soon as it finishes bearing that same year. Till the old plants under or mow them short and spread mulch over them to kill them.

Plant Junebearers for Jam Sessions; Everbearers for Nibbling

Sun-warmed strawberries are one of the biggest pleasures of the home garden. But too many or too few berries aren't much fun. Select the right plants to start with to tailor your harvest.

Junebearers. These are the overachievers of the strawberry family. They make lots of runners and lots of berries all at once. If that's what you want, you just can't beat Junebearers. Choose a cultivar with multiple disease resistance.

Everbearers. These produce a few runners and a modest quantity of berries spread over the whole season. Pick an old-fashioned cultivar like 'Quinalt' or go with alpine strawberries. "Day-neutral" cultivars are not a good low-maintenance choice.

Give Crowded Strawberries a Haircut and a Dose of Old News

If you grow Junebearers, your plants may seem bent on crowding themselves out of existence. Compensate for this self-destructive trait by revving up your power mower for a once-a-year, done-before-you-know-it renovation.

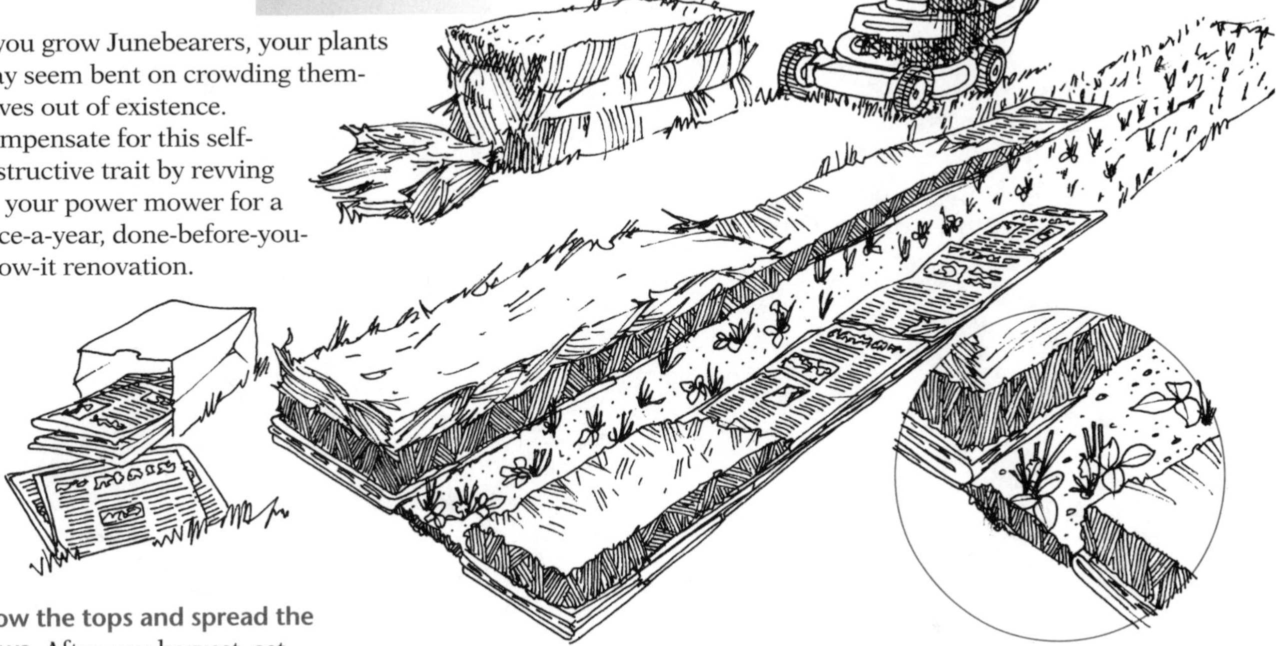

Mow the tops and spread the news. After you harvest, set your mower at about 2 inches, snap on the grass catcher, and chop off all those leaves. Dump the clippings into the compost.

Cover the edges of the bed with sections of newspaper at least four sheets thick. Leave just a 6- to 10-inch-wide strip of mowed plants uncovered down the middle of the bed. Hold the paper down with handfuls of soil or compost.

Layer on compost, then mulch and water. Shovel a ½-inch layer of compost over the chopped-off plants in the unpapered strip. Then cover the whole bed (paper and compost-covered strip) with 2 inches of loose straw mulch. Finally, give the whole bed a good soaking, and you're done until next year.

THEY AIN'T CALLED STRAWBERRIES FOR NOTHING

Beat the strawberry-patch-turned-weed-patch problem before it rears its ugly head. Mulch around newly planted strawberries with 4 to 6 inches of straw or other organic mulch. The straw also keeps your berries clean and ready to pop into your mouth. But weed-deterring mulch may prevent runners from rooting and filling in the row. If so, open a little hole in the mulch with your fingers where you want a new plant. Poke the end of a runner down against the soil in the hole. Nature will take it from there.

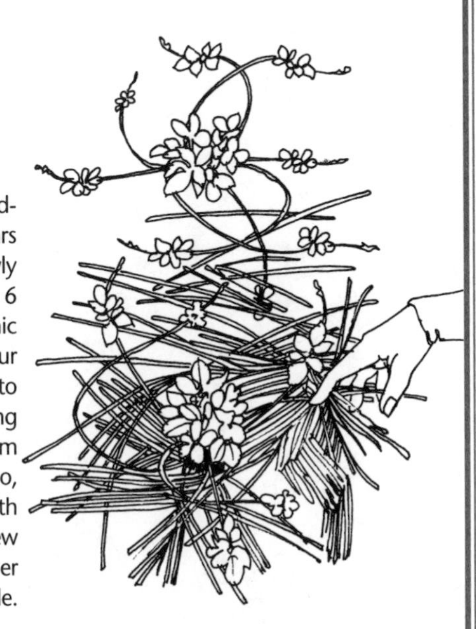

Teach Your Blackberries and Raspberries to Stay Put

Blackberries and raspberries make great backyard fruit crops. Not only is their fruit delicious and abundant, the plants are also easy to grow. But they are generally thorny and can spread rampantly. Here are two things to do to make them welcome residents in your yard.

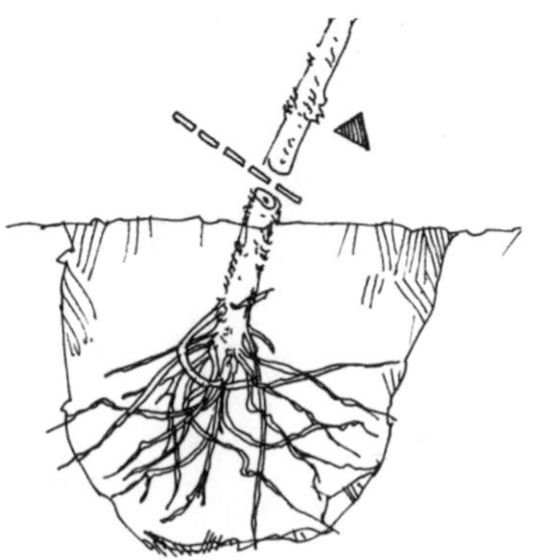

Plant bareroot brambles in early spring. When planting, set the dormant canes 1 to 2 inches deeper than they were grown. Then cut them back to 1 inch from the ground. Dispose of the prunings, and you'll have less chance of disease problems later.

Give them enough room to start with. If you don't give blackberries and raspberries room at planting time, you'll curse them later as you try to squeeze around the plants to pick or mow. Plant raspberries and thorny blackberries 3 feet apart in a row. Plant thornless blackberries 6 feet apart in a row. Leave at least a 5-foot aisle between rows so you'll be able to get between them to mow and pick.

Show your brambles who's in charge. Curb the spreading tendencies of raspberries and blackberries right from the start. To make sure you end up with a manageable row, not an impenetrable scratchy patch, draw an imaginary 1-foot-wide strip with your new berries right down the middle. Mow the area outside that 1-foot-wide row regularly (seed it with slow-growing grass or let nature provide). Every time you mow you'll effortlessly nip off any suckers that sprout outside their designated row. No stooping, no sweat.

Tame a Wild or Out-of-Hand Berry Patch

Do you like to take a walk on the wild side and pick some berries on a summer afternoon? But you only wish the patch had more edge and less unreachable middle? Well, make some more edges! Next winter spend an afternoon cutting some 6-foot-wide paths right through the center of the patch with your power mower and/or some long handled loppers. (If it's a really big patch, rent a brush cutter or hire a farmer with a mower that will chop up the old canes at the same time.) Mow your new paths periodically to keep them open if you like, and enjoy next summer's berry picking.

Take the "Ouch!" Out of Picking Bramble Fruits

If a thorny embrace isn't your idea of a good time, try one or more of these painless ideas.

Go thorn-free. Select cultivars with no or few thorns and avoid a sticky issue. Try 'Chester' or 'Navaho' for thorn-free blackberries. Boysenberries, Loganberries, and Youngberries all come in thornless versions, too. Look for 'Canby' or 'Mammoth Red' for almost thornless red raspberry harvests.

Stake it to 'em. Black raspberries and thornless blackberries don't spread much but stay in neat clumps. This is not to say they still don't try to reach out and grab you. Pound a metal fence post in right next to each clump. Tie the canes to the post with a sturdy loop of twine every year in late winter.

Round 'em up. Red and yellow raspberries spread underground to make a solid row (or patch if you let them). Avoid scratches from nodding canes with the easy-to-build V-trellis shown above.

1. To make this V-trellis, pound pairs of 8-foot metal fence posts into the ground at an angle. They should be about 1½ to 2 feet apart at the bottom, 3½ feet apart at the top, and 6 feet high. You'll need one pair at each end of your row for rows up to 30 feet long.

2. Add a sturdy anchor post at either end of the row.

3. Use wire or plastic bailing twine to string the trellis. You'll need two wires, one 2½ feet and one 4½ feet from the ground.

4. Every year, cut off the canes that have fruited and tie the remaining canes loosely to the trellis in late winter. See "Easy Pruning for Raspberries and Blackberries" on page 156.

Pick Fast with a 2-Handed Picker

A sawed-off gallon-size plastic jug is just the thing for a hands-free picking bucket. Use scissors to remove the top, leaving the handle intact. Slip your belt through the handle, fasten it, and voilà—an instant picking aid you can't drop or kick over.

Pick firm berries such as blueberries and gooseberries right into the jug. Soft berries such as raspberries will crush if they are piled more than four deep. Put a pint or half-pint container in the bottom of the jug, and swap it for an empty one whenever it's full.

Easy Pruning for Raspberries and Blackberries

Two or three short pruning sessions a year (depending on what kind of berries you have) is all it takes to tame your brambles. In return, you get easier picking with fewer scratches, and your plants will stay healthier.

Simple Summer Snips

▲ **Cut off used-up canes.** Bramble canes die after they make their summer fruit crop. So, after you harvest those last few fruits, pull out your trusty clippers. Clip off all the canes that had fruit on them as close to the ground as possible. *Don't* cut off canes that haven't made fruit yet; they hold next year's berries-in-the-making. *Fall berry pickers take note:* If your red or yellow raspberries offer you fruit in late summer and fall, *don't* cut off those canes. They still have a summer crop of berries in them.

▼ **Pinch back thornless blackberries and black raspberries.** Left alone, these types grow long, arching canes. Pinch them back when they're young and you'll get more fruit and suffer fewer entanglements. When the canes are about waist-high, snip off the top few inches. The clipped canes will grow many side branches that will bear lots of fruit next summer.

Early Spring Mulch Renewal

If you are keeping your berries in bounds by mowing on either side of the rows, there is just one place weeds can raise their ugly heads: right in your berry row (where you least want them). Spend a few minutes after you've pruned your raspberries and blackberries adding some mulch to slow down these weeds.

Start by sprinkling a bit of compost on the row if you have some to spare. Then work 4 to 6 inches of loose organic mulch in around the canes. Straw is good for mulching berries; so are the rough wood chips you can often get free from road crews.

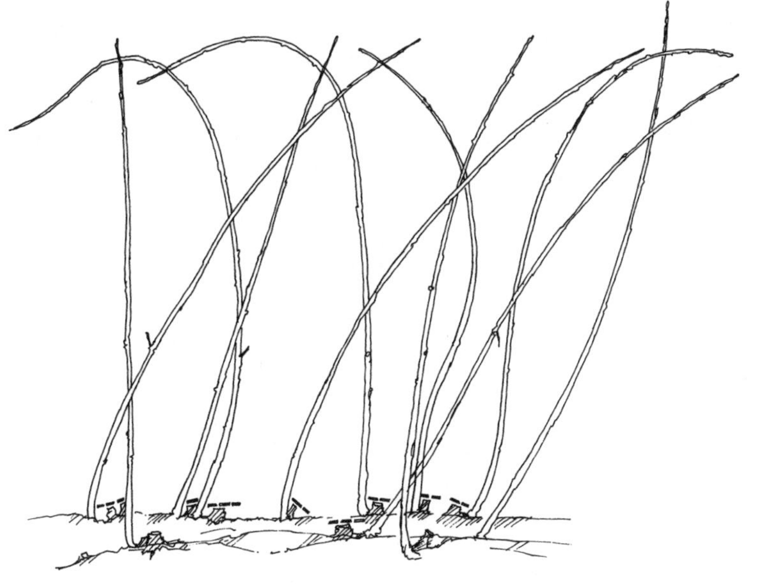

Late-Winter Thinning

On a nice day in late winter or early spring, spend a few minutes with your clippers in your berry patch. Start by cutting off any fruited-out canes you didn't remove after harvest last summer. Then cut off any skinny or bent-over canes. Finally, follow the appropriate set of instructions at right.

▲ **Red and yellow raspberries and thorny blackberries.** Thin the remaining canes to leave four canes per foot of row. Don't snip off the tips of the canes unless they were winter-killed.

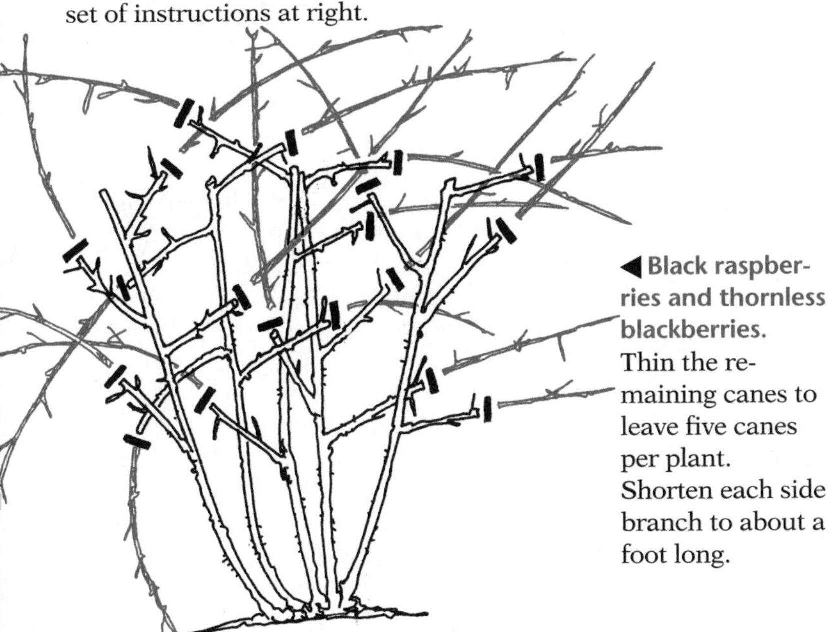

◀ **Black raspberries and thornless blackberries.** Thin the remaining canes to leave five canes per plant. Shorten each side branch to about a foot long.

Give Berry-Robbing Birds the Brush-Off

After weeks of watching them ripen, the last thing you want is bird-pecked berries. Try these tips for keeping the berries whole—and wholly for you.

Location. Plant near a door or path you use frequently. Human traffic discourages birds better than a scarecrow.

Tabby tracks. Entice a cat to lounge about in the berry patch. A puss in full view is a much more effective bird deterrent than a clever hunter hiding in the bushes.

Netting. Lightweight plastic netting keeps out birds (they will pick through it if it's too close to the fruit, though). Use a large piece and anchor it all around with boards or rocks so the winged thieves can't sneak under and have a feast. Or gather the edges around the base of a bush and tie it shut like a sack. Remove for harvest, then replace until next picking time.

Cage. Beat the netting blues by building a wooden cage frame with a door around the bush(es). Staple wire mesh or netting over it—it will last for years.

Train Grapes High and Let Gravity Do the Work

You can make this workhorse of a trellis from 4 × 4 timbers as shown here. To make a longer-lasting one, you'll need three 8-foot lengths of metal or PVC pipe, and two 90-degree elbows to connect them. To erect it, connect the pipes with the elbows, dig two 2-foot-deep postholes, and then set up the trellis.

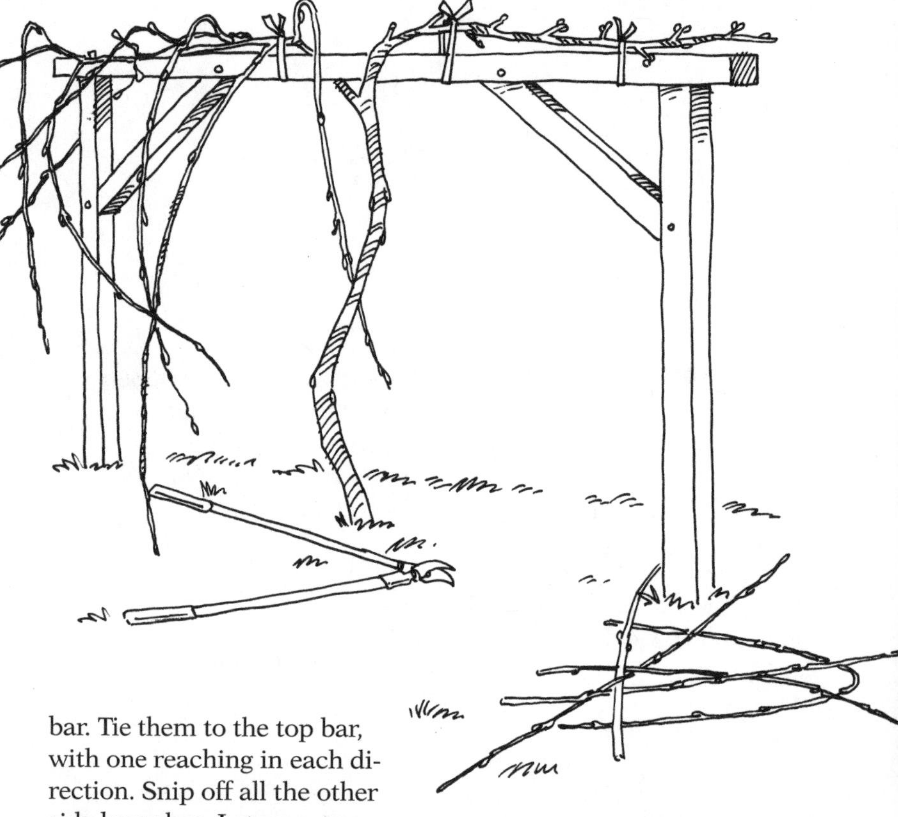

Gardeners often try to convince grapes to grow up a fence trellis, but vines don't always grow up. This means you spend your spare time tucking and tying stray shoots up all summer long. Use the following simple method and spend your summer lying down and sipping grapeade instead.

Getting Started

1. **Build a sturdy frame.** You can build the long-lasting, one-vine trellis shown here in just a few hours.

2. **Grow a tall trunk.** Plant your vine under the middle of the trellis. (Choose a hardy, disease-resistant cultivar suited to your area.) Tie a length of twine to the center of the top bar and tie the other end loosely near the base of the vine. Let the strongest shoot climb the twine. Remove any other shoots that form. Snip off the tip of the chosen shoot when it reaches the top bar.

3. **Grow two main branches.** Lots of side branches will sprout after you cut off the tip of the upright shoot. Choose two sturdy ones near the top bar. Tie them to the top bar, with one reaching in each direction. Snip off all the other side branches. Let your two chosen branches grow until they reach the ends of the top bar. Then clip off the tips.

Growing Happily Ever After

1. **Do nothing all spring and summer.** As new shoots grow, their weight will pull them gently downward. Sit back and watch the fruit swell. Come fall, pick and enjoy. (And tell your friends how hard you worked to raise those grapes.)

2. **Do a winter haircut.** Get out your clippers on a sunny day in late winter and spend a few minutes getting your vine ready for spring. Check the ties that hold the main branches to the top bar and loosen or replace them as needed. Cut off any shoots that sprouted from the trunk below the top bar. Then cut all the hanging shoots back to leave two buds on each (the stubs will be about 4 inches long).

3. **Continue to grow happily ever after.** Alternate summer watching and winter pruning every year. As the vines age, cut off a few of the oldest stubs each winter to thin things out.

Converting An Old Vine

If you already have a grapevine, it's not hard to change it over to this training method.

1. **Check the support system.** If your vine already has a sturdy trellis with a wire 5 to 6 feet high, you can use that. If not, build one over the vine as described earlier.

2. **Hack it back.** Grapevines are very forgiving, so get out a saw and some clippers on a nice day in late winter and have at it. Cut your vine back to the top of the current trunk. Or, if the current trunk is badly twisted or lying on the ground, cut it off a few inches above the soil line. Next summer train one of the new shoots as you would a newly planted vine.

Sprinkle Sulfur for Great Blueberries

Blueberries are well known as acid-soil lovers. If your soil isn't very acid (pH 5.0 or higher), by nature your blueberries may suffer. Sprinkle a handful of elemental sulfur under each plant every spring to make sure things stay nice for your plants.

Oh-So-Simple Pruning for Blueberries

You can harvest good crops of blueberries for years without ever having to prune them. But, if you'd like to boost your crop a bit or think a bit of pruning is warranted, here's what to do.

Highbush and mid-high blueberries. Cut off a few branches that are 5 or more years old at ground level each winter. Also remove any dead branches or ones that are leaning severely.

Lowbush blueberries. These ground-hugging plants spread by suckers. The easiest way to prune them is to divide your patch in half and mow one half right down to the ground every winter. Alternate halves each year and you'll always have one patch busily growing back while the other patch is productively fruiting.

Plant an Edible Hedge and Throw Away Your Hedge Clippers

Need a hedge, but hate the repeated shearing it needs to stay neat? Wish you had room for some berry bushes, but can't figure out where to fit them in? Solve two problems with one low-maintenance solution: Replace your hedge with a closely spaced row of berries. Gooseberries or currants make a nice low hedge; thorny cultivars discourage trespassers. Blueberries or bush cherries make a taller, informal hedge. Raspberries and blackberries make a great narrow screen if you tie them to a fence.

Keep your hedge well back from driveways and sidewalks so dropped fruit won't land on the pavement. You may want to consult with your neighbors if the hedge will butt up against their property—offer them half the fruits, or plant away from the line and keep a mowed path along the actual property line to beat back wandering suckers.

CHAPTER 16

Herbs

Herbs the Low-Maintenance Way

HERBS ARE NATURALS in your low-maintenance garden. Whatever your yard is like—hot and dry, or moist and shady—there are tough herbs just waiting to go to work for you. And herbs don't just stand around looking great—nothing puts life into food like your own freshly snipped herbs.

So stop struggling with finicky plants and set your sights on herbs instead. This chapter gives you some no-nonsense tips for succeeding with herbs and suggests specific herbs for challenging landscape sites. You'll also find suggestions for where to plant herbs for minimum maintenance and easy ways to start your own plants.

No-Nonsense Tips for Growing Herbs

It's hard to imagine plants that are easier to grow than herbs. All they ask for is six or more hours of sun per day and average to good garden soil, and they're on their way. Hardy perennial herbs, like garlic chives, mint, and thyme, are probably the easiest herbs to grow. Once planted, they come back year after year and eventually establish large attractive clumps. Annual herbs must be replanted each year but are well worth the effort. Use these tips to get your herb garden off to a great start.

Start with transplants. If you only need one or two plants (which is plenty for most herbs), transplants are your best bet. They'll have a head start on weeds, and you won't have to spend time thinning seedlings.

Well-drained soil means no-fuss herbs. If there's one key to growing healthy herbs, it's providing them with well-drained soil. Whatever type of soil you have, before you plant turn plenty of compost or other organic material into the planting site. Organic matter will improve drainage in waterlogged clay soils and hold water in sandy ones. You can also grow your herbs in raised beds or containers.

Hold the manure. Herbs don't need rich soil or fertilizer to grow well. In fact, too-rich soil just encourages rampant, less flavorful growth. A little compost mulch every few years is all the feeding most herbs require.

Use your herbs. Regular trimming keeps new tender growth coming, so clip all season. If you have more herbs than you can cook with, use the aromatic clippings as mulch.

Give perennials a fall haircut. Regular harvesting should take care of all the pruning perennial herbs need. If they look scraggly at the end of the season, cut them back by about a third and remove old or dead wood. Check again in spring and remove any dead wood. After three to five years, many perennial herbs lose vigor and should be divided or replaced. See "Simple Steps for Propagating Herbs" on page 164 for ways to divide herbs—it's a good way to increase your plantings fast.

It Pays to Be Choosy When It Comes to Culinary Herbs

Not all herb plants are created equal. Use these suggestions so you don't get burned with a tasteless look-alike.

Grow from seeds. Annual herbs are easy to grow from seed, and you can expect good results from most any seed packet. Growing perennials from seed is more of a gamble; in general, it's easier and more reliable to start with transplants. Don't try to grow tarragon or oregano from seeds at all since these seed-grown plants are usually flavorless.

Sniff before you buy. Put potential purchases to the rub-'n'-sniff test. Rub a leaf between your fingers; if it doesn't have a good, strong aroma like the herb you're looking for, don't waste your time and money on it. This test also works for seedlings: When you thin, leave the most fragrant plants.

Buy smart. For the best selection, look for specialty growers in your area. Or order from one of the many mail-order herb nurseries. See "Sources" on page 355 for a list.

Plant Herbs for Quick Problem-Spot Solutions

Herbs are tough plants you can turn to for solving landscape problems. For shady sites, try angelica, lemon balm, mint, and sweet cicely. Sweet woodruff and violets make super low-growing groundcovers in shady areas.

Many herbs, including sage, oregano, rosemary, lavender, santolina, and horehound, thrive in dry, sun-baked sites. Thymes make outstanding, colorful groundcovers in hot, dry conditions.

Herbs can provide quick-and-easy camouflage for eyesores, too. Hide an old tree stump with a planting of mint or cover a broken-down concrete wall with a cascade of thyme, for example.

Grow an Easy-Care, Elegant Herb Garden

A formal herb garden can take hours of fussing and trimming to keep it looking its best. With a little planning, you can keep all the elegance and eliminate all the work by trading in tightly clipped shapes for soft, natural ones. This garden features fragrant herbs that will stay neat and create waves of color with little or no pruning. To create your own fragrant refuge, select and arrange plants by height to create wavelike clumps.

This planting mixes annuals and perennials in a variety of heights and forms. Bee balm and yarrow provide a backdrop for the bench. Calendulas and garlic chives bloom under the birdbath, while rose geraniums, parsley, purple sage, lemon thyme, and piccola basil make a pleasant tapestry of color and form on the opposite side.

Don't Fuss with an Herb Garden, Grow Your Herbs with Vegetables

Why take care of two separate gardens when one will do? A super-easy way to grow annual herbs is to simply plant them in rows with your annual vegetables. There's room in most vegetable gardens for perennial herbs such as sage and chives, too: Plant them with your other perennial crops such as asparagus or rhubarb, away from the path of the tiller.

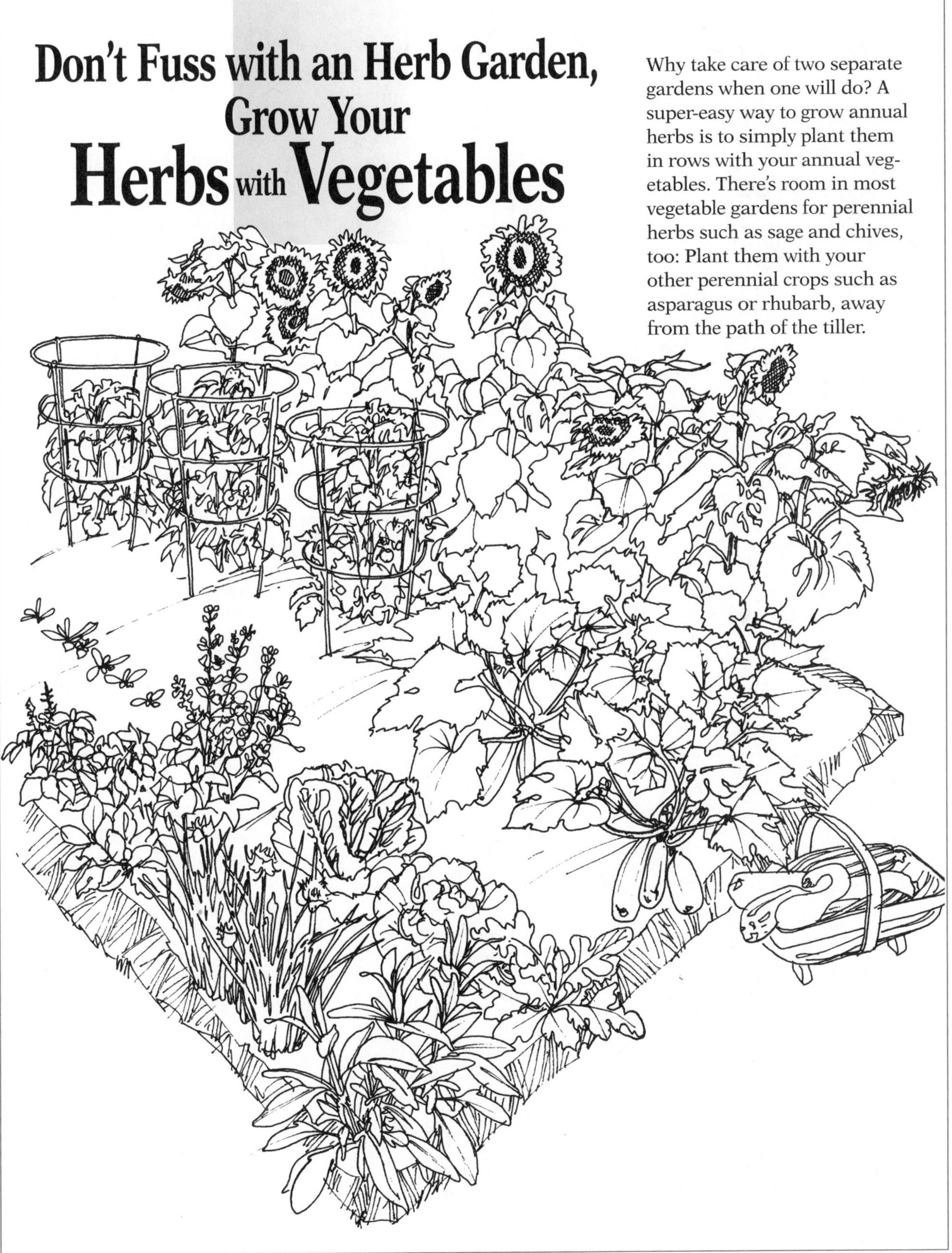

Plant a Drain Tile Herb Garden

Large ceramic drain tiles are great containers for herbs. Mix and match heights for a multi-tiered effect, or select all one height. Like any other type of container, they're a great way to grow herbs on a poorly drained site. Or consider planting invasive herbs such as mint in them to keep them out of everything else.

For best results, bury the base of each drain tile about 6 inches in the soil. For an easier and faster result with tiles under 1½ feet tall, just set the tiles directly on the soil. Be sure to level the site so each tile is stable.

Next, fill the tiles with potting mix and plant. Choose a mix designed for large containers or mix equal parts houseplant soil and perlite or vermiculite. Stir in a cup of compost per tile and water well to settle the potting mix. Leave 1 inch of headroom below the rim to make watering easy. Since containers dry out more quickly than in-ground plantings, water often so the mix never dries out. Monthly feeding with 2 tablespoons fish emulsion and 1 tablespoon seaweed per gallon of water will keep your drain tile garden growing strongly.

Simple Steps for Propagating Herbs

Propagating herbs is easy and rewarding, whether you need to divide a clump of herbs that's gotten too large or want to share a plant with a neighbor. For no-fuss propagation, stick to division and layering. Here's what you need to know to master these easy techniques.

Easy herb division. The best time to divide herbs is in early spring just before plants start to grow, but you can also wait until fall. To make replanting easier on your herbs, wait for a cloudy, windless day to work. Plants will be less stressed and will recover quickly. It helps to protect the newly divided plants from strong sunlight and provide extra water for a few days.

When you divide, dig up the entire clump with a garden fork or spade. Plants like oregano and mint form dense mats that are easiest to divide with a sharp shovel. For clump-forming herbs like chives, lift and water the clumps well. Then pull them apart with your hands and replant; each new clump should have three to five small bulbs to make a strong plant.

For an easy, no-dig approach to division, look for rooted sections around the edges of a

Easy Ways to Hold Onto Just-Picked Flavor

Stocking your kitchen with garden-fresh herbs for the winter doesn't have to take much of your precious time. Just use the tips below.

Strip the leaves later. Dry bunches of herbs through the season in a warm, dry place. Use rubber bands to bundle the bunches. Straightened-out paper clips make handy hangers for bundles. Stuff dry bunches of herbs into large airtight containers and label them. You can strip the herbs from the stalks in the fall when you have more time. To retain flavor, don't crumble the dried leaves until ready to use in cooking.

Make herb cubes for next-to-fresh flavor. Juicy leaves like basil freeze easier than they dry. Basil retains better flavor when it's frozen, too. To make herb cubes, puree leaves in the blender with enough water to make a slurry. Pour the slurry into ice cube trays and freeze. Pop out the cubes and store in plastic bags. Add herb cubes to soups and stews as needed.

Freeze leaves whole for fast flavor. If you're really short of time, strip leaves from stems, pack them in self-closing bags, and freeze. Be sure to label frozen herbs—they'll all look the same once they're frozen.

Use Your Car for Easy, One-Day Drying

Do you want dried herbs for winter without lots of effort? Pick a dry, sunny day when herbs are ready to pick. The best time of day to harvest is just after the morning dew has dried, but any time when the leaves are dry and clean is fine. Lay some newspaper in the back of your car. Spread the herbs on the newspaper, then cover them with another layer of newspaper. Close the car windows and let the sun do the rest. Herbs should be crackly dry by the end of the day.

To quickly mince herbs, put a handful of leaves in a teacup and snip them up with scissors. Or hold a bunch of herbs over a teacup in one hand and cut them up with the other.

clump, slice them off with a trowel, and pot them up or transplant them.

Layering. An easy way to root woody herbs like sage and lavender is to encourage them to form new roots through a process called layering. In early summer, select two or three branches near the base of the mother plant that are long enough to lay on the ground. Bend them over and strip the leaves off where the stems touch the soil. Press each stem firmly into the soil, anchor it with a U-shaped metal pin made from a piece of clothes hanger, and cover the pinned stem with soil. Keep the covering soil moist all season and you should have rooted plants to dig up, cut off the mother plant, and transplant in the fall.

Compost

Stooling or mound layering is a simple way to propagate woody herbs like lavender, rosemary, and thyme. Heap 3 to 5 inches of compost or loose soil over the crown of the herb in spring. Roots will sprout from the covered stems. After several weeks, when they are well rooted, gently brush away the mound of soil, cut the stems off, and plant each piece where you want a new plant.

Quick and Tasty Salads

Herbs look as good as they taste, so why hide them in the backyard? For an ornamental and edible salad bar right outside your door, try growing sage, garlic chives, basil, marjoram, tarragon, and other herbs next to greens like lettuce, chard, and arugula.

Edible flowers such as nasturtiums add color to the design—and your salads, too. To make your garden as convenient as it is attractive, choose a handy location, such as just outside the front door. That way you can easily step outside and harvest salad greens and herbs just minutes before mealtime.

Sit Back and Watch These Herbs Plant Themselves

Instead of direct seeding, thinning and fussing every year, let herbs replant themselves. Plant them once in an out-of-the-way place and each year let some of the flowers go to seed.

To get your reseeding patch started, wait until the soil warms up and prepare a seedbed outdoors where the plants are to grow. Then sow the seed and keep the area moist until the seeds pop up.

Each year, let some of the plants go to seed for a crop in fall and/or the following spring. Don't pile a lot of mulch over the seeds or they won't germinate when the weather cools off in late summer. This technique is also good for fussy herbs like angelica that only grow from just-ripened seed.

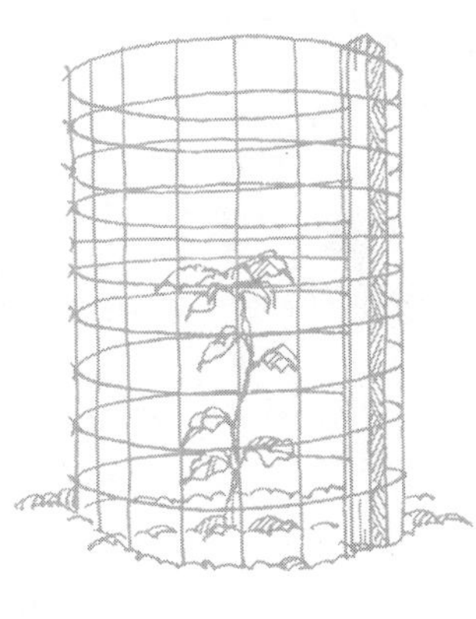

CHAPTER 17

Trellising and Training

Trellising and Training the Low-Maintenance Way

SPENDING THE TIME to trellis and train your vegetable crops doesn't sound much like low maintenance, but it's a case of a stitch in time saving nine. Trellising plants keeps the fruits off the ground and out of reach of sow bugs, ground beetles, and soil-dwelling fungi so you can harvest more and better vegetables with fewer plants. And because little of the harvest is wasted, you don't have to spend as much money on seed or as much time planting it. Trellised crops also take up less space in the garden, and that means less digging, weeding, watering, mulching, and fertilizing. Insect and disease problems are readily visible at eye level, too, and handpicking pests is less of a strain. Finally, picking vegetables is faster and easier when you don't have to bend to do it.

Fortunately, you don't have to spend much time or money to build all the trellises your garden needs. You'll find a variety of easy-to-make trellises in this chapter that will let you start your garden growing vertically in a matter of minutes.

Make a Trellis in 10 Minutes with Garden Netting

◀ **Make a sturdy A-frame trellis.** Heavier crops like pole beans, melons, cucumbers, pumpkins, and squash need an extra-sturdy trellis so the weight of their vines doesn't cause the netting to sag or the stakes to lean. An A-frame trellis made of wood stakes works fine. For the ends, use two stakes joined by crosspieces at the top and near the bottom, as shown. Join the two ends by nailing a crosspiece across the top. Hammer the stakes into the ground, then drape the netting over the crosspiece and anchor it with rocks, bricks, or U-shaped wire. (Or, for a neater look, drape the netting before attaching the crosspieces, as shown.)

Plastic or nylon garden netting is a godsend for low-maintenance gardeners. Peas, cucumbers, and pole beans, which climb by twining or with tendrils, will scramble up the netting with no help from you. For peas, 1-inch mesh is fine; use 4- to 6-inch mesh for larger vegetables like pole beans, melons, cucumbers, and squash. Use rocks, bricks, or U-shaped wire anchors to hold the bottom of the net in place. When the crop is finished, just pull up these trellises and move the netting elsewhere in the garden. Or roll and store it for next season.

▶ **Ten-minute pea trellis.** Pea vines will quickly cover both sides of this foolproof trellis. To make it, all you do is use a staple gun to attach netting to the top of two 5- or 6-foot tall tomato stakes or 2 × 2s. Then hammer the stakes into the soil. You can also secure the netting with twist ties or plastic-coated wire.

Bend It Here, Bend It There to Make a Simple Zigzag Trellis

This simple zigzag fence trellis is a good solution for cucumbers, squash, gourds, and melons. You can plant on both sides of the trellis, so it saves space in the garden. It also allows better air circulation than two parallel trellises.

You'll need an 8-foot section of stiff garden-fence wire that will allow a 2 × 4 grid to stand without sagging. Although fencing is usually sold in rolls, your building-supply store may be willing to sell you a smaller section.

1. **Bend.** Wearing boots and using a board as a straightedge, bend the 8-foot length of fencing in half.

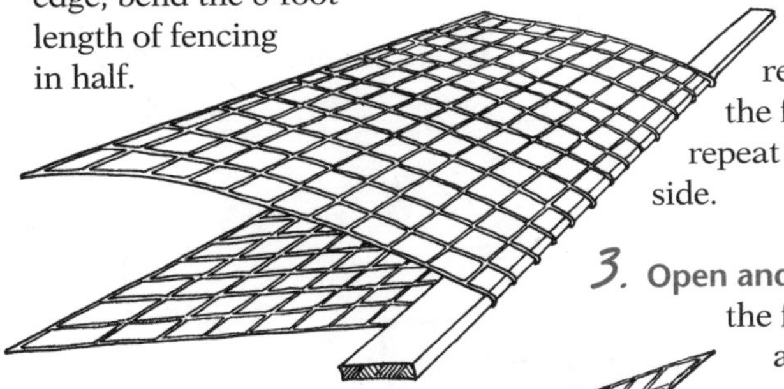

2. **Bend again.** Again using the board, bend back a quarter of the fence in the opposite direction. Then flip the fence over and repeat with the other side.

3. **Open and install.** Open the four panels into a wide zigzag and stand the trellis in the garden. Anchor it with stakes and plastic-coated wire at the ends.

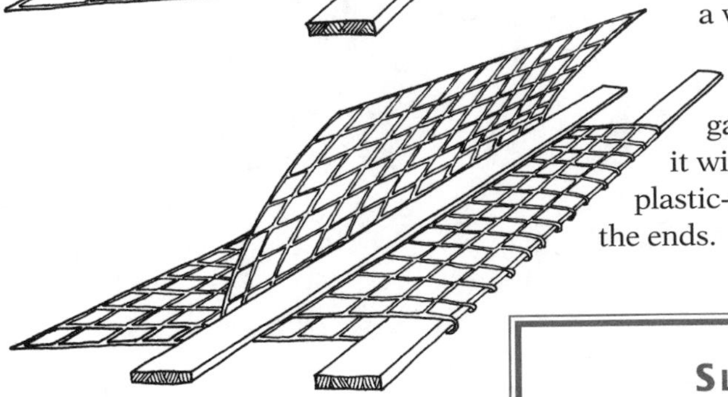

Sling Up Your Crops with Panty Hose

Support heavy fruit like ripening melons in slings of recycled panty hose. Cut off the legs of the panty hose, then cut each leg in half. Gently tuck the squash, pumpkin, or melon into the stretchable fabric, then loosely knot the sling to the trellis, allowing enough room for the fruit to grow and expand.

Build a Simple Lattice Trellis

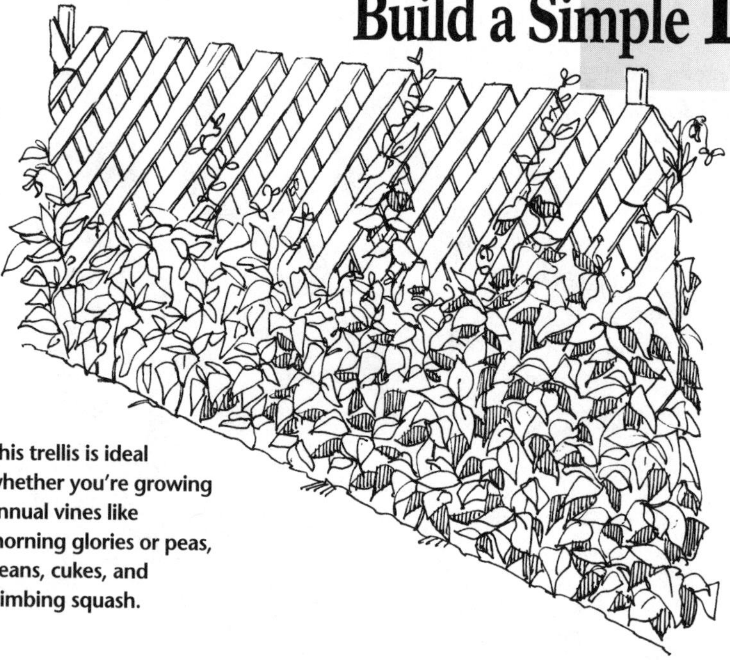

This trellis is ideal whether you're growing annual vines like morning glories or peas, beans, cukes, and climbing squash.

For a simple trellis that's as attractive as it is functional, start with a 4-foot-wide section of lattice (available at home centers and building-supply stores) and two metal or wooden fence posts. (Lightweight stapled lattice is strong enough to support all but the heaviest garden crops.) To erect it, just set the posts and attach the lattice—either with nails, staples, or lengths of plastic-coated wire. Since lattice casts shade, keep it on the north side of the garden to avoid blocking sun to other crops, or use it to provide light shade for summer lettuces.

TAKE-IT-EASY TIP!

Plan Before You Build

No matter what kind of trellis you decide on, you'll save time and aggravation if you plan before you build. Once you have a design in mind, check that scrap wood pile, or plan a trip to the building-supply store for materials. Don't forget to consider how you'll attach the netting or wire to the frame.

Make sure your trellis will be sturdy enough so it won't collapse under the weight of a heavy crop. An A-frame can be freestanding or anchored by its legs in the ground. A short vertical trellis can be anchored by sticking its legs in the soil. A 3-foot length of metal pipe, driven 6 to 12 inches into the ground, provides backbone to a tall vertical trellis.

Use Found Objects for Quick-Fix Trellises

Everything from lawn chairs to gates can be used to support a vining crop—plants aren't particular. Here are a few out-of-the-ordinary instant "trellises" that enterprising gardeners use.

The coffee-can prop. Get good fruit off the ground by setting it on top of overturned coffee cans. This works well with pumpkins and melons.

Bedtime story. Scrounge around for a child's outgrown "bed tent." Once the fabric is removed, the plastic framework makes a quick, lightweight trellis for the garden. Anchor the bottom with U-shaped metal pins, then attach strings or netting.

TV time. Plant a 4- to 6-foot-long metal or plastic pipe 1 foot deep in the ground, then slip an old TV antenna in the top. Pole beans, limas, or gourds can easily climb the pole and stretch out on the tines of the antenna.

Don't Train and Tie Tomatoes, Cage Them

Tomato cages eliminate the tedious time spent staking, tying, and training tomatoes. But store-bought cages are flimsy and prone to toppling. Here's a stable, long-lasting cage you can make with concrete-reinforcing wire, available at building-supply stores.

1. **Cut.** Wearing sturdy gloves, use heavy bolt cutters to cut an 8-foot length of concrete-reinforcing wire. Cut off the bottom wire to leave prongs for support in the soil.

2. **Roll.** Roll the wire into a cage and wire the sides together using plastic-coated wire or the ends of the reinforcing wire.

3. **Install.** To anchor the cage over planted tomatoes, push the bottom prongs firmly into the soil. One or two stakes attached on either side will lend added support to keep the cage from toppling under heavy fruit loads.

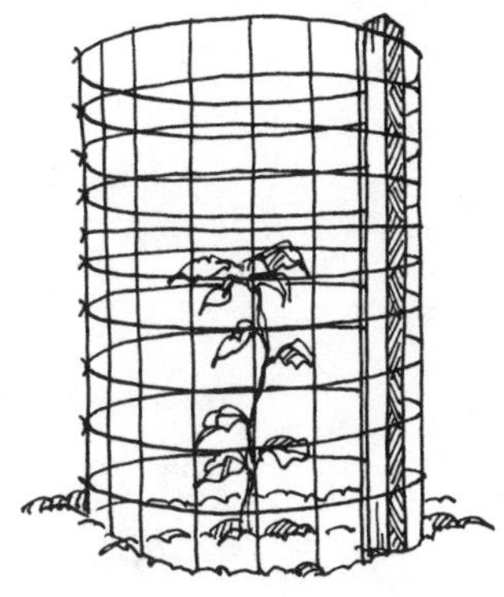

For a quick and easy tomato trellis, lay an expandable aluminum or wooden laundry rack on its side, pull it out, and tap in a stake at each end to make sure it stays open. Then set tomatoes between the Xs. The framework of the rack will corral the vines, and the top bar (once the side of the rack) will hold the tomatoes off the ground.

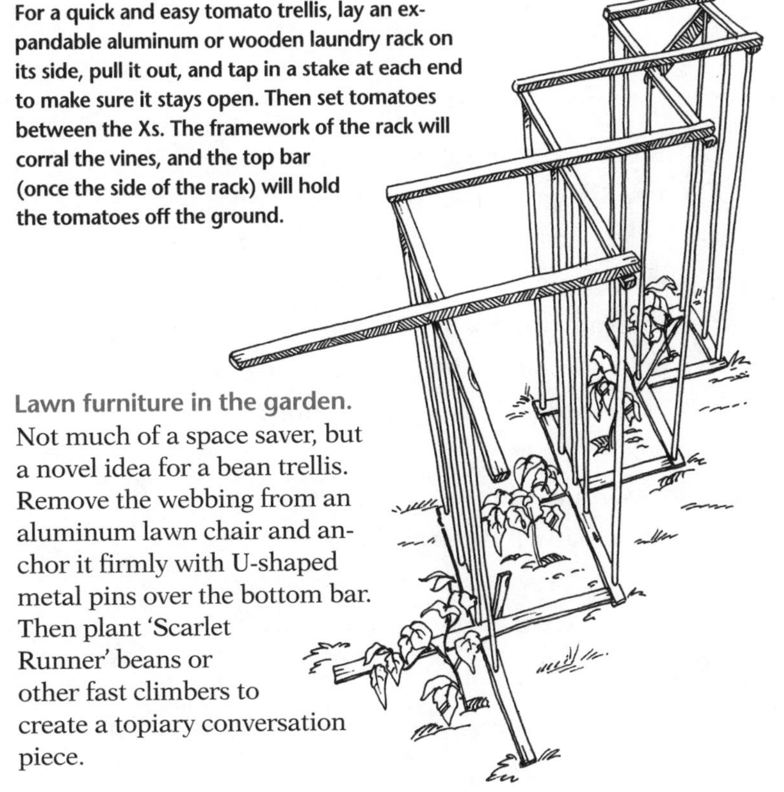

Lawn furniture in the garden. Not much of a space saver, but a novel idea for a bean trellis. Remove the webbing from an aluminum lawn chair and anchor it firmly with U-shaped metal pins over the bottom bar. Then plant 'Scarlet Runner' beans or other fast climbers to create a topiary conversation piece.

Chapter 18

Harvesting

Make the Most of What You Pick

Stretch Your Harvest with Season Extenders

Become a Quicker Picker

Use Basic Tools as Handy Harvest Helpers

Smart Tips for Handling Non-Prime Produce

Quick Tricks in the Kitchen

Stretch Your Storage Time

Containers and Wraps That Make Food Last

Give Your Fresh Veggies Fresh Air

Just-Right Harvesting Guide

Harvesting the Low-Maintenance Way

A BIG PART of hassle-free harvesting actually happens months ahead of time, when you plant your garden. For example, at planting time you could choose cultivars that are ready to pick at different times, so you don't have to harvest everything at once. But once it's time to pick, a little planning and organization go a long way toward speeding up the harvest.

The pages that follow include ideas for quick picking, as well as pointers on how and when to harvest for peak flavor. And just in case you have to harvest early, or a few crops slip past their prime before you can get to them, you'll find suggestions for fast, tasty ways to prepare non-prime produce.

Good Timing Helps You Make the Most of What You Pick

Harvesting right can be one of the most time-saving things you can do in your garden. Not only will you make the most of your gardening efforts by picking produce when it tastes the best, but letting your harvest get out of control always means extra work. And cleaning up rotten fruit, pulling bolted plants, and hauling waste to the compost pile is unpleasant work at best.

Harvesting when weather conditions favor good flavor is an easy way to make sure you get the most from what you pick. Because heat and strong sunlight make plants lose water, your produce will be the most succulent if you harvest when the weather is cool and not too bright—in the morning or evening, or on a cloudy day. As an added plus, produce that's harvested during the cooler parts of the day is cooler, so it will chill faster when refrigerated and stay fresh longer.

Try to harvest when the plants are dry so you don't inadvertently carry diseases through the garden. (Disease-causing fungi spread from plant to plant through the garden in water droplets.)

Some Don't Like It Hot

Some crops can't take prolonged heat; it ruins their taste. Vegetables that are touchy about heat include broccoli, cauliflower, lettuce, peas, and radishes. Plan to pick them if a week or more of hot weather—temperatures higher than about 80°F—is about to set in.

Warm temperatures cause them to bolt, or send up a flower stalk. Generally it's best to send crops that have bolted directly to the compost pile. If you take the time to bring them into the kitchen, you'll find that radishes grown in too much hot weather are very hot, while bolted broccoli and cauliflower will no longer have the crunchy heads they're grown for. Bolted lettuce leaves are bitter.

Set Your Picking Priorities

Good flavor can be fleeting; some crops pass their prime nearly overnight, while others stay stable for a week or two. If you are in a time crunch, first check the fruits and vegetables that won't wait, then the ones that are more patient. If you're not sure what crops most need your attention, check the "Crop Harvesting Schedule" on this page.

You'll find harvesting at the right time means less waste—and that's good news for your plants and for your wallet.

Crop Harvesting Schedule

When to Harvest	Crops
Daily	Beans, green and filet Beets Blackberries Corn Cucumbers Peas Raspberries Zucchini
Weekly	Eggplants Leeks Melons Peppers Tomatoes
As Needed	Beans, dry Carrots Brussels sprouts Kale Parsnips Potatoes Winter squash

Stretch Out Your Harvest with Simple Season Extenders

It takes just a bit of added effort to coax an extra-long harvest from many plants. What's in it for you? Sometimes weeks of harvest from plants you'd otherwise have to replace.

To get more from lettuce and other greens, for example, just remove tender outer leaves as you need them, leaving the rest of the plant to continue growing. When you harvest broccoli and cabbage, leave a few inches of stalk and a few lower leaves to encourage the plant to produce sideshoots—they'll be smaller but just as edible.

Oh-So-Simple Frost Protection

Protecting plants from an early frost is another way to extend your season and it doesn't have to take much more than a few minutes of your time. Providing temporary frost protection is a good way to buy time if the crop isn't ready to pick or you just don't have time to harvest. Often, a killing frost is followed by several weeks of warmer weather, so you may only have to protect plants for a night or two to extend the season by several weeks.

The quickest method is to cover the plants with sheets, blankets, or plastic on nights when frost threatens. It's primitive, but it works. Of course, you'll want to keep lightweight covers from blowing away by anchoring loose corners with rocks or bricks, or by resting dead branches over the top. Just be sure not to smash the plants in your efforts to save them. Avoid crushing especially delicate plants by placing a tomato cage over them before throwing on the cloth or plastic. Use clothespins to clip the cover to the framework.

Another method is to make a tent over a grouping of plants, using the same tent-making technique you perfected as a child: Tie a clothesline to supports on either end of the grouping—garden stakes or the backs of lawn chairs will do. Then throw a blanket, tarp, or other covering over the clothesline and anchor the corners with rocks.

For an easy but more permanent solution to frost and cold, cover cool-season vegetables like beets and greens with a 6-inch layer of loose straw or leaves. You'll have fresh produce into winter.

Become a Quicker Picker

Take a few moments during a post-planting lull to get organized. This way, once crops are ready, you can make the most out of every harvesting minute. Think about ways you can save steps and handle your produce fewer times. Here are some proven shortcuts to get you started; see how many more you can come up with.

Slip into your shoes. Keep an old pair of slip-on shoes near the door so you don't waste valuable picking time hunting for footwear. Kick them off on your way back in so you don't have to clean dirt off the floor.

Pack while you pick. Carry along plastic bags and containers and pack the produce while you're in the garden. When you get to the kitchen, put the goods directly into the refrigerator. For more storage ideas, see "Containers and Wraps that Make Food Last" on page 178.

Chill in the garden. If you'll be in the garden for more than half an hour, take along an ice chest and chill peas, corn, broccoli,

Use **Basic Tools** as Handy Harvest Helpers

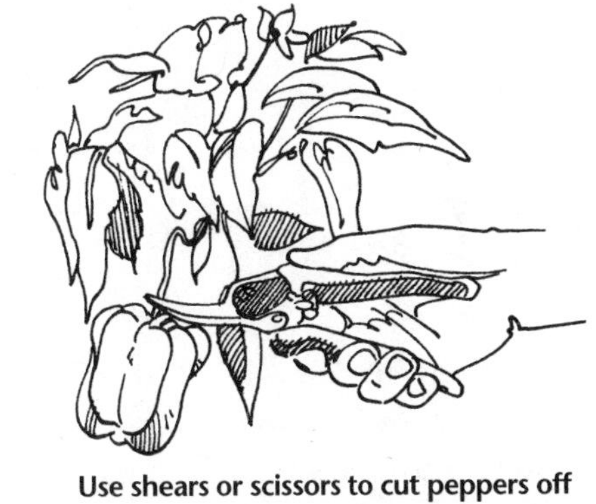

Use shears or scissors to cut peppers off the plant when you harvest. Yanking at the fruit isn't just frustrating and time-consuming; it also damages the plant because it leads to broken stems and disturbed roots.

When it comes to tools, the fewer the better. You don't want to feel like a one-man band clattering your way to the garden. For most picking jobs, your hands are sufficient—you may want to wear gloves when harvesting crops that are scratchy or smelly though.

Take along a knife for harvesting thick-stalked crops like broccoli and cabbage, as well as leafy crops like lettuce. Use scissors or pruning shears to cut the stems of peppers, okra, and other crops that don't pull off easily. If you'll be harvesting potatoes and other root crops, carry a spade or garden fork; if the soil is dry, you'll make the job easier by moistening it slightly before digging. If you have tree fruit to pick, consider investing in a long-handled fruit picker to save you from struggling with ladders. See "Pick Fast with a 2-Handed Picker" on page 155 to learn how to make your own picking tool.

A sharp knife makes it easy to harvest lettuce, whether you're taking individual leaves or the entire plant. A pocket knife or an old, but still sharp, kitchen knife is also fine for harvesting broccoli, cabbage, or cauliflower.

and delicate greens and fruits; otherwise, they'll fade fast.

Sort the good from the bad. Carry an extra bucket for damaged fruits and vegetables, and toss them into it as you pick them. By sorting the good from the bad right away, you don't have to touch each piece again in the kitchen.

Clean up outside. Wash greens or produce you plan to eat right away while outside to prevent a mess in the kitchen. Fill a bucket with cold water, or use the kids' wading pool. While you're at it, pick off and compost the inedible parts like stems and husks.

To make digging root crops easier, moisten dry soil with a sprinkle from the hose before you dig. To keep from damaging the crop with your spade or fork, start digging several inches away from the base of the plant.

Smart Tips for Handling Pre- or Post-Prime Produce

If you have to harvest a little early because frost threatens, or if wet weather keeps you out of the garden during a critical week, you can still make the best of your produce. Here are a few suggestions; for more ideas on handling specific crops, see the "Just-Right Harvesting Guide" on page 179.

Try these not-so-tough tricks. Conquer toughness in cookable vegetables by dicing, grating, or shredding them. Then sauté, stir-fry, or add to soup, stew, or egg dishes.

Puree not-quite-prime produce. Some vegetables are well suited, either cooked or raw, to being pureed with tomato juice to make a vegetable cocktail. Which ones you use is a matter of preference; for starters, try sweet peppers, celery, carrots, and a bit of onion.

Turn them into soup. Make a soup base by boiling vegetables until they're very soft. Strain the broth and compost the vegetables. Don't use members of the crucifer family, such as broccoli and cauliflower—their flavor is too strong.

Put up jam or jelly. Make jam or jelly from berries that aren't quite ripe.

Puree post-prime fruit. Any fruit past its prime can be pureed, then served over ice cream or mixed with fruit juice and chilled for a cooling summer beverage.

Add it to the soup. Make soup from carrots, peas, potatoes—even cucumbers. Also add pureed vegetables to soup stock.

Bake it. Make breads or muffins from apples, blueberries, tomatoes, carrots, or zucchini.

Make compost. Add rotten produce to the compost pile. The rejects decompose to form great fertilizer, and you keep diseases and insects off the plant.

TAKE-IT-EASY TIP!

Don't Chop When You Store

When you pick fresh produce, don't bother chopping those veggies into bite-size bits until you're ready to eat. Produce lasts longer uncut since less surface area is exposed to dry air and organisms that cause decay.

Quick Tricks in the Kitchen

Produce is most flavorful and tender when picked at its prime—and picking produce at its peak also saves you time and work in the kitchen.

You can serve many fresh vegetables raw or give them a light steaming. By picking produce at the right time, you'll have fewer tough stems or leaves to discard, so less goes to waste and you get more food on the table.

Washing Can Wait

When faced with a bushel of muddy produce fresh from the garden, you may be tempted to scrub the lot of it—using up your evening and messing up the kitchen in the process. Fortunately, you don't need to—in fact, in most cases you shouldn't. Washing most vegetables and fruits before storing makes them vulnerable to rot. It's better to wash produce right before you use it.

There are a few exceptions. Take a few moments to briskly but briefly swish greens—such as lettuce, chard, spinach, endive, and kale—in cool water, then shake off the excess and roll them in a towel before putting them into a plastic bag and then into the refrigerator. Cucumbers can be washed beforehand; so can leeks, which hide dirt in their layers.

Stretch Your Storage Time

With a little attention to how you wrap and refrigerate your produce, you'll increase its storage life. Fortunately, proper storage isn't complicated since most produce needs the same treatment: a plastic container or wrap, and a temperature of about 35°F. The few exceptions are listed in the right-hand column below. (Note that the best storage temperatures are cooler than the average refrigerator, which is generally somewhat warmer than 35°F.) Check this list to find out how to store your produce properly and how long you can expect it to last.

Cold and Moist

To get the maximum storage from the vegetables listed below, keep them near freezing in a refrigerator. Store in a plastic container or wrap.

Asparagus	2 weeks
Beets	1–3 months
Blueberries	2 weeks
Broccoli	3 weeks
Brussels sprouts	1 month
Cabbage (early maturing)	3–6 weeks
Cabbage (late maturing)	3–4 months
Carrots (tops removed)	4–6 months
Cauliflower	2–3 weeks
Collards	2–3 weeks
Corn	4–8 days
Kale	2–3 weeks
Lettuce	2 weeks
Onions (green)	2–3 weeks
Parsnips	2–6 months
Radishes	2–3 weeks
Turnip greens	2–3 weeks
Turnip roots	4–5 months

Cool and Moist

Keep the following vegetables cold but not freezing—a root cellar or basement that stays about 40°F is ideal. Keep most vegetables listed in a plastic container or wrap; potatoes store better loose so they don't get moldy—and be sure to keep them in the dark.

Beans, green	1 week
Cucumbers	10–14 days
Eggplants	1 week
Peppers, sweet	2–3 weeks
Potatoes, Irish	4–6 months
Squash, summer	7–10 days
Watermelons	2–3 weeks

Cool and Dry

The following vegetables need cool—about 40°F—and dry conditions for best storage. Try keeping them in an attic or unheated room, and don't put them in plastic containers or wrap.

Onions	2 months
Pumpkins	2–5 months
Squash, winter	2–4 months
Tomatoes (ripe)	1 week
Tomatoes (unripe)	Up to 1 month

Containers and Wraps That Make Food Last

After putting in effort to grow and harvest, you don't want to watch fresh produce turn to smelly slime. The secret to keeping produce fresh as long as possible is to store it at the right temperature and humidity. Fortunately, you don't need a root cellar and a humidifier. Plastic and a refrigerator are all it takes.

Plastic keeps produce from drying out. You can use rigid plastic containers, plastic bags, or plastic wrap. Plastic containers, besides being reusable, can be stacked in the fridge and protect delicate produce like berries from being smashed.

Sealable plastic bags take up less space and are also reusable. The kind with tiny holes that let out excess moisture are especially good for lettuce, scallions, and other watery vegetables (you may find a cloth equivalent in catalogs or in the produce section at the grocery store). If you don't want to invest in sealable bags, you can use the ones you bring produce home in from the grocery store, but they are thinner, hard to clean, and don't hold up as well when reused.

Refrigeration is less complicated. You either want to use it—which is usually the case—or you don't. And if you do, you just need to remember that some vegetables can't take the coldest part of the fridge and should be stored in the warmest part of the refrigerator (generally in the drawer marked "vegetables.") See "Stretch Your Storage Time" on page 177 for specific recommendations.

Indoor Ripening Tips for Tip-Top Tomatoes

Here's an easy way to quickly ripen not-quite-ripe tomatoes: Put them in a plastic bag with a banana, orange, or apple. The fruit gives off ethylene gas, which hastens ripening. For more gradual ripening, store tomatoes in a brown paper bag out of direct sun. If you have to pick all the remaining fruit on your plants to keep them from freezing at the end of the season, try wrapping them individually in newspaper and storing them in a cool, dry place. All the fruit that has started to turn a lighter shade of green while still on the plant will ripen indoors.

Give Your Fresh Veggies Fresh Air

Does your fresh produce become overripe before you use it? The culprit is the ethylene gas that your fruits and vegetables give off as they mature. The gas isn't harmful, but it speeds up the ripening process unless you can get rid of it.

Use cloth bags or plastic bags with holes in them to help vent ethylene away from stored produce. Or to extend your storage time even more, try packaging that absorbs and removes ethylene. Plastic bags and wraps made with a mineral called oya stone have this unique ability.

Oya stone bags were developed by the Evert-Fresh Corporation of Houston, Texas, and are available in health food stores and groceries. The stone pulls ethylene away from your produce and breathable plastic lets it escape from the package. The packaging has a slightly rough feel, different from any other storage bag you've seen. But your produce will stay fresh longer.

Just-Right Harvesting Guide

Picking when the crop is ready gives it the best flavor and texture. It also saves time since you don't have to ripen too-early produce indoors or prepare too-late produce to compensate for its shortcomings. This table tells you when prime time is for popular vegetables and fruits. For crops that change quality as they age but are still edible, you'll also find suggestions for easy ways to prepare them before and after their peak quality. Produce that goes straight from being good to being garbage can still be useful—in the compost pile.

Crop	When to Harvest	How to Harvest	Non-Prime Uses
Apples	When fruit is full size, has turned color, and pulls readily from the branch.	Twist off, leaving the stem on the apple. Handle carefully to prevent bruises.	Applesauce or apple cider.
Asparagus	When spears are 5–8 inches long, with firm, closed heads.	Snap off the tender, usable portion by bending the spear over at ground level.	If stalks become tough with age, peel off outer layer before steaming. Or make soup.
Beans, dry	When leaves turn yellow and begin to fall.	Pull up or cut off the plants and let dry, indoors or out, on a sheet of cloth or plastic. The pods split when dry, making it easy to remove the beans.	If bean seeds are green (not mature), shell, refrigerate, and cook them within a few weeks—don't try to dry them.
Beans, green or snap	When pods snap when you bend them, but before seeds plump in the pod. Pod length varies with cultivar.	If you'll eat the beans within a day or two, pinch or snip off the stem end to remove the pod from the plant so you don't have to cut it off in the kitchen.	If beans are too young to snap, lightly steam and serve with butter or sesame oil. Old pods are tough and require extra cooking time.
Beets	When roots are at least 1½ inches in diameter.	Loosen soil with a spade, then lift beets. To keep the juices from running out, twist off, don't cut, the leafy top when ready to eat either top or root.	Tiny beet thinnings can be cooked and eaten with the tender greens. Shred large, tough beets for borscht with plenty of low-fat sour cream or plain yogurt.
Blueberries	A week or two after the berries turn blue.	Cup your hands under fruit clusters and tickle them with your thumbs. Ripe berries will fall off into your hands.	Jelly if too early (the fruit is still tart), juice if too late.
Broccoli	Harvest main head when it is well developed but buds are still tight. Harvest side shoots while the buds are still tight.	Cut off main head 4–6 inches below the head, leaving the main stem to encourage smaller but equally edible sideshoots. Cut sideshoots about 4 inches from the top.	Broccoli heads are still edible after the buds start to open. Cut into small pieces and stir-fry.

(continued)

Just-Right Harvesting Guide—Continued

Crop	When to Harvest	How to Harvest	Non-Prime Uses
Brussels sprouts	When sprouts are tight and ½–1½ inches in diameter. Sprouts at the bottom of the stalk are ready before those at the top. Can harvest after frosts.	Twist or cut sprouts from the stem, starting at the base and working up.	Compost.
Cabbage	When head is full and tight; size depends on the cultivar. Harvest immediately if head starts to bulge—it may split.	Cut head off near the base, leaving the lower leaves to encourage small edible sprouts.	Split heads are edible but must be used before they start to rot. Shred and sauté with onion, apple, and a fruity vinegar.
Carrots	Baby carrots when they turn orange; other types vary. As the predicted harvest date approaches, pull out a few to see if the size is right.	Loosen the soil with a spading fork and pull the roots.	Old carrots are woody and less sweet. Make them into carrot juice or carrot bread.
Cauliflower	When head is 6–8 inches in diameter and firm—usually 1–2 weeks after the head first appears in the leaves.	Cut the whole head from the stem.	Once the head looks like rice, compost it.
Celery	When stalks reach desired size.	Cut off the whole plant at soil level, or remove individual outer stalks to encourage more growth in the center.	Older stalks can get pithy. Chop fine and use in soup or relish.
Chard	Leaves are best when 3–10 inches long.	Cut off leaves as you need them, or harvest the whole plant 1 inch above the ground.	Cook older leaves after removing tough parts of the stem.
Corn	Pick when milky juice spurts out when you pierce a plump kernel with a fingernail. If the juice is clear, wait a few days. If no juice spurts out, it's overripe.	If you'll eat it right away, save kitchen mess by husking the ear while it's on the plant, then twisting off the ear. If you'll store the corn, twist it off the plant husk and all.	If you miss the milk stage, add ears to the compost pile or cut the kernels off and use them in soup.
Cucumbers	While cucumbers are still immature and small. Length varies with type and cultivar. Seeds should be small and soft.	Hold the stem with one hand and pull the fruits from the vine with the other hand.	Over-mature cucumbers turn yellow and have hard seeds. Discard seeds and skin and use the flesh in soup, stuff the shell with tuna or chicken salad, or make pickles.

Crop	When to Harvest	How to Harvest	Non-Prime Uses
Eggplant	When skin is firm and shiny and seeds are soft and white. When you press the skin, it should leave a dent that fills in slowly.	Use a knife to cut the fruit with about 1 inch of stem.	Maturing fruits develop hard seeds and become bitter. Slice thinly, place in a colander, sprinkling each layer with kosher salt to draw out the bitterness. After 30 minutes, rinse and pat dry, then cook.
Grapes	When the grapes are firm and taste good.	Cut cluster from the vine with pruners.	Make not-quite-sweet grapes into jelly. Overripe grapes can be made into juice.
Kale	Whenever leaves are large enough to use, even after frost.	Harvest individual leaves from the outside, or harvest the whole plant.	Old leaves become tough. Slice thin and sauté or steam until soft.
Leeks	As needed, before frost.	Loosen soil with a spading fork and pull individual plants.	Older leeks may get tough. Chop the white parts for soup, or slice thin and stir-fry.
Lettuce	Once leaves are large enough for salads; or once heads are firm for heading cultivars.	Pick outer leaves, or cut the whole plant off at the soil level.	Bolted lettuce is bitter; compost it.
Melons	Let melons ripen on the vine for best flavor. The rind turns from green to yellow, tan, or white and the end away from the stem feels soft when pressed.	When ripe, many melons "slip" or separate easily from the stem. Gently lift the fruit off of the stem; if you have to tug, it's not ready.	Overripe fruits are soft and less flavorful. Make them into juice or cold soup.
Okra	When pods are about 2 inches long.	Cut pods off with a sharp knife.	Big okra pods are gooey and the seeds tough. Chop and add to gumbo. Compost if the stem is hard to cut.
Onions	For green onions (scallions), when the leaves are long enough for your purposes and the bulb isn't much wider than the leaves. For bulbs, after the leaves have dried and fallen over.	Pull green onions. Dig up bulbs, toss on the lawn or other non-soil surface, and let dry in the sun for a day. Then let cure for 2–3 weeks in a dry place with good air circulation.	Some green onions will grow into bulb onions, others will overwinter and sprout again in spring. If bulb onions go to seed, harvest and use immediately.
Parsnips	When needed in fall, before the ground freezes solid, or before leaves sprout in spring.	Loosen soil deeply with a spading fork and dig roots.	Large roots may be hollow or pithy. Chop fine, cook, and mash or puree them.

(continued)

Just-Right Harvesting Guide—Continued

Crop	When to Harvest	How to Harvest	Non-Prime Uses
Peaches	When fruits show their mature color, taste sweet, and separate easily from the branch.	Gently grasp the fruit and twist upward. Handle carefully to prevent bruises.	Overripe fruits are soft. Make them into sauce to serve over ice cream.
Pears	Harvest most pears when the fruit is full-size but still hard, after it turns from dark to light green. Harvest 'Seckle' and Asian cultivars when they are sweet and fully colored.	Pull from the branch with an upward twist.	Tree-ripened pears may be soft and gritty. Try them poached or made into pear sauce or applesauce.
Peas	Pick snow peas when pods are full-length but seeds haven't plumped up. Harvest sugar snap peas once the seeds swell. Harvest English peas—the ones you remove from the pod—when seeds are mature but not hard, and pods have lost their shine. Pick right before you plan to eat them. Harvest early if a heat wave is coming.	Pull from plant. Plan on three harvests during about a one-week period. For the last picking, pull up the plant and pluck the pods while you sit someplace comfortable.	Snow peas will be shell peas if you wait (but you may want to pick and compost them so more young pods keep coming). Snap peas may get tough, but they still taste good—just cook old ones a little longer. Add overripe shell peas to soup.
Peppers	Harvest while fruits are green or fully colored but before the skin starts to shrivel. Wait until the skin is firm and seeds have formed. Sweet peppers are sweetest and hot peppers are hottest when they change color.	Cut fruits from plant, leaving a bit of stem attached. Wear gloves when harvesting hot peppers and keep your hands off your face.	Ripe "green" peppers are good and sweet; try them sautéed. Dry ripe hot peppers that start to shrivel and grind them for seasoning.
Potatoes	Harvest new potatoes when they are large enough for your purposes. Dig gently with your fingers to see how large they are. Harvest potatoes to store once the skins don't peel off easily when you rub them with your finger or after the vines die back.	Dig, being careful not to pierce the potatoes' skin. Protect potatoes from light. Cure storage potatoes in a dark, humid place at 60° to 65°F for two weeks. Then store at 40°F.	Compost or plant green potatoes. Rub sprouts off stored potatoes before using.
Radishes	When root diameter is ½–1 inch. Radishes plump up quickly.	Pull up the whole plant.	Old radishes are hot and pithy; compost them.

Crop	When to Harvest	How to Harvest	Non-Prime Uses
Raspberries	When berry is its mature color and pulls easily from the plant.	Pull, leaving the white core on the plant.	Overripe fruits are soft. Puree them and pour over ice cream or add to a fruit drink.
Spinach	When leaves are the size you need.	Pick outer leaves as needed, or cut the whole plant off at, or just below, soil level. Pick all leaves when plants start to bolt.	Older leaves are tougher and may be bitter but can be chopped and cooked.
Squash, summer	Harvest summer squashes when they are 4–6 inches long while the skin is very tender.	Cut from plant, leaving a bit of stem on the fruit.	Too-big summer squash is seedy and tough. Compost seeds and skin. Grate and sauté flesh, hollow it out and stuff with cooked vegetables and cheese, or make into quick bread.
Squash, winter (including pumpkins)	Pick winter squashes when the stem is woody and the skin is too hard to pierce with a fingernail, but before frost.	Cut from vine leaving a few inches of stem attached. Cure winter squash in a dark place at 80° to 85°F for 10 days. Store at 50 to 55°F.	Pick open male blossoms and stuff with herbed ricotta cheese. Cook and eat immature fruits like summer squash. Use frost-nipped fruits as soon as possible.
Strawberries	When berries are fully red.	Pinch stem off above berry. If you plan to cook them immediately, leave the green caps on the stem and pick just the berries.	Overripe fruits are soft. Puree or make a milkshake.
Tomatoes	After the tomatoes develop full color but are still firm.	Pull off all fruits before frost.	Use overripe tomatoes for sauce or fresh juice. Ripen fruits that have started to turn color in a dark, dry place at room temperature. Slice green tomatoes, dip in batter, and fry, or chop and pickle.
Turnips	When roots are 1–2 inches in diameter.	Loosen soil and pull roots.	Large roots may be pithy or hot. Grate or dice before cooking.
Watermelon	When the rind becomes rougher and less glossy, the underside turns from green to white or yellow, and the tendril next to the fruit stem turns brown.	Hold vine with one hand and pull or cut fruit off vine.	Overripe fruits have very soft, juicy flesh. Compost or boil the juice down for pancake syrup.

PART 3

Saving Time in

he Lawn and Landscape

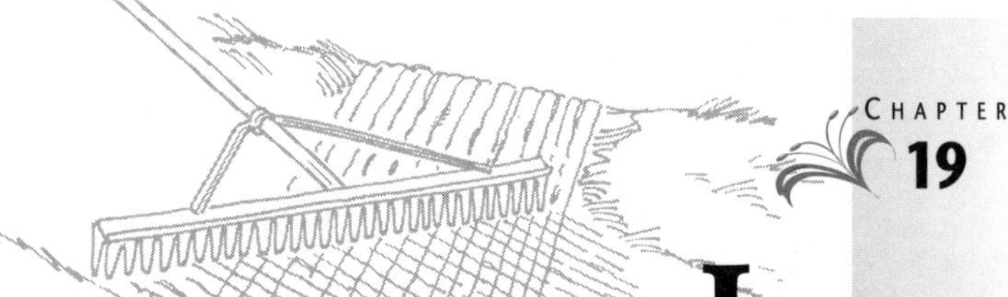

CHAPTER 19

Lawns and Groundcovers

- Keep Grass in Check
- Tame the Mowing Monster
- Regular Mower Maintenance
- Speed Mowing Time with a Bigger Mower
- Quit Vacuuming Your Lawn—Feed Your Soil
- Keep Weeds at Bay by Reseeding
- Grow Grasses You Can Count On
- Get to Know Good Groundcovers
- Getting Groundcovers Going
- Tackle Tough Sites with Groundcovers

Lawns and Groundcovers the Low-Maintenance Way

LAWN GRASSES AND GROUNDCOVERS go hand in hand in the low-maintenance landscape. Nothing beats a lawn for a durable place to play or a smooth, green swath to set off flower beds. But lawn grasses perform best in full sun on fertile, well-drained soils. That's where groundcovers come in. Nothing beats them for care-free plantings on tough-to-mow sites—or to reduce high-care grass.

In this chapter, you'll learn how to reduce the time you spend on your lawn by examining your equipment, grass choices, and routine care. You'll also find out how modifying old habits will help you cut lawn care. Finally, you'll learn to recognize parts of your landscape better suited for groundcovers than for turf grasses.

Keep Grass in Check with Edging and Mulch

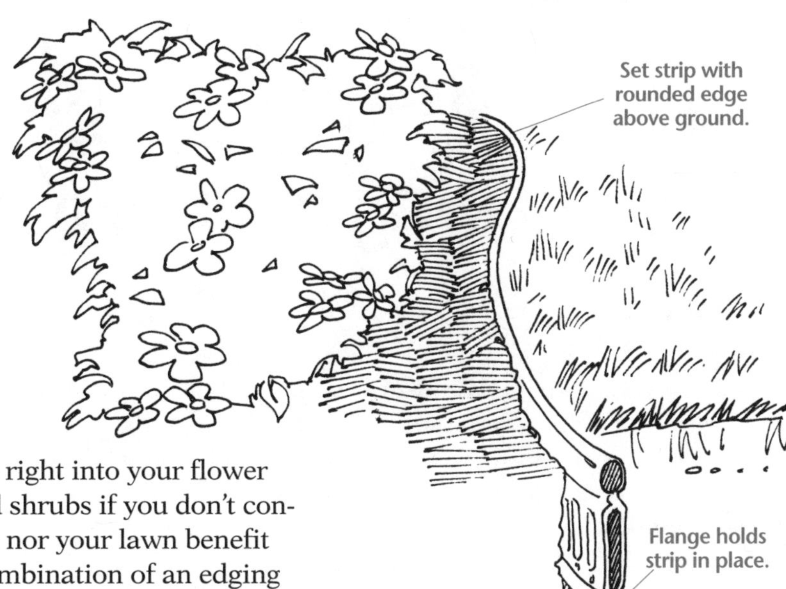

A vigorously growing lawn will grow right into your flower beds and up to the bases of trees and shrubs if you don't control it. Neither your trees and shrubs nor your lawn benefit from the resulting competition. A combination of an edging barrier and mulch around plants and plantings will keep the grass where you want it. It will also protect other plants from too-close encounters with mowers and trimmers.

To install edging strips, start with thick, good-quality edging; you'll find a variety of edging strips at local garden centers and nurseries. Thick edging is easier to install and will last the longest. Deeper edging stays in the ground better. Here's how to go about installing your edging.

1. Use a garden hose, rope, or a line drawn with sand or lime to outline the area you want to edge. Keep curves gentle and avoid sharp corners.

2. Use straight pieces of plastic edging if possible. Warm coiled edging in the sun for easier straightening.

3. Dig a straight-edged trench that's as deep as your edging. To save yourself work on a large installation, consider renting a power trencher.

4. Working from one end, loosely install the entire length of edging with the rounded edge just above the soil line. Backfill just enough to hold the edging in place. The edging should stay in the trench without any pressure. Tight curves or forced fits will pop out later.

5. Inspect the installation, make any minor adjustments, then backfill and firm the soil around the edging. Water the area thoroughly for uniform settling and firming.

6. Check edging strips annually to make sure spreading weeds or grass haven't grown over them. Mow over the top of the strip, with one wheel in the bed and one in the lawn. This lets you mow and trim at the same time. Keep the garden mulched to control spreading weeds.

TAKE-IT-EASY TIP!

Go Forward to Find Hard-to-Mow Spots

If you're spending a lot of your mowing time dragging your mower backward or throwing it into reverse, chances are you're mowing in some too-tight spaces. Try to complete an entire mowing session without backing up. Evaluate any unmown areas as candidates for replacement with no-mow plants.

Methods to Help You Tame the Mowing Monster

Letting your grass grow a little taller contributes to the overall health of your lawn by promoting stronger, deeper roots.

Most of us give up far too much of our limited free time to cutting grass. But if you want a traditional-looking lawn, mowing is a necessary evil that can consume large portions of your time from spring to fall. Short of giving up your lawn entirely, there are ways to make mowing easier, quicker, and more efficient.

The amount of time you spend mowing is a direct result of the vigor and layout of your lawn, as well as the kind of mower you use. Since a healthy, vigorous lawn can grow fairly aggressively, you're more likely to reduce mowing time by mowing more efficiently than by mowing less often. Try any or all of the following tips to make your mowing quicker and easier.

Repair or replace awkward spots. Level out rough spots in your lawn to allow your mower to travel more easily. Keep grassy areas at least three times the width of your mower to allow for easy turning. Fill smaller or tough-to-mow sites with groundcovers.

Mow frequently. Mow often enough to remove no more than one-third of the leaf blade at one time. Frequent mowing reduces clipping clutter, snips off germinating weeds, grinds leaves, and promotes dense turf. The mower will move quickly over the lawn, too.

Bumps and dips in your lawn make mowing harder and cause scalped spots where the mower's blade gets too close to the ground. To smooth your way to easier mowing, remove existing sod with a sharp spade or sod lifter. Then, shave soil from high spots and fill in low ones to level them with the surrounding soil. Mound added soil slightly to allow for settling. Finally, replace sod, and water until muddy. Keep the area moist until gentle tugging shows that the sod has rerooted.

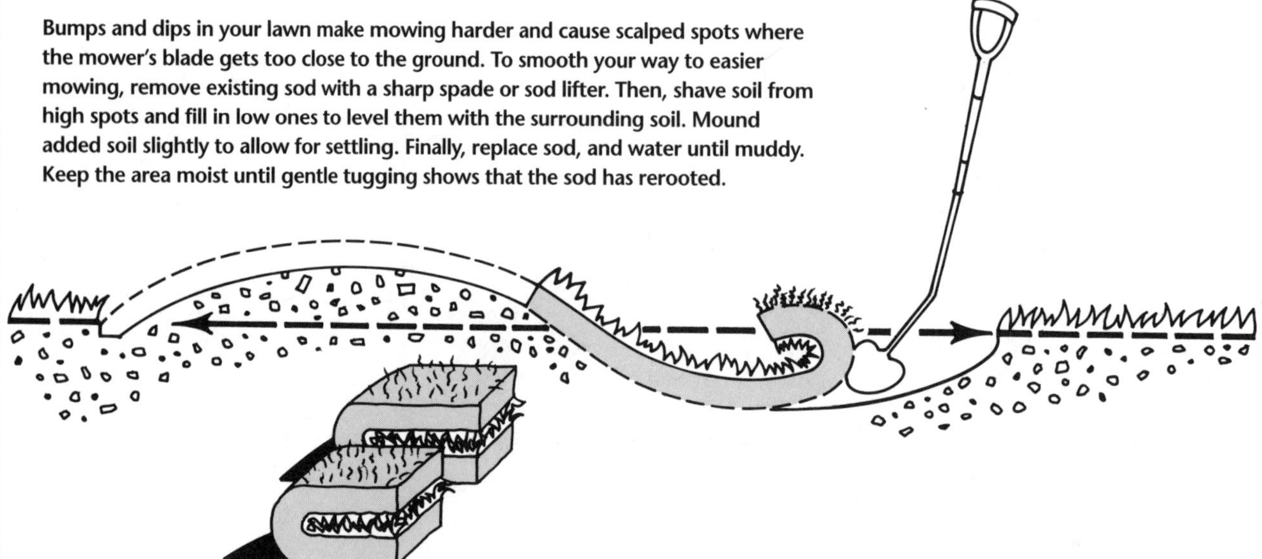

Mow high. Set your mower blade to a height of about $2\frac{1}{2}$ inches for most grasses; higher for fescues and St. Augustine grass. Tall grass smothers prostrate weeds, captures more sunshine, and roots more deeply to reach nutrients and water.

Use the proper tool. A properly sized mower with adequate power will speed up the mowing process. It's also a pleasure to use equipment that performs a chore quickly and easily.

Let clippings lie. Save yourself work and return moisture and nutrients to your lawn: Let cut grass lie where it falls.

Add water during dry spells. Water enough to keep the grass alive during droughts without bringing it out of heat-induced dormancy. Drought stress makes lawns susceptible to invasion by weeds, diseases, and pests. When watering is necessary, apply 1 to 2 inches by recording the time it takes for your sprinker to fill a pan to that depth. Select sprinklers that adjust for complete coverage and distribute a large quantity of water quickly. Use programmable timers to water late at night when water pressure is high and winds are minimal.

Avoid overfertilizing. The lush new growth that results from generous applications of nitrogen is disease-prone and requires frequent mowing. A healthy lawn may get by with little more than the clippings produced when you mow, plus one or two top-dressings with compost or other organic fertilizer each growing season.

Accept and encourage diversity. Diseases, insects, and other stresses have less impact on lawns that have a mixture of grasses, along with weeds like clover.

Eliminate obstacles and trimming. Shape plantings and borders so you can guide the mower around them without excessive turning or stopping.

Consolidate plantings. Plant shrubs and trees in groups and mulch or plant beds of groundcovers around them. It's much easier to mow around the edge of a group of plants than to mow around each plant individually.

Prune offending branches. Ducking and dodging as you mow slows your progress and is dangerous—you're not paying attention to your mower if there's a tree branch in your face. Keep trees and shrubs pruned appropriately to give you access with the mower, or plant no-mow plants beneath obstructing limbs.

Make follow-up trimming obsolete. Use perennials and groundcovers that hang over the edge of the lawn around tree trunks or along buildings. Let your mower's deck slip under the overhanging leaves to cut the grass right to its hidden edge. Install mowing strips around plantings to eliminate trimming after you mow. See "Keep Grass in Check with Edging and Mulch" on page 187 for directions.

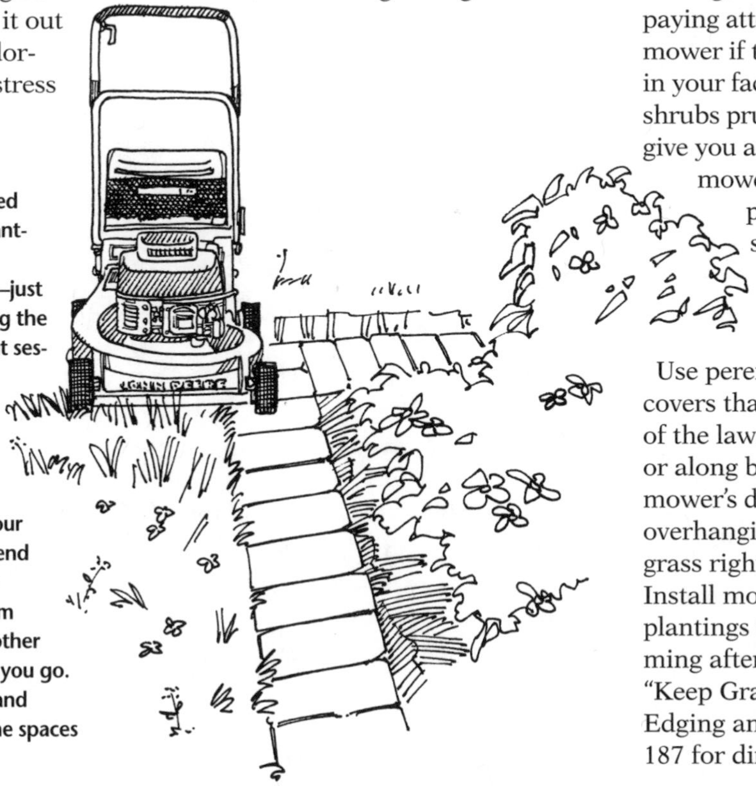

Mowing strips installed around landscape plantings make trimming around them a snap—just run your mower along the strip and forget about sessions with a string trimmer. To install a brick mowing strip, use a sharp spade to dig a brick-size trench around your bed. Starting at one end of the trench, lay the bricks in, butting them snugly against each other and leveling them as you go. Backfill as necessary and sweep dry soil into the spaces between the bricks.

Minimize Frustration with Regular Mower Maintenance

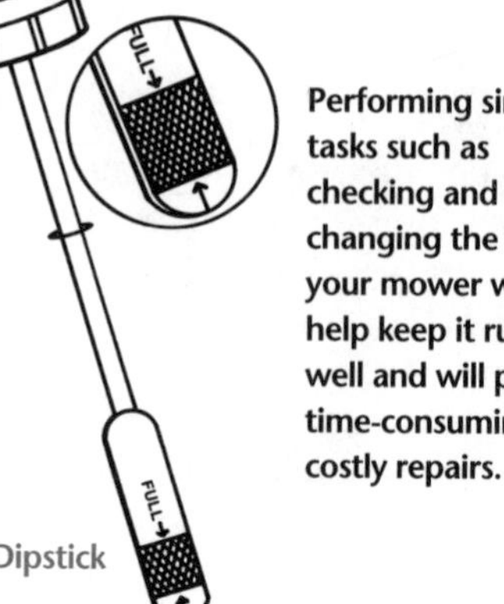

Performing simple tasks such as checking and changing the oil in your mower will help keep it running well and will prevent time-consuming, costly repairs.

Few things are as frustrating as having a lawn in need of mowing and a mower that won't work. Performing regular maintenance on your mower or having a mechanic maintain it for you is a small investment that can prevent major mowing headaches.

Check the oil. Do this while the mower is on level ground, before you start the engine. Fill to the appropriate level for your mower's engine. Change engine oil when it's warm—contaminants are suspended and the oil will flow easily.

Keep filters clean. Clean foam filters in warm, soapy water. When they're dry, squeeze enough oil through them to lightly coat the entire filter. Gently tap and blow dirt out of pleated paper filters. Replace them when the paper discolors significantly.

Keep belts and chains snug. Check belts for cracks or glazing. Keep spares on hand even if you don't change them yourself so you don't have to wait for parts to be ordered and shipped.

Keep the mower clean. Use a leaf blower or shop vacuum to remove dust and debris from the mower deck and engine compartment. While you wash the mower, look for loose hardware or other potential problems. Avoid getting water on ignition parts, or the mower will have to dry before it will start.

Lubricate chains, bearings, and bushings. Check the owner's manual for locations and lubricant specifications.

Keep blades sharp. Sharp blades cut cleaner with less power. Removing the blades frequently for sharpening will keep them from becoming stuck on.

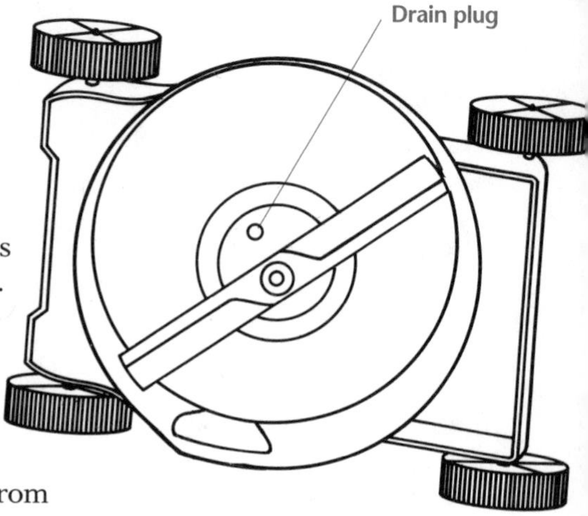

Speed Mowing Time with a Bigger Mower

If you have a large lawn to cut, buying a bigger mower is a straightforward way to reduce the time you spend mowing. And a larger mower with a larger engine will do the job more efficiently than a small machine that's running for a longer time.

When shopping, consider overall mower size, deck size and location, maneuverability, engine size, comfort, and cost. Mower features to consider as you shop include cutting deck placement, the power source that moves the mower (you or the engine), pull start vs. electric start, the engine's capacity relative to the work it has to do, and overall comfort and ease of use. Use this list of mower types to help you find the mower that's right for you and your lawn.

Quit Vacuuming Your Lawn and Feed Your Soil Instead

Leaves or clippings can smother lawn grasses, but you don't have to spend hours vacuuming or raking them up and hauling them away. Instead, use your mower to grind them up into small particles so they can settle into the soil and decompose. You'll not only eliminate most raking, but you'll also be enriching the soil with organic matter.

You can actually treat your lawn like a giant sheet composting site. Throw anything the lawn mower will handle onto the lawn, then pulverize it. Rake up resistant material when you're finished and remove it to the compost pile. Use these tips to make the most of your mower as a soil-enriching power mulcher.

Mow often. Take care of leaves before they build up and clog the mower. The added mowing time is minimal, and you'll no longer have leaf disposal.

Keep the blade sharp. A sharp blade pulverizes effectively.

Clean the air filter frequently. Dry, dusty leaves will plug the filter quickly. Make sure that you clean your filter often, especially after mowing leaves, which produce more dust.

Circle inward. Use a side-discharge mower to blow leaves into a row, then mow the row to grind the leaves into tiny pieces and disperse them to the outside over the lawn.

Circle outward. For heavy leaf cover, start in the middle of an area and discharge the leaves to the outside for dispersal or pickup around the edges.

Make light work of leaf lifting. If you need to rake up leaves, rake them onto a large tarp for easy transport. Leaves are light when dry; grab the corners of the tarp to tote large quantities.

Mulching mowers. Mulching mowers (or mulching modifications to bagging mowers) chop clippings and leaves into fine pieces, reducing grass residue and allowing easier cleanup. They don't work well in grass that is too tall or wet.

Bagging mowers. These machines pulverize grass, leaves, and debris while vacuuming the lawn. Bagging takes more time than allowing the clippings to fall back on the lawn, but it provides a useful material for mulching or composting. Look for bags that are large, easy to put on and take off, and easy to empty. Find a mower that bags when necessary, but also mulches or discharges effectively.

Intermediate mowers. Sized between homeowner models and mowers used by maintenance crews, some intermediate mowers offer a sulky option and may be used either as a large walk-behind or a rider.

Riding mowers. Riding mowers generally have larger decks than their walk-behind counterparts and travel faster than a comfortable walking speed. Riders come in different sizes and configurations, so find one that meets your specific needs.

Do You Need a Garden Tractor?

Garden tractors provide many of the advantages of riding lawn mowers, with the added versatility of attachments like rotary tillers, snowblowers, grading blades, or even hydraulic loader buckets. If you need that variety of equipment, a garden tractor saves time and storage space because you only have to maintain one engine. If you have no need for these attachments or the tractor's towing capability, you may not want a large, clumsy tractor as a lawn mower.

Keep Weeds at Bay by Reseeding

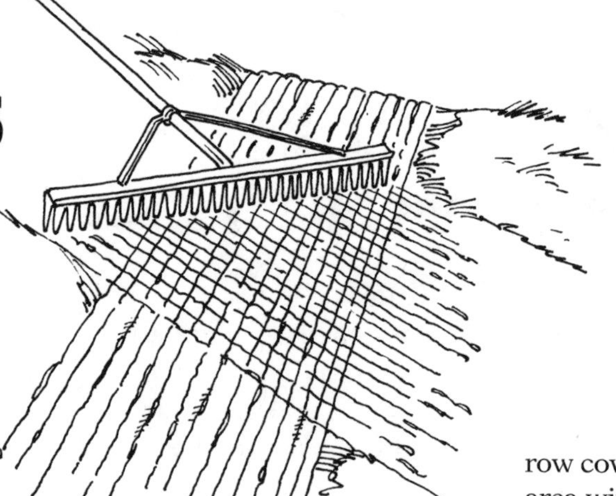

Grass seed germinates best when it has good contact with the soil. Prepare the soil in areas you want to reseed, then use a rake to scratch lots of shallow furrows in the soil before you sow your seed.

Keep weeds from colonizing your lawn by reseeding bare or sparsely covered patches. For best results, seed in late summer when soils are warm and weed seed has already germinated. Here's how.

Remove existing vegetation. Remove weeds and existing grass with a sharp spade, sod lifter, or scuffle hoe. Rough the soil to a depth of at least 1 inch, using a rake or cultivator for small areas and a rotary tiller for large ones. Level the soil with the surrounding area, then rake from several directions to make many crossing furrow lines. Grass seed germinates best in grooves, so make plenty of them.

Sow your grass seed. To increase germination, protect the seed from hungry birds, and prevent it from washing away in rain, lightly mulch the area with straw. Or tack a floating row cover over the seeded area with rocks or bent lengths of wire until the grass begins to sprout. Water gently to wet the top ½ inch of soil, then keep the area moist, but not soggy, until your seedlings are ready for mowing.

Mow when most of the area needs it. Don't wait too long to mow or taller grass will shade the remaining new seedlings. After three mowings, treat the newly seeded area like an established lawn.

Grow Grasses You Can Count On

Whether you are installing a new lawn or renovating an existing one, use the following tips to select the best grass for your lawn.

Suit your local growing conditions. Northern, cool-season lawns are commonly composed of bluegrass, ryegrass, or fescues. Warm-season lawns most often contain zoysia, St. Augustine, centipede, bahia, and bermuda grasses. Check with your county's extension office or garden centers to get up-to-date recommendations on the best grasses for your area.

Pick the best cultivars. Look for lawn grass cultivars with drought tolerance, disease resistance, and other low-maintenance characteristics. There are also dwarf or slow-growing cultivars that need less mowing.

Plant endophyte-enhanced grasses. For a lawn that resists pests, try a grass that contains endophytes, fungi that live in plants without causing harm. In grasses, these fungi confer resistance to leaf-eating pests like chinch bugs, sod webworms, and armyworms. Cultivars of fine fescues, tall turf-type fescues, and perennial ryegrasses are currently available. Choose seed mixes that contain at least 50 percent endophyte-enhanced seed for maximum protection; buy fresh seed to ensure that the fungus is viable.

Get to Know Good Groundcovers

Cut your lawn maintenance time to the bone by filling troublesome spots with groundcovering plants other than lawn grasses. Many plants tolerate mowing and foot traffic and make excellent lawn replacements. Some will cover the ground and enhance your landscape with flowers or wildlife-attracting fruits.

Start by looking at plantings in your neighborhood to see which groundcovers do well in your area. Also seek recommendations from fellow gardeners or knowledgeable nursery and garden-center employees. Use the checklist below to help you choose plants that will cover the ground where grass won't do.

☑ Match plant choices to site conditions such as available light, available water, soil type on the site, heat and cold, and traffic.

☑ Mowing tolerance is important if the mower routinely strays into the groundcover area.

☑ Plants that spread via above- or below-ground roots or stems will fill an area quicker than clump-forming plants.

☑ Evergreen groundcovers look good year-round and offer the most soil protection where erosion is a concern.

☑ Dense growth discourages weeds.

☑ In terms of appearance, choose groundcovers based on leaf texture and color. Consider flowers as a short-term bonus feature.

☑ Insects and diseases can ravage mass plantings. Select plants that have a proven track record in your area. Mix groundcovers to avoid problems of a single species.

Don't Pave with Plants

Grass and other groundcovers are poor substitutes for pavement. If you have a heavily traveled area where plants will not grow, install a path instead. Wood chips, gravel, cobblestone, flagstone, brick, and concrete can all provide attractive, functional, and low-maintenance walkways. Check local availability, cost, durability, and methods of installation. Use perennials to soften the edges of your walk or to mask exposed areas.

Getting Groundcovers Going

Thick, weed-smothering patches of groundcover start with thorough soil preparation, especially in difficult sites. Preparing the soil helps get your groundcovers growing quickly and gives them a head start on weeds.

Start by removing existing sod or undesirable growth from your site. Prepare the soil as you would for any good garden planting—till deeply and add organic amendments. (You'll find several soil preparation methods to choose from in Chapter 2.) Smooth the soil surface with a garden rake and break up any remaining clods. Water to settle the soil, and you're ready for planting.

Space plants according to their growth rate and size at maturity. Plant fast-growing perennials, ornamental grasses, and other herbaceous plants 1 to 3 feet apart; junipers and other woody plants 3 feet apart.

Mulch the site after planting to control weeds and reduce moisture loss. Water thoroughly. Groundcovers need regular watering until they are well established, which will take an entire growing season for woody plants. Keep weeds pulled to avoid competition.

Tackle Tough Sites with Terrific Groundcovers

Dry, shady sites, such as the spaces under shade trees and shrubs, beneath eaves, and on shaded slopes, are some of the toughest challenges a gardener faces. But before you despair of having anything grow in the dry, bare spots beneath your trees, try some of the perennial groundcovers listed below. You'll find more groundcovers in Chapter 21.

Herbs as Groundcovers

Low-growing herbs such as dainty-but-tough thymes and free-ranging mints can make excellent groundcovers. While covering the ground quite adequately, herbs offer bonuses that grass lacks. Tread on them or nick them with trimmers, and they'll perfume the air for you. And they're perfect when you're in a pinch for something to season tonight's dinner with! Good groundcovering herbs include Roman chamomile (*Chamaemelum nobile*), thymes (*Thymus* spp. and cvs.), pennyroyal (*Mentha pulegium*) and other mints (*Mentha* spp.), and wild strawberries (*Fragaria virginiana*).

Groundcovers for Dry Shade

Lawn grasses never grow well in shade, especially dry shade. Instead of struggling to maintain lawn under such conditions, replace it with swaths of groundcovers that will thrive like those listed below. Water plants regularly until they're established.

Ajuga (*Ajuga reptans*): Green, purple, or variegated leaves; 4–6 inches tall. Zones 4–8.

Common periwinkle (*Vinca minor*): Shiny, dark green foliage with blue or white flowers; 4–6 inches tall. Zones 4–9.

Epimediums (*Epimedium* spp.): Evergreen or semi-evergreen foliage; 6–12 inches tall, depending on species. Zones 3–8.

Lily-of-the-valley (*Convallaria majalis*): Lush foliage and fragrant white flowers in spring; 6–8 inches tall. Zones 2–8.

Lilyturfs (*Liriope* spp.): Green grasslike foliage with purple or white spikes of flowers; 1½ feet tall. Zones 5–9.

Wintercreeper (*Euonymus fortunei*): Glossy evergreen leaves; 4–6 inches tall; will climb trees. Zones 4–8.

Yellow archangel (*Lamiastrum galeobdolon*): Green leaves marked with silver; 8–14 inches tall. Zones 4–9.

Groundcovers for Soggy Sites

Soggy spots are a trial when planted in lawn grasses—if grass will grow in them, they're always too wet to mow. Instead, fill moist spots with groundcovers that will enjoy the dampness. The plants below will thrive in moist to wet soil in sun or shade.

Astilbes (*Astilbe* spp.): Fernlike foliage with white, pink, or red flowers; 1–4 feet tall, depending on species. Zones 3–8.

Creeping Jenny (*Lysimachia nummularia*): Small rounded leaves with yellow flowers; 2–4 inches tall. Zones 3–8.

Hostas (*Hosta* spp.): Foliage in many sizes and shades of green, many variegated types, with white or lavender flowers in summer; 6 inches–4 feet tall, depending on cultivar. Zones 3–8.

Lady's-mantle (*Alchemilla mollis*): Pale green foliage with yellow-green flowers; 1 foot tall. Zones 3–8.

Violets (*Viola* spp.): Green, heart-shaped leaves with white, blue, or lavender flowers; 6–12 inches tall. Zones 3–9.

Many ferns also thrive in wet soil, including sensitive fern (*Onoclea sensibilis*), cinnamon fern (*Osmunda cinnamomea*), and ostrich ferns (*Matteuccia* spp.).

CHAPTER 20

Low-Maintenance Garden Projects

The Right Tool Saves You Time

If Wood Is Good, Is Plastic Fantastic?

Hardware for Low-Maintenance Results

What to Do about Decay

Difference in Lumber Dimensions

Raising Beds Lowers Labor

Pave the Way to Garden Pleasures

Basic Paving Installation

Tame a Water Hazard with a Simple Span

Step-by-Step Steps

Steps Can Ease Your Ups and Downs

A Low-Care, Easy-to-Build Deck

Projects the Low-Maintenance Way

GARDENERS TEND TO THINK of their landscapes in terms of the plants in them, but other elements make a beautiful, easy-care landscape. Structures, the hardscape within the landscape, are an important part of a low-maintenance landscape. They can add interest and drama to your garden. For example, steps and walkways make it easy to stroll through a garden—and care for it, too. Decks and patios actually are low-maintenance groundcovers—they don't need mowing, watering, or weeding and have the added advantage of creating living spaces that you can enjoy.

In this chapter, you'll find projects that will help you reduce garden maintenance in the long run. You can buy or pay someone else to build them for you, but if you're the least bit handy, you can complete most of them in a weekend. We've also suggested tools and hardware that you'll find useful for simple projects.

The Right Tool Saves You Time

Electric drill

Twist drill bit

Masonry bit

Spade bit

You don't need to own a lot of tools to successfully tackle outdoor projects for your home. Every job can be done with the right hand tools, but often a portable electric tool will save you a great deal of effort and time. The few electric tools you need are fairly inexpensive and usually easier to use than their hand-powered counterparts. Price, of course, depends upon quality, but you won't need heavy-duty professional-model tools, which are the most expensive. You may be surprised at how inexpensive some of these tools are, although cheap tools generally are no bargain. Shop for moderately priced tools produced by recognized manufacturers to get quality that will suit your level of use.

Electric drill. The most helpful tool is an electric drill. Choose a 3/8-inch, variable speed, reversible drill. The 3/8 refers to the size of the chuck opening, where the drill bit goes. A 1/4-inch drill is too small to hold larger bits that you may want to use. A reversible drill allows you to reverse the direction of the bit to remove screws or back the drill out of a hole you're drilling. Most drills offer both forward and reverse modes.

With the drill, you need drill bits, which are least expensive when purchased in sets. Regular twist drill bits for drilling metal are fine for most wood uses. Inexpensive spade bits are good for larger holes, and masonry bits are necessary for any masonry drilling you do.

A Word to the Wise

Read user instructions carefully before operating any power equipment. Wear eye and hearing protection while using your tools, and never operate them without the appropriate safety guards and devices in place. When using a tool for the first time, or before you start a new project, make a few practice cuts on scrap wood to familiarize yourself with the tool.

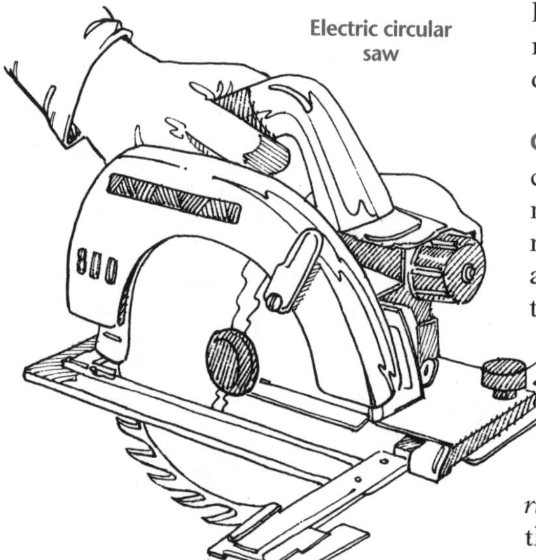

Circular saw. A portable circular saw makes fast work of most sawing jobs. Blades range from 6 to 8 inches in diameter, with 7 1/4 inches being typical. Circular saws are very versatile since both the depth and the angle of cut are adjustable.

Guides allow accurate lengthwise cutting (known as *ripping*) along a board, although most cuts with a circular saw are made freehand. On portable circular saws, the blade rotates from the bottom of the work through to the top, toward you, then down again. This motion pulls the saw down into the work as you move the saw away from you along the cutting line. Because the blade moves this way, you should cut plywood with the good face down to minimize splintering.

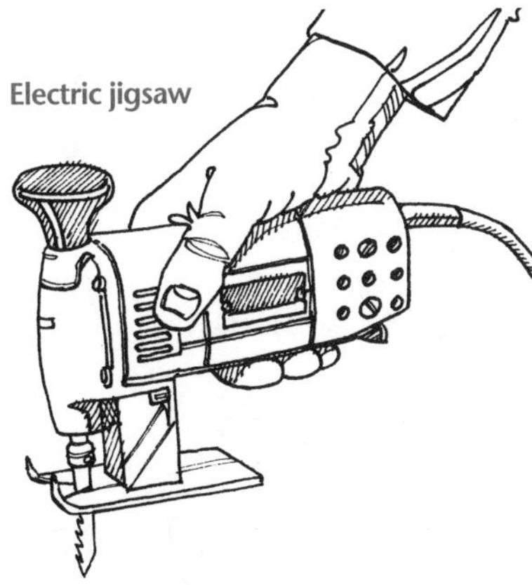

Electric jigsaw

Electric jigsaw. Portable electric jigsaws, or saber saws, don't cut as fast as circular saws, but they can make a variety of cuts, including curves. The thin saw blade, reciprocating up and down at high speed, can follow a tight radius to cut inside or outside curves.

On most models, an adjustable shoe that presses against the workpiece allows you to make cuts of various angles. With the proper blades, jigsaws can also cut brass, aluminum, and soft metals. To make cuts in enclosed areas, insert the saw blade in a hole drilled in the waste area.

If Wood Is Good, Is Plastic Fantastic?

Plastic "wood" is not quite ready to take over the building construction industry, but the time seems right for this product that turns trash into useful products. Considering that it does not rot, splinter, burn easily, or become food for insect pests, it is easy to see you might want to consider plastic wood for some of your landscaping needs.

You can saw, drill, and screw into plastic wood using normal woodworking tools; some manufacturers recommend using carbide saw blades to reduce heat and friction while working with plastic wood. Produced mainly from recycled high-density polyethylene (HDPE), plastic wood comes in a few different colors and configurations—landscape "timbers," boards, and kits for specific items such as planters or benches. A few manufacturers mix sawdust with the plastic wood to give it a more wood-like consistency.

Plastic wood's primary drawback is its lack of strength. Even the large "timber" sizes are not intended for structural purposes. But for some furniture applications and in many landscape uses, that doesn't matter. While plastic wood is actually about 25 percent heavier than wood, plastic wood products are often considerably lighter because they are formed with a hollow core, so one person can handle them easily.

In the landscape, plastic wood's main uses are as edging and border timbers, planters, fencing, picnic tables and benches, compost bins, and play equipment. For many of these items, the manufacturers reinforce the plastic with nonplastic components to increase their strength.

Look at the manufacturer's specifications for any plastic wood product before you buy to be sure it can do the job you intend it to do. Weigh the benefits of plastic wood, such as the ease with which it can be cleaned, with potential drawbacks. For example, nails and screws in plastic wood tend to pull out, making joining difficult. You may need to drill holes and bolt members together, or use special fasteners recommended by the manufacturer.

As the recycled plastic market continues to swell with soda bottles and grocery bags, it's likely that the variety and quality of plastic wood products will continue to increase. Consider them when choosing materials for your landscape; in the right applications, plastic wood products can serve you maintenance-free and indefinitely.

Choose Your Hardware for Low-Maintenance Results

The metal hardware that holds together your outdoor projects is subject to the same weather extremes as the lumber, and you should choose it with that in mind. Make sure all your hardware connections are galvanized or otherwise coated to prevent rust. Rust weakens hardware over time and leaves unattractive dark stains on wood.

Screws and nails. *Common nails* have great shear strength, but tend to work loose over time. *Spiral-* or *twist-shank* nails have greater holding power. Screws hold even better than nails, but you'll need to do some drilling to provide pilot holes for the threads and clearance for the unthreaded shanks. Choose brass, stainless steel, or plated screws for outdoor jobs.

Heavy-duty hardware. For heavy-duty holding jobs, such as in a deck, you need sturdier hardware. A *lag screw* or bolt is a large screw with a bolt-type, hexagonal head that allows you to drive it into a predrilled hole with a wrench.

Carriage bolts and *machine bolts* make extremely strong connections. Because of their different head configurations, the machine bolt needs a washer, while the carriage bolt does not. Both need predrilled clearance holes.

Use *expansion bolts* to secure wood to masonry, such as concrete or brick. Tap the anchor section into a predrilled hole in the masonry. When the bolt is threaded into it, the anchor expands it to secure the connection.

Timber connectors. You can connect large timbers to one another with metal fittings made just for this purpose. A *beam-to-post connector* has flanges that let you nail it to the top of a post; other flanges provide a site for nailing on a beam. *Joist connectors* allow you to hang a 2 × 8 or larger joist from a header joist.

Other hardware connectors and fittings are available. A trip to your local home-supply store can help you become familiar with them before you begin a project.

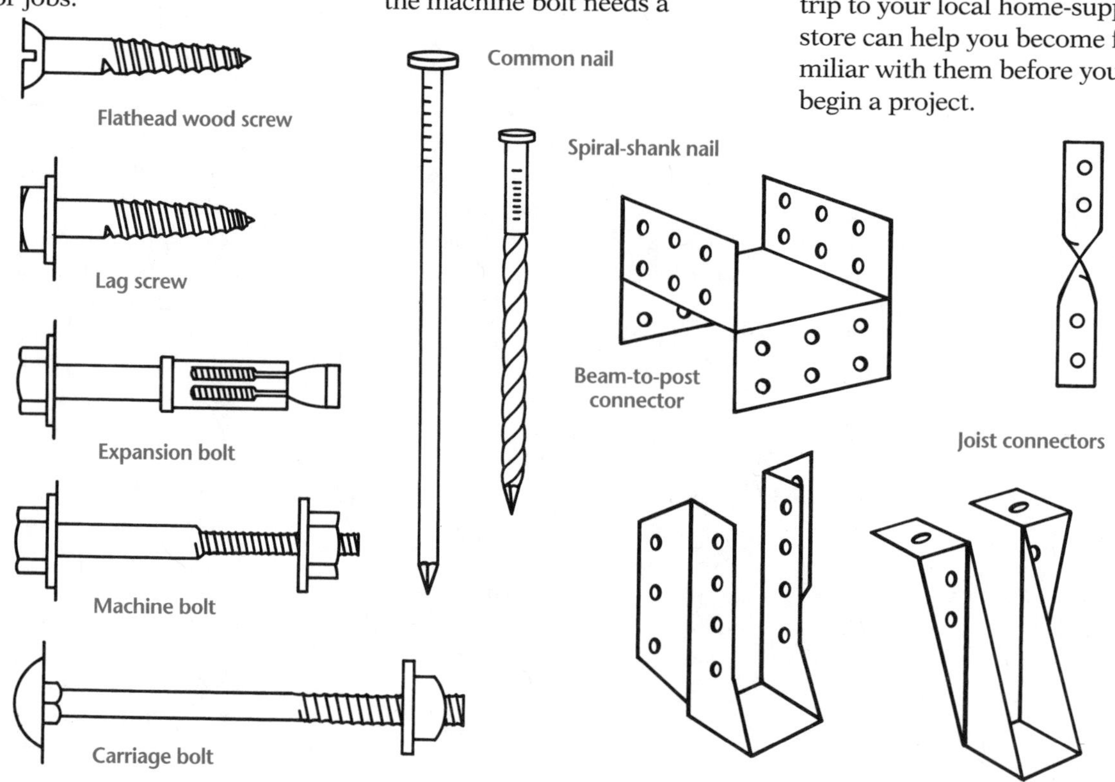

What to Do about Decay

Exposing wood to weather creates opportunities for fungi and wood-boring insects to feast on your projects. Protecting wooden structures from such attacks can prove tricky for gardeners who don't want to fill their landscape with toxic products. The alternative—building projects with wood harvested from rainforests or old-growth stands of redwood—is equally undesirable.

You can build the projects in this book out of pretty much any wood that's available at your local lumberyard. Protect your projects from moisture by applying a finish. This is especially important for wood that's in constant contact with soil and for any places where moisture might be trapped next to the wood. Wooden structures that have little soil contact and that dry quickly (because water drains off of them) after a rain are less prone to rotting.

When choosing materials for structures that will be in contact with the soil, such as raised beds, edgings, or compost bins, consider using a building material other than wood.

Cinder blocks, cement or plastic edgings, and recycled plastic "lumber" are all excellent alternatives to even the most decay-resistant lumber for such uses. If you choose to use wood in soil-contact situations, do as much as you can to prevent rot. Select decay-resistant lumber like red cedar or redwood.

A two-coat method of sealing out moisture offers additional protection: Apply a penetrating sealer, such as Thompson's Wood Protector, followed by a coat of high-quality exterior paint.

Nail Size Guide

To buy the right size nail for every job, use this size guide to translate penny sizes into inches.

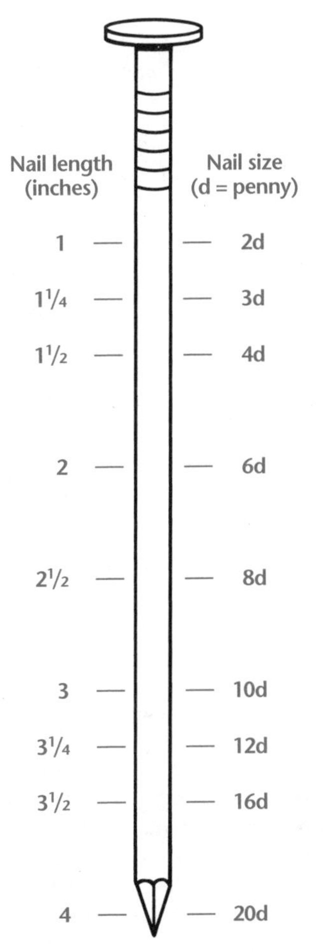

Difference in Lumber Dimensions

When planning a project, keep in mind that the nominal sizes of wood are not the actual dry, dressed sizes. This will affect the size of the hardware you buy. This table shows the differences in dimensions in standard construction lumber. For example, a 2 × 4 is actually 1½ × 3½ inches.

Nominal Dry Size (inches)	Actual Size (inches)
1	¾
2	1½
4	3½
6	5½
8	7¼
10	9¼
12	11¼

Raising Beds Lowers Labor

Building raised beds is an easy project that can save lots of work over the life of your garden. Plants growing in raised beds benefit from improved drainage, reduced competition from encroaching weeds, and fluffy, uncompacted soil. Raised beds enable you to work in your garden earlier in the spring and prevent perennials from suffering in soggy winter soils.

A well-planned raised bed is no more than 5 feet wide, so you can easily work from either side without walking in it and compacting the soil.

Choosing the Right Materials

You can frame your beds with any number of materials, although it's possible to make raised beds without frames simply by amending and mounding the soil. Most gardeners base their choice on availability and aesthetics. If you're framing front-yard flower beds, you may choose to shape your beds with materials that match your home, such as brick or stone. In less visible locations, you can reduce your costs by using cinder blocks or other locally available building materials. A one- or two-high frame of cinder blocks, staked at the corners and periodically along the walls, creates an effective raised bed with a ready-made bench all around the garden.

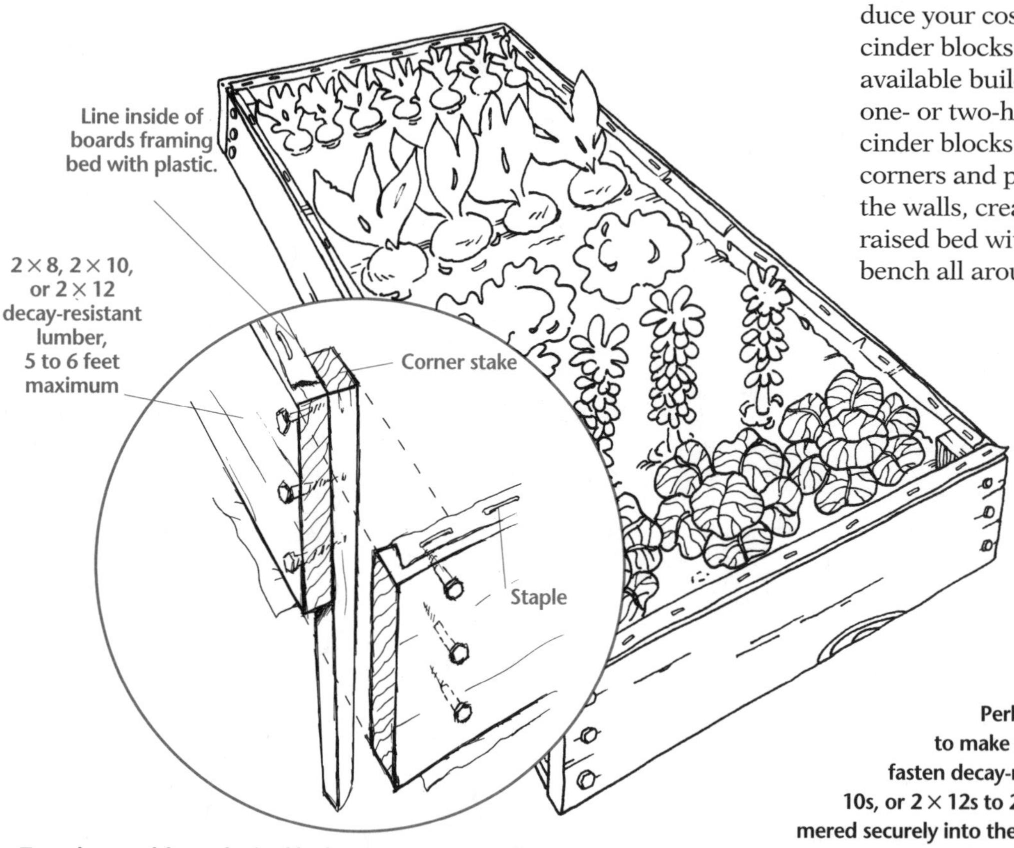

Perhaps the easiest way to make a raised bed is to fasten decay-resistant 2 × 8s, 2 × 10s, or 2 × 12s to 2 × 2 stakes hammered securely into the ground at each corner. You can nail the framing boards to the stakes, but attaching them with bolts or lag screws makes your beds more durable and less likely to pull apart. You can create several raised beds in a few hours with this method.

To make wood-framed raised beds more permanent, line the inside of the boards with sheets of inexpensive polypropylene plastic. Fold the plastic around the boards and staple it in place before you bolt the boards to the stakes.

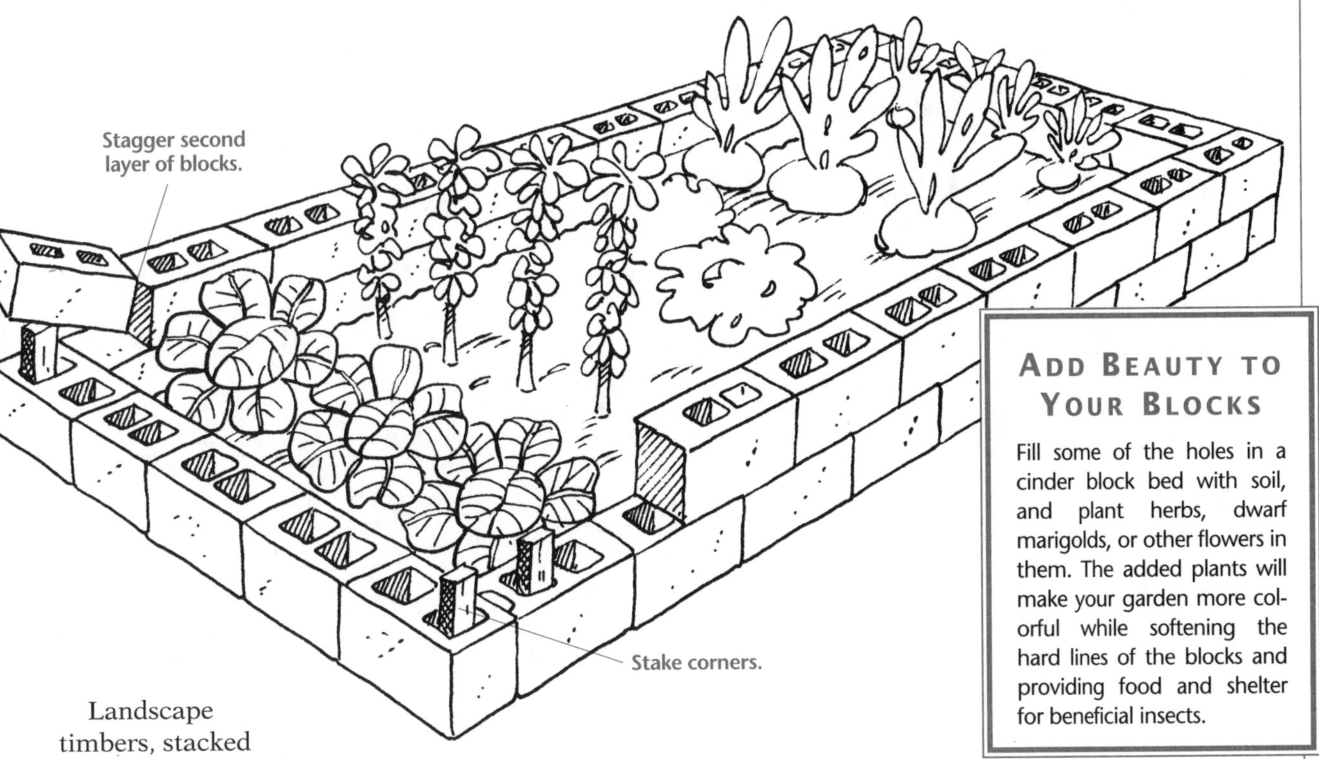

Add Beauty to Your Blocks

Fill some of the holes in a cinder block bed with soil, and plant herbs, dwarf marigolds, or other flowers in them. The added plants will make your garden more colorful while softening the hard lines of the blocks and providing food and shelter for beneficial insects.

Landscape timbers, stacked and pinned together, are another good option. Stack timbers two or three deep to form the beds, overlapping them at the corners to tie the sides together. Drill holes in the timbers and stake down through the upper timbers into the lower ones as you build. If the length of your bed requires you to butt timbers end to end, stagger the placement of these joints, as well as lapping the corners.

Building Raised Beds: Simple Steps to Success

Whether you're building with wood, brick, or stone, start by roughly staking out the area you want the bed to cover. Remove any existing vegetation, then turn and amend the soil within the bed before you frame it.

1. **Measure your beds.** Measure across each end to get the exact width, and pace off or measure with a tape the distance along the sides. If you're framing the bed with standard-size planks, like 2 × 10s, it's easiest to let the length of the boards determine the length of the bed.

2. **Check the angles.** For structural stability and visual appeal, you'll want your beds to be square to rectangular—with 90 degree corners. To check this, measure corner to corner diagonally across the outline of the bed. Your bed is rectangular if the diagonal measurements are equal. Measure with a string if your tape measure is too short.

3. **Smooth the soil where the frame will rest.** If you're framing with brick, dig a shallow trench and line it with a 1-inch layer of coarse sand to provide a stable base.

4. **Install the frame.** Build brick beds either dry or with mortar. If you mortar your bricks, stretch a string between two stakes as a straight edge guide, and use a 2- to 3-foot-long carpenter's level to keep them on the horizontal. If you're building with stones, you can stack them directly on top of the soil, although a shallow trench will give them added stability. Stack the stones so that they slant slightly inward toward the center of the bed.

5. **Fill your bed.** Use compost, soil, and other organic matter.

Pave the Way to Garden Pleasures

Although most gardeners prefer plants to paving, there are many places in the landscape where paving is useful, appropriate, and labor saving. Installing a paved path once, for example, is a much better use of your time than repeatedly working to maintain part of your lawn that's trampled by traffic.

Find the Right Paving for Your Project

Start your paving project with a mental design. Consider how you'll use the paved area. As a patio? A lightly traveled path? How big is the area you want to pave? Choose paving that harmonizes with your home and is appropriate for the intended uses. You can install some paving materials, such as bricks, in different ways to create varying visual effects. For a large paved surface, you might choose to combine different materials to make it look more interesting.

Asphalt, bricks, concrete, stones, tiles, and wood are all types of paving that may find a place in a home landscape. While you can install most paving options yourself, you may choose to hire a contractor to install some types, such as asphalt and large-scale concrete projects. One advantage of brick and precast concrete pavers is that you can install paving at your own pace. You can finish your project in a day or gradually, as you have time to work on it.

Concrete. Concrete is a familiar and inexpensive paving. It is durable, needs little or no maintenance, and is more versatile than most people realize. You can vary its color, or seed it with stones to change its texture. It is unforgiving, however, and preparation before pouring is critical since you can not stop once you have begun.

Concrete requires sturdy forms to hold its weight in place while it hardens, and you must have tools, such as edgers and floats, to give the

Basic Paving Installation

Paving materials vary a great deal from region to region, based on what's available, but installation techniques for most materials are very similar. In areas where the ground freezes in the winter, lay paving on 2 inches of leveled sand over a base of 4 to 6 inches of tamped gravel. Where the ground does not freeze, you can install paving on a layer of leveled sand without the layer of gravel beneath it. Pour concrete directly on sand, eliminating the gravel. Stone patterns, tiles, and edgings are usually set in a 1-inch-deep mortar bed over sand.

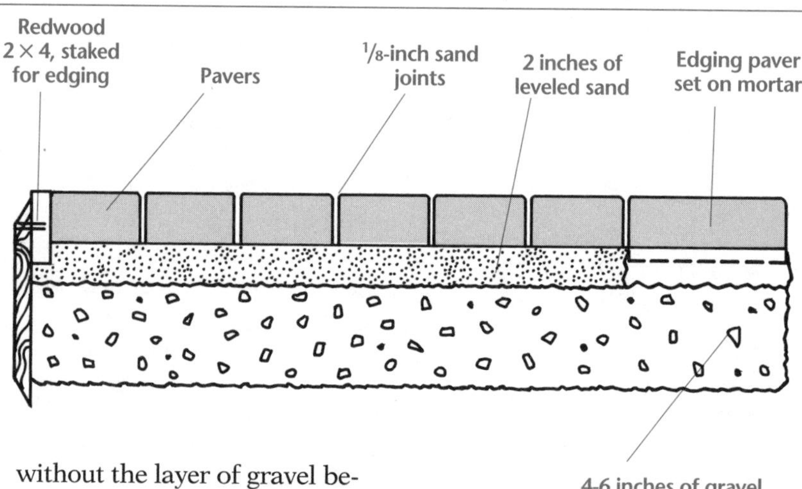

surface the proper finish. You can mix concrete in a wheelbarrow or trough, or you can rent a portable motorized mixer.

Running bond

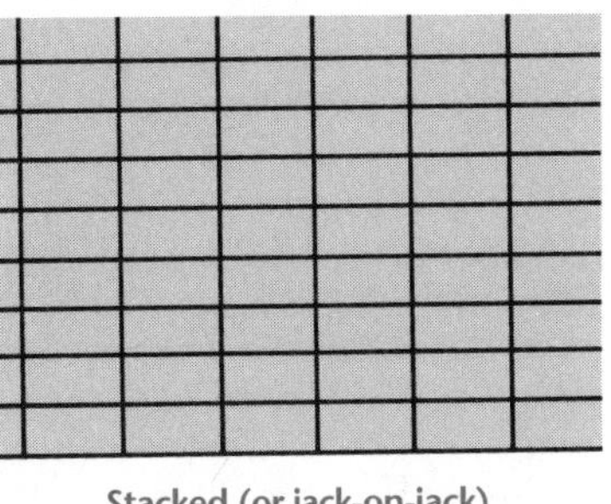
Stacked (or jack-on-jack)

Brick. Brick paving is one of the best choices for do-it-yourself home projects. Bricks come in a variety of colors and textures, and they are easy to plan with. Brick paving absorbs moisture so it dries quickly after a rain, doesn't become slippery, and stays cool in summer.

It is relatively simple to estimate the amount of material and cost because of the uniform size (about 2 × 4 × 8 inches), which is compact and easy to handle. You can lay bricks in many patterns; mixing patterns adds interest to large paved areas and helps define borders.

Basket weave

Diagonal herringbone

Add a Layer of Prevention

If you're laying pavers over sand rather than setting them in mortar, it's worth your time to put a weed-blocking barrier over the sand. You can use landscape fabric, cardboard, layers of newspaper, or any other light-excluding materials, as long as you keep the surface level. Although it adds a step to your paving installation, it will keep weeds from coming up through your pavement for years to come.

Precast pavers. Precast concrete pavers offer another easy-to-install paving option. They come in many colors and shapes, and are dense, durable, and of uniform size. Some styles fit together in interlocking geometric patterns. Install precast pavers on a base of sand over gravel, with sand joints between pavers. Some styles are shaped with holes in them that allow you to grow grass or other groundcovers over the paved area.

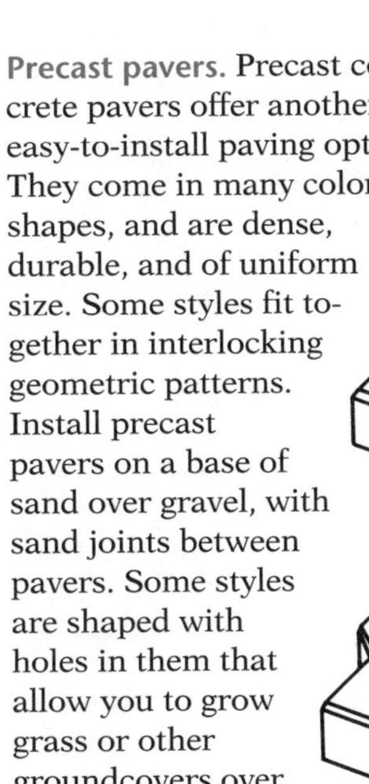

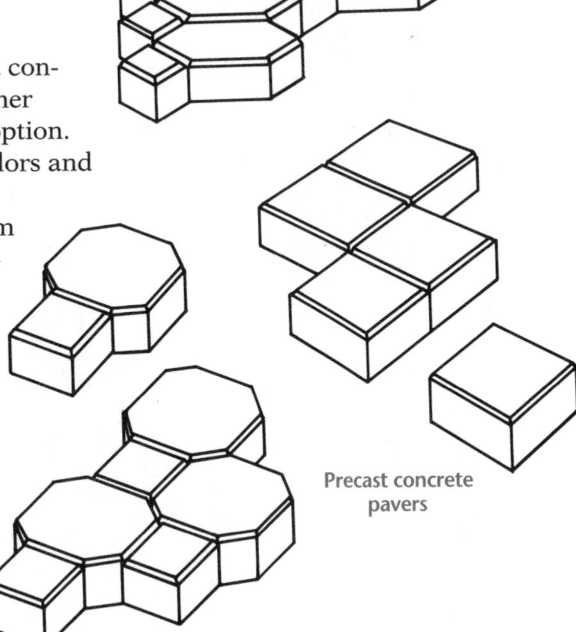
Precast concrete pavers

(continued)

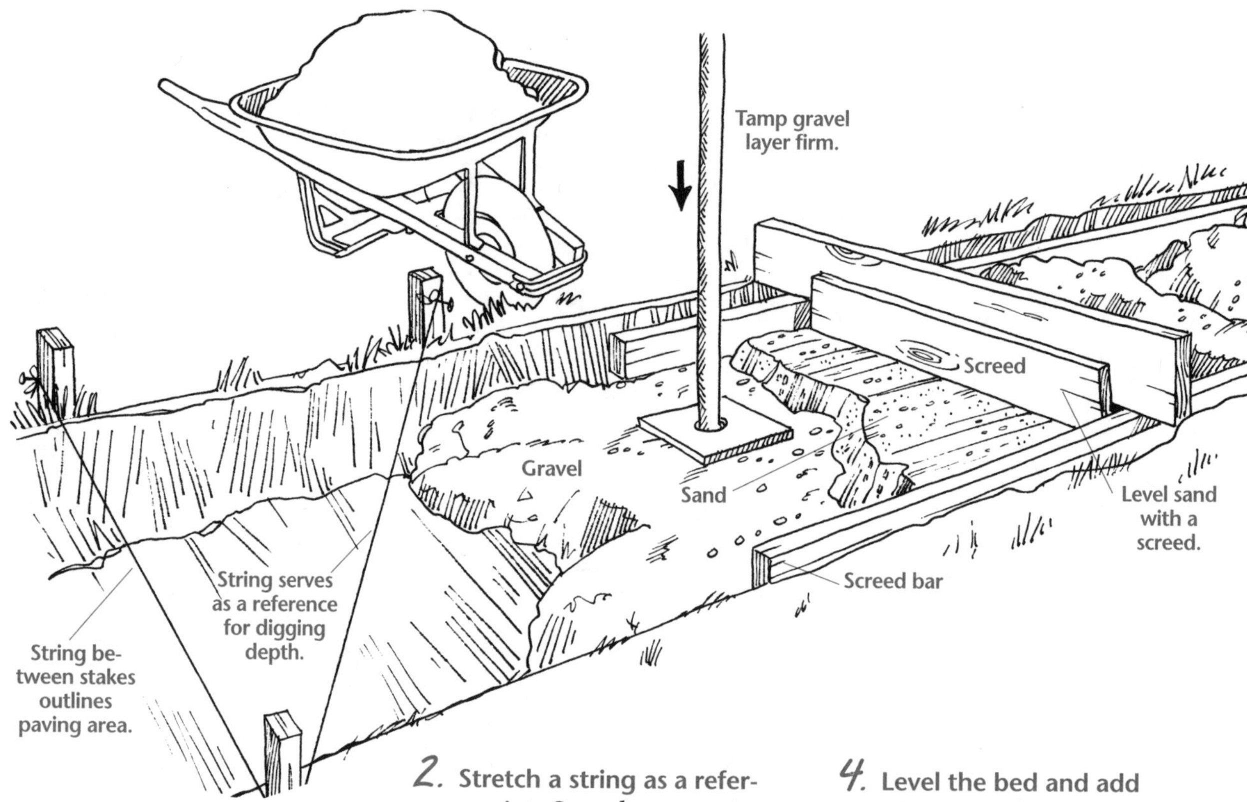

Paving Installation: Careful Planning Smooths the Way

1. **Outline the area you plan to pave.** Use a string stretched between stakes to outline the area and serve as a digging guide. It also will help you determine the amount of material you'll need. Use a hose to design curved edges or draw them on the ground with lime or bonemeal. Measure frequently with your tape measure to maintain equal distances between edges.

If you're installing a walkway, skip to Step 5 and install edging strips to serve as your digging guide.

2. **Stretch a string as a reference point.** Stretch your string a few inches to a foot above the ground and use a line or carpenter's level to level it. The string will serve as a reference point as you dig out the bed for your paving and base materials. If you're installing a paved area next to your house, slightly slope the strings away from the house for drainage—about 1½ inches for every 8 feet.

3. **Excavate the site.** Measure down from your strings to help keep the bed level as you dig. Remove enough soil to accommodate the depth of your base materials plus your paving. Stretch a string diagonally across the area and measure down from it to check the depth of the bed in the middle of the site. Add more stakes and stretch more strings as needed.

4. **Level the bed and add gravel.** Use a rake to level the bed, then add gravel. Use a hand tamper or mechanical compactor to firm it and remove air pockets.

5. **Add sand and level it.** Lay 2 inches of coarse sand over the gravel and level it with a *screed,* a straightedge that you pull across the sand at a constant height. It knocks down high spots and lets you see where to fill in low spots.

Screed bars work like rails that the long, straight screed slides over. For wide areas like patios, lay lengths of 2 × 2s on the gravel base to provide screed bars for the sand. If you are installing a path that has an edging, it can serve as the screed bars. Nail a board that fits between your edgings to a longer board that will lay across them to smooth the sand base in a path.

Tools Needed for Paving Installation

- ☑ Broom
- ☑ Carpenter's level
- ☑ Hammer and nails
- ☑ Hand or machine compactor
- ☑ Rake
- ☑ Rubber mallet
- ☑ Saw
- ☑ Shovel
- ☑ String and stakes
- ☑ Tape measure
- ☑ Wheelbarrow

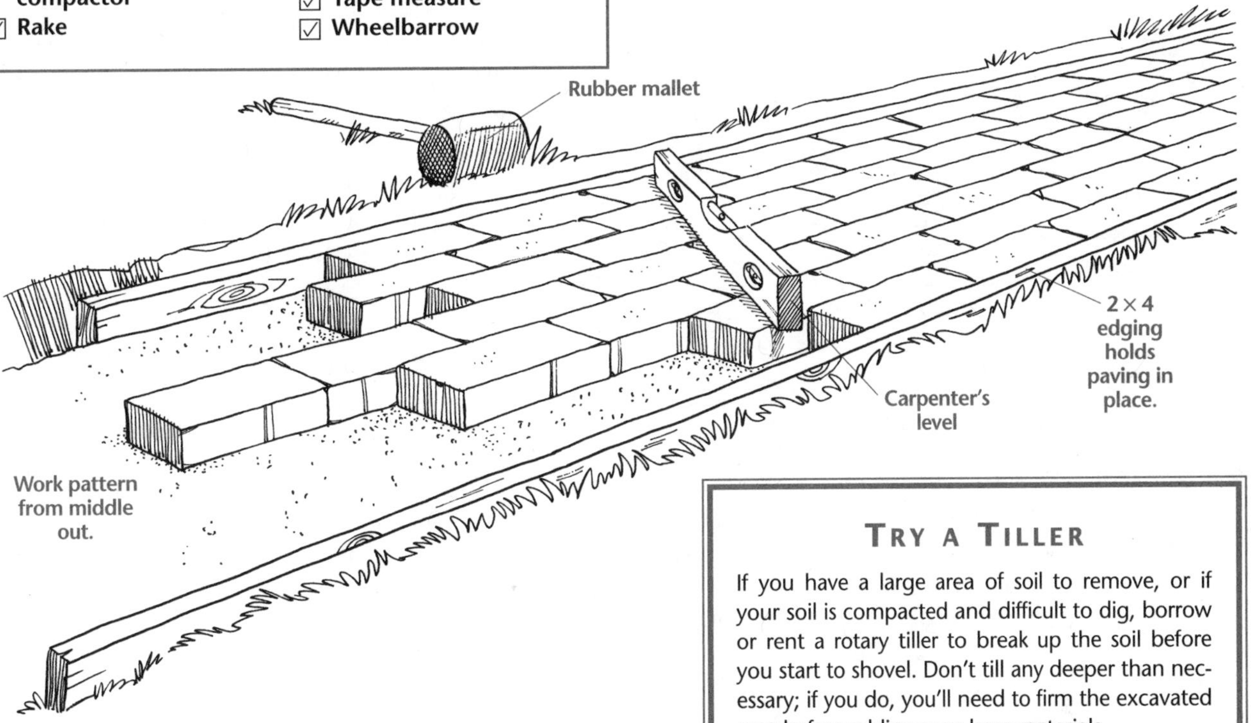

Try a Tiller

If you have a large area of soil to remove, or if your soil is compacted and difficult to dig, borrow or rent a rotary tiller to break up the soil before you start to shovel. Don't till any deeper than necessary; if you do, you'll need to firm the excavated area before adding your base materials.

6. **Set the pavers.** Once the sand is level, begin setting your pavers, leaving about ⅛ inch of space between each of your bricks, precast concrete pavers, or tiles. Work the pattern from the middle out toward the edges, so any discrepancies are less noticeable or can be accounted for if cutting is necessary. Measure frequently to ensure the pattern is straight. It's easy to pry up stones, bricks, or pavers and reset them as needed. A rubber mallet for easing the pavers into position and a level for ensuring their evenness are handy at this stage.

7. **Install edging.** An edging will hold your paving in place and define the paved area. You can use a redwood 2 × 4 set on edge and staked firmly in place, a row of bricks set on edge, or heavier paving units made specifically to serve as edging. The edge paving can be set in a mortar base to help hold the entire project together.

Edging usually completes the installation, but for a walkway it may come at the beginning. Set with the top at final grade, it serves as both a digging guide and as screed bars for leveling the sand. Maintain exact measurements between edgings in this case so paving units fit. A temporary, moveable edging set on grade can also serve as screeding.

8. **Spread fine sand over the finished paving.** Sweep it into the cracks until they are full. Sprinkle the paving with a garden hose, then repeat with more sand.

Tame a Water Hazard with a Simple Span

A permanently wet area in your landscape can be quite a nuisance if it interferes with your movement about the yard. A simple footbridge, built from 4 × 4 beams set on precast concrete piers, can get you over the soggy site and on your way in no time.

First, measure the distance you wish to span to determine what size beams you need. The span is from the center of one concrete pier to the next, with the beams on edge. Mark the location of the bridge with string stretched between stakes and leveled with a line level. Two 4 × 4 beams set 4 feet apart on center can span 6 feet; 4 × 6s can span 8 feet; and 4 × 8s can span 11 feet.

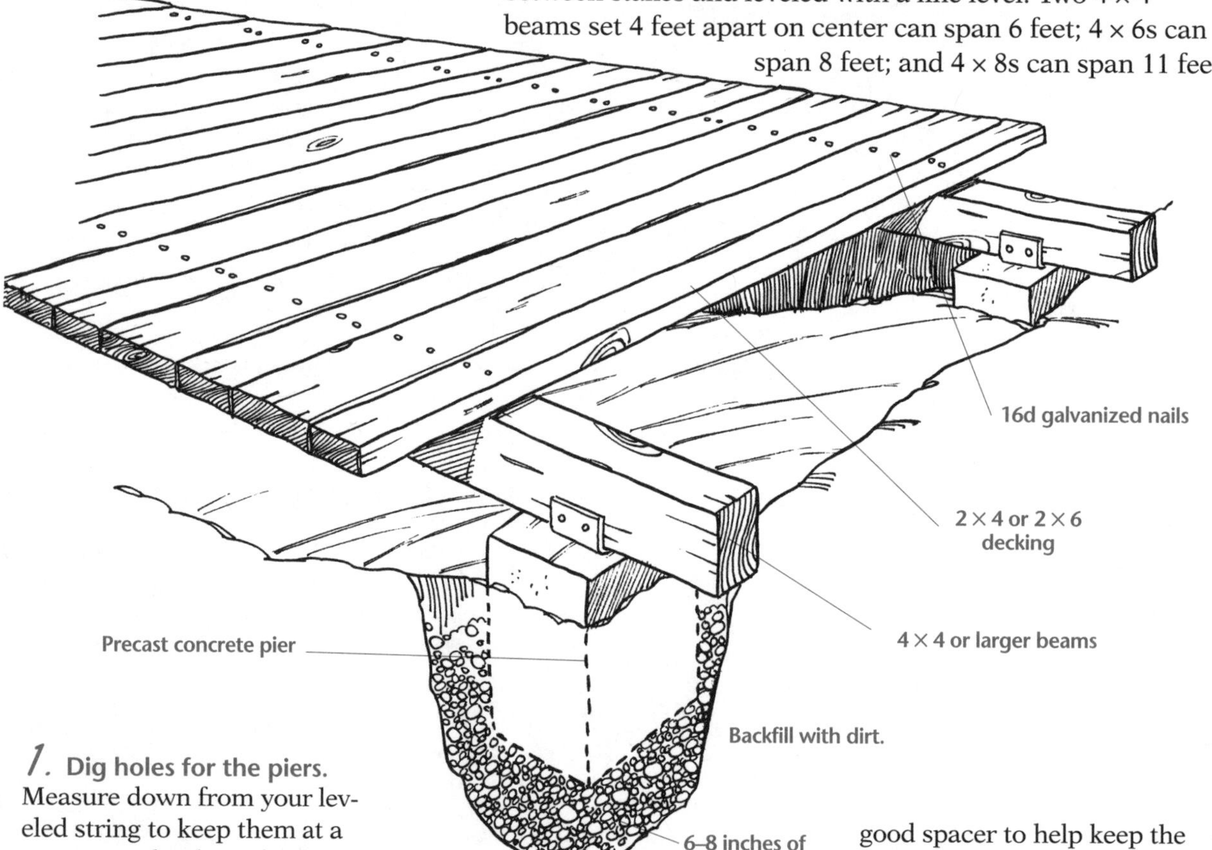

1. **Dig holes for the piers.** Measure down from your leveled string to keep them at a consistent depth. Make the holes deep enough to hold a 6- to 8-inch gravel base beneath each pier.

2. **Add gravel to the holes and level the piers.** Then fill with dirt around the piers to grade.

3. **Set your beams.** Set your beams into the nailing blocks or hardware cast in place on top of the piers and nail them into place.

4. **Nail down the decking.** Nail 2 × 4s or 2 × 6s across the beams to form the deck of the bridge. Leave 3/16 inch of space between each deck board for drainage—a 16d nail makes a good spacer to help keep the right distance between boards. You can cut all the decking to the exact length before nailing it to the beams, or leave it about an inch too long. Use a straightedge (such as one of the deck boards) to align the ends of the decking on one side as you nail it down. After the boards are attached, use a portable circular saw to cut the other ends straight.

Step-by-Step Steps

To transform a slippery slope into easy-to-use steps, you'll first need to know the rise and run of the slope. To measure the *rise,* hold a 2 × 4 or a long pole horizontal and level, with one end resting at the top of the slope. Measure the distance straight down from your pole to the bottom of the slope. To measure the *run,* place a pole upright and level at the bottom of the slope, and measure the horizontal distance to the top of the slope.

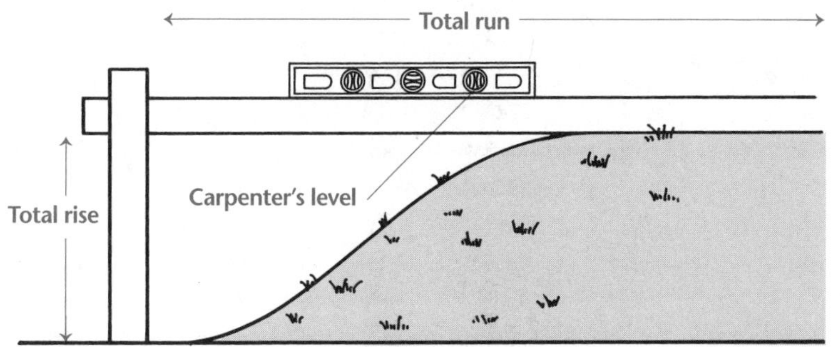

Now do some simple math to see how many steps you'll need. Divide the rise of the slope by the desired height of each step. The result is the number of steps. Now divide the run of the slope by the number of steps to find the length of each tread. Check the table below to see if your treads and risers are properly proportioned; if not, adjust your numbers until you achieve the right balance.

Tread-to-Riser Relationships

Use these recommendations to design steps that will be easy to negotiate.

Tread (inches)	Riser (inches)
19	4
18	$4\frac{1}{2}$
17	5
15	$5\frac{1}{2}$
14	6
13	$6\frac{1}{2}$
12	7

Steps Can Ease Your Ups and Downs

Steps add an inviting aspect to the landscape and create transitions from one part of your yard to another. They also save you the hassles (and hazards) of scrambling up and down slopes and offer a solution for steep, hard-to-mow areas. Well-planned steps are safe and easy to use because they maintain the right proportions between treads (the part you walk on) and risers (the vertical parts). Steps on gentle slopes work best with low risers and wide treads, while steeper slopes need taller risers and narrower treads. Use the method shown on this page to find the total rise and run for your slope. With that information, you can work out how many steps you need and how much material it will take to build them.

Let your steps conform generally to the slope rather than trying to shape the slope to fit the steps. It means less work for you and a more comfortable climb. To make your steps easier to use, plan for a width of at least 4 to 5 feet, if your site and materials will allow it. Be flexible with your design, letting the treads extend over flat areas to form short pathways where the slope flattens, then rises again.

(continued)

1, 2, 3 Basic Step Installation

Follow these steps to install yours. See "Step Options" on this page for specifics on materials you can use.

1. **Mark the risers.** Use stakes to mark both ends of each riser. Use a shovel to shape the slope into rough soil steps, using the stakes as guides. You may need a pick or mattock to accomplish this task.

The tread of each step is just a short section of paving. Leave enough space between risers for the necessary gravel and/or sand base, in addition to the depth of the tread material.

2. **Install the steps.** Work from the bottom to the top of the slope. Alternately set risers and treads in place. Use a carpenter's level to keep them horizontal.

3. **Grade the site.** After the steps are installed, grade the soil on either side to slope naturally down to the steps. Border your steps with stones or plantings of perennials, herbs, groundcovers, or low shrubs to give them a finished look that's easy to maintain.

Step Options

Timber steps. Steps constructed with 4 × 6 timbers for risers are the simplest to build. You can stack two 4 × 4 timbers together to make risers for steeper slopes. Drill into the timbers and tie them to the soil with galvanized metal stakes or spikes (basically huge nails).

Brick or concrete steps. You could also make the risers from bricks or from concrete poured into simple forms. Pave the treads with brick, gravel, wood chips, or groundcovering plants. If you choose to make brick treads, set them in a base of 1½ to 2 inches of mortar over 3 to 4 inches of gravel. Treads of gravel and other loose materials will require edging to keep them in place.

Stone steps. Fieldstone steps with risers of smaller stones look natural in informal landscapes. This type of step can wind more easily because of the varying size of the components. To make wider steps, set two or more fieldstones side by side on a wider bed of small stone risers. For stability, set the small stones in a mortar bed with at

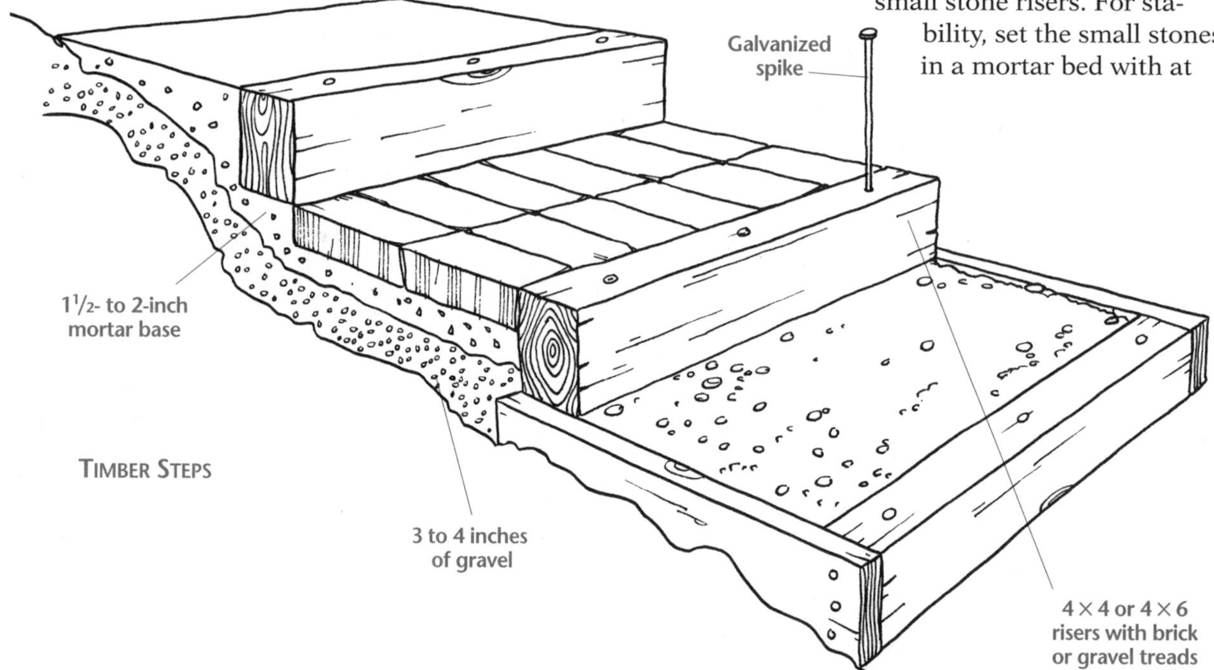

TIMBER STEPS

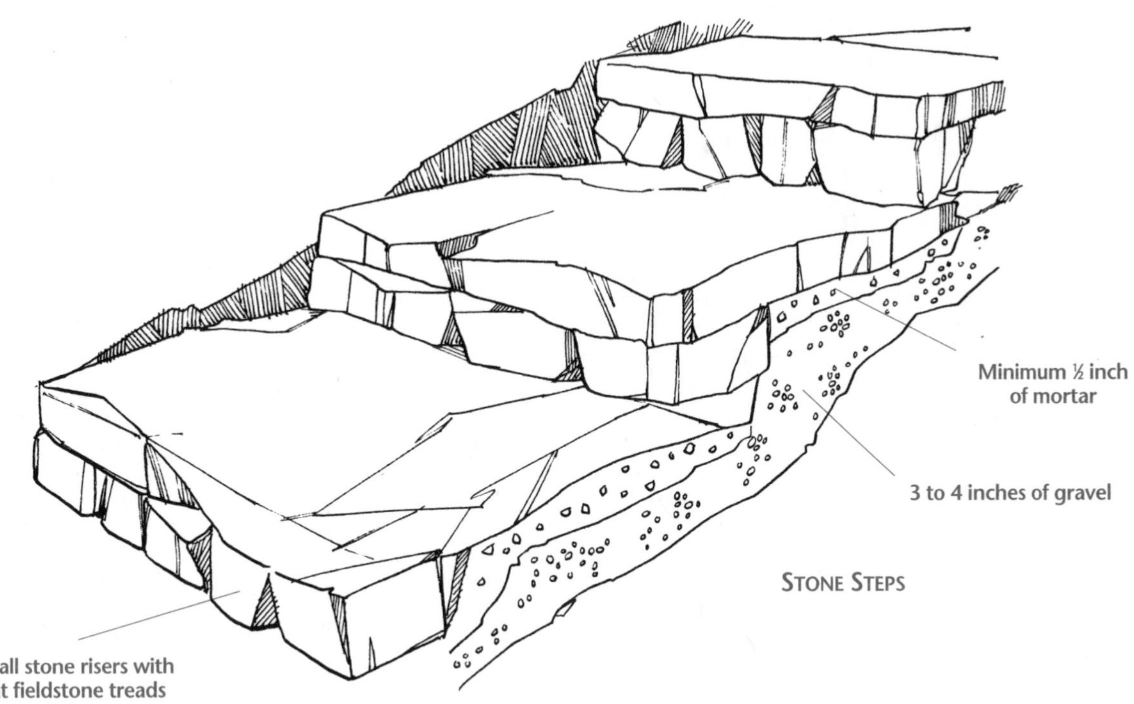

STONE STEPS

least ½ inch of mortar between the small stones and the fieldstone cap. As with brick treads, lay the mortar on top of 3 to 4 inches of gravel. If you don't want to see the mortar, rake it from the face of the joints before it sets completely. You could also use bricks to form the risers for these steps, or stack two fieldstones with mortar beneath and between them. Set the bricks and slate in mortar beds underlaid with gravel.

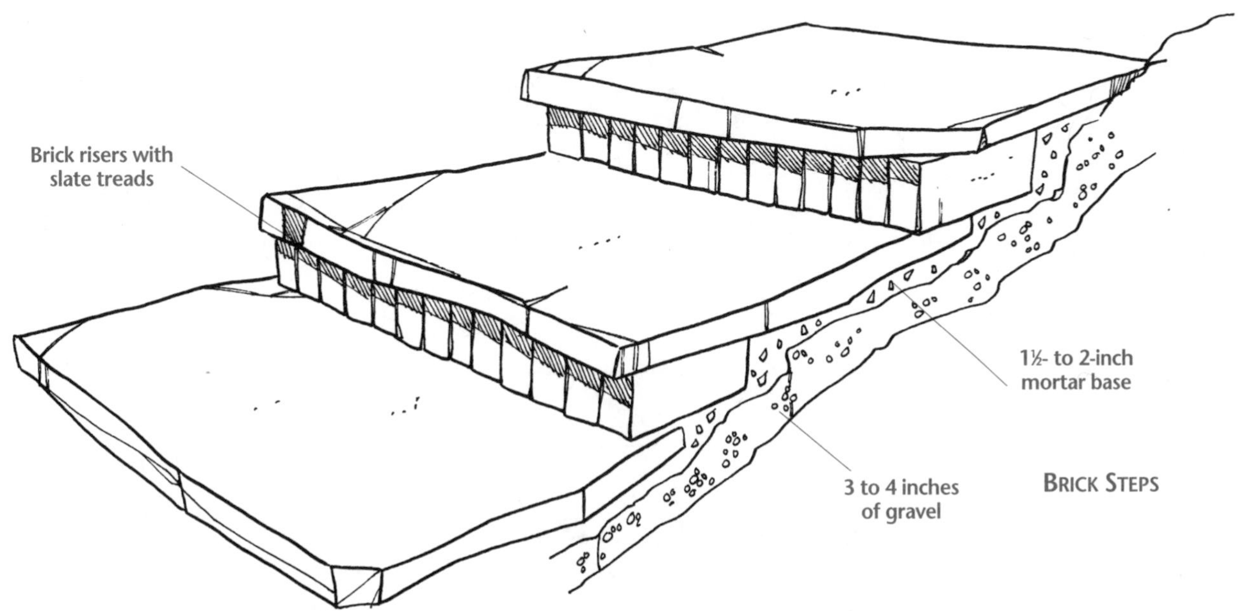

BRICK STEPS

Enhance Your Yard with a Low-Care, Easy-to-Build Deck

Building a deck is not automatically a major investment involving a contractor. You can add a simple deck to your landscape in about a weekend, using tools you probably have at home. Size and place the deck to suit your needs—since it's freestanding, it can go anywhere. Precast concrete piers support the deck's 4 × 4 beams; these are topped by a deck of 2 × 6s.

Begin by deciding where you want your deck. Check the site for sun, drainage, and slope of the land. It's okay if the site slopes slightly, but the more level it is the better. If you're building your deck next to your house, any slope should be away from the house.

Decide on the size of your deck and make a plan, similar to the one shown below, to help you figure out how many beams, piers, and deck boards you need. Space your beams (the distance the deck boards must span) no more than 3 feet apart on center (from the center of one beam to the center of the next). Keep the space between the piers, along the length of beams, no more than 5 to 6 feet on center. If your deck is next to your house, leave a ½- to 1-inch gap between the deck and the house.

Do a Little Make-Sure Math

Make certain the layout of your deck is rectangular. From one corner stake (stake A), measure 3 feet out along the outlining length of string toward another stake (stake B); fold a piece of masking tape over the string to mark that point. From stake A, measure 4 feet along the string toward the stake at the other corner (stake C); mark that point with a second piece of tape. Measuring from tape mark to tape mark across the hypotenuse of the triangle, the distance should be exactly 5 feet. If it is not, adjust the position of stake B or C until the measurement is 5 feet and your deck is a true rectangle.

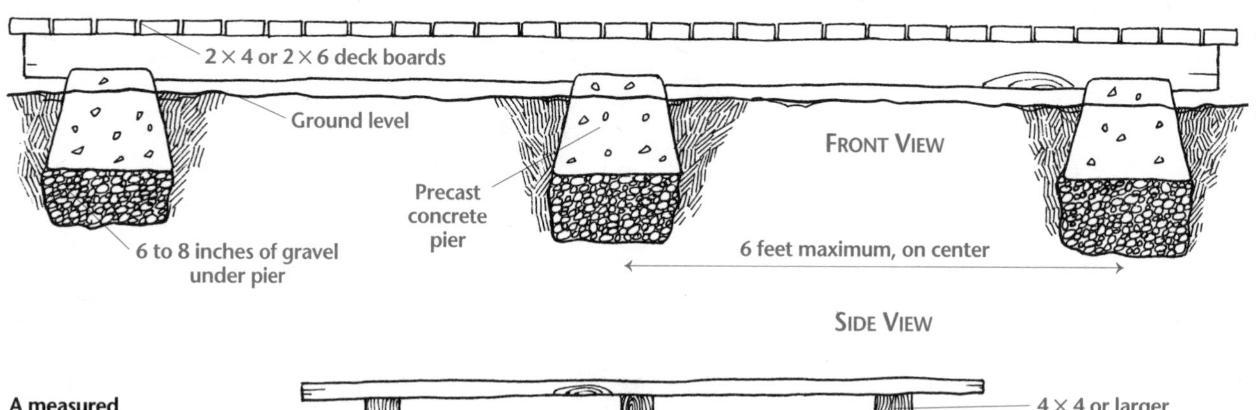

A measured drawing of the front and side views of your deck will help you determine how many piers, beams, and 2 × 6 deck boards you'll need.

Simple Steps to an Easy Deck

1. **Lay out your deck with stakes and string.** Use two stakes to mark each corner; place one about 6 inches out on a straight line with one side and the other stake 6 inches out on a line with the other side. When you stretch strings between the stakes, the strings will cross at the corners of the deck and form its outline.

Stretch string between the stakes and level it with a carpenter's level or, preferably, a line level. The string helps you visualize the deck, determine where you need to add or remove soil, and level the piers. Remove all sod in the deck area.

2. **Lay out the piers.** Working from your drawing, measure in from the strings and lay out the piers. Drive a stake to mark the center of each pier position. Set the piers back from the edges of the deck to keep them out of sight.

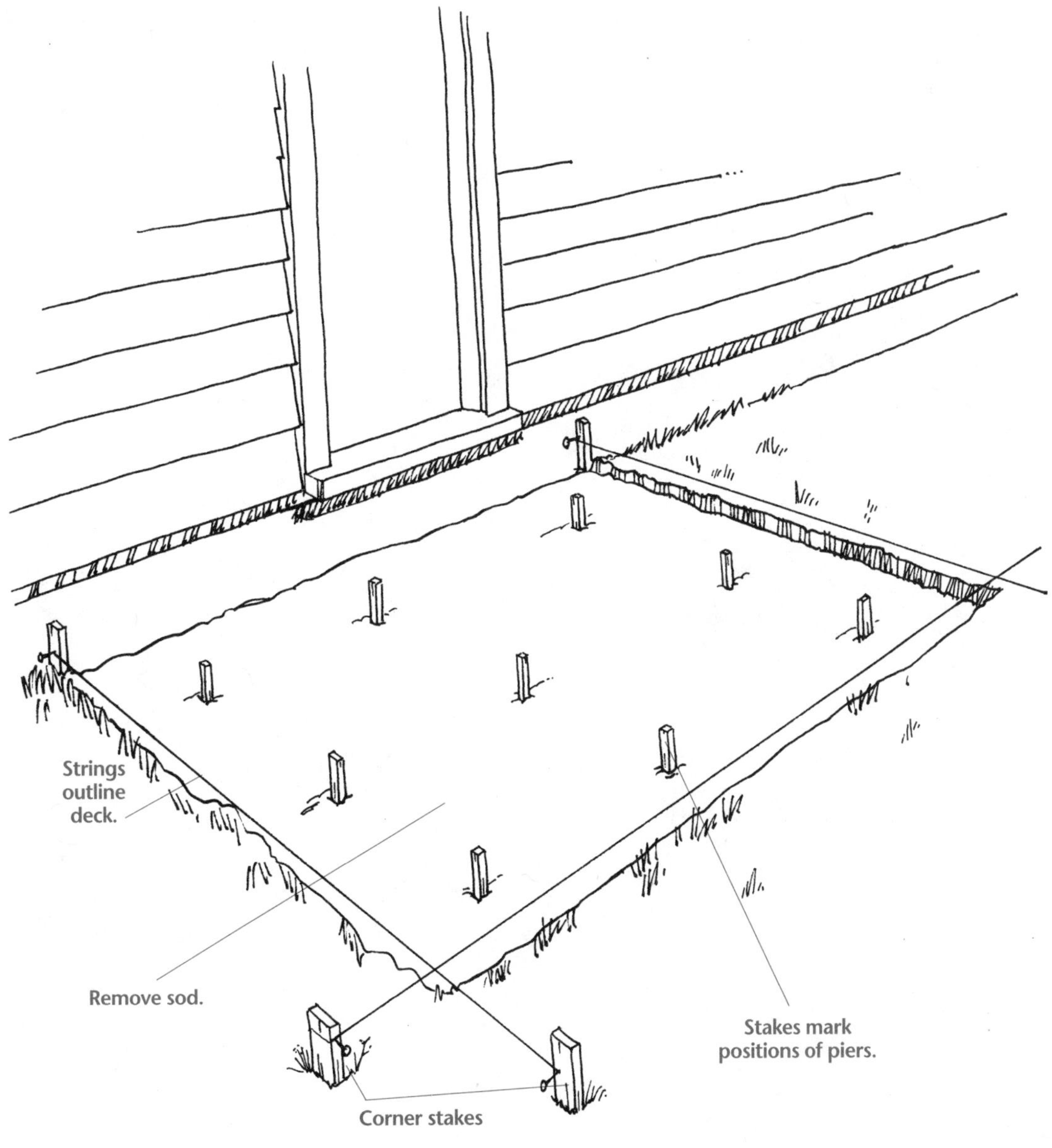

(continued)

3. **Dig a hole for each pier.** Dig deep enough to accommodate a 6- to 8-inch gravel base plus most of the height of the pier. Stretch additional strings, as needed, to help you position your holes and measure the depth to dig. Remove the soil in a wheelbarrow, add gravel to each hole, and tamp the gravel to remove any air pockets. If you don't have a good tamper handy, use the end of one of your 4 × 4 beams. In areas where the ground does not freeze in the winter, you can set your piers in smaller holes with just a 2-inch layer of sand in the bottom.

4. **Set the precast piers onto the gravel.** Adjust the height, level, and exact alignment according to string lines and a carpenter's level. Backfill with soil around the piers. Check the accuracy of your work with a tape measure from time to time to make sure the piers are spaced properly.

5. **Spread landscape fabric.** To prevent grass and weeds from growing up between the deck boards, spread landscape fabric or other light-blocking material over the area. Cut an X in the fabric over each pier and pull it down snugly around them.

6. **Saw the 4 × 4 beams to length.** Lay them across the

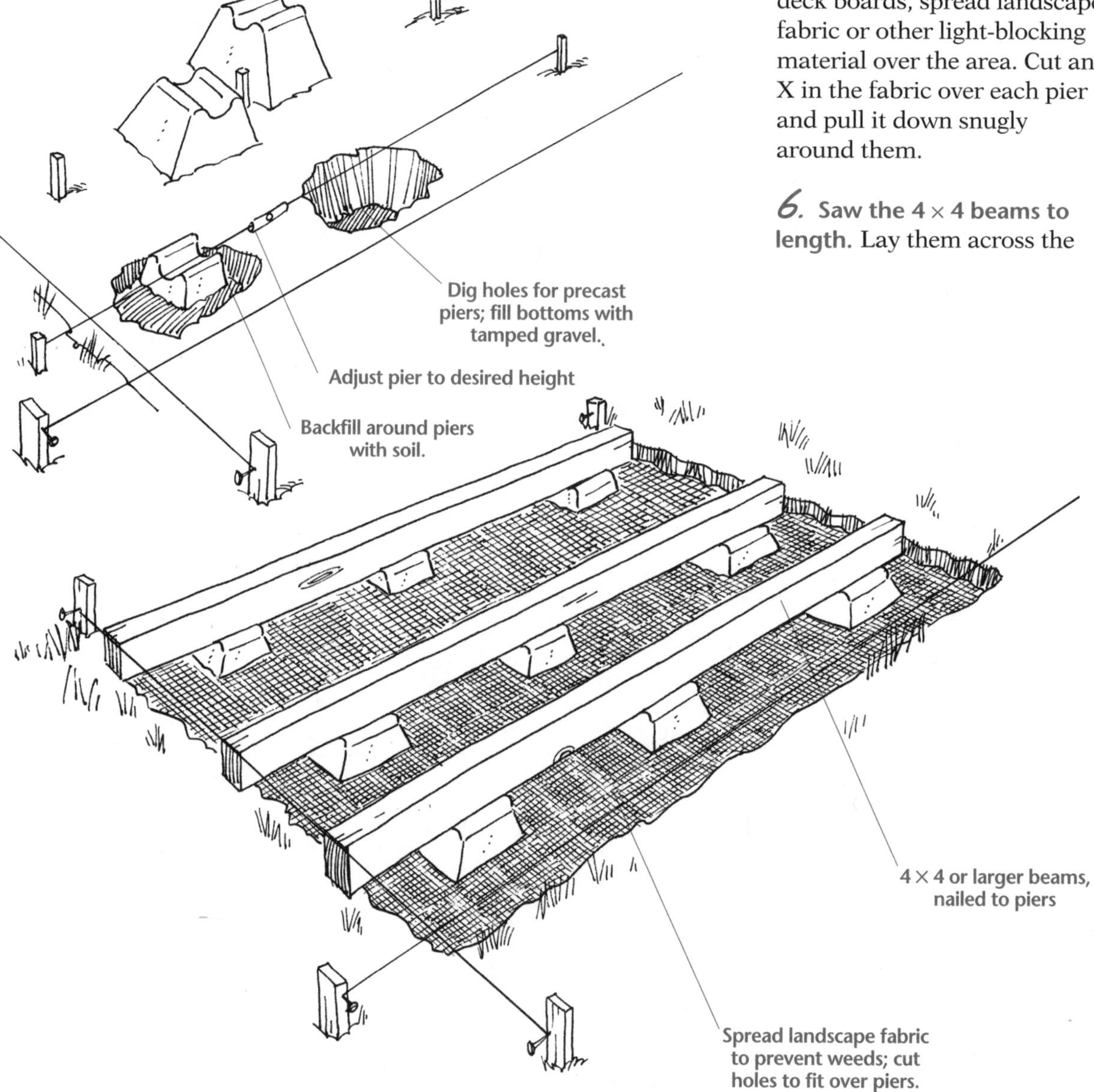

piers and nail them in place. Each pier will have a wooden nail block or metal hardware precast in it for nailing the beam. Align the ends of the beams with a string or a straightedge, or by careful measurement.

7. Nail on the decking.

Laying out the decking can be tricky, but with a small deck you can lay out the boards before nailing them. Snap chalk lines as nailing guides, then attach each 2 × 6 deck board to the beams with two 16d galvanized nails at each beam. You can use ring-shank or twist nails for stronger hold. Use a 16d nail to space between the boards as you nail them. Let the first and last deck boards overhang the ends of the beams about an inch. You can adjust this somewhat, or adjust the spacing between the boards to make them fit evenly. If necessary, you can narrow the width of one board to fit the width of the last space.

As you work, use a straightedge to align all the deck boards on one end; let the other end extend slightly long. After all the boards are nailed in place, measure from each side of the deck and snap a chalk line to mark the edge of the boards. Cut along this line with a portable circular saw to even the ends. Soften up this hard edge with a rasp. Stain and/or seal the cut ends and your deck is complete.

Ease Stain and Sealer Applications

If you want to stain and/or seal your deck, it's easier to do it before you nail the boards to the beams. This ensures that you get an even coating on all surfaces and gives the deck better protection from the elements.

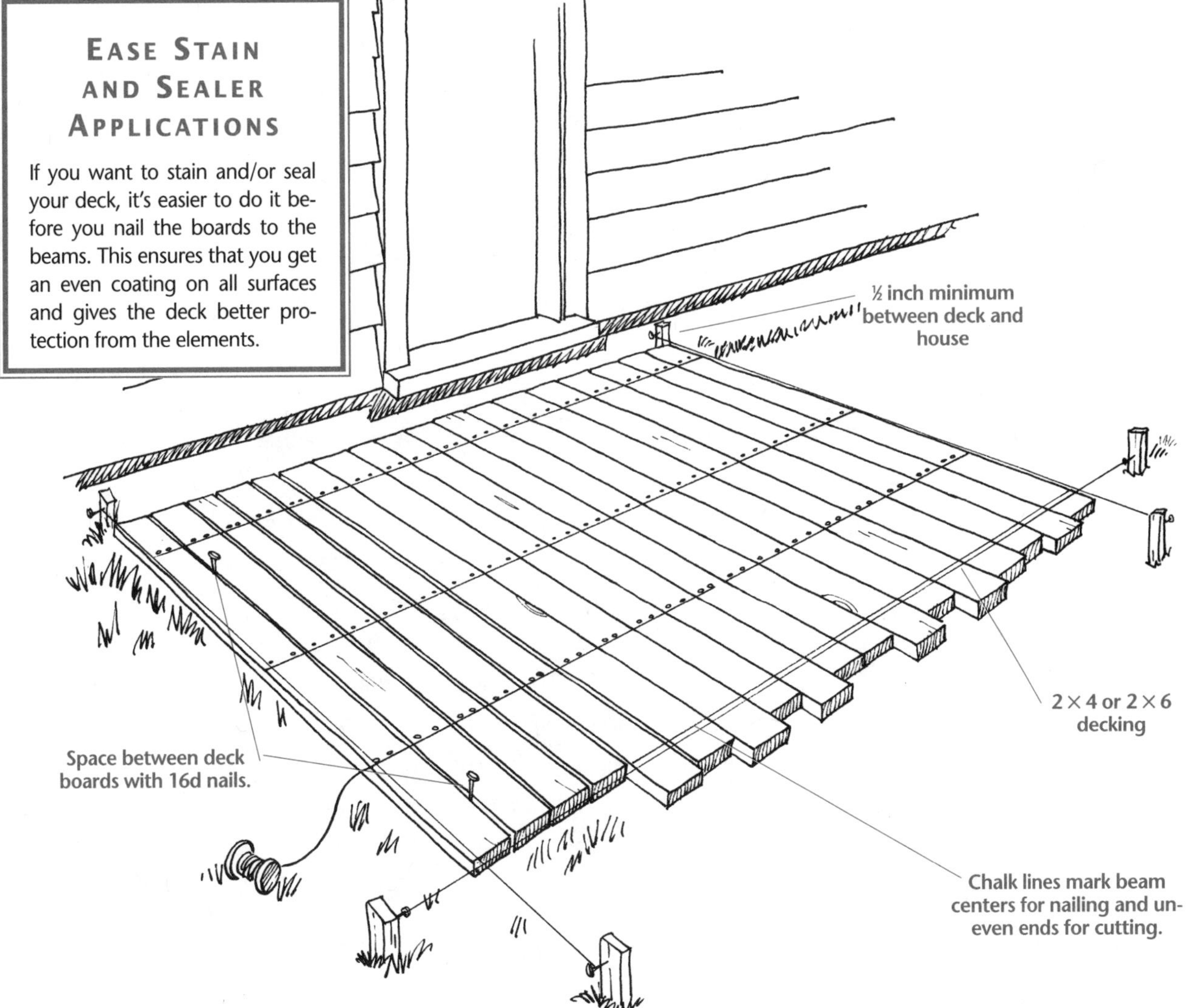

CHAPTER 21

Problem Sites: Quick Solutions to Your Yard's Trouble Spots

Problem Sites the Low-Maintenance Way

THE EASIEST WAY to solve a problem is to turn it into an opportunity. Do you have a soggy swale or a parched slope in your yard? Just match the right plants to your conditions and let them transform your eyesore into an easy-care garden. Matchmaking beats every other method of improving your site because all you have to do is plant.

If you want to grow vegetables or have some favorite plants that need special conditions, don't despair. There are plenty of ways to simplify site improvement. Look over the easy techniques for fixing problem sites in this chapter. Before you head for the garden, take a look at Chapters 2 and 6. They offer the best all-around methods for improving any site using compost and mulch.

SHADY-SITE SOLUTIONS

Stop struggling with your dark area, and take advantage of what it can offer you instead. Whether you're dealing with dry or moist shade, you've got a perfect spot for a dazzling wildflower and woodland plant garden.

If shade is so dense that rain can't reach the ground and even wildflowers struggle, there are simple ways to let light and water in. Check the tips below for methods to thin dense plantings, techniques for planting under trees, and even ways to turn sparse shaded lawn areas into lush groundcover blankets. These easy techniques guarantee shade flowers will thrive and your maintenance chores will fade away.

To Pick Care-Free Plants, It Pays to Know Your Shade

You'll turn your shady problem site into an easy-care triumph if you remember that not all shade is created equal. A site can have light, filtered shade or deep, dark shade, for example. For a low-maintenance garden that looks great, too, all you really need to know is where you have heavy shade—the most difficult site for plants—and where you have partial shade. Then choose the plants that thrive in the conditions you have. Look through the list of "Care-Free Plants for Shade" on page 216 for specific recommendations.

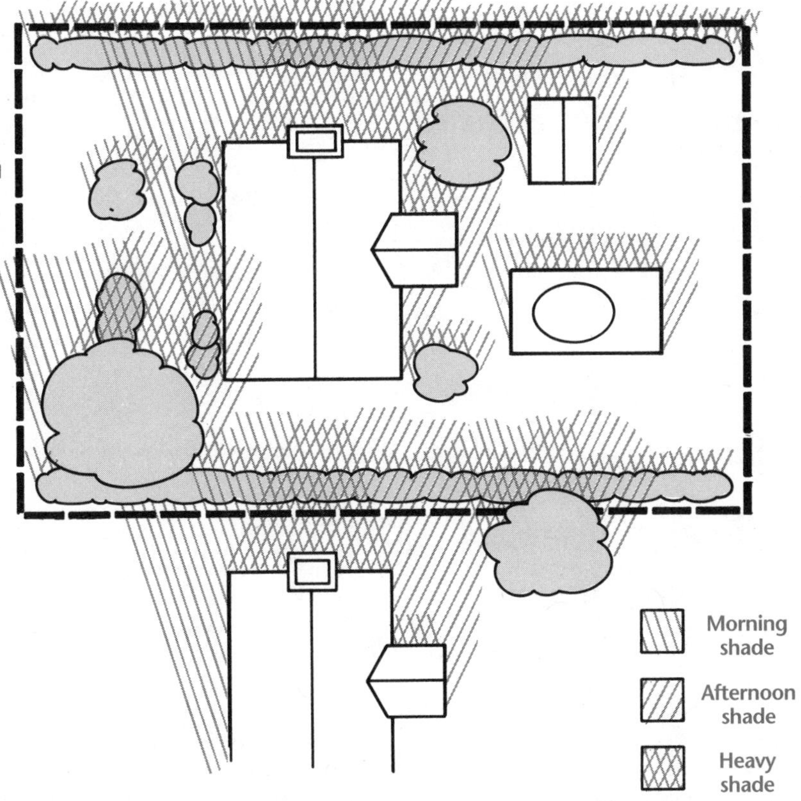

Start solving shady-site problems by identifying spots that receive different amounts of shade during the day. Sketching patterns of shade and shadow on a rough map of your yard is a good way to get a realistic picture of what parts of the garden are in shade all day or only part of the day. For best results, mark partially and heavily shaded areas in your landscape at different times of day and during different seasons.

Care-Free Plants for Shade

Plenty of gorgeous plants thrive in shady sites. Welcome them and you can say good-bye to the sun lovers that languish and increase maintenance. Groundcovers, for example, give you lots of options for the dark shade under trees. See "Fuss-Free Flowers for Shady Sites" on page 306 for more plants that thrive in shade.

If your site gets a few hours of morning sun each day, you'll have even more choices since many plants enjoy partial shade. Use sun lovers for sites that blaze with afternoon sun—shade lovers may burn.

Groundcovers for Heavy or Partial Shade

Big blue lilyturf (*Liriope muscari*): Strap-shaped evergreen leaves; spikes of violet or white flowers in summer. Zones 6–9.

Canada wild ginger (*Asarum canadense*): Creeping plant; velvety, heart-shaped leaves; red, juglike flowers hidden by foliage. Zones 3–8.

Common periwinkle (*Vinca minor*): Trailer with small, glossy leaves; lavender-blue flowers in spring. Zones 4–9.

English ivy (*Hedera helix*): Low creeper with glossy, lobed evergreen leaves. Zones 4–9.

Epimediums (*Epimedium* spp.): Tough creeper with wiry stems; glossy, compound leaves; spurred red, yellow, white, or pink flowers in spring. Zones 3–8.

Japanese pachysandra (*Pachysandra terminalis*): Spreads rapidly by rhizomes; glossy evergreen leaves; white flowers in late spring. Zones 4–9.

Spotted lamium (*Lamium maculatum*): Spreads by creeping stems clothed in silver leaves with central green stripe; pink or white flowers. Zones 3–8.

Yellow archangel (*Lamiastrum galeobdolon*): Upright spreader with silver-mottled leaves; yellow flowers. Zones 4–9.

Perennials for Heavy Shade

Fringed bleeding heart (*Dicentra eximia*): Bushy plant with blue-green ferny foliage; pink heart-shaped flowers. Zones 3–9.

Lady fern (*Athyrium filix-femina*): Lacy, bright green leaves emerge from a creeping rhizome. Zones 2–9.

Lenten rose (*Helleborus orientalis*): Clumps of compound evergreen leaves; clusters of white, pink, rose, or purple flowers in early spring. Zones 4–9.

Hostas (*Hosta* spp.): Foliage plants with showy leaves in a variety of shapes from lance-like to heart-shaped; leaf colors include green, blue, yellow, and variegated; showy lavender or white flowers. Zones 3–9.

Siberian bugloss (*Brunnera macrophylla*): Heart-shaped leaves; blue flowers similar to forget-me-nots in early spring. Zones 3–8.

Variegated Solomon's seal (*Polygonatum odoratum* 'Variegatum'): Tall plant with oval leaves outlined in white that rise up the stem like rungs of a ladder; nodding, fragrant bell-shaped flowers. Zones 3–9.

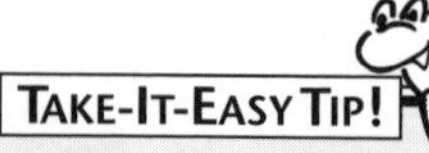

TAKE-IT-EASY TIP!

Simplify Tree Care with Mulch

Some shady areas defy gardening attempts, and that's when mulch makes the easiest groundcover of all. A layer of bark mulch can give you a care-free, weed-free surface instantly; it's especially good for unsociable sites like under black walnut trees or the heavy shade of southern magnolias. Spread mulch all the way out to the drip line for easier mowing, no weeding, and happier trees.

Perennials for Partial Shade

Allegheny foamflower (*Tiarella cordifolia*): Creeping groundcover with maplelike evergreen leaves; short spikes of fuzzy white flowers in spring. Zones 3–8.

Astilbes (*Astilbe* spp.): Clumps of attractive, divided foliage; airy plumes of flowers in all shades of pink and red, plus white in late spring and summer. Zones 3–9.

Bloodroot (*Sanguinaria canadensis*): Clumps of starry white flowers in spring, followed by gray-green, deeply lobed leaves. Zones 3–8.

Bugbanes (*Cimicifuga* spp.): Tall plants with huge divided leaves; narrow spikes of fuzzy white flowers in summer. Zones 3–8.

Columbines (*Aquilegia* spp.): Mounding plant with lacy foliage; spurred flowers bloom blue, white, yellow, red, and bicolor in spring or early summer. Zones 3–9.

Cranesbills (*Geranium* spp.): Mounded plants with rounded, lobed leaves; saucer- or cup-shaped flowers in blue, pink, purple, or white. Zones 3–8.

Heartleaf bergenia (*Bergenia cordifolia*): Large, leathery leaves; clusters of waxy pink bell-like flowers in spring. Zones 3–9.

Siberian iris (*Iris sibirica*): Clumps of narrow, sword-shaped leaves; blue, purple, yellow, white, or bicolor flowers in early summer. Zones 2–9.

Prune Unruly Shrubs into Well-Behaved Trees

Instead of taking giant shade-casting shrubs like lilacs, rhododendrons, and burning bush out of the ground, turn them into small trees with a pair of pruning shears and a saw. Prune out suckers and dead or damaged wood, then choose one to three of the healthiest, best-formed stems for the trunks of your new tree. Remove the other stems and then shape and thin the crown of your new tree. Now you'll have enough room, light, and air circulation for your shade garden to thrive.

Plant Bulbs for Shade-Loving Spring Color

Spots under large trees generally get plenty of sun in spring but are plunged into darkness as the trees leaf out. Brighten up these shady spots by filling them with bulbs such as daffodils, snowdrops, and crocuses. Spring bulbs are perfect for such summer-shaded sites because they bloom early, make all the food they need, then disappear as the shadows are closing in. Also, add shade-tolerant groundcovers like hostas, vinca, and those listed in "Care-Free Plants for Shade" on the opposite page; they'll fill in the site after the bulbs fade.

Maintenance Is a Breeze When You Plant under Trees

Get rid of miserable mowing and weeding chores in a hurry with clumps of quick-growing groundcovers. Buy large pots or flats of well-rooted plants and break them into large pieces for the quickest coverage and the shortest planting time.

The best way to put a stop to maintenance under trees is to replace struggling lawn grass and weeds with shade- and drought-tolerant groundcovers. Prepare planting pockets to give groundcovers a good start; they won't ask you for anything more.

Planting pockets make happy homes for plants under trees. Explore the area under your trees with a hand trowel before you plant groundcovers. Find open areas between established tree roots, then dig small holes or "pockets" for plants.

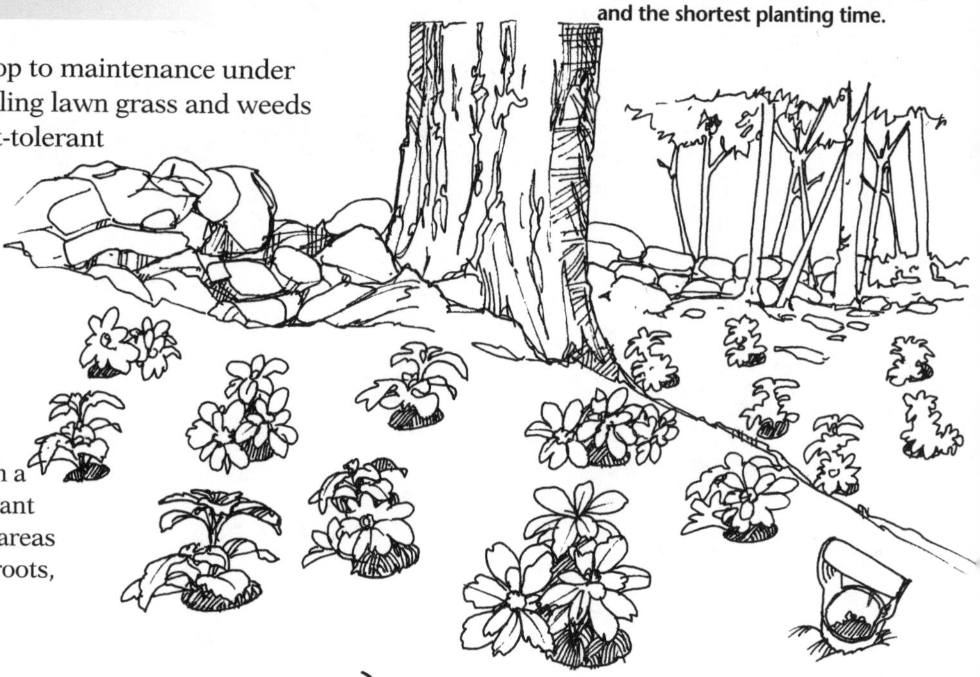

If you've got shallow-rooted trees such as maples and beeches, there will be lots of fibrous roots to work around. Trees like oaks, with deep roots, will have more root-free places to plant. Whichever type of tree you're dealing with, take care not to damage large roots and do not remove more than 5 percent of smaller roots while planting.

Add just enough compost to fill your holes and bring new plants up to the original soil level. Never bury the crown of a tree or it will decline. Oaks are particularly vulnerable. Any damage to oak roots during the growing season may make them susceptible to oak wilt. Other trees to handle with care include sugar maple and basswood.

Plant drought-tolerant groundcovers and let nature handle the watering. Irrigation helps your new plants, but altering the natural moisture regime or adding too much water may kill your trees. Choose plants that can compete with tree roots for water, so they can fend for themselves without additional drinks from you.

Try big blue lilyturf (*Liriope muscari*), lungworts (*Pulmonaria* spp.), Japanese pachysandra (*Pachysandra terminalis*), and yellow archangel (*Lamiastrum galeobdolon*). Bulbous plants also thrive in dry shade; after blooming in spring they go dormant, so they don't have to compete for water. Try spring beauties (*Claytonia virginica*), scillas, and crocuses.

Brighten Too-Shady Spots with Pruning Shears

When shade is too deep, lighten the dark recesses of your yard by opening up your tree or shrub canopy. Remove branches to allow light and water to reach your plants. For large trees, have an arborist do the work for you. If you have smaller plants, consider these shade-lightening techniques. See Chapter 9 for more helpful tree and shrub pruning tips.

Add light by keeping trees healthy. Broken or diseased branches threaten the health of your trees and cast shade. Start any pruning project by removing them.

Raise the roof. Remove drooping or low-hanging branches that make you feel closed in. Raising the canopy allows more light in and increases air circulation. Carefully choose the branches you remove, and balance the form of the tree as you go.

Let the sun shine in. Open up densly branched trees by removing branches that cross, are too crowded, grow upward, or have narrow crotch angles. It's best to work from the bottom up and from the inside out, so you can preserve the graceful lines of the main limbs.

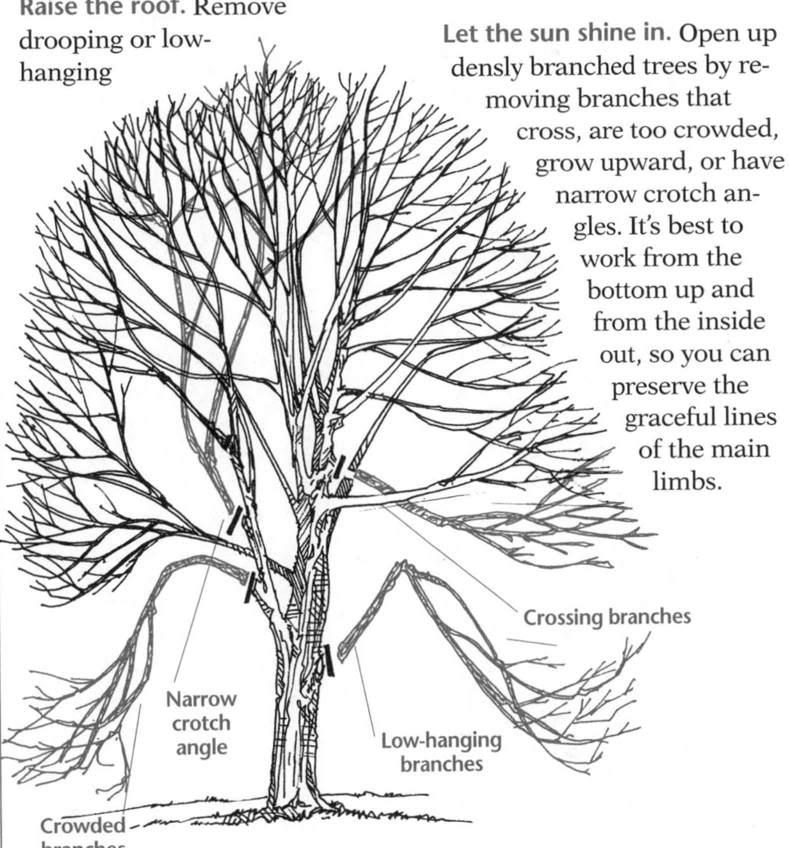

WET-SITE SOLUTIONS

Soggy sites and heavy wet soil may seem like a liability, but some of the most beautiful shrubs and perennials that we grow actually prefer constant moisture. Most wet-site plants are adaptable and will grow well under drier garden conditions. Give them the moisture they love, though, and they develop to their full potential and look their stunning best. Another great thing about wet sites—you won't have to water your plants, so maintenance chores are easier. If you have a soggy spot, what you've really got is a chance to make a unique and beautiful garden that can fend for itself. If your moisture is in the wrong place, don't pout. There are plants to sop up the excess and ways to direct water where it's wanted.

Bridges Make It Easy to Work on Wet Sites

A low spot, drainage swale, or ditch makes a great low-maintenance garden spot, but only if you can get to it. A simple plank bridge takes only moments to build and will give you easy access.

Nail two rough, decay-resistant 2 × 10 or 2 × 12 planks side by side onto short lengths of decay resistant 2 × 4s. (See "What to Do about Decay" on page 199 for information on protecting your wooden bridge from rot.) On level ground, the plank material can be from 10 to 16 feet long, depending upon the amount of wet land you need to span. Butt two or three plank walkways end to end if necessary. If the ground is not exactly flat or the path turns, make shorter walkways.

Space the 2 × 4s about 48 inches apart, and secure each plank to the 2 × 4s with three 16d nails. Rough wood works best since it prevents slipping and is slightly thicker (stronger) than planed wood.

Plant Ponds from Dry Ground

Stay dry *and* get your pond or water garden planted by dropping plants into the water from your pool's edges. If your pond is sizable, you can do it from the comfort and safety of a boat. To plant, place divisions of hardy water plants in small pieces of burlap, add soil and a stone, and loosely tie the edges together. Then drop plant bundles from a dry spot. Your wrapped plants will sink to the bottom where the weight of the rock and soil will keep it in place while the new plants take hold. Young roots have no trouble growing through the burlap. By the time the plants are established, the burlap will have rotted away.

Eliminate Water Worries with Plants, Not Drainage Projects

The usual solution to a soggy site is to drain it, but you'll get better results for a lot less effort if you plant it. A low spot with damp soil is quite an asset once it's surrounded with astilbes, irises, ferns, and other moisture lovers. And plants are great for soaking up excess water around your foundation or in your yard. You've got the option of putting plants where the water is or bringing water to where the plants are. Using excess water will save you from watering chores and bills.

Plant thirsty plants beside leaky spots. The well-drained conditions found around foundations are perfect for plants like mint and lavender. Their spreading roots will slurp up water before it has a chance to drip down your basement wall.

Ship extra water to where plants can use it. If your water problem is bigger than a foundation planting can handle, slope the soil away from your house at the rate of 1 inch every 4 feet. To help the water move, construct a gentle swale or channel to carry the water away from the house.

Direct water through the yard to a spot that is already low, like your wet-site garden. The extra water will help ensure that the water-loving plants you've planted will get the moisture they need.

Plant moist areas. Many moisture lovers like a combination of lots of water and good drainage. Rather than planting them in a drainage ditch or shallow pond, cover the area *around* your wet spot. Plants set along banks get the drainage they need and the moisture they crave. In return, you'll get less maintenance—no more difficult mowing areas and wet weedy spots. See "Plants That Prefer Moist Sites" on page 222 for plants to try.

Plant wet spots. Consider a water garden for sites that are constantly under water. There are lots of plants to choose from, including cannas, irises, water lilies, and a huge variety of bog plants. Your best bet is to visit a water gardening nursery or browse through water gardening catalogs. They can supply you with recommendations for the easiest plants to grow in your area. See "Sources" on page 355 for a list of catalogs.

Compost Helps You Avoid Watering Seasonally Wet Sites

If your moist garden turns into a desert in summer, you'll spend lots of time with a hose—unless you can find a way to hold more water in the soil. One application of organic matter in spring will improve your soil's water-holding capacity and add nutrients to help plants endure the stress of dry summer conditions. Spread 3 to 4 inches of compost or rotted manure over the entire bed and incorporate it thoroughly with a tiller or a spading fork.

Cover Wet Spots without Losing Control of Rampant Plants

Invasive plants are great for crowding weeds or overgrown grass out of soggy sites, but not if they take over nearby garden or lawn areas. To save time chasing runaway groundcovers or grasses, plant them in containers.

A galvanized iron pail, bucket, or plastic tub will rein in spreading roots and keep plants where you want them. Cut the bottom out to allow for good drainage. Or, buy strips of 18- or 24-inch-wide aluminum or galvanized steel at a hardware store. The length depends on the size of the container you need. An average container size is 2 feet in diameter; for that size, you need 6 feet of length. Join the ends together and sink the cylinder into the ground.

Plants That Prefer Moist Sites

The better you are at matching plants to your growing site, the less you'll have to care for them. Fortunately, when it comes to moist sites, there are lots of plant choices. All of the plants listed below are perfect for growing around wet areas where they'll get plenty of moisture and good drainage. Plants that can actually be planted in swampy areas are marked with an asterisk (*).

Perennials

Astilbes (*Astilbe* spp.): Summer-blooming perennials with airy plumes of fuzzy flowers in shades of white, pink, purple, and red. Zones 3–8.

Bee balm (*Monarda didyma*): Fragrant, lance-shaped leaves; dense heads of red, purple, pink, or white flowers in summer. Zones 4–8.

Cinnamon fern (*Osmunda cinnamomea*): Large, graceful plants with arching fronds. Zones 3–10.

Cord grass (*Spartina* spp.): Graceful grasses with long, arching blades and stiff, treelike flower spikes. Variegated forms are available. Zones 3–8.*

Daylilies (*Hemerocallis* spp.): Straplike leaves and cheery lilylike flowers in shades of red, orange, and yellow. Flowers last a day, but plants bloom for nearly a month in summer. Zones 3–9.

Golden-rays (*Ligularia* spp.): Bold foliage plants with rounded or spear-shaped leaves and clusters of tall spikes of yellow flowers in summer. Zones 3–8.*

Gooseneck loosestrife (*Lysimachia clethroides*): Wiry stems clothed in shiny, bright green leaves; drooping spikes of white flowers. Zones 3–8.

Hibiscus (*Hibiscus* spp.): Dinner-plate-size flowers open for only a day, but plants stay in bloom for over a month. Flowers may be white, red, or pink. Zones 4–9.

Hostas (*Hosta* spp.): Foliage plant with clumps of heart- or lance-shaped leaves in shades of green, blue, and yellow, many with white or yellow variegations; fragrant white or lavender flowers. Zones 3–8.

Joe-Pye weed (*Eupatorium* spp.): Large plants with whorled leaves; huge heads of pink flowers in midsummer. Zones 3–8.

Lobelias (*Lobelia* spp.): Summer- and fall-blooming

plants with elliptical to lance-shaped leaves; tall spikes of red or blue flowers. Zones 3–9, depending on species.

Marsh marigold (*Caltha palustris*): Spring-blooming wildflower with 1-inch butter yellow flowers and deep green, rounded leaves. Plants go dormant after flowering. Zones 2–8.*

Obedient plant (*Physostegia virginiana*): Stiffly upright stems; spikes of tubular pink, rose, or white flowers in late summer. Zones 3–9.

Queen-of-the-prairie (*Filipendula rubra*): Stately perennial with bold, palmately lobed leaves and large pink plumes that resemble cotton candy. Plants bloom 4–6 feet high in summer. Zones 3–9.

Rodgersias (*Rodgersia* spp.): Foliage perennials with large, imposing compound leaves and fuzzy white or pink flowers that resemble astilbes. Zones 4–7.

Siberian iris (*Iris sibirica*): Narrow, upright foliage and dainty flowers in all shades of blue and purple, as well as rose, yellow, and white. Zones 2–9.*

Smartweeds (*Polygonum* spp.): Groundcovers with shiny, lance-shaped leaves; dense spikes of small, beadlike pink, rose, or white flowers. Zones 3–8.

Stoke's aster (*Stokesia laevis*): Showy plant with long, slender basal leaves; open clusters of blue or white flowers in summer. Zones 5–9.

Swamp sunflower (*Helianthus angustifolius*): Tall plant with linear leaves; masses of 3-inch, bright yellow sunflowers in fall. Zones 5–9.

Turtleheads (*Chelone* spp.): Tall, autumn-blooming plants with narrow leaves and unique, inflated pink or white flowers that resemble the head of a turtle. Zones 3–8.*

Yellow flag (*Iris pseudacorus*): Tall iris to 4 feet with broad, straplike leaves; delicate yellow flowers in late spring and early summer. Thrives when roots are submerged. Zones 4–9.*

Yellow loosestrife (*Lysimachia punctata*): Whorls of felted leaves; tiers of starry, bright yellow flowers. Zones 4–8.

Shrubs and Trees

American planetree (*Platanus occidentalis*): Large tree with starry, palmate leaves and beautiful, mottled white bark; fuzzy, round seedpods in summer. Zones 4–9.

Bald cypress (*Taxodium distichum*): Large conifer that drops its feathery leaves in fall; rounded cones. Tolerates swampy sites. Zones 4–8.*

Green ash (*Fraxinus pennsylvanica*): Medium to large, fast-growing tree with glossy, compound leaves and furrowed bark; clear yellow fall color. Zones 3–9.

Red maple (*Acer rubrum*): Tall tree with smooth gray bark when it is young; star-shaped, lobed leaves turn flaming red in autumn. Zones 3–9.

Red-osier dogwood (*Cornus sericea*): Creeping shrub valuable for its bright red winter twigs; clusters of small white flowers in spring, followed by white berries. Zones 2–8.

Silver maple (*Acer saccharinum*): Large, fast-growing tree with deeply lobed leaves and shaggy, mature bark. Zones 3–9.

Spicebush (*Lindera benzoin*): Large shrub with elliptical leaves that emit a pungent odor when crushed; yellow fall color. Yellow flowers in early spring are followed by fragrant red berries. Zones 4–9.

Summersweet (*Clethra alnifolia*): Medium-size shrub with dark green leaves; summer spires of fragrant white flowers. Plants spread by creeping stems to form tight colonies. Thrives in swamps and bogs. Zones 4–10.*

Sweetspire (*Itea virginica*): Small to medium-size shrub with glossy green foliage, red fall color, and drooping spires of fragrant white flowers in summer. Thrives in wet sites. Zones 5–9.*

SLOPING-SITE SOLUTIONS

If pushing and pulling your lawn mower up slopes isn't your idea of fun, put a stop to steep-site maintenance with mulch and fast-growing plants. A cover of mulch helps conserve moisture, which is usually short on slopes. It also keeps weeds from taking over and breaks the force of driving raindrops. A combination of groundcovers, perennials with spreading roots, and dense mats of leaves can quickly replace hard-to-mow grass or cover bare or weedy banks. Spreading plants help hold the soil in place, too, and soak up rain that would otherwise wash steep areas away.

Evade Planting Problems on Slopes with Erosion Mats

Spreading groundcovers will eliminate your mowing and weeding chores fast if you anchor plants with fabric mats for a quick start. You can easily hold soil and new roots in place with erosion control mats made of burlap, wool mat, or paper. Avoid landscape fabric since you want a mat that biodegrades.

Buy enough fabric to cover the slope—or just part of it, if you'd rather work at it bit by bit. Roll the burlap or mats out and secure them to the slope with wire pins. Set plants out where you want them. Then lift each container and cut an X with a sharp knife to make a hole large enough for the root ball. Fold the edges back, dig a hole, and plant. Then, fold the edges back around the plant. Once you've finished planting, mulch over the new planting to disguise the fabric and conserve valuable moisture.

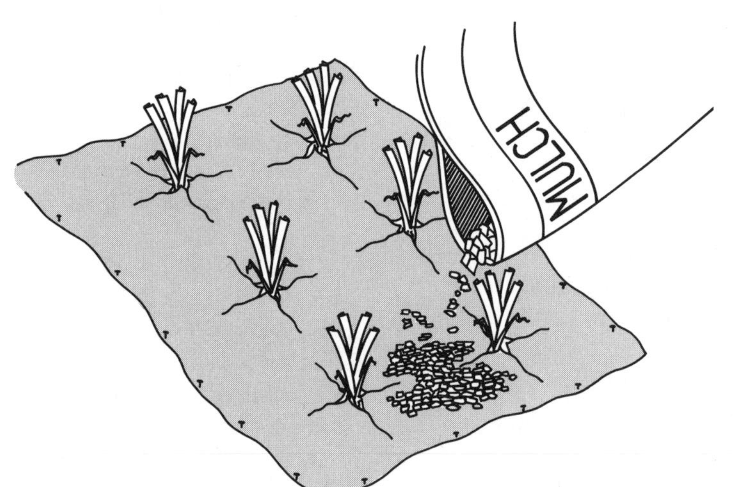

Level Rocky Slopes with Terrace Gardens

Do you spend more time slipping and sliding off your steep slope than gardening? Level your planting area with rock terraces and save all that wear and tear. Stone terraces will take some work, but once you're done, you won't have to worry about you or your plants rolling down hill. You won't have as many water worries either, since the level beds will hold moisture instead of letting it run away.

Plan on low walls (less than 3 feet tall) since they're simpler to build and work around. If you have a very steep slope, you'll need more than one terrace. Figure out how many terraces you'll need by following the directions for installing stairs on pages 207–209. Just substitute terrace height for step height; the math is the same.

1. **Mark the height and length of the wall.** Use stakes and string to mark the top edge of each wall. They'll serve as guidelines for laying the stones, so make sure the string is level.

2. **Lay the walls.** Start with the lowest wall and work back toward the top of the slope. Dig out a little soil and place stones so they sit firmly on the ground. Add layers of stone until you reach the string. Slope the walls backward slightly to give them stability.

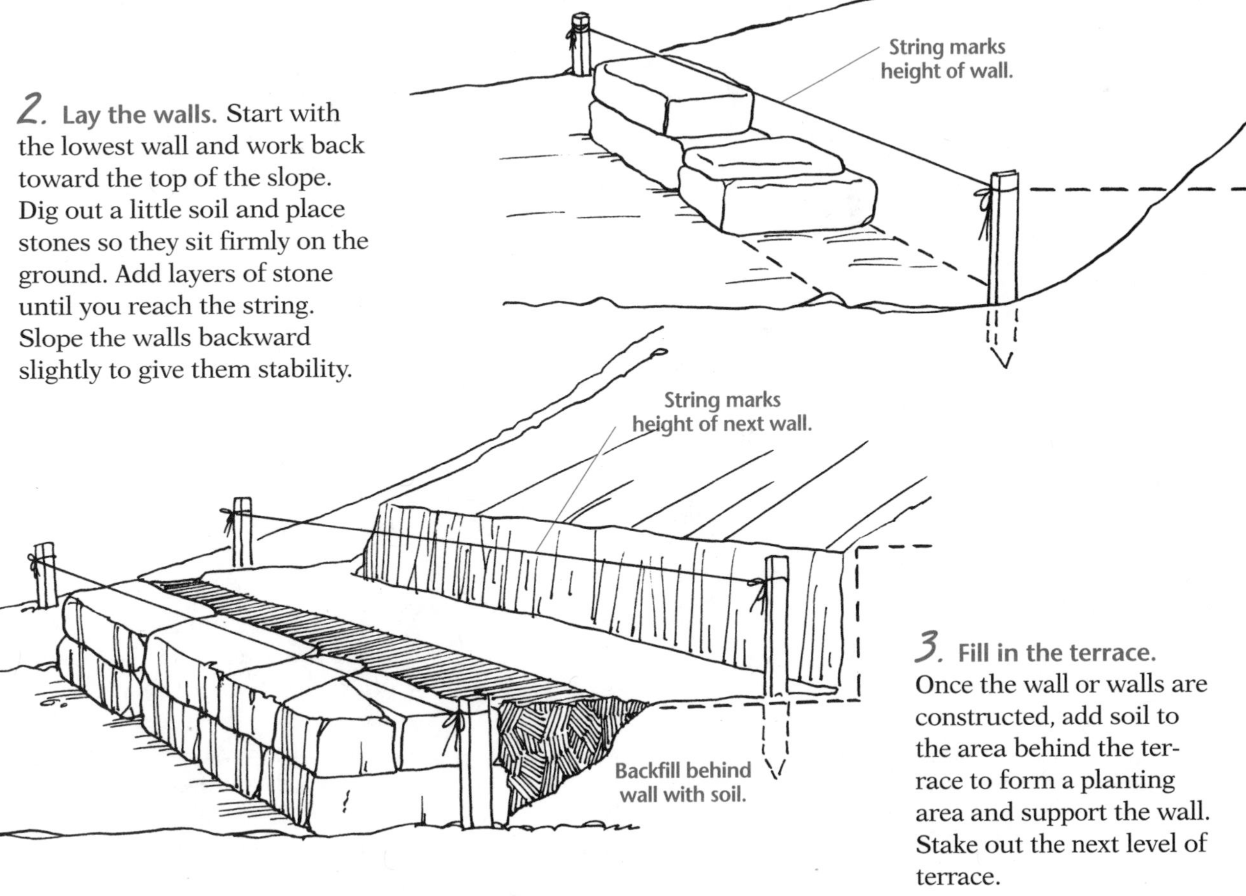

3. **Fill in the terrace.** Once the wall or walls are constructed, add soil to the area behind the terrace to form a planting area and support the wall. Stake out the next level of terrace.

Try Stepping Stones for Easy Access to Slopes

Strolling up a garden slope step by step sure beats scrambling your way up, clinging to rocks and plants. If you've fought your slope long enough, start saving energy with stepping stones.

Start by walking up your slope at a comfortable pace to find the most convenient height and width for stepping stones. Then follow the instructions below for easy placement. When you're done, plant low-growing groundcovers beside the steps so you won't have to fight off weeds or mud.

1. **Dig in.** Remove 2 or 3 inches of dirt from the area where you'll place the stones.

2. **Level it.** Put down a ½-inch layer of sand or gravel so you have a flat surface on which to place the stones.

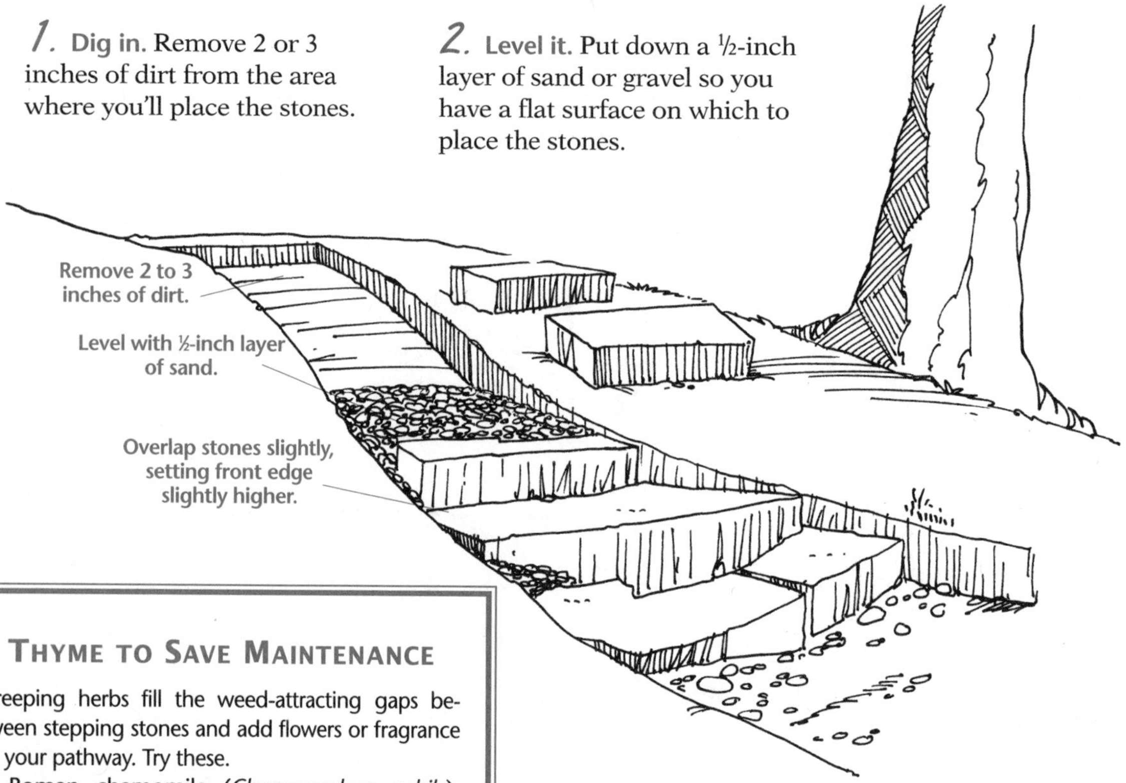

3. **Set the stones.** Start at the bottom of the slope and place stepping stones so the front edge is slightly higher than the back for stability. Place the next rock so it overlaps the first one just a bit. Continue overlapping stones until you reach the top.

Thyme to Save Maintenance

Creeping herbs fill the weed-attracting gaps between stepping stones and add flowers or fragrance to your pathway. Try these.

Roman chamomile (*Chamaemelum nobile*): Feathery foliage, daisylike flowers; 6–9 inches tall.

Creeping germander (*Teucrium chamaedrys* 'Prostratum'): Pink flowers; 5–8 inches tall.

Creeping thyme (*Thymus praecox* subsp. *arcticus*): Purple flowers; 4–6 inches tall.

Woolly thyme (*Thymus pseudolanuginosis*): Pink flowers; fuzzy foliage; 2 inches tall.

Mother-of-thyme (*Thymus serpyllum*): Red flowers; 3 inches tall.

Tough Plants for Sunny Slopes

Drought-tolerant groundcovers, herbs, ornamental grasses, and shrubs are the best candidates to survive the dry conditions often found on slippery slopes. Cover your slope with a mix of them and you'll never have to struggle with awkward mowing or weed-covered banks again. They'll also hold the soil in place and encourage water to percolate down into the soil instead of running off it.

All the plants listed below will thrive in full sun with the well-drained soil that sloping sites provide.

Groundcovers

Bugleweed (*Ajuga reptans*): Ground-hugging, 4–6 inches high; dark green leaves with blue, white, or pink flowers. Zones 4–9.

Maiden pinks (*Dianthus deltoides*): Narrow, blue-green leaves; pink or white flowers; 6–12 inches high. Zones 3–9.

Perennial candytuft (*Iberis sempervirens*): Dark, evergreen leaves; flat, bright white flower clusters in spring; 6–12 inches high. Zones 3–9.

Stonecrops (*Sedum* spp.): Thick, waxy leaves; pink, white, or yellow flowers; 2–15 inches high, depending on species. Zones 3–8.

Wintercreeper (*Euonymous fortunei*): Trailing or climbing evergreen plant; many types with variegated leaves. Zones 4–9.

Herbs

Lavender cotton (*Santolina chamaecyparissus*): Gray-green foliage; yellow buttonlike flowers; 1–2 feet high. Zones 6–8.

Thymes (*Thymus* spp.): Creeping, fragrant-leaved; 1–12 inches high; tiny white or pink flowers. Zones 5–9.

Wild marjoram (*Origanum vulgare*): Bushy; 1–2 feet high; white flowers. Also called oregano, but not all plants have scented leaves. For true oregano, buy from specialists and/or rub and sniff the foliage before you buy. Zones 5–9.

Ornamental Grasses

Blue fescue (*Festuca cinerea*): Clump-forming; 6–12 inches high; blue-green foliage. Zones 4–9.

Little bluestem (*Schizachyrium scoparium*): Clump-forming; 2–5 feet high; light green foliage. Zones 3–10.

Side oats grammagrass (*Bouteloua curtipendula*): Clump-forming, 1–2 feet high; gray-green foliage. Zones 4–9.

Shrubs

Cotoneasters (*Cotoneaster* spp.): Many species, ranging from creeping 1–2 feet high to large shrubs reaching 12 feet or more. Small, dark green leaves, white flowers, and red fruit. Some species are evergreen. Zones 5–9, depending on species.

Junipers (*Juniperus* spp.): Needle-leaved evergreen available in many forms, from prostrate, 6-inch-tall types to large trees. Select a species or cultivar that matures at the height that's best for the site. Zones 3–9, depending on species.

Northern bayberry (*Myrica pensylvanica*): Gray-green leaves and waxy berries, both very aromatic; 3–10 feet high. Zones 3–9.

St.-John's-wort (*Hypericum* spp.): Evergreen or semi-evergreen shrubs with oval leaves and yellow flowers. Zones 4–9, depending on species.

Staghorn sumac (*Rhus typhina*): Shrub to small tree; 10–30 feet high. Large, fernlike leaves. Zones 4–8.

Tough Plants for Shady Slopes

Slopes planted in lawn grass are a headache whether they're in sun or shade. If you have a shady slope, replace the grass with one of these easy-care, shade-loving groundcovers.

Ajuga (*Ajuga reptans*): Creeping plants with green, bronze, or variegated foliage; blue, pink, or white flowers; 3–6 inches high. Zones 3–9.

Common periwinkle (*Vinca minor*): Evergreen plant with small, dark green leaves; lavender-blue or white flowers; 4–6 inches tall. Zones 4–9.

English ivy (*Hedera helix*): Evergreen vine; 6–8 inches high when creeping on the ground; will climb trees to 50 feet. Zones 5–9.

Epimediums (*Epimedium* spp.): Spreading plant with evergreen or semievergreen leaves; small yellow, pink, bronze, or white flowers in early spring; 5–12 inches high. Zones 3–8.

Japanese pachysandra (*Pachysandra terminalis*): Plant with glossy green leaves that spreads by runners; white flowers; 6–9 inches tall. Zones 5–9.

Help Plants Spread to Save on Planting

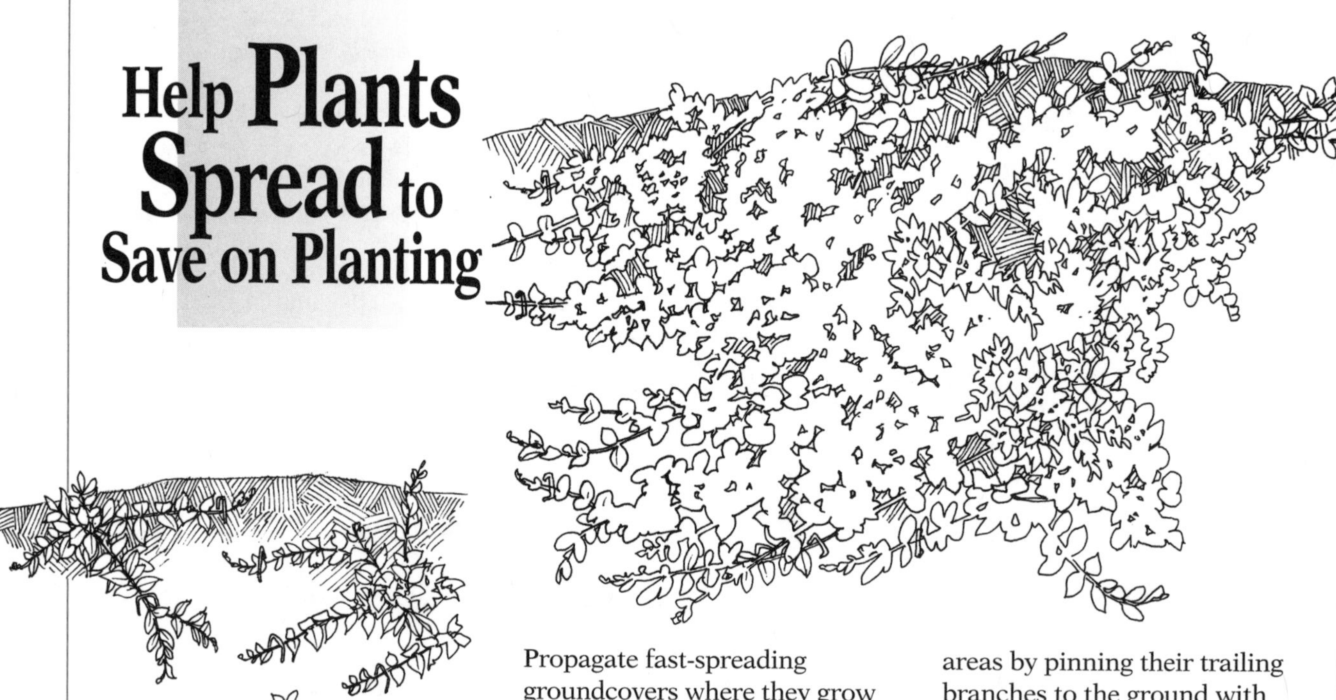

Propagate fast-spreading groundcovers where they grow and you can cut your planting time in half. Start by planting half as many parent plants as you need to cover your slope. When they are growing well, help them spread over the bare areas by pinning their trailing branches to the ground with wire. Keep pinning branches as they grow until the area is covered. Stems will form roots—and ultimately new plants—wherever they contact the ground.

Dry-Site Solutions

If you're stuck with a sun-parched spot with baked-dry soil, you probably think endless work is the only way to turn it into a garden. Not so!

Choose the right plants and easy soil improvement methods, and you can create a thriving garden without breaking your back. For lowest maintenance, plant only drought-tolerant plants with sturdy roots. They're the ones that can survive soil that cracks and shrinks when moisture evaporates.

If you crave a wider range of flowers and have no other garden spot, mulch and add soil amendments like compost or well-rotted manure to help hold soil moisture in. Consider installing a soaker-hose irrigation system if time is short and you have existing plants that are thirsty now.

Whichever way you decide to handle your dry site, this section will give you all the plant recommendations and tips you need to transform a dusty site into a delectable one.

Let Soaker Hoses Water for You

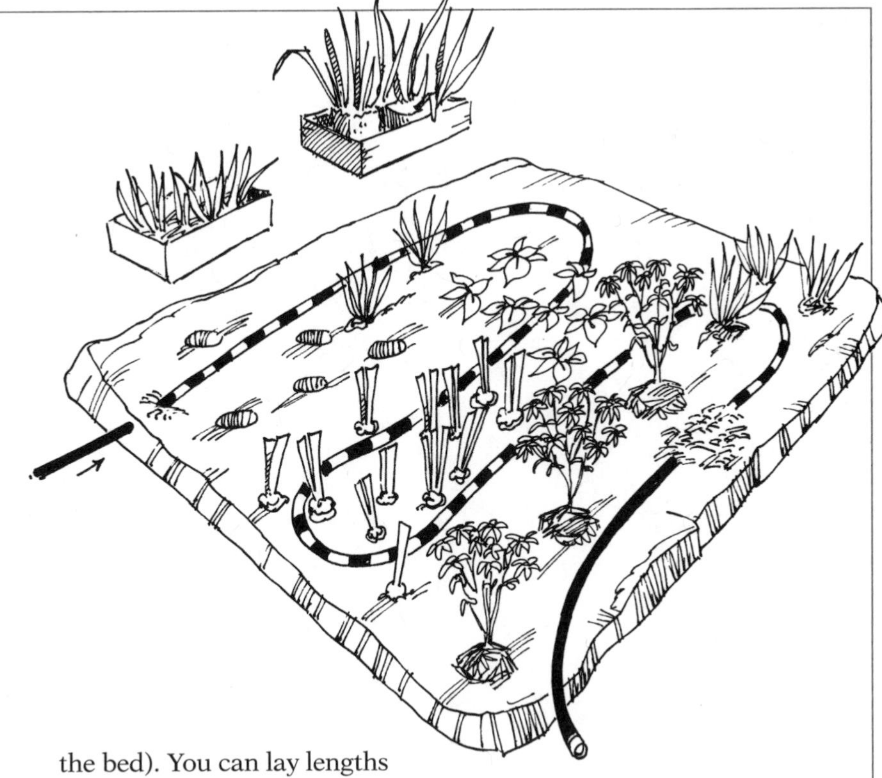

Soaker hoses water by slowly dripping water onto the soil. For easy watering, snake them through beds in spring so they'll drip water onto shrubs, perennials, and other plants. Then cover them with mulch and leave them in place all season instead of dragging them around from bed to bed. You may need a length of regular hose to attach them to a faucet (otherwise they'll drip water between your faucet and the bed). You can lay lengths of soaker hoses in different dry beds that need regular watering and just move your length of regular hose. Use quick-release hose couplers to make moving your hose a snap. See the illustration on page 72 for more on quick-release couplers.

Shade Structures Screen Out Scalding Sun

On a hot, exposed site, the sun's rays can bake your soil dry and suck up all available moisture. Planting trees provides a long-term solution for a too-sunny site. But if you need immediate relief, erect a shelter to keep your plants—and you—from turning crispy. A shade shelter will keep the soil and your plants cooler and moister so you'll have fewer watering chores. A layer of mulch on the soil will provide added protection and help retain even more water in the soil.

You can create an easy shade structure by twining vines and branches into a bower or by building an open-ended shelter from latticework. If you need to cover a large area, build an arbor with a series of parallel posts or columns as supports and an open roof of wooden cross-rafters. Plant it with vigorous climbing vines like Virginia creeper (*Parthenocissus quinquefolia*), trumpet vine (*Campsis radicans*), or five-leaf akebia (*Akebia quinata*). They'll clamber up support posts to throw a quick cover of shade.

For a super-simple structure, try building a lath house using wood posts or metal bars to form the outline of a roof and sides. Cover the structure with thin, narrow strips of wood, set close together but not touching—the closer they are, the more shade they'll cast.

Make Planting Dry Sites a Snap

What's the easiest way to prepare a dry site for planting? Choose tough, drought-tolerant plants that like your garden spot the way it is, and you'll nearly avoid the task altogether. That way, all you need do is clear the weeds away, dig up the site with a garden fork or spade, and plant. Water after you plant, and be sure to water regularly until the plants are established.

Use the tips below to prepare a dry-soil site for less stalwart plants, improve the soil on an existing site, and make even drought-tolerant plants happier.

Moisturize before you dig. Don't try to dig soil that's dry as dust. Not only will it destroy the soil structure, but dry soil is physically harder to dig than moist soil is. Two days before you want to prepare the soil on a dry site, water it thoroughly. Then check the amount of moisture in the soil before you dig. Pick up a handful of soil and squeeze it. It should clump together but crumble easily when you press on it with your thumb. If it doesn't crumble easily, it's too wet; wait a day and test the soil again. If it won't clump together, add some more water before you dig.

Defy dry soil with mulch. A 2-inch layer of any organic mulch such as shredded or chipped bark or shredded leaves helps the soil hold on to precious moisture. Keeping bare garden spots covered with mulch also helps cool the soil and makes it easier to work with.

Add organic matter. The more organic matter in your soil, the more moisture it will hold. It's just that simple. A layer of organic mulch will gradually add organic matter to the soil as it decomposes. To speed up the process without too much extra work, treat your dry site to an annual application of compost, composted manure, or humus. Don't bother to dig it into the soil, just spread it over the site and top it with a new layer of mulch. The earthworms and other soil organisms will work it down into the soil for you.

Make mulch and plants improve dry sites for you. Use a thick (8- to 10-inch) layer of organic mulch and a planting of sod-busting flowers or vegetables to work dry soil. The mulch adds nutrients and humus to your site as it decomposes, and plant roots break up the hard crusted soil. See "Mulch and Grow Better Soil" on page 55 for details on this super soil-restoring system.

Moisturize dry sites with soaker hoses. Garden spots close to the house are often very dry. To turn such sites into happy homes for plants that can't tolerate dust-bowl conditions, lay soaker hoses out over the site and cover them with a layer of mulch to help conserve water. A quarter-turn of the faucet is all it takes to water any time during the growing season. Soaker hoses operate under low pressure, so water drips into dry ground slowly without runoff. Use a timer to turn hoses on and off to make watering a really low-maintenance task.

Stock up on soaker hoses. Instead of hauling your soaker hoses from site to site all summer long, buy enough soaker hoses to water all your beds. Set them out in spring and leave them in place until fall. That way, you'll only need to turn a spigot to water all summer. Cover soaker hoses with mulch for the perfect solution to bone-dry ornamental plantings like those around your house foundation.

To make moving your main hose from soaker hose to soaker hose a snap, buy quick-release hose couplers for your watering system. That way, you can move your main hose just by clicking it off one soaker hose and onto another. For more on quick-release hose couplers, see "Make Your Hoses Behave with Handy Hose Tamers" on page 72.

Eliminate Watering Chores by Redirecting Runoff

Most yards are sloped to drain water toward the street, which wastes water your plants could use—water that could save you from dragging hoses around. Keep your dry sites moist by redirecting excess water to your lawn or gardens. Use shallow channels or swales to move water from downspouts and paved surfaces to thirsty garden sites.

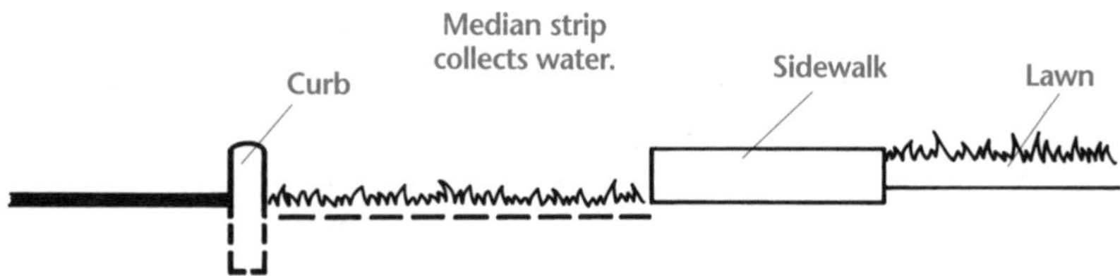

Send water where the plants are. You can collect water that runs off paved areas like sidewalks and flows into the street, too. To water a lawn with excess runoff, for example, lower the lawn so it's below the paved area—just as the median strip planting is below the sidewalk and curb in the drawing at left. Extra water will run into the median strip and keep grass lush, instead of rushing over it into the street. It's a job to strip your sod, remove a few inches of soil, and resod, but you'll put an end to water worries once and for all.

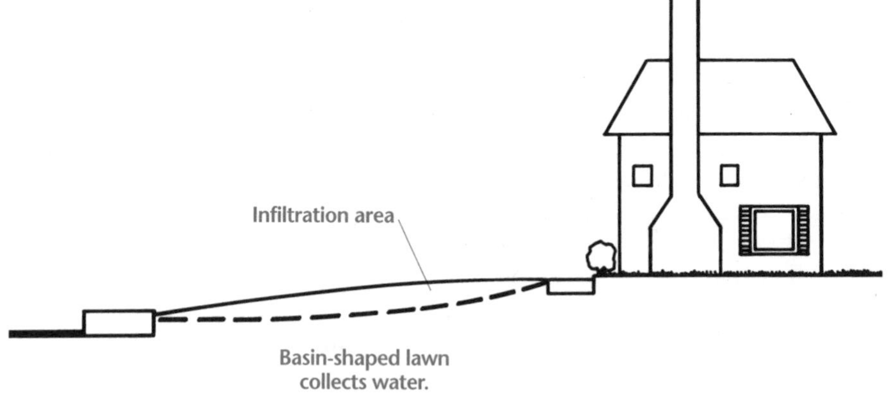

Sculpt your yard. If lots of water runs through your yard, capture and use it instead of watching it wash uselessly through your grass and gardens into the sewer. You'll stop soil erosion and save on watering chores in the process. Choose a broad, level area of lawn as your "infiltration area." This is where you'll gather water and allow it to soak into the ground.

Create a bowl with sides that slope gradually toward the center. Try a slope of 1 foot for every 20 feet so it won't look too obvious. If the basin is accepting water from a huge roof and lots of pavement, it should be at least 10 × 10 feet, and 6 inches deep. If you don't have that much space, make a smaller basin that fits your yard; even a little one will help you hold and use escaping water.

Perfect Perennials for Dry Clay Soil

Choose your plants carefully to assure no-fuss success in dry clay soil. The shrinking and swelling of clay as it dries and rehydrates wreaks havoc on tender roots. The plants listed below have tough roots that will stand up to clay soil.

Blue false indigo (*Baptisia australis*): Broad, shrublike plant with three rounded leaflets per leaf; spikes of deep blue, pea-shaped flowers; 3 feet high. Zones 3–9.

Butterfly weed (*Asclepias tuberosa*): Hairy stems with narrow, lance-shaped leaves; flat clusters of bright orange flowers; 1–2½ feet high. Zones 3–9.

Daylilies (*Hemerocallis* spp.): Straplike leaves; cheery, funnel-shaped flowers of all colors except blue; 1–6 feet high, depending on species and cultivar. Zones 2–9.

Gayfeathers (*Liatris* spp.): Leafy stems; tall purple flower spikes; 6 inches–6 feet high, depending on species. Zones 3–9.

Globe thistle (*Echinops ritro*): Showy spiny leaves; rounded heads of small, steel blue flowers; 3–5 feet high. Zones 3–8.

Purple coneflower (*Echinacea purpurea*): Coarse leaves; daisylike purple flowers with persistent central cones; 2–4 feet high. Zones 3–8.

Torch lilies (*Kniphofia* spp.): Grassy leaves; spikes of fiery flowers; 1–5 feet high, depending on cultivar. Zones 5–9.

Willow blue star (*Amsonia tabernaemontana*): Shrubby plant with glossy, lance-shaped leaves; small, starry blue flowers; 3 feet high. Zones 3–9.

Yuccas (*Yucca* spp.): Stiff, swordlike leaves; waxy white flowers; 4–15 feet high, depending on species. Zones 3–10.

Easy-to-Grow Annuals for Dry Sites

Annual plants, by nature, are adaptable. They bloom tirelessly and produce seed each fall when the parent plant dies. The annuals below grow naturally in hot, dry climates.

California poppy (*Eschscholzia californica*): Delicate, gray-green dissected leaves; showy, cuplike orange flowers.

Calliopsis (*Coreopsis tinctoria*): Narrow leaves; showy red and orange flowers in airy clusters.

Dahlberg daisy (*Dyssodia tenuiloba*): Delicate dissected foliage; dozens of small yellow-orange daisies all summer.

Four-o'clock (*Mirabilis jalapa*): Bright green, pointed oval leaves; fragrant tubular flowers open in the afternoon; colors include red, crimson, magenta, yellow, and white.

Gazanias (*Gazania* spp.): Tufts of neat, compound foliage; lots of starry, 2-inch daisies in reds, yellows, and oranges.

Joseph's-coat (*Amaranthus tricolor*): Tall, covered with pointed oval leaves; long, fuzzy tail-like flower spikes.

Rose moss (*Portulaca grandiflora*): Succulent foliage stores water for lean times; 2-inch yellow, red, pink, or white single or double flowers.

Snow-on-the-mountain (*Euphorbia marginata*): Tall, leafy stems crowned with small flowers; snow white and green bracts.

Dependable, Drought-Tolerant Trees and Shrubs

If drought regularly strikes your site, look for plants that thrive in poor, dry soil. There are drought-tolerant trees and shrubs for every site, from meadows to woods. For the easiest success, pick the ones that thrive in a spot most like yours.

Bayberries (*Myrica* spp.): Large shrubs with narrow, aromatic leaves; fragrant berries; grow on dry dunes and in fields; 5–12 feet high. Zones 2–6.

Black chokeberry (*Aronia melanocarpa*): Medium-size shrub with glossy, oval leaves; clusters of small white flowers with pink stamens; black fruits in summer; grows in extremely dry sites as well as in moist soil; 3–5 feet high. Zones 3–8.

Bush honeysuckle (*Diervilla lonicera*): Small, creeping shrub with handsome, pointed leaves; small clusters of yellow flowers; fall color is yellow; grows in dry to moist open woods; 3–5 feet high. Zones 3–7.

Butterfly bush (*Buddleia davidii*): Large arching shrubs with showy flowers in shades of purple, white, pink, blue, and red; may be killed to ground in cold-winter areas; flowers on new growth; grow in full sun in well-drained soil; 5–10 feet high. Zones 6–8.

Ceanothus (*Ceanothus* spp.): Small to medium-size shrubs with attractive oval leaves; foamy clusters of small flowers; grow in dry prairies, meadows, or on windswept mountainsides; 3–4 feet high. Zones 4–8.

Common hackberry (*Celtis occidentalis*): Tree with rounded to oval crown and pointed leaves; small, hard, black fruits; grows on dry river terraces and in old fields; tolerates limey soils; 40–60 feet high. Zones 2–9.

Devil's-walking stick (*Aralia spinosa*): Large shrub with huge tropical-looking compound leaves; clusters of small yellow flowers and purple berries; grows in dry fields from thick creeping stems; 10–20 feet high. Zones 4–9.

Ginkgo (*Ginkgo biloba*): Huge tree; unique, fan-shaped leaves turn gold in fall; stinky fruit—plant male trees only; extremely drought-tolerant and long lived; grows in almost any full-sun situation; 50–80 feet high. Zones 3–8.

Golden-rain tree (*Koelreuteria paniculata*): Medium to large tree with spreading, rounded crown of bright green compound leaves; midsummer sprays of yellow flowers; yellow fall foliage; flowers best in full sun; endures dry soil, heat, and air pollution; to 50 feet high. Zones 5–9.

Gray dogwood (*Cornus racemosa*): Medium to large shrub that forms broad colonies; small flattened clusters of ivory-colored flowers, followed by white berries; grows in dry, open woods and fields; 10–15 feet high. Zones 4–8.

Hickories (*Carya* spp.): Large tree with smooth, gray bark and large, compound leaves; hard, edible nuts; grows in dry woods; 50–75 feet high. Zones 4–9.

Junipers (*Juniperus* spp.): Evergreens with shrubby or treelike forms, depending on the species; needles may be green, gray, or blue; grow in fields and on slopes and rock outcroppings; 2 inches–60 feet high, depending on cultivar. Zones 3–9.

Oaks (*Quercus* spp.): Large trees with graceful forms, neat foliage, and acorns; grow in dry to moist woods; 50–80 feet high. Zones 3–9.

Pines (*Pinus* spp.): Adaptable evergreens for dry sites and poor soil; needle color varies by species; grow well in disturbed sites and on open soils in full sun; 20–60 feet high. Zones 3–7.

Sumacs (*Rhus* spp.): Large spreading shrubs; bold compound leaves turn flaming red in fall; attractive red fruits; grow at the edge of woodlands, in old fields, and along roadsides; 15–25 feet high. Zones 3–8.

WINDY-SITE SOLUTIONS

When wind seems like your garden's enemy, sucking moisture from leaves and roots, breaking branches, and knocking down flowers, block it with a windbreak. You have lots of choices, from building a fence to planting living barricades of perennials, grasses, trees, or shrubs. When you use windbreaks to protect plantings near your house, you'll notice an added benefit, too—lower heating and cooling bills! And if a windbreak isn't your style, there are plants that tolerate drought and high winds without any fussing from you.

Reduce Yard Maintenance Year-Round with Windbreaks

Put a stop to summer and winter winds that howl across your yard, drying and breaking your plants. You'll have fewer plant replacements and watering chores since there's less evaporation.

Plants are ideal for slowing down the air. They're flexible so they absorb the wind force and form an extended zone of calm air behind them. Plants do allow *some* air circulation; after all, you don't want a hermetically sealed yard. Light breezes help keep pests and diseases under control and cool you in summer.

Put windbreaks where the wind blows. Prevailing winter and summer winds blow from different directions. Make sure you place your windbreak where it blocks the most troublesome winds. Winter winds generally blow from the northwest and west, so to be most effective, your windbreak should stretch along the north and west side of your property.

Use fast- and slow-growing plants. If you plant only rapidly growing plants in your windbreak, you'll get maximum protection in the shortest time. But most fast-growing plants don't live very long—you'll be replanting soon unless you mix some long-lived, slower-growing trees in from the start. Cut out the fast-growing trees as they decline so there's room for the long-lasting ones. For best results and year-round effectiveness, combine deciduous and evergreen trees and shrubs.

Pick a height that protects your plants. The height depends on how much area you want to protect. A windbreak cuts the force of the wind behind it for an area that extends five times the height of the windbreak. You may want less height for summer windbreaks because they'll shade nearby garden plants. Don't make summer windbreaks much taller than the flowers they're protecting; then you can plant right up to the windbreak.

Stretch windbreaks beyond the garden or house. For really effective wind protection, extend the planting 50 feet beyond either side of the area you want to protect. If you don't have that much room, just plant as far as you can.

Space plants as wide apart as their mature width. If a shrub grows 6 feet wide, space the plants 6 feet apart. Lower branches need light or they'll die out, so don't plant them too close. Keep them alive for the best wind protection.

Simple Windbreaks That Suit Your Schedule

Throw out your windy-site maintenance cares along with the elaborate windbreak plans that call for hundreds of plants. All you need is a fence—or just 1 to 3 rows of plants—to direct the wind away and break its force as it moves across your property.

Fences make the fastest windbreaks. When time or space is short, a wooden fence makes a quick and effective windbreak. You don't have to wait for plants to grow to get protection from hot or icy blasts. Fences are especially good when there isn't room or light enough for windbreak plants. They'll cut down on noise pollution, too, if that's a problem. A 6-foot fence will provide 30 feet of wind protection—plenty for most gardens.

Make the fence slightly porous by spacing the slats an inch or so apart. This allows some wind to pass through the fence so plants behind it get good air circulation. It also keeps your fence from getting clobbered with the full force of each wind blast. If you plan to cover the fence with vines, use lattice or place the slats 3 to 4 inches apart to allow wind to pass through.

Use one-row windbreaks for small properties. A single staggered row of evergreens makes a low-maintenance windbreak for small yards. Place plants closer than you would in a normal planting, just 10 feet apart for 30-foot-tall trees. Staggering the planting breaks the force of the wind better than a single straight row.

Use three-row windbreaks for large properties. When you've got lots of space to protect, add one row of small trees (20 to 30 feet tall), and one of small shrubs (4 to 8 feet tall) in front of your row of evergreens (30 to 60 feet tall).

The branches and leaves of the smaller plants help slow the wind as it blows through them. If you've got the time and space, add a row of mixed grasses and flowers along the outside of the windbreak. The varied sizes and shapes of plants diffuse the wind more and more as it penetrates each successive barrier.

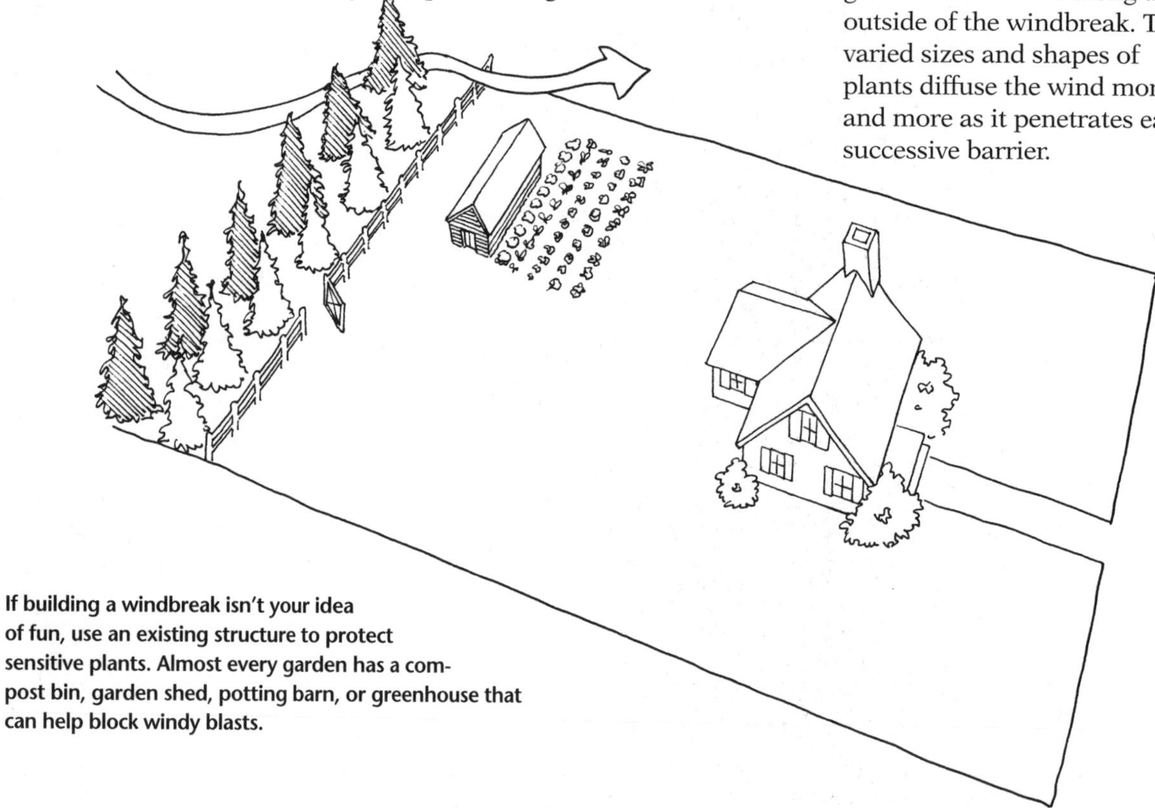

If building a windbreak isn't your idea of fun, use an existing structure to protect sensitive plants. Almost every garden has a compost bin, garden shed, potting barn, or greenhouse that can help block windy blasts.

Large Plants Make Easy Windbreaks for Delicate Flowers

Fragile flowers fade when they're battered by high winds. But not if you shield them with tall perennial flowers or grasses. Choose plants with stiff, erect stems that can stand up to the wind, or thin, flexible ones that bend without breaking. Place large plants on the windward side of more fragile flowers to protect them from hot summer winds or winter snows.

Place the clumps in a zigzag row on 3-foot centers for fast, effective wind protection that allows room for growth. You can plant wind-sensitive plants 2 to 3 feet from the grasses on the leeward side.

Plant Windbreaks for Free Pest Control

How can windbreaks control pests? By attracting birds and other wildlife that munch on insects in your garden. It doesn't take any more work to plant a windbreak that wildlife like. Any trees and shrubs provide resting, nesting, and feeding sites. Include fruiting shrubs and trees such as crabapples (*Malus* spp.), elderberries (*Sambucus* spp.) serviceberries (*Amelanchier* spp.) and viburnums (*Viburnum* spp.) to make your site most attractive.

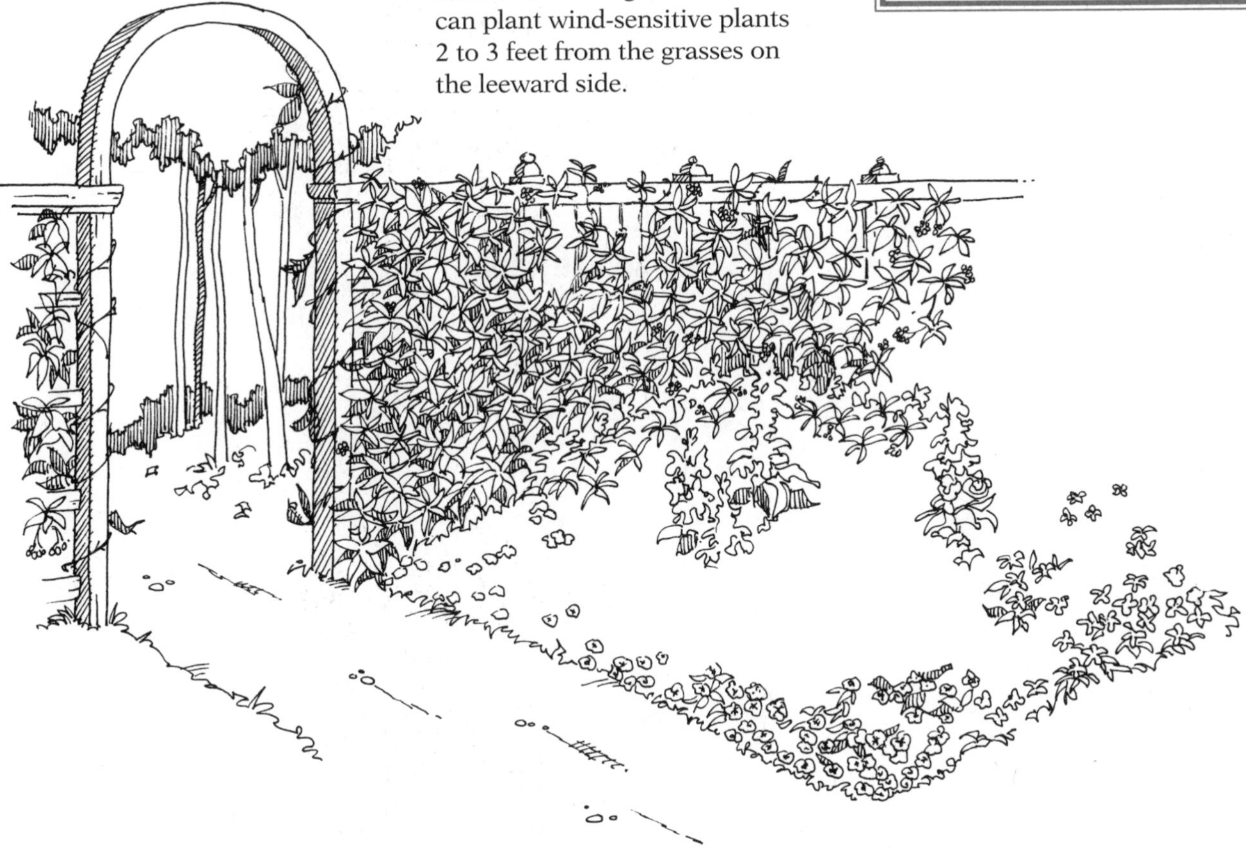

If dry summer winds parch your plants, protect them with a fast-growing vine. A simple trellis or fence makes a perfect support structure. Plant vines thickly and train them up your fence to establish a dense cover quickly. Choose small-leaved plants that stand up to wind, such as American bittersweet (*Celastrus scandens*), silver lace vine (*Polygonum aubertii*), or trumpet honeysuckle (*Lonicera sempervirens*). See "20 Versatile Vines" on page 330 for more recommendations.

Tough Plants for Exposed, Windy Sites

Cope with constant breezes and windy knolls by choosing plants that are both flexible and beautiful. The perennials and grasses listed below will bend with the wind and spring back in place when storms are over. Also see "Dependable, Drought-Tolerant Trees and Shrubs" on page 234.

Grasses

Feather reed grass (*Calamagrostis acutiflora*): Upright, tufted grass; narrow flower spikes held above the foliage; seed heads persist into winter; 18–24 inches high. Zones 3–9.

Little bluestem (*Schizachyrium scoparium*): Small grass with dense, upright stems clothed in cottony tufts in late summer; 2–5 feet high. Zones 3–8.

Switch grass (*Panicum virgatum*): Open, clumping plant with drooping leaves; airy sprays of small flowers; 4–7 feet high. Zones 2–9.

Perennials

Blazing-star (*Liatris* spp.): Stout stems clothed in narrow, grassy leaves; dense spikes of purple flowers; 3–5 feet high. Zones 3–8.

Coneflowers (*Rudbeckia* spp.): Rough, hairy leaves; yellow daisylike flowers with brown or green domed centers; 1½–6 feet high. Zones 3–9.

Purple coneflower (*Echinacea purpurea*): Large, purple daisylike flowers with raised central cone; 2–4 feet high. Zones 3–8.

Sunflowers (*Helianthus* spp.): Floriferous plants with bright yellow flowers on leafy stems; 4–8 feet high. Zones 3–8.

Threadleaf coreopsis (*Coreopsis verticillata*): Fine, needlelike leaves; yellow, daisylike flowers; 1–3 feet high. Zones 3–9.

Trees and Shrubs

Alders (*Alnus* spp.): Large shrubs or small trees with dense, upright branches and large, rough leaves; 40–60 feet high. Zones 3–8.

Basswood (*Tilia americana*): Tall, oval tree with large, rounded leaves. Medium to fast growth when young; 60–80 feet high. Zones 2–8.

Eastern white pine (*Pinus strobus*): Graceful evergreen; full, fast-growing when young; open, slower-growing later; 50–80 feet high. Zones 3–8.

Green ash (*Fraxinus pennsylvanica*): Large tree with compound leaves that turn yellow in autumn; 50–80 feet high. Zones 3–9.

Junipers (*Juniperus* spp.): Large evergreen shrubs or small trees; 2 inches–60 feet high, depending on cultivar. Zones 2–9.

Norway spruce (*Picea abies*): Dense conical to oval evergreen with pendulous branches. Young plants grow fast, but rate slows as plants mature; 40–60 feet high. Zones 2–8.

Oaks (*Quercus* spp.): Majestic, upright oval or spreading trees with broad, lobed leaves. Medium to slow growth rate; 50–80 feet high. Zones 3–10, depending on species.

Poplars (*Populus* spp.): Medium-size trees with foliage that rustles pleasantly in wind to mask noise pollution; 40–70 feet high. Zones 2–8, depending on species.

Red maple (*Acer rubrum*): Large tree; fairly fast growing when young, but stronger than other maples; very adaptable; 40–60 feet high. Zones 3–9.

Rugosa rose (*Rosa rugosa*): Tough, adaptable shrub for extreme climates and salty sites; rose-pink or white flowers in summer; 4–7 feet high. Zones 2–7.

Viburnums (*Viburnum* spp.): Rounded to oval shrubs with dense branches; medium to large leaves; rounded flower clusters followed by berries; 2–15 feet high. Zones 2–9, depending on species.

Willows (*Salix* spp.): Shrubs or trees with dense, flexible branches that rustle in wind; 10–100 feet high, depending on species. Zones 2–9, depending on species.

HIGH-TRAFFIC SOLUTIONS

Do kids, dogs, mail carriers, and paper deliverers always cut across your yard, killing the grass and compacting the soil? When gentle reminders and even threats fail to elicit any response, it's time to plant a traffic-control garden.

In the pages that follow, you'll find solutions for sites that seem destined to be trodden. You'll learn how to add a path to usher traffic through the garden and find strategies for blocking trails where paths don't seem to work. A few plants will serve as a friendly reminder not to cut across your property or to stay on a path.

Pavers as Saviors

If you have a whole herd of people and pets tromping through a planting, get their feet off the soil by providing pavers or stepping stones. Heavy feet compact the soil and collapse the spaces that hold the air and water plants need to grow. Use pavers to take the brunt of the pressure so the soil stays loose and friable.

Make sure the pavers are close enough to provide a continuous walking surface. If you are using stepping stones, each one should be large enough for your entire foot. There is nothing worse than teetering on a tiny stone while trying to keep from falling into the garden.

Choose a material that fits with the other elements in the garden or with the house. If your house is brick, stick with brick. If you have a stone terrace, use the same stone for the path or pavers. For choices and installation instructions, see "Pave the Way to Garden Pleasures"on page 202.

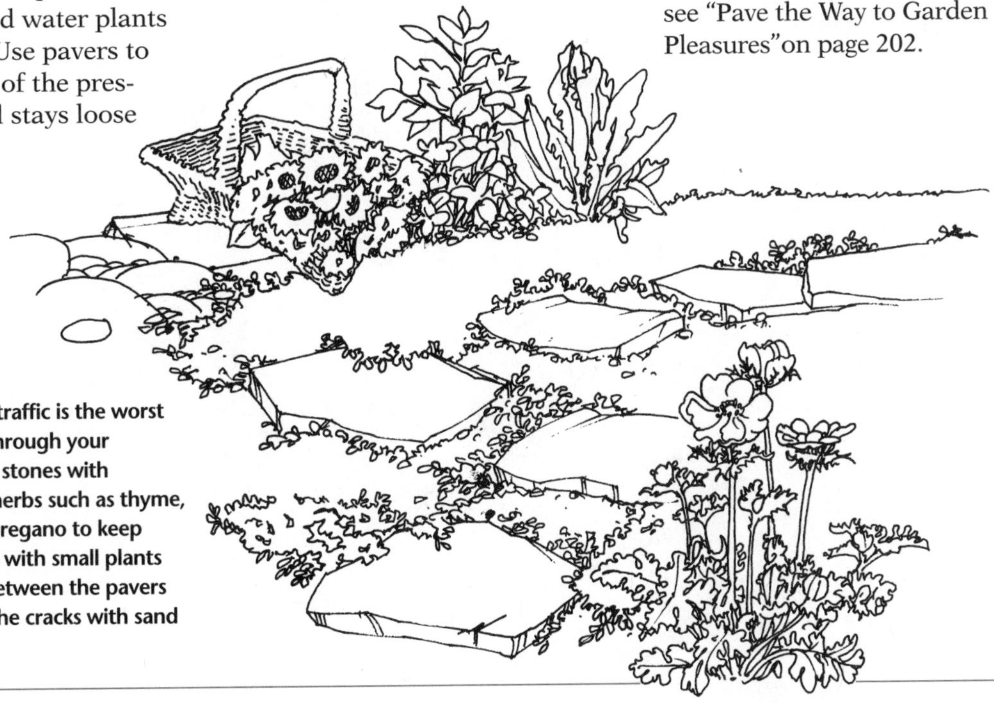

Set pavers where traffic is the worst to guide visitors through your garden. Surround stones with groundcovers or herbs such as thyme, pennyroyal, and oregano to keep weeds away. Start with small plants and place them between the pavers before you fill in the cracks with sand or soil.

Pots and Plants Stop Traffic in Its Tracks

If a path through your garden resembles an interstate highway, you may need to block it off with plants. Flowers in pots make an easy-to-grow barrier for areas where the soil is extremely compacted from traffic. For large or persistent pathways, tough hedges make impassable obstacles.

Pots plug up shortcuts. For the best barriers and the least maintenance, choose substantial containers at least 2 to 3 feet across and equally high. Small pots are easily overlooked and dry out quickly. Fill pots with exuberant plantings of tall plants to create fullness. Use large perennials—at least 2 feet tall—or even shrubs.

Hedges ensure that shortcuts are short-lived. The most important consideration for a barrier hedge is dense growth so trees and shrubs provide a visual as well as a physical barrier. In most cases, mild-mannered plants like arborvitaes (*Thuja* spp.), yews (*Taxus* spp.), or European hornbeams (*Carpinus betulus*) will do the trick. But in areas with relentless invasions, you may have to put a wire fence down the center of the shrub border to make sure no one plows through it. As a last resort, use thorny shrub selections like false holly (*Osmanthus heterophyllus*) and true hollies (*Ilex* spp.). For a list of more good hedge plants, see Chapters 26 and 31.

Let Yard and Garden Paths Show You Where *Not* to Grow

Instead of spending loads of money to repair trampled turf and flattened flowers, take a minute to see what they're trying to tell you. Invariably, new and old yards begin to show signs of preferred travel routes and shortcuts. Anyone who uses your yard frequently will wear away the soil and a path will develop.

You can spend loads of time, money, and effort fighting the pathmakers—erecting barriers, replacing plants or grass, and issuing dire warnings—or you can join them. Instead of forcing people to move in ways they don't want to, let these "cow paths" show you where to put walkways. You'll save yourself more than a few headaches if you place walks or trails where they are most needed, and then develop your lawn and gardens around them. Here are some pathmaking tips to help guide you.

The most direct route is usually the best. This is especially true for utilitarian paths used to take out the garbage or walk to the compost pile, vegetable garden, or driveway.

Don't put in a lot of unneccesary twists and bends—you'll only be tempting the shortcutters who use your yard. A gentle curve is nice if your style is informal, but if the garden is formal, get to the point and make the path straight.

Select the best width. The width of the path depends on its position and intended use. If the path is the main approach to your house, you'll want it 4 to 5 feet wide so two people can walk comfortably abreast. If the path is an intimate walkway through the garden, 2 feet is wide enough for one person. For simple maintenance, a 1-foot-wide path may do the trick, but you'll need 3 feet if you intend to bring a wheelbarrow in with you.

Use stepping stones for cut-throughs. If your kids or the mail carrier tend to cut through a flower bed to get to the house next door, add a couple of stepping stones to guide their way and keep them off the soil.

The same thing goes for a path that cuts through a flower bed in the backyard to a neighbor's house. Containers of flowers or small shrubs on either side of the path will help direct traffic toward the stepping stones and off your flowers.

Let garden paths meander. Of course, you don't want a ramrod-straight path running through a wildflower or shade garden. But traffic patterns can help you design even a winding garden path.

Let the routes you use to do things like care for your garden or walk to a bench in the shade establish the basic location of the path. Then adjust the curves and direction to keep visitors away from hazards like low-hanging branches and roots or rocks they could trip over. Be sure your path winds past special plants you want them to see and enjoy.

To direct traffic, mulch your path with a material that contrasts with your garden—shredded bark, for example, if you use leaves on your beds.

PART 4

Saving Time with

Smart Plant Choices

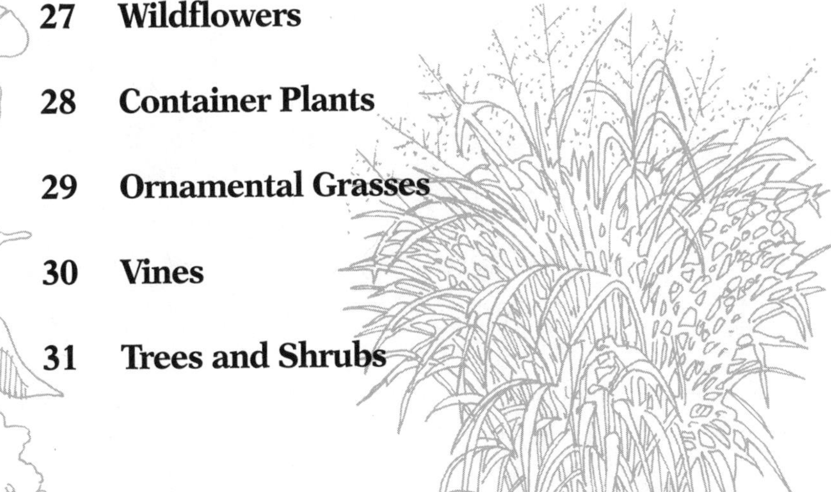

CHAPTER 22

Flowers

Flowers the Low-Maintenance Way

FLOWERS can be great care consumers, but few of us would want to be without them. The instant or anticipated charm of beautiful blossoms is a big incentive for clearing space in the schedule for flower gardening. For example, who objects to taking time to plant a six-pack of colorful zinnias or petunias? Designing flower gardens may seem like an intimidating task, but in this chapter you'll find simple guidelines to follow that can take most of the fuss out of garden design. With forethought and smart plant choices, you can create gorgeous plantings that don't demand lots of maintenance. In some cases, planting well-designed flower beds can even reduce the amount of time you usually spend on other routine yard chores, such as mowing the lawn or trimming around trees.

A Credo for Low-Work Gardening: Don't Fight Your Site

A near-holy commandment for the low-maintenance gardener is: Match the plant to the site. Instead of trying to change difficult conditions with soil amendments or raised beds, select plants that will thrive as is. Most common garden annuals—and many herbs—are suited only for average to good soil and good drainage. But among the huge selection of flowering perennials, bulbs, vines, and grasses available, you're sure to find plants suited to any garden situation. It makes sense to use those that will thrive instead of those that will struggle for survival.

For example, broaden your garden horizons with wildflowers, like the ones shown here, that are naturally suited to difficult conditions. Do a little homework before buying, and search out nearby nurseries or specialty-seed sources. Buy seeds in single-species packets, not prepackaged mixes, for better impact and to avoid later thinning. You'll find many more suggestions of plants for difficult sites in Chapter 21.

Turk's-cap lily (*Lilium martagon*)

Ironweed (*Vernonia* spp.)

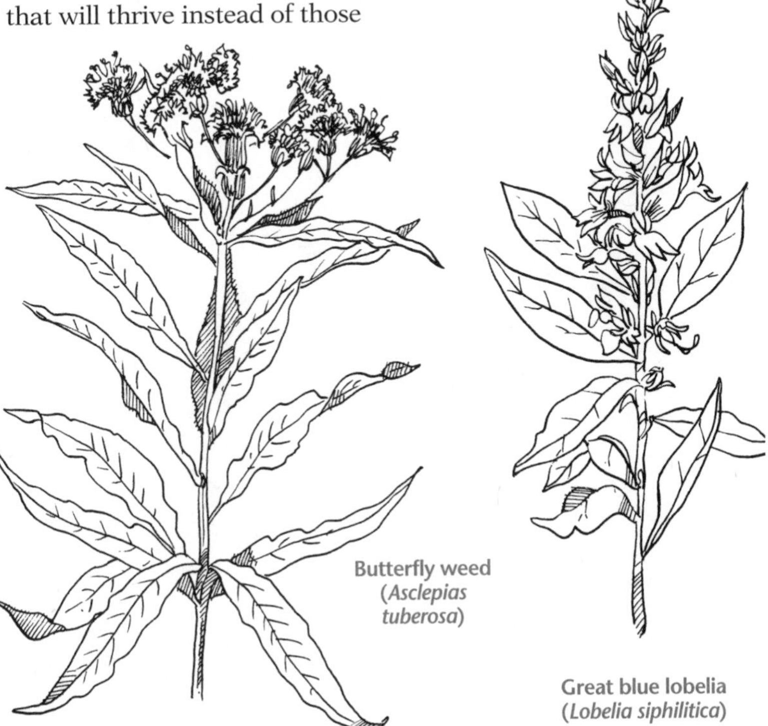

Butterfly weed (*Asclepias tuberosa*)

Great blue lobelia (*Lobelia siphilitica*)

Naturally adapted wildflowers are a great low-maintenance solution for difficult sites. Brilliant orange butterfly weed thrives in dry, nutrient-poor, loose, or sandy soils; great blue lobelia and Turk's-cap lily need moisture and some shade; deep-rooted ironweed flourishes in heavy clay.

Whether Controlled or Care-Free, Flowers Can Be Nearly Maintenance-Free

Flower gardens can have a neat, controlled look, with every plant assigned its own particular place. Or, they can run with a looser rein, creating an informal "country garden" look, with perennials spreading at will and self-sowers filling in the gaps with charming serendipity. Whether you prefer neat or nonchalant is a matter of personal choice. Either type is effective in the low-care landscape. Home landscapes often have opportunities for both types of flower garden—perhaps a disciplined, refined planting as the main display bed, and a wilder bunch out by the mailbox.

The most important thing to remember is to choose plants that suit your style. For a semiformal garden, you'll want plants like irises and hostas that know their place; if you plant self-sowers or fast spreaders, you'll spend hours on hands and knees trying to keep things under control. For the freewheeling flower bed, focus on plants that fill in fast, like yarrows, and that drop their seeds with abandon, like cosmos, so that the design of the garden is always an unexpected pleasure.

▼ **Keep formal beds manicured with mulch.** Formal and semiformal gardens are unforgiving of imperfection. Weeds stand out accusatorily in a formal bed. But a controlled planting of well-behaved flowers is still within reach of low-maintenance gardeners, thanks to the miracle of mulch. Mulch smothers weeds and cuts down on watering, two big time-eaters. Plants in semiformal and formal gardens typically have a bit of open space around them, which can be an invitation to weed invasions. Make mulch your best friend, reapplying it whenever new populations of weeds crop up. Once you have a good layer of mulch down, you'll find that weeds yield easily to hand-pulling or a scuffle hoe.

▼ **Cultivate the country look.** The informal jumble of a country garden is a good look for low-care gardeners. Combine reliable perennials, such as bee balms (*Monarda* spp.) and monkshoods (*Aconitum* spp.), with self-sowing annuals and biennials. A low-care garden should include plenty of annuals for color that lasts for weeks, often until frost. Choose annuals that resow themselves year after year. The serendipity of self-sown flowers is a part of the country garden's charm.

Invest in Plants for a Quick-Start Garden

Starting a flower garden by buying plants is more expensive than starting from seed, especially when perennials cost $3 a pot and more. But if you can afford it, it's a great time saver and a good start to a successful garden. You can install plants exactly where you want them, avoiding transplanting and thinning chores.

One-gallon pots—or even three-gallon pots—filled with healthy, vigorous perennials are mighty tempting, but your budget will be better off if you can resist the instant gratification. Four-inch starter pots of perennials may not give you as good a display their first year, but they're a great buy for gardeners on a budget. By the end of the season, the small plants will have caught up to their high-priced brothers, and by next year you probably won't be able to tell the difference.

Rent-a-Greenhouse

Flowers, especially perennials, can be slow and small when started from seed, and they take careful nurturing under lights—not exactly a low-maintenance prospect. But the mom-and-pop greenhouse in your neighborhood can often be persuaded to start a flat of seeds for you. In a commercial establishment it's little trouble, though at home it's high-care. A 50-50 split of the plants from your seed is a typical trade, or you can work out other arrangements.

Keep Mowing in Mind When You Design

Before you fill your yard with flowers, think about the physical layout of your beds and borders. Carefully planned flower plantings will eliminate some of that weekend drudge work behind the mower, but randomly placed beds can mean *extra* mowing woes.

Plan for flowering slopes. If you've been spending your Saturday mornings dragging a lawn mower up and down that bank behind the mailbox, replace that high-maintenance lawn grass with thick groundcovering perennials like daylilies (*Hemerocallis* spp.), creeping phlox (*Phlox stolonifera*), or pinks (*Dianthus* spp.). Be sure to mulch heavily until the plants are established to prevent weeds from contaminating the plot.

Size pathways to fit your mower. Keep the width of your mower in mind when designing the layout of your flower beds and borders. Allow enough space around and between beds for convenient access, according to the width of your mower deck. Few things are as frustrating—or as time-consuming—as having to add one last pass with the lawn mower to remove a final 6-inch strip of grass. If your mower cuts a 3-foot-wide

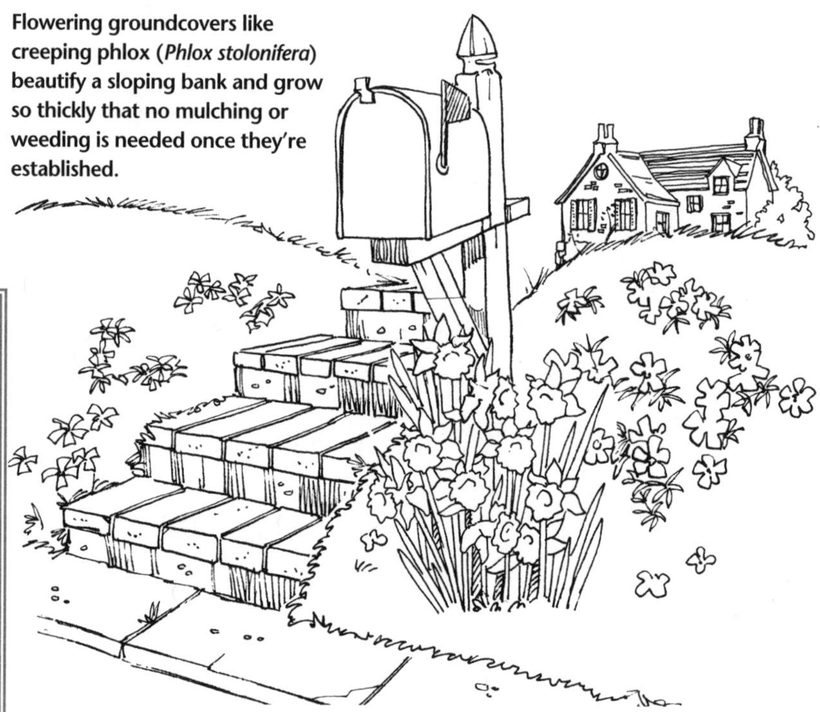

Flowering groundcovers like creeping phlox (*Phlox stolonifera*) beautify a sloping bank and grow so thickly that no mulching or weeding is needed once they're established.

swath, a 5- or 5½-foot-wide path will be just the right size, allowing some overlap between passes. A smaller 2-foot-wide cutting deck requires a path sized accordingly.

Don't make yourself cut corners. Formal, geometric beds and borders with straight edges and sharp corners are a higher maintenance design than flowing, free-form, informal shapes. Maneuvering your mower around angled turns takes more time and thought than whizzing along the edge of a curved border.

Merge beds to minimize mowing. Combining several small flower beds into one large planting is another way to finish mowing faster. Integrate isolated landscape shrubs into the planting, too, to eliminate the need for mowing around each one. If you have several rose bushes dotted along the front walk, for instance, an underplanting of lavender, alyssum, and creeping thyme will make the roses look less naked and create a small, romantic garden.

Rescue isolated shrubs like specimen roses and eliminate exacting mowing by tying the shrubs together with an underplanting of flowers.

Smothering Sod Lets You Spread Your Beds

Like the old Roman Empire, flower gardens have a way of expanding year by year, swallowing lawn as they grow. Turning turf into flowers is one of the more daunting tasks that a low-maintenance gardener faces, but there is an easy way: Simply smother your grass.

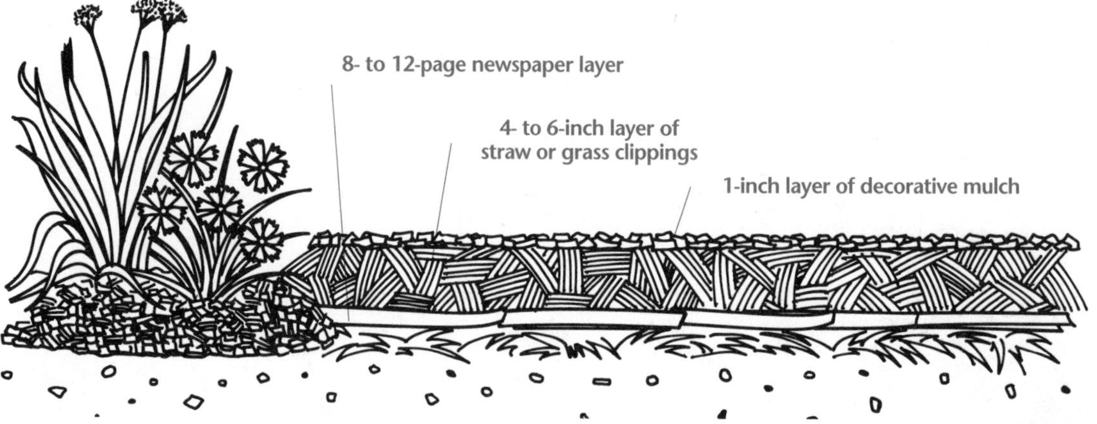

By applying a super-thick or very dense layer of mulch to the intended flower bed, you are blocking light and air from the grass plants beneath, which eventually give up and die. Eight to twelve-page sections of newspaper are an effective smothering device. Wet the newspaper with a garden hose to keep it from blowing away as you work. Apply the sections with plenty of overlap so that desperate grass can't force its way through to the air. Then blanket the newspapers with several inches of organic mulch such as aged straw or grass clippings. Top with a thin layer of fine decorative mulch if desired, such as shredded bark or buckwheat hulls. Wet it well. Wait at least three weeks, then plant the bed with perennials or annuals from containers, pulling the mulch aside to dig a planting hole. Remove any grass roots from the backfill. Water thoroughly, and apply 2 inches of mulch around the new plants. By the time the deep mulch rots down at the end of the season, the grass should be dead. Earthworms attracted by the mulch will make the soil below loose and friable.

Create a new flower bed with this technique or use it to expand an existing one. To expand a bed, just start your newspaper and mulch layer on the edge of the existing bed. Be sure to overlap the edges thoroughly so weeds don't show up between the two.

Simple Shortcuts for Combining Colors

For most gardeners, planning isn't as much fun as doing. Figuring out color schemes and plant combinations can be frustrating and time-consuming. Dispense with complicated plans and simplify your beds and borders by planting in large blocks of color. You'll get a bigger effect by planting a dozen or more of the same plant to fill a large stretch than you will by mixing plants or colors.

Limit your beds and borders to three main colors to make selecting and placing plants easier and more satisfying. Yellow, white, pink, blue, purple, and gray or silver are effective in any threesome combination. Red and orange are often difficult to weave into the garden. Here are some other simple solutions for using color in your garden.

Settle color clashes with white. There's an easy, no-dig way to soften clashing colors in the garden—separate the clashing combatants with neutral white-flowered annuals. Here's how it works: If your brilliant pink astilbes and bright orange lilies have surprised you by blooming at the same time, fill in between them with white-flowered annuals like impatiens or sweet alyssum to soften and separate the colors. You can move one of the offending colors in the spring or fall, when it's not in bloom. Or separate them permanently with white-flowered perennials that will be in bloom at the same time. Silver-foliaged plants like dusty miller also have the same effect.

Make your yard bigger with blue. It's true, cool colors like blue make things seem farther away than they really are. A garden of blue, soft pink, and white will make your yard seem larger than one planted in red, orange, and yellow. All without having to take care of another square inch.

Start color combinations on your doorstep. Can't decide what color would be right for your garden? How about selecting a color that matches or complements your house's trim? Plant mounds of lavender-blue bellflowers (*Campanula* spp.), spiky clumps of deep violet salvia 'East Friesland', and tall purple Canterbury bells (*C. medium*) beside the stoop to accent a teal-colored door. Remember to keep things in balance—a garden the same color as the house adds nothing to the overall effect. Mustard siding? Yellow flowers would be too much; go with blues instead.

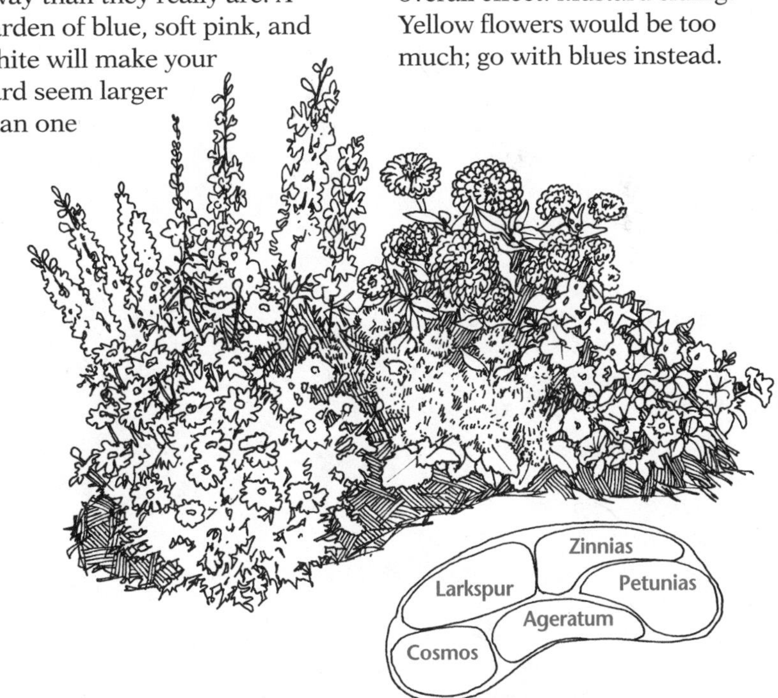

This annual bed uses a block of hot orange direct-seeded Klondike-type cosmos, followed by a block of soft blue dwarf ageratum bought as bedding plants, then a block of white multiflora petunias, set in as bedding plants. Tall red zinnias and deep blue larkspur, both direct-seeded, add height behind.

A Word to the Wise: Think Twice before Planting Invasives

Many of the most-expert experts scorn invasive perennials (plants that spread vigorously), but it's all a matter of perspective. If you want a balanced planting in a mixed border, or if you have a small garden, invasives can quickly become major headaches. But if you want to fill a new bed in a hurry or plant an easy-care area, they're a great choice.

When you want hurry-up-and-grow plants, look for perennials that are *stoloniferous*, which means they spread by creeping underground stems. These plants often grow so thickly that they crowd out competing weeds.

Invasive perennials vary in their rate of aggressiveness. Lamb's-ears (*Stachys byzantina*), for instance, is a fairly well-mannered spreader that expands slowly and can be easily kept in line. But a single plant of one of the fastest-spreading perennials, the native sunflower known as Jerusalem artichoke (*Helianthus tuberosus*), can colonize a 4-foot-wide area in just a single year, and its brittle tubers are nearly impossible to remove completely once it gets going.

Some invasives are easy to control by hand-pulling, but others are insistent growers that spring back no matter how often you pull. You're not doing yourself any favors by planting these eager beavers where they'll need to be brought back into bounds a few years down the line. Save them for areas that are isolated from your less-agressive plants, or use them to create a no-care flower bed along a sidewalk fence. To preserve good neighbor relations, don't plant aggressive invasives near property boundaries.

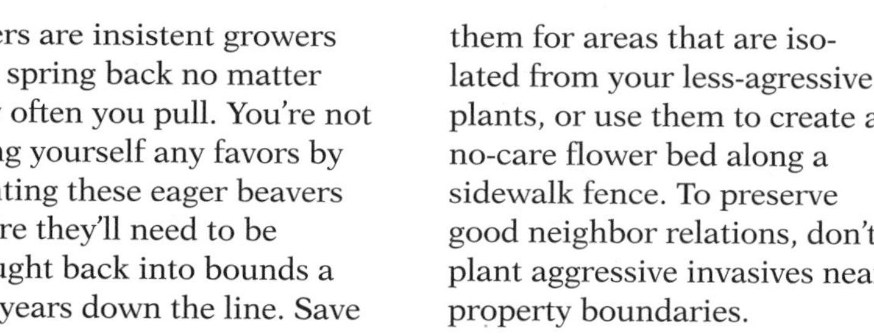

White-flowered sweet woodruff (*Galium odoratum*) and naturalized violets are a good combination for shade.

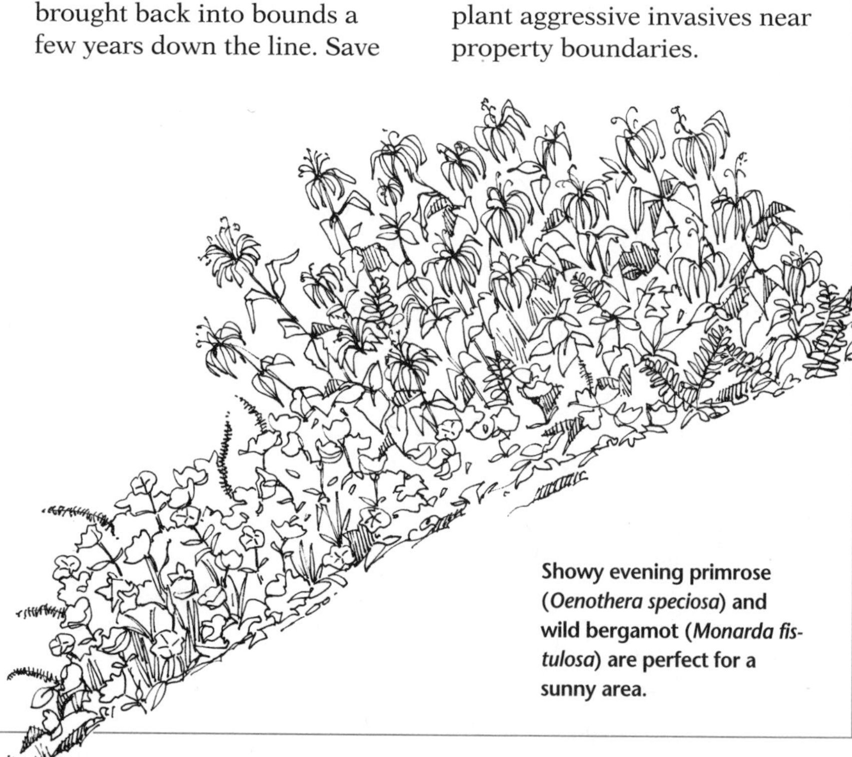

Showy evening primrose (*Oenothera speciosa*) and wild bergamot (*Monarda fistulosa*) are perfect for a sunny area.

Is Deadheading Worth Your While?

Peach-leaved bellflower (*Campanula persicifolia*) bears stalks of lovely, soft, lavender-blue flowers, but when blooms fade, blossoms brown quickly and hang on the plant like old laundry. Balloon flower (*Platycodon* spp.) is another perennial that doesn't "self clean." Many gardeners accept faded flowers in the garden, but if you prefer a neat look, you may be better off replacing these plants with those of neater habit. For example, some annuals, such as begonias and Madagascar periwinkle (*Catharanthus roseus*), drop faded flowers and bloom continuously.

On the other hand, many gardeners find deadheading—removing tired and dying flowers—an agreeable chore that doesn't take much time. Even the most dedicated low-maintenance gardener probably won't eliminate daffodils or daylilies from the garden because of their tendency to hang onto faded flowers.

When you do deadhead, suit your technique to the plant. Pinch or clip off old blooms on plants like pansies that have thin stems. Brittle stems, like those on salvia, are easy to break off with the flick of a wrist. Or deflower salvias, petunias, marigolds, and other flowers that bloom all at once in a hurry with hedge clippers.

Twiggy Support for Top-Heavy Flowers

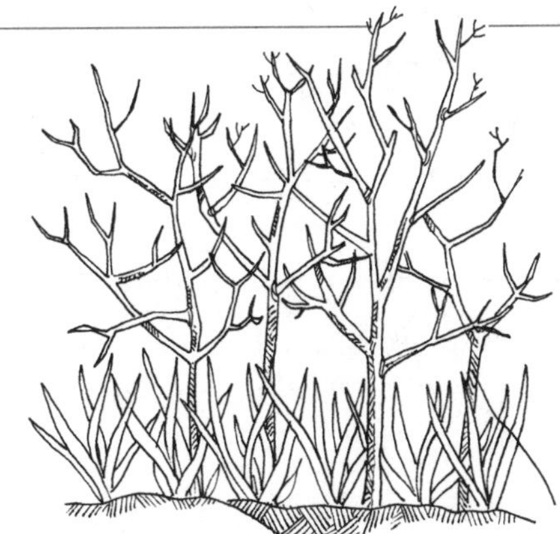

In the formal or semiformal garden, a flower that leans with the wind or its own weight may need a little help to straighten its backbone. A twiggy clipping makes an ideal plant support for flopsy annuals such as spider flower (*Cleome hasslerana*). Such clippings are easy to handle and blend right in among the plants. Strip any leaves off the clippings and leave them to dry in the sun for a day or two. (Otherwise, they may put out roots and begin to grow when you stick them in the garden). Poke the dry branches into the soil so that they are well anchored. Put brush in place earlier in the season for prone-to-leaning perennials, such as delphiniums, so that flower stems grow up through it.

CHAPTER 23

Annuals

Make Hassle-Free Beds for Annuals

Cure Landscape Problems Fast with Annuals

Choose Annuals That Don't Need a Babysitter

Enlist Annuals in the Weed War

Keep 'em Blooming with Quick Pruning

Choose Flowers That Replant Themselves

Get More for Your Buck with Flats

Annuals the Low-Maintenance Way

NOTHING BEATS ANNUALS when you want bold, colorful results in a hurry. They're easy to come by (just check any garden shop or supermarket in spring), easy to plant, and easy to grow. They come in a huge variety of flower types, colors, textures, and sizes to fit every garden. And when you start with inexpensive bedding plants, they start out looking great, and their bright flowers keep going and going all season long.

But annuals are much more than pretty flowers you can use to add a spot of color around a flagpole or along the driveway. In this chapter, you'll not only learn how to grow annuals with the least work possible, you'll find out how to put them to work for you in the landscape. Discover how to use annuals to hide ugly views, revive old plantings, call attention to your home, battle weeds, and even help you direct traffic. And when the growing season is over, you won't have to fuss with pruning and protecting tender plants, just yank annuals out of the ground. Their shallow roots, fleshy stems, and succulent leaves make them easy to pull and completely compostable.

Make Hassle-Free Beds for Annuals

Do you like the bold splash of color annual beds offer but wonder if you're up to the work? Don't worry, annuals are tough and adaptable and will bloom their heads off even in soil that's not ideal. Here's a bare-bones approach to making annual beds.

Build planting islands. Most annuals have shallow, fibrous roots, so you won't have to spend time digging or tilling deep beds. To get your annuals off to a good start, water the soil if it's dry to make your job easier, and dig up any woody weeds on the site. Then turn the soil to a shovel's depth. A shovel or digging fork works fine to loosen up a few inches of soil. Then make mounds of compost or potting soil to raise the area up slightly and you're ready to plant.

Make the most of mulch. Top every annual bed with up to 4 inches of organic mulch such as shredded bark to control weeds, retain moisture, and create a finished look. It's a one-step maintenance plan.

BEFORE

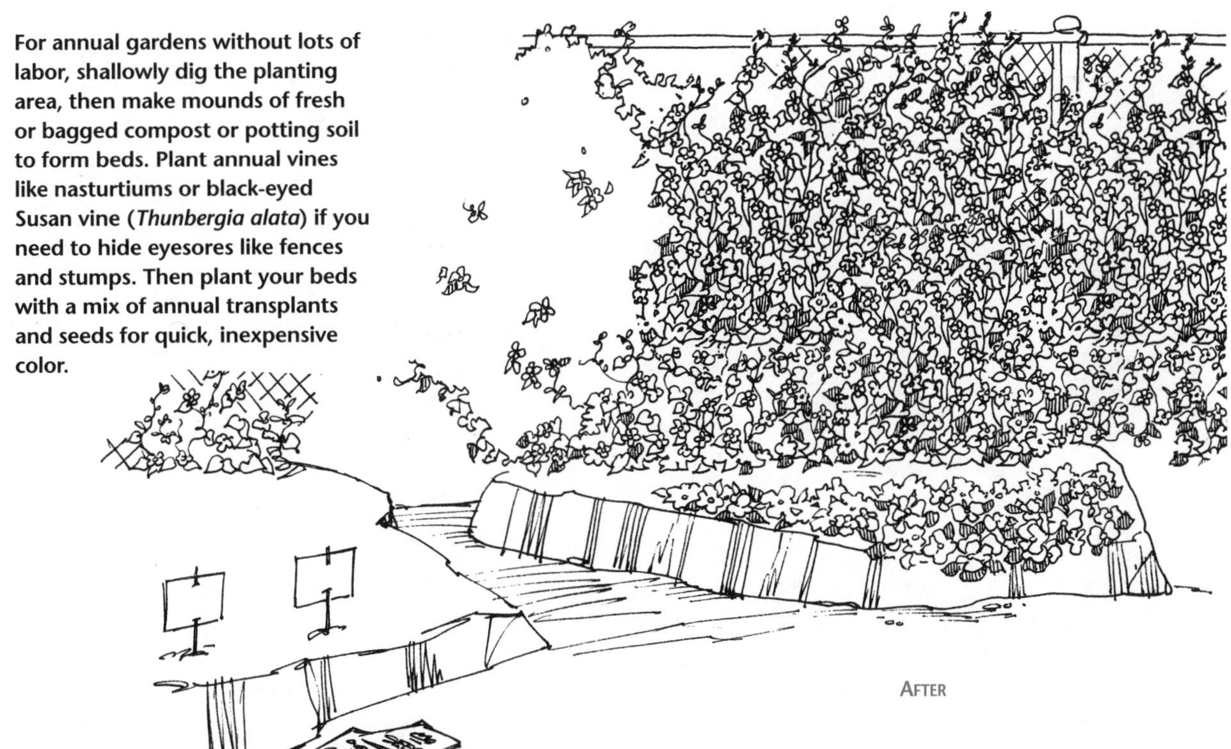

AFTER

For annual gardens without lots of labor, shallowly dig the planting area, then make mounds of fresh or bagged compost or potting soil to form beds. Plant annual vines like nasturtiums or black-eyed Susan vine (*Thunbergia alata*) if you need to hide eyesores like fences and stumps. Then plant your beds with a mix of annual transplants and seeds for quick, inexpensive color.

Cure Landscape Problems Fast with Annuals

Whether your garden is new or well established, there comes a time when it needs a quick face-lift. Fortunately, you don't have to resort to major surgery. Unsightly views, barren homesites, and garden hot spots all respond to annual therapy.

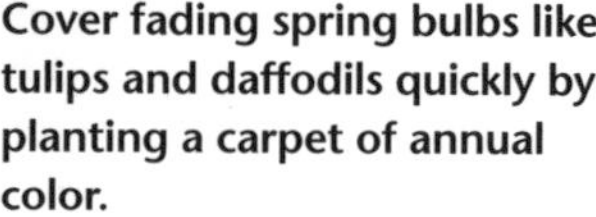

Cover fading spring bulbs like tulips and daffodils quickly by planting a carpet of annual color.

Brightly colored annuals can add pizzazz to your lifeless foundation planting. Choose vibrant flowers like salvia, zinnias, and marigolds to fill in between ho-hum shrubs.

A dose of annuals calms clashing colors. When bulbs or flowering shrubs bloom in colors you didn't expect (imagine orange lilies and pink astilbe against a red brick house!), don't panic—surround them with a planting of white-flowered or silver-leaved annuals. These neutral-color plants will give quick relief by toning down flowers that are just too bright.

Plant an instant facelift. Dull, boring foundation plantings are a fact of life in many landscapes. To cover up sparse areas and dead spots in foundation plantings, or to spruce up for a special event, plant annuals. Mix them among your shrubs to fill in gaps, add bright accents, and create an interesting mix of textures. Or simply plant annuals in front of foundation plantings. For an extra-quick spot of color when you don't have time to plant, place a few pots or hanging baskets of colorful annuals like petunias or wax begonias on the front porch.

Direct traffic with annuals. Well-placed annual beds not only liven up plantings, they also define space and direct traffic in your yard. You can line a path or mark off a bed with a row of annuals, for example. Or use plantings of brightly colored annuals to keep visitors from cutting through a bed you're trying to restore, welcome them to the front door, or warn them where they shouldn't step.

Dress up leggy landscape plants with flowers. There's nothing attractive about leggy

Impatiens are great plants for dressing up a leggy hedge like this one. Not only will they thrive in shade, they'll discourage shortcutters from tromping through your planting.

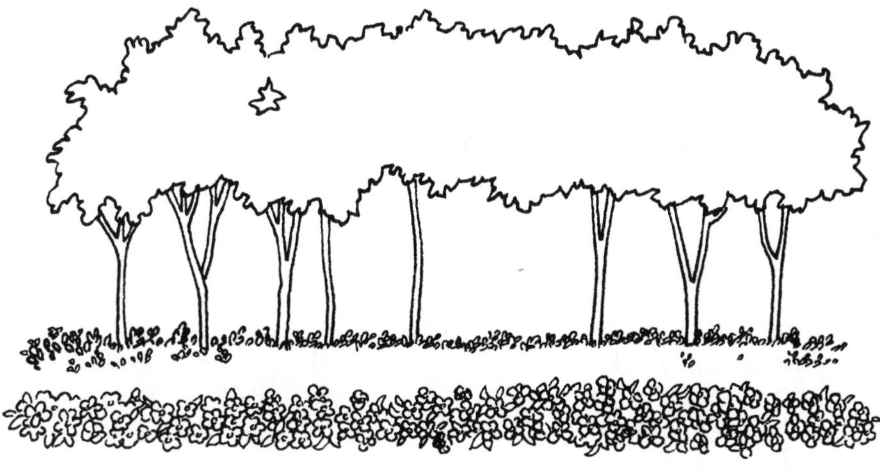

hedges or foundation plants. The bare stems, combined with scraggly grass or weeds underneath, are an eyesore, pure and simple. You can use annuals to dress up leggy plantings in a hurry—or to surround and dress up any tree or shrub planting.

Use quick coverups for ugly views. It's an easy matter to screen that old shed, falling-down fence, or the neighbor's old car with annuals such as sunflowers, amaranth, tall zinnias, cosmos, or spider flowers (*Cleome hasslerana*).

Grow instant shade with annual vines. Nothing beats annual vines for fast, inexpensive shade. You can grow new annual vines to make shady spaces or use them for quick cover while slower-growing perennial vines become large enough for permanent shade. Try morning glories (*Ipomoea* spp.), gourds, cup-and-saucer vine (*Cobaea scandens*), moonflower (*Ipomoea alba*), hyacinth bean (*Dolichos lablab*), cypress vine (*I. quamoclit*), scarlet runner beans (*Phaseolus coccineus*), and black-eyed Susan vine (*Thunbergia alata*).

Measure Out and Plant with Ease

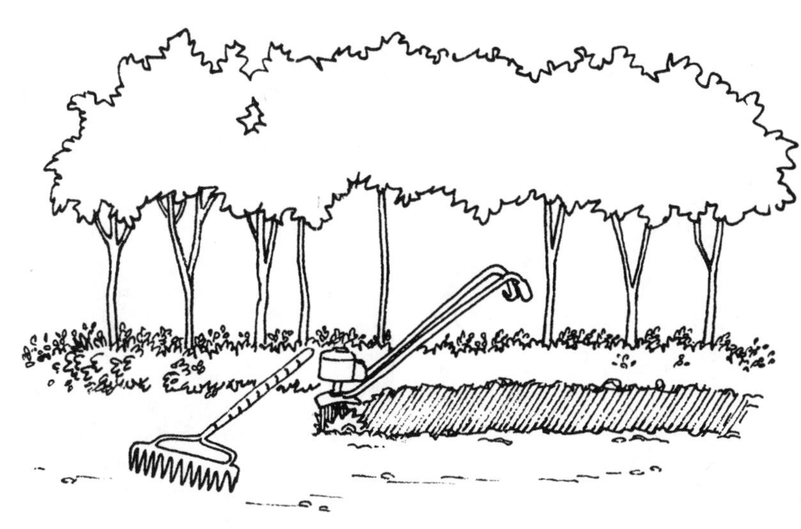

To add a bed of annuals in front of an existing planting, measure out from trunks about 2 feet so you won't damage the roots, and dig or till a shallow trench on all sides of the tree line. If you uncover too many roots 2 feet from your planting, move out farther. Add compost or other organic matter, rake lightly, then plant.

A garden rake with markings at 6-inch intervals makes a convenient yardstick.

Choose Annuals That Don't Need a Babysitter

Pick the right plants and you won't have to fuss with constant feeding, watering, and cleaning. The annual favorites listed below can fend for themselves, and most have flowers that drop neatly after blooming so you don't need to deadhead. Just provide the right amount of light, water well when you plant them, surround them with 3 to 4 inches of mulch, and enjoy.

Partial to full shade. Browallia (*Browallia speciosa*), coleus (*Coleus × hybridus*), impatiens (*Impatiens wallerana*), polka-dot plant (*Hypoestes phyllostachya*), wax begonias (*Begonia* Semperflorens-Cultorum hybrid), wishbone flower (*Torenia fournieri*).

Full sun. Cleome (*Cleome spinosa*), globe amaranth (*Gomphrena globosa*), Joseph's-coat (*Amaranthus tricolor*), Madagascar periwinkle (*Catharanthus roseus*), Melampodium (*Melampodium leucanthum*), rose moss (*Portulaca grandiflora*), narrowleaf zinnia (*Zinnia angustifolia*, also sold as *Z. linearis*).

Enlist Annuals in the Weed War

Everyone who's ever planted a new groundcover or perennial bed shares one problem: new plantings need time to grow together. While you're waiting, weeds will try to fill the spaces between plants. Fortunately, you can fight them off with trailing annuals such as sweet alyssum, Madagascar periwinkle, and verbena. They'll fill in gaps until the slower-growing perennial groundcovers have grown large enough to fill the space on their own. In perennial gardens, you can plant annuals to fill in the gaps—trailing ones for the front and a variety of annuals with different heights, colors, and textures for the rest of the garden. The annuals will shade out weeds, add color, and prevent erosion.

Get perennial groundcover plantings off to a weed-free start by mulching them at planting time, then interplanting with creeping annuals. Here, sweet alyssum is being interplanted with vinca.

Keep 'em Blooming with Quick Pruning

Annuals will bloom all summer long if you pick off spent flowers to keep them from going to seed. But picking off each flower as it fades can take an eternity. What to do?

Instead of spending hours picking spent posies, use hedge shears to slice off whole swaths of spent flowers fast and send them right into bloom again. Try shearing marigolds, petunias, primroses, zinnias, annual lupines, and other annuals that hold their blooms upright and tend to open all at once.

Choose Flowers That Replant Themselves

Plan for the ultimate in low-maintenance by growing annuals that reseed in your garden. All you have to do is plant them once, and they'll return year after year on their own.

To encourage your plants to reseed, cut back on water as the last blossoms fade. When flower heads dry, crush them to release seeds into the planting bed. If you live in an area where winters are too rough for reseeding, let plants set seed, then pluck the dried blossoms and store them in a cool, dry, place in plastic bags. Replant in spring.

Early each spring, watch for seedlings from your reseeders. Let them grow to 2 inches tall before thinning the stand. Transplant extra plants directly to other flower beds on a cloudy day, or just pluck them and add to the compost pile.

Reseeding annuals are especially popular for cottage gardens. To get them started, prepare a seedbed where you want the plants to grow and just scatter the seeds. Here are some of the most reliable reseeders.

Baby-blue-eyes (*Nemophila menziesii*) with blue cup-shaped flowers; cleome (*Cleome hasslerana*) with airy pink, purple, or white blooms; cornflower (*Centaurea cyanus*) with pale blue button flowers; and flowering tobacco (*Nicotiana alata*), in shades of pink, purple, red, or white. Try garden balsam (*Impatiens balsamina*), four-o'clocks (*Mirabilis jalapa*), and cosmos (*Cosmos bipinnatus*) for pink, red, white, and yellow blooms; Johnny-jump-up (*Viola tricolor*) for tricolored flowers, love-in-a-mist (*Nigella damascena*) for blooms of blue, pink, purple, or white; sweet alyssum (*Lobularia maritima*) for clusters of tiny pink, purple, or white flowers; and larkspurs (*Consolida* spp.) for spikes of blue, pink, purple, red, or white.

There's no rule that you can't add reseeding herbs to your garden as well. Try dill and cilantro (whose tasty seeds are the herb coriander) for ferny foliage and delicate flowers.

Get More for Your Buck with Flats of Annuals

Nothing beats annuals for getting a big color impact with a minimum of work. If you start with transplants, you can literally plant an instant garden. And for the biggest impact, buying annuals by the flat makes lots of sense. You not only get the best price per plant, but you can create bold patterns of color that will dress up your yard in a hurry. Buying in flats—or at least six-packs—also helps you concentrate on a limited color scheme, so you'll avoid the confusing mishmash of conflicting colors, sizes, and shapes that results from planting lots of different annuals.

▲ **Unify your landscape with color.** If you have several small flower beds, you *could* put a different planting in each one. But to create a unified design, repeat the same planting beside the front door or around a lamppost, column, or mailbox. Masses of a single color will draw attention to your entryway, while the repetition between beds soothes the eye.

▼ **Create a sheet of color.** For another quick and dramatic display, plant a flower bed using a single flat of 24 to 36 annual plants. Sloping your bed slightly from back to front will show off your flowers to best advantage. Stand at the top of the bed and use a garden rake to pull up soil until it elevates the bed about 6 inches for every 6 feet.

CHAPTER 24

Bulbs

Bulbs the Low-Maintenance Way

FLOWERING BULBS are so easy and undemanding that every low-maintenance garden should include them. Hardy bulbs, such as daffodils and crocuses, are true workhorses in a low-maintenance garden. So-called tender bulbs, such as caladiums, cannas, and tuberous begonias, are pretty tough customers, too.

In this chapter, you'll find techniques for succeeding with a variety of bulbs and bulblike plants. After all, what could be easier than a ready-to-grow flower that comes prepackaged with its own food source and blooms over a period of years?

Let Nature Take Its Course in No-Care Bulb Plantings

In an informal landscape, an utterly easy way to use bulbs is to naturalize them. Naturalizing involves planting bulbs into your existing landscape so that they look as if they grew there on their own. For best effect, group them in drifts rather than straight rows. Best of all, once the bulbs are planted and established, your efforts are over.

Good locations for naturalizing bulbs include grassy banks, meadows, property edges, around shrubs, and open woodlands. For naturalizing in your lawn, try small, low-growing bulbs such as crocuses, glory-of-the-snow (*Chionodoxa luciliae*), grape hyacinths (*Muscari* spp.), Grecian windflowers (*Anemone blanda*), striped squills (*Puschkinia scilloides*), miniature narcissus cultivars, netted irises (*Iris reticulata*), Siberian squills (*Scilla siberica*), snowdrops (*Galanthus* spp.), and spring starflowers (*Ipheion uniflorum*).

Go with Plumbago

Tough, fast-growing plumbago (*Ceratostigma plumbaginoides*) is a creeping, semi-woody perennial that makes a great groundcovering companion for bulbs. Combine it with mid- to late-spring bloomers that will put on a show until the plumbago's new growth begins to expand in late spring. Or, for a fall floral display, interplant plumbago with fall-blooming bulbs like autumn crocuses (*Colchicum* spp.) or winter daffodil (*Sternbergia lutea*). Plumbago's bright blue blossoms appear in late summer and carry on into fall, making it an excellent complement for autumn bulbs.

Keys to Success with Naturalized Plantings

- Use large quantities of small bulbs for visual impact.

- Plant in loosely defined drifts, leaving space between the bulbs; they'll fill in by naturally dividing and seeding. One way to arrange them quickly is to lightly toss the bulbs and plant them where they land.

- One kind, one color is always effective. At most, limit yourself to two or three species or flower colors in one area.

- Let the bulbs' foliage ripen. When bulbs are planted into lawn, leave the lawn uncut until the bulbs' foliage matures, or subsequent years' flowers will be diminished or even eliminated.

- Keep species' site preferences in mind when you plant. Try crocuses in sunny areas, Siberian squills and daffodils in partial shade, and woodland natives such as winter aconites (*Eranthis* spp.) and trout lilies (*Erythronium* spp.) in shadier locations.

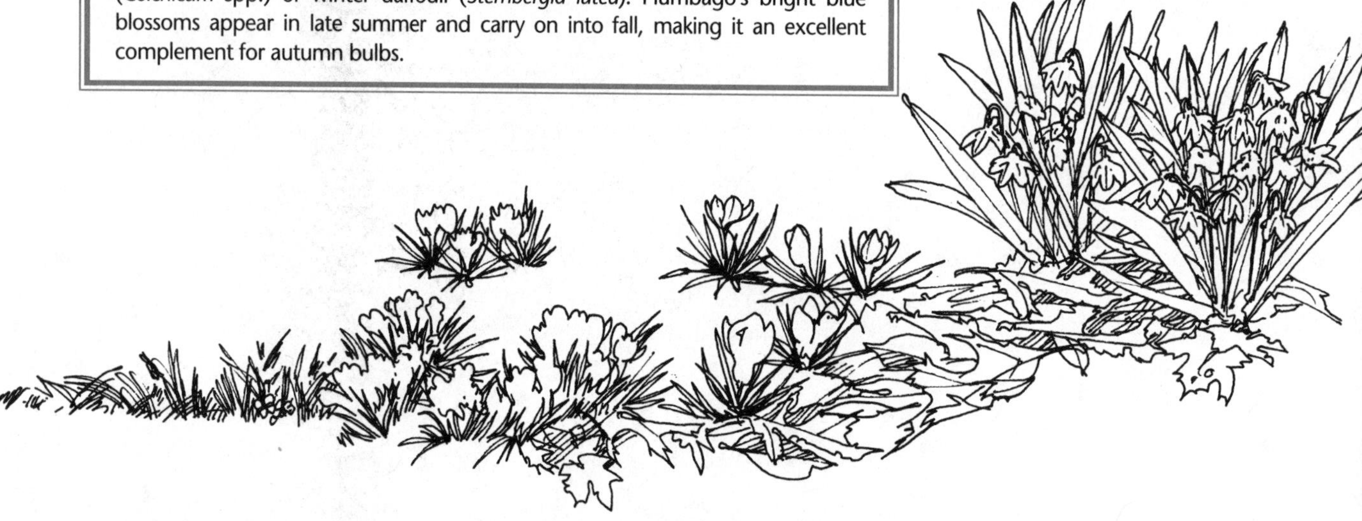

- Match form to function. Formal-looking bulbs can seem out of place in informal plantings. Try grape hyacinths (*Muscari* spp.) instead of stiffly upright Dutch hyacinths (*Hyacinthus orientalis* cultivars); tuck species tulips into your landscape rather than their hybridized offspring.

- Top-dress naturalized bulb plantings with compost or dried manure. Apply in spring, just as the leaves start to emerge, and again in early fall to nourish future flowers.

TAKE-IT-EASY TIP!

Leave the Leaves Alone!

Resist the temptation to "do something" about the fading foliage of past-bloom spring bulbs. Don't braid it. Don't tie it up. Don't cut it down. This only makes more work for you at the expense of your bulbs' good health. Leaves create food to replenish bulbs for the following year's growth and form the flowers you're looking forward to next spring. Besides, they'll be gone soon. The leaves of spring bulbs usually disappear a month after flowering, although daffodil foliage may remain six weeks or longer.

8 Hints to Help You Buy the Best Bulbs

Starting out with healthy bulbs gets your garden off to a good start and helps keep maintenance at a minimum. Vigorous plants look better and are better able to resist pests and diseases, all with little effort on your part. Use these tips to get the best bulb buys.

1. Consider the source. Buying bulbs locally lets you handpick each one, ensuring that you'll get the best they have to offer. However, mail-order companies that specialize in bulbs will have a greater selection. They may offer reduced prices for large quantities of bulbs.

2. Consider the service. Look for local suppliers that sell bulbs *at* planting time, not months before. Reputable mail-order firms will ship bulbs to you at the proper planting time for your area and guarantee bulb quality.

3. Shop early in the season. Placing mail orders early ensures the bulbs you want will be available and that they'll arrive at the proper time for planting. Local retailers will have the best selection early in the planting season.

4. Select bulbs that like your locale. Check with garden retailers and your county's extension office to learn which bulbs are right for your region. Remember that winter survival is only half the battle—some bulbs suffer when temperatures soar. Look for bulbs that will endure your local conditions.

5. Buy the biggest bulbs. With bulbs, you get what you pay for. Larger bulbs—often called "top size," "jumbo," or "double-nosed"—deliver the best flowers and are more likely to produce new bulbs to increase your flower planting. And they don't take any longer to plant than small bulbs.

6. Weigh your decisions. Buy solid bulbs that seem heavy for their size. Soft, lightweight bulbs will grow poorly, if at all.

7. Inspect and reject. Don't worry about small tears in the outer covering of bulbs as long as the protective skin is still there. Reject any bulbs that are moldy or showing signs of rot.

8. Watch out for wild ones. Collecting bulbs from their native wild habitats has endangered many species. If you buy species bulbs rather than cultivars, ask if they were nursery propagated. If you can't get a satisfactory answer, shop someplace else.

Buying Time for Your Tulips

Among the hardy bulbs, tulips tend to be short-lived perennials, sometimes producing only a couple years of bloom. Given the cost of bulbs and the effort of installing them, this gradual petering out can be a big disappointment. But not all tulips are fickle—some will return tirelessly for several years, and there are ways to encourage them.

Plant *species* tulips (or *botanical* tulips). These early-bloomers outlive their hybrid counterparts. Or select cultivars with a reputation for being long-lasting; they're sometimes sold as "perennial tulips." (Three years is perennial in hot climates; they'll last longer in cooler areas.) Plant cultivar tulip bulbs deeply, 8 to 10 inches below the soil.

Plant Combinations Bring Out the Best in Your Bulbs

In addition to keeping your bulbs healthy so they look their best, there are other ways to make the most of blooming bulbs in your landscape. By assembling some easy plant combinations, you can use bulbs to add color and sparkle to your gardens—without a lot of hassle.

Let late-blooming perennials hide fading bulb foliage, as daylilies do for these drumstick chives (*Allium sphaerocephalum*).

Complement and contrast. In a spring garden, between the bulbs, set out low-growing flowers that bloom at the same time as your bulbs. Good bulb companions include pansies, Johnny-jump-ups, wallflowers (*Cheiranthus cheiri*), and forget-me-nots (*Myosotis* spp.). You can also combine taller bulbs like tulips with smaller bulbs like grape hyacinths.

Use flowering trees or shrubs with your bulbs to supply contrasting colors. Try blue squills (*Hyacinthoides non-scriptus*) or glory-of-the-snow (*Chionodoxa luciliae*) near yellow forsythias, or yellow daffodils near white-flowered crabapples.

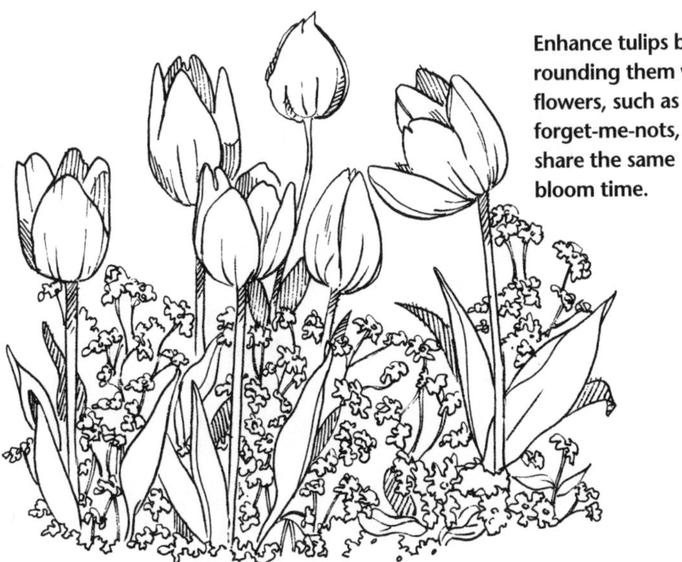

Enhance tulips by surrounding them with flowers, such as these forget-me-nots, that share the same bloom time.

Combine and cover. Plant your bulbs among spring-flowering perennials such as basket-of-gold (*Aurinia saxatilis*), purple rock cress (*Aubrieta deltoidea*), or perennial candytuft (*Iberis sempervirens*). Since spring bulbs virtually disappear from view when their tops die back, perennials planted adjacent to the bulbs can serve as markers to remind you not to dig there later in the season.

Later-blooming perennials that emerge as your bulbs are flowering won't detract from the bulb flowers, yet they'll fill the aboveground spaces left by the bulbs and help to conceal the dying bulb foliage. Many perennials can fill this role, including daylilies, baby's-breath, hostas, and ferns.

Dig In and Double Your Bulbs

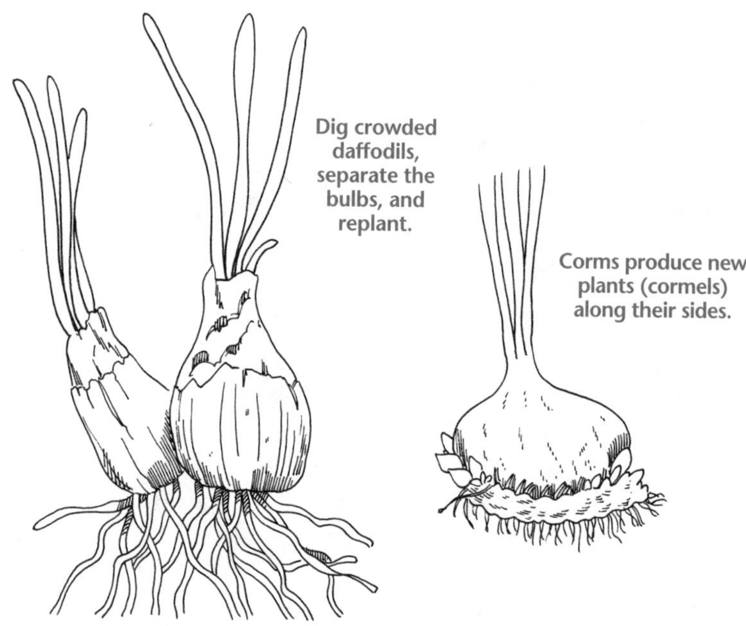

An added bulb bonus is their ability to multiply. Without your spending another penny, bulbs such as daffodils and crocuses will increase in number over the years.

If the number of flowers a bulb planting produces begins to decline over the years but there's lots of foliage evident, the bulbs have multiplied, creating a cluster of small, closely spaced bulbs.

After the foliage has faded, dig and separate the bulbs. Replant them right away, at the proper spacing. Given more space, they'll soon grow to flowering size again.

Get Maximum Impact with Minimum Effort

It's as easy to plant a garden of bulbs that blooms for months on end as it is one that blooms for only a few fleeting weeks. Why? Although most hardy bulbs flower in the spring, they don't all flower at the same time. So to make the most of your planting time, it pays to plant an assortment of different bulbs.

For example, some small bulbs like snowdrops and crocuses begin blooming in late winter, while some tulips may not finish flowering until early summer.

One good place to start is to look for the season of bloom in the descriptions of bulbs when you shop, whether you're looking in a local garden center or a catalog. You'll find ratings like "very early spring," "early spring," "mid-spring," and "late spring," for example. To get the longest bloom possible, select some from each season.

Don't just consider different species of bulbs like crocuses and tulips, either. Many bulbs, including daffodils, tulips, and lilies, have a wide variety of species and cultivars that bloom at different seasons, too. You can buy tulips, for example, that will bloom in late winter to very early spring, mid-spring, and late spring to early summer.

Also try using microclimates on your property to vary the bloom time of your bulbs—even if they're all the same cultivars. Microclimates are variations in the prevailing conditions that are caused by factors such as topography, shade, or proximity to buildings. For example, bulbs planted in a site with southern exposure will bloom earlier than the same species planted in a north-facing spot.

Tools to Make Bulb Planting a Breeze

Planting is easiest when you use the tool that works best for you and for the planting design you've chosen. For naturalizing small bulbs in a lawn or other groundcover, a narrow-blade trowel works well, as does a naturalizing tool. An auger attachment for your power drill eases the process of making individual holes for larger bulbs, while a spade is useful for digging a large hole to hold several bulbs.

Spade. For excellent effect and a well-prepared planting site, use a classic garden spade to excavate a large hole that will hold many bulbs.

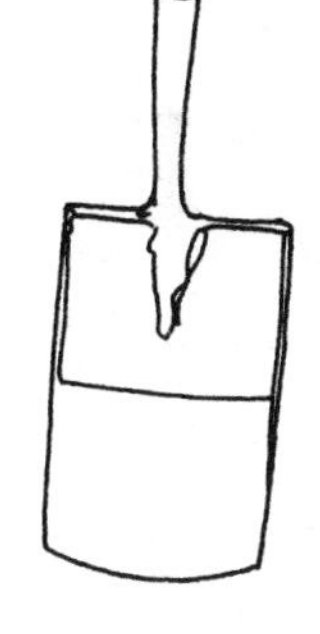

Bulb planters. Both long- and short-handled bulb planters are useful tools for making individual holes for larger bulbs.

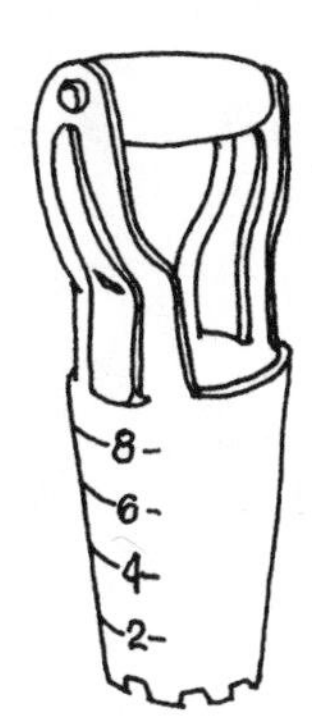

Naturalizing tool. This crowbarlike tool gives you lots of leverage when planting small bulbs in your lawn. Use it much as you would a trowel, but without the bending—just use your foot to push the soil back after planting each bulb.

Trowel. Stab your trowel, daggerlike, into the soil and pull it toward you to open up a planting hole for a small bulb. Then remove it and tuck the bulb in by pressing the soil back into place.

Auger. Turn your power drill into a bulb planter with an auger, which is also useful for digging holes for larger bulbs.

Smaller Hyacinths Stand Taller

Your efforts (and money) may seem wasted if spring winds and rains topple the top-heavy blooms of the large hyacinth bulbs you planted last fall. Here's a case where smaller bulbs are better: The smaller blooms produced by medium-size hyacinth bulbs are less likely to fall prey to blustery spring weather. Reserve your biggest bulbs for indoor pots, and plant medium-size bulbs for a more durable garden display.

Increase Daffodils' "Face Value" with Good Site Selection

You wouldn't hang your favorite painting facing the wall. Likewise, when you plant daffodils, you want to see their faces—the open, cup-shaped sides of the flowers—not their backs.

When selecting a planting site for daffodils, it's helpful to know that their open blooms will turn toward the direction from which the strongest sunlight comes—usually south to west. Think about where you'll be when you're looking at your daffodils—at your window, perhaps, or coming up your front walk, and position plantings accordingly.

A Simple Guideline for Planting Depth and Spacing

In general, plant bulbs at a depth three to four times their height. Space large bulbs 5 to 6 inches apart and small bulbs 1 to 3 inches apart. Although all of the structures shown here are referred to as bulbs, they represent a variety of underground storage structures—corms, tubers, tuberous roots, fleshy rhizomes, and true bulbs—that share similar cultural requirements.

Which End Up?

When you're planting bulbs, make sure to give them the best start by planting them right side up. Generally, place them in your prepared hole with the pointed tip up. If your bulb doesn't have a point, don't despair. Remember the second rule of bulb planting: When in doubt, plant it sideways. The bulb knows which way is up and will have less to overcome from being sideways in its hole than if you plant it upside down.

Plant Dutch iris bulbs 2–6 inches deep.

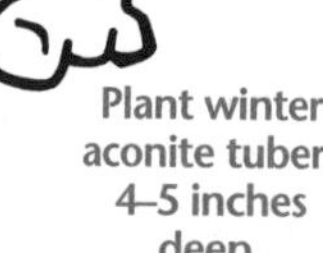
Plant winter aconite tubers 4–5 inches deep.

Plant canna rhizomes 3–5 inches deep.

Plant crocus corms 4–5 inches deep.

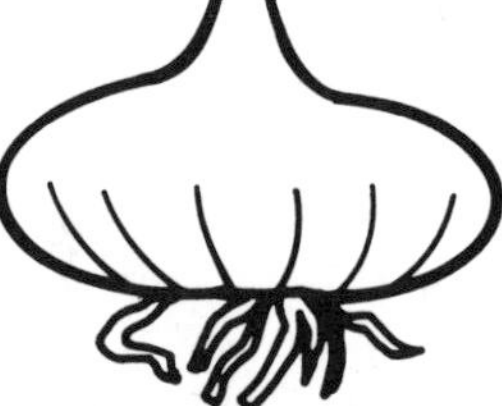
Plant gladiolus corms 3–8 inches deep.

Plant daffodil bulbs 4–5 inches deep.

Plant lily bulbs 12–15 inches deep.

Terrific Techniques for Planting Bulbs

Whatever tool you use to prepare your site, don't skimp on the size of the hole and don't overcrowd. Bulbs planted at the proper depth and spacing live longer and are less subject to injuries from animals or cultivating tools. Try some of the tips that follow to create effective bulb displays throughout your yard.

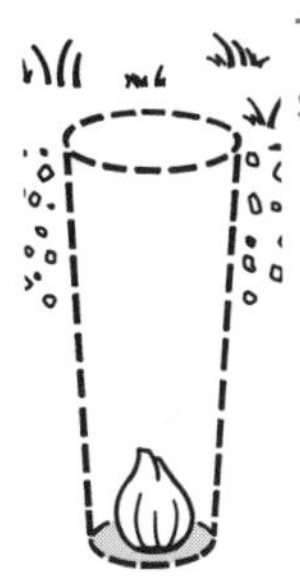

Tuck in bulbs with single holes. To tuck bulbs between existing plants, such as in a perennial garden, use a spade, auger, or bulb planter to make individual holes.

Plant 'em together if you have the room. If you're planting lots of bulbs in an area that's free of other plants, simply dig a hole to the proper depth and space a group of them out over the bottom of the hole. This planting method maximizes the impact of their blooms and saves you from digging several individual holes.

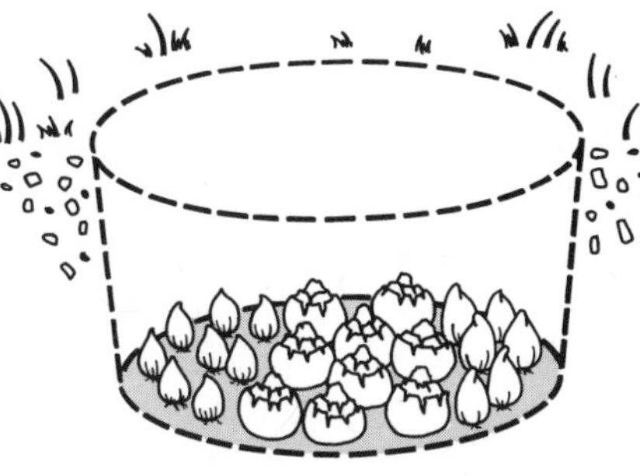

Plant colorful beds of bulbs in planting areas. You can combine different bulbs and flower colors to create colorful designs anywhere in your yard. For best results, excavate and prepare the entire planting area all at once. Then work out your color and spacing by arranging the bulbs in the bottom of the hole before you cover them.

After planting, water thoroughly to firm the soil and to stimulate root growth. Top-dress the planting with organic fertilizer or compost. If the weeks following planting are dry, water periodically until the ground freezes. Apply mulch in late autumn to keep soil temperatures from fluctuating. Although nothing is visible above ground, vital root growth is occurring below the soil.

Try layering a planting of different-size bulbs. For a lot of pizzazz in a limited space, you can use bulbs with coinciding bloom times for a spectacular one-shot show, or with consecutive bloom, as shown above, for a longer-lasting display. Plant large bulbs deeply, medium-size bulbs above them, and small bulbs an inch or two below the soil surface. Choose bulbs that do not need frequent division; otherwise you may have to dig up the whole planting or put up with diminished flowering from bulbs that have multiplied.

The layered planting of crocuses, Spanish bluebells, and lilies shown will add color to the garden from early spring into midsummer. The lilies will hide the fading leaves of the earlier-blooming bulbs. Be sure to offset bulbs slightly from one layer to the next, as shown above, and leave enough soil in between the layers for normal root growth.

Let Soil Temperatures Tell You When to Plant Hardy Bulbs

Fall-planted bulbs need time to put down roots in a new site *before* the ground freezes for winter. In order to bloom properly, they also need a period of cold, but not freezing, temperatures, called a chilling requirement. Here's an easy guideline you can use to make sure you satisfy both these requirements when you plant: Wait until the soil temperature 6 inches beneath the surface is below 60°F.

This means planting in September in Zones 2–3; in September to early October in Zones 4–5; in October to early November in Zones 6–7; in November to early December in Zone 8; and in December in Zone 9. In regions with mild winters, bulbs like tulips are often given a cold treatment by refrigeration before they are sold for planting in early winter.

Success Starts with Soil Smarts

Almost all bulbs need a soil with good drainage, moderate fertility, and a pH value slightly acid to neutral (pH of 6.0 to 7.2). But good drainage isn't always easy to come by.

If your sandy soil does not retain water well (drains too quickly), make your intended bulb site more amenable before you plant by adding compost or other organic matter to help it hold moisture.

In heavy clay or poorly drained soils, use organic matter to improve drainage. Planting in raised beds or on slopes also helps create better drainage for your bulbs.

Bulbs Bloom Best in Sites Where the Sun Shines Bright

Your bulbs will give you the greatest effect for your effort if you plant them in a sunny site. Most bulbs need strong light to grow and flower well. But if your summer yard looks shady, don't despair. Go for early-flowering spring bulbs that do most of their growing before deciduous trees and shrubs extend their leaves. These bulbs won't grow in sites with heavy, permanent shade, however, such as under evergreens.

Crocuses, daffodils, glory-of-the-snow (*Chionodoxa luciliae*), snowdrops (*Galanthus* spp.), and squills (*Scilla* spp.), as well as early tulip cultivars, are all early bloomers that are quite happy in woodland gardens and other sites with summer shade. And don't miss the chance to deck a woodland garden with these bulbs that will grow in light to partial shade: Checkered lily (*Fritillaria meleagris*), hardy cyclamen (*Cyclamen hederifolium*), trout lilies (*Erythronium* spp.), snowdrops (*Galanthus* spp.), Spanish bluebells (*Hyacinthoides hispanicus*, formerly called *Endymion hispanicus* or *Scilla campanulata*), and winter aconite (*Eranthis hyemalis*).

Help Your Bulbs Live Long and Prosper

Once hardy bulbs are in the ground, they don't need much care. However, there are a few techniques that will pay off by adding years of healthy, vigorous growth to your bulbs' lives.

- Select sound, healthy bulbs and plant them properly.
- Spread about ¼ inch of dried manure over the top of your bulb plantings in spring, just as foliage is beginning to emerge, and again in early fall.
- Mulch plantings to protect the soil, preserve moisture, and prevent weed seeds from germinating. Mulch also keeps mud from splashing on flowers.
- Remove spent flowers from bulbs before seed heads form. This enables each bulb to store food for next year's flowers instead of forming seeds.
- Plant large bulbs like tulips and daffodils at the deep end of the recommended range to slow their rate of multiplication, since the smaller bulbs that result may take several years to reach flowering size.
- Plant lilies with their roots in the shade by mulching the root zone, planting groundcovers around them, or selecting sites where other plants or structures shade the roots without blocking sun from the foliage.
- In warm-winter zones, plant bulbs at the deepest end of the recommended range to avoid soil temperature shifts and too-early warming of the soil in spring.
- Select planting sites carefully. While most spring bulbs grow well in full sun in cooler climates, they often do better in light shade in hot climates.

Simple Ways to Hide Bulb Bare Spots

Like your spring bulb garden, but dread a bare plot later in the season? Try one of these simple techniques to keep your soil covered and your garden looking its best.

Groundcovers that bloom with your bulbs, such as vinca with miniature daffodils, make a nice combination in any spot.

Grow bulbs with annuals. Sow or set shallow-rooted annuals such as marigolds, snapdragons, or wax begonias above bulbs as they are going dormant. This gives summer cover and color to your bulb site.

Cover your bulbs with groundcovers. Before making this choice, think about how the groundcover will look when the bulbs are blooming. Will it flower at the same time? Will the flower colors complement each other? Good groundcovers to use with bulbs include bugleweed (*Ajuga reptans*), creeping Jenny (*Lysimachia nummularia*), spotted lamium (*Lamium maculatum*), thyme, vinca (*Vinca minor*), and wintercreeper (*Euonymus fortunei*). Or try barren strawberry (*Waldsteinia* spp.), English ivy (*Hedera helix*), pachysandra, and prostrate junipers over large, deeply planted bulbs.

Tips to Protect Your Bulbs from Beasts

Cute but pesky animals may decide that your bulb plantings are buffet tables located for their convenience. If chipmunks or voles eat up your bulbs, squirrels dig them up, or rabbits, woodchucks, deer, or birds munch on their flowers or foliage, try these techniques to end the tasting.

Plant bulbs that animals don't like. Even hungry animals leave poisonous daffodil bulbs alone; squills (*Scilla* spp.) and snowdrops (*Galanthus* spp.) are reported to be similarly unbothered. And the skunky scent of fritillaries (*Fritillaria* spp.) repels mice, squirrels, and voles from bulb plantings.

Put up a good defense. Take measures to prevent animal problems before they start. Put your bulbs in the ground inside a wire basket or cage—they'll still be able to send out roots and shoots into the soil, but animals won't be able to get to the bulbs. Or place sharp gravel around the bulbs at planting to discourage underground diners. Lay wire mesh on the soil surface above your bulb planting to keep squirrels from digging them up.

Stop Forgotten Bulb Syndrome

Once spring bulbs have flowered and faded from the scene, it's easy to forget they're there. To protect dormant bulbs from errant shovels, use some sort of marker or map to note their positions.

Grape hyacinths make great markers for other spring flowering bulbs because they have foliage in the fall when other bulbs are invisible aboveground. If you combine your bulbs with other perennials, you can let the perennials mark your bulbs for you.

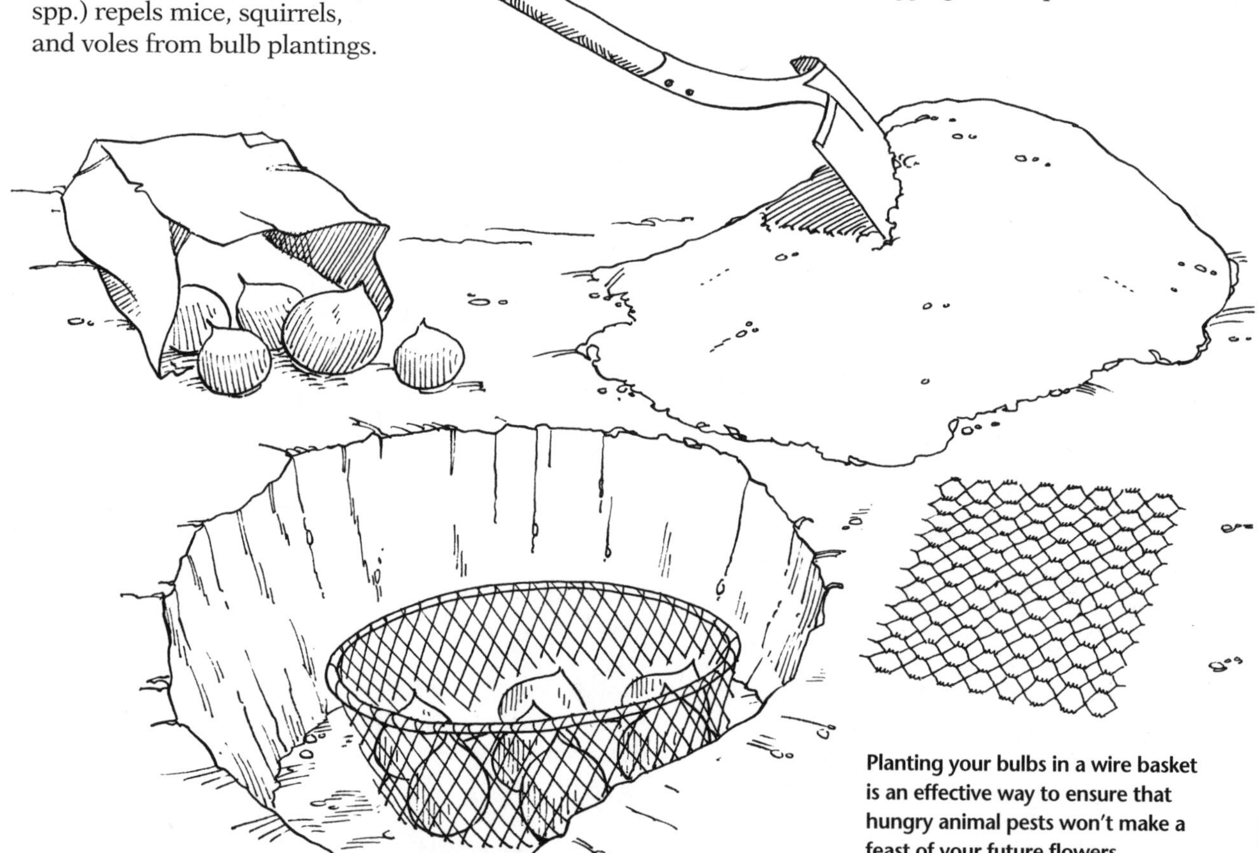

Planting your bulbs in a wire basket is an effective way to ensure that hungry animal pests won't make a feast of your future flowers.

Take Time to Try Tender Bulbs

In comparison to their hardy counterparts, tender bulbs can hardly be considered low maintenance. However, many gardeners don't mind the extra effort it takes to grow tender bulbs. Among them are excellent plants for shady sites, such as tuberous begonias, caladiums, and calla lilies (*Calla* spp.). Gladiolus are tender bulbs that make great cut flowers; dahlias add valuable late-season color.

North of Zone 9, you can handle tender bulbs a couple of ways. For minimal effort, treat tender bulbs as annuals—purchase fresh stock each year and grow them for one season only. Plant them at the proper depth after the soil warms up in spring.

If purchasing them each year is too costly, save money by overwintering them—moving them to a warmer location. Bring potted bulbs indoors and allow them to rest; dig bulbs planted in the garden, then store them using one of the methods shown here. Overwintering tender bulbs takes time but saves the expense of using them as annuals in cold-winter areas.

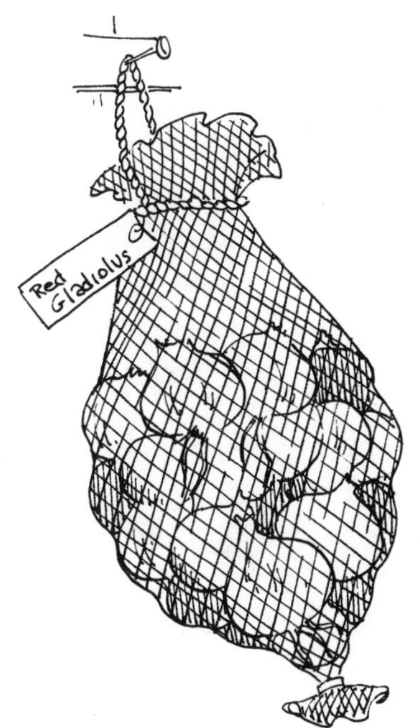

Hang glads for good air circulation. To store gladiolus corms, shake off the soil and remove the foliage just above the corm. Break off the shriveled old corm under the new one and hang the new corms in plastic mesh bags in a dry, cool (around 45°F) spot.

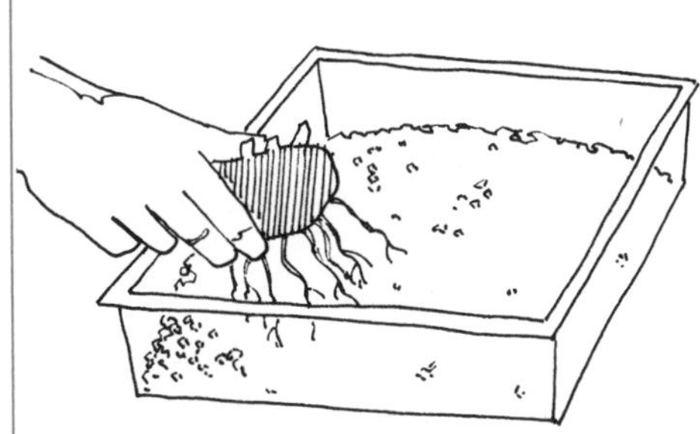

Store tuberous begonias in vermiculite. After digging tuberous begonias, let the plants dry for a week or so, then cut the stems to just above the tuber. Let stem stubs dry completely, shake the soil off the tubers, and store them in vermiculite, dry peat, or sharp sand at 45° to 55°F.

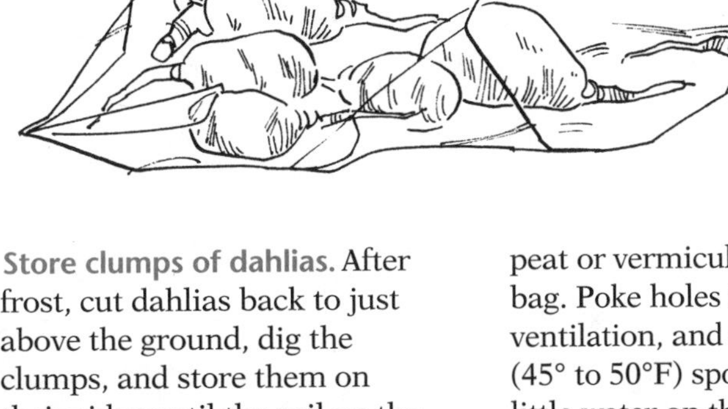

Store clumps of dahlias. After frost, cut dahlias back to just above the ground, dig the clumps, and store them on their sides until the soil on the tubers dries. Store entire clumps with the soil still on them, or remove the soil and store them in barely moist peat or vermiculite in a plastic bag. Poke holes in the bag for ventilation, and store in a cool (45° to 50°F) spot. Sprinkle a little water on the peat or vermiculite during the winter if the roots wither. In spring cut the clumps up, making sure each piece has a pinkish "eye."

CHAPTER 25

Perennials

Perennials the Low-Maintenance Way

Do you go to retail centers each spring and drive home with flats of annual flowers? Plant perennials this year and skip the spring pilgrimage evermore. In this chapter, you'll find out how perennials transform maintenance headaches like fencelines or other hard-to-mow areas into easy-care color spots. If you have an unlandscaped yard, perennials give quick, colorful effects while trees and shrubs grow. Perennials also give you a bounty of flowers for fresh and dried bouquets.

And many perennials spread, self-sow, or are easy to divide, so you can fill your yard with flowers without spending a fortune.

Perennials: Perfect Landscape Problem Solvers

Where can perennials solve problems in your landscape? Just about anywhere. Blanket the ground under large trees with tough, shade-tolerant hostas or astilbes. Then you can forget about trying to get grass to grow there. Better yet, no more mowing around those trees! Perennials around the feet of your shrubs also decrease mowing and mulching headaches. Just think of it this way: The more perennials you plant, the less lawn you mow. How about sloping areas or rocky sites where nothing seems to grow well? Perennials such as sedums and pinks (*Dianthus* spp.) will thrive there, too.

Fencerows are a natural choice for perennial plantings. Tending to grass along a fence is a tedious chore. It's hard to mow, and afterward, you still have to clip with a trimmer or grass shears. And there are probably weeds to pull as well to finish the job. But a grouping of perennials planted against a fence looks terrific. The fence provides a backdrop, and the perennials don't need mowing or tiresome trimming.

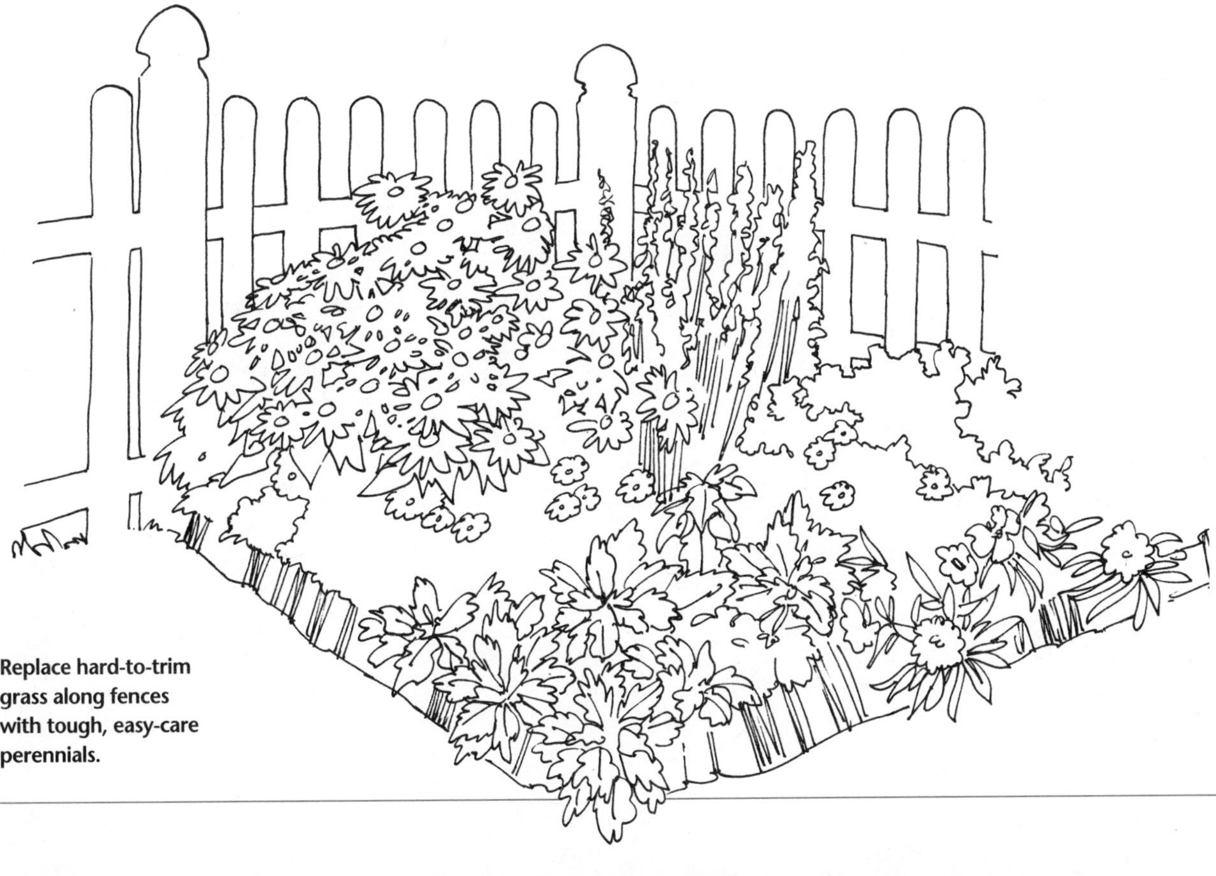

Replace hard-to-trim grass along fences with tough, easy-care perennials.

Get the Best Bargain for Your Perennial Bucks

Perennial plants are for sale almost everywhere you look. It's no small challenge to keep plant-shopping time to a minimum and get the best value for your money. Wherever you shop, the most important rule in choosing perennials is to choose plants that match your site. Take a little time to learn about your site's conditions. Then use garden reference books or pick the brains of the staff at a reputable nursery to find a selection of perennials that will grow well in the area you want to plant.

Plant-Shopping Savvy

When shopping for perennials locally, don't be lured by seasonal displays at megastores. Avoid the inferior-quality plants you'll inevitably find there. Make a stop at a reputable nursery or garden center instead. Because their reputation depends on the quality of the plants they sell, these professionals will help you make good choices.

Keep these tips in mind when picking out your plants.

Choose plants with few or no open flowers. These plants will establish themselves quickly in your garden. And you'll get to enjoy all their flowers, not just ones that open after you plant.

Choose plants with vigorous roots. What's below the soil is more important than what's on top. When you shop, tip the plant out of its container and examine the soil mass. The soil should be moist, and you should see roots growing through it. No soil should fall away from the roots.

Choose well-fed, pest- and disease-free plants. Look for healthy green leaves. Avoid plants with leaves that have spots, brown edges, mottling, or signs of insect pests (be sure to check undersides of leaves for these). Yellow leaves on lower parts of stems indicate starving plants. Choose bushy plants or plants with many growing points emerging from the soil rather than leggy ones that have only one or two unbranched stalks.

Mail-Order Madness

When you get one mail-order catalog, you get them all, and plant catalogs are no exception. Here's how to winnow out the good from the bad and ugly in mail-order catalogs.

Don't fall for the hype. Beware of catalogs that make unrealistic claims for the plants they offer, like "Grows anywhere!" or "Blooms all summer!" Instead, look for specialty catalogs, which offer better plants than catalogs that sell everything from vegetable seeds to flowering shrubs.

Go for the facts. Pick out catalogs that include lots of useful information, such as hardiness zones, cultural requirements, and realistic periods of bloom for the plants offered.

Check size before you buy. Pay close attention to the size or grade of plants being offered for sale, information that is skillfully hidden in some catalogs. Don't just compare prices: Check whether you'll receive bareroot plants, plants in small pots, or larger container-grown plants. Some mail-order companies sell perennials in 3-inch pots—their prices may seem cheaper than most, but you'll be getting very small plants. Avoid catalogs that don't clearly explain how they pack and ship plants.

Don't be fooled by pretty pictures. Some of the best mail-order companies send out relatively plain, unillustrated lists. You can always rely on a good reference book to find out what plants look like. Remember, as a customer, you're paying for those expensive glossy catalogs.

A Shopper's Guide to Perennials

Once you've decided which perennials you want to grow, you have to decide *how* to buy them. Mail-order perennials frequently are shipped bareroot—the roots are soilless, wrapped in absorbent packing material. You can also buy small plants in 2- or 4-inch pots, or bigger plants in containers as large as 1 gallon. Here are some pros and cons of each type of plant.

Perennials Sold As	Advantages	Disadvantages
Bareroot plants	Best size-to-price ratio; largest selection of species and cultivars from mail-order catalogs.	Viability may suffer if poorly shipped; need to be planted when received; can't be planted in summer or fall (fall planting okay in Zones 8 and 9).
Small containerized plants	Less expensive; can be planted spring or summer with proper care; can be maintained for a short time until you're ready to plant.	Often suffer if shipped; usually not vigorous enough to plant in fall; greater chance that plants will die after planting than with other types; usually require two years to reach blooming size.
Large containerized plants	Best viability; will bloom in the year planted; can be planted spring, summer, or fall with proper care; easy to maintain until you're ready to plant.	Most expensive; some companies remove large plants from pots before shipping to reduce shipping costs—plants need immediate watering on arrival and must be potted up or planted without delay.

Heed These Timing Tips for No-Fail Planting

Buying perennial plants can take a hefty bite from your gardening budget. Container-grown perennials may cost as little as $3 or as much as $30. Bareroot plants are cheaper but also more finicky to establish. Planting at the right time is free insurance that your plants will establish themselves quickly and grow well.

Container-grown perennials. You can plant container-grown perennials in spring, summer, or fall. If you plant in summer, take special pains to water the young plants while they get established. Spring is the preferred time to plant container-grown perennials in Zones 3–7, but fall is the best time to plant in Zones 8–10.

Bareroot perennials. Plant bareroot plants only in spring if you live in Zone 7 or north; fall plantings invariably rot rather than root. Plant bareroot plants only in fall in Zones 8–10. Cooler temperatures and more generous rainfall through the winter will help your perennials get a grip, while brutally hot, dry summers can fry plants.

Proper Soil Prep Prevents Perennial Maintenance Problems

With perennials, "spend time now to save time later" should be your motto. More than any other type of plant, perennial performance depends on good soil preparation before planting. Improving the soil before planting is the true low-maintenance approach with perennials. Your work at the outset will pay you back year after year with quick-to-establish, flourishing plants that live longer and need less care.

Resist the temptation to quickly dig holes and stick the plants in. If your soil is heavy clay, this creates a bathtub effect, where water flows from the surrounding heavier soil into the lighter, more porous soil in the planting holes. The result is weak, sickly looking—or even drowned—plants.

So just what *should* you do? If you're willing to wait, you can take a passive approach that requires more waiting, but less muscle power. See "Make a Garden The Nearly No-Dig Way" on page 13. But if you want to plant perennials within the week, here's what's in store.

1. If you're planting an area that was formerly lawn, start by using a flat spade to cut through and remove the sod. If it's a weedy area, dig out the perennial weeds.

2. Loosen the top 6 to 8 inches of the soil by digging or tilling. Test the soil pH and correct it if necessary. In general, perennials grow best when soil pH is between 6.0 and 7.0.

3. Cover the area with 1 to 3 inches of compost. Using a digging fork, work the compost into the top several inches of the soil.

See "For Speedy Soil Improvement, You'll Have to Dig In" on page 18 for more details on site preparation. And remember: One afternoon's work digging a bed can save you from the frustrations of a failed garden full of unhappy plants. It's a small investment of time that pays off in ten or more years of low-maintenance pleasure enjoying the colors, textures, and fragrances of a perennial garden.

Pamper Perennials at Planting

With soil prep complete and plants lovingly selected, planting perennials is a relatively routine affair. But take a few extra minutes to plant right so your plants settle into their new homes quickly and successfully. It will mean a better-looking, quick-to-maintain garden down the line because your plants will grow strongly and beat out weeds that want to share their space.

There are some important differences between planting techniques for bareroot perennials and container perennials. Bareroot perennials often have a tangled clump of roots. If you just plop that tangled mass in a planting hole, the roots have a hard time spreading out through the soil. The plant will be slow to establish itself. But by using the simple soil cone planting technique shown at right, you can give your plants a head start in their new home.

Planting container perennials is a snap, but be sure to follow the simple instructions at right for best results.

Bareroot Perennials

1. Soak the roots of bareroot plants in lukewarm water for an hour or so before you plant. Dig the planting hole, then shape a cone of loose soil in the bottom of the hole. After soaking, remove all packing material from around the roots and trim off any broken or rotted roots.

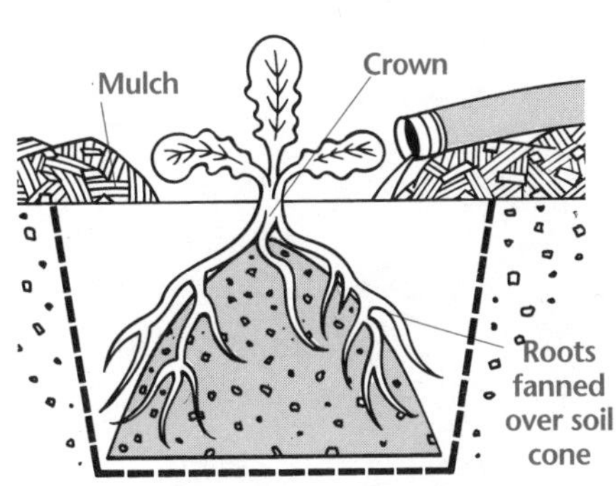

2. Fan the roots out over the soil cone. Make sure that the plant is set as the same depth as it grew in the nursery. You can probably determine this by looking for the area where the color changes on the plant stems. If not, set the plant so that the crown (the point where the roots and topgrowth meet) is at soil level. Fill in the hole and top the soil surface with a fine organic mulch such as shredded leaves. Give newly planted plants a slow, deep soaking.

Container-Grown Perennials

1. After digging the planting hole, gently slip the plant out of its container. Take a minute to tease out or cut through some of the roots. This will stimulate the roots to grow out into the surrounding soil, producing a stronger, healthier plant in the long run.

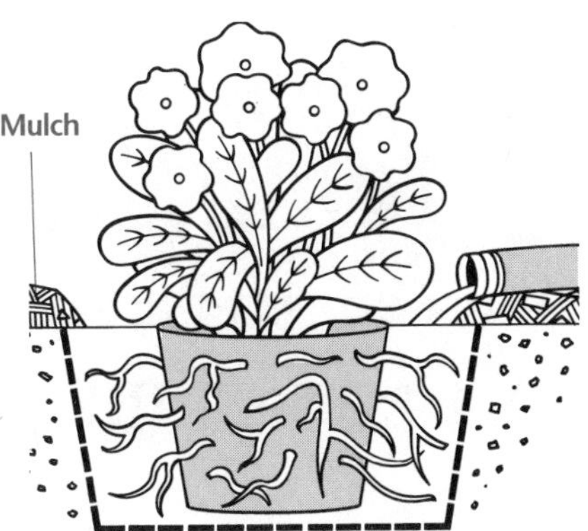

2. Set the plant in the hole and check the position of the crown. It should be at or just above soil level (to allow for some settling of the soil after planting). Then fill in the hole, spread mulch around the plant, and water it in well.

After you plant, put an identification label next to each plant. Most perennials come with a label that you can transfer right into the garden along with the plant. If not, take a minute to write one and put it in place. The foliage will soon cover the less sightly labels.

You may think it will be easy to recognize and remember each plant, but memory is all too fallible! Using labels now will save you from spending time paging through records or catalogs to identify the plants.

A Balanced Meal for Perennials

If you plant perennials in well-prepared soil, they'll grow just fine with no additional fertilizer at all for two years or even longer. If and when you do feed your perennials, use a fertilizer with at least twice as much phosphorus as nitrogen. (If your plants get too much nitrogen, they'll be all foliage and no flowers.) Good organic fertilizers for perennials are bonemeal and fish meal. Just broadcast them around your plants and scratch them into the soil surface. Check package directions to determine the amount to apply.

With Perennials, There's No Need to Be a Neatnik

Hard frosts bring an end to the beauty of blossoms in perennial gardens. But that doesn't necessarily mean that you have to cut down and clean up. Don't be a neatnik: Leave your perennials in place! It not only saves time but also makes the garden a pretty sight through the winter. The "skeletons" of ornamental grasses and perennials like showy stonecrop (*Sedum spectabile*) will catch the snow in attractive ways. Plus, leaving the dry tops in place helps protect the crowns from cold.

When spring comes again, though, surely it will be time to clean out the garden, right? Not so fast! Cutting off old growth in early spring certainly tidies things up, but it's *not* mandatory for the survival of your plants. Flowering plants in the wild survive nicely without anyone tidying them up. Last year's dry leaves and stalks may look unkempt in early spring, but as the season progresses, most of the foliage fades away on its own. What's happening, of course, is that it's breaking down into compost on the spot, helping your soil and saving you time. So only do spring cleanup if *you* like the look of a tidier garden.

Perennials with Stalwart Stems Don't Need Staking

Choosing dwarf cultivars of tall perennials is one easy way to avoid the task of staking. But for the back of a flower bed or border, there's no substitute for the grandeur of tall perennials. So how to deal with the tendency of tall perennials to flop?

One option is to pair floppy plants with a perennial that will provide natural support. Interplanting lily bulbs with perennials, as shown, is a terrific way to support the lilies without having to stake them. The perennial foliage will also hide the lily stalks as they die off. By using groups of Asiatic, regal, and oriental lilies, you can have lilies blooming from June through August. Pair lilies and perennials either by coordinating their flower colors or by planning for them to bloom at different times.

Another option is to choose tall plants with sturdy stems that withstand wind or beating rain. Here are several that resist flopping: 'Bridal Veil' and

Asiatic lilies and baby's-breath (*Gypsophila paniculata*)

'Ostrich Plume' astilbes (*Astilbe* × *arendsii* 'Bridal Veil' and *A. thunbergii* 'Ostrich Plume'); queen-of-the-prairie (*Filipendula rubra* 'Venusta'); sunflower heliopsis (*Heliopsis helianthoides*); torch lilies (*Kniphofia* spp.); gayfeathers (*Liatris* spp.); Russian sage (*Perovskia atriplicifolia*); and mulleins (*Verbascum* spp.)

Or, simply choose perennials that look just as pretty when allowed to cascade, such as boltonia (*Boltonia asteroides*), cardinal flower (*Lobelia cardinalis*), common sneezeweed (*Helenium autumnale*), white gaura (*Gaura lindheimeri*), and New England aster (*Aster novae-angliae*).

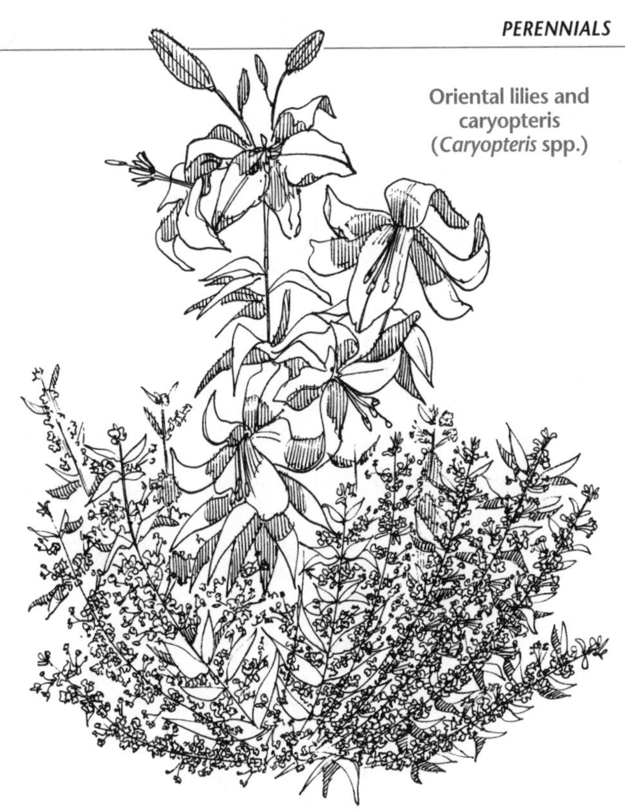

Oriental lilies and caryopteris (*Caryopteris* spp.)

Regal lilies (*Lilium regale*) and queen-of-the-prairie (*Filipendula rubra*)

Asiatic lilies and hostas (*Hosta* spp.)

Fast Pruning Fixes for Perennial Flowers

When perennials fade or fall over before the growing season ends, look to pruning for a pick-me-up. You don't have to resort to replacement flowers or staking when one swift clipping will get them back in line.

Giant fall-blooming plants like 10-foot-tall Maximilian sunflower (*Helianthus maximiliani*) will flop all over if you let them reach their mature height. Cut back your staking chores by cutting the plants back by half in early summer. They'll still reach 6 feet tall by fall.

Don't let good flowers go to seed. Pruning off old blooms—a process called deadheading—prolongs flowering and keeps perennials and annuals from wasting energy setting seed. Use hand shears to cut widely spaced flowers back until the stems are hidden by foliage. Speed up the process for close-set flowers by using hedge clippers. If you want plants to reseed, let the seed ripen from a few flowers at the end of the season.

Cut stakes and string out of your garden. Some fall-blooming perennials like asters and chrysanthemums can get too tall for their own good. One option is to use stakes and strings to support their heavy, floppy stems. But a quick cut early in the season lets you skip the hassle of maneuvering string around uncooperative stems later on. Snip the tops off leggy perennials in early summer with a pair of hedge shears. They'll come back shorter and bushier in plenty of time to bloom. Be sure to do your trimming by about the 4th of July; otherwise, you may be cutting off flower buds as you go, ruining the fall blooms.

Choose Dressy Mulch to Show Off Perennials

Mulch is essential to keep your perennial beds low maintenance because mulching reduces the need for weeding and watering. But straw and newspaper just aren't chic and stylish enough for mulching perennials. Use a fine-textured mulch, like rotted sawdust, shredded leaves, buckwheat hulls, or ground corncobs. Weed-free compost or composted manure are also fine, and they offer the added bonus of a gentle feeding at the same time. Shredded bark is okay, too, but will look a little chunky around small perennials.

Multiply Your Plants While Dividing Your Budget

Preparing to divide. Dig up the plant, getting as much of the root mass as you can. For the maximum number of divisions, gently wash the roots with water to remove the soil so you can see all the "plantlets" individually.

Planting perennials is a great way to reduce long-term garden maintenance, but some gardeners can't afford the investment for a large planting. Dividing perennials is an easy way to fill your garden quickly, revitalize overgrown or overcrowded plants, and save a lot of money in the process.

It's amazing how many plants you can get from an established clump of vigorous perennials like hostas. Consider that one run-of-the-mill hosta plant in a 1-gallon container can cost $8 or more. By dividing, you can produce 10 or 20 free plants for a half-hour's work. That means you can take on maintenance-reducing projects—like a large hosta planting under shade trees—that might otherwise be too expensive for you to afford.

The best times to divide perennials are early spring and fall. But if that doesn't suit your schedule, you can divide at other times of year. Just be sure the plant isn't flowering when you divide it. If the plant is growing actively, cut back the foliage by half before dividing.

Dividing fibrous roots. Insert a knife between the growing points of the crown and cut into individual pieces.

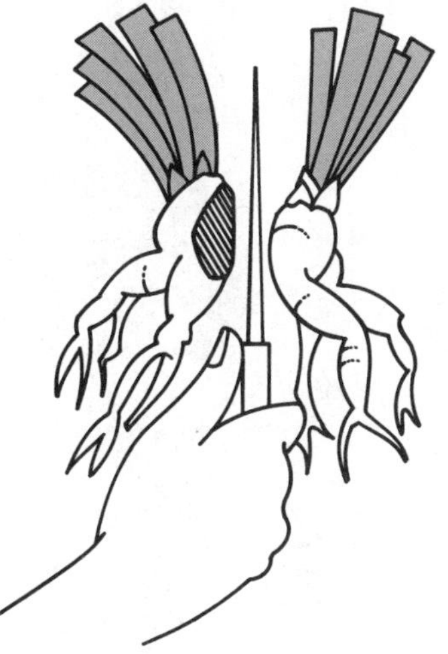

Dividing fleshy roots. Cut through the roots with a knife. There should be at least one growing "eye" on each root piece.

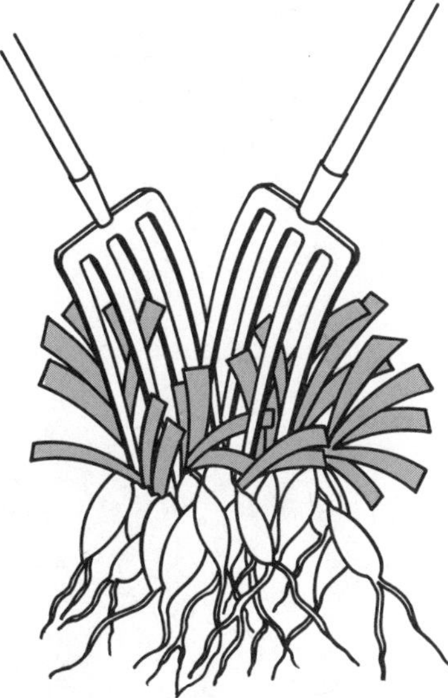

Dividing tough clumps. When a knife won't do, use two garden forks placed back to back to pry the crown into pieces.

If You Don't Dig Digging, Try Dig-Less Division

Dividing perennials without lifting entire clumps from the ground is easy and will produce three to five new plants per clump.

If your goal is to get more plants with minimum work, try dividing without digging up the mother plant. For tough perennials like daylilies and Siberian iris, cut back the foliage by half (unless it's early spring or late fall), and use a sharp-edged spade to cut the mature clump into sections right in the ground. Then use a garden fork to lift the peripheral sections. Transplant those pieces and replace the soil around the central piece. Don't forget to water everything in thoroughly, including the piece you didn't move.

With smaller, tender perennials, you can often get a few divisions just by feeling around the edges of the clump with your fingers and teasing away a rooted piece.

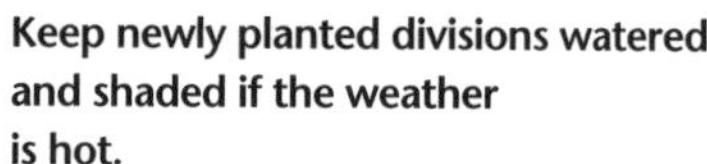

Keep newly planted divisions watered and shaded if the weather is hot.

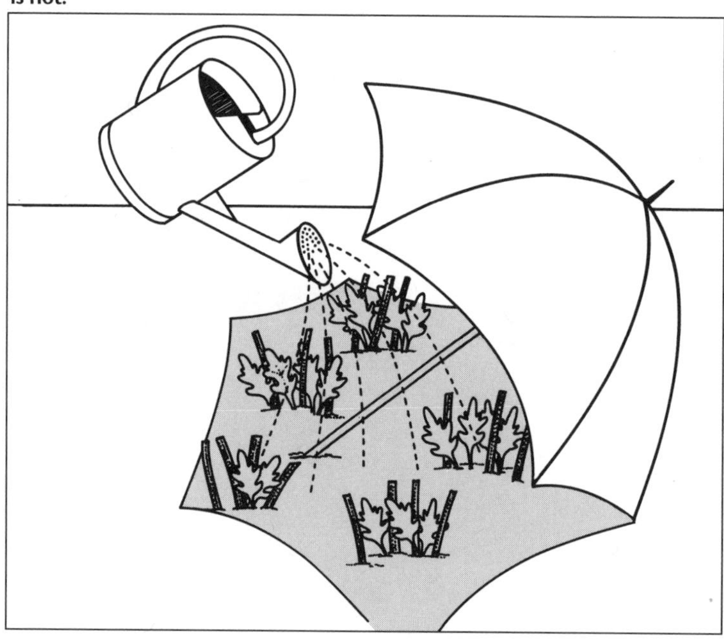

Feeling in the soil for rooted stems should work for most perennials that have underground stems, such as catmint or asters. You can also try it on oriental poppies and a host of other plants.

Perennials for Gardeners Who Don't Do Division

Dividing is a great way to increase your plant population, but what if you don't want or need more perennials? All of the perennials listed below will thrive for years without dividing. In addition to tips on when they could be divided, you'll find a description of the type of site that will make them happy for years.

Baby's-breath (*Gypsophila paniculata*): Difficult to divide. Rich, moist, neutral to alkaline soil. Zones 3–9.

Black snakeroot (*Cimicifuga racemosa*): Slow-growing; divide only in fall if absolutely necessary. Rich, moist soil in sun or shade. Zones 3–8.

False indigos (*Baptisia* spp.): Deep-rooted; move only if plants grow too large for their site. Rich, moist soil in full sun or light shade. Zones 3–9.

Gas plant (*Dictamnus albus*): Difficult to transplant. Rich, well-drained soil in full sun to part shade. Zones 3–8.

Globe thistle (*Echinops ritro*): Seldom need division; to propagate, remove a rosette from side of main clump. Sandy or loamy soil in full sun. Zones 3–8.

Goat's beards (*Aruncus* spp.): Move in spring and cut roots with sharp knife. Rich, moist soil in part shade. Zones 3–7.

Hellebores (*Helleborus* spp.): Divide only if necessary. Evenly moist, well-drained soil in part shade. Zones 4–9.

Monkshoods (*Aconitum* spp.): Disturb only if plants are overcrowded. Rich, well-drained soil in full sun. Zones 3–7.

Oriental poppy (*Papaver orientale*): Dig and divide brittle roots in late summer if plants become overcrowded. Rich, moist, well-drained soil in full sun. Zones 2–7.

Peonies (*Paeonia* spp.): Thick, deep, fleshy roots are difficult to divide. Rich, moist, well-drained soil in full sun to light shade. Zones 3–8.

Sea hollies (*Eryngium* spp.): Difficult to divide because of taproot. Well-drained soil in full sun. Zones 3–8.

Sea lavender (*Limonium latifolium*): Plants establish slowly; avoid dividing them. Rich, well-drained soil in full sun to light shade. Zones 3–9.

White gaura (*Gaura lindheimeri*): Seldom needs division. Moist, well-drained soil in full sun. Zones 5–9.

Select Seed-Producing Perennials for Easy Plant Propagation

Some perennials self-sow modestly. They produce enough seed to provide you with extra plants or give your garden that informal cottage look, but not so much as to be weedy.

The simple trick to encouraging self-sowers is to leave the soil around the plants bare. Seeds need to contact bare ground to germinate; they'll germinate poorly in mulch. You can pot up the seedlings or just let them fill in the bed.

Try some of these reliable reseeders: Columbines (*Aquilegia* spp.), Siberian bugloss (*Brunnera macrophylla*), red valerian (*Centranthus ruber*), common foxglove (*Digitalis purpurea*), purple coneflower (*Echinacea purpurea*), white gaura (*Gaura lindheimeri*), lobelias (*Lobelia* spp.) and balloon flower (*Platycodon grandiflorus*). Strawberry foxglove (*Digitalis* × *mertonensis*) is a hybrid foxglove that self-sows and comes true from seed.

Beef Up Bloom Times
and Focus on Foliage for Great, No-Fuss Perennial Gardens

It's easy to create a perennial garden that's bursting with flowers in May and June. Early spring and summer are prime bloom times for many popular perennials. Keeping your garden colorful and varied through summer and fall is a greater challenge. But by making smart plant choices, you can create a perennial garden that looks great from spring to fall. To get the most color for the least effort, choose long-blooming perennials. Also try interplanting early- and late-blooming perennials, and include perennials with attractive, long-lasting foliage.

Long bloomers. There are many excellent plants that bloom virtually all summer. Sometimes it's just a matter of knowing which cultivar to ask for. For example, some bleeding heart species and cultivars are spring bloomers only. But fringed bleeding heart (*Dicentra eximia*) blooms through the summer—'Luxuriant' is an especially fine cultivar. Other perennials with exceptionally long bloom seasons include balloon flower (*Platycodon grandiflorus*), 'Butterfly Blue' pincushion flower (*Scabiosa caucasica* 'Butterfly Blue'), yellow corydalis (*Corydalis lutea*), and white gaura (*Gaura lindheimeri*). How to separate the long from the short bloomers? Here's where a knowledgeable nursery owner can offer invaluable advice.

Another way to extend bloom season is to select several different cultivars of a particular plant. Read through the daylily offerings of a well-stocked perennials nursery, for example. You'll find daylilies with bloom seasons that are described as early, midseason, and late. All you need to do to extend your daylily display from a few weeks to two months or more is select cultivars from each of the categories. Daffodils, tulips, peonies, irises, and chrysanthemums are just some of the other plants that provide this option.

Interplanting can be as simple as combining one early bloomer with one late bloomer. Here, pasqueflowers (*Anemone pulsatilla*) provide color and interest while butterfly weed (*Asclepias tuberosa*) gets established. After the pasqueflowers finish blooming, the tall butterfly weed flowerstalks push through the ferny pasqueflower foliage.

Interplanting. When your heart is set on a plant with a short bloom season, look for a plant with a different blooming season as a companion. For example, oriental poppies have a notoriously short, but glorious, bloom season. They disappear shortly after flowering, leaving large gaps in the garden. Instead of giving them up altogether, combine them with plants that will fill the spaces they leave, such as baby's-breath (*Gypsophila paniculata*), boltonia (*Boltonia asteroides*), and Russian sage (*Perovskia *atriplicifolia*). See the illustrations on the opposite page for another example of interplanting.

Foliage plants. Some perennials are a lot stronger in the foliage department than others. For example, hostas are grown primarily for their foliage. Bethlehem sage (*Pulmonaria saccharata* 'Mrs. Moon') has handsome leaves that persist for the entire season—long after the spring flowers are gone. Epimediums (*Epimedium* spp.) are wonderful shade plants that are nearly evergreen in the south. And baptisias (*Baptisia* spp.) offer great mounds of blue-green foliage all summer. Coral bells (*Heuchera* spp.) have beautiful foliage, and many types also have attractive flowers.

Try 'Palace Purple' heuchera (*H. micrantha* var. *diversifolia* 'Palace Purple') and 'Snow Angel' heuchera (*H. sanguinea* 'Snow Angel'). Other strong foliage candidates include lady's-mantle (*Alchemilla mollis*), heartleaf bergenia (*Bergenia cordifolia*), meadow rues (*Thalictrum* spp.), and sedums (*Sedum* spp.).

Instead of spending your summer worrying about fading foliage, stick to plants with foliage that remains attractive for much of the season. A garden planted with bee balm and yarrow, for example, may look great in early summer but leaves a lot to be desired by the time autumn rolls around. Mix them with foliage that is longer lasting, like yuccas, ornamental grasses, butterfly bush (*Buddleia* spp.), grape leaf anemone (*Anemone vitifolia* 'Robustissima'), or New England asters (*Aster novae-angliae*).

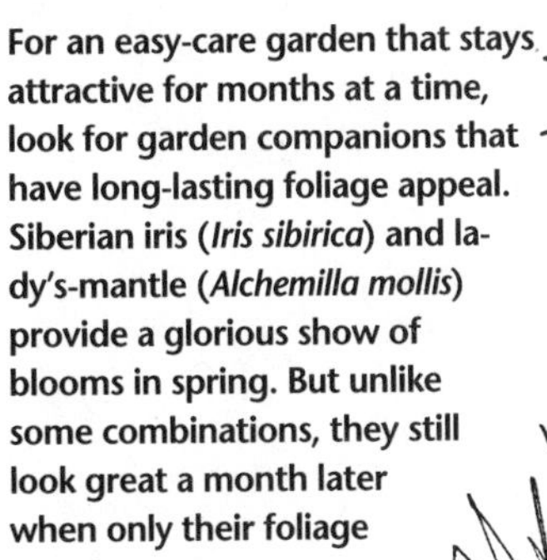

For an easy-care garden that stays attractive for months at a time, look for garden companions that have long-lasting foliage appeal. Siberian iris (*Iris sibirica*) and lady's-mantle (*Alchemilla mollis*) provide a glorious show of blooms in spring. But unlike some combinations, they still look great a month later when only their foliage remains.

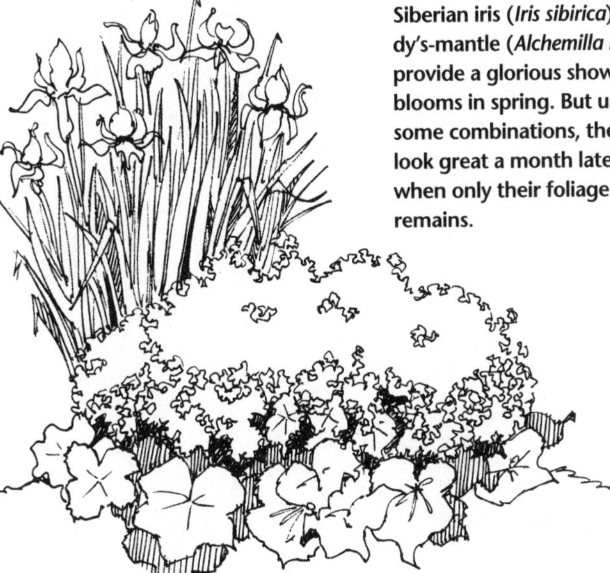

For Extra-Long Color, Plant Annuals with Your Perennials

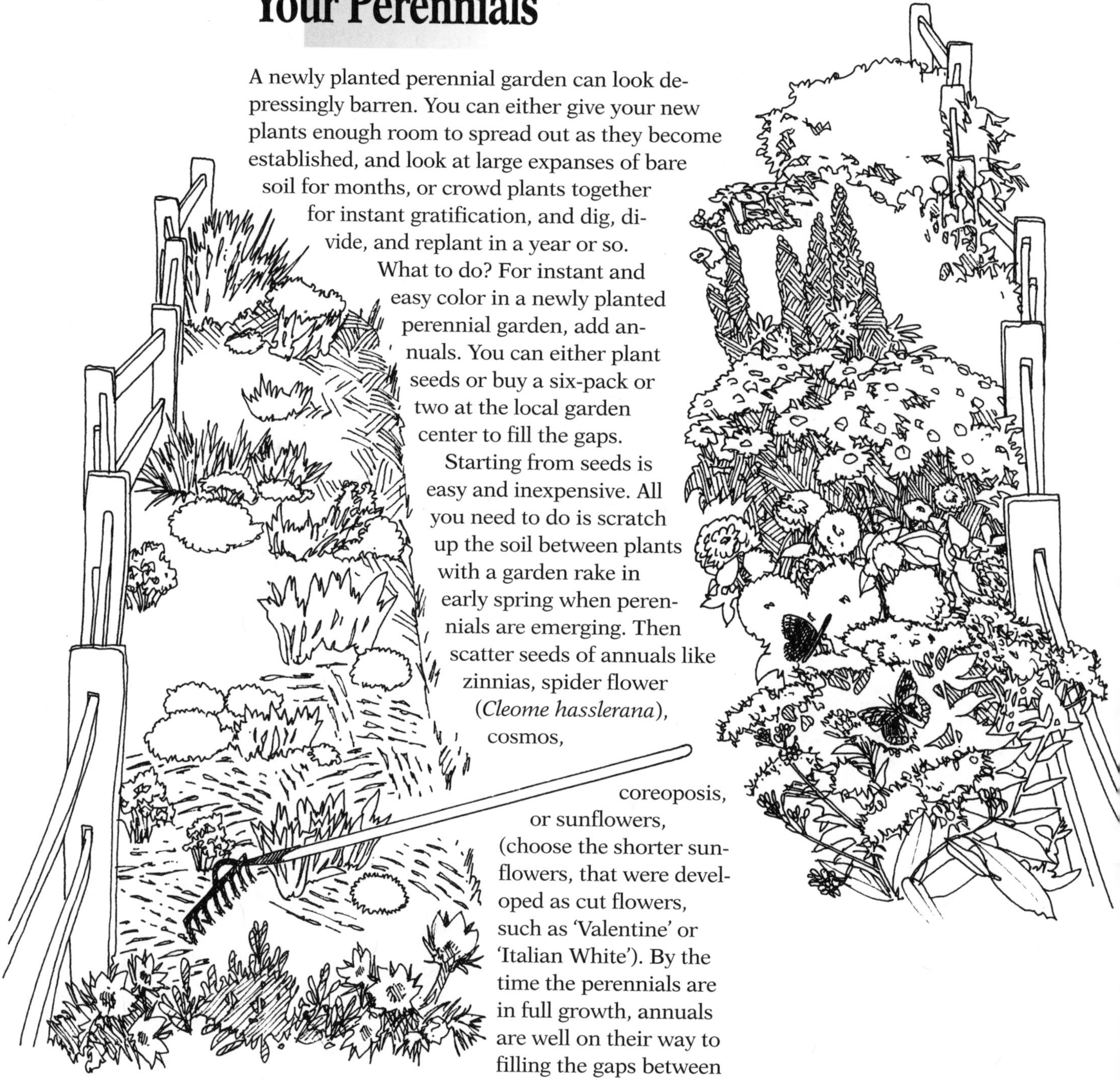

A newly planted perennial garden can look depressingly barren. You can either give your new plants enough room to spread out as they become established, and look at large expanses of bare soil for months, or crowd plants together for instant gratification, and dig, divide, and replant in a year or so.

What to do? For instant and easy color in a newly planted perennial garden, add annuals. You can either plant seeds or buy a six-pack or two at the local garden center to fill the gaps.

Starting from seeds is easy and inexpensive. All you need to do is scratch up the soil between plants with a garden rake in early spring when perennials are emerging. Then scatter seeds of annuals like zinnias, spider flower (*Cleome hasslerana*), cosmos, coreoposis, or sunflowers, (choose the shorter sunflowers, that were developed as cut flowers, such as 'Valentine' or 'Italian White'). By the time the perennials are in full growth, annuals are well on their way to filling the gaps between them.

25 Terrific Low-Maintenance Perennials

The following perennials are fantastic choices for your low-maintenance garden. Their foliage looks good all season long and many of them flower for months. They rarely suffer from pests or diseases and are not too picky about soil. Best of all, none of them need pinching or staking to look their best. For more low-maintenance perennials to solve specific planting problems, see Chapter 21.

Name	Description	Comments
Achillea spp. (yarrows)	Ferny, blue-gray foliage; flat-topped clusters of white, pink, red, or yellow flowers up to 5 inches across in summer; 2–4 feet tall. Zones 3–9.	Full sun to light shade; drought-tolerant. Choose shorter cultivars with medium-size flower clusters to avoid flopping stems. Choose between quick- or slow-spreading types to suit your needs.
Amsonia tabernaemontana (willow blue star)	Clusters of pale blue, star-shaped flowers in spring and early summer; narrow, lance-shaped leaves; 1–3 feet tall. Zones 3–9.	Full sun to partial shade; average to rich, evenly moist soil. Mass plants to make a hedge or low screen. Foliage colors yellow to orange in fall.
Aster novae-angliae and *A. novi-belgii* (New England and New York asters)	Bloom in late summer and fall; cover themselves with blue, purple, pink, red, or white 2-inch, daisylike flowers; 1–6 feet tall. Zones 3–8.	Full sun to light shade; need evenly moist soil. Choose short cultivars to avoid flopping stems. Divide every 3–4 years. Plant with showy stonecrop and ornamental grasses for fall color.
Astilbe spp. (astilbes)	Fluffy plumes of tiny white, pink, red, or maroon flowers in early summer; glossy foliage; some have red-tinged leaves; 1–4 feet tall. Zones 4–8.	Light to full shade; need evenly moist soil. Divide clumps every 3–4 years. Plant with hostas and pulmonarias.
Baptisia australis (blue false indigo)	Spikes of indigo blue pealike flowers appear in late spring and early summer above rounded, blue-green foliage; 2–4 feet tall. Zones 3–9.	Full sun to light shade; drought-tolerant once established. Showy, gray-black seedpods add interest in fall and winter.
Campanula carpatica (Carpathian harebell)	Neat, mounded plants bear single blue or white bell-shaped flowers up to 2 inches across in spring and summer; 8–18 inches tall. Zones 3–8.	Full sun to part shade. Spreads very slowly. May self-sow. Perfect for edges of flower beds. Combine with pink cranesbills (*Geranium* spp.).
Coreopsis verticillata (threadleaf coreopsis)	Needlelike leaves and loads of yellow, 2-inch, daisylike flowers borne from early summer through frost; 1–3 feet tall. Zones 3–9.	Full sun to light shade; drought-tolerant once established. If site stays evenly moist, try planting with *C. rosea*, its pale pink twin. Divide if clump starts to die in the center.
Dicentra eximia (fringed bleeding heart)	Bushy plants with blue-green, fernlike foliage and clusters of pink or white heart-shaped flowers throughout spring and summer; 10–18 inches tall. Zones 3–9.	Light shade; needs evenly moist soil. Divide overgrown clumps if flowering is reduced. Looks great with hostas.

(continued)

25 Terrific Low-Maintenance Perennials—Continued

Name	Description	Comments
Echinacea spp. (purple coneflowers)	Bold 2–5-inch daisies with white, pink, and purple petals and cone-shape orange-brown centers that shine in the mid- and late summer garden; 2–4 feet tall. Zones 3–8.	Full sun to light shade; drought-tolerant once established. Resents division. May self-seed.
Geranium sanguineum var. *striatum* (Lancaster cranesbill)	Delightful hardy perennial covered with single pink flowers with darker pink veins from spring until frost; 8–12 inches tall. Zones 3–8.	Full sun to moderate shade; drought-tolerant once established. May self-seed or be divided. Try other hardy cranesbills (*Geranium* spp.) for blue, purple, and white flowers. Foliage turns an attractive red in fall.
Hemerocallis hybrids (modern daylily cultivars)	Popular perennials with flowers in every color but blue. Lilylike blooms blaze in summer; strap-shaped foliage is handsome all season; 18 inches–5 feet tall. Zones vary depending on species.	Sun to moderate shade; drought-tolerant once established. Each flower lasts but a day: Look for cultivars with a long bloom period to extend the display. Choose cultivars with small, single flowers since their faded flowers are inconspicuous and drop off unaided. Cut off any seed pods after flowering is finished. Combine with daffodils for two gardens in one space.
Heuchera × *brizoides* (hybrid coral bells)	Dainty clusters of tiny red, pink, or white bells dance above neat mounds of evergreen leaves in late spring through summer; 1–2½ feet tall. Zones 3–8.	Full sun to light shade; need evenly moist soil. Divide every 3–4 years as plants grow themselves out of the ground. Try planting with cranesbills (*Geranium* spp.)
Hosta hybrids (hostas, funkias)	Indispensable perennials grown primarily for their wide range of foliage colors and markings; tall spikes of white or purple flowers, some quite fragrant, provide an extra show in summer; 6 inches–3 feet tall. Zones 3–8.	Light to full shade; needs evenly moist soil. Cut off flowerstalks after bloom. Combine cultivars with different leaf colors and patterns for interesting shade gardens.
Iberis sempervirens (perennial candytuft)	Mat-forming perennial with dark, evergreen leaves; plants are nearly covered with clusters of white flowers in early spring; 6–12 inches tall. Zones 3–9.	Full sun to light shade. Cut back by one-third with hedge shears at least every few years after flowering. Pair with bright spring bulbs for a knockout display.
Iris sibirica (Siberian iris)	Delicate 2–3 inch white, yellow, blue, purple, or bicolor flowers float above clumps of swordlike foliage in early summer; 1–3 feet tall. Zones 2–9.	Full sun to partial shade; needs evenly moist soil. Divide only if bloom is reduced by crowding. Nip off seed heads after flowering. A natural near water, or combine with peonies.
Monarda didyma (bee balm)	Crowns of white, pink, scarlet, or maroon flowers punctuate the summer garden and prove irresistible to hummingbirds; green or maroon-tinted foliage is pleasantly aromatic; 2–4 feet tall. Zones 4–8.	Full sun to partial shade; needs evenly moist soil. Divide every three years to keep plants vigorous and prevent them from spreading. Or plant in a naturalistic area and let them run wild. Wild bergamot (*M. fistulosa*) sports soft lavender-pink flowers.

Name	Description	Comments
Nepeta × faassenii (catmint)	Spikes of violet-blue flowers rise from the gray-green foliage in spring and summer. 1½–3 feet tall. Zones 3–8.	Full sun to light shade. Cut back by one-half after flowering to neaten plant and encourage more flowers to form. Great planted with yarrows.
Oenothera macrocarpon (Ozark sundrops, formerly known as *O. missouriensis,* Missouri primrose)	Showy lemon yellow flowers, 3–4 inches across, in late spring and early summer, continuing throughout the season; 6–12 inches tall. Zones 4–8.	Full sun to light shade; heat- and drought-tolerant. Spreads slowly via creeping roots to form a dense clump.
Paeonia lactiflora (common garden peony)	Hardy, long-lived perennials with large, silken-petaled flowers that grace late spring gardens with vivid splotches of white, pink, or red; shiny foliage remains attractive through summer; 2–3 feet tall. Zones 2–8.	Full sun to light shade; needs good drainage. Divide if bloom is reduced. Choose single cultivars or shorter, small-flowered double cultivars that won't tip over or produce unattractive gobs of wilted petals. Clip off spent flowerstalks after flowering.
Platycodon grandiflorus (balloon flower)	Bright blue, 2- to 3-inch-wide flowers open from inflated, balloonlike buds in early to mid-summer; 2–3 feet tall. Zones 3–8.	Full sun to light shade; drought-tolerant once established. New shoots are slow to emerge in spring. Self-sows without being a nuisance.
Pulmonaria saccharata (Bethlehem sage)	Clusters of pink buds and blue, pink, or white flowers appear in early spring; silver-spotted green leaves remain attractive all season; 9–18 inches tall. Zones 3–8.	Partial to full shade; drought-tolerant once established. Combine with spring bulbs and fringed bleeding heart for a delightful shade garden.
Rudbeckia fulgida (orange coneflower)	These hardy, adaptable "black-eyed Susans" provide 2-inch yellow daisies for the summer garden; 1½–3 feet tall. Zones 3–9.	Full sun to light shade. Divide every 3 years. Pair with purple coneflowers and showy stonecrop for a late summer display.
Salvia × superba (violet sage)	Stiff spikes of blue to violet flowers make a bold display from early to midsummer; 1½–3½ feet tall. Zones 4–7.	Full sun to light shade; drought-tolerant once established. Shear off faded flower spikes to encourage new growth and more flowers. Combines well with yarrows and coreopsis.
Sedum spectabile (showy stonecrop)	Tiny pink flowers in huge, flat-topped clusters provide months of color in summer and fall. The gray-green foliage looks fine all season long; 1–2 feet tall. Zones 3–9.	Full sun; very drought-resistant. Divide if clumps fall apart during the season. Looks nice planted with ornamental grasses and coneflowers.
Veronica spicata (spike speedwell)	Spikes of pink, blue or white flowers arise in summer over narrow, gray-green leaves; 1–3 feet tall. Zones 3–8.	Full sun or light shade in well-drained soil; heat- and drought-tolerant.

Chapter 26
Roses

Guidelines for Feeding and Watering Roses

Pick a Problem-Free Site for Your Roses

No-Nonsense Guidelines for Planting Roses

Plan a Low-Maintenance Rose-Filled Landscape

Plant Rugged Rugosas and Other Old Roses

Start Out Right: Pick the Best Plants

A Low-Work Pruning Primer

Painless Rose Propagation

Search and Destroy Rootstock Suckers

A Practical Guide to Managing Rose Diseases

Manage Rose Pests the Low-Maintenance Way

Roses the Low-Maintenance Way

There's good news for rose lovers. You can fill your yard and garden with beautiful, fragrant roses without having to strap yourself to a sprayer or pamper prima donnas. In fact, there's a whole world of fabulous roses that resist or tolerate diseases, don't need much pruning, and can do without winter protection in all but the most brutal climates. Many of the best roses for low-maintenance landscapes are shrub roses, which bloom year after year with little or no fertilizing, pruning, or pampering.

In this chapter, you'll learn how to select, grow, and use easy-care roses throughout your landcape. They make great low-maintenance additions to every sunny yard—as hedges, specimen plants, additions to flower beds and borders, and even groundcovers. So read on—and welcome to the world of roses.

Keep-It-Simple Guidelines for Feeding and Watering Roses

Once established, roses thrive with much less care than you'd think, provided you choose your roses and the site carefully. For least-work watering, plan on using a soaker hose or more sophisticated drip irrigation system. See Chapter 8 for more on watering.

Most rose-feeding regimens are designed around the needs of finicky hybrid teas, but most shrub roses will bloom year after year with no fertilizer at all other than an annual application of rotted manure or compost. If you prefer to "push" your shrub roses a bit for more and bigger blooms, feed them once in early spring and again in June with a mixture of 2 parts alfalfa meal, 1 part blood meal, 1 part bonemeal, 1 part fish meal, and 1 part cottonseed meal. Scratch a couple of cups into the soil around each rose.

Pruning a Newly Planted Rose

Take a moment to prune your rose's canes back by one-third to one-half, even though the canes will already appear pruned by the nursery. Pruning ensures vigorous heavy growth in balance with the reduced root mass of the bareroot rose. Always cut just above an outward-facing bud.

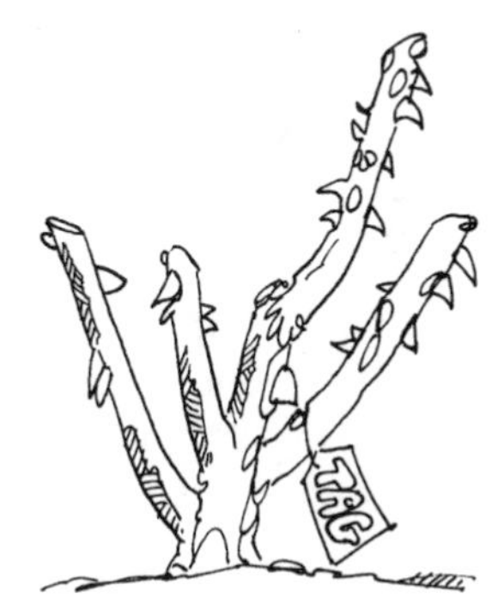

Pick a Problem-Free Site for Your Roses

When you look for sites to grow roses, think about vegetables. Why? Because roses grow best in the conditions that keep vegetables happiest: They generally need full sun, good air circulation, and rich, well-drained soil. Roses growing in dank, shady spots won't bloom well and are more prone to diseases. Also avoid extremely exposed sites subject to drying winter winds.

Beware of obvious low spots, and of zones around large paved areas like driveways or patios. If the paved surface is sloped toward your future rose bed, rainwater will drain right onto your roses. If your chosen site is poorly drained and you can't think of a better spot, build raised beds to raise your roses above drainage problems.

Also avoid sites where you have removed a rose, even if it was thriving. Pick a spot at least a few feet to one side of where the old rose stood.

Take a Look at Soil Type

Most roses thrive in rich, well-drained soil amended with plenty of organic matter. If you have clay soil, add 4 to 6 inches of any well-rotted organic matter and 1 inch of coarse (builder's) sand to your rose area and incorporate thoroughly. If you're planting several roses, renovate the whole area; if you're planting a single rose, renovate a 3-foot circle. If you have a loamy or sandy soil, skip the sand but add the organic matter. Sandy soil may require even more organic matter to improve moisture retention. For more on evaluating soil, see Chapter 2.

No-Nonsense Guidelines for Planting Roses

Plant roses just as you would any other shrub, whether you are dealing with bareroot or container-grown roses. See Chapter 5 for directions. Use the tips below to ensure your roses get off to an extra-healthy start.

Inspect bareroot roses promptly. As soon as bareroot roses arrive, unpack them and plunge their roots into a bucket of water. Your plants should arrive fully dormant; if new growth is already emerging, notify the supplier immediately. A bareroot rose that is pushing out new growth in its packing material is at considerable risk when making the transition to the garden.

Plant as soon as you can. Plant bareroot roses immediately. If you can't, dig a trench in a shady spot and bury your roses' roots up to where the canes emerge, then water thoroughly. Plant them in a permanent location within a week. While planting, never allow the roots to dry out. Keep plants handy in a bucket of water or very moist sawdust or leaves.

Soak containerized roses before you plant. Soak containers in a bucket of water before you plant; the soilless mix most roses are grown in will resist wetting if you water only after planting.

Locate the bud union before you decide how deep to plant. Whether you're planting bareroot or container-grown roses, look for the slightly swollen crook or discontinuity between the roots and where the canes emerge that indicates a bud union. (Most roses are grafted onto a separate rootstock to speed propagation. Own-root roses are generally superior to budded ones, but aren't widely available because they are more difficult and expensive to propagate.) To protect it from cold and help prevent the rootstock from suckering, plant the rose so the bud union is 2 to 4 inches below ground level.

Water thoroughly. Fill the basin around newly planted roses and allow it to drain several times. Then plunge the end of the hose into the loose soil around the rose to fill air pockets, which can sound the death knell for new roses. Give newly-planted roses 1 to 1½ inches of water a week and check soil moisture frequently by plunging your fingers into the soil to see if it is either too wet or too dry.

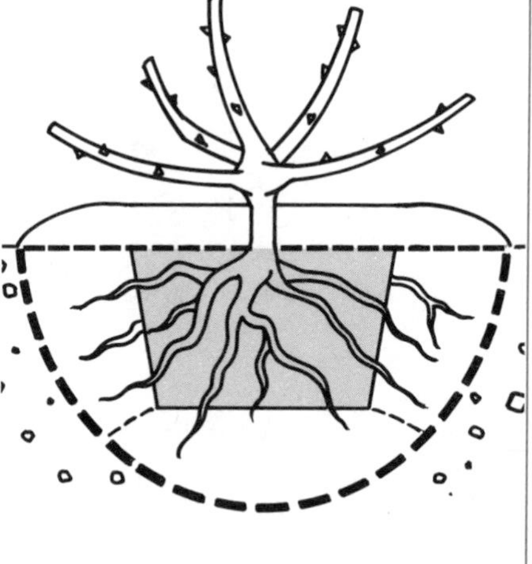

Container-grown roses will often have their bud unions above soil level in the pot. Ignore this; plant the rose just as deeply as you would if it were bareroot. Plant own-root or *ungrafted* roses as you would any plant—at the same level as it was growing in the nursery.

Plan a Low-Maintenance Rose-Filled Landscape

Fussy formal rose gardens are guaranteed maintenance headaches and they're often difficult to integrate into modern landscapes, anyway. Since healthy, hardy roses come in so many sizes and forms, use them throughout your landscape. Here's how.

Mix roses with shrubs, perennials, or herbs. Roses look great as part of a mixed shrub border and are classic companions in herb or perennial gardens. Scattering roses around helps minimize disease problems, too. Easy-care shrub roses like rugosas, and other old roses listed in "Plant Rugged Rugosas and Other Old Roses" on page 296 are perfect for this purpose. Roses in the Parkland and Explorer series are also especially hardy and bloom profusely. Other roses to consider for flower borders include 'The Fairy', 'Nearly Wild', and 'Mary Rose'.

Choose carefree roses for hedges. Many shrub roses make great barrier plantings or informal, no-shear hedges. Try rugosa roses (*Rosa rugosa*), old-fashioned shrub roses like 'Stanwell Perpetual', *R. alba* cultivars, or modern shrub roses like 'Carefree Beauty'.

Plant a rose foundation. Roses can provide a refreshing alternative to the usually dull foundation plants. (You may need to amend the soil in this usually alkaline area with a bit of sulfur to put the pH in the 6.0 to 7.0 range roses prefer.)

Cover with climbers. Climbing or rambling roses can clamber along fences, up trellises, and even over dead trees or other objects. They'll smother low objects with little effort from you. If you want a rose to climb on your house or a garden fence or wall, you'll need to invest time training it. Recommended hardy, healthy climbers include 'William Baffin', 'Dortmund', 'New Dawn', and 'John Cabot'.

Use roses as groundcover. For great groundcover, what could be better than attractive, hardy roses that flower continually and are disease- and drought-resistant to boot! Plant them on a hard-to-mow slope, along the driveway, or on any other sunny area you're tired of mowing. Try any roses from the Pavement series, or memorial rose and its cultivars (*Rosa wichuraiana*), along with 'Sea Foam', 'The Fairy', and 'Max Graf'.

Climbing or rambling roses can perform garden magic by smothering unsightly objects. Plant them next to a decrepit barbeque grill or propane tank, and watch it disappear.

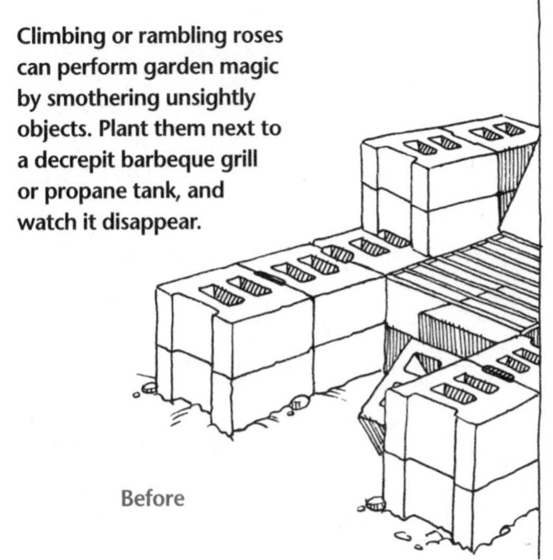

Before

After

Grow Healthy Yellow Roses

Yellow roses are notoriously susceptible to blackspot, but if you love yellow roses, don't despair. Try one or all of these yellow roses, which have little or no blackspot susceptibility and are hardy as well: The yellow rose of Texas (*Rosa* × *harisonii*); *Rosa eglanteria* 'Goldbusch'; *Rosa rugosa* 'Agnes'; *Rosa spinosissima* 'Aicha', 'Fruhlingstag', 'Fruhlingsgold', 'Hazeldean', and 'Old Yellow Scotch'; Father Hugo's rose (*Rosa hugonis*); and *Rosa xanthina* 'Canary Bird'.

Plant Rugged Rugosas and Other Old Roses

If you have room for only one type of rose in your landscape, choose rugosas. Tough as nails, tolerant of drought and salt spray, and immune to disease, they don't get tougher than this. Rugosas are hardy to at least Zone 4; some are hardy to Zone 2. Add continuous bloom from spring until frost, heavenly fragrance, great fall foliage color, and huge hips good for jam-making, and you have the best all-around rose there is.

Rugosas come in many colors—from magenta through white. They also range in size from low groundcovers to 6-foot hedges. Some of the best are 'Blanc Double de Coubert', 'Fru Dagmar Hastrup', 'Therese Bugnet', 'Hansa', and 'Delicata'. Avoid 'Conrad F. Meyer', 'Topaz Jewel', and 'Rose a la Parfum de l'Hay.'

Tough Old Roses

Many old roses make great additions to low-maintenance landscapes. With the exception of the albas, the old roses listed below are seldom troubled by diseases. You may get a bit of blackspot or mildew on them, but not enough to warrant intervention.

Gallicas. These oldest roses in cultivation are upright, about 4 feet tall, with flowers in shades of pink, crimson, mauve, or purple. Foliage is dark green and slightly susceptible to mildew. Try 'Charles de Mills', 'Belle de Crecy', 'Cardinal de Richelieu', and 'Empress Josephine'.

Damasks. Source of attar of roses, these grow to 5 feet and have clear pink flowers and apple green to gray-green foliage that is seldom troubled by disease. Recommended damasks include 'Celsiana', 'Madame Hardy', 'Ispahan', and 'Autumn Damask', which reflowers in the fall.

Albas. Disease-free shrubs to 6 feet or more, albas have beautiful gray-green foliage and fragrant pale to shell pink or white flowers. They tolerate light shade. Try 'Maiden's Blush', 'Felicité Parmentier,' 'Celestial', 'Mme. LeGras de St. Germain,' and 'Alba Maxima.'

Centifolias. Known as the "cabbage roses" for their many- petaled blossoms, centifolias have disease-resistant foliage, fragrant pink, white, mauve, or purple flowers, and grow to 5 feet. Recommended cultivars include 'Tour de Malakoff' and 'Fantin-Latour'.

Start Out Right with Roses: Pick the Best Plants

The single most important thing you can do to have low-maintenance roses is to choose ones that are hardy, disease-resistant, and disease-tolerant from the start. Don't be fooled by plants at your local garden center that look disease-free: Most nurseries use fertilizers and pesticides to ensure that their plants look their best. Roses that look great under this high-input system won't hold up or be trouble-free in your low-maintenance one.

Take the time to search out some of the superior roses listed in this chapter. Many are available from mail-order nurseries (see "Sources" on page 355); well-stocked garden centers also carry more and more of them every year.

A Low-Work Pruning Primer

The good news about pruning roses is that most shrub roses will grow and flower even if you never prune them. But, if you have the time, some judicious pruning will increase the size and number of flowers and keep the plant more vigorous and well-shaped. The best time to prune is very early spring, before new growth emerges. Here's how.

Remove deadwood. At this time of year, you will be able to tell by their darker bark which canes have been winter-killed. If you're in doubt, scratch the cane with your fingernail. The "skin" of a live cane will scratch easily and the tissue beneath will be green. Prune well into live tissue and, as always, cut just above an outward-facing bud. Remove any completely dead canes at ground level.

Remove spindly growth. Remove any spindly growth and any canes that are crossing or badly congested. If your rose is growing taller than you'd like, head back the tallest canes individually, but never use hedge trimmers to give roses a "buzz job." Not only are you making unnecessary work for yourself, but you will cause your rose to become full and leafy on top and bare below—and minimize flowering to boot.

Take steps to rejuvenate overgrown roses. Take a firm hand to overgrown shrub roses that have lots of deadwood, or that are scraggly or out of bounds.

In very early spring, remove all deadwood and prune away half of the oldest canes at the base of the plant. Also remove crossing branches that crowd the center of the plant.

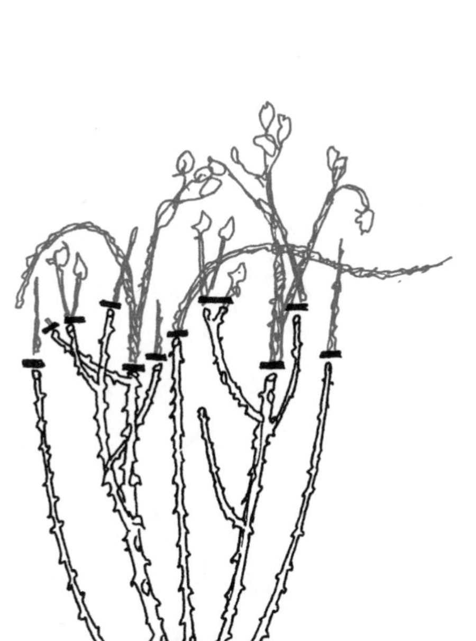

As a final step, cut all the remaining growth back by half. Be sure to cut just above an outward-facing bud.

Painless Rose Propagation

It's easy to propagate many kinds of roses. Layering, shown here, is an ideal method. Shrub roses, ramblers, climbers, and groundcover roses can be easily propagated right in the garden by layering.

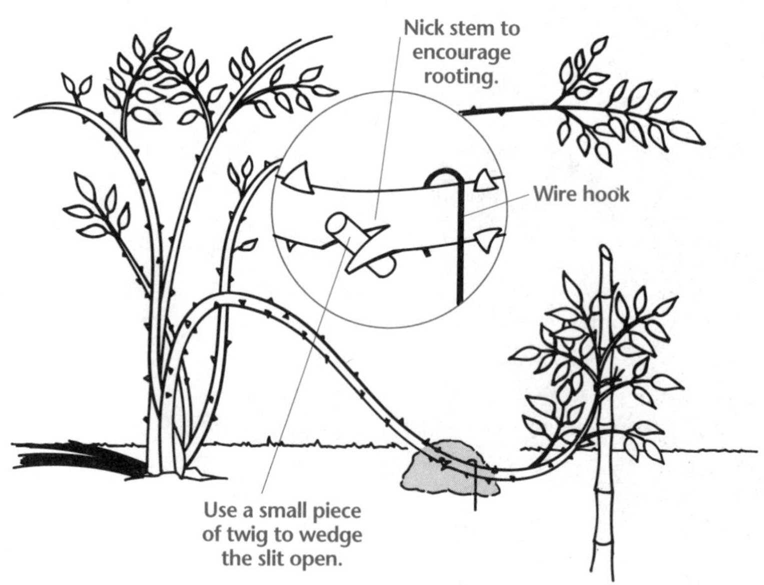

Roses with flexible stems are easy to layer right in the garden. Just bend the stem to the ground, loosen the soil where the stem meets the earth, and nick the stem with a sharp knife, as shown. Hold the stem in place with a wire hook and mound soil or a mixture of sand and peat over it. Stake the stem tip and keep the area moist; your new plant should be rooted in 6 to 8 weeks.

Simple Suckers

Rugosa roses, many species roses, and some roses that are

Search and Destroy Rootstock Suckers

The only absolutely essential pruning roses need is removal of rootstock suckers. These occur when the rootstock on which your rose is grafted sends up its own shoots, when what it's supposed to do is just stay down there in the ground and serve as roots for the grafted top. If you don't remove them, they'll likely crowd out the much-more-desirable rose grafted on top. The illustration gives tips on recognizing and removing rootstock suckers.

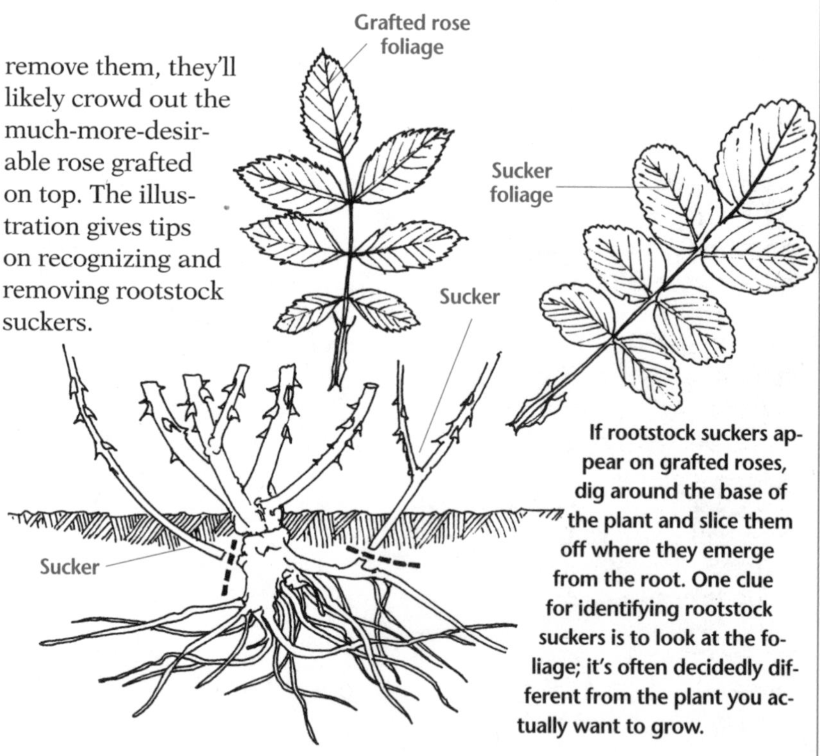

If rootstock suckers appear on grafted roses, dig around the base of the plant and slice them off where they emerge from the root. One clue for identifying rootstock suckers is to look at the foliage; it's often decidedly different from the plant you actually want to grow.

grown on their own roots will send up suckers surrounding the original plant. To convert these into a ready source of new plants, check to make sure the suckers are coming from the top graft and not the rootstock of a grafted rose. (See the illustration below if you have trouble telling the difference.) Then simply use a sharp spade to cut the suckers and their roots free from the mother plant. Cut the tops of your divisions back by two-thirds and plant in a new location. Water thoroughly and keep new divisions shaded for the first couple of weeks if the weather is hot.

Just How Deadly Are Rose Diseases?

Blackspot is by far the most serious rose disease because, when severe, it causes almost complete defoliation. The rose must then put out all new growth, exhausting its reserves. When this occurs repeatedly or in late summer, the rose often will succumb over the winter. Mild blackspot, however (on less than 50 percent of the leaves), can be tolerated by most roses with no ill effect except on the distraught gardener. Mildew almost never seriously compromises the survival of a rose; its major harm is cosmetic. So take a more relaxed and tolerant attitude toward mildew and milder cases of blackspot.

A Practical Guide to Managing Rose Diseases

You don't have to spend your summer strapped to a sprayer to keep diseases from destroying your roses. Use the tips below to minimize disease problems.

Stay away from susceptible roses. Most modern hybrid teas and floribundas have been bred without regard for disease resistance and, as a result, are terribly susceptible to blackspot and mildew. Your number-one line of defense against these plagues is to stay away from susceptible roses. See "Plant Rugosas and Other Old Roses" on page 296 for a host of disease-resistant roses to choose from.

Fight diseases with site selection. Moisture on rose foliage and poor air circulation favor disease organisms; a site with good air circulation helps control both problems.

Keep foliage dry when you water. When you water your roses, try not to get water on their foliage. Also water early in the day so any water on the leaves will dry quickly. Soaker hoses spread underneath the mulch are an excellent way to water roses.

Dispose of problems. Always burn or dispose of all prunings along with dead foliage that has dropped from your roses.

Fight disease with mulch. Applying a new layer of mulch each spring helps bury overwintering fungal spores and keep them from germinating.

Disease Remedies

Use the following techniques for controlling the most common rose diseases.

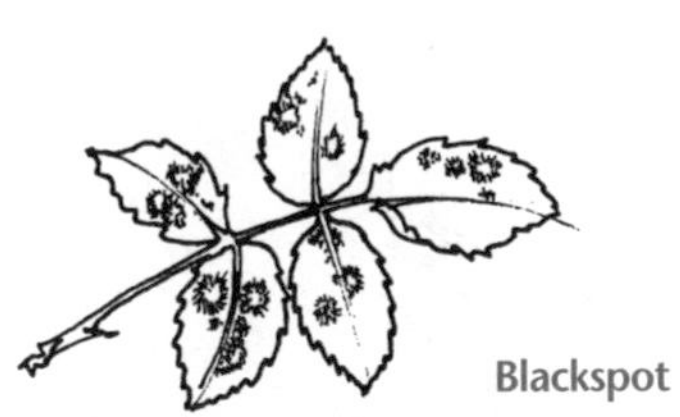

Blackspot

Blackspot. Remove and burn all infected foliage both on and off the plant. Then, as anomalous as this sounds, apply overhead irrigation at night for about 5 hours. Repeat at 10-day intervals. According to rose expert Peter Beales, this will wash spores off and away from the plants sufficiently to control the disease. Use a solution of

(continued)

1 ounce of baking soda in 10 gallons of water as a preventive. As a last resort, dust or spray with wettable sulfur, adding a few drops of liquid soap as a spreader if spraying. Apply sulfur on an overcast day.

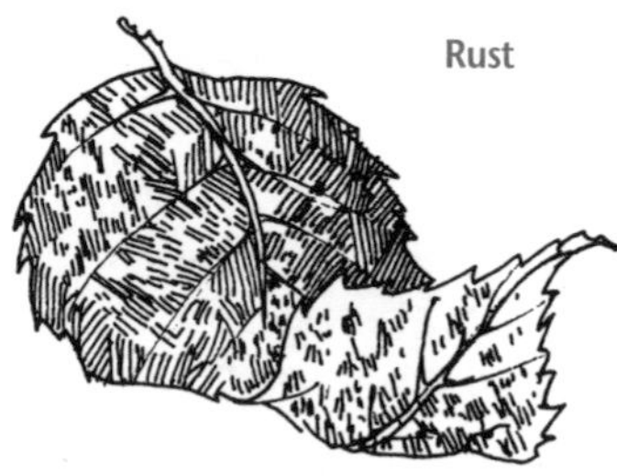

Rust. Look for leaves with orange spots on their undersides and light yellow spots on their upper surfaces. Remove and burn all infected foliage. Apply new mulch. As a last resort, apply sulfur as for blackspot.

Mildew. Since mildew first appears on the terminal growth, remove the terminals affected. Mildew spores, unlike blackspot, don't germinate readily in wet conditions, so you can syringe or hose the plant off thoroughly, being careful not to splash nearby roses. Spray at regular intervals with baking soda as a preventive, as for blackspot. Minimize fertilization with nitrogen-rich materials. As a last resort, spray or dust with sulfur.

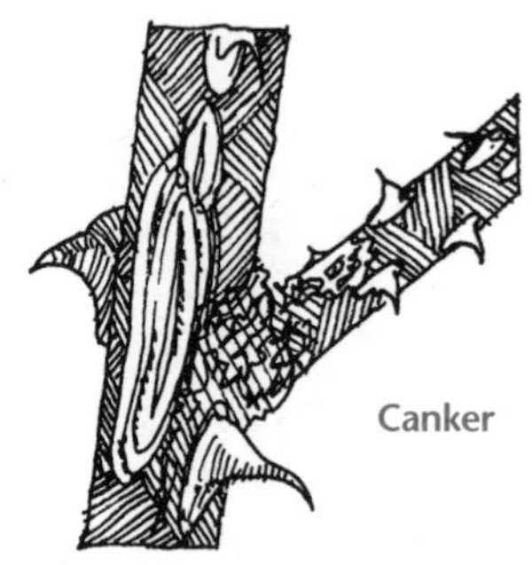

Canker. Using very sharp shears, remove all affected canes below the swollen, discolored area. Be sure to cut back to healthy growth, and disinfect pruners in rubbing alcohol between cuts.

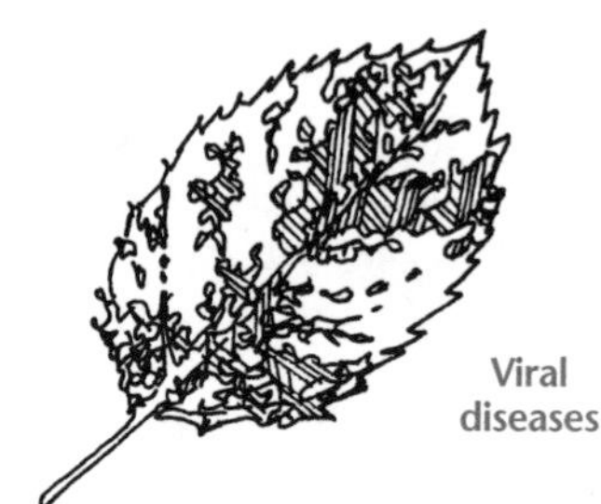

Viral diseases. There is no cure for viral diseases like mosaic, which won't kill your rose but will weaken it. Destroy any plants that display circular yellow-green mottling on their foliage or that develop inexplicably curled leaves and stunted growth. Mosaic is spread during propagation of roses in the nursery. Inspect all plants carefully before you make your purchase.

Manage Rose Pests the Low-Maintenance Way

If you see insect damage on your roses, don't panic. You can keep pest problems to a minimum by using a simple combination of organic methods and benign neglect. Just follow the suggestions below.

Encourage birds and beneficials. Wild and weedy areas that are left undisturbed host a myriad of insects and birds, both of which are natural predators that keep rose pests under control. Don't just depend on birdseed to attract birds: Plant a diversity of plants in your landscape to provide food and nesting sites for birds. Hang nesting boxes and consider keeping your garden shed or garage door open in spring and summer to accommodate the barn swallows and phoebes that might want to raise a family there. They more than pay for the inconvenience with the insects they eat. For tips on attracting them, see "Persuade Beneficials to Become Resident Pest-Control Experts" on page 106.

Stay away from sprays. Even organically acceptable insect sprays like rotenone or insecticidal soap affect beneficial insects. For example, even soap sprays kill ladybug larvae feeding on the inevitable infestation of aphids in early June. If you maintain a hands-off policy, the ladybugs should have the situation under control within two to three weeks, and your roses will have suffered only temporary and very minimal damage.

Pest Control

Here's help for the most common rose pests you're likely to encounter.

Beetles. Handpick beetles, which chew holes in flowers and leaves, early in the morning. To catch a lot at once, place a sheet under the plant and tap the plant lightly with a stick, then gather the fallen beetles and drop them into a jar of soapy water. Control beetle grubs by applying milky disease to the lawn and soil around roses. Beetle traps attract the pests: If you use them, place them at least 50 feet downwind from roses.

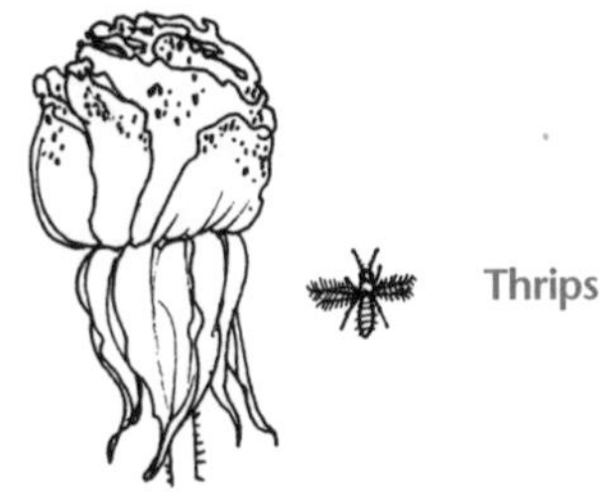

Thrips. Thrips cause petal edges to turn brown and buds to remain unopened. The easiest way control them is to cut off and burn affected flowers.

Rose midges. These tiny pests cause buds and leaves to blacken and die. To control them, cut off and burn affected tissue.

Aphids. Clusters of aphids attack new growth in spring, causing disfigured buds and blooms. Prune away and destroy severely infested branches. Wash pests off plants with strong sprays of water. If infestations are persistent, spray with insecticidal soap.

Rose slugs. Skeletonized foliage and sluglike larvae on undersides of leaves signal rose slugs. Dislodge the pests with a jet of water; wear gloves if you handpick. If infestations are persistent, spray with insecticidal soap.

Rose chafers. Handpick these pests that feast on flowers and skeletonize foliage. Then tent plants with cheesecloth or floating row covers for a couple of weeks.

Chapter 27

Wildflowers

Plan Ahead for Trouble-Free Gardens

Layer Your Flowers for Effective Displays

Fuss-Free Flowers for Sunny Sites

Fuss-Free Flowers for Shady Sites

Turn That Lawn into a Wildflower Meadow

Turn Fallen Leaves into Mower-Made Mulch

Transform a Wet Spot into a Bog Garden

Wildflowers the Low-Maintenance Way

PLANTING WILDFLOWERS is a practical and very beautiful way to reduce the maintenance your yard requires. There are beautiful native wildflowers in every region of the country. Just look around you in fields and along roadsides in spring, summer, or fall, and you'll spot the blooms of native wildflowers. Think about it—these natives cope routinely with droughts and spells of heavy rain, cold, and blazing sun and return year after year with a profusion of blooms. All with no effort from any gardener. Why not put them to work in your yard?

This chapter will give you hints for succeeding with wildflowers and suggest some plants to try in various sites. It also tells you, step by step, how to develop a beautiful, low-maintenance perennial wildflower meadow.

Plan Ahead for Trouble-Free Wildflower Gardens

Growing wildflowers is a snap if you take time to plan before you start. Here's what you need to know to get started.

Let your site tell you which wildflowers to plant. Why torture yourself or your plants by trying to grow sun lovers in part shade, or moisture lovers on a dry site? Avoid the extra work it takes to fight with Nature, and work *with* her instead. You'll find some suggestions for picking site-suitable wildflowers on the next few pages. For more ideas and information, consult one of the books on growing wildflowers listed in "Recommended Reading" on page 358. Or look at catalogs that specialize in wildflowers.

Mulch. Mulching saves lots of weeding and watering time. This is especially true when you are getting a new planting established. Pile 3 to 4 inches of organic mulch around, but not touching, your plants.

Pack your garden with plants. Fill your wildflower garden so there won't be room for weeds to grow between the plants once they're mature.

Layer Your Flowers for Effective Displays

Take a cue from roadside tapestries made of tall sunflowers and goldenrod, supported by sprawling fall asters. Plant your natives with the tallest plants at the back of the bed, medium-height ones in the middle, and the low-growing sprawlers at the front. The plants can lean on each other for support, and you'll still be able to see all the flowers.

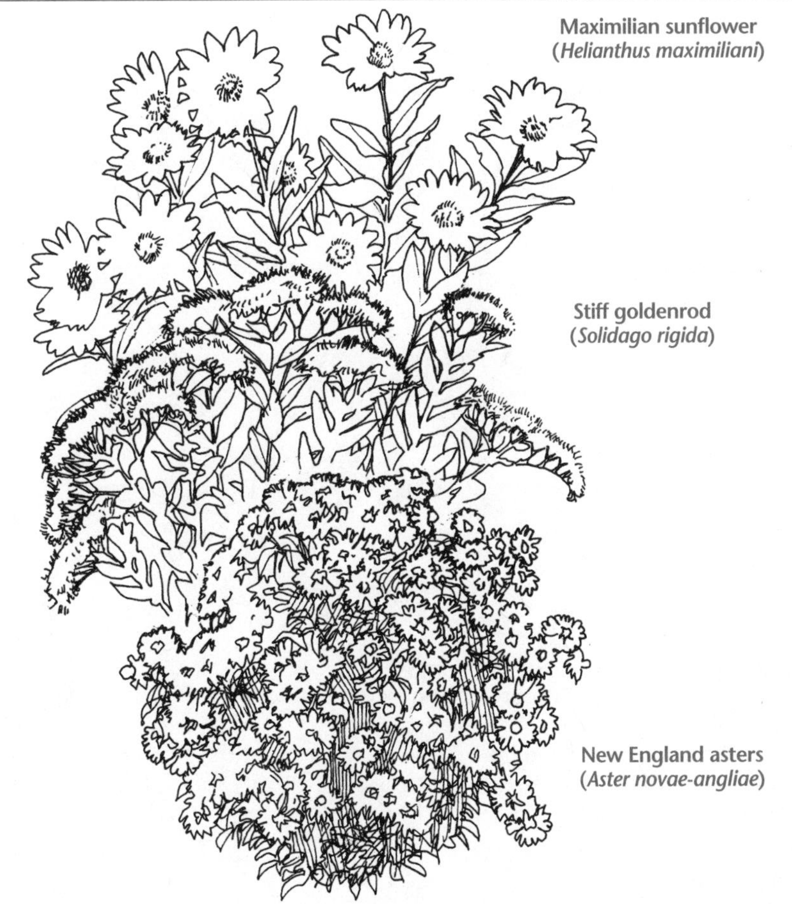

Fuss-Free Flowers for Sunny Sites

Even if you don't know their names, you're probably familiar with many wildflowers that thrive in full sun. You've seen these tough survivors blooming in riotous abandon along roadsides and neglected fields, in soils that range from heavy clay to mixtures of sand and rocks. Here are some of the easiest sun worshipers to grow.

Black-eyed Susan (*Rudbeckia hirta*): Yellow-orange daisy flowers with dark brown centers from summer through fall; 2–3 feet high. Zones 4–8.

Blue false indigo (*Baptisia australis*): Spires of indigo-blue flowers in early summer; attractive seedpods; 2–4 feet high. Zones 3–9.

Blue flag iris (*Iris versicolor*): Blue flowers in late spring to midsummer; 2–3 feet high. Will take light shade; needs moist to saturated soil. Zones 2–7.

Boltonia (*Boltonia asteroides*): Tiny white daisy flowers from late summer through fall; 4–6 feet high. Zones 3–9.

Butterfly weed (*Asclepias tuberosa*): Clusters of deep orange blooms in late spring through summer; 2–3 feet high. Grow from seed; avoid transplanting. Zones 3–9.

Button gayfeather (*Liatris aspera*): Tall, fuzzy spikes of lavender blooms in summer; 4–6 feet high Easy to grow from seed. Zones 3–9.

Canada lily (*Lilium canadense*): Nodding, bell-shaped yellow or red blossoms in summer; 4–5 feet high. Will grow in wet areas. Zones 3–7.

Downy phlox (*Phlox pilosa*): Clusters of pink to purple flowers in spring; 1–2 feet high. Zones 5–10.

Foxglove penstemon (*Penstemon digitalis*): White to purple-tinged flowers in late spring through early summer; 2–5 feet high. Zones 4–8.

Hairy beardtongue (*Penstemon hirsutus*): Purplish to violet flowers in late spring through early summer; 2–3 feet high. Self-sows freely. Zones 4–8.

Kansas gayfeather (*Liatris pycnostachya*): Tall, fuzzy spikes of lavender blooms in summer; 3–5 feet high. Zones 3–9.

Lance-leaved coreopsis (*Coreopsis lanceolata*): Yellow daisy flowers borne from late spring into summer; 1–2 feet high. Spreads. Zones 3–8.

Marsh mallow (*Hibiscus moscheutos* subsp. *palustris*): Large pink, white, or red flowers in summer; 4–8 feet high. Zones 5–10.

Wildflowers provide a beautiful way to cover hard-to-mow slopes. Choose drought-tolerant plants with strong, mat-forming roots to bind the soil. Yarrows and native grasses work well. Or plant non-spreading wildflowers and fill in between them with a fibrous-rooted plant like verbena.

Maryland gold aster (*Chrysopsis mariana*; may be listed as *Heterotheca mariana*): Bright yellow daisy flowers from late summer through fall; 1–3 feet high. Zones 4–9.

Maximilian sunflower (*Helianthus maximiliani*): Clusters of 3-inch yellow daisies in late summer and fall; 4–10 feet high. Zones 3–8.

Mexican hat (*Ratibida columnifera*): Yellow daisy flowers with dark brown, cone-shaped centers from summer through fall; 1–4 feet high. Easy to grow from seed. Zones 2–10.

Mouse-ear coreopsis (*Coreopsis auriculata*): Bright, golden yellow daisy flowers in spring; 1–2 feet high. Spreads; will grow in shade. Zones 4–9.

New England aster (*Aster novae-angliae*): Purple daisy flowers with yellow centers from late summer to fall; 3–6 feet high. Divide in late fall. Zones 3–8.

Ozark sundrops (*Oenothera missouriensis*). Bright yellow flowers from summer through fall; interesting seedpods; 6–12 inches high. Zones 4–8.

Pale coneflower (*Echinacea pallida*): Large, pale rose daisy flowers from summer through fall; 3–4 feet high. Zones 4–8.

Purple coneflower (*Echinacea purpurea*): Large, reddish purple daisy flowers with bright golden cones in the center from summer through fall; 2–4 feet high. Zones 3–8.

Rose verbena (*Verbena canadensis*): Clusters of tiny, rose-colored blooms in spring and summer; 8–18 inches high. Zones 4–10.

Small's beardtongue (*Penstemon smallii*): Purplish pink blossoms in late spring through early summer; 2–2½ feet high. Self-sows freely; will grow in shade. Zones 6–8.

Stiff goldenrod (*Solidago rigida*): Large heads of small golden-yellow flowers in fall; 3–5 feet high. Zones 3–9.

Tall ironweed (*Vernonia altissima*): Purple flower heads in late summer through fall; 3–10 feet high. Zones 4–8.

White gaura (*Gaura lindheimeri*): White to pinkish blossoms in summer through fall; 3–4 feet high. Zones 5–9.

Wild bergamot (*Monarda fistulosa*): Topknots of light lavender flowers in late summer; 2–5 feet high. Zones 3–9.

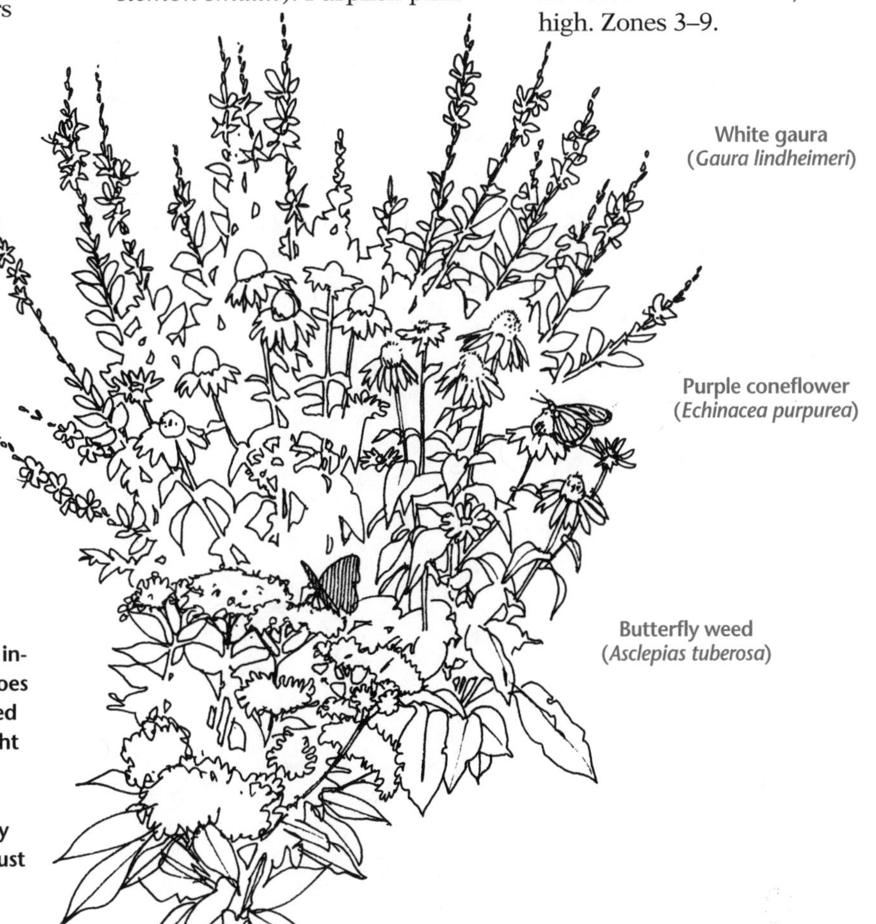

Does your sunny site have thin, infertile soil that's full of rocks? Does it get muddy in spring and baked dry in summer's heat? Don't fight it. Plant it with sturdy roadside wildflowers like white gaura, purple coneflower, and butterfly weed. They'll like your garden just the way it is.

Fuss-Free Flowers for Shady Sites

If you have even a small group of deciduous trees, you can make the space under them into a charming woodland garden. As a rule, woodland natives prefer moist, humusy soil that's well-drained and not soggy. Many wildflowers bloom before the trees leaf out fully in the spring, but you'll still be able to enjoy a few flowers and a wide variety of foliage all summer long.

Once established, a woodland garden is very undemanding. Fallen leaves provide a natural mulch. Shade from the trees keeps the soil from drying out, so you'll spend less time watering. Here are some of the easiest shade lovers to grow.

Black snakeroot (*Cimicifuga racemosa*): Airy spikes of white flowers in summer followed by blue-black berries in fall; 3–8 feet high. Zones 3–8.

Bloodroot (*Sanguinaria canadensis*): Snowy white blooms in early spring; 4–8 inches high. Self-sows freely. Zones 3–9.

Canada violet (*Viola canadensis*): White blossoms in spring and early summer; 6–12 inches high. Zones 3–8.

Cardinal flower (*Lobelia cardinalis*): Spikes of scarlet blossoms in late summer through fall; 2–5 feet high. Will grow in sun; insists on moist soil. Zones 2–9.

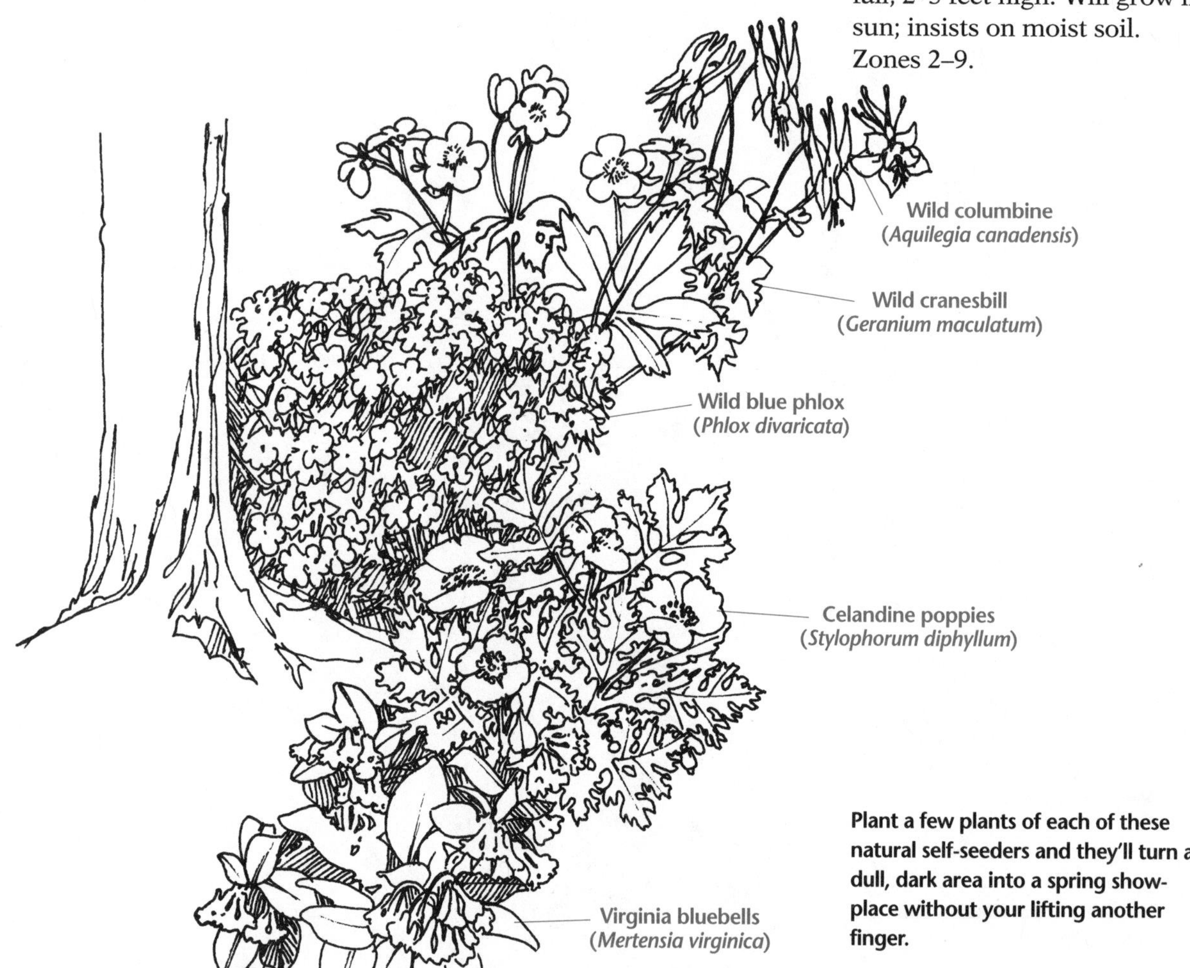

Plant a few plants of each of these natural self-seeders and they'll turn a dull, dark area into a spring showplace without your lifting another finger.

Celandine poppy (*Stylophorum diphyllum*): Deep yellow flowers in spring; 12–18 inches high. Self-sows freely. Zones 4–9.

Creeping polemonium (*Polemonium reptans*): Clusters of deep blue blossoms in spring; 8–16 inches high. Self-sows freely. Zones 2–8.

Crested iris (*Iris cristata*): Pale blue flowers with orange crests in spring; 2–8 inches high. Spreads. Zones 3–9.

Fringed bleeding heart (*Dicentra eximia*): Clusters of pink heart-shaped flowers in early spring through summer; 10–18 inches high. Will grow in almost full sun. Zones 3–9.

Jack-in-the-pulpit (*Arisaema triphyllum*): Striped green-and-purple hooded blossoms in spring, followed by bright orange-red berries in fall; 1–3 feet high. Zones 3–9.

Large-flowered bellwort (*Uvularia grandiflora*): Nodding pale yellow blossoms in spring; 12–18 inches high. Spreads. Zones 3–8.

Ohio spiderwort (*Tradescantia ohiensis*): Blue to rose or nearly white flowers in spring; 2–3 feet high. Will also grow in full sun. Zones 3–9.

Red fire pink (*Silene virginica*): Clusters of bright scarlet flowers in late spring and early summer; 6–20 inches high. Zones 3–9.

Shooting-star (*Dodecatheon meadia*): Nodding clusters of dart-shaped pink flowers in spring; 6–20 inches high. Zones 4–8.

Turk's-cap lily (*Lilium superbum*): Nodding red-orange blooms in summer; 4–7 feet high. Will grow in wet places. Zones 4–9.

Virginia bluebells (*Mertensia virginica*): Clusters of nodding blue and pink buds that open into blue trumpet-shaped blooms in spring; 1–2 feet high. Self-sows. Zones 3–9.

Wild blue phlox (*Phlox divaricata*): Clusters of blue to almost white flowers in spring; 10–15 inches high. Self-sows freely. Zones 3–9.

Wild columbine (*Aquilegia canadensis*): Nodding red and yellow flowers in spring; 1–3 feet high. Self–sows readily. Zones 3–8.

Wild cranesbill (*Geranium maculatum*): Light violet-colored blossoms in spring; 1–2 feet high. Self-seeds freely. Zones 4–8.

Willow blue star (*Amsonia tabernaemontana*): Clusters of light blue star flowers in spring; 1–3 feet high. Will take some sun. Zones 3–9.

Instead of pampering grass on shady sites where it won't grow happily, get off the mowing merry-go-round. Try tucking woodland wildflowers in around the roots of trees for a natural, easy-care groundcover.

Large-flowered bellwort (*Uvularia grandiflora*)

Canada violets (*Viola canadensis*)

Turn That Time-Consuming Lawn into a Wildflower Meadow

Why spend your summers sweating behind your mower breathing exhaust fumes? Wouldn't you rather sit back and watch flowers blow in the breeze instead? Replacing a lawn with meadow wildflowers is a great way to cut down on mowing chores. Once established, a wildflower meadow needs no fertilizer, little water, and just one mowing a year. If your site gets six to eight hours of sun a day, you can grow a meadow. Just follow these steps.

Start small. Planting a successful meadow involves some hands-on work. If you've set your sights on a huge expanse of meadow, break the project into smaller sections and start one section each year until the entire area is complete.

Mow. Cut any existing vegetation as close to the ground as possible in midsummer. Rake and remove the clippings.

Till. Turn under any remaining vegetation. Give the roots and weed seeds a week or two to sprout. Then till again, but only about 1 inch deep this time. Repeat the waiting and shallow tilling 3 or 4 more times until very few new weeds appear.

Plant. Once you have a clean seedbed, you are ready to plant. The best time to plant in Zone 3 and warmer is about one month before your first killing frost in the fall. In colder zones, or if fall is not a good time for you, plant as soon as the soil can be worked in the spring.

Broadcast seed, walk on it to press it in, and sprinkle a very light layer of straw over the area to help keep the soil from drying out. Or set transplants and water them in.

Water. Keep the seedlings or transplants moist until they are established (usually about 4 to 6 weeks).

Mulch. Right after you set out plants, or as soon as seedlings are large enough to identify, mulch the meadow with 3 to 4 inches of organic mulch.

Weed. Walk through the meadow occasionally the first year and pull out any unwanted plants.

Mow. Starting the year after planting, your meadow will need to be mowed once a year in early spring. Use a string trimmer or scythe and cut 4 to 6 inches above the ground so you won't disturb the crowns of the plants. Use a bush hog to mow large meadow areas.

Pale coneflower (*Echinacea pallida*)

ie dropseed (*olus heterolepis*)

Get the Best Meadow Flowers the First Time Around

A well-planned perennial meadow is a thing of beauty for many years. Don't skimp when it comes to selecting plants and buying seed; you'll just end up lavishing time and energy on plants that won't thrive. Here's how to set the stage for success.

Choose a regional mix. Most seed companies and nurseries offer both wildflower and grass-and-wildflower mixes that are designed for specific parts of the country. Some of the plants will thrive in your area; others won't. If this doesn't bother you, a mix is an easy way to go. Avoid "instant meadow" mixes, which are mostly annual flowers, as well as inexpensive generic wildflower mixes—you will be disappointed with them in the long run.

Blend your own mix. Your best bet is to purchase flowers and grasses suited to your site. The easiest way is to read the descriptions in nursery catalogs to find wildflowers and grasses that thrive in your conditions. Then think about bloom times and choose carefully so you'll always have something in flower.

If you like adventure, try making up your list by roaming the countryside around your house with a wildflower guidebook in one hand and a notebook in the other. Write down what you find in bloom in various seasons. You can then order the seed from a catalog or go back later and collect seed from the local plants.

Save on Weeding Time: Choose Aggressive Wildflowers

If you're trying to start a meadow and you don't have much time, a mix of aggressive wildflowers may be just the ticket. You won't have the variety you might get in a more carefully planned and developed meadow, but you will get a flower-filled meadow fast.

Try vigorous perennials like common yarrow (*Achillea millefolium*), Queen-Anne's-lace (*Daucus carota* var. *carota*), dame's rocket (*Hesperis matronalis*), oxeye daisy (*Chrysanthemum leucanthemum*), and showy evening primrose (*Oenothera speciosa*). In two or three years, they will take over and choke out any other weeds or flowers in the area with very little help from you.

Turn Fallen Leaves into Easy Mower-Made Mulch

Chopped leaves make an ideal mulch for a wildflower garden—especially a woodland one. If you have a side-discharge mower, try this technique to chop and spread leaves while you mow.

Start mowing your leaf-covered yard on the opposite side from and parallel to the garden bed you want to mulch. Keep the discharge pointed toward the garden and make forward and backward passes moving gradually toward the garden. You'll create a moving windrow of chopped and rechopped leaves. As you finally mow along the garden, the last of the shredded leaves will be blown into place.

If your mower doesn't have a side discharge or the leaves and garden are far apart, use your bagging mower. Just snap on the bagger and mow your leaf-covered lawn. Empty the instant mulch onto the beds where you want it.

Transform a Problem Wet Spot into a Beautiful Bog Garden

If you have a wet spot where the mower always bogs down in the mud, don't spend another aggravating afternoon or lose sleep thinking up ways to drain your own personal wetland. Fill it with wildflowers that love bogs and wet places, and turn the potential mud hole into a beautiful low-care garden instead.

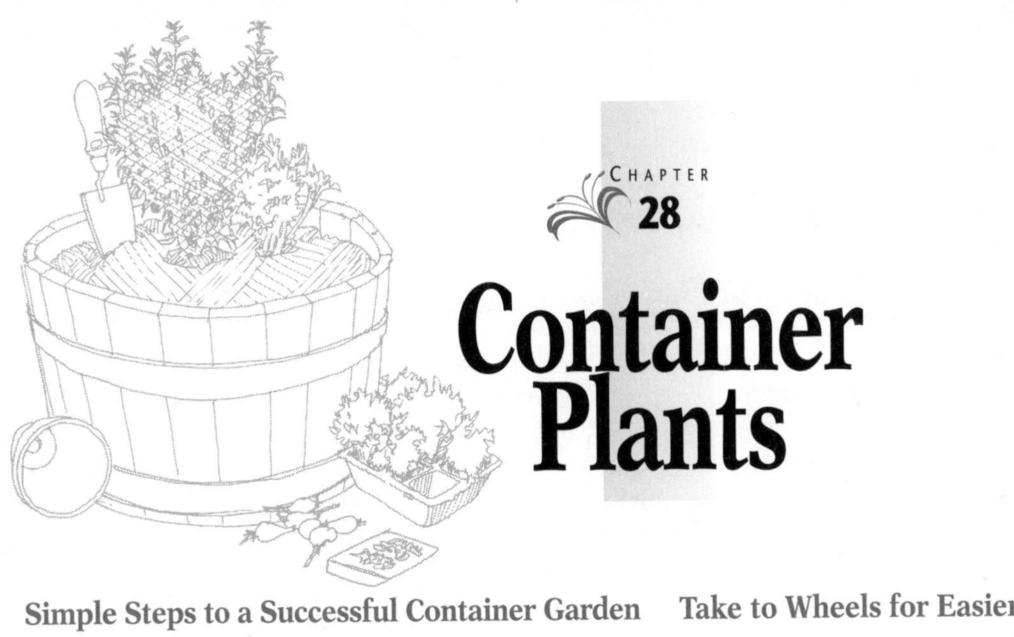

Chapter 28

Container Plants

- Simple Steps to a Successful Container Garden
- Container Options
- Build a Space- and Labor-Saving Vegetable Box
- What Plants Need
- Keep Herbs Close at Hand
- Take to Wheels for Easier Plant Care
- Wick Away Indoor Water Cares
- Household Items Keep Plants from Drowning
- Best Bets for Least-Work Potted Plants
- Grow Patio Pots for Year-Round Interest

Container Plants the Low-Maintenance Way

WHETHER YOU'RE GROWING tubs of herbs and vegetables on the deck or houseplants in a sunny window, growing plants in containers adds a dimension to gardening that's hard to pass up. Growing plants in pots lets you move plants at will: You can easily bring a cherished tender herb like rosemary indoors to protect it from winter cold or grow an ever-changing display of flowers on a deck or patio. It also puts you in control of the growing conditions. You can garden if the soil is lousy, plant when you have the time, and use every available space. With containers, you can take advantage of light and moisture wherever you find them—in sunny stairwells and steamy bathrooms, under trees, or out front beside your driveway.

In this chapter, you'll find tips and techniques for making container gardening even more enjoyable than it already is.

Simple Steps to a Successful Container Garden

It doesn't take much to keep container plants happy. Since you control the soil, water, and light, it's easy to provide perfect growing conditions. For the best results and the least hassle, group plants with similar needs in a single container. If you mix sun-loving flowers with shade lovers, or mix plants that need lots of water with those that don't, you'll drive yourself crazy trying to keep all of them happy and healthy.

Grow Great Plants with the Right Soil Mix

Choose a commercial container mix or make your own to get potted plants started right. A good mix drains well, retains moisture, and provides support for your container plant. Experiment with a few to find the one that's right for your plants. Or buy a mix and doctor it.

For a good do-it-yourself mix, combine 1 part potting soil and 2 parts organic matter—compost, shredded bark, leaf mold, or any material large enough to improve drainage and lend stability. Sharp sand, used by masons (available at most lumberyards), is another good option.

You can tailor it to fit your watering habits, too. If you like to water often, use sharp sand to increase drainage in your mix; if you grow on the dry side, add organic matter like compost to hold moisture between waterings.

Container Options

The sky's the limit when it comes to choosing containers for your plants to grow in. Of course, there are hundreds of conventional containers to choose from. Explore as many as you can think of.

But don't just stop there. Container gardening means recycling. Plant in leftover pieces of pipe from plumbing projects, drain tiles that have been stood on end, rusty wheelbarrows, used tires, old bird cages—anything can become a planter/conversation piece in your garden. Where openings can't hold soil, make a liner of burlap or plastic screen.

Let There Be the Right Amount of Light

You can make any container plant happy. Move pots to the shade if the sun gets too bright, or set them in the sun if that's what your plants prefer. Cluster sun lovers together in a hot spot so you can water them with a quick once-over. Let shade-tolerant combinations grace bare spots under trees and in dark corners.

Add Water and Let the Plants Grow

Once plants are potted and placed in an area with adequate light, all they need is water. Give them the right amount when they need it, and you'll have healthy plants and few maintenance chores.

Use the knuckle test to know when to water clay or plastic containers. Stick your finger into the soil down to the first knuckle. If your fingertip is dry, it's time to water. How much is enough? Irrigate every pot until water flows out the bottom. If your plant drains into a saucer, throw out the excess.

Because container-grown plants have restricted root space, they're often nutrient-stressed. To keep your container garden growing vigorously, plan on feeding regularly. Compost tea, liquid kelp, or fish emulsion are all fine fertilizers for container plants that you can apply when you water. As a rule, water at *half* the strength recommended on the container *twice* as often.

Build a Space- and Labor-Saving Vegetable Box

Wooden fruit or vegetable crates from the grocery store—or their plastic equivalent, milk or storage crates—make great no-till vegetable garden boxes. If you grow in these handy containers, you won't have to wait for soil to warm up or for the weather to improve; whenever you're ready to plant, the conditions are right.

▲**Start your crate garden with burlap.** Before filling your crates with your favorite soil mix and amendments, line them with burlap to keep soil from escaping. Then moisten the soil and start planting.

◀**Just plant and grow.** Small plastic milk crates are great for plants like lettuce and basil. For tall tomatoes or climbing cucumbers, use a wooden vegetable crate with a wire support. To make a simple support, after planting staple a 6-foot-tall section of hog wire (fencing with 4-inch squares) around the outside of the box. Attach it to itself for extra strength. Plants can lean or climb on the wire.

What Plants Need

When conditions aren't right, plants let you know—all you have to do is take a look at their leaves. A few commonsense cultural practices will cure most container plant problems.

Pale, stretched-out, spindly plants. Give these plants a brighter spot. If lower leaves turn yellow, water less often and feed with fish emulsion or another soluble fertilizer at a half-strength rate for two waterings to get them going again.

Plants that wilt even with adequate watering. Plants with this symptom may have root problems. Pull the plant out of its pot and take a look at the roots. If roots have filled all available space, divide the plant, repot it in new soil, and resume routine care. If roots are few or rotting, repot and let the soil dry between waterings.

Keep Herbs Close at Hand

When you're cooking, the last thing you have is time to waste. The sauce simmers, pasta's ready to serve, and you need some parsley. You don't have time to change shoes and tromp out to the garden. Turn instead to a convenient half-barrel filled with your favorite fresh herbs. A traditional strawberry pot works great, too; plant separate herbs in pockets on the jar's sides and they'll all have enough room to grow. Be sure to water from both the top and sides. When you need an herb, just snip off a sprig with scissors.

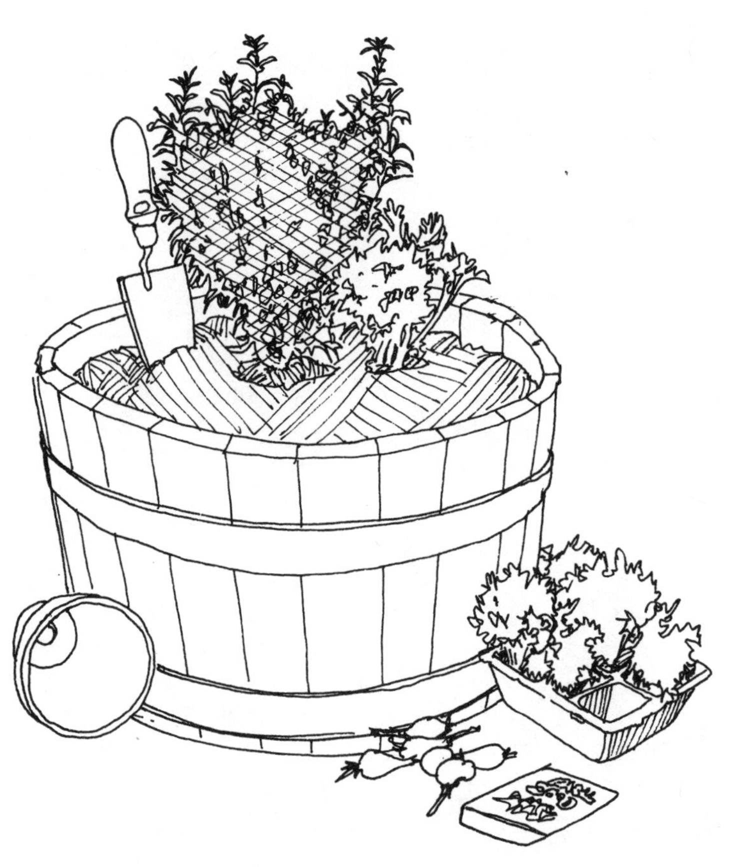

Take to Wheels for Easier Plant Care

Mobile gardening may not be an automotive trend, but putting containers on wheels lets you move them easily. Three-wheel steel dollies from your local hardware store make it easy to wheel huge pots about—whether you need to bring tender tropicals inside when seasons change or move large houseplants where you can water or spray safely away from carpets and furniture. Or bolt casters on a circle of plywood or other material. A wagon makes a great tool for rolling sun-loving annuals out to your shady patio to quickly decorate for a party. Or use it to move pot-grown tomatoes to safety when frost threatens.

TAKE-IT-EASY TIP!

Get Rolling for Easy Repotting

Wheels make container gardening easier at repotting time. Mix soil in your wheelbarrow or garden cart or just open a bag of commercial planting mix and dump it into a wagon. Put empty pots, trowel, and gloves in your new mobile potting bench, and get rolling. By taking the soil to the containers instead of dragging them to the soil, you save time—and your back.

Wick Away Indoor Water Cares

Containers with built-in reservoirs and wicks, and soil additives designed to conserve moisture, are modern technology's answer to tedious watering chores. Lots of "self-watering" pots work quite well. You can also make your own wick system, as shown here.

Some plant care professionals use encapsulated moisture products to conserve water in container plantings. These water-absorbing polymers swell up to hold extra moisture and release it later. Other less expensive substances, like peat moss, vermiculite, and perlite, do the job as well or better in home environments.

▶ **Insert wicks when you pot.** Cotton wicks, pieces of wool or cotton yarn, and strips of panty hose all make fine wicks. Insert them halfway up the container, through the drainage hole, when you pot.

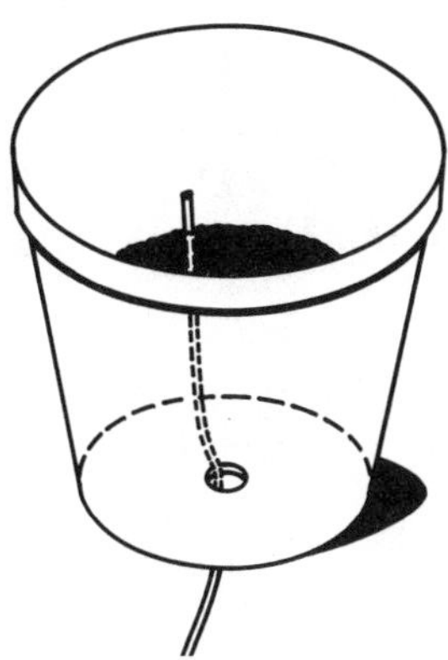

◀ **Watering made easy.** To water, just fill the reservoir. Until you're sure your wick system is working properly, also check the soil regularly to make sure it's damp enough.

▶ **Buy wick waterers.** Many companies offer pots with built-in wick-watering systems. These have a reservoir, a tube to fill it, a wick that runs up into the medium, and often a water-level indicator.

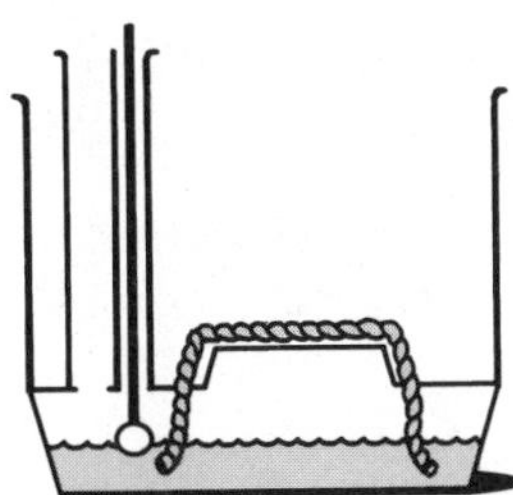

Use Household Items to Keep Plants from Drowning

A saucerful of water can mean root rot or death for plants like rosemary that demand well-drained soil. Try these tips for getting rid of that water without breaking your back.

Remove excess water with a plastic turkey baster and you won't have to lift heavy pots.

Elevate pots slightly on blocks, sponges, or hard plastic chocks so they can drain instead of being flooded by a saucerful of water.

Best Bets for Least-Work Potted Plants

Successful container gardens start with plants that like container life. Use these tips to find the best plants for your potted garden.

Look for drought-tolerant plants. Drought-tolerant herbs, ornamental grasses, annuals such as geraniums and marigolds, and many perennials, including daylilies, sedums, and hardy cacti (*Opuntia* spp.), make fine container residents. Fleshy leaves are a good clue to go by when you're looking for drought-tolerant plants: Plants that have them, like sedums, can hold on to water better than plants with thin, papery leaves.

Select dwarf shrubs and trees. You'll find a wide variety of dwarf shrubs and trees to choose from at well-stocked nurseries and garden centers. Dwarf cultivars generally have smaller root systems, grow slowly, and keep pleasing proportions for years. Those qualities translate into less work for you since they'll rarely need pruning or repotting.

Grow fruits, vegetables, and herbs. You can grow dwarf fruit trees, herbs, and a wide variety of vegetables (compact cultivars are best) on a sunny site in a variety of tubs and pots. Lettuce and other salad greens will perform well in a half-day of sun.

Try tropicals. Shallow-rooted tropical foliage plants seem to defy gravity. The huge leaves that emerge from small root systems make them ideal for growing in pots.

Plant groundcovers. Groundcovers provide living mulch beneath potted trees, suppress weeds, and often deliver bonus blooms. Try annual groundcovers like sweet alyssum, evergreen ones like creeping junipers, or flowering perennials like creeping thymes, sedums, or hen-and-chicks.

Grow flowers to keep your garden colorful. Perennials and annuals keep container plantings blooming nonstop until frost. If you're growing a potted tree that blooms in spring, put summer and fall-flowering perennials in the same container to extend the bloom. Or grow several smaller pots of perennials and bring them front and center while they're flowering. Annuals have shallow root systems that make them terrific companions to any container plant. Try sweet alyssum, coleus, impatiens, petunias, or marigolds, just for starters.

Plant sprawlers to dress up containers. Quick color and instant cover change even worn or stained containers into flower-filled beauties. Any plants that cascade or sprawl, like petunias, vinca, creeping thyme, and trailing junipers make good choices since their foliage drapes and decorates any pot. And don't forget annual vines like black-eyed Susan vine (*Thunbergia alata*). Plant a pot of each, or mix and match.

Make friends with invasive plants. Put unmanageable mints and intrusive bamboos in half-barrels on a patio or in plastic pots or bottomless buckets set in the ground. Sink pots of bog plants into the sides of water gardens; they'll get needed moisture without troubling fish and filter systems.

Grow Patio Pots for Year-Round Interest

It doesn't take lots of space, plants, or bother to decorate your deck, patio, or porch with nonstop color. Fill a large, sturdy container with a variety of plants chosen for their hardy habits, successive seasonal color, contrasting textures, and eye-pleasing forms. It can stay outside all year to brighten your landscape in every season.

Select a small tree or shrub with attractive winter twigs, evergreen foliage, or colorful berries, add bulbs to bloom in spring, a perennial plant to flower during the summer, and an evergreen groundcover to complement the planting and keep weeds away.

Enjoy year-round color and texture with a tub planted with a Japanese maple, coral bells, vinca, and crocuses.

For easy planting, place the plant with the largest rootball first, followed by medium-size, small, and finally groundcover plants.

CHAPTER 29

Ornamental Grasses

Ornamental Grasses the Low-Maintenance Way

It's time to get to know the grasses you cut only once a year: the ornamental ones. They don't need supplemental watering once established, the more vigorous types can hold their own against weeds, and they're rarely troubled by diseases or insects. Best of all, ornamental grasses are truly plants for all seasons. In autumn, many dry to beautiful shades of tan and ochre. Others are evergreen or semi-evergreen.

Some ornamental grasses quickly grow to the size of large shrubs, making them great choices for quick landscape effect. Yet as vigorous as they are, the best of them don't need dividing. And no pruning headaches—just cut them down to the ground once a year in early spring.

With Grasses, It Pays to Know When They Grow

Most ornamental grasses will grow nearly anywhere, but knowing a little about their likes and dislikes will help you select the best ones for your site and situation. For gardeners, grasses fall into two general groups, as determined by their season of active growth: Warm-season grasses grow during the summer; cool-season ones during cooler months.

(continued)

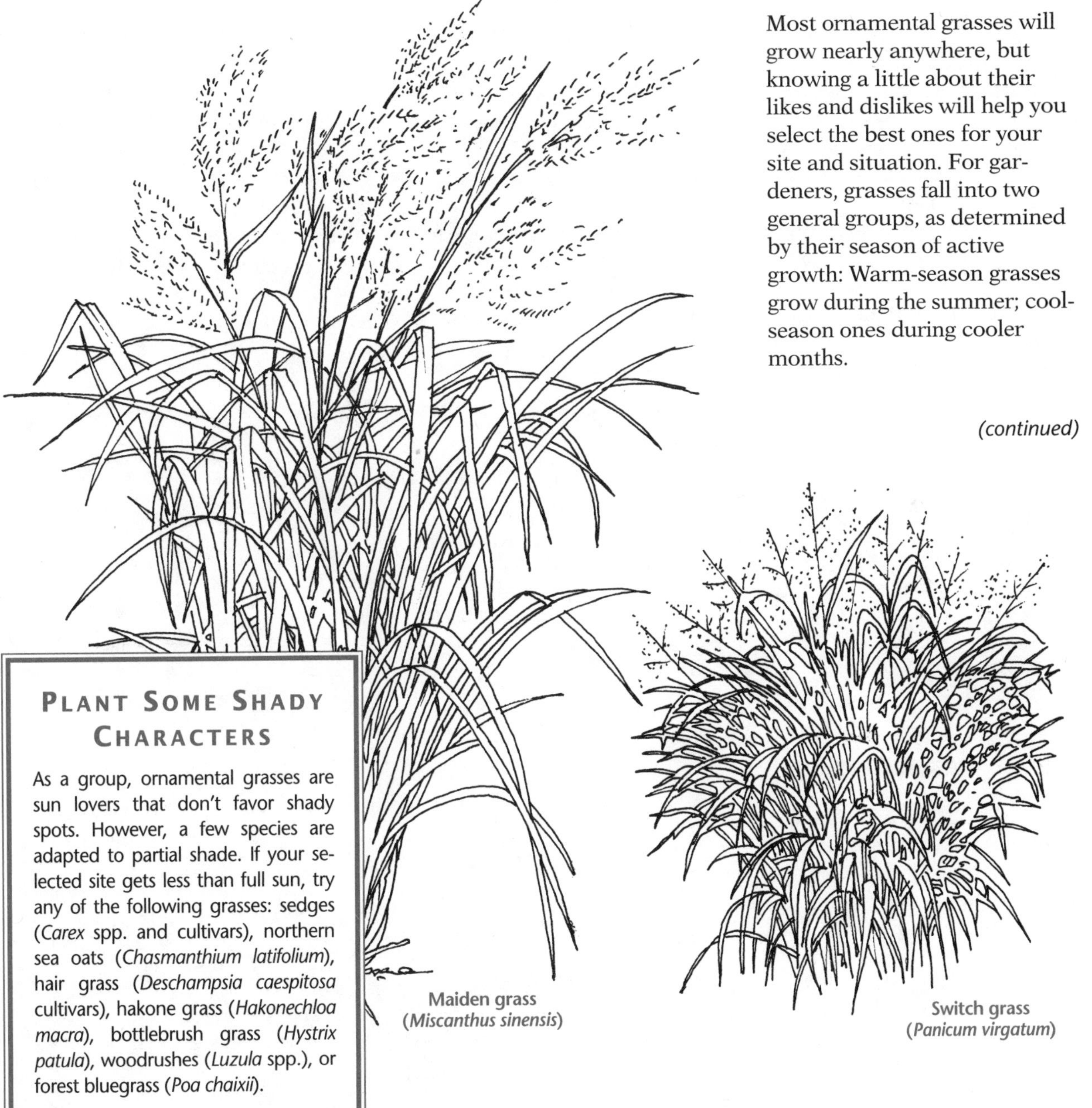

Maiden grass (*Miscanthus sinensis*)

Switch grass (*Panicum virgatum*)

Plant Some Shady Characters

As a group, ornamental grasses are sun lovers that don't favor shady spots. However, a few species are adapted to partial shade. If your selected site gets less than full sun, try any of the following grasses: sedges (*Carex* spp. and cultivars), northern sea oats (*Chasmanthium latifolium*), hair grass (*Deschampsia caespitosa* cultivars), hakone grass (*Hakonechloa macra*), bottlebrush grass (*Hystrix patula*), woodrushes (*Luzula* spp.), or forest bluegrass (*Poa chaixii*).

Although both groups include great low-maintenance plants, warm-season grasses require even less work to grow than cool-season ones. Here are some general characteristics of each group to keep in mind as you select grasses for your landscape.

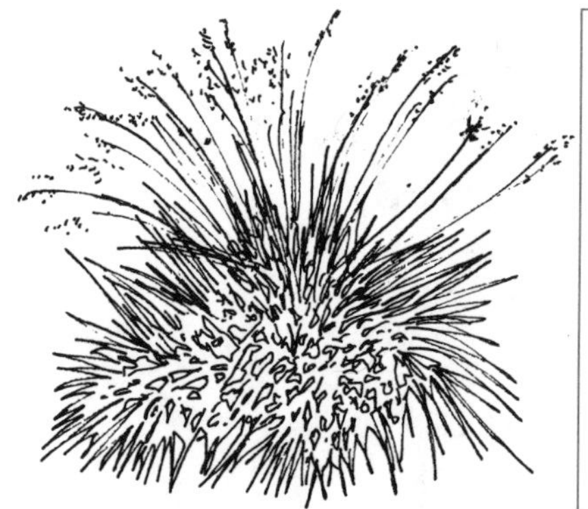
Blue oat grass (*Helictotrichon sempervirens*)

Warm-Season Grasses

Late spring and summer are the main growing seasons for warm-season grasses. They bloom from June through September, depending on the species. In winter, their foliage turns attractive shades of buff and tan. Generally, they are more tolerant of clay soils and poor drainage and rarely need dividing. Once a year in early spring, they need to be cut to within a few inches of the ground.

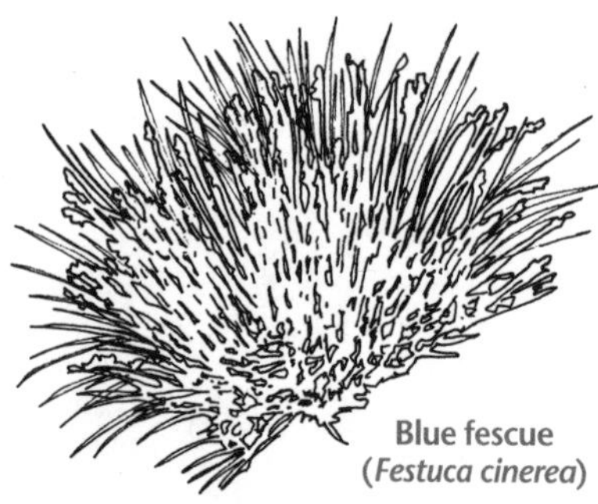
Blue fescue (*Festuca cinerea*)

Cool-Season Grasses

These grow actively during the cool seasons of the year—primarily spring and fall, winter in mild areas. Their foliage is often evergreen or semi-evergreen, and they bloom in spring or early summer. As a result, they provide landscape interest when warm-season grasses are least effective. Cool-season grasses are fussier about soil, though. In general, they need better drainage and are less tolerant of heavy clay than warm-season grasses.

Cool-season grasses generally aren't cut back completely in early spring, as warm-season ones are. Instead, they need more selective trimming and cleaning up at winter's end. Because they tend to die out in the center of the clump, they need dividing every two or three years.

You'll find many outstanding warm-season and cool-season grasses to choose from in "Ornamental Grasses for Special Sites" on page 324; just look down the "Description" column of the table and you'll find the growing habit of each grass listed first.

Corralling Aggressive Spreaders

Keep bamboos and ornamental grasses that spread aggressively under control by planting them inside a concrete culvert, a large garbage can with the bottom cut out, or another type of "container." The container should extend to a depth of 2 to 3 feet. Leave a 2-inch rim above the soil to control wandering aboveground stems.

Dividing Grasses Large and Small

The good news about dividing ornamental grasses is you may never need to do it. Cool-season grasses need dividing every two to three years, as new growth begins to appear in fall, winter, or early spring. Warm-season grasses almost never need dividing, but if you want more plants or need to improve the spacing in an overcrowded planting, tackle the project after you've given them their annual haircut in spring.

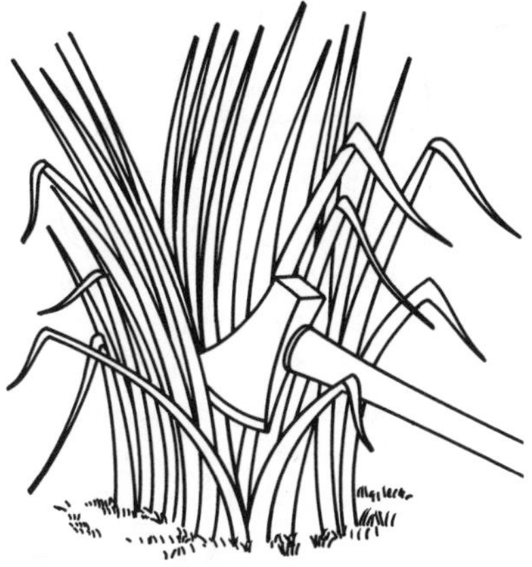

▲ **Get-tough division for large grasses.** You'll need to use an ax, or a wedge and a small sledgehammer, to divide large warm-season grasses. Cut the crown into several hunks, then pry the hunks out with a shovel and transplant them. If you only need a division or two, pry them off the side of the clump.

Dividing large clumps of ornamental grasses isn't a job for the faint-hearted. The easiest way to tackle the task is to do it right in the ground, as shown above. If you want to separate the clump into small divisions with three to five growing points each, however, you'll need to dig out the clump and wash off the soil so you can see what you're doing. Although it's more time-consuming, you won't believe how many grass plants you can get from a clump this way.

▼ **Simple division for smaller grasses.** Dividing cool-season grasses and small clumps of warm-season ones is relatively easy. Use a spade to lift small clumps of grasses from the soil, then rinse the roots clean with a hose. Slice away dead areas and divide the actively growing sections with a sturdy knife or a spade. Then replant or pot up the divisions.

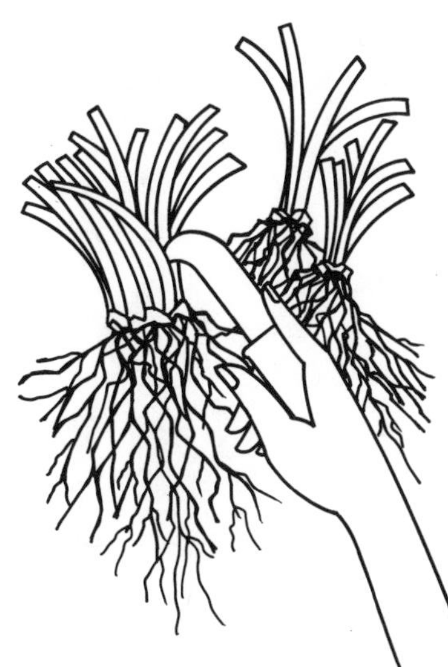

Grasses as Groundcovers

Grasses with spreading habits are generally too invasive for a perennial garden, but they make excellent groundcovers. Grow them alone or combine them in beds with other aggressive groundcovers. It's best to plan a site that will help you keep them in bounds without extra work. Regular mowing around a planting of them will help as well. For example, groundcover grasses are perfect for island beds surrounded by lawn, or sites with lawn on one side and a road or pond on the other. Or plant them in containers sunk in the soil, as shown on the opposite page.

You'll find many outstanding grasses to use as groundcovers in "Ornamental Grasses for Special Sites" on page 324; just read down the "Special Uses" column of the table and look for plants with spreading habits.

You can also use clump-forming grasses as groundcovers; just plant them on even centers as you would a vegetable garden that's been planted intensively. On shady sites, try this technique with the grasslike sedges (*Carex* spp.) and woodrushes (*Luzula* spp.). On sunny ones, try quaking grass (*Briza media*), fescues (*Festuca* cultivars), tufted hairgrass (*Deschampsia caespitosa*), blue oat grass (*Helictotrichon sempervirens*), and fountain grass (*Pennisetum alopecuroides*).

Basic Grass Care for Bountiful Results

Ornamental grasses have a plant-it-and-forget it quality that assures them a place in the heart of every gardener. Once you've chosen grasses suited to your site conditions and landscape, planting and care are simple matters. Soil preparation is largely unnecessary, particularly if you stick with the warm-season grasses. Except for requiring full sun, these grasses really don't care where you put them. Below, you'll find what little you need to know to grow a landscape full of lush, healthy, low-maintenance ornamental grasses.

Planting Grasses

About the only thing you need to do to prepare an area for grasses is remove any existing vegetation and plant. Since most ornamental grasses don't ever need to be divided, planting them properly the first time really pays off. You can plant containerized grasses any time from spring through fall, but you'll minimize watering chores if you plant early or late enough for your new grass to catch spring or fall rains.

Dig your grasses a good home. Plant your grasses in holes that are about twice as wide as the containers. Spread a mixture of soil and compost in the hole, then settle the plant so its crown is about 1 to 2 inches above the soil line. Refill the hole with soil and compost, and water thoroughly to settle the plant in place.

Planting pot-grown grasses. After removing an ornamental grass from its pot, use a knife to score the roots around the outside of the root ball. Or tease them out with a screwdriver. This encourages the roots to branch and spread out in all directions.

Handling bareroot grasses. If you've ordered bareroot grasses from a mail-order nursery, unpack and inspect them as soon as they arrive from the nursery. Each plant should have at least two or three culms (growing points). Do not accept plants consisting of a single culm; they have a high failure rate. The root system should look husky. Scratch the skin of a root with your fingernail; the tissue beneath should appear whitish, not brown or black. Blackened tissue means the roots are dead. If anything looks bad, notify the nursery immediately. Cool-season grasses, especially, are prone to arrive in poor condition.

Use a knife to score the roots of a pot-grown grass.

Plant bareroot grasses immediately. If you can't plant right away, settle them temporarily in containers of potting soil, water thoroughly, and keep them in a shady place. When you plant them permanently, dig a hole wide and deep enough to accommodate the roots. Fan out the roots over a cone of soil, and plant them so the crown is about an inch below the soil surface. After planting, water thoroughly and mulch.

Caring for Your Grasses

Once they're established, your grasses will thrive almost in spite of you. Except for the first couple of months after planting or during prolonged drought, they will do fine without any additional water.

Fertilizing is entirely optional. If you're feeling extravagant, give your grasses a spring feeding with a high-nitrogen fertilizer, such as blood meal, or anything you would use on your lawn. Apply the fertilizer around the clump, not on top of it, and water it in thoroughly.

The only other care your grasses need is their once-yearly trimming. Cool-season grasses are evergreen and don't need a dramatic spring clean-up like warm-season grasses. Just clean them up each spring by cutting off browned foliage. Give warm-season grasses a spring crew cut to clear the way for new growth and get the most landscape interest from your grasses.

nt in a hole ice as wide as e container, then tle the plant so the wn is 1 to 2 inches ove the soil line.

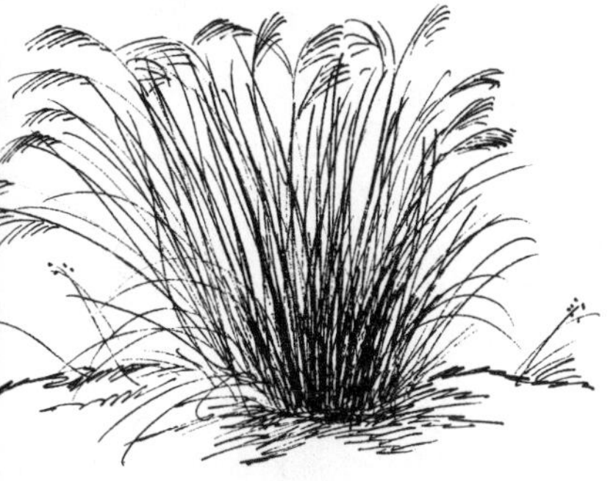

The late-summer flowers of warm-season grasses have tough stems and seed heads that dry to lovely shades of buff in autumn. They add beautiful texture and color to the winter landscape. Wait until spring to cut these grasses down so you don't miss the show.

In early spring, use pruning shears, hedge trimmers, a metal-blade weed trimmer, or a chain saw to cut your warm-season grasses to a few inches above ground level. New growth will emerge as soon as the weather warms.

Give 'em Room to Grow

Grasses form big clumps, and one of the most common mistakes is planting them too close together. When planting warm-season grasses, be sure to pick a site large enough to accommodate their size at maturity. That way, you'll only need to divide them if you want more plants for another part of your landscape. Here's a useful rule of thumb: Allow as much space between grasses as their mature height. For example, leave 5 feet of space between a grass that grows 5 feet tall and its neighbors.

Another common mistake is to plant clumps of grasses as individual specimens in the lawn. Not only does this create a spotty-looking design, it also creates more obstacles to mow around. To simplify your mowing and get more visual impact from your grasses, group them together or combine them with perennials or shrubs. When combining grasses with other plants, remember the rule of thumb about spacing. Resist the temptation to crowd other plants around them; you'll only have to move them in a year or two.

Ornamental Grasses for Special Sites

To find the best ornamental grasses for your garden, look through the list below. (You'll find true grasses and related grasslike plants listed.) For each, you'll find the season of growth, height, hardiness, and suggestions for special uses. Grasses grow well in full sun with average to rich well-drained soil, but many grasses can also grow well in problem sites—like heavy clay soil. Ornamental grasses make great additions to low-maintenance landscapes since they're so easy to care for, and because they'll grow in sites where other plants might need special pampering or special advance soil preparation in order to thrive.

Name	Description	Special Uses
Andropogon gerardii (big bluestem)	Warm-season grass. Blue-green to silvery foliage; purplish flower spikes. Height: 4–7+ feet. Zone 4.	Clump-forming habit. Will grow in heavy clay soil; tolerates drought.
Bouteloua spp. (grammagrass)	Warm-season grasses. Gray-green, fine-textured foliage; interesting, one-sided flower heads. Height: 1–2 feet. Zone 4.	Clump-forming habit. Withstand mowing. Will grow in heavy clay or sandy soil; withstand drought.
Briza media (quaking grass)	Cool-season grass. Evergreen foliage with attractive seed heads. Height: 1–1½ feet. Zone 4.	Clump-forming habit. Will tolerate a wide range of soils provided it has moisture.
Calamagrostis arundinacea 'Karl Foerster' (Foerster's feather reed grass)	Cool-season grass. Arching foliage with tall, brown to golden flower spikes; evergreen in mild climates. Height: 2–4 feet. Zone 5.	Clump-forming habit. Will grow in heavy clay soil and poorly drained or wet sites.
Carex spp. and cultivars (sedges)	Cool-season growers. Fine-textured, arching foliage in blue, green, silvery, or variegated; many are evergreen. Height: 6 inches–3 feet. Many species hardy to Zone 5.	Clump-forming habit. Will grow in shade, heavy clay soil, and poorly drained or wet sites. *C. morrowii* (Japanese sedge) and *C. sylvatica* (forest sedge) withstand drought.
Chasmanthium latifolium (Northern sea oats)	Warm-season grass. Bamboolike foliage with attractive seed heads. Height: 2–3 feet. Zone 5.	Clump-forming habit. Will grow in shade, sandy soil, and poorly drained or wet sites; withstands drought.
Erianthus ravennae (ravenna grass)	Warm-season grass. Gray-green foliage with silvery flowers. Height: Foliage 4–5 feet; flowers 8–12 feet. Zone 6.	Clump-forming habit. Will grow in poorly drained or wet sites; withstands drought.
Festuca cinerea (blue fescue)	Cool-season grass. (Formerly *F. ovinia* 'Glauca'.) Blue-green foliage; evergreen. Height: 8–18 inches. Most to Zone 4.	Clump-forming habit. Will grow in sandy, well-drained soil; withstands drought.

Name	Description	Special Uses
Glyceria maxima 'Variegata' (variegated manna grass)	Warm-season grass. Foliage striped creamy yellow. Height: 2–3 feet. Zone 5.	Vigorous spreading habit. Will grow in poorly drained or wet sites.
Helictotrichon sempervirens (blue oat grass)	Cool-season grass. Blue-green foliage; evergreen. Height: 12–18 inches. Zone 4.	Clump-forming habit. Will grow in sandy soil; withstands drought.
Juncus spp. (rushes)	Cool-season growers. Semi-evergreen foliage; many have attractive seed heads. Height: 1–4 feet, depending on species. Some to Zone 4.	Clump-forming habit. Will grow in poorly drained or wet sites.
Luzula sylvatica (greater woodrush)	Cool-season grower. Mounds of matlike evergreen foliage. Height: 8–12 inches. Zone 4.	Clump-forming habit. Will grow in shade, heavy clay soil, and poorly drained or wet sites.
Miscanthus sinensis (maiden grass)	Warm-season grass. Dense clumps of arching foliage; attractive seed heads. Height: 5–6 feet. Zone 5.	Clump-forming habit. Will grow in heavy clay soil and poorly drained or wet sites; 'Gracillimus' withstands drought.
Panicum virgatum (switch grass)	Warm-season grass. Green to gray-green foliage; showy seed heads. Height: 4–7 feet. Zone 5.	Clump-forming habit. Will grow in heavy clay soil and poorly drained or wet sites; withstands drought.
Pennisetum alopecuroides (fountain grass)	Warm-season grass. Mounds of arching foliage; showy seed heads. Height: 2–3 feet. Zone 6.	Clump-forming habit. Will grow in heavy clay soil; withstands drought.
Phalaris arundinacea var. *picta* (white-striped ribbon grass)	Warm-season grass. Foliage striped with green and white. Height: 2–3 feet. Zone 4.	Spreading habit. Will grow in heavy clay soil and poorly drained or wet sites; withstands drought.
Schizachyrium scoparium (little bluestem)	Warm-season grass. Light green foliage topped by fluffy seed heads. Height: 2–3 feet. Zone 3	Clump-forming habit. Will grow in sandy soil; withstands drought. 'Blaze' has especially vibrant fall color.
Sorghastrum nutans (Indian grass)	Warm-season grass. Medium green foliage with attractive seed heads. Height: 2–3 feet. Zone 4.	Clump-forming habit. Will grow in heavy clay or sandy soil and poorly drained or wet sites.
Spartina pectinata 'Aureomarginata' (golden-edged prairie cord grass)	Warm-season grass. Green foliage edged in yellow. Height: 3–6 feet. Zone 4.	Spreading habit; can be invasive in moist soil. Will grow in heavy clay soil and poorly drained or wet sites.
Sporobolus heterolepis (prairie dropseed)	Warm-season grass. Fine-textured foliage; attractive seed heads. Height: 2–3 feet. Zone 3.	Clump-forming habit. Will grow in sandy soil; withstands drought.

Bamboos Are Low-Maintenance Grasses, Too

Bamboos are among the most versatile, beautiful, and low-maintenance plants in the grass family. They are pest- and disease-free, too. Their only drawback—one that can be used to advantage in some situations—is that many of them are aggressive spreaders. Keep them in bounds by planting them inside an underground barrier, as shown on page 320. Or select a site with natural barriers. For example, use bamboo as an erosion-controlling groundcover on a slope between a pond and a lawn, or between a lawn and a road. Mowing will control bamboo shoots on the lawn side. Another simple solution is to plant bamboo as a specimen in your lawn and just contain it by mowing around it. But watch out if there is an unmowed zone beyond the lawn; bamboo stolons can travel 20 to 30 feet.

Following is a list of recommended spreading bamboos.

Black bamboo (*Phyllostachys nigra*): 25 feet tall; Zone 6, Zone 5 in sheltered location.

Dwarf green-stripe bamboo (*Pleioblastus viridi-striatus*): 2 feet tall; Zone 5.

Dwarf white-stripe bamboo (*Pleioblastus variegatus*): 1–2 feet tall; Zone 5.

Kuma bamboo (*Sasa veitchii*): Plant in shade; 3 feet tall; Zone 5.

Pygmy bamboo (*Arundinaria pygmaea*): Excellent low groundcover; Zone 5.

Yellow-groove bamboo (*Phyllostachys aureosulcata*): 25 feet tall; Zone 5.

Or choose a nonspreading bamboo, especially cultivars of the clump-forming fargesias (*Fargesia* spp.), which are evergreen and hardy to Zone 5.

Grow a Grass Windbreak

For quick shelter on the windy side of a perennial planting, ornamental grasses are an easy answer. A row of clump-forming grasses like maiden grass (*Miscanthus sinensis*) behind a perennial planting will shield your perennials from wind and look great, too.

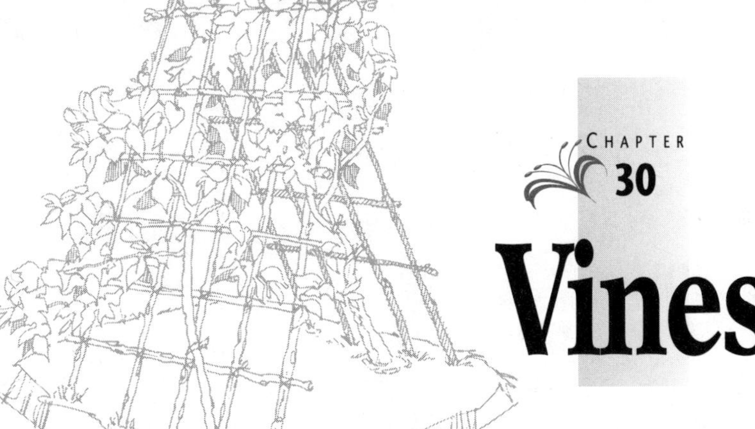

CHAPTER 30

Vines

Ask What Vines Can Do for You

Plant Vines to Hide Eyesores Fast

Vines Thrive When the Site Is Right

20 Versatile Vines

Quick and Painless Pruning for Vines

Give New Vines a Quick Trim

Restyle an Old Vine

Pruning Mature Vines

Easy Ways to Help Your Vines Climb

Grow Your Own Awning

Create a Quick Wildlife Garden

Vines the Low-Maintenance Way

If you'd like to spruce up your landscape in a hurry, try planting vines. Whether you want an easy-to-erect privacy screen, a simple way to hide a landscape eyesore, or just a quick burst of color, vines offer easy solutions to a host of landscaping challenges. Not only are they easy to grow, but their vigorous spreading nature also means they'll provide spectacular effects with little help from you. All they need is the right site and something to climb up, cling to, or scramble over. For an especially effective display—without any extra work—plant vines that offer colorful flowers, fruits, or bright leaves for autumn interest.

This chapter will help you choose easy-care, pest-free vines. You'll also learn easy ways to help them climb and thrive. Worried about having to build elaborate support structures for vines? Stop worrying! You'll find ideas for easy trellises, too.

Ask What Vines Can Do for You

Have you been struggling with landscape bugaboos like an unmowable lawn area, a garden the size of a postage stamp, or spots that are plagued with too much sun or shade? Forget about costly landscape renovations; let vines solve site and exposure problems for you.

Add height to small gardens. Vines are a great way to add height in gardens large or small. They can also provide an alternative to expensive, slow-growing trees. They're great for providing an evergreen backdrop without adding too much shade. And their interesting leaf shadows and colorful blooms can add a whole new care-free dimension to small gardens. They can scale trellises, walls, or the trunks of existing trees to draw the eye up. Or let them drape over entryways and porches to create a sense of mystery.

Light up shady areas. To brighten a dark spot without trimming all your trees back, try vines with variegated foliage. Look for English ivy and wintercreeper with gold or white borders or streaks. Hardy kiwi (*Actinidia kolomikta*) has white and pink flushed leaves; variegated Japanese honeysuckle (*Lonicera Japonica* 'Aureo-reticulata') has leaves marked with yellow. For best color, provide a spot with partial sun. Depend on the flowers of climbing hydrangea to brighten up very shady areas.

Replace lawn grass. If you have an area where grass won't grow or where you just don't want to have to mow, consider using a vine as a groundcover. English ivy works well in such a situation, as does wintercreeper and climbing hydrangea.

Shade a porch, pergola, or summerhouse. What if you need cool shade and privacy *fast* during the lazy days of summer, but you want sunshine for warmth in winter? No problem! Choose a vine that loses its leaves in winter, such as Dutchman's-pipe, hardy kiwi, or grapes. Or, choose an annual vine that will die back with the first hard frost, such as one of the morning glories.

Plant Vines to Hide Eyesores Fast

Is there an object in your landscape that you'd like to have disappear in a hurry? Vigorous vines can work magic when it comes to screening ugly architectural or landscape features quickly and painlessly. So to put your eyesore out of sight and out of mind, choose the vine vanishing act you like best.

Cover a chain-link fence. If your backyard is surrounded by a bare chain-link fence, why not dress it up with vines? Perennial vines, like trumpet honeysuckle, will hide it from view but may take a while to get established. As a "quick

Vines Thrive When the Site Is Right

Do a little site research before you plant if you want to grow vines that will make your landscape look marvelous. For the best results with the least work, choose vines that are adapted to the site and soil conditions in your garden. That way, your vines will have the conditions they need to thrive, and you won't spend any extra time improving or changing the site. Use the questions below to help you evalutate your site and narrow your hunt for the perfect vine. Turn to "20 Versatile Vines" on page 330 for more on the vines mentioned below.

What's your light like? The amount of light a site receives helps dictate which vines will grow best there. Morning glories and black-eyed Susan vines need a site with full sun, while silver lace vine requires only a half-day of sun. Boston ivy, grapes, trumpet vine, and Dutchman's-pipe are equally happy in sun or shade. (Flowering types will bloom less in shade, though.) And English ivy and climbing hydrangea prefer shady spots. You'll find directions on evaluating the amount of sun and shade that falls on your property on page 215.

How does your soil stack up? Before you decide what vines to plant, find out if the soil on your site is rich or poor. Then select a vine that will thrive in the soil you have. That way, you won't have to fertilize and amend your soil to match the needs of a particular vine. Vines such as five-leaf akebia, porcelain vine, and grapes need fertile soil and will languish in poor sites. Others, such as hardy kiwi, grow too vigorously in rich soil and are best grown in infertile soil. Trumpet vine, English ivy, Boston ivy, and wintercreeper are not so particular and wilI take almost any soil type. See "Find Out What Your Soil Needs Most" on page 15 for instructions on evaluating your soil.

Does your dirt drain? Drainage is another soil characteristic to consider. Wisteria and some hybrid clematis must have good drainage to perform well; five-leaf akebia and hardy kiwi are more tolerant. See "Test Soil Drainage" on page 15 for a simple test you can use to evaluate drainage.

Where's your water? Most vines are drought-tolerant, but you may need to think about the moisture needs of a vine before choosing it for your site. For example, grapes need enough moisture during their growing season to form plump fruits. Clematis also needs large amounts of water. Use these vines if you have a moist, well-drained site, or make sure you have easy access to a water supply in case of drought.

fix," plant fast-growing annual vines, such as hyacinth beans or morning glories, to add cover the first year.

Hide a hideous air conditioner. You can make an ugly air conditioner disappear with a screen of trelliswork and a mix of evergreen and annual vines. (Be sure to keep the trellis and vines 1 foot away from top discharge models; 6 feet away from side discharge ones.) The annuals will give you an almost instant screen and even some colorful flowers; the evergreens will give long-lasting cover.

Make a tree stump—or tree—disappear. Instead of paying to have a dead tree or tree stump removed, just make it disappear with vines. Hiding a tree stump is easy—just plant an evergreen trailing vine such as English ivy or wintercreeper around it. Within no time the stump will be history. To turn a dead tree into an attractive addition to the landscape, use it as a support for trumpet honeysuckle or wisteria.

20 Versatile Vines

To find the perfect easy-to-grow vine for your site, look through the list below. For easy matchmaking, you'll find a description of each vine's features, size, and hardiness, as well as details on the best sites to grow it. All of the vines are deciduous unless indicated otherwise.

Name	Description	Comments
Actinidia kolomikta (hardy kiwi)	Twining perennial. Attractive foliage blushed with white and pink. White or green blooms in summer. Size: 20 feet. Zone 4.	Full sun or part shade; poor to average soil. Works well on trellises, arbors, and climbing trees. *A. arguta* bears edible fruit.
Akebia quinata (five-leaf akebia)	Twining perennial. Semi-evergreen foliage. Fragrant, purplish flowers. Fruits are purple and sausagelike. Size: 30 feet. Zone 4.	Sun or light shade; average, well-drained soil; dry or moist conditions. Gives quick coverage; provides lacy coverage on fences and latticework.
Ampelopsis brevipedunculata (porcelain vine)	Perennial climbing by tendrils. Lacy, dark green foliage. Tiny white blooms. Fall berries turn lilac, green, blue, then black. Size: 25 feet or more. Zone 4.	Sun or light shade; average, well-drained soil. Evergreen in the South; deciduous in colder climes. Excellent for covering a wall or pergola.
Aristolochia durior (Dutchman's-pipe)	Twining perennial. Large, coarse leaves. Unusual pipe-shaped blooms. Size: 30 feet. Zone 4.	Sun or part shade; prefers rich, moist soil. Fast-growing; makes a good porch-screening vine and works well on trellises.
Campsis radicans (trumpet vine)	Clinging perennial. Medium green leaves. Trumpet-shaped orange blossoms. Size: 30–40 feet. Zone 4.	Sun; any soil; pollution-tolerant. Needs no aid to climb; a nice addition to fences or arbors. A favorite of hummingbirds.
Celastrus scandens (American bittersweet)	Twining perennial. Light green leaves; greenish to yellowish flowers. Grown for its scarlet seeds and colorful autumn foliage. Size: 20 feet. Zone 2.	Sun or light shade; poor or rocky ground. Does well on walls, banks. Plant male and female plants to ensure fruit; use stems of dried fruit for arrangements.
Clematis spp. (clematis)	Twining perennials. Attractive leaves. Pink, blue, purple, white, or yellow blooms. Size: 5–30 feet, depending on species. Hardiness depends on species; some hardy to Zone 4.	Fertile, moist, well-drained soil; mulch to keep roots cool. Some hybrids are difficult to grow. Many species, including sweet autumn clematis (*C. maximowicziana*), and virgin's bower (*C. virginiana*) are easy to grow. Use on fences, arbors, mailboxes, and trees.
Dolichos lablab (hyacinth bean)	Twining annual. Leaves in threes. Pretty purple pealike flowers and edible pods in summer. Size: 15 feet or more.	Sun and warm conditions; thrives in Zone 7 or further south; start indoors further north; average soil. Provides a delightful tracery on a trellis or lattice; resembles runner bean.
Euonymus fortunei (wintercreeper)	Clinging perennial. Glossy evergreen leaves. Small whitish flowers. Deep orange-red fall berries. Size: 40 feet or more. Zone 5.	Sun or shade; any soil except wet. 'Variegatus' has particularly attractive white-bordered leaves. Use on walls.

Name	Description	Comments
Gelsemium sempervirens (Carolina jessamine)	Twining perennial. Glossy evergreen foliage. Clusters of bright yellow, trumpet-shaped blooms in spring. Size: 10–20 feet. Zone 7.	Sun or light shade; prefers rich, moist, well-drained soil but will tolerate average soil. Great for trellises, fences, and mailboxes.
Hedera helix (English ivy)	Clinging perennial. Glossy evergreen foliage. Clusters of tiny greenish flowers. Size: 100 feet. Zone 5.	Light to heavy shade; rich, moist, well-drained soil. Climbs surfaces like stone walls and brick buildings without support.
Hydrangea anomala subsp. *petiolaris* (climbing hydrangea)	Clinging perennial. Shiny, deep green foliage. Showy, lacy, whitish flower heads. Attractive cinnamon-colored bark. Size: 75 feet. Zone 4.	Sun or shade; rich, moist, well-drained soil. Clings by small rootlike holdfasts; needs no support. Great for buildings and walls and to train up trees.
Ipomoea spp. (morning glories)	Twining perennials grown as annuals; perennials in Zones 8–9. Species vary widely; all bear trumpet-shaped blue, purple, pink, red, or white blossoms. Size: 8–20 feet, depending on species.	Sun; any well-drained soil. Start from seed in early spring; give quick coverage; interplant with perennial foliage vines.
Lonicera sempervirens (trumpet honeysuckle)	Twining perennial. Native vine; shiny, semi-evergreen foliage; scarlet blossoms. Size: 20–50 feet. Zone 4.	Sun or shade; average, moist, well-drained soil. Blossoms loved by hummingbirds; is beautiful on mailboxes, fences, trellises.
Parthenocissus quinquefolia (Virginia creeper)	Climbing perennial. Broad, deciduous leaves cut into five leaflets; gorgeous reddish-purple fall coloration; tiny bluish-black fruit. Size: 60 feet. Zone 3.	Sun or shade; any type of soil; tolerates wind and pollution. Needs a rough surface on which to climb; good for climbing trees or covering walls.
Parthenocissus tricuspidata (Boston ivy)	Clinging perennial. Glossy foliage turns brilliant scarlet in fall; blue-black fruit. Size: 50 feet. Zone 4.	Sun or shade; any soil type; prefers moist but tolerates dry sites. Excellent for urban buildings; pollution-tolerant; attaches itself to stone and brick with no support.
Polygonum aubertii (silver lace vine)	Twining perennial. Long, lance-shaped leaves; clouds of tiny white blossoms in late summer. Size: 20–30 feet. Zone 4.	Sun or shade; poor to average soil; tolerates dry conditions. Valued for its fast growth; good cover for fences and arbors.
Thunbergia alata (black-eyed Susan vine)	Twining perennial grown as annual. Triangular leaves; summer blooms in orange-yellow, white, or cream with dark purple throats. Size: 6–10 feet.	Sun; average soil. Popular in hanging baskets and on low trellises. Direct-seed in place when weather warms.
Vitis spp. (grapes)	Twining perennials. All produce fruit in fall; some delicious, others inedible. Size: to 90 feet, depending on species. Zones 4–8, depending on species.	Sun or light shade; average, well-drained soil (but will tolerate poorer soil). Offers welcome summer shade for porches and grows well on arbors and pergolas.
Wisteria floribunda (Japanese wisteria)	Twining perennial. Dark green foliage with many leaflets. Fragrant lavender blooms in spring. Size: 30 feet or more. Zone 4.	Sun; average, well-drained soil. Good for use on pergolas and summer houses; needs a strong support structure and help climbing.

Quick and Painless Pruning for Vines

Don't let the thought of pruning strike fear into your heart; perennial vines only *look* hard to prune. In fact, it only takes a few cuts once a year to maintain their shape, curb excess growth, and remove damaged or unhealthy shoots. One rule to remember when you're giving your vines their annual trim is to always cut back to a bud, a lateral branch, or the main trunk. Be careful not to leave stubs—they may die back and cause decay in the healthy branch.

Prune When the Time Is Right

For most flowering vines, the right time to trim is when you have the time. Unless you're doing drastic pruning, which is best done when plants are dormant, you can shape your plants in any season.

If time isn't a concern and you want the most flowers you can possibly get, arrange your pruning schedule to suit your vines. Prune all early spring flowering vines—including wisteria, Carolina jessamine, clematis, and trumpet honeysuckle—just after they finish blooming. If you prune before they bloom in early spring, you'll snip off flowers along with the branches.

Vines that flower in late spring to summer bloom on the current year's growth, so prune them in the spring. This early pruning will encourage new growth, which leads to more flowers. Examples are American bittersweet and silver lace vine.

Grapevines need yearly pruning in mid- to late winter before the sap rises. Merely cut each shoot of last year's growth back to one or two buds.

Give New Vines a Quick Trim

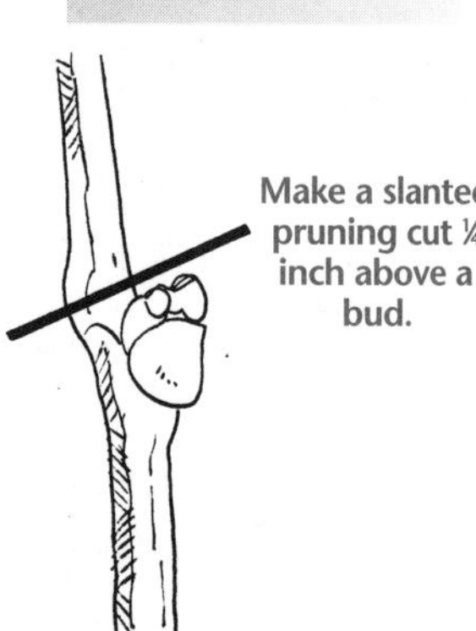

Make a slanted pruning cut ¼ inch above a bud.

To get newly planted woody vines off to a good start, give them a haircut at planting time. Start by cutting the topgrowth back by half. This gives the roots a chance to develop sufficiently to support the topgrowth. When you prune, always make a slanted cut just above a bud, as shown at left. Trimming topgrowth stimulates side branches to grow more vigorously, so you'll get a sturdier framework to support future growth.

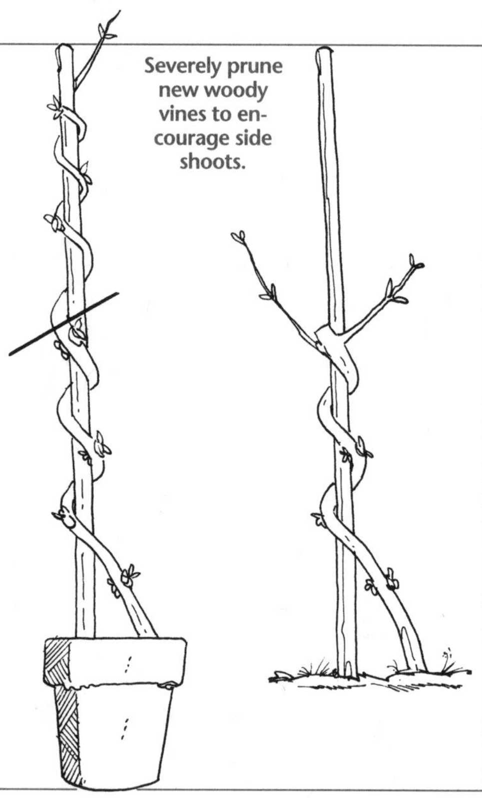

Severely prune new woody vines to encourage side shoots.

Restyle an Old Vine

It takes drastic action to rejuvenate and reshape an old or neglected vine, but it doesn't have to take lots of effort. Simply spread the process out over three or more years.

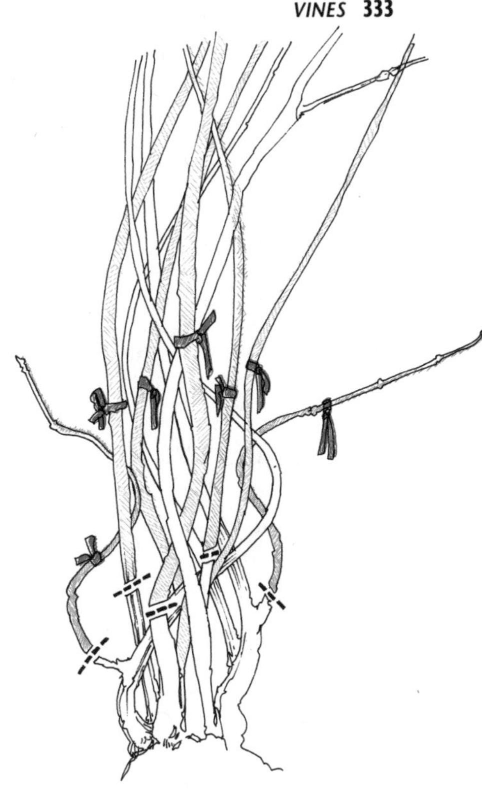

Year one. Don't do *any* pruning in the first year. Instead, observe your vine carefully during the growing season and decide which parts should go. Remove dead, diseased, and overgrown branches. To make pruning easy, tie colored tape or string around branches you plan to remove. These markers make it easy to find unwanted branches when pruning season arrives.

Year two. Start the pruning portion of your renovation when the plant is dormant, in late winter or early spring. That way, it's easy to see what you're doing because there aren't any leaves—at least on deciduous vines. It's also easier on the vine since it isn't growing actively. Thin out a few of the oldest, toughest stems first by cutting them back to 6 to 12 inches above the ground. New shoots will sprout in spring; when they reach 6 to 12 inches long, prune the tips to encourage branching.

Year three. Prune again the following late winter or early spring. Remove a few more of the remaining unruly stems as you did in year two. You can continue renovation pruning into a fourth year or until you bring the vine back to the size and shape you want.

Pruning Mature Vines

You can do light pruning to shape a mature vine whenever you have the time. Snip back the straggly shoots that give your plant a messy look, and thin out any dead, broken, or diseased wood. If your vine needs lots of pruning, wait until it's dormant before tackling the task.

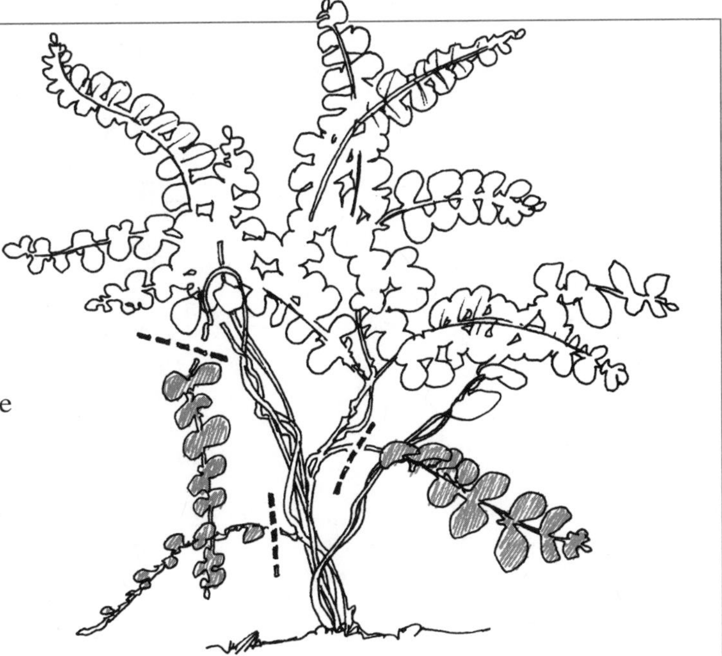

Easy Ways to Help Your Vines Climb

Before you invest time and money constructing elaborate trellises and arbors, look around your yard. Plants already growing in your yard can make perfect vine supports. You can also use inexpensive pipes—either metal or PVC—along with a variety of found materials to make great-looking, easy-to-build trellises.

Pick your favorite "trellis" pictured here, or use your imagination and combine them to make use of materials you have on hand. For example, interlace a framework of pipe with saplings, or rope it together with twine or vines. (You may need to tuck the vines in and out a bit as they grow to get the desired effect.)

▶ **Train up a tree.** Let's face it, there are ways to support vines that are as easy as pie. Just look around when you drive in the country and you'll see vines scrambling happily up tree trunks all over the place. Why not give it a try at home? Just plant a climber at the base of a favorite tree, give it some strings or a temporary trellis to help it get up to the lowest branches, and sit back and watch it go. Some good examples would be clematis trained up a fruit tree, or climbing hydrangea in an oak. Or let lightweight trailing vines, such as black-eyed Susan vine or clematis, drape themselves over shrubs in your garden or meander their way among your perennials.

Stick with annual vines or well-mannered perennials if you try this technique. Evergreen vines, like English ivy, and extremely vigorous growers, like trumpet vine, can smother plants they cover.

▲ **Make a sapling tent.** You'll need about 20 saplings, bamboo poles, or extra-long tomato stakes. Lash pairs together at the top. Add a "ridge pole" on top and lash it in place. Then tie crosspieces in place down the sides, parallel to the ridge pole, to add stability and help the vines climb. Have someone help you stand the tent up, then spread the legs, push them into the soil, and plant your vines at the base.

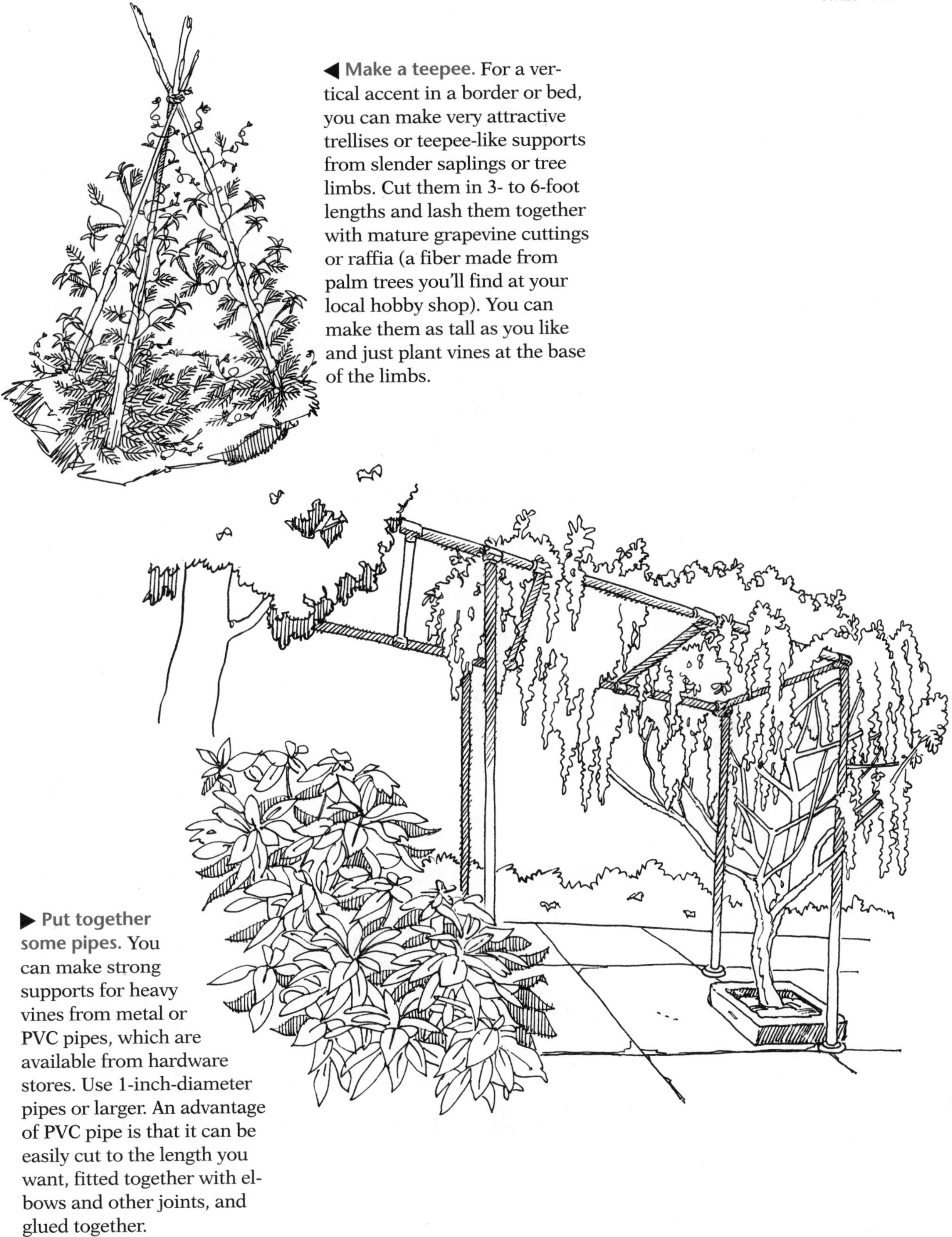

◀ **Make a teepee.** For a vertical accent in a border or bed, you can make very attractive trellises or teepee-like supports from slender saplings or tree limbs. Cut them in 3- to 6-foot lengths and lash them together with mature grapevine cuttings or raffia (a fiber made from palm trees you'll find at your local hobby shop). You can make them as tall as you like and just plant vines at the base of the limbs.

▶ **Put together some pipes.** You can make strong supports for heavy vines from metal or PVC pipes, which are available from hardware stores. Use 1-inch-diameter pipes or larger. An advantage of PVC pipe is that it can be easily cut to the length you want, fitted together with elbows and other joints, and glued together.

(continued)

◀ **String up an annual.** Slender twining annual vines, such as morning-glories and black-eyed Susan vines (*Thunbergia alata*), can be trained on sturdy twine as their sole support. Or give them some twine so they can work their way up to an awning or a piece of latticework. Just put a stake in the ground and attach the twine to it, then attach the other end of the twine to the farthest point you want the vine to reach.

▶ **Adapt a trellis.** When you want to cover a specific eyesore like a downspout, a standard flat trellis may not do the job. To make it hide more than one side, simply take two strips of cedar trellis as long as the downspout is high, nail them together at right angles, then butt them against the wall to which the downspout is attached. This way, you can cover a downspout with a vine without actually having it climb directly on it.

Grow Your Own Awning

You can easily turn your hot, sunny porch into a cool retreat. All you need is a vigorous vine. Salvage an old awning frame, as shown, or attach a metal bar to your porch. Cover the framework with chicken wire and train a Boston ivy (*Parthenocissus tricuspidata*) or Dutchman's-pipe (*Aristolochia durior*) up it to create a beautiful, shady nook. Or use a silver lace vine (*Polygonum aubertii*) and watch your framework vanish in a froth of foliage and blossoms.

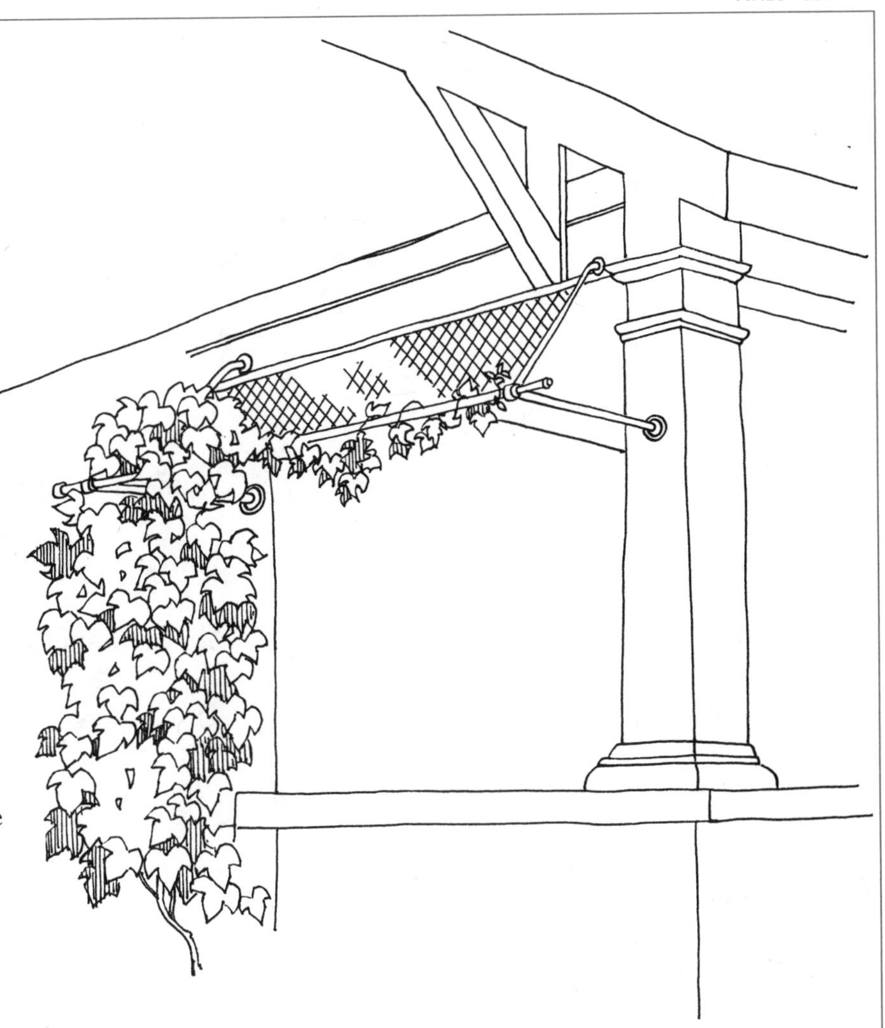

Create a Quick Wildlife Garden

Vines make a perfect centerpiece for a garden designed to attract birds, butterflies, and other wildlife. Hummingbirds are drawn to colorful blooming vines with tubular flowers. They're especially fond of the color red, so they adore cypress vine (*Ipomoea quamoclit*) and trumpet honeysuckle (*Lonicera sempervirens*). They also favor orange trumpet vine (*Campsis radicans*).

For attracting butterflies, try planting cypress vine, sweet peas (*Lathyrus latifolius*), wisteria, or Japanese honeysuckle (*Lonicera japonica*). Plant wild passionflower (*Passiflora incarnata*), too, since it's a food plant for the caterpillar of the gulf fritillary. You'll see quite a show as the adult butterfly lays its eggs and caterpillars hatch out. You can expect some munched leaves, but it's a small price to pay for a front row seat at a butterfly drama.

Chapter 31

Trees and Shrubs

Trees and Shrubs the Low-Maintenance Way

Few landscape options require as little maintenance as a planting of well-chosen and carefully planted trees and shrubs. But before you rush to fill your yard with trees and shrubs, note those important qualifiers: *Well-chosen and carefully planted.*

In this chapter, you'll learn how to choose healthy trees and shrubs that will thrive in your landscape. Since trees and shrubs are a long-term investment that can either be carefree or add loads of maintenance nightmares, it pays to do a little research, ask questions, and choose carefully. You'll also learn how to plant and care for your trees and shrubs properly.

10 Tips for Easy Trees and Shrubs

1. Choose disease- and pest-resistant species and cultivars. Check with nursery owners and your county's extension office to find out which plants are best for your area.

2. Choose plants adapted to your site's soil, exposure, and other conditions. A tree that is stressed by factors such as drought, poor soil, or not being adapted to the site you've selected is more susceptible to pests and diseases that otherwise might not trouble it.

3. Choose plants whose mature size and form fit your spot. A tree whose size and shape are suited to your spot won't need pruning. A large tree in a small space will overwhelm the landscape and pose expensive problems such as limbs overhanging your roof or blocking windows.

4. Buy from reputable nurseries. Plants from grocery and hardware store lots are usually inferior and poorly cared for.

5. Give your plants room to grow. Space them far enough apart to allow them to reach full size without crowding.

6. Choose drip irrigation where watering is required.

7. Choose trees with small or winter-persistent leaves to minimize fall raking chores.

8. Make mowing easier by consolidating trees and shrubs in islands or borders rather than dotting your yard.

9. Underplant trees and shrubs with groundcovers or shade-tolerant perennials to minimize mulching chores.

10. Mulch around trees without underplantings to prevent weeds and mowing hassles.

Smart Shopping: Look Out for Losers

Healthy, vigorous trees that resist pests and shrug off diseases are a joy in any landscape. Unfortunately, when you shop, it pays to remember that the most widely available trees aren't always best to plant. Trees that originally had few problems can develop them if they are too widely planted because pests or diseases move in to take advantage of the dense populations.

To avoid a problem, stay away from the "losers" listed here. Although some have appropriate uses, their troubles largely outweigh their benefits.

American mountain ash (*Sorbus americana*)

Cockspur hawthorn (*Crataegus crus-galli*)

English oak (*Quercus robur*)

European mountain ash (*Sorbus aucuparia*)

European white birch (*Betula pendula*)

Flowering crabapple (*Malus* cultivars). Disease-resistant crabapples are available, but disease-prone cultivars are sold.

Lombardy poplar (*Populus nigra* 'Italica')

Purple plums (*Prunus cerasifera* cultivars)

Russian olive (*Eleagnus angustifolia*)

Siberian elm (*Ulmus pumila*)

Silver maple (*Acer saccharinum*)

Thornless honey locust (*Gleditsia triacanthos* var. *inermis*)

White ash (*Fraxinus americana*)

White poplar (*Populus alba*)

Save Work with Wise Buys

Woody plants are the durable goods of your landscape. Each one represents a long-term investment that helps determine how attractive and how easy to maintain your property is. With a healthy start and a small, but consistent, amount of care, the trees and shrubs you plant in your yard will become an enduring source of shade, shelter, and beauty.

Because trees and shrubs are such long-term investments, it makes sense to shop carefully when you choose them. Taking time to make smart selections not only ensures that you're satisfied with the plants you've chosen, it also helps reduce the amount of care you'll need to provide over their long lives.

Start with the Seller

Your low-maintenance tree or shrub begins its life in a nursery. Make sure the nursery you buy from, whether mail-order or local, has a reputation for quality plants and intelligent service.

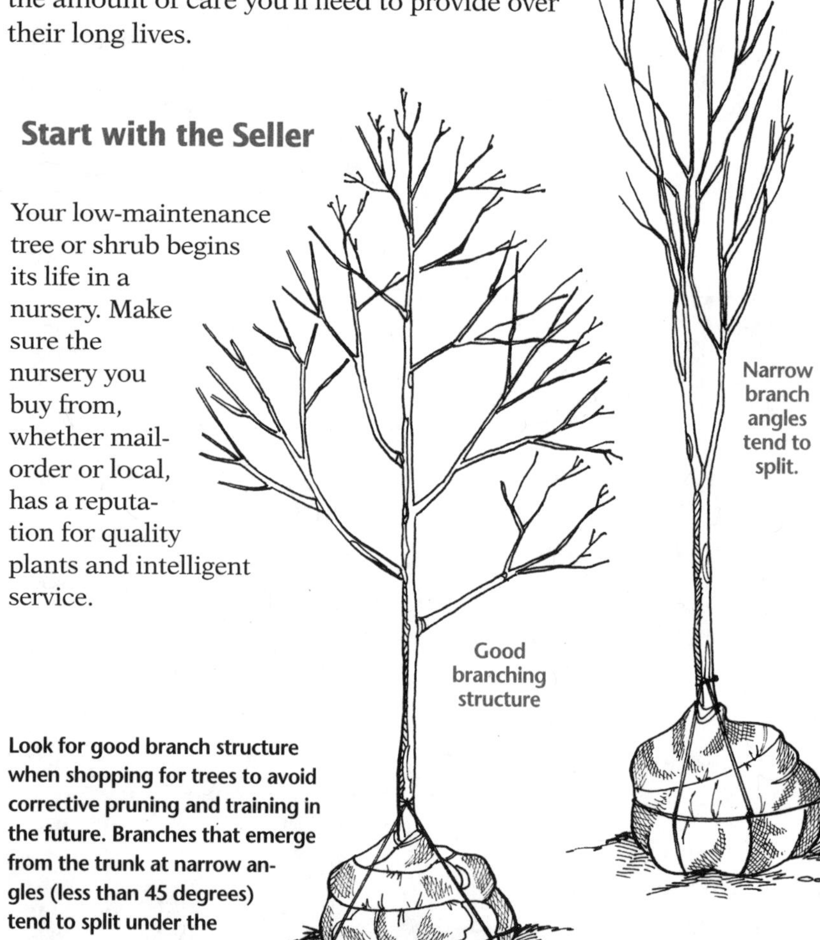

Look for good branch structure when shopping for trees to avoid corrective pruning and training in the future. Branches that emerge from the trunk at narrow angles (less than 45 degrees) tend to split under the weight of snow and ice.

Figure out just what and how many plants you need before you buy. This clear idea is your best protection against impulse buying. Before you shop, call around to find which nurseries have the plants you're looking for, what size they are, how they've been grown, and how much they cost.

Inspect and Detect

At the nursery, inspect each prospective purchase thoroughly. Here's what to look for.

• Examine leaves, stems, and bark for signs of disease or insects.

• Choose plants with foliage that's turgid and green, not drooping or yellowed.

• Inspect the roots, too. If the plant is in a container, tip it out carefully or ask nursery personnel to do this for you. No soil should fall away from the root ball, and a vigorous mass of roots should be visible at the soil surfaces that were covered by the pot.

• Check the moisture of the growth medium. An extremely dry root ball may mean that the plant has been poorly cared for and unnecessarily stressed.

• Finally, make sure the individual plant you've chosen has good form. A misshapen plant will at least require more pruning and shaping, and at worst may never outgrow its homeliness.

Make Sure Roots Measure Up

Balled-and-burlapped (B&B) trees and shrubs are field grown, usually dug while dormant, and their root balls wrapped with burlap. The biggest hazard of buying a B&B tree is that it may have an undersize root ball. The rule of thumb is that the root ball should be 1 foot in diameter for every inch of the trunk's diameter at its base. There is no comparable rule for shrubs, but the bigger the ball, the faster the plant will establish. Undersize root balls are a bigger hazard for trees, whose roots extend far beyond their driplines. The average B&B tree retains only 5 percent of its original root mass.

Look for Signs of Life

If a B&B plant is dormant, scratch its bark in a few places to make sure that it is alive throughout. Live bark scratches easily to reveal green tissue beneath. Ask nursery personnel to pull back the burlap to let you check for root girdling, a condition in which a plant's own circling roots can choke it to death. Inspect the root ball for signs of cracking, and touch the soil to see that it's moist. Don't buy a plant with a cracked or crumbled root ball.

If the root ball is wrapped in rotproof burlap, ask if the nursery will remove it and rewrap the ball in untreated burlap. This will allow you to plant without removing the wrapping.

Stay Away from Stranglers

Girdling roots can cause your trees and shrubs to mysteriously decline and die. Check new tree and shrub purchases for signs of circling roots. As a plant grows, such roots can tighten around its stem, gradually cutting off its supply of water and nutrients.

Girdling roots can cut off the food supply to trees.

Avoid plants that have filled pots with circling roots.

Trees (and Shrubs) to Go: Have Them Your Way

You can buy woody plants in the following three forms: bareroot, containerized, or balled-and-burlapped (B&B). Each option offers advantages and disadvantages in terms of its effect on planting and aftercare. Use this table to help you choose how you'd like to purchase your plants and to guide you in caring for any plants you buy, no matter how they arrive.

Form	Advantages	Disadvantages
Bareroot	Least expensive; cheapest to ship via mail order.	Need immediate planting or heeling in; may arrive with insufficient root mass to allow growth; careful packing and shipping required to ensure plants don't dry out; for spring or fall planting only.
Containerized	Established root mass; easy to maintain if you can't plant right away; can plant any time during growing season if aftercare is adequate; less expensive than same size plant balled-and-burlapped.	Some plants slow to root out into soil; soilless mix around roots resists watering even after planting; more expensive than bareroot.
Balled-and-burlapped (B&B)	Usually heartier than comparably sized containerized plants; already hardened to outdoor conditions; permits planting of larger plants; usually establish more quickly.	Heavy and more difficult to transport and handle; most expensive; if wrapped in rotproof burlap (usually dyed green), must be unwrapped; large size of plant in relation to rootball may necessitate staking.

Make Your Trees Work Harder: Look for 4-Season Appeal

Real landscape workhorses don't just sit there and grow, they also add visual appeal—with flowers, fruits, fall color, form, and/or attractive bark. Their blossoms or unusual foliage may allow you to spend less time tending annuals or perennials as sources of color. Their fruits may lure birds or other wildlife to brighten your yard and entertain your family.

Paint a cheery tableau outside a window with a combination of evergreen and fruit-laden shrubs. Shrubs with persistent fruits add color and attract birds to the winter landscape. An added bonus: Many make great cutting materials for holiday wreaths and arrangements.

Hedge Your Bets against High Hedge Maintenance

Lowering the amount of maintenance your landscape needs doesn't mean giving up on hedges. It simply requires you to give up on the notion that a hedge must be closely clipped and geometrical—pruned to within an inch of its life—to keep it under control and tidy. In addition to the huge amount of maintenance they require, clipped, formal hedges all too often end up top-heavy, their shaded lower foliage dropping off to reveal the unsightly, knobby knees beneath.

Instead of slipping into this time-worn, high-maintenance groove, give yourself an attitude adjustment and plan on an informal, low-maintenance hedge. The plants listed below make excellent informal hedges; they maintain a natural unshorn shape that is upright to mildly arching with little or no pruning.

For evergreen hedges, consider one of the new hybrid boxwoods—*Buxus* 'Green Gem', 'Green Velvet', or 'Green Mountain', which are all hardy from Zones 5 to 8. Hollies also make fine evergreen hedges. Consider *Ilex glabra* 'Nordic' ('Nordic' inkberry), hardy in Zones 5 to 9, or one of the blue hollies, especially *Ilex* × *meserveae* 'Blue Prince' and 'Blue Princess', hardy in Zones 5 to 8. (Plant one 'Blue Prince' for every several 'Blue Princess' plants to get berries.)

Plants for Deciduous Hedges

'Brilliantissima' red chokeberry (*Aronia arbutifolia* 'Brilliantissima'). Zones 4–9.

Korean barberry (*Berberis koreana*). Zones 3–8.

Mentor barberry (*Berberis* × *mentorensis*). Zones 5–9.

Nanking cherry (*Prunus tomentosa*). Zones 3–5.

Regel privet (*Ligustrum obtusifolium* var. *regelianum*). Zones 4–8.

Rugosa roses (*Rosa rugosa* cultivars). Zones 3–7.

Summersweet (*Clethra alnifolia*). Zones 5–9.

Winter honeysuckle (*Lonicera fragrantissima*). Zones 5–9.

'Winter Red' winterberry (*Ilex verticillata* 'Winter Red'). Zones 4–9.

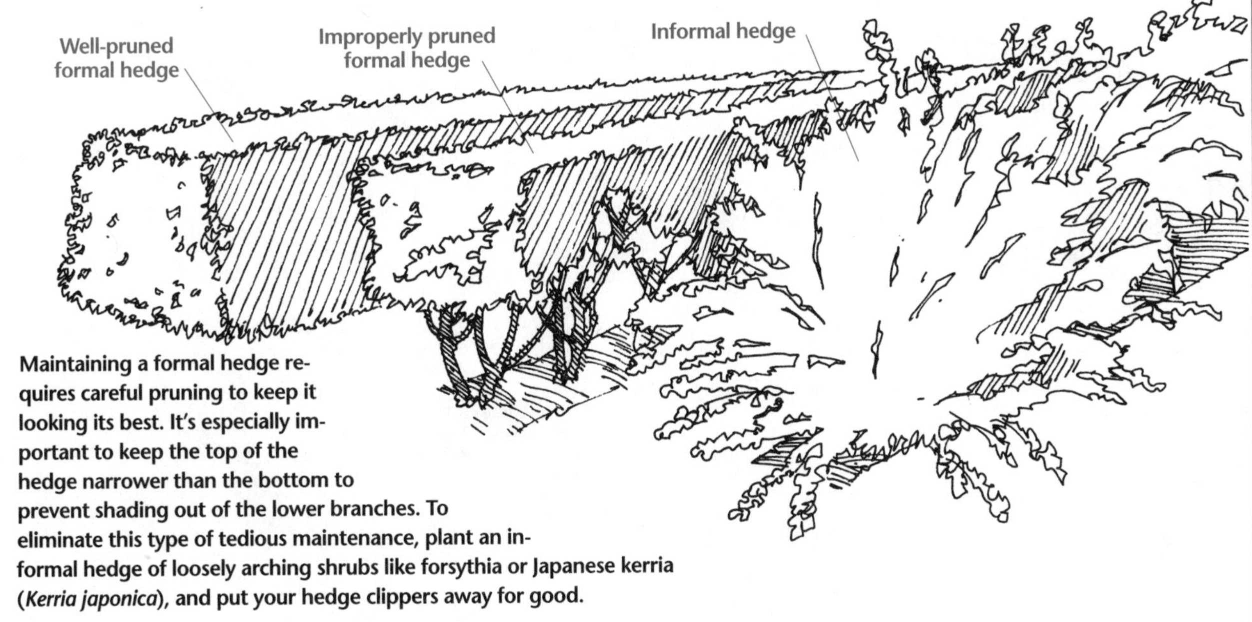

Maintaining a formal hedge requires careful pruning to keep it looking its best. It's especially important to keep the top of the hedge narrower than the bottom to prevent shading out of the lower branches. To eliminate this type of tedious maintenance, plant an informal hedge of loosely arching shrubs like forsythia or Japanese kerria (*Kerria japonica*), and put your hedge clippers away for good.

Keep Maintenance in Mind at Planting Time

You can plant a yard full of easy-care, low-maintenance trees and shrubs and still end up with a maintenance nightmare. That's because the design you choose for your plantings can have a big effect on how much work they'll take to maintain. Keep these design principles in mind when you're deciding where to plant new trees and shrubs.

Plant islands for easy maintenance. Instead of scattering plantings, group trees together into freeform islands in the lawn. Underplant with shade-tolerant shrubs and groundcovers, then mulch for low-maintenance planting you'll enjoy for years to come. Use edging strips to keep lawn grass from overtaking your islands, and mow around them with a single pass of the mower. See page 189 for more on mowing strips.

Eliminate fenceline hassles with mixed plantings. Plantings of trees, shrubs, groundcovers, and easy-care perennials can eliminate tedious weeding and trimming along fences. Just select plants suited to the site, then plant and mulch. If you need to be able to paint your fence occasionally or need access to plantings from the back, leave a 2-foot maintenance path between fence and plantings.

Prudent Planting Pays Off

Planting properly will save you scores of hours of maintenance in the future. It can also save you money replacing plants that perish because they were poorly planted. Follow the suggestions below to get your trees and shrubs off to a great start.

Whether you're planting bareroot, containerized, or balled-and-burlapped (B&B) stock, prepare the planting area before you dig your hole. Remove all unwanted vegetation and turn and loosen the soil. Soil requirements of different trees and shrubs vary widely. Whenever possible, match the plant to your existing soil. If your soil is inadequate for the plant you've chosen, incorporate soil amendments over the entire planting area, not just in the planting hole. When planting a single shrub, renovate an area at least 3 feet in diameter. For a tree, renovate an area at least 5 feet in diameter.

Planting Bareroot Stock

Mail-order trees and shrubs are usually shipped bareroot in spring. Here's how to plant them.

Inspect your plants as soon as they arrive. Bareroot plants should be carefully packed in moist materials, and their bark should show no signs of shriveling. The roots should look husky and healthy. If the root mass looks extremely small for the size of the plant, contact the nursery immediately and register your dissatisfaction.

Take care before planting. After unpacking them, soak your plants in a bucket of water or weak compost tea for 12 to 24 hours. If you can't plant immediately, bury them almost completely in a shady spot for no more than a week (a process called "heeling in"). Trim all broken or damaged roots, and prune back the top by one-third to one-half before you plant. Never allow the roots to dry out, even for a few minutes.

Plant well. Spread the roots of bareroot plants over a mound of soil in the bottom of the planting hole. Look for a soil line on the stem and use it as a planting depth guide, as shown. Backfill carefully with unamended soil, making sure that finely crumbled soil is in contact with the roots. Pat the soil down firmly around the roots, form a basin around the plant, and water several times after planting, plunging the hose end underground to fill air pockets. Apply a 2-inch layer of mulch around the plant to conserve water and control weeds.

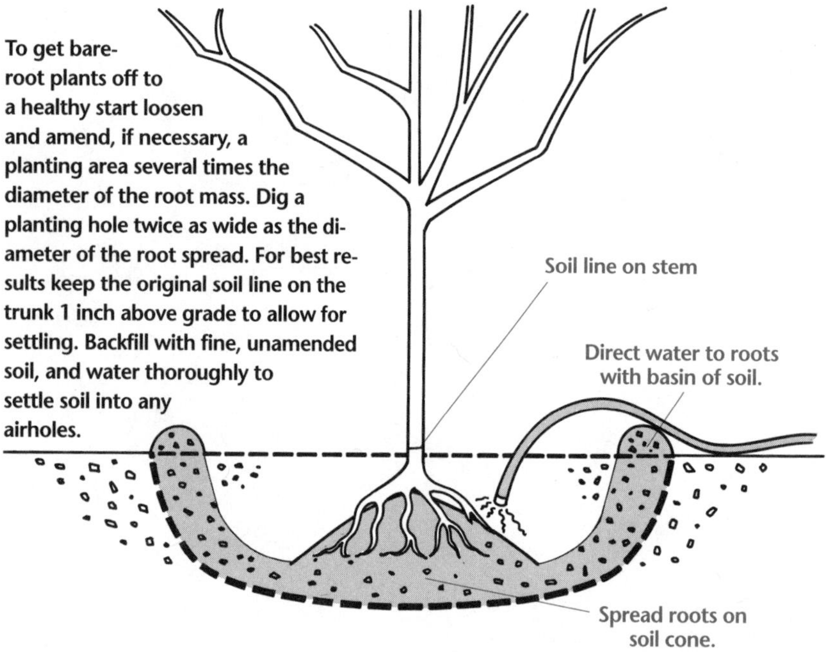

To get bareroot plants off to a healthy start loosen and amend, if necessary, a planting area several times the diameter of the root mass. Dig a planting hole twice as wide as the diameter of the root spread. For best results keep the original soil line on the trunk 1 inch above grade to allow for settling. Backfill with fine, unamended soil, and water thoroughly to settle soil into any airholes.

Planting Containerized Stock

Use these tips to get container-grown trees and shrubs off to a good start.

Soak before planting. Plunge each container into a bucket of water until the root ball is saturated.

Score the roots. Use a knife or screwdriver to cut the roots to a depth of ½ inch at intervals around the container. This encourages the roots to grow outward into the soil.

Dig the right hole. Dig a planting hole about twice as wide as the container, deep enough so that the surface of the root ball will be just below soil level. If drainage is poor, make the hole shallower so you have to mound the soil around the plant to cover it. Place the root ball on a slightly elevated platform of soil in the bottom of the hole. The surrounding moat will collect water to be wicked up from the bottom of the root ball—water tends to flow around the soilless mix used in most containers.

Planting Balled-and-Burlapped Stock

Here's how to get B&B plants in the soil and off to a good start.

Always support the root ball. Never move a B&B plant by grasping the trunk or stem. Doing so requires the roots to support the weight of the soil and will break them. Use a dolly or a cart to move B&B plants too heavy to carry easily. Make sure the root ball is moist, but not wet, before you plant.

Check the burlap. Check to see if your plant is wrapped in a plastic burlap material or true burlap, which is biodegradable. Remove plastic burlap entirely; it can restrict root growth. Also cut away planting "cages" that may contain the roots. Real burlap will wick moisture away from the roots if it's exposed, so pull it partially away from the ball and bury it when you backfill.

Study the roots to dig the right hole. Dig a hole two to three times as wide as the root ball, and deep enough so that the uppermost roots emerging from the stem are just below soil level. Open the burlap slightly and pull away enough soil to locate these roots. In the process of digging the plant, additional soil is sometimes thrown on top of the ball. For this reason, it's easy to inadvertently plant B&B stock much too deeply. Especially in heavy soils, this is one of the most common causes of death in B&B plants. In very heavy soils, dig the hole shallow enough so that you must mound the soil around the upper third of the root ball.

Pull back burlap to expose uppermost roots.

Roll or gently lower the ball into the hole. Dropping B&B stock can fracture the root ball and seriously compromise the plant.

Backfill carefully, making sure that there is good soil contact around the ball. Form a basin of soil around the plant and water thoroughly several times.

TAKE-IT-EASY TIP!

Stop! Don't Stake

Don't **automatically stake your newly planted trees. Studies have shown that unstaked trees establish stronger roots and tops.** ***Do*** **stake newly planted trees that are on extremely windy sites. It's also a good idea to loosely stake trees planted near heavily trafficked sites—it protects them from jostling.**

Plan for Post-Planting Care

Your new tree or shrub is most vulnerable in its first year of life. Use this simple post-planting care checklist to get your plants off to a vigorous start.

Water, water, water. Inadequate watering is the number-one cause of new plant death. Most new plants need about an inch of water per week during the first growing season.

Mulch. Keep an adequate layer of mulch around your new plant to prevent weed competition.

Feed. When the plant puts out new growth, feed it with some weak manure tea or compost tea. Or just pull back the mulch and apply a layer of compost or rotted manure around the root zone. Replace the mulch over it.

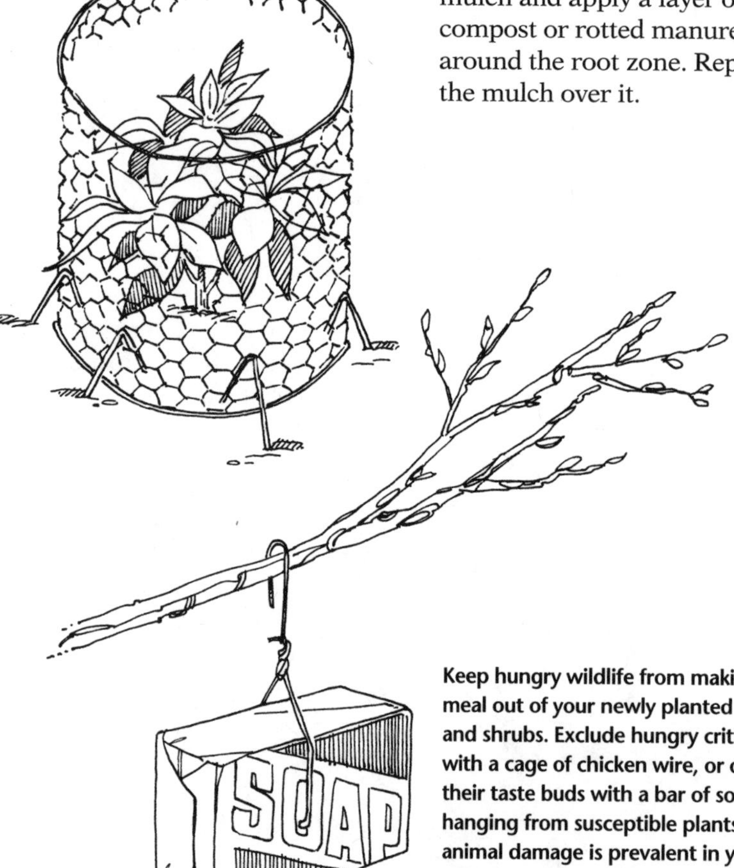

Keep hungry wildlife from making a meal out of your newly planted trees and shrubs. Exclude hungry critters with a cage of chicken wire, or offend their taste buds with a bar of soap hanging from susceptible plants. If animal damage is prevalent in your area, check your deterrents regularly to make sure they're doing the job.

Minimal Maintenance Methods

A well-chosen, carefully planted tree or shrub will need little maintenance beyond its early years. In most cases, your plant will flourish surprisingly well with benign neglect. But you may occasionally need to intervene. Here's a rundown of the care you can expect and tips for minimizing it.

Watering

After the first year, your trees and shrubs should not need supplemental watering, except during periods of unusual drought. The exceptions are azaleas and rhododendrons, which need steady moisture to look their best. If you can't keep them well watered, you'll be better off without them.

If you want to plant in a dry spot, choose plants adapted to drought. If your spot is boggy, choose wet-tolerant plants.

If you want to install an irrigation system for your trees and shrubs, stay away from overhead irrigation. Opt instead for one of the many drip irrigation systems available. See Chapter 8 for more on efficient watering techniques.

Pruning

The best way to minimize pruning maintenance is to put

yourself through an attitude adjustment. Forget about closely shorn globes, cones, and gumdrops. Focus instead on the graceful beauty of a shrub's natural form and learn to appreciate it. Disabuse yourself of the notion that all plants need pruning to make them look "neat" or to keep them under control. Choose shrubs and trees whose ultimate form and size are suited to the spot you have in mind.

Stop, don't top! Never, ever perform—or have performed—on your trees the disgraceful disfigurement known as "topping." This practice causes dangerous, weak-wooded trees that decline gradually and eventually die. If a tree is interfering with power lines, remove individual limbs, transplant the tree, or cut it down.

Leave limbing in limbo. Forget about "limbing up" your evergreens. This practice of removing the lower limbs of evergreens spoils their graceful form and creates more mowing for you. Let those branches sweep the ground and they'll provide their own mulch zone around the tree.

Occasionally, of course, the need to do some light pruning will arise. You'll find low-maintenance pruning tips and techniques in Chapter 9.

Fertilizing

Most trees and shrubs will grow just fine—albeit more slowly—without any fertilization. Applying 3 to 4 inches of compost to the root zone once or twice a year is helpful. Occasionally, in very lean soil, more help is needed. Manure tea gives a quick boost to starving plants; a mulch of grass clippings provides a more slowly released nitrogen supply.

Grow them lean and mean. Too much nitrogen fertilizer promotes lush growth that is very tender and disease susceptible. Even resistant trees and shrubs can fall prone to diseases like fire blight on a nitrogen-rich diet. In Zones 3 through 7, withhold nitrogen fertilizer from your woody plants after the 4th of July to give new growth from the spring a chance to "harden" and to curtail additional lush, tender growth.

Think Small

Instead of planting a full-size tree, consider the trees listed here. They range from 10 to 25 feet tall—just right for filling in a limited-space landscape with little or no pruning.

You can screen an area quickly and easily with multistemmed plants. In this list, trees with multitrunk tendencies are marked with an asterisk (*).

Callery pears (*Pyrus calleryana* cultivars, especially 'Aristocrat' and 'Autumn Blaze'). Zones 4–8.

Chinese dogwood (*Cornus kousa* var. *chinensis* cultivars). Zones 5–8.

Crape myrtles (*Lagerstroemia indica* hybrids and cultivars)*. Zones 7–9.

Downy serviceberry (*Amelanchier arborea*)*. Zones 4–9.

Eastern redbud (*Cercis canadensis*). Zones 4–9.

Flowering crabapples (*Malus* cultivars). Zones 3–8.

Japanese snowbell (*Styrax japonicus*). Zones 5–8.

Japanese stewartia (*Stewartia pseudocamellia*). Zones 5–8.

Japanese tree lilac (*Syringa reticulata*). Zones 3–7.

Mountain silverbell (*Halesia monticola*)*. Zones 5–9.

Pagoda dogwood (*Cornus alternifolia*). Zones 3–7.

Star magnolia (*Magnolia stellata*)*. Zones 3–8.

White fringe tree (*Chionanthus virginicus*)*. Zones 3–9.

The Secret's in the Soil: Rhododendrons and Azaleas Demystified

There's no denying the beauty and versatility of rhododendrons and azaleas. Their bountiful, beautiful flowers and attractive, often evergreen foliage make them a welcome addition to nearly any landscape. It's no wonder that so many gardeners are willing to struggle against less-than-ideal conditions to grow them.

If rhododendrons and azaleas are must-have plants in your landscape, pay close attention: Rules about careful siting go doubly for these plants. Although they are neither more tender nor more difficult to grow than many other landscape plants, rhododendrons are very particular about the conditions they grow in. Success is a matter of choosing plants appropriate to your area, preparing the soil adequately, and supplying adequate moisture.

In the mid-Atlantic, the South, or the Pacific Northwest, soil and weather conditions make it relatively easy to grow just about any and all rhododendrons and azaleas. Gardeners in other regions need to exercise more care in selecting plants and sites. In northern zones, for example, it's important to steer clear of selections whose flower buds are not hardy enough to withstand the cold. After all, what's the use of growing a rhododendron that never blooms?

Choose a site in partial shade for your rhododendrons and azaleas. Shelter them from drying winter winds benefits evergreen types. But don't try to grow rhodies under maples; their greedy roots won't give timid rhododendrons a chance.

Dig in for Success

If you want to grow rhododendrons and azaleas in anything less than their native moist, rich, woodland soil, there's no getting around doing some soil preparation. If you have clay soil, add equal parts of coarse sand and organic matter (leaf mold, compost, pine bark,

An evergreen screen can help create a just-right site for your rhododendrons. Position rhododendrons to let taller evergreens shade them from damaging winter sun and block at least some winter wind. But that's not the only benefit of this neighborly arrangement—the evergreens' needles make an excellent acidic mulch for the rhododendrons, too.

rotted manure, or rotted sawdust) and incorporate thoroughly. Add plenty of amendments, so that the resulting area is mounded up a few inches. Test the soil pH. If it's above 6.0, incorporate sulfur to bring it down into the 5.0 to 6.0 range. Plant your rhododendrons and mulch with 3 to 4 inches of pine bark, rotted sawdust, or pine needles. Spread out the roots on the surface of the root ball to stimulate them to grow outward, something rhododendrons' roots are very slow to do.

In sandy soils, forget about adding sand, but double up on the organic matter. Avoid creating a mound that will contribute to the already rapid drainage. Sandy soils are often acidic; don't routinely add sulfur without checking the pH.

Have a source of water handy, as rhododendrons need pretty constant moisture throughout summer. Drip irrigation is best. And remember to water evergreen rhododendrons thoroughly before the ground freezes to help ward off winter desiccation.

HEED THIS ALKALINE ALERT!

The soil around a house foundation is almost always alkaline and therefore not suited to growing acid-loving plants. Putting plants such as rhododendrons and their relatives in such a site sentences you to a rigorous maintenance routine to keep the soil pH low enough to satisfy their needs. Without regular soil modification, your plants will grow poorly and make other maintenance tasks for you. Save yourself a lot of work by saving your rhododendrons for more appropriate sites.

For Problem-Free Evergreens, Heed These Tips

Needled evergreens are among the most widely planted trees and shrubs. As with many popular plants, they have been heavily overplanted and often badly used. Use the tips below to minimize problems.

Choose carefully. Pines, in particular, have become host to a plethora of pests. Minimize problems by consulting with experts on the most durable evergreens for your area. Also ask about evergreen alternatives to the most commonly planted spruces and pines.

Avoid streetside sites. Many pines and most spruce cannot tolerate salt spray from vehicles whooshing along a salted street in winter. Browning foliage on the street side of a planting is a surefire sign of salt damage.

Shelter plants from winter winds. Pick a site that is sheltered from prevailing winter winds, which can shrivel evergreens' foliage. And place them away from south-facing windows so they don't block welcome winter sun.

Consider size at maturity. Whether you're planting spruces, pines, yews, or junipers, don't be fooled by their cute, compact forms in containers. It's all too easy to take a small plant home, plop it in place next to your foundation, and end up shearing and hacking at it to keep it in bounds for the rest of its life. To avoid future pruning nightmares, look at height and spread, and space plants accordingly. Fill in between small plants with perennials or groundcovers for a finished look while you wait for plants to grow.

Buy plants that behave. If you need a low-growing or compact plant for a special site, don't depend on pruning—look for cultivars of evergreens that will mature at the height you want. Cultivars of creeping juniper (*Juniperus horizontalis*) and western red cedar (*J. scopulorum*) mature at heights from several inches to 1½ feet. Low-growing pines, spruces, and yews are also avaible, so don't settle for what's most commonly available.

USDA Plant Hardiness Zone Map

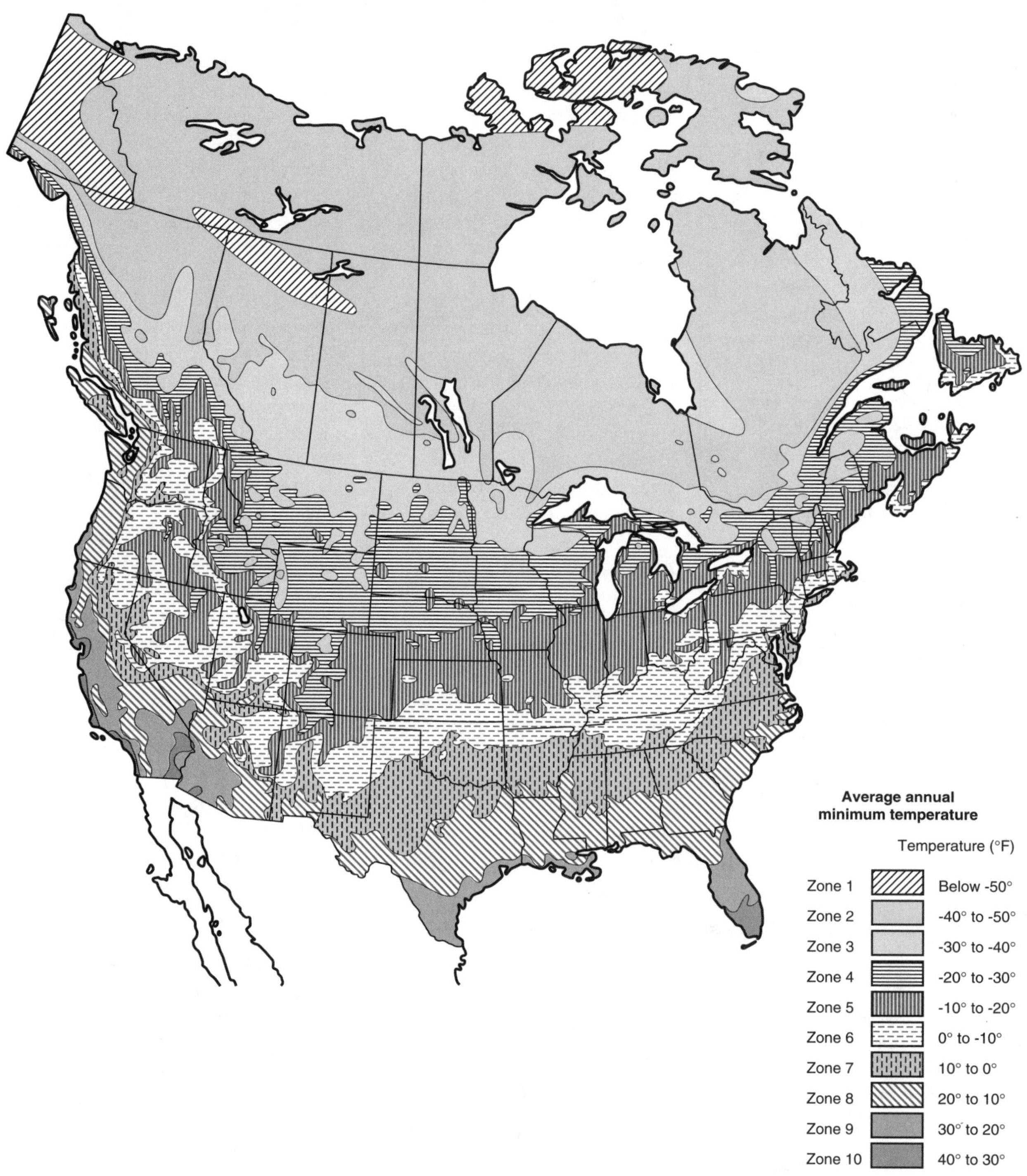

Sources

Bulbs

The following businesses specialize in flowering bulbs.

The Daffodil Mart
Route 3, Box 794
Gloucester, VA 23061

Dutch Gardens
P.O. Box 200
Adelphia, NJ 07710

John Scheepers, Inc.
P.O. Box 700
Bantam, CT 06750

McClure & Zimmerman
P.O. Box 368
108 West Winnebago Street
Friesland, WI 53935

Van Bourgondien Bros., Inc.
P.O. Box A
245 Farmingdale Road
Babylon, NY 11702

Vandenberg
1 Black Meadow Road
Chester, NY 10918

Flowers and Ornamental Grasses

The following companies offer a wide range of annual and perennial flowers, and ornamental grasses. Many also offer roses.

W. Atlee Burpee & Co.
300 Park Avenue
Warminster, PA 18974

Bluestone Perennials
7211 Middle Ridge Road
Madison, OH 44057

Hastings
P.O. Box 115535
Atlanta, GA 30302

Jackson & Perkins
P.O Box 1028
Medford, OR 97501

Kurt Bluemel, Inc.
2740 Greene Lane
Baldwin, MD 21013

Milaeger's Gardens
4838 Douglas Avenue
Racine, WI 53402-2498

Park Seed Co.
P.O. Box 31
Greenwood, SC 29647

Thompson & Morgan, Inc.
P.O. Box 1308
Jackson, NJ 08527

Wayside Gardens
1 Garden Lane
Hodges, SC 29695

White Flower Farm
P.O. Box 50
Route 63
Litchfield, CT 06759-0050

Fruit

The following companies specialize in tree fruits, small fruits, and berries.

Ahrens Nursery & Plant Labs
P.O. Box 145
Huntingburg, IN 47542

Bear Creek Nursery
P.O. Box 411
Northport, WA 99157

Edible Landscaping
P.O. Box 77
Afton, VA 22920

Henry Leuthardt Nurseries, Inc.
P.O. Box 666
East Moriches, NY 11940

Hopkins Citrus and Rare Fruit Nursery
5200 S.W. 160th Avenue
Fort Lauderdale, FL 33331

New York State Fruit Testing Cooperative Assoc. Inc.
P.O. Box 462
Geneva, NY 14456-0462

North Star Gardens
19060 Manning Trail North
Marine on St. Croix, MN 55047

Raintree Nursery
391 Butts Road
Morton, WA 98356

St. Lawrence Nurseries
Rural Route 5, Box 324
Potsdam, NY 13676

Southmeadow Fruit Gardens
Box SM
Lakeside, MI 49116

Stark Bros. Nurseries & Orchards Co.
Highway 54
Louisiana, MO 63353

Whitman Farms
3995 Gibson Road NW
Salem, OR 97304

Gardening Equipment and Supplies

The following companies sell products including organic fertilizers, composting equipment, animal repellents, beneficial insects, sprayers, tillers, row cover and shading materials, irrigation equipment, hand tools, and carts. Some also sell seeds and/or plants.

Bountiful Gardens
19550 Walker Road
Willits, CA 95490

DripWorks
380 Maple Street
Willits, CA 95490

Gardener's Supply Co.
128 Intervale Road
Burlington, VT 05401

Gardens Alive!
5100 Schenley Place
Lawrenceburg, IN 47025

Harmony Farm Supply
P.O. Box 460
Graton, CA 95444

A. M. Leonard, Inc.
P.O. Box 816
Piqua, OH 45356

Necessary Trading Co.
P.O. Box 305
422 Salem Avenue
New Castle, VA 24127

Peaceful Valley Farm Supply Co.
P.O. Box 2209
Grass Valley, CA 95945

Pest Management Supply
311 River Drive
Hadley, MA 01035

Raindrip, Inc.
21305 Itasca Street
Chatsworth, CA 91311

The Urban Farmer Store
2833 Vicente Street
San Francisco, CA 94116

Herbs and Unusual Plants

The following companies specialize in herbs and heirloom or hard-to-find plants.

The Gourmet Gardener
8650 College Boulevard
Overland Park, KS 66210

J. L. Hudson, Seedsman
P.O. Box 1058
Redwood City, CA 94064

Le Jardin du Gourmet
P.O. Box 75
St. Johnsbury Center, VT 05863

Meadowbrook Herb Garden Catalog
P.O. Box 578
Fairfield, CT 06430

Native Seeds/SEARCH
2509 North Campbell Avenue #325
Tucson, AZ 85719

Sandy Mush Herb Nursery
Route 2, Surrett Cove Road
Leicester, NC 28748

Seed Savers Exchange
3076 North Winn Road
Decorah, IA 52101

Seeds Blüm
Idaho City Stage
Boise, ID 83706

Seeds Trust High Altitude Gardens
P.O. Box 4619
Ketchum, ID 83340

Well-Sweep Herb Farm
317 Mount Bethel Road
Port Murray, NJ 07865

Trees and Shrubs

The following nurseries offer a broad selection of woody plants and vines; most sell perennials as well.

Appalachian Gardens
P.O. Box 82
410 Westview Avenue
Waynesboro, PA 17268

Forestfarm
990 Tetherow Road
Williams, OR 97544

Mellinger's, Inc.
2310 West South Range Road
North Lima, OH 44452

Owen Farms
2951 Curve-Nankipoo Road
Route 3, Box 158-A
Ripley, TN 38063

Roslyn Nursery
211 Burrs Lane
Dix Hills, NY 11746

Springhill Nurseries
6523 North Galena Road
P.O. Box 1758
Peoria, IL 61656-1758

Wayside Gardens
1 Garden Lane
Hodges, SC 29695

Vegetables

These businesses range from small suppliers of specialty vegetables to large companies that sell vegetable, herb, and flower seeds, as well as seed-starting equipment and supplies.

W. Atlee Burpee & Co.
300 Park Avenue
Warminster, PA 18974

The Cook's Garden
P.O. Box 535
Londonderry, VT 05148

DeGiorgi Seed Co.
6011 N Street
Omaha, NE 68117

Harris Seeds
P.O. Box 22960
Rochester, NY 14692

Ed Hume Seeds, Inc.
P.O. Box 1450
Kent, WA 98035

Johnny's Selected Seeds
2580 Foss Hill Road
Albion, ME 04910

J. W. Jung Seed Co.
335 South High Street
Randolph, WI 53957

Nichols Garden Nursery
1190 North Pacific Highway
Albany, OR 97321

Park Seed Co.
P.O Box 31
Greenwood, SC 29647

Piedmont Plant Co.
P.O. Box 424
Albany, GA 31703

Pinetree Garden Seeds
Route 100
New Gloucester, ME 04260

Redwood City Seed Co.
P.O. Box 361
Redwood City, CA 94064

Shepherd's Garden Seeds
6116 Highway 9
Felton, CA 95018

Stokes Seeds, Inc.
Box 548
Buffalo, NY 14240

Sunrise Enterprises
P.O. Box 330058
West Hartford, CT 06133-0058

Territorial Seed Co.
P.O. Box 157
Cottage Grove, OR 97424

Tomato Growers Supply Co.
P.O. Box 2237
Fort Myers, FL 33902

Water Garden Plants and Supplies

These businesses offer a comprehensive selection of plants and supplies for water gardens.

Lilypons Water Garden
P.O. Box 10
6800 Lilypons Road
Buckeystown, MD 21717

William Tricker, Inc.
7125 Tanglewood Drive
Independence, OH 44131

Wildflowers and Native Plants

The following companies sell seeds and/or plants of wildflowers and other native species.

Applewood Seed Co.
5380 Vivian Street
Arvada, CO 80002

Clyde Robin Seed Co.
3670 Enterprise Avenue
Hayward, CA 94545

Native Seeds, Inc.
14590 Triadelphia Mill Road
Dayton, MD 21306

Niche Gardens
1111 Dawson Road
Chapel Hill, NC 27516

Plants of the Southwest
Route 6, Box 11-A
Santa Fe, NM 87501

Prairie Nursery
P.O. Box 306
Westfield, WI 53964

Wildseed Farms, Inc.
P.O. Box 308
Eagle Lake, TX 77434

Woodlanders, Inc.
1128 Colleton Avenue
Aiken, SC 29801

Recommended Reading

Container Gardening

Stevens, David, and Kenneth A. Beckett. *The Contained Garden: A Complete Illustrated Guide to Growing Plants, Flowers, Fruits, and Vegetables Outdoors in Pots.* New York: Penguin USA, Studio Books, 1983.

Bales, Suzanne F. *Burpee Container Gardening.* New York: Prentice Hall General Reference and Travel, 1993.

General Gardening

Binetti, Marianne. *Tips for Carefree Landscapes.* Pownal, Vt.: Storey Communications, Inc., 1990.

Bartholomew, Mel. *Square Foot Gardening.* Emmaus, Pa.: Rodale Press, 1981.

Bradley, Fern Marshall, and Barbara W. Ellis, eds. *Rodale's All-New Encyclopedia of Organic Gardening.* Emmaus, Pa.: Rodale Press, 1992.

Hynes, Erin, and Susan McClure. *Rodale's Successful Organic Gardening: Low-Maintenance Landscaping.* Emmaus, Pa.: Rodale Press, 1994.

Kourik, Robert. *Drip Irrigation for Every Landscape and All Climates.* Santa Rosa, Calif.: Metamorphic Press, 1992.

Medic, Kris. *Rodale's Successful Organic Gardening: Pruning.* Emmaus, Pa.: Rodale Press, 1995.

Michalak, Patricia S., and Cass Peterson. *Rodale's Successful Organic Gardening: Vegetables.* Emmaus, Pa.: Rodale Press, 1993.

Herbs

Hylton, William H., and Claire Kowalchik, eds. *Rodale's Illustrated Encyclopedia of Herbs.* Emmaus, Pa.: Rodale Press, 1987.

Michalak, Patricia S. *Rodale's Successful Organic Gardening: Herbs.* Emmaus, Pa.: Rodale Press, 1993.

Grasses

Greenlee, John. *The Encyclopedia of Ornamental Grasses.* Emmaus, Pa.: Rodale Press, 1992.

Taylor's Guide Staff. *Taylor's Guide to Ground Covers, Vines, and Grasses.* Boston: Houghton Mifflin Co., 1987.

Pest and Disease Control

Borror, Donald J., and Richard E. White. *A Field Guide to the Insects of America North of Mexico.* The Peterson Field Guide Series. Boston: Houghton Mifflin, 1970.

Carr, Anna. *Rodale's Color Handbook of Garden Insects.* Emmaus, Pa.: Rodale Press, 1979.

Ellis, Barbara W. and Fern Marshall Bradley, *The Organic Gardener's Handbook of Natural Insect and Disease Control.* Emmaus, Pa.: Rodale Press, 1992.

Fisher, Bill. *Growers Weed Identification Handbook.* Oakland, Calif.: ANR Publications, 1985.

McClure, Susan, and Sally Roth. *Rodale's Successful Organic Gardening: Companion Planting.* Emmaus, Pa.: Rodale Press, 1994.

Michalak, Patricia S., and Linda A. Gilkeson. *Rodale's Successful Organic Gardening: Controlling Pests and Diseases.* Emmaus, Pa.: Rodale Press, 1994.

Smith, Miranda, and Anna Carr. *Rodale's Garden Insect, Disease and Weed Identification Guide.* Emmaus, Pa.: Rodale Press, 1988.

Wildflowers

Imes, Rick. *Wildflowers: How to Identify Flowers in the Wild and How to Grow Them in Your Garden.* Emmaus, Pa.: Rodale Press, 1992.

Johnson, Lady Bird, and Carlton B. Lees. *Wildflowers Across America.* New York: Abbeville Press, 1988.

Credits

Writers

C. Colston Burrell is a garden designer, writer, and photographer whose design business, Native Landscapes, specializes in the use of native plants and perennials. Cole is co-author of *Rodale's Illustrated Encyclopedia of Perennials*.

Matthew Cheever is a horticulturist and owner of Evergreen, a landscape design and maintenance company in Milton, Wisconsin.

Barrie Crawford is the author of *For the Love of Wild Flowers* and co-author of *The Gardens of Two Sisters*. She gives workshops on wildflowers at Callaway Gardens in Pine Mountain, Georgia.

Erin Hynes is a freelance garden writer from Austin, Texas. She has a master's degree in weed science from Pennsylvania State University.

Tina James hosted an organic growing series for Maryland Public Television and wrote a book on the same topic called *Gardening from the Heart*.

Barbara Kaczorowski is a horticulturist, landscape designer, and co-owner of Accent Gardens, a landscape design and installation firm in Cicero, Indiana.

Ruth Kvaalen is a horticulturist, freelance garden writer, and photographer. She tends her garden in West Lafayette, Indiana.

Nel Newman is a freelance writer, horticulturist, and master gardener. She publishes a newsletter called *Garden Tips*. Her garden grows on 1.3 acres in midtown Jackson, Mississippi.

David Page owns and operates a furniture-building shop in Swarthmore, Pennsylvania. He has a masters of fine arts degree in furniture design and woodworking from Rhode Island School of Design.

Sally Roth is a contributing editor of *Fine Gardening* magazine, publisher of the nature and gardening journal *A Letter from the Country,* and nature columnist for the *Sunday Evansville Courier.*

Editors

Barbara W. Ellis has a bachelor's degree from Kenyon College and a bachelor's degree in horticulture from Ohio State University. She is a former publications director/editor for *American Horticulturist* and is former managing editor of garden books at Rodale Press.

Joan Benjamin is an associate editor of garden books at Rodale Press. She has a bachelor's degree in agriculture from the University of Missouri and a master's degree in public horticulture administration from the University of Delaware's Longwood Graduate Program.

Deborah L. Martin has a bachelor's degree in horticultural writing from Purdue University and has worked as a Cooperative Extension agent for urban gardeners in Indianapolis. She is an associate editor at Rodale Press.

Contributing Editors

Fern Marshall Bradley has a bachelor's degree in plant science from Cornell University and a master's degree in horticulture from Rutgers University. She has managed an organic market garden and is an editor at Rodale Press.

Jean M. A. Nick has a bachelor's degree in biology from Smith College and a master's degree in horticulture from Rutgers University. She has extensive experience in the commercial greenhouse industry and is an associate editor at Rodale Press.

Special Thanks

Lee Reich, Ph.D., is the author of *Uncommon Fruits Worthy of Attention* and *A Northeast Gardener's Year.*

Nancy Ondra is a senior associate editor of garden books at Rodale Press who has a passion for variegated foliage.

Ken Burton is a senior associate editor of woodworking books who built himself a workshop of straw.

Index

Note: Page references in *italic* indicate tables. **Boldface** references indicate photographs or illustrations.

D

G

H

I

J

N

O

P

Q

R

Y

Z